To Make the Hands Impure

To Make the Hands Impure

Art, Ethical Adventure, the Difficult and the Holy

ADAM ZACHARY NEWTON

FORDHAM UNIVERSITY PRESS   *New York* 2015

Copyright © 2015 Fordham University Press

Fordham University Press has no responsibility for the persistence or accuracy of URLs for external or third-party Internet websites referred to in this publication and does not guarantee that any content on such websites is, or will remain, accurate or appropriate.

Fordham University Press also publishes its books in a variety of electronic formats. Some content that appears in print may not be available in electronic books.

Visit us online at www.fordhampress.com.

Library of Congress Cataloging-in-Publication Data

Newton, Adam Zachary, author.
    To make the hands impure : art, ethical adventure, the difficult and the holy / Adam Zachary Newton.
        pages cm
    Includes bibliographical references and index.
    ISBN 978-0-8232-6351-6 (hardback) — ISBN 978-0-8232-6352-3 (paper)
    1. Philosophy, Modern—20th century.   2. Philosophy, Modern—21st century.   3. Art and morals.   4. Ethics in literature.   5. Reader-response criticism.   6. Lévinas, Emmanuel—Criticism and interpretation.
    I. Title.
    B5800.N395 2014
    190—dc23

                                                                        2014029448

Printed in the United States of America

17 16 15   5 4 3 2 1

First edition

For Miriam, abundantly

איר גאַנצן זאַפֿט טראָפֿן ניט פֿאַגיסן
האָט ער פֿאַמעלעך, ווי מען טראָנט אַ כּוס

מיט וויין אין ביידע פֿולע הענט די פּלוים
געבראַכט דער וויַב און איידל צוגעטראָגן
צו אירע ליפֿן

A tu lado vivirán y se hablarán
como cuando estás conmigo

"כל חפֿץ טוב שיש בביתי טלי אותו..."
אין חפֿץ טוב לי בעולם יותר ממך

CONTENTS

DOG EARS FOUR-A-PENNY The wares in a bookshop look completely unread. On the other hand, a school-boy's Latin dictionary looks read to the point of tatters. . . . Our problem is to alter the [owned] book in a reasonably short time so that anybody looking at it will conclude that its owner has practically lived, supped and slept with it for many months. You can, if you like, talk about designing a machine driven by a small but efficient petrol motor that would "read" any book in five minutes, the equivalent of five years or ten years' "reading" being obtained by merely turning a knob. This, however, is the cheap, soulless approach of the times we live in. No machine can do the same work as the soft human fingers. The trained and experienced book-handler is the only real solution of this contemporary social problem. What does he do? How does he work? What would he charge? How many types of handling would there be?

* * *

'Popular Handling—Each volume to be well and truly handled, four leaves in each to be dog-eared, and a tram ticket, cloak-room docket or other comparable article inserted in each as a forgotten book-mark . . .

'Premier Handling—Each volume to be thoroughly handled, eight leaves in each to be dog-eared, a suitable passage in not less than 25 volumes to be underlined in red pencil . . .

'De Luxe Handling—Each volume to be mauled savagely, the spines of the smaller volumes to be damaged in a manner that will give the impression that they have been carried around in pockets, a passage in every volume to be underlined in red pencil with an exclamation or interrogation mark inserted in the margin opposite, not less than 30 volumes to be treated with old coffee, tea, porter or whiskey stains, and not less than five volumes to be inscribed with forged signatures of the authors. . . .'

The latest racket we have on hands is the *Myles na gCopaleen Book Club*. You join this and are spared the nerve-wracking bother of choosing your own books. We do the choosing for you, and, when you get the book, it is *ready—rubbed*, i.e., subjected free of charge to our expert handlers. You are spared the trouble of soiling and mauling it.

Myles na gCopaleen (Flann O'Brien)

Meaningful Adjacencies

In responding by a manual act of presence (*graphein*) to bodily acts of presence, in delivering over to verbal or plastic form that of the spirit which comes to attest to itself, [art does] not procure for us new objects to consider, but rather a new source of restlessness.

—Jean-Louis Chrétien

The human, as we now understand, cannot be grasped and saved unless that other part of itself, the share of things, is restored to it.

—Bruno Latour

For it is held in the hand and drawn into the movement of practical life. . . . It is as if the soul were an arm which one of the worlds—whether the real or the ideal—stretches out so that it may seize the other and join it to itself, and be grasped by and joined to it.

—Georg Simmel

NAMES

What I saw had little to do with cemeteries as one thinks of them; instead, before me lay a wilderness of graves, neglected for years, crumbling and gradually sinking into the ground amidst tall grass and wild flowers under the shade of trees, which trembled in the slight movement of the air. Here and there a stone placed on the top of a grave witnessed that someone must have visited one of the dead— who could say how long ago. It was not possible to decipher all of the chiseled inscriptions, but the names I could still read—Hamburger, Kissinger, Wertheimer, Friedländer, Arnsber, Auerbach, Grunwald, Leuthhold, Seeligmann, Frank, Hertz, Goldstau, Baumblatt, and Blumenthal—made me think that perhaps there was nothing the Germans begrudged the Jews so much as their beautiful names, so intimately bound up with the country they lived in and with its language. A shock of recognition shot through me at the grave of Maier Stern, who died on the 18th of May, my own birthday; and I was touched, in a way I knew I could never quite fathom, by the symbol of the writer's quill on the stone of Friederike Halbleib, who departed this life on the 28th of March 1912. I imagined her pen in hand, all by herself, bent with bated breath over her work; and now, as I write these lines, it feels as if *I* had lost her, and as if *I* could not get over the loss despite the many years that have passed since her departure. I stayed in the Jewish cemetery till the afternoon, walking up and down the rows of graves, reading the names of the dead.

W. G. Sebald, *The Emigrants*

Take this as a moment of *anagnorisis*—a recognition scene, long after Aristotle.[1] But let us take it also as a scene of reading. Although it begins with an attempt at deciphering, the passage quite deliberately escorts us into a different precinct: *what happens to us when we read*, or, as we might also say, *what our reading makes happen*. Granted, it is probably more customary to think of what we do when standing before a headstone as something other than "reading." It is not quite scanning, which we routinely perform when we see a billboard or sign. Nor does it quite approximate decoding, which is what the character Pip does at the beginning of Charles Dickens's *Great Expectations*, when, too young to read, he construes the shapes of the lettering on the headstones that mark his dead parents' and siblings' graves as indicating what those persons must have looked like, an emblematic tutorial in the vagaries of icon, index, and symbol.[2] I would propose that it more closely resembles what we do when we see or search a face: that is, we recognize and (potentially) *acknowledge* it.

But Sebald's narrator *does* indeed read, as he moves reflectively from headstone to headstone, noting the cultural specificity of surname (these are not his people). By recording those names for us, he even more-than-names them; he shelters them, so to speak, in what the philosopher Jean-Louis Chrétien evocatively named "an ark of speech."[3] If "there was nothing the Germans begrudged the Jews so much as their beautiful names, so intimately bound up with the country they lived in and with its language," then here, in this place of bereavement and potential oblivion, those names—like the living presences the biblical Noah is commanded to collect and preserve—are gathered and welcomed through a gratuitous act of hospitality, which takes the form of reciting and recounting them.

Further, Sebald's narrator gives himself license to perform the kind of personating, imaginative acts while writing fiction that we routinely exercise as its readers. Fantasizing from the incised quill on the gravestone to an imagined pen in the hand of the deceased, her loss—the loss *of* her—uncannily becomes *his*. We should therefore not think it accidental that the grave which prompts such transferential merger belongs to a *writer*, its headstone displaying a graphic symbol evidently more vivid, more "esemplastic" (in Coleridge's sense of shaping and unifying power),[4] for the narrator's imagination than even his own birthdate he sees inscribed upon another gravestone.

What I would especially invite us to notice in this poignant moment of vagary in Sebald's book is its careful concatenation of names—names that are evidently read, perhaps even pronounced in succession and thereby connected to one another. It is long a matter of national custom for public monuments to the dead, in particular victims of collective calamity, to display their names in memorialization. The Fishermen's and Fishermen's Wives Memorials in Gloucester Harbor, Mass.; the traveling AIDS Memorial Quilt; the Field of Empty Chairs at the Oklahoma City National Memorial; the Cenotaph in Hiroshima Peace Park; the Wall of Names at the Kigali Memorial Center and the Nyanza Wall of Memory, Rwanda; dissident artist Ai Weiwei's sound piece "Remembrance for Names of the Student Earthquake Victims Found by the Citizens' Investigation," whose anonymous voices recite the names of 5,385 children killed in collapsing school buildings during the 2008 Sichuan earthquake;[5] the Wall at the Vietnam Veterans Memorial; and most recently, the bronze rectangular facades at the National September 11 Memorial, designed by Michael Arad: in all these cases, as Maya Lin often explained the philosophy behind her design for the Vietnam Veterans' Wall, "The names would become the memorial."[6]

At the VVM, the 58,272 names of American soldiers killed in action in Southeast Asia are engraved chronologically on the granite wall according to the date of the casualty. At the Oklahoma City Memorial, the 168 names inscribed on empty chairs are grouped according to the floor on which each person was located at the time of the bombing, and also according to the blast pattern. The names in the NAMES Project AIDS Quilt appear haphazardly and are frequently neither the legal nor official name but rather those of private usage: nicknames, affectionate sobriquets.[7] Other memorials list names in the most common and democratic manner: alphabetically.

It is in this regard—the logic of name placement—that Michael Arad's September 11 Memorial, *Reflecting Absence*, is unique. Around the perimeter of the two colossal cubic voids that mark the footprints of the destroyed trade towers, ringed by waterfalls cascading into a sunken pool that encloses a smaller, central draining pool, is a bronze balustrade containing one-hundred and fifty-two five-foot by ten-foot panels on which are inscribed the names of the 2,977 victims from 90 countries of the plane crashes and collapsed towers.[8] Each name was finished by hand. In addition to nine category groupings by North and South Towers, the four airline flights downed on September 11, "first responders," and the six victims of the February 26, 1993, WTC bombing, they are arranged according to a three-tiered system called "meaningful adjacencies." The names of colleagues or fellow employees on the bronze panels may be placed alongside each other, like the eleven firefighters of New York City Fire Department Ladder 3 or the seventy-three employees of Windows on the World; so may those of relatives, friends, and even people who had only happened to meet on the morning of September 11. Name adjacency depends on patterns of affiliation. The entire arrangement was complex enough to require an algorithm in order to sort out the multiple permutations of nearness.[9]

This site, too, while it may have "little to do with cemeteries as one thinks of them," *is* most certainly a cemetery, even if the graves are denied the consolation and regard of individuation. Were one, like Sebald's narrator, to walk up and down reading the names of the dead ensemble, the pattern of organization would not be immediately obvious, except insofar as they are comprehended by the organizing categories of flight number or municipal agency, and so on. Indeed, to *read* those meaningful adjacencies, to create a kind of syntax for them that is not just stochastic—like the random adjacency of names and faces in the days following September 11 on posted flyers that pleaded, "Have you seen this person?"—one would need to be aware of their meanings, and their adjacency, in advance.

"There is obviously no text less in need of commentary than a list of names," says Emmanuel Levinas mordantly in one of his *Talmudic Readings*, intending quite the opposite sense.[10] For Sebald's narrator, any coherence to be read into the wilderness of gravestones has to do with the beautiful German-Jewish names inscribed upon them. So, to the casual observer, do the 2,983 names, especially because they are not alphabetically grouped, appear only randomly arranged. Like the narrator in *The Emigrants*, a visitor to the September 11 Memorial can absorb, intone, litanize the names as a pure collectivity, not so differently from the way those names are read out publically on each anniversary: the martyred dead.

Yet, as incisions, the names can also be *felt*: fingered (each panel is kept heated or cooled, depending on the season), caressed, and—as one of Levinas's Talmudic readings expresses a very distinctive modality of touch—"rubbed." In this case, rubbing means not only palpation but also *frottage*: tracing the textured surface of the incised names with pencil and paper, and thus exporting them from public space into private communions.[11] "One must 'rub' the text to arrive at the life it conceals," Levinas writes, implying a dual exposure: of book to self and self to book. And even if the metaphor specifically describes the sort of vigorous *literary* reading that, almost like circumcision, delaminates and thus unconceals, it is hard to conceive a more apt formulation in regard to the incised parapet of the September 11 Memorial for the human desire to bring the dead back through the tactile immediacy of their written names. As Levinas has remarked of Talmudic discourse generally, such frictional commerce with inscription participates in "an extreme attention to the Real."[12] Or, to take a small liberty with his own translation of the *mishnah* from tractate *Avot* (6:2) that stands as the epigraph to *Difficile Liberté*: "**lisibilité** sur les tables de pierre."

No less than Sebald's excruciatingly personal meditation on the grand scale of loss, Arad's *Reflecting Absence* stages, by means of its particular "pattern language,"[13] what this book will call an *ethics of reading*. Meaningful adjacencies are gifts of proximity. They stage Sebald's gesture—not just harboring, by recording, names in an ark of speech, but carefully preserving affiliations among them. And precisely because reading is so intimately connected with *touching* at this memorial, a tenderness of sentiment and memory that is also a tendering—of hand or penciled paper—it "takes place" in the literal sense of the phrase, so dependent is it on location and vicinity. If one were to demur, however, and say that scanning, caressing, pronouncing, or communing with hundreds of names does not approximate "reading" according to conventional practice—certainly not what we recognize as literary or scriptural reading, or even at the mechanical levels of saccade and lineation—Sebald's narrator invites us to consider how it may aspire to be or become so.[14] For in *The Emigrants*, too, a structure of "reflecting absences" guides and underpins the text's *ethical* reception.

THE PLACE OF ETHICS

My working definition of ethics fastened to the event of reading will acquire mass and density in the chapters that follow. From the Sebald and Arad scenes of "reading" re-staged here, it modulates to the more ethically intimate (certain post-Freudian schools will prefer "extimate") situation I call "the book in hand." But, for the moment, Levinas's own formula from *Totality and Infinity* can suffice for an outline: "We name this calling into question of my spontaneity by the presence of the Other, ethics" (43). "Ethics" is thus a matter of a certain *pressure* on presence. In this book, such pressure becomes tactile, and thus literalized. To have one's spontaneity called into question is to be disturbed or arrested in the freedom and naturalness of one's movements: in a word, *impeached*. In the directed sense I give to this Levinasian claim of troubled spontaneity in the act of reading, it is to *feel* a certain kind of book that reposes in one's hands as if one were thus to become responsible for it. "Ethics," in a (doubled) word, becomes a matter of *tact*—of both touch and regard.

And yet, such Levinasian ethics obviously gesture toward the metaphysical. In a significant aside, Jacques Derrida twice in print recalls a remark Levinas once made to him, "They say that I, that it's ethics I'm interested in. No. What interests me is *the holy*."[15] And in an interview from 1986, Levinas himself confesses, "The word ethics is Greek. Nowadays, above all, I think much more about holiness, the holiness of the face of the Other or the holiness of my obligation as such."[16] Holiness (*sainteté*) *may* signify religiosity, but in Levinas's usage, it does so less in relation to religion as myth than as textual tradition and the correlative practice of study and reading. Accordingly, I would like to consider one dimension for an ethics of reading as underwritten or superimposed by this "holy," in the distinctive sense Levinas attaches to it and as I clarify in successive chapters.

On the other face of the coin, the category of "the secular" need not be defined either antinomially (e.g., in Charles Taylor's "subtraction theory" whereby secularization records the liberating loss of prior, misleading fidelities), or even neutrally in relation to its counterpart, but rather as "the secular-and-*other*."[17] This would be the way in which the mundane (like Hebrew *ḥol*, meaning the weekdays other than the Sabbath) is already marked, shadowed, and inscribed by the exalted (as *qodesh*, in Hebrew, means "set apart from"). The traversal between these domains is what this book names "The

Difficult and the Holy." Being discourses in potentially *contiguous*, even *contaminated* reading,[18] literature and scripture can be said thus to be *touched* by and to *touch* each other.

How exactly do the passage from Sebald's book and Arad's two 212-foot by 212-foot engraved tetragons lend themselves still more to that definition and that traversal between sacred and secular spaces? As to the first, the definitional question of ethics, Sylvia Benso reminds us in her book *The Face of Things* of Heidegger's observation that the etonym of ethics originally denoted a "dwelling place" or haunt; accordingly, Levinasian ethics thus corresponds to "a locative description, not a normative procedure."[19] It both *locates*, in refining coordinates of place time, and it serves as a *location*, a *topos*: it demarcates a certain terrain, like a national memorial in lower Manhattan at which we read the names of the dead, and potentially at least, reflect upon the ethical implications of that act of reading. We "make contact with" such a place—as in Gen. 28:11, where the Hebrew verb-root פגע, midrashically understood, can also connote "entreaty."

As either a place or the opening of a space "where distance is revealed, where a difference is maintained," ethics thus locates its actors, problems, and potential effects: "a space neither neutral nor pre-constituted, where the encounter with what is other can be said to *take place*."[20] That "taking place" is a relation Levinas names "proximity." In ingeniously chosen figures, Levinas will speak in his book *Otherwise Than Being* of the trope of the "one-for-the-other [as an] accord, a chord, which is possible only as an arpeggio" rather than a collapsing of distance between self and other which, paradoxically, yields a cleavage, "like two vowels in a dieresis, maintaining a hiatus without elision" (70).

While more obviously spatial on a literal plane, Sebald's and Arad's stagings of reading, each in its own way but arpeggiated together, open such a chordal set of coordinates, especially when we consider that Levinas also portrays ethical relation rhetorically, as taking place in and through language. Located *there* is thus an order of potential merger or usurpation—e.g., "and now, as I write these lines, it feels as if *I* had lost her"—the curved space, in Levinas's phrase,[21] where the ethical subject is *altered*, othered and made different, by the neighbor.

What the "traversal of these two domains," from difficult to holy, might mean is something we can track in this additional passage from *The Emigrants*, when the narrator's peregrination in Kissingen concludes:

> . . . but it was only when I was about to leave that I discovered a more recent gravestone, not far from the locked gate, on which were the names of Lily and Lazarus Lanzberg, and of Fritz and Luisa Ferber. I assume Ferber's Uncle Leo had it erected there. The inscription says that Lazarus Lanzberg died in Theresienstadt in 1942, and that Fritz and Luisa were deported, their fate unknown, in November 1942. Only Lily, who took her own life, lies in that grave. I stood before it for a

long time, not knowing what I should think; but before I left I placed a stone on the grave, according to custom. (225)

As I hinted earlier, these are not his people: They are Jews, he is not. Our narrator is here only because his friend Max Ferber has passed along to him the memoirs of his mother, Luisa Ferber, née Lanzberg. He has journeyed himself to the Jewish cemetery in Kissingen solely because these memoirs were vouchsafed to him, memoirs which were written in the shadow of impending doom by Luisa Lanzberg and which, consequently, reach back to recall a childhood and youth spent in Steinach in lower Franconia and Bad Kissingen. Their author, so we are informed, is not even interred in the grave the narrator stands before, a negative instance of what Levinas calls *les imprévus de l'histoire* or "unforeseen history." And yet, the narrator feels compelled to follow her (or her name) *here*, in this spot. Max Ferber has previously confessed to him his own haunted sense of responsibility, having had to read his mother's writing twice:

> On that second occasion, the memoirs, which at points were truly wonderful, had seemed to him like one of those evil German fairy tales in which, once you are under the spell, you have to carry on to the finish, till your heart breaks, with whatever work you have begun—in this case, the remembering, writing and reading (193).

Elsewhere, I have written about this passage at length, explaining that very far from being an evil German fairy tale, the memoirs are a German-Jewish chronicle inserted within an expatriate German memoir that enframes it.[22] Its rhetorical logic is that of *errance*, where even to be home is to be dislocated, mobilized elsewhere, and where one is drawn out of oneself, toward the elsewhere, toward the other. Noting the horrendous scythe that was the Holocaust, in this case, the Terezín camp-ghetto; noting family connections, most of which have now been severed by it, in the nexus of Ferbers and Lanzbergs; noting, thus, the chime of names that all begin with the letter "L": Lily, Lazarus, Luisa, and Leo; noting his own disquieted arrest; noting, finally and decorously, a small act of *ḥesed* (lovingkindness) performed—"but before I left I placed a stone on the grave, according to custom"—a religious custom not the narrator's but one that he honors just the same: all this, its play of presence and absence, of recognition and responsiveness, of contact made and unmade, follows from the spatial act of "walking up and down the rows of graves, *reading the names of the dead.*"

The *placing* of the stone, particularly, marks when the narrator finally touches what he has, until that point, only discreetly regarded; it concretizes through the hand the attitude of "saddened tenderness": "that reality always extends further than any subjectivity can reach, even further than the ethical relation to which tenderness offers some access" (Benso, 179). I propose that we take it also as a sign for Sebald's readers, for us. "How are we to be *affected*?" is the question to which such an act distantly calls our attention. In so doing, it calls reading itself into question, in the Levinasian sense, arresting the free exercise of its "spontaneity." It holds us, if we let it. It is a small jewel of tact in the doubled sense of touch and regard, a tendering that communicates attentiveness.

Inside this book that we read is a memoir. The book's narrator has tracked the place and byways the memoir narrates. We, his readers, track his tracking, in turn. This is how a book like *The Emigrants* works, this is its mimetic machinery: it stages an ethics of reading for us, and we, in turn, are prompted to perform our own version of it—or at least are placed in a position to reflect upon that staging. Potentially, again, *our* work of "remembering, writing, and reading" mimes the narrator's own, who has already modeled an ethics of remembering, of writing, and of reading. How might we be said, thus, to be *altered* as readers? Into what relationship of contiguity are we thus drawn by grasping such a work, tracing its tracings, reading the names of the martyred dead that it reads, and how are we thus "joined" to its project?

At this moment in Sebald's book, not so very different from the scene of quasi-reading and its contiguities we are asked to transact at Arad's memorial,[23] the question also becomes: into what meaningful adjacency are we ourselves thus drawn, reading in others' footsteps and traces, and how, in being joined to its project, could we be said, ethically, to "have made something happen?" But aren't we free to do nothing? Is that not the exact meaning of our autonomy, our separateness, out "just thereness?" After all, it is not as though we are faced with a human body in extremis, or a legal case, or a practical, "real-world" problem that requires our intervention. Moreover, if we are witnesses, do we even attest to the witnessing in any visible, accountable way? Reading Sebald's book, we are, presumably, alone and secluded, or at least insulated from the world. All we are doing is holding a book in our hands. At Arad's memorial, while we are in public view, we are (except by the security presence), left mostly unwatched and thus safely anonymous. Where does ethics "take place" in either of these examples?

A conventional humanist defense might say that perhaps the ethical lies in merely being "touched, in a way I knew I could never quite fathom," as Sebald's narrator expresses it—safely positioning us between the notional and the emotional. For isn't that one of an artwork's cathartic purposes, and one reason we raise monuments to the dead: to touch us, unfathomably, and maybe purge us therefore of pity, of fear, or of just the casualness that we take to be our natural relationship to the world?[24] In the face of such demurrals, I want to propose another set of possible consequences.

Beyond affect or pathos, beyond spontaneity defended and preserved, we are given the chance to *enact* something by being asked to make connections, even if the traces are ultimately ineffable. When we *read* the names engraved upon the September 11 Memorial more than just record them, we open a space for proximity to them, as does Sebald's narrator when he recites the names and tracks the personal histories that make up the Ferber-Lanzberg family.[25] While Sebald's narrator is not asked to sign an affidavit after departing the Kissingen cemetery, nor are we after visiting Arad's memorial, stones have been left to make contact with graves in the former, and we, if we wish, can touch the latter and physicalize it to a greater degree of permanence by penciling it—the way one does commonly when one needs to retrieve lost information.

Literary theorist and philosopher Mikhail Bakhtin will call such conscious and participatory presence an act of ответственность ("answerability"), a fair copy of a life instead of a draft version, a signature below the content of an obligation that certifies it. Philosopher Stanley Cavell will call it "acknowledgment": a declaration of presentness and frontedness. For Levinas, proximity disturbs us even before we have the opportunity to choose or initiate it. Arad's "meaningful adjacencies" thus prompt a deliberateness of agency on the part of its visitors, since, as for Sebald's pointed connectiveness of name and family (both individual and ethnocultural), the meaning behind the adjacencies is a *narrative* one, the personal stories "behind the stories" related by victims' families, stories that are effectively unavailable to us. Behind or under the names, in other words (like textures brought back through penciled rubbing) repose narratives: another reason not only to be *touched* but also to *touch*—to agitate or caress by hand, as if making physical contact with the surfaces granted virtual access to the depths, the absences, underneath.[26]

The ethics of reading in both these examples also suggests a certain *ritual* sensibility or practice, a "religious essence of language . . . which all literature awaits or commemorates," as Levinas puts it in his introduction to *Beyond the Verse.* In an early essay from 1937—before, that is, the Lanzberg-Ferbers met their fate—Levinas wrote, "as though, in the world where technology has cleared a way for us without resistance, the ritual constantly marked a pause, as though it interrupted for an instant the current that constantly connects us to things."[27] Moreover, in each instance (*The Emigrants* and *Reflecting Absence*), signifying signs (proper names) illustrate more than the transfer of information, the confirmation of identity. True, engraved names may seem to represent the very apotheosis of language that is fixed and petrified; "an epitaph," writes Anne Carson lapidarily, "is something placed upon a grave: a σῶμα that becomes a σῆμα, a body that is made into a sign."[28]

And yet, the bare record of "nothing more than the name of the Deceased with the date of birth and death" can prompt the deepest veneration; or so William Wordsworth attests in the third of his eloquent essays on epitaphs (1810).

> I know not how far the Reader may be in sympathy with me, but more awful thoughts of rights conferred, of hopes awakened, of remembrances stealing away or vanishing were imparted to my mind by that Inscription there before my eyes than by any other that it has ever been my lot to meet with upon a Tomb-stone.[29]

Over and above an indicative *Said* (*le Dit*), Levinas will insist that such recording of names thus, more important, constitutes an expressive *Saying* (*le Dire*), an always reanimated interlocution: "a sign given of this giving of signs . . . in proximity and sincerity . . . an *approach* to and a *contact* with the neighbor."[30] Or, as Wordsworth renders the solidarity inscribed by an epitaph "that thus lovingly solicits regard" (173): "this is prolonged companionship, however shadowy" (190).

THE ARGUMENT OF THIS BOOK

On display in these two memorial texts by Sebald and Arad, or through transactions prompted of their readers, then, are some of the tropes to be developed over the eight chapters of this book. They are (1) *corporeality*—making palpable contact with the literary artifact in one's hands; 2) the *tact* inside of tactility; (3) *ethical proximity*—the nearness and enigmatic tug of meaningful adjacency that stops short of coincidence (4) *difficult reading*—a semiotic order not transparently apprehended, as in Arad's network of multiple tangencies and affiliations linking the memorialized dead of September 11; (5) *limit cases* that constellate the previous elements in relief, from which, then, one may work backward toward norm or definition; and finally, (6) a "coming and going" (*va-et-vient*) between the everyday and the holy.[31]

Not on display in Arad's text, however, and analogous to the chiseled inscriptions in the Kissingen cemetery that *cannot* be made out by Sebald's narrator, are the names of thirty-six known undocumented workers, most Latino—delivery persons, waiters, cleaners, cooks and possibly those of homeless New Yorkers—who may also have perished at the World Trade Center on September 11.[32] In their case, a different reckoning and a different order of difficulty is demanded for an assemblage of names that, while listed elsewhere, do not share in the recognition of a national public memorial.[33]

Here, "ethics" means three things: (1) the supplement that challenges any systematic totality, (2) a Saying ("a modality of approach and contact," in Levinas's phrase) that exceeds the Said ("a system of nouns identifying entities"),[34] and (3) the limit-point of communication where the ethical event becomes ever more exigent. The fact that, in the absence of legally binding social identities, some names elude the reading, tracing, touching, and rubbing of embodied encounter (no inscription on bronze exists for them) would seem to return us to something like the wilderness of graves in the Kissingen cemetery—where material acknowledgment simply fails and where no "book of signs" can be held in the hand. What recognition scene, after all, can transpire here?

An analogy suggests itself with the intentional poetics of the "counter-monument" trend by German artists and architects commemorating the *Shoah*. For example, Jochen Gerz's "invisible" Holocaust Memorial, *2146 Steine—Mahnmal Gegen Rassismus* (1993), consists of pavement stones in front of Saarbrücken Castle that were inscribed and dated with the names of all the Jewish cemeteries in use in Germany before the war (the one that Sebald's narrator visits, among them), and then replaced engraved side down so that the names—and indeed the memorial itself—remained entirely concealed. The congregational communities, for which the proper names were already token remembrances, were thus made, in effect, to "go missing" yet again as a provocation to both memory and the limits of representation. The memorial itself was engineered in stealth under the cover of night, so that even its construction amounted to a trace-structure.[35]

And yet, the "*desaparecidos*" of September 11 may be quintessential figures of ethical (not to mention, political) alterity, unmemorialized though they may be. "I opened . . . he had disappeared," quotes Levinas in *Otherwise Than Being* from the *Song of Songs*,[36] in order to underscore how, through such disappearance (the trace, however, of a presencing, rather than an absence), one enters the ethical order and becomes invested as a responsible subject.[37] Even if the claim is one to which we can never adequately respond, we thereby become answerable—a common point at which the ethical projects of Emmanuel Levinas, Mikhail Bakhtin, and Stanley Cavell all happen to converge.

In this way, one's responsivity to the other person "break[s] forth" in advance of recognition or identification.[38] But further, beyond the Levinasian, Cavellian, Bakhtinian philosophical limit, when it comes to those who have been marginalized or excluded, or whose inclusion does not coextend with their proper names, to be answerable means that, "I am under obligation to offer up predicates that 'give [them] countenance,'"[39] even if that means the merest, or bare, recognition. I must, in other words, touch them somehow and figure them forth.

Sebald's and Arad's stagings of presence and absence, including the ethical remainder of illegible headstones and unrecorded victims' names, represents one of several limit-cases for the questions of remembering, writing, and reading that this book will seek to explore and for which our attendance and agency as readers in each case become a necessary dimension. These are questions for secular text and for scripture alike, for both art and ethical adventure—whose practical effects, as this book's title expresses one formula for the relationship between writing and human touch, *make the hands impure*. Known rabbinically as *metamei et ha'yadayim* (substantive, *tum'at yadayim*) that formula will be advanced in the introductory section, "Laws of Tact and Genre," which samples analyses of the corporeal by Jean-Luc Nancy, Jean-Louis Chrétien, and Jacques Derrida and opens the question of embodiment for the special situation of the book in hand.

This book divides into three parts: "Hands" (three chapters), "Genres" (three chapters), and "Languages" (one chapter), framed by this prologue, an introduction, and epilogue. A précis of the successive chapters together with a brief word on method follow. Each chapter will add another face to a multisided ethics of reading by angling it at a slightly different slant, while sustaining the focus on tact or touch. The trope of *book in hand* undergoes a series of modulations throughout: from the plain, hard facts of book physicality in Chapter 3, revisited in Chapter 5; to a set of aural or acoustic particulars placed in contiguous relation in Chapter 4; to the spatial situation of uniquely proximate bodies in Chapter 6; to a scene "before the bookcase" in Chapter 7, where language and translation are the stuff of alphabet, grapheme, and script, columns of text like a "string of black pearls."

Chapter 1, "Pledge, Turn, Prestige: Emmanuel Levinas and Edward Said," begins the argument in earnest by considering two orders of proximity: the status of the literary artwork in relation to sacred text or Holy Scripture, and the task of criticism as espoused by two formidable late twentieth-century humanists, Emmanuel Levinas and Edward Said. The chapter's title initiates a discussion of art's relation to magic; Georges Poulet's analysis of "the book" in his essay "The Phenomenology of Reading" and an early essay on aesthetics by Levinas, "Art and its Shadow" set the stage for a juxtaposition of Levinas and Said, in which Said's essays on religious and secular criticism in "The World, the Text, and the Critic," and later writings like "Timeliness and Lateness" and *Humanism and Democratic Criticism*, are interread with several of Levinas's *lectures talmudiques*.

Chapter 2 begins with a fuller explanation of *tum'at yadayim* and ends, contrapuntally, with Said's reading of Conrad's *Nostromo* from *Beginnings: Intention and Method* (1975) in dialogue with Levinas's Talmudic reading "Promised Land of Permitted Land" from 1965. Art and ethical adventure, the difficult and the holy, are traced in suspended dialectic, such that each becomes the other's uncanny neighbor. The sacred and secular, much like the "rub" between tradition and modernity that gives many of the authors and their writings discussed in this book their kinetic friction, become mobilized as partners in conversations rather than fixed at diametric poles. The coupling of Saidian and Levinasian critical consciousnesses, improbable as it may at first appear, obeys a similar logic.

Following that dialogical model, Chapter 3, "Henry Darger, Blaise Pascal, and the Book in Hand," examines the limit-case of what we might call *écriture trouvé*: found writing that has fallen into the hands and under the critical gaze of unintended readers. "Touch" and "tact" in the sense developed in the book's Introduction, provide a fulcrum for exposition. The twinning of religious and secular currents continues in this chapter, and the pairing of figures is purposefully off-kilter: mathematician and inventor, philosopher and pietist Blaise Pascal and "author, artist, sorry saint, protector of children" Henry Darger. Each figure serves to illustrate the pathos of authority and molestation (Edward Said's terms for an originating act of creative will and subsequent encroachments upon it by time and convention), as they impinge upon authorial intention and method. Their coupling is illuminated with recourse to Levinasian tropes of sensibility and "friction" in sympathetic resonance with Walter Benjamin's more familiar notion of aura.

Chapters 4–6, subtitled "Ethics of Reading" I–III, consist of separate treatments of Levinas, Bakhtin, and Cavell, a troika of philosophical anthropologies originally proposed in my first book, *Narrative Ethics* (indeed, such polyphony was as much the *subject* of that book as either narrative or ethics). What was braided there as an ethical thematics, however, the present study prefers to treat both individually and non-thematically. Each chapter situates its philosopher-reader against the background of a particular genre: the Talmud, the Novel, and Tragic drama/film, respectively. Chapter

4, "Levinas and the Talmud," coordinates two essays from *Difficult Freedom* (1976) not typically discussed together: "Name of a Dog" and Signature." Returning to questions about story first proposed in *Narrative Ethics*, this coupling is embedded in a chain of linked narrative "extracts." The chapter's second part also draws from Levinas's body of essays, aligning his final *lecture talmudique*, "Who Is One-Self" (1989) and a meditation on R. Ḥayyim of Volozhin from *In the Time of Nations* (1988).

Chapter 5, "Bakhtin and the Novel," examines the earliest major work of Mikhail Bakhtin, *Toward a Philosophy of the Deed* (1919) and an unfinished essay in aesthetic phenomenology, "Author and Hero in Aesthetic Activity" (1920–23), along with some of his very last writings from the 1970s, including "Toward a Methodology of the Human Sciences." Bakhtinian themes for an ethics of reading will be teased out by revisiting the limit-cases of Darger and Pascal, with attention once again to the question of the corporeal for acts of reading.

In Chapter 6, "Cavell and Theater/Cinema," the recurrent question of embodiment is transposed to the situation of *isolated sitting in the presence of others*, through a discussion of Stanley Cavell's aesthetic philosophy specific to the media of performance and personation, film and theater. *The World Viewed*, Cavell's 1971 book on cinema, and "The Avoidance of Love," his 1969 essay on *King Lear*, provide a new scaffold for an ethics of reading, reconceived as a drama of co-presence and witnessing.

Chapter 7 corresponds itself to the third major part of the book, "Languages." Its title, "Abyss, Volcano, and the Frozen Swirl of Words" incorporates metaphors drawn from essays by Gershom Scholem and Emmanuel Levinas about the *Aktualisierung* ("actualization") or *Verweltlichung* ("secularization") of Hebrew in the twentieth century. Restaging the interplay of "difficult" and "holy," the chapter groups together a set of modernist essays about translation and language in its material aspect: "*Gilui v'khisui balashon*," ("Revealment and Concealment in Language") from 1915, by Ḥayyim Naḥman Bialik; "*Bekenntnis über unsere Sprache*" ("Confession on the Subject of Our Language"), a 1926 "letter" from Gershom Scholem dedicated to Franz Rosenzweig; and Rosenzweig's 1926 and 1925 essays, *Die Schrift und Luther* ("Scripture and Luther") and *Neuhebräisch? Anlässlich der Übersetzung von Spinozas Kritik*.

The chapter is bookended by excerpts from Bialik's 1904 poem *Lifnei aron ha-sefarim* ("Before the Bookcase") and the remarkable hymn to the Hebrew language from 1946, *Ḥaquqot otiyyotayikh* ("Engraved Are Your Letters") by the American Hebraist Abraham Regelson. Walter Benjamin's 1916 essay, "On Language as Such and the Language of Man" and the 1923 essay on translation serve as points of reference, along with Levinas's "Poetry and Resurrection: Notes on Agnon" from 1976. "The Eyes of Language: The Abyss and the Volcano," Derrida's fervent and ingenious 1986 essay analyzing the Scholem letter, and *Monolingualism of the Other*, his 1996 text on Rosenzweig, provide a postmodern counterpoint. An epilogue reenlists Levinas for a final inventory of examples.

Each of the three chapters on Levinas, Bakhtin, and Cavell begins by emphasizing their performances as *readers*—a trebled orientation to Talmud, Novel, and Theater/Film. To that extent, the pressure placed on those performances attempts to discern the force for each of the book in hand—even when, in Cavell's case, the "book" takes the form of a movie theater, or in the Levinas chapter, a shepherding of individual vocables, "an attentive readiness for of sounds to occur." My method throughout the book prefers block quotation to paraphrase, a choice that derives in part from a scruple to let texts speak for themselves and be heard in their own voice, in part from a predilection for criticism as counterpoint. In a similar spirit, the sometimes copious chapter notes reflect a compunction that is equally the legacy of rabbinic custom— *ha'omer davar b'shem omro* ("one who says something in the name of the person who originally said it")—and the *habitus* of modern scholarship.

PROXIMITIES

As such, *To Make the Hands Impure* represents the fifth in a series of connected projects. While they have differed widely in content, each has proposed an ethical practice of reading across a range of disciplinary areas.[40] Unfolded from book to book, the cycle is unified by a common signature methodology, something I have variously called "facing," "neighboring," or "proximity," terminology (loosely) adapted from the writings of Emmanuel Levinas. The figure of Levinas has loomed large over the entire enterprise, no matter the particular disciplinary vectors of each book. But I have also described that same method as "dialogical," in the spirit of Bakhtin's favored practice, and as an expression of the Cavellian concept of "acknowledgment." In the present book, I revisit all three figures, partly in allegiance to the original vision of *Narrative Ethics* but also to sustain a methodological difference from alternate models of ethical criticism or rhetorical ethics in current vogue.[41]

In doing so, I am importing signature locutions from the thought-ventures of Levinas, Bakhtin, and Cavell, and applying them outside the bounds of philosophy to an interpretive project that crosses a variety of disciplinary borders. Ecologically speaking and as an academic project, *To Make the Hands Impure* thus seeks to articulate tangencies between the literary humanities and Jewish studies.[42] Whether I thus translate or traduce is a not-insignificant question for both my own declared ethical agency and for the industry of scholarship on all three figures that understands its critical imperative to be disciplinarily driven. To sharpen the point, let me now invoke one literary theorist whose declared métier is ethics (he is citing yet another): "the only people to whom we should listen on the topic of ethics are those who are evidently embarrassed by their talk."

> For literary critics at least, this embarrassment can, or should, stem from taking
> ourselves as spokespersons for self-congratulatory values in reading that are

extremely difficult to state in any public language. And with this embarrassment there probably ought be some self-disgust, since our claims to understand and use ethics seek a self-promoting and perhaps unwarranted dignity for what we do, while they also displace the domain or thrills and fascinations and quirky sensualities that may be in fact what we produce for our clients.[43]

Charles Altieri's claim here is manifestly oriented toward "ethics talk" as "values talk," but the nested structure of citation that imposes its own ethical burden is perhaps even more noteworthy, at least for my own book's purposes.[44] In *To Make the Hands Impure*, "ethical *values*" are *not* what an ethics of reading primarily addresses. The ethics of reading across this book's range of chapters denotes neither the moral content nor even the moral imagination of a text or a textual tradition. Nor does it concern itself with whether this or that text is licit or illicit, virtuous and thus advantageous for its readers, or else deleterious in some way (objectionable on one moral ground or another), and thus insalubrious. Sustaining the rhetorical force of Altieri's admonition, I appeal instead, for my version of ethics talk, to the efficacy of one of Levinas's favored tropes, "proximity."

Levinas's, Bakhtin's, and Cavell's ethical philosophies are all sober perfectionist endeavors. Even though each is passionately attached to the power of a text or a canonical tradition—the *Talmud Bavli*, Shakespearean tragedy, prose fiction and poetry—their respective ethical enterprises ultimately push off the texts they may analyze in order to locate themselves *outside the text* with respect to actual interpersonal encounter in the world. I take it as granted that the two symbolic orders, the interpersonal and the intertextual, do not in any strict way correspond—that is, an ethics of reading can only mime an ethics of personhood or of action.[45] Consequently, my own emphasis on the act of reading itself at best *approximates* expressly philosophical or metaphysical insights by transposing them to quite another hermeneutic plane.

Levinas's, Bakhtin's and Cavell's ethical projects nonetheless all but command their readers to *enact*, by themselves, these authors' own finely etched acts of interpretive engagement. And indeed, as I treat these three figures here, they are positioned as first and foremost *authors and readers* over and above philosophers—hence, the warrant for my own rhetorical moves as purposefully *proximate*. It is also why this book's final chapter considers more closely the insinuating question of *translation* for a poetics of contiguity, of linguistic systems abiding side-by-side. Hence also, my preference for the trope of *staging*, where individual readings are as much a function of the framing as of the framed.

To tarry with Levinas for a moment: even an explanatory account of his philosophical thought (there are many book-length "introductions") is freighted with vying descriptive categories. Is it transcendental or a lived immediacy, or both? Does it correspond to a phenomenology or a hermeneutics, or both?[46] Is it an anthropology or a metaphorics? A critical theology or constructivist postphilosophy? Is it Hebrew or

Greek? Which genealogy, which history of ideas, is most apposite for contextualizing its stake in what Jürgen Habermas calls the (Western, Hellenic-Germanic) philosophical discourse of modernity: a distinctly postmodern tradition, or a more restrictively Judaic one, instead? And then, *which* Judaic one, exactly: rabbinic-Talmudic, *Wissenschaftlich*-modern, or even Mitnagdic-pietistic?[47] While they may stand over Levinasian philosophy *ab ovo usque ad mala*, these are not, however, questions that my book will tackle. Nevertheless, one may still wonder whether they do not still inflect the specific questions about reading explored here.

To that end, let me offer a clear statement of purpose about method. Strictly speaking, pairing texts and making them ostensibly co-present does not obey the "asymmetric" structure that Levinas's rigorous ethical syntax of proximity would demand. The pairing, for example, of philosopher Blaise Pascal and outsider artist Henry Darger is certainly eccentric; but the conjunction, as I outline it in Chapter 3, does *not* correspond, in Levinas's model of transcendent ethical relation between persons, to the exclusively vertical axis where "height" (master and teacher) and "destitution" (widow and orphan) define the condition of alterity.[48] This represents but one example of the hindrance to be encountered in a free application of Levinas's philosophical thought to the situation of reading or to reading practice(s). Or rather, one is free to do so; but the freedom would be less than "difficult," in Levinas's (a)stringent sense. Yet, it is less in Levinas's thought (or, for that matter, Cavell's or Bakhtin's) that this book invests its particular ethical claims than in his own *practice*—but not quite a philosophy—of reading.[49]

I refer to this practice and its critical premises as a *staging*, just as I understand the praxis of both scriptural and secular works, of Talmudic and literary texts alike, as a *self-staging*, a testing of premises, an actualization of intention and design.[50] To read, in Levinasian fashion, is to *stage* transmission and the task of interpretation, in the various lexicographic senses that word connotes: to exhibit or present, to produce or mount, to arrange and carry out. Latin *staticum* is the etymon for all these transitive meanings, and in the spirit of Levinas, reading can be erected as "a place for standing," as much a mode of accountability as of positioning. Staging texts or traditions on the blocked space of nearness can also be construed as an exercise in sonority—as a programmatically *contrapuntal* criticism is commonly associated with the work of Edward Said, a resonating space for the harmonic possibilities of orchestrated readings.

To read in this fashion, with the critic stationed at the podium as conductor or ensconced in his booth like a sound-engineer, is thus to read *after* Levinas, *after* Bakhtin, and *after* Cavell. My attraction to the concept of "staging" makes additional sense as it likewise resonates with Bakhtin's focus on the speaking person in the novel (a staging of discourse) and with Cavell's preoccupation with dramas that are quite literally staged or viewed.[51] By way of defending this conceit—the rhetorical idiom of "in Levinasian fashion"—I cite an anecdote related by Salomon Malka in his biography of Levinas, which conveys what I intend in this book as a general principle of *approximation*:

> We spoke one day about the names of God as they are found in Jewish tradition.
> There was one he did not know, namely *Kavyakhol*, which I told him my father
> used sometimes [: a] word . . . found in rabbinic literature. Literally it means:
> "Making necessary allowances." Or more simply, "So to speak." So to speak. Like
> an Otherwise said. Or an otherwise than being. He liked the expression very
> much. He repeated *Kavyakhol, Kavyakhol,* like a candy melting in his mouth.[52]

This "as it were" or "so to speak" is the rabbinic counterpart to the *comme si* ("as if")
in Levinas's own philosophical rhetoric—"sheltering the nominative from the predicate," as Susan Yager expresses it in a lovely phrase, "giving us 'not knowing, but
proximity.'"[53]

Accordingly, when I invoke Stanley Cavell's signature notions of acknowledgment
and staged witnessing in a theater to describe the ethical conditions that impinge
upon the act of reading, or his trope of "attunement" to elaborate my own textual
pairings; or when I transpose Bakhtin's language of "outsideness" and "the hero" from
the strictly textual plane to the scene of reading, I take an acknowledged, but I think,
permitted liberty. If the attempted result in each case succeeds as an *altered reading*—
in the double sense of the practice or event of reading "made other" and the changed
contours of one text in pointed coordination with another—one feels the Levinasian
or Cavellian or Bakhtinian warrant.[54] That is to say, I have tried to contrive a critical
practice that draws close to Levinas, Cavell, and Bakhtin but stops short of parroting
or "applying" them. At bottom, I agree with critic James Wood that most, if not all,
criticism (including the fully philosophical or quasi-philosophical kind) "is itself
metaphorical in movement, because it deals in likeness."[55] The likeness there—the
proximity—bridges authorial description and our critical redescription of it; it lies
between the writer's textual imagination and the imagination we exercise as readers,
listeners, or viewers.

A model for what I have in mind here can be found in Desmond Manderson's aptly
titled book on tort jurisprudence, *Proximity, Levinas, and the Soul of Law.* Manderson
follows two rules of thumb that parallel this book's method:

1. He discovers and configures a deep co-implication between a Levinasian
   concept—in this case, ethical proximity—and the modern concept of
   negligence or "duty of care" in common law spelled out paradigmatically
   by Lord Atkins's judgment in *Donoghue v. Stevenson* (1932) as "the neighbor
   principle," and revisited more recently by the High Court of Australia in
   tort cases from 1984 to 2000 at whose heart is a jurisprudential reformula-
   tion of the neighbor principle as legal *proximity.*

2. He explains Levinas's concept with regular reference to artworks, both verbal and plastic: Borges's story *"El acercamiento a Almotásim,"* Antony Gormley's concept piece *Field for the British Isles* (1993), and Henry Moore's sculpture *Moon Head* (1964).

The first of these loose parallels, "The Approach to al-Mu'tasim," is a characteristically Borgesian text more or less encapsulated by its title, a fictitious novel by a Hindu barrister about a law student whose life becomes "the insatiable search for a human soul by means of the delicate glimmerings of reflections this soul has left in others."[56] "The man called Al Mu'tasim," whoever he is, is never found or arrived at, but rather, is only approached through a set of traces—the literary transposition of Levinas's trope of *l'approche* or *la proximité*. Similarly, Gormley's *Field for the British Isles*, a sculpture comprising forty thousand clay figurines with eyeholes, made by a hundred or so people from the community around the Ibstock brick factory where the figures were kiln-fired, gives concrete expression to the Levinasian trope of *visage*, described by the artist as "twenty-five tons of clay energised by fire, sensitised by touch and made conscious by being given eyes . . . a field of gazes which looks at the observer making him or her its subject."[57]

Both these examples depend on thematization: an artwork is made to translate a philosophical concept. Manderson's explanation for his third point of reference, however, comes closest to my own purposes here, for it speaks to the critical act of pairing itself as bringing something about:

> We should not be surprised at he juxtaposition of these two works, of the Levinas of 1961 with the Moore of 1964. It is not a question of intention, the conscious appropriation and interpretation of the ideas of others to serve our purposes. But neither is the juxtaposition of artist and philosopher a coincidence. It is an instance of proximity itself, of a breath one feels before one is conscious of its presence. . . . The connection between the perspectives of Emmanuel Levinas and Henry Moore—between the discoursing mouth of the one and the sculpting hand of the other—lies in their proximity: the head and the hand have contaminated each other infinitely, not totally. (180)[58]

In parallel fashion, the coupling in this book of works *as* lessons in proximity—manuscripts by Darger and Pascal, essays in criticism by Levinas and Said, a passage about a cemetery from a novel by Sebald and a memorial by Arad that *houses* a cemetery at Ground Zero, the *Talmud Bavli* and a Conrad novel—pairings such as these lend themselves to this same notion of altered reading, of the "holy" and "difficult" as neighbor-strangers. As Manderson pinpoints instructive affinities between the legal doctrine of Proximity and ethical *proximité*, so, through analogies with or between the "case studies" he finds in art, he attempts "not to illustrate something but to learn something" (20). This book aspires to a similar logic of practice.

Likeness *shared* by Levinas, Cavell, Bakhtin in contraposition is quite another matter, however, since the three do not approximate each other either biographically or culturally, notwithstanding various contiguities of thought. In arranging their respective discursive timbres, the critic-revoicer is perhaps better understood as a kind of audio equalizer: Edward Said would say, "a contrapuntalist," Bakhtin, a "polyphonist," and Cavell, an agent of "directed motion."[59] At any rate, the challenge of such inter-reading resists the easy harmonies of unison, of "recolored and reassembled" sound. Scoring for any likenesses, negotiating between dialogic forces alternately authoritative and internally persuasive (Bakhtin); across the range of sonorities that attune strings to wood (Levinas); the trick is to find the right pitches of voice (Cavell), the instructive syncopation and resonance-cum dissonance in the elaboration of that counterpoint.[60] Call it criticism's art of the fugue, its experiment in two-part invention.

So far in this book, that off-rhyme practice has taken the textual form of the Sebald passage from *The Emigrants* sounding against Arad's September 11 Memorial. It informs the contraposition of Nancy, Derrida, and Chrétien in the introductory chapter, Said and Levinas in Chapters 1 and 2, Pascal and Henry Darger in Chapter 3, the two of them again with Bakhtin in Chapter 5, Cavell's reflections on film and a movie by Martin Scorsese in Chapter 6, and the more polyphonic ensemble of Bialik, Scholem, Rosenzweig, Levinas, and Derrida in Chapter 7. Since Levinas's voice is by far the dominant one in this assemblage, I feel I should venture a final word about its presence in my work overall.

THE LEVINAS EFFECT

I would hardly be alone in remarking on the polymorphous recourse to Emmanuel Levinas in the current world of academic ventures. In 1996, Colin Davis's *Introduction to Levinas* coined the phrase "Levinas effect" to describe the expansive application of his work to multiple fields: "the ability of the Levinassian text to appear differently to each of its readers [which] colours acts of both appropriation and criticism."[61] I am not sure the fault lies with the text's absorptive or adhesive properties, however. "To make the hands impure"—a formulation that I freely acknowledge *I* adapt here with license—possesses a peculiarly apt valence for the "colouring" that eclectic or tendentious approaches to Levinas imprint on his body of work. The following example is representative: "Finally, and perhaps to the chagrin of Levinas, I'd like to suggest that the radically exterior Levinasian ethical subject is always a *junkie,* moving constantly outside itself in the diachronic movement of desire."[62] The chagrin is perhaps not Levinas's alone.

At the same time, however, it must be acknowledged that few intellectual figures open onto so many different horizons of thought and endeavor, due to the varied predilections Levinas himself indulged, but also to the contiguous character of the ethical enterprise itself.[63] Confining it strictly to Levinas's avowed concerns, we would have to say that it touches on ethical metaphysics, philosophy, Jewish philosophy and Judaism, theology, aesthetics, biblical and rabbinic source texts, the Holocaust, and what he called "the holy." That his thought also demonstrates tangents to politics and history, law, medicine, and business, pedagogy, literary and cultural studies, film and photography, psychology and psychoanalysis, multilingualism and translation, conflict resolution and interreligious dialogue, bioethics and environmental ethics, anthropology and sociology, ancient philosophy and modern intellectual history; that it lends itself, as well, to rapprochement with a host of figures across a range of different discourses as his complementary (or non-congruent) *others*: all this bespeaks a protean body of work and the plenitude of its possible applications, which may well be unique for all that.[64]

A kind of secular Torah in need of always-renewed exegesis, Levinas's work continues to generate a steady stream of academic monographs. While perhaps no specialized treatment has the last word, the best, in my view, are Abrahamic like Manderson's rather than Odyssean; they leave home rather than return to it. Many either address a guild readership or (re)introduce Levinas to wider audiences; a few mobilize Levinas's own work outside and elsewhere as so many other-directed "essays on exteriority"— the subtitle, in fact, of *Totality and Infinity*. That particular orientation describes this book's own approach and method, which also affords an opportunity to revisit a methodological apparatus from my first book and recalibrate some of its beveled edges. While the plaiting, as I styled it then, of Levinas, Cavell, and Bakhtin is one I still take a certain pride in having devised, I believe the distinct strands now call for stricter differentiation.

ACKNOWLEDGMENTS

> Le discours interrompu rattrapant ses propres ruptures, c'est le livre. Mais les livres
> ont leurs propres destins, ils appartiennent à un monde qu'ils n'englobent pas, mais
> qu'ils reconnaissent en s'écrivant et en s'imprimant et en se et en se faisant préfacer
> et en se faisant précéder d'avant-propos. Ils s'interrompent et en appellent à
> d'autres livres et s'interprètent en fin de compte dans un dire distinct du dit.
> (*Autrement qu'être ou au-delà de l'essence*, 217)

> A book is interrupted discourse catching up with its own breaks. But books have
> their fate; they belong to a world they do not include, but recognize by being
> written and printed and by being prefaced and getting themselves preceded with
> forewords. They are interrupted, and call for other books and in the end are
> interpreted in a saying distinct from the said. (*Otherwise Than Being; Or, Beyond
> Essence*, 171)[65]

I quoted the preceding passage as an epigraph to *Narrative Ethics*, whose fate, not surprisingly, was the very corrigibility to which Levinas attests. No less than Levinas's own books, or those of any author, mine called for other books in turn, ensuring that the dialogical work it sought to model exceeded its given limitations in method or imagination. Said calls this the dialectic of authority and molestation. It happens that some of that molestation or interruption was practiced by the successive books I myself felt compelled to write, each a further attempt to "exscribe" Levinasian thought as the ethics of reading.

To that degree, *To Make the Hands Impure* represents the latest installment in an ongoing critical "intrigue" or "adventure," Levinas's specialized words for plot.[66] The first suggests entanglement (as in its cognate, "intricacy"), while the second conveys the sense of something happening to someone—both, then, apt descriptions for a storyline I have, evidently, yet to unravel fully. But as this prologue has now reached its limit and calls for interruption, let me do so by recording my acknowledgments before turning to the introductory chapter about rabbinic and postmodern accounts of touch.

In *Totality and Infinity*, Levinas observes that, "the first teaching of the teacher is [the] very presence as teacher from which representation comes" (100). I must therefore single out and thank Jo Keroes, whose liberal presence got me started on my professional way after the nearly decade-long fermata of fingering a taxi's steering wheel by day and the book in hand at night. Levinas also speaks of "a being taught in a non-maieutic fashion" (204); and for that gift of exteriority, I thank Philip Fisher, who trained me to discern how it is books themselves that teach us how to read them. I have benefited subsequently from a number of such presences, some of whom were my colleagues, some my students, and some the literary critical company kept outside the classroom, many of whose names appear in the bibliography and footnotes to this book. I owe them all my gratitude.

My experiences in middle school in the Bronx, New York, were perhaps the most formative of all, as I have been bidden recently to revisit. There, I think I first learned to connect ethics and reading, even if that connection was embodied, strangely enough, as fetish rather than (difficult) freedom, and even if it took the next twenty years to discover truer, more faithful symbioses once I took up the vocation of teaching myself, where what one wants is not one's own voice back in copy speech (Frost), but countertext, original response.

In his preface to *Totality and Infinity*, Levinas also identifies the influence on that work of German-Jewish philosopher Franz Rosenzweig as *trop souvent présént dans ce livre etre cité* ("too often present to be cited"). In the language of midrash: *mashal le-mah ha-davar domeh* (to what is this to be compared)? As far as my own book is concerned, and certainly beyond its borders, such powers of ubiquity and influence, as endlessly intriguing as they are adventurous, belong ultimately to my wife, Miriam Udel. That Levinas elsewhere calls this kind of indebtedness "liturgical" is only too fitting for someone so gifted at fusing the work of a religious textual tradition—its *ergon*—to the humane public spaces—the *leiton*—within which she practices the teaching vocation. I locate myself there as well, for I am that beneficiary of the "very presence as teacher" who is also fortunate enough to be her life companion.

Expressed midrashically,

אמר בשם ר' אחא, יו"ד שנטל הקב"ה מאמנו שרה שנקראה שרי ניתן חציו על שרה וחציו על אברהם

Rabbi Huna said, quoting Rabbi Aḥa: The letter ׳ *yod* removed from Sarai's name (to make "Sarah" in Gen. 17) was divided into two letters; one ה *hei* was added to Abram (to make "Abraham") and the other ה *hei* to Sarah (*Talmud Yerushalmi*, Tractate *Sanhedrin* 13a; also *Midrash Rabbah* 47:1).

Because letters also signify numbers in Hebrew, the numerical value of the subtracted ׳ (10) was divided into two supplements of ה (5) and then distributed between husband and wife. Yet, it was from her that this new enhancement to both names became even possible; he became amplified, became more than himself, only due to *her* plenitude, her capaciousness, her expanse. "The faithful return grace not for what they receive but for the very fact that they can return grace"[67]: this, for Levinas, defines liturgy, and just so it names my own boundless gratitude to my wife in *das Wunder umschliesst die Beide* ("the very heart of wonder").[68]

Part of the manifestly idiosyncratic nature of my project lies in the fact that its topic—the ethics of reading as the touch of the book in one's hand—holds *it* to a peculiar (and for its readers, a peculiarly self-conscious), standard. I must therefore acknowledge David Suchoff for his incomparable advocacy and tact. Likewise, no book so conceived could have enjoyed a more responsive hermeneutic of generosity than was bestowed by my extraordinary readers at Fordham University Press, whose editorial staff—Thomas Lay, Eric Newman, Katie Sweeney, and Kem Crimmins—were also exemplary. The late Helen Tartar, whom I knew all too briefly, deserves my special gratitude for her receptivity and vision for the book; I am saddened that she could not see—and handle—it in print. Danielle McClellan, Gregory McNamee, Natalie Reitano, Ann Peters, David Lavinsky, Harry Ballan, Carl Feit, R. Saul Berman, and Adrienne Asch *a'h* graciously extended editorial advice, encouragement, curiosity, and sonority when one or all were needed.

Typically, a book of this length and scope takes shape in installments and over time: preliminary article-versions of individual chapters, conference presentations, venues for scholarly colloquy, a skein of interlocutors for the various strands of the project itself are the norm for incubation. The writing of this book is *durchkomponiert*, and took shape in a burst of concentrated intensity once the flow temporarily dammed up by administrative responsibilities was released. I am therefore grateful to the Tam Institute for Jewish Studies at Emory University for the semester's residence that made the writing of these pages possible, and to the Provost's office of Yeshiva University, for the term leave and subvention funds that made their publication feasible.

Finally, on a campus visit in which some of this book's postulates were provisionally circulated, an isolated lesson in tact stood out that enabled their felt sense to be brought home most hauntingly. Through the fortuitous pairing of two items from the library's special collection, Abraham Joshua Heschel's 1933 *Anmelde Buch* from the Hochschule für die Wissenschaft des Judentums, and his 1935 *Arbeitsbuch* (Nazi identity document) briefly passed through my hands. For the few moments while I fingered them, I was their custodian, superadding my touch, stained—and arrested—by theirs.

Laws of Tact and Genre

Writing, in its essence, touches upon the body.

—Jean-Luc Nancy

All books in the Bible defile the hands.

—*Mishnah Yadayim* 3:5

For the meaning of the voice perishes with the sound; truth latent in the mind is wisdom that is hid and treasure that is not seen; but truth which shines forth in books desires to manifest itself to every impressionable sense. It commends itself to the sight when it is read, to the hearing when it is heard, and moreover in a manner to the touch, when it suffers itself to be transcribed, bound, corrected, and preserved.

—Richard de Bury, *Philobiblion* (1345)

"Those are very expensive books."

"Don't be so nervous, John. People are supposed to touch them."

"There is touching," John said sententiously, "and there is touching."

—Philip Roth, *Goodbye, Columbus*

TACTILITY AND REVERENCE

In the now-severely reduced Jewish population on the island of Cuba (a high estimate of 1500 persons out of eleven million total), it was not uncommon for the quorum of ten required for public prayer in the small Orthodox synagogue of Havana to consist of "*ocho hombres, la Torah, y Dios*," with the Torah scroll—and God—standing in for the missing men.[1] In Havana's Conservative Sinagoga Bet Shalom (also known as "El Patronato"), the situation used to be even starker: "For more than 30 years, the daily minyan usually consisted of seven elderly men and three Torah scrolls placed in chairs in a small chapel."[2]

While skirting the outer boundary of a decidedly anti-idolatrous system of belief and practice, this phenomenon (albeit irregular and obviously still exclusionary toward women), exemplifies a deep relationship between human subject and material entity in Jewish religious self-understanding.[3] Ritual objects in daily use such as *tzitzit* (fringes) and *tefillin* are the objects of tactile reverence when kissed at specified junctures during prayer; so are *mezuzot* (doorway scrolls), when persons come and go, and *sefarim* (religious books) when taken up or put down. Women, whose possibilities for ritual object-relations in Jewish worship are curtailed, nevertheless perform a quintessentially Levinasian gesture of proximity, when, after Sabbath candles are lit, they circle their hands as if to spread the flame's light that can't be touched.[4]

In the world of ceremonial practice, a *sefer* Torah is a consecrated artifact accorded maximal dignity and modesty: covered when not in immediate use; always handed, received and held with the right hand; never shown one's back if it can be helped, or left unattended; carried erect during its procession while the congregation rises in turn; distinguished by reverential pointing and mimed touching when elevated after recitation.[5] With a scroll—that fusion of *nomos* and sacred history—thus enabled to "count" as if it were another person in prayer, what do we deduce about the contiguous boundary of scripture and self more generally? How, in short, do persons and scrolls converge?

On the occasion of his father's *yortsayt* in 1959, Rabbi Joseph B. Soloveitchik gave a lecture in Yiddish entitled "A Yid iz Geglaykhn tzu a Seyfer Toyre" (A Jew Is Likened to a Torah Scroll), which entertained that very question. The lecture's first half examines the relevant halakhic sources (tractates *Shabbat*, *Megillah*, *Bava Kama*, *Kiddushin*, *Berakhot*, *Sanhedrin*, and *Yoma* in the *Talmud Bavli*) that establish what R. Soloveitchik calls the "axiomatic" analogy between human person and inscribed parchment.[6] In the second, more philosophical portion of the lecture, that analogy prompts a more expansive consideration of the concept *qedushat yisrael* (the holiness of the human):

> A Torah scroll does not absorb any holiness from the text alone, despite the fact that the words comprise the Word of God. For only the human act sanctifies, creates holiness. We require [in the production of Torah scrolls, *tefillin*, and *mezuzot*] that the processing of the parchment be done for the sake of the *mitzvah* and that the writing be done for the sake of the *mitzvah*.[7]

This processing (known as *'ibbud*) which allows the ink to be absorbed onto the parchment surface, and this inscription, (both construed as *li-shemah*, "done for the sake of the *mitzvah*") differ from and complement one another as do "external" Torah scroll and "internal" Torah scroll.[8] Just as the various *halakhot* oblige the mechanical act of writing to be sanctified through calligraphy "which reflects the characteristic features and qualities of that person—their emotional spurts, visions and dreams, pride and falls, happiness and grief, courage and despair, and fear and excitement for redemption"—so a scribe is obliged to "enunciate a word before it is written down"[9] (the Torah being declaimed as it is inscribed), thus translating a wholly internal "personal, living Torah" into an embodied and transpersonal scroll.

> When a person pours into his handwriting all of what his soul contains, he fills the cold, black letters, written on dead parchment, with holiness. At that point, the ink is transformed into a black fire and the parchment into a white fire. The parchment and the letters are uplifted with human passion, warmed with the human soul, and become holy. Even the Holy Names cannot be raised to the level of holiness if a human being does not sanctify the four letters of the Names. In a word, holiness in all realms cannot be realized without human initiative.[10]

R. Soloveitchik's analysis stops short of the parallel construction from the reverse direction, as it were, of contaminable transmission between Torah scroll and person that rabbinic law codifies under the category of *tum'at yadayim*, "impurity of the hands." But along with the picture of communal worship where scrolls can double for persons, it sets the stage for a modulation from the realm of resemblance or analogy to an actual contact-zone where touch makes all the difference. What R. Soloveitchik describes as the dialectical flow of inside/outside—"That [potential] sanctity in the externalities, which waits to be imbued into the objective-concrete forms of place, time, parchment, and letters, is born in the subjective internalities of human existence: everything that exists on the outside exists on the inside"[11]—I wish to reframe as the stuff of contiguity and tactility: of the *side-by-side*.[12] First, however, let me introduce a few specifics about what the *Halakhah* means by impurity in order to lay groundwork for a fuller treatment in Chapter 2.

TUM'AH (טומאה)

The Sages of the Oral Torah enacted several categories of prohibited tactile contact according to descending degrees and character of ritual uncleanness, as derived from biblical proscription. If, for instance, a utensil touches a corpse of a non-kosher animal (or a kosher animal not ritually slaughtered), it has the status of "first-degree" impurity (*rishon*) and can transmit impurity to the "second-degree" (*sheni*).[13] But halakhic properties of purity and impurity do not follow from notions of defilement in any obvious sense, since *tum'ah* is entirely intangible. Rather, we might see the distinction between them as situated on a fault-line between life and death, or between integral and particulate. Whole, complete, organic entities "contract" and thus transmit impurity. A corpse, a dead creature on the order of an insect or lizard, and human semen typify three halakhic sources of *tum'ah* ("impurity"), which transmit it in turn to four categories of entities: persons, articles (utensils or clothing), foodstuffs, and liquids.

But strangely enough, among contaminant articles and objects, books and scrolls of Holy Writing (*sifrei/kitvei haqodesh*) were also decreed to possess the capacity, as the Sages expressed it, "to make the hands impure" (*metamei yadayim*).[14] Correlatively, human hands themselves were also accorded a special status according to their propensity to busy themselves with things.[15] Such classification ensured that holy objects like *terumah* (a raised offering) or *qodesh* (a hallowed vessel) not be handled casually and be accorded the proper respect commanded by their *qedushah*, or holiness. Were they to be touched by impure hands (or by ritually clean rinsed hands from which one's attention becomes diverted) they would be rendered unfit; the hands themselves required ritual ablution or immersion in a *mikveh*.

And yet, counterintuitively, holy books possessed the power to taint persons, not the other way around.[16] One might think that "touch" generally should be the relevant halakhic category here.[17] Hebrew נגיעה /*negiah*—more properly, קרבה/*qrevah* ("coming near") in earlier sources—refers by custom to physical contact between the sexes (*la'arayot* and *b'derekh ḥiba*) as biblically proscribed in two Levitical commandments and elaborated further by the *Bavli* (*bShabbat* 13a), Maimonides's *Mishneh Torah* (*Is-surei Biah* 21), and later law codes, e.g., *Shulḥan 'Arukh* (*Even HaEzer* 20–21).[18]

An etiology for *tuma't yadayim* in the *Bavli*, Tractate *Shabbat 14a*, foregrounds a detail about storage places for Torah scrolls in the Mishnaic period. The customary practice was to stow them with *terumah*, sanctified grain, since both were considered ritually holy. However, because vermin would eat the grain (which consequently had to be destroyed) and gnaw on the scrolls, the latter were given the status of *sheni l'tum'ah* (second-degree impurity) and stored elsewhere.[19] Scholars have been understandably piqued by the linguistic apotropaism that thus transforms defilement into a sign of sanctity.

An alternate exposition in *bMegillah* that more closely follows Tractate *Yadayim* in the Mishnah proposes that the classification has to do instead with the texts' intrinsic *qedushah* (their "aura," so to speak), which had a direct consequence for the all-important question of canonicity. Could books that did not mention the name of God, for instance like Song of Songs and The Book of Esther, or that skirted close to non-Jewish philosophies, like Ecclesiastes, be included alongside the Torah and the Prophets at part of the biblical text corpus?[20]

By a somewhat roundabout operation, just as holiness (of scripture) became attached to a strictly cultic concern for purity (of object), criteria for canonicity became connected to those for sanctity and purity, and the sign of Scripture's authorized status became its capacity to make the hands impure. Texts not intrinsically holy, that do not reveal "the voice of God" and that the Mishnah calls *hamiram*—like the works of Homer (*Yad.* 4:6) or the book of *Ben Sira* (Tosefta on *Yad.* 2:13)[21]—were thus decreed *not* to defile the hands.

And so, against the background of a sanctified canon read and understood in conjunction with a codified system of law, the formulation also came to mark the borderline between one kind of text (scriptural, holy, sacred) and another (worldly, secular, "merely" literary). Rabbinical commentary even elaborates the distinction in discussions about the status of translations from Hebrew to other languages, debating whether acts of translation retain the religious qualities of the original and whether such change of state might not profane them somehow.[22]

How might we moderns think about the paradox of a holy scripture that not only contaminates or pollutes but also does so in counterintuitive relation to everyday texts—let's call them literature—that do not thus transmit "defilement?" Following the track laid out by R. Soloveitchik, we can think about a Torah scroll's intrinsic holiness as not only embodying divine speech but also as a function of *embodiment* itself in its interhuman dimension.[23] In parallel, Emmanuel Levinas, two of whose Talmudic readings discussed in the next chapter comment on *tum'at yadayim*, will identify the Torah as a "holy writing before being a sacred text."

The Torah represents an always renewable exegesis and transmission rather than "the dogmatic narration of some supernatural or sacred origin," precisely because it coordinates one self with its others, "commands and vows" me to them.[24] In his interview with Phillip Nemo from 1984 that discusses the power of secular literature, Levinas attests to the book in hand as expressing an especially formative relation: "I think that in the great fear of bookishness, one underestimates the "ontological" reference of the human to the book that is commonly taken for a source of information, a "tool" of learning, a handbook, whereas it is rather a modality of our being" (*Ethics and Infinity*, 21).[25]

It is against this background of Levinas's and R. Soloveitchik's metaphysical canvases that we might visualize the prayer services at the synagogue in Havana: seven persons softly intoning prayer in stationary position, mutually adjacent, vouchsafed to each other and to God at that moment because along with them, three stationary and erect Torah scrolls complete their collectivity.

Albeit on the more specialized plane of canonized scripture, the ritual phenomenon of "impurity of the hands" similarly situates person and text in immediate, even continuous material relation. *Tum'at yadayim* as connected with *sifrei haqodesh* thus anticipates R. Soloveitchik's and Levinas's arguments that inscription is fundamentally bound up with the interhuman, or the human with the holy. It also suggests a transferential property of exposition and commentary inasmuch as a Torah scroll (or canonized scripture) does not exist secluded from human contact—an inert totem or untouchable sacral object—but, on the contrary, is *imbued* with touch as the sanctifying effect of transitivity for reading eyes, reciting mouths, listening ears, and hands that hold.[26]

To put the question another way and thus articulate the boundary between religious practice on the one hand, and the sacred-inside (or alongside)-the secular that we see in Sebald's and Arad's aesthetic designs on the other: what happens when a work reposes in my hands or when it "holds" me holding it; when I thus touch or am touched? What sort of *alteration* (ethical othering) follows from being neighbored to it, and it to me, in sensible proximity? What phenomenological meaning can be assigned to those book-holding hands,[27] even in the baldly instrumental instances of e-books and tablets, keystrokes and mouse clicks in a digital future that aspires to be "frictionless," where media technology—not completely unlike scrolls of the law—effectively stands in for human presence against an ostensibly "platform-neutral" horizon?[28]

What is so singular about the combination of hand and book, each its own metonym of the human, the two together conducting a circuit of tactile, cognitive, and affective energies? Finally, how and where do we mark a boundary that philosopher Jean-Luc Nancy would call *partagé*, both shared and sheared, conjoining and disjunctive, contiguous at the limit-point of embodiment where persons and material texts converge on each other? Those are some of the inquiries this book undertakes. While I elaborate the concept of *tum'at yadayim* at much greater length in the next chapter, I would like to dwell just a little longer here on the specifically *corporeal* connection between book and hand by briefly considering examples from literary fiction, and then segue to a contemporary discourse on the sense of touch in work by Jean-Luc Nancy, Jacques Derrida, and Jean-Louis Chrétien.

BOOKS IN HANDS

One of the less obtrusive but still vividly tactile scenes involving hands in Charles Dickens's truly hands-obsessed novel *Great Expectations*[29] features "the Educational scheme of course established by Mr. Wopsle's great-aunt," in which "the pupils formed in line and buzzingly passed a ragged book from hand to hand."

> The book had an alphabet in it, some figures and tables, and a little spelling—that is to say, it had had once. As soon as this volume began to circulate, Mr. Wopsle's great-aunt fell into a state of coma; arising either from sleep or a rheumatic paroxysm. The pupils then entered among themselves upon a competitive examination on the subject of Boots, with the view of ascertaining who could tread the hardest upon whose toes. This mental exercise lasted until Biddy made a rush at them and distributed three defaced Bibles (shaped as if they had been unskillfully cut off the chump-end of something), more illegibly printed at the best than any curiosities of literature I have since met with, speckled all over with ironmould, and having various specimens of the insect world smashed between their leaves.[30]

Here, the book in hand is an illegible, moldy relic and part of the general chaos, staged in inverse proportion of material and cultural value to the book Dickens's *readers* are holding in their hands just then—making the irony of a defaced Bible *inside* the novel all the more piquant. Half a century later, Walter Benjamin's *Berliner Kindheit um Neunzehnhundert*, allows us to witness a second scene of classroom reading, materially different from Pip's recollection:

> My favorites came from the school library. They were distributed in the lower classes. The teacher would call my name, and the book then made its way from bench to bench; one boy passed it on to another, or else it traveled over the heads

until it came to rest with me, the student who had raised his hand. Its pages bore
traces of the fingers that had turned them. The bit of corded fabric that finished off
the binding, and that stuck out above and below, was dirty. But it was the spine,
above all, that had had things to endure—so much so, that the two halves of the
cover slid out of place themselves, and the edge of the volume formed ridges and
terraces. Hanging on its pages, however, like Indian summer on the branches of
the trees, were sometimes fragile threads of a net in which I had once become
tangled when learning to read.[31]

Where the books Pip recalls are obliterated by human contact or disuse, the book
in Benjamin's memoir bears the impress (fingerprints or yellowed paper) of the hands
in which it has been deposited and through which, transferred. As Marina Levina
nicely observes, the book's passage from desk to desk—its transmission—follows conspicuously upon a call, an address.[32] Arriving in Benjamin's child hands, its pages hold
out the possibility of "entanglement": "*ich einst bein Lesenlernern mich* verstrickt *hatte*."
Both scenes, negatively in the first instance and with more emulative force in the
second, illustrate what I mean by "transitivity."

Two last tangents will drive the point home. When the telegraphist heroine of
Henry James's 1898 novella *In the Cage* reads and marks—by actually tallying—the
words in a message handed to her by a customer to whom she has become attached,
the narrator tells us that "she indeed felt her progressive pencil, dabbing as if with a
quick caress, the marks of his own, put life into every stroke."[33] Telegraph messages
are not novels or even novellas, to be sure; yet, James has framed the one by the example
of the other. If Braille and other glyph-based writing systems that require the press of
fingertips to make meaning necessarily abandon eyesight for touch as the sense-faculty
that "reads," then this *dabbing as if with a quick caress* all but forces into consciousness
the customarily unactivated tactility with which we read books by *disregarding* their
materiality.

For, we precisely *do not* count or progressively pencil ("dab") the words that accumulate across the page in front of us—graphemes whose strokes nevertheless solicit
a mode of caress, like tracing, that we naturally withhold. And as to the finger-work
demanded by Braille itself (and in distant echo of Levinas): "I have read and re-read
it," wrote Helen Keller of her Bible, "until in many parts the pages have faded
out—I mean, my fingers have rubbed off the dots, and I must supply whole verses
from memory."[34] John Macy, Keller's biographer, captures such a moment for us from
the poignant vantage of the eavesdrop: "The time that one of Miss Keller's friends realizes most strongly that she is blind, is when he comes on her suddenly in the dark
and hears the rustle of her fingers across the page."[35]

As it happens, the advent of Braille parallels a development in nineteenth-century
book culture implicitly evoked by the other three preceding scenes of reading,
which Leah Price, in *How To Do Things with Books in Victorian Britain*, has dubbed

"nonreading." One form it took in narrative poetics was that of "novelistic narrators replacing the mental act of reading by the manual gesture of holding, in order to repudiate the omniscience that could penetrate characters' thoughts."[36] Price also explains the related and relatively new phenomenon of readers becoming touch-averse:

> By the nineteenth century . . . the cheapening of both paper and literacy opened the less pleasant possibility of bumping into one's social inferiors within the readership of a particular book, or the handlership of a particular copy of a book. The traditional fear that a text might poison its readers' minds was now joined by a newer anxiety that poor, sick, or dirty fellow handlers might infect their bodies (15).

Such apotropaic sensibilities confirm, albeit negatively, the felt power of the book in hand—something that in this highly police-procedural moment of ours in popular culture we could imagine along the lines of CSI Library of Congress, where computer graphics take us into the permeable layers of page and book-cover to isolate the various "sedimentations" (Levinas's term) of human DNA.[37] More positively conveyed by an intimate relationship to books which Dickens's and Benjamin's scenes of instruction merely hint at, modernity becomes the marketplace where book's outsides begin to matter as much as their insides, or as Price puts it, a "book's material properties trump its textual content when its value (whether for use or for resale) lies in attributes orthogonal to its legibility" (8). Furthermore, as Price points out in her reading of *David Copperfield,* the Soloveitchikian analogy between person and Torah scroll finds its secular Victorian update in Dickens's multiple figurations of the human as a kind of parchment to be marked, impressed, and scarred.

> Here again, however, Dickens's metaphors draw fine distinctions between writing surfaces: the novel's media ecology reduces David to a manuscript only after assimilating him to something more like a published book bound between boards labeled not with his name but with the sign "HE BITES." (103)[38]

But Dickens's and Benjamin's scenes of formative culture, mediated by James and spiritualized by Keller at her Bible, also gesture back toward premodern precedents, when we bring to mind a set of reading practices founded upon the scriptural over and above the literary-commercial. During the Christian Middle Ages, for example, the high watermark of so much rabbinical commentary[39], writers were unabashed about the bodily interpenetration of person and book, already figured for them by incarnation, eucharist, and transfiguration in the Gospels.[40] Dante, the author of *Piers Plowman*, Richard of Bury, and Peter of Celle are just some of the many figures for whom books had faces, texts were ingestible, codices were to be "rubbed."

In a congruent Jewish commentarial tradition, it was customary for authors to be merged with the titles of their books, for example, the *Sefat Emet*, the *Ha-emek Davar*, the *Mei Shiloach*, and the *Kli Yakar*, which is how they are routinely referred to today in traditional circles of Jewish learning (as, likewise, in the folios of the tractate *Megillah* in the *Bavli*, Esther the person and Esther the biblical book are referred to interchangeably by the Talmudic masters). But the Dickens, Benjamin, and James examples also identify the modern by making that peculiar rapprochement between inside and outside or self and object wholly prosaic and secular.

Philosophers have long been intrigued by the same quotidian bifold. Since Aristotle through Descartes and Kant and after, the Western philosophical tradition has typically assigned the body both an inside and an outside, independent of whether a soul reposes within: inner and outer senses, for example, as Kant classified them in his *Anthropologie in Pragmatischer Hinsicht* (1833).[41] In twentieth-century philosophy (Husserl, Franck, and Merleau-Ponty, for example), the sense of touch has been analyzed as either limited instrumentality or expansive horizon of perception and experience, a basic disposition or structure of intentionality; theorists like Michel Foucault and Judith Butler break with the phenomenological tradition, staging or engaging the body as a "site" of sociohistorical relations that are produced or regulated, and as a vehicle of performative, "citational" self-staging.[42]

In the next section, I turn, instead, to a different strand of contemporary philosophies on touch and the body—one that, anticipated by Helen Keller's touch-reading, will enable us to begin fleshing out the *tact* in contact, the radical primacy of transitivity,[43] and set the stage for the analysis in ensuing chapters.

TOUCH: NANCY

As a particularly resistant, strange, and elusive "modality of being"—the body and touch *after* Levinas, we could say—embodiment and materiality are the special burden of two books by French philosophers from the intellectual generation succeeding Levinas's: Jean-Luc Nancy's *Corpus* and Jacques Derrida's commentary, *On Touching: Jean-Luc Nancy*. In place of no doubt more familiar and expected language for the book in hand like inscription or intimacy, Derrida and Nancy prefer, rather, to speak in terms of "exscription" and "extimacy," coinages designed to emphasize the element of exteriority each wishes to bring out in any operation of touch or tangency.

"The ontological body has yet to be thought" (15), Nancy exclaims almost in echo of Levinas. "How, then, are we to touch upon the body, rather than signify it or make it signify?" (9)—that is, if we take embodiment to constitute, in its moments, externality as such; if the body is the confounding rather than the articulation of sense boundaries; if the body marks "a limit point," if it "keeps its secret"; if "the body is a *tonus*, a tension or tending"; and if "bodies are differences . . . first and always other . . . elsewhere [and] from elsewhere?"[44]

Toward an answer, his book constructs what he calls alternately a *corpus partes extra partes* ("a stammering body of bits and pieces") and a *technē* and "anatomy" for material being that links it directly to the act or event of writing/reading.[45] For this linkage Nancy coins the word *exscription*, a property of outsidedness common to both writing and the body that manifests itself in interruptions: "tangential points, touches, intersections, dislocations" (11).[46] This crossing point represents the shared coefficient Nancy identifies as "tact."

> A touching, a tact, like an address: a writer doesn't touch by grasping, by taking in hand (from *begreifen* = seizing, taking over, Germans for "conceiving") but touches by way of addressing himself, sending himself to the touch of something outside, hidden, displaced, spaced. His very touch, which is certainly his touch, is in principle withdrawn, spaced, displaced. It *is:* the foreign contact drawn near, with the foreigner remaining foreign in the contact (remaining a stranger *to* contact *in* contact: that's the whole point about touching, the touch of bodies). This is how writing is addressed. Writing is thinking addressed, thinking sent to the body, sent, that is, to the very thing that displaces, estranges it . . . . "Ontology of the body" = exscription of being. Existence addressed to an outside (*there*, where there's no address, no destination; and yet (but how?) someone does the receiving: myself, you, us bodies, finally). (19)[47]

Let us imagine a practical instance of Nancy's theorization (one we have seen anticipated in the previous section by the brief allusion to "caress" in James's *In the Cage*). When W. G. Sebald's narrator says, "I was touched [Ger. *angerührt*, like Levinas's *sollicité*, "agitated, roused" but, as in English, connoting the doubled sense of "tact"] in a way I knew I could never quite fathom, by the symbol of the writer's quill on the stone of Friederike Halbleib,"[48] the abstract formulations of touch, tact, and writing as an address "to an outside" poignantly come home to us; indeed, their iconic personalization by Sebald has the capacity to touch us in turn, and we both note and mimic the *staging* of tact.

To be "touched," like Sebald's narrator, of course, is to be emotionally affected, stirred, *angerührt*—as in Levinas's understanding of sensibility as exposure. The coordination of both corporeal and affective-emotional senses in the word for "touch" in more than one language is worth pondering. Very simply, "we have to see reading as something that's not deciphering: touching, rather, and being touched." Again, "Writing, reading: a matter of tact" (87).[49] Finally, from the related essay "On the Soul" which ties together touch and emotion: "we can add another word, as well: *commotion,* being set in motion with" (135). Touch, tact, commotion: as a heuristic vocabulary, Nancy's helps us to see why examples like Sebald and Arad impress themselves upon us.

When enacted as the rubbing of victims' names at the September 11 Memorial, writing and reading *tangibly* become matters of tact, of palpation, agitation, and caress. And thus perhaps most fittingly in regard to the texts of both Arad and Sebald as I have aligned them, Nancy will speak of the relationship between bodies and space as "the milieu of a *proximity*" where there is in fact no *mi-lieu* ("between place"), if *milieu* means immersion, "a diffuse or infuse generality."[50] "In sum," Nancy says, "we're in the *technē* of the *neighbor*" (91). Bodies share or enact "compearance": they come together in the world.[51]

Nancy's exposition of the corporeal is additionally helpful to us here for its suggestive implications for the question of a canon or corpus of texts that authorizes inclusion or exclusion and that eventually comes to closure; "coming together" just *is* that contact for which the book in hand figures that closure and its cordon of sanctity/defilement. "To touch upon what's closed is already to open it. Perhaps there's only ever an opening by way of a touching or a touch. And to open—to touch—is not to tear, dismember, destroy" ("On the Soul," 123).[52]

Each of the discursive moments from Nancy's writing that I have quoted glosses *The Emigrants* and *Reflecting Absence*, as they severally look ahead to the authors and works I introduce later in the book. In the aggregate, they provide conceptual language that bridges material facts and the agency we perform as reader/writers and as bearers of certain traditions, worldly as well as sacred—work that, in turn, locates and positions us in time and history.

TACT: DERRIDA

But they have also acted as a provocation to Nancy's fellow philosopher and friend, Jacques Derrida. Derrida's book-length response to *Corpus* picks up on Nancy's inquiry—how are we to touch upon the body?—by "touching upon" the sense of touch itself, the "haptocentric tradition" that takes shape in Christian theology and European philosophy alike.[53] For our purposes, I will briefly touch upon Chapter 4 of *Le Toucher*, "The Untouchable; or the Vow of Abstinence," specifically, its initial structuring around the thrice-repeated declaration, "For there is a law of tact," slightly changed through iteration: "*Il y a la loi du tact*" and "*Il y a là loi du tact.*"

This iterative trick—repeating a statement and thereby subtly altering it—is a technique Derrida also deployed in an essay from three decades previous, "The Law of Genre"; a comparison of the two texts in this regard proves instructive. Especially since the macro-structure of my own book quite depends on the "fleshing out" of the tactile in direct relation to the organizing category of genre, I want to use these reflections on Derrida's twin laws of tact and genre because, as with Nancy's vocabulary for the tactile, they help outline a conceptual space within which to think pure-and-impure, sacred (holy)- and-quotidian, in specific relation to the book in hand: reading as the agency of touch.

"The Law of Genre" (1980) begins like this: "Genres are not to be mixed. I will not mix genres." Derrida then twice repeats the formula in somewhat slightly altered form. He then suggests, without his having framed them more straightforwardly, that each of those propositional speech acts could be taken in at least two senses: as, on the one hand, future-tense constative announcements and, on the other, as "sharp orders," performative promises, or oaths. He elaborates:

> As soon as the word "genre" is sounded, as soon as it is heard, as soon as one attempts to conceive it, a limit is drawn[;] as soon as genre announces itself, one must respect a norm, one must not cross a line of demarcation, one must not risk impurity, anomaly, or monstrosity. . . . If a genre is what it is, or if it is supposed to be what it is destined to be by virtue of its *telos*, then "genres are not to be mixed"; one should not mix genres, one owes it to oneself not to get mixed up in mixing genres. Or, more rigorously: genres should not intermix. And if it should happen that they do intermix, by accident or through transgression, by mistake or through a lapse, then this should confirm, since, after all, we are speaking of "mixing," the essential purity of their identity. This purity belongs to the typical axiom: it is a law of the law of genre. . . . And suppose for a moment that it were impossible not to mix genres. What if there were, lodged within the heart of the law itself, a law of impurity or a principle of contamination? . . . Before going about putting a certain example to the test, I shall attempt to formulate, in a manner as elliptical, economical, and formal as possible, what I shall call the law of the law of genre. It is precisely a principle of contamination, a law of impurity, a parasitical economy.[54]

What follows is a classic deconstructive operation. No text lives outside the particular genre specifying the distinctive trait that earns that same text or similar ones formal belonging; and yet, the distinguishing mark—the legal criterion—of that genre does not itself ostensibly "belong" to the genre. We might demonstrate Derrida's technical point this way: the difference between the scene of name-reading in Sebald's memoir-novel-travelogue (itself, a blurring of genres), and the scene of name-reading that Arad's memorial creates—narration and literary detail in the first instance, public communion and "rubbings" in the other—does not itself *belong* to either genre.

The respective identifying features certainly work to identify the particular genre at hand, a literary fiction entitled *The Emigrants* and a national memorial entitled *Reflecting Absence*. But the mark that says "novel" on the front or back covers of *The Emigrants* or that says "memorial" on the website or signage for *Reflecting Absence* is neither novelistic nor part of the architectural language of memorials; it is what makes the mark "remarkable," in Derrida's analysis, which also accounts for its peculiar "taint" and implicitly introduces the shadow of contamination or impurity.

Once the mark is included as part of that particular work, the work's "membership," its participation in the genre it exemplifies, becomes contaminated. The work is no longer a pure example of its class. The mark of membership is thus present and on the outside; but it is also absent (from the category or genre within which features are designated by it) and on the inside (a trace or imprint *within* each of the genre's features). As Derrida expresses the paradox, "the remark of belonging does not belong. It belongs without belonging. . . . It gathers together the corpus, and at the same time, in the same blinking of an eye, keeps it from closing, from identifying itself with itself" (65).

The rhetorical (or better, textualist), operation Derrida conducts through this line of argument, in accordance with the general trends of Derridean style, will not satisfy detractors. The conclusions can seem either forced or trivial.[55] But his larger and, I believe, consequential point is twofold: (1) nested within the law—the purifying agency—of (literary) genre resides an engine of impurity—"the law of the law"—that enables genre and taxonomy to function in the first place: it founds but at the same time undoes them; (2) Law itself (the archetypical institution for distinguishing, codifying, and ruling) is predicated on something that escapes its regulatory apparatus, that originates outside its grammar and syntax, "a conceptual impurity that is the condition for the claim of purity."[56] Derrida calls this mechanism of internal deconstitution, the *genre-clause* and the legal principle he wishes to derive from it, the "law of participation without membership." Both law and clause prevent a "Novel" or a "Memorial" that so indicates itself as ever entirely (purely) belonging to itself. For "what is at stake, in effect, is exemplarity and its whole enigma which works through the logic of the example" (59).

Each of the chapters that follow situates its overarching concerns with touch and the ethics of reading in respect to a given genre, and thus to the logic of example. "Talmudic tractate and *lecture talmudique*," "novel," "stage/film," "literary-philosophical essay" are the names of those four genres. Each genre, in turn, correlates with a distinct critical voice: Levinas in Chapter 4, Mikhail Bakhtin in Chapter 5, Stanley Cavell in Chapter 6, and the polyphonic chorus of Bialik, Scholem, Rosenzweig, and Agnon in Chapter 7. In regard to the first three, each author not only concentrates his exegetical energies on a particular rhetorical domain, but each also could be said to "reside" within that rhetorical world and its gravitational pull, as the specific genre itself exercises a dynamic force on his critical attention and intellection.

The Talmud, the Novel, Theater and Cinema—the world anatomized and codified, the world made prosaic, the world witnessed and viewed. Through these three proscenium arches, Levinas's, Bakhtin's and Cavell's respective critical consciousnesses are thus *staged*, each genre serving as *metteur en scène* for the dramas of exteriority, outsideness (вненачодимость), and separateness privileged by each of their philosophies.[57]

Chapters 1 and 2, on religious and secular criticism (Said and Levinas) and Chapter 3, on "private" writing by Blaise Pascal and Henry Darger (revisited in Chapter 5), develop another set of reflections about genre and tact—specifically, on how the one constrains, obliges, and troubles the other. But for all these separate expositions of genre, I wish to keep Derrida's point about porosity and "contamination" in the foreground. When I say that each of these rhetorical domains invites an ethics of reading, when I assume that the notion of a reading practice makes Levinasian, Bakhtinian, and Cavellian examples tangent to each other, I am suggesting that reading "impurely" *just is* the condition of modernity.

Moreover, within the layered canvas of this book, Levinas's, Bakhtin's, and Cavell's "hands" act, as it were, like *pentimenti* for the performative acts of reading inscribed by my own critic's hand; just so, the discursive forms of novel, tragedic drama/film, and Talmudic reading should be regarded in palimpsest, so many underwritings of each other. To think Conrad and Vico together, as Edward Said does,[58] or to dialectize Hebrew-Aramaic and Greek like Levinas, is, I think, to accept "the law of genre" as a first principle—as Vico, Conrad, and a certain midrashic sensibility peculiar to rabbinic exegesis already intimate on their own. Reading the Talmud together with Conrad, which I do at the end of Chapter 2, merely extends that same principle one level up, reframing the contiguities yet again. And as demonstrated by the linkage of Levinas and Said in the next chapter, the concept of genre likewise helps me to make tangential the two orders of "the difficult and the holy," by thinking together secular and religious bodies of text, literature and scripture.

The Emigrants and *Reflective Absence* have already supplied us with exemplary hybrids of genre.[59] Sebald's composite work conjoins novel, memoir, travelogue, and photograph album, each separate genre bordering and touching upon the others. Arad's memorial is part cenotaph, part revenant (it occupies the "footprints" of the destroyed twin towers), part monument, part catalogue of names, part "touchpad." Genres, as Derrida insists, cannot help but touch and mix (although touching, it should be said, need not be coterminous with mixing).

On Touching underlines the fact that Nancy's *Corpus* itself is structured around contiguity as a formal principle, the paradoxical bridge in the Christian mythos between *Hoc est enim corpus meum* ("Here is my body") and *Noli me tangere* ("Don't touch me"). And where Nancy privileges Christian religion in its aspect of flesh and blood, Derrida keeps returning to its paradoxical fusion of the corporeal and transcendental. Likewise, touch marks the crossing-point of sensible and intelligible, where the touchable intersects the untouchable; the pre-Christian figure of Psyche (figuring prominently in *Corpus* and *The Birth to Presence*) captures a similar paradox: tangible, yet untouchable. The tangent between presented body and prohibited touch[60] Derrida calls "the law of tact," in echo, we can now see, of his idiosyncratic exposition of the "law of genre."

As the genre clause enables mixing what shall not be mixed, so the law of tact discloses the untouchability of touch, the non-tactility of tact—an *espacement*, partition, and "slip"—the law that says, "one must touch without touching," which we can take as a (frustrated) gesture toward transcendence and the infinite as well as a stubborn reminder of the physical, the flesh-and-blood body.[61] Both laws also disclose the logic of exemplarity, which in Derrida's *On Touching* takes the form of metonymy, of part for whole (i.e., hand for person).

> For there is a law of tact. Perhaps the law is always a law of tact. . . . And one should understand tact, not in the common sense of the tactile, but in the sense of knowing how to touch *without* touching, without touching *too much*, where touching is already too much. Tact touches on the origin of the law. Just barely.

> At the limit. By essence, structure, and situation, the endurance of a limit as such consists in touching *without* touching the outline of a limit. (67)

Touching constitutes a limit-experience: "is finitude, period" (298). Moreover, as with genre (and with law, generally),

> It is touching that touches upon the limit, its own "proper-improper" limit, that is to say, on the untouchable on whose border it touches. . . . To touch is to touch a border, however deeply one may penetrate, and it is thus to touch by approaching indefinitely the inaccessible of whatever remains beyond the border, on the other side." (297)

Intangibility (the "*cannot*-touch") and untouchability ("the *must*-not-touch") are brought together as two orders mediated by "the *différence* of tact" (298).

> Between two given orders—yes, given as given as much as ordered (do touch but *do not* touch, in no way, do touch *without* touching, do touch *but* to watch out and avoid any contact)—it in effect installs a relationship that is at the same time *conjunctive* and *disjunctive.* Worse than that, it brings into contact both contradictory orders (do so and do not do), thus exposing them to contamination and contagion. But what it thus brings into contact, or rather contiguity, *partes extra partes*, is first of all contact *and* non-contact (68).

Again, to those less impressed by Derrida's philosophical style (and *Le Toucher* is a late text), the point may seem more paranomastic than profound. Tact, as a species of propriety, implies a discreet distance from touch-as-contact; and yet the word itself says "touch." A paradox! But also perhaps an adumbration of the essential ambivalence of the concept and of the difficulty in drawing a line between something and its contrary.

As was the case in the essay on genre, Law, the domain of regulatory statement and practice and the agency of discrimination and purification, is rendered paradoxical through the instability of a given law whose definitional burden is difference. Law—let us say, for example, the practical, ritually specific apparatus of *Halakhah* in respect to defilement—guards against "touching, affecting, corrupting" (67); that is its raison d'être. And yet, by prohibiting or abstaining from, by marking a limit, the interdiction also sets a tripwire. The pure and the impure, holiness and profanation might be tactfully distinguished, and yet to do so also risks bringing them into conjunction, tracing a circuit of transmissibility and contamination. One should understand tact here, Derrida says, beyond simply the tactile, "in the sense of knowing how to touch *without* touching, without touching *too much,* where touching is already too much" (67).[62] To touch is to touch a border, and therefore to approach what lies beyond.

Nancy's definition of writing follows a similar logic, as we have seen. As "exscription," writing "comes out of itself"; it stands exposed—to itself and to the world—and it goes toward an outside. (In an interview, Nancy defined that word as "the fact that writing indicates its own outside, is decanted and shows things."[63]) For Nancy and Derrida alike, touch, tact, and writing are not accomplished facts but rather expressions of yearning—affective experiences that approximate contact rather than simply bring it about.[64] They happen as if on a border or at a discrete point of contact.

"When I lift these bricks, stones, concrete blocks," writes Michel Serres, "I exist entirely in my hands and arms and my soul in its density is at home there but, at the same time, my hand is lost in the grainy body of the pebbles" (*The Five Senses*, 25). The *book-in-our hands,* it seems to me, physicalizes this syncope in the most familiar yet still mysterious way. It marks the site of tangency that invites, licenses, or wards away imaginative penetration and indwelling. This is the *tact*, the *contingency*, the *impertinence*, of reading.

TOUCH: CHRÉTIEN

When Derrida quotes philosopher and theologian Jean-Louis Chrétien's citations of Merleau-Ponty (i.e., "To touch is to touch oneself") and Henri Maldiney (i.e., "In touching things, we touch ourselves to them, as it were; we are simultaneously touching and touched"), he sees more than just the doubling of transitivity (touching others) and reflexivity (self-touch); he discerns the *scandal* of touch, if it can be put that way, its strange impurity as both concept and event. And thus does again Derrida's reframing of Nancy's deconstruction of a (largely Christian) tradition of touch resemble his analysis of genre, law being a major point of reference in each.[65]

When one looks back at Chrétien's *The Call and the Response,* from which Derrida quotes, we see an analysis of touch that traces it back to Aristotle's analysis in *De Anima*, where it becomes the primary sense for any organism because of its immediacy and pervasiveness. And yet, as Chrétien shows (and Nancy and Derrida, after him) it is never as straightforward or simple as we may think. Indeed, Aristotle himself labeled the sense of touch both "unfindable" and "hyperbolic." Extrapolating thus, from Aristotle by way of Aquinas, Chrétien insists, "we must lay bare the fact that touch is never bare" (125), and, "This undiscoverable sense is also an unnamable and oftentimes unnamed, sense" (91).

Chrétien explains that touch is not merely contact between one surface and another; instead, some other three-dimensional medium is always interposed (air, water), which "constitutes an untouchable element in touch, a skin or membrane that separates the skin from things but cannot be felt" (88). Phenomenologically speaking, the medium of touch expressed or felt as adherence, friction, contact can be accounted for as much in terms of distance as proximity. "To touch is to approach or to be approached; far from elevating touch to a new level, maximal contiguity, if materialized, would only impoverish it" (89).

This is the implicit lesson of the September 11 Memorial, I think, one that is brought out even more overtly in the passage from *The Emigrants.* Touching never gets us quite close enough. Degrees of nearness are really all that can be achieved or hoped for.[66] Proximity—groping—defines our relation to things, to human others, indeed, to ourselves; for while we may completely subsist in and through touch, we never quite "feel" the body that expresses sensitivities of the flesh: physical need, desire, and even basic autonomic function.

The quintessential sensory vehicle for human connection and interconnectedness, the *hand*[67] is both weighted and ineffably fragile *because* it serves as a medium of contact with otherness—contact with what is other, but also contact *as* what is other— like the uncanny neighboring of "here is my body" and "do not touch me" within the same rhetorical space.[68] The hands that hold a book, the book that lies within one's hands: this is one of those special meeting places, a unique one in fact, where intimacy and otherness establish a singular contact.

"WHAT WOULD GIVE ONE THE RIGHT TO TOUCH IT?"

Contact between hand and text resides in the quotidian, we know; what could be more everyday than the act of reading but also so various in its applications? No doubt, this explains some of the motivation behind the famous collection of photographs by André Kertész's *On Reading*, or the many depictions of readers through centuries of pictorial art: *Moça com Livro*, *Mädchen mit einem Buch*, *Jeune fille lisant*.[69] Yet, what the Rabbis of the Talmud attest to is that the very touch that intervenes not implausibly relates to contagion. Why? מפני שהידים הן עסקניות "Because hands are always restless" (*mTohorot* 7:8, *bShabbat* 14a).

Whether it is hand that touches text or text, hand, a sign is registered for canonical inclusion/exclusion. Touch, reminds Chrétien, is never bare; "the foreign contact drawn near, with the foreigner remaining foreign in the contact," says Nancy. This represents the photo negative, so to speak, to the kinship relation, the cross-relatedness, that R. Soloveitchik highlights in that same tradition when he examines the likeness it admits between sanctifying person and Torah scroll.

In respect to *tum'at yadayim* as a ritual category for the sacral power of that scroll, however, Chrétien's notion of "transitivity" or Nancy's and Derrida's "tact" are probably better understood as *transfer*. How "contamination"—etymologically, the coming together of L. "*con*" (with) and "*tangere*" (touch) to signify "coming together" itself—came to signify "rendered impure by contact or mixture," is an intriguing story. Defilement quite obviously results when two surfaces come together and mingle; pollution comes from blending, aggregating, and in an archaic sense (not surprisingly), sexual commerce and interbreeding. The genealogical sketch of Chrétien-Nancy-Derrida outlined here helps us understand how "the logic of the limit" pertains to the book's sequence of limit-cases, and, moreover, casts a clarifying light on the decision to export the rabbinic formulation "to make the hands impure," in order to refract the various kinds of texts and genres I have assembled here.[70]

But while deeply invested in religious experience and the transcendent, neither *Corpus* nor *On Touching* (nor *L'appel et la response*, for that matter) betrays any particular knowledge of Judaic concerns with touch, transmission, and embodiment (R. Soloveitchik's *yortsayt* lecture would have offered an intriguing companion piece). Nor do they extend their "tactilist" and haptic concerns, their review of Western philosophy's penchant for "*humainisme*" (Derrida), to the special circumstances of the book in hand. But when Derrida ventures, "Suppose one were to reach there, what would give one the right to touch it?" (131), touching, an "impertinent pertinence" restricted to a mere point or by tangent, is explicitly connected to longing, to the wish to press further: to touch *upon* and to penetrate. I would consequently like to keep this insight about desire in the foreground and in the minds of my readers, as we proceed to more concerted acts of reading in the chapters that follow.

For, as applied to reading and its various practices, the question Derrida poses may be asked in relation to quite different sorts of texts, to holy scripture no less than to fiction, film, or philosophy. When, for example, a poem or novel nudges readers' imagination through "hand [or "hands-on"] instruction," in Elaine Scarry's interesting phrase, we are introduced to a literary-cognitive training in grasp, caress, and palpability.[71] But, the difference between Jane Eyre's holding a book which is then thrown directly at her within the plot of Charlotte Brontë's novel, and our grasping *Jane Eyre* in the time and space of reading is the difference between an imagined property of authorial instruction—what Scarry calls "dreaming-by-the-book"—and the burden of a felt object upon our person, which then *bears* on us.[72]

And yet, a book is more than a thing, greater than just gear or instrument. "We must also realize," writes Roger Chartier, that reading is always a practice embodied in gestures, spaces, and habits."[73] This is the lesson to be drawn from the example we began with, synagogue-worship in Havana, Cuba, where we can see transitivity at work in the flesh and in black and white. If a Torah scroll can join the community of persons and thus, by itself, serve to fulfill the statutory mandate of communal prayer, then perhaps we too easily construe our relation to the texts we bear in hand, the texts that accompany us side-by-side, marking the seam between corporeal, worldly event and the enigma of tact. At the end of *Otherwise Than Being; Or, Beyond Essence*, Levinas calls such taken-for-grantedness to account in one of his most gem-like *formules*: "This relaxation of virility without cowardice is needed for the little cruelty our hands repudiate" (185). It is, of course, *our hands* that are empowered to slacken and let go ("*répudièrent*" connoting a dissolution of bonds)—even, perhaps especially, in the act of taking hold and enfolding.[74] The next chapter explores some of these ideas further by looking at the task of criticism as practiced respectively by Edward Said and Emmanuel Levinas. It begins, however, in the spirit of a scroll substituted for a person, with a magic trick.

PART ONE

Hands

CHAPTER I

Pledge, Turn, Prestige

Worldliness and Sanctity in Edward Said and Emmanuel Levinas

Apparently, he likes the tear (*déchirure*) but detests contamination.

—Jacques Derrida on Emmanuel Levinas

Indeed, nothing is more mobile, more impertinent, more restless than the hand.

—Emmanuel Levinas

Here is an ambition (which the Zahirites have to an intense degree) on the part of readers and writers to grasp texts as objects whose interpretation—by virtue of the exactness of their situation in the world—*has already commenced* and are objects already constrained by, and constraining, their interpretation. . . . (Incidentally, one of the strengths of Zahirite theory is that it dispels the illusion that a surface reading is anything but difficult.)

—Edward Said

TOUCHING ON MAGIC: LEVINAS

Every great magic trick consists of three parts or acts. The first part is called "The Pledge." The magician shows you something ordinary: a deck of cards, a bird or a man. He shows you this object. Perhaps he asks you to inspect it to see if it is indeed real, unaltered, normal. But of course, it probably isn't. The second act is called "The Turn." The magician takes the ordinary something and makes it do something extraordinary. Now you're looking for the secret, but you won't find it, because of course you're not really looking. You don't want to know. You want to be fooled. But you wouldn't clap yet. Because making something disappear isn't enough; you have to bring it back. That's why every magic trick has a third act, the hardest part, the part we call "The Prestige."

So, in the familiarly glottalized timbre of actor Michael Caine's voiceover, begins *The Prestige*, Christopher Nolan's 2006 film about illusions and dueling illusionists. As John Cutter, ingénieur to both stage magicians and plots, speaks (to us?), we are

45

shown a bird—real, unaltered, normal; the same bird placed in a cage; the same cage suddenly collapsed under an enveloping veil; the same veil then removed to reveal neither bird nor cage; and finally, the payoff or "Prestige": to the delighted eyes of a young girl, the object is brought back—quite literally, a bird-in-the-hand. We recognize the trick as the classic parlor effect known as the "vanishing" (or "flying") bird-cage," which is revisited several times in the course of the plot, as is Cutter's patter.

But intercut with this brief riddling of the magician's code, through the sleight of hand that is cinematic montage (for every film editor is a "cutter"), we glimpse another interrupted sequence that tells a major piece of the movie's storyline. Like other Nolan films—*Memento*, *Inception*, and *Insomnia*, for example—intricate narrative structure accompanies a reflexive meta-plot or self-allegory: artwork as manipulation, as magic, as mirror, as maze, as misdirection, as mimesis. Like those films, *The Prestige* fully exploits what Walter Benjamin called the "optical unconscious,"[1] a latent cinematic possibility in the "dream factory" ever since that industry's . . . inception. George Méliès, the first "cinemagician"—two of whose early shorts, *The Conjuror* (1899) and *The Vanishing Lady* (1896) anticipate Nolan's film—and Orson Welles—whom Nolan has cited as an influence—represent just two famous figures standing over *The Prestige* as antecedents in the tradition of filmic art as flimflam. To cite them here is merely to underscore the deep relation between movies and magic, a relation we revisit, along with Méliès, in Chapter 6.[2]

In Nolan's film, *Pledge, Turn, Prestige* not only serves to elucidate the workings of stage-magic. It also slyly anticipates the three-part plot of the movie itself. Part patter, part prose-poem, part explanation, part plot summary, Cutter's elucidation is the kind of double-talk associated with a not wholly reliable narrator whose vocation happens to be the inventing and engineering of tricks.[3] If, analytically speaking, "magic is the dramatization of explanation more than it is the engineering of effects," then Cutter's three-act explanation opens onto the performative horizon of craft and artificing that magicians call "the real work"—"the complete activity, the accumulated practice, the total summing up of tradition and ideas—what makes a magic effect magical."[4]

What goes unwitnessed by the little girl instructed by Cutter, however, is the fate of the original bird, which is crushed to death in the collapsed cage in order to facilitate the illusion. Mimesis as *Prestige* is costly: nothing is ever really brought back whole once it is pledged.[5] This is the darker implication of Cutter's instruction, and the essence of the interpolated plot sequence we see glimpses of—which is perhaps why we don't want to know and prefer, rather, to be fooled. Manipulated and subject to sleight, the object-in-hand—like the film we happen to be watching—never really stays *unaltered*.

I begin this chapter with Nolan's film because I want to speculate on two related matters: (1) art as its own complex apparatus of conjuring, and (2) the agency of those performing magicians we know as critics. If we thus employ a little stagecraft ourselves and throw its voice, *Pledge, Turn, Prestige* has yet another story to tell. In the ensuing pages, it will take shape through a counterpoint between certain reflections on text, reading, and the role of the critic. Specifically, we will track philosopher Emmanuel Levinas and literary theorist Edward Said as each practices his respective vocation of (quasi-)religious and (predominantly) secular criticism.

Let that story begin, however, with criticism's repurposed version of the vanishing birdcage (minus the misdirection). What follows is an excerpt from an essay about the acts of reading and criticism, voice-over by Georges Poulet, a critic-philosopher on the oblique to Saidian and Levinasian postures alike.[6]

> Books are objects. On a table, on bookshelves, in store windows, they wait for someone to come and deliver them from their materiality, from their immobility. When I see them on display, I look at them as I would at animals for sale, kept in little cages, and so obviously hoping for a buyer. For—there is no doubting it—animals do know that their fate depends on a human intervention, thanks to which they will be delivered from the shame of being treated as objects. Isn't the same true of books? Made of paper and ink, they lie where they are put, until the moment some one shows an interest in them. They wait. Are they aware that an act of man might suddenly transform their existence? They appear to be lit up with that hope. Read me, they seem to say. I find it hard to resist their appeal. (53)[7]

If books seem to share something palpable with the animate world of captive pets (like, say, a bird in a flying birdcage), they share much less with their inanimate fellows—statues or vases, for instance.[8]

> Buy a vase, take it home, put it on your table or your mantel, and, after a while, it will allow itself to be made a part of your household. But it will be no less a vase, for that. On the other hand, take a book, and you will find it offering, opening itself. It is this openness of the book which I find so moving. A book is not shut in by its contours, is not walled-up as in a fortress. It asks nothing better than to exist outside itself, or to let you exist in it. In short, the extraordinary fact in the case of a book is the falling away of the barriers between you and it. You are inside it; it is inside you; there is no longer either outside or inside (54).

Poulet's 1969 essay "The Phenomenology of Reading" marks a fault line in the history of modern literary criticism and theory, and it was first given under the title "Criticism and the Experience of Interiority" for the famous Johns Hopkins conference "The Languages of Criticism and the Sciences of Man," sharing space over that fault line with ground-breaking presentations by Jacques Derrida, Jacques Lacan, and Roland Barthes. It has been the subject of numerous critiques and commentaries since. My own contribution here consists merely in discerning what could be called a three-act drama—not quite *Pledge, Turn, Prestige*, but close enough.

Thus, Act I: once the book is opened, it ceases to be a material reality and is converted into the reader's consciousness: "Unheard-of, I say. Unheard-of, first, is the disappearance of the 'object.' Where is the book I held in my hands? It is still there, and at the same time it is there no longer, it is nowhere" (54). Act II: "*Je est un autre*," in Rimbaud's famous ungrammaticality; the reading consciousness is *alter*ed.

> This is the remarkable transformation wrought in me through the act of reading. Not only does it cause the physical objects around me to disappear, including the very book I am reading, but it replaces those external objects with a congeries of mental objects in close rapport with my own consciousness. . . . I am someone who happens to have as objects of his own thought, thoughts which are part of a book I am reading, and which are therefore the cogitations of another. They are the thoughts of another, and yet it is I who am their subject. The situation is even more astonishing than the one noted above. I am thinking the thoughts of another. (55)

Finally, Act III: the reader's annexed or usurped consciousness and its full participation in the artwork cede to the disenchanted work we call criticism.

> Thus I often have the impression, while reading, of simply witnessing an action which at the same time concerns and yet does not concern me. This provokes a certain feeling of surprise within me. I am a consciousness astonished by an existence which is not mine, but which I experience as though it were mine. This astonished consciousness is in fact the consciousness of the critic: the consciousness of a being who is allowed to apprehend as its own what is happening in the consciousness of another being. Aware of a certain gap, disclosing a feeling of identity, but of identity within difference, critical consciousness does not necessarily imply the total disappearance of the critic's mind in the mind to be criticized. (60)

Et voilà: *Pledge, Turn, Prestige* transposed (with a little liberty) to the plane of textuality, along with the semi-magical agency exercised by critical consciousness in the act-event of reading.

How does Poulet, in turn, help us to think about further implications of John Cutter's formula? Let us *bring it back* and see. Consider it now as an *ars poetica* for the workings of art, generally. For, all artistic enterprise—"the complete activity, accumulated practice, summing up of tradition"—is founded on something like the formula of a pledge, a turn, and a prestige, is it not? Architecture stakes a pledge on the transformation of space and surrounding element into social structure and habitation. Music stakes a pledge on mechanical waves of pressure realized in ordered configurations of frequency and pitch, duration and interval that enable song and rhythmic pulse. The plastic arts stake a pledge on the materiality of stone and wood, glass and textile, pigment and canvas rendered into design, pattern, image, and form. Dance stakes a pledge on the human body posed and mobilized through performance and social contact. Cinema (is there a more deceptive practice?) stakes a pledge on the illusion of movement generated by twenty-four frames per second, not to mention the *bricolage* of those cutter-magicians we know as editors; and like theater, film stakes a pledge on the stylized impersonation of person. Last but not least, literary and verbal representation stakes a pledge on language as both artifact and expression, and on the uncanny circuit of address between writers and readers.

And for each *pledge* in the history of these traditions, crafts, and practices, there is a corresponding *turn*: the artist takes something ordinary—a townhouse, say—and makes it extraordinary—like Antonio Gaudi's Casa Batlló or Casa Milà. Likewise, for each—by some *thing* being brought back, smuggled in, or shown always to have been there even in disguise—there is the third act, the *prestige*. Diego Velázquez's *Las Meninas* and Beethoven's *Diabelli Variations*, Orson Welles's *Citizen Kane* and Elizabeth Bishop's "One Art," Julio Cortázar's *Rayuela* (*Hopscotch*) and short fiction by Robert Walser severally work this magic. Art presents itself, wills some change in form, the production of some effect or consequence, and finally rematerializes either itself or its objects.

"A work of art," wrote poet-critic Paul Valéry in his essay on Leonardo da Vinci, "should always teach us that we haven't previously seen what we are seeing"—a truism, as far as it goes.[9] But from the Parmenidean tradition, as transmitted by Plato on down and cleverly postmodernized by a work like Nolan's *The Prestige,* we also discover that the prestige of artistic mimesis never comes scot-free. This is the tutorial in ambivalent recognition engineered by literary narration from the Hebrew Bible to *Middlemarch*, from the *Odyssey* to Ford's *The Good Soldier* or Borges's "Deutsches Requiem."[10] When seeing amounts to "enchanted looking," in Stephen Greenblatt's phrase,[11] art has worked its magic on the "sensate skin of the real"[12] even while the frame looms; a spell has been cast, a charmed circle drawn.

An example, now (of the book in hand, no less), from that incomparable literary transmogrifier, Bruno Schulz:

> The salesgirls slip ever more rapidly between the rows of books, grey and parch-mentlike, yet full of dark pigment in their debauched faces, the dark pigment of brunettes, a glistening, greasy blackness which lurks in their eyes, and then darts out of them along a sleeking, zigzagging cockroach path. But also in their scorched blushes, in the piquant stigmata of their beauty-spots, the shy indications of dark down, do they disclose their breed of black, clotted blood. That colouring with its too-intense force, that dense and aromatic mocha, seems to smear the books they take into their olivaceous hands. Their touch seems to run on the pages and leave a dark rainfall of freckles in the air, a streak of snuff, like the rousing, bestial aroma of a puffball.[13]

Here is one difference between art and magic, however: what in the performance of a magic trick is typically or even necessarily experienced as a sequence—pledge, *then* turn, *then* prestige—in art is almost always synchronous. The ordinary, the extraordinary, the ordinary brought back, but coextensive:

He was like a magic mill, into whose hoppers the bran of empty hours was poured, bursting into bloom in its mechanism with all the colours and aromas of oriental spices. But we, having grown accustomed to that metaphysical prestidigitator's magnificent jugglery, were inclined to take for granted the blessing of his sovereign magic which had delivered us from the lethargy of our empty days and nights.[14]

Art *may* aspire to the condition of music, according to the famous Paterian dictum,[15] but as a sibling to the magic trick, it perhaps more fittingly aspires to the condition of cinema—still images given the illusion of movement.[16] From a formal or materialist point of view, at least, this "give" or play can be said to be *art's* "real work." It is also what Levinas calls the commerce of "reality and its shadow."

Indeed, according to the early essay of the same name, art's non-Schulzian relation to reality—its *real* work—corresponds to that of a beguiled predator who abandons "the prey for the shadow."[17] If only subliminally, Levinas's figure reminds us of the proverb in which the falcon-in-hand exceeds the value of any prey in the bush—not to mention the fate of the bird made expendable though John Cutter's legerdemain in Nolan's *The Prestige*. "Total alterity in which a being presents itself out of itself, does not shine forth in the *form* by which things are given to us, for beneath form things conceal themselves" (*Totality and Infinity*, 192). This pressure on the form of things—"seen *in* the light as silhouettes or profiles" (140)[18]—or on form itself as a kind of shadowy companion to the Real, is consistent with Levinas's sober critique of the aesthetic from the 1940s, where (modern) art is explained as the substitution of an image for an object, doubling and thus "allegorizing" it, a function of what he there calls *the sensible*: "being insofar as it resembles itself, insofar as . . . it casts a shadow" (8).

Art signifies fabulation in the etymological sense of composing fables: as humans are seen not only through the figural animals of Aesop or La Fontaine but *as* those animals, which "stop and fill up thought," so art institutes "an ambiguous commerce with reality in which reality does not refer to itself but to its reflection" (6), its image. Art's exemplary form, then, is plastic image and statuary because it "immobilizes" what it represents; as rhythm and musicality, however, it invites "participation," a negatively-tinged term in the early philosophical writings whose synonyms are "incantation" and "captivation."[19] Platonically, Levinas conjures the penumbral world of the aesthetic as a sphere of "Non-truth": "the very event of obscuring, a descent of the night, and invasion of shadow" (3)

In turn and in the spirit of his friend Maurice Blanchot, Levinas will characterize the artist as a "nomad . . . wandering . . . as in a desert [where] one can find no place to reside."[20] Temporally, art transpires in the *entretemps*, "the meanwhile," a suspended space of permanent interruption. Spatially, like the naked world of things themselves, art is experienced laterally, not frontally, as expressed in *Totality and Infinity*, "already abdicating to the hand which seeks its vulnerable point, which already ruse and industry, reaches for it obliquely" (160). In this domain, objects "receive a borrowed light" (74). They are manipulated, and do not present themselves. This, for Levinas, is the sum of art's *Prestige*.

Crucially, *hands* mark the site of ruse and industry, of magic: "that dense and aromatic mocha, seems to smear the books they take into their olivaceous hands." Or more obviously (from another Bruno Schulz story entitled "Kometa" (The Comet), this quasi-Spinozist moment[21]:

> "*Panta rei!*" he cried, demonstrating with movements of his hands the eternal
> circulation of substance. For a long time he had wanted to mobilise the hidden
> power which circulates within it, to melt its rigidity and clear its path to thorough
> penetration, transfusion, and universal circulation, its only true nature.[22]

Thus, the very form of things, as an artistic desideratum, exerts or establishes a magic of its own—as *placing* and *graspability*, as the weak gravitational field of *meubles* ("movables")—and it is not by accident that Levinas conspicuously tethers art to that realm, e.g., "the exceptional structure of aesthetic existence evokes this singular term *magic*" (3) and further, "all the power of the contemporary novel—its art-magic—is perhaps due to this way of seeing inwardness from the outside" (11) and finally, "magic, recognized everywhere as the devil's part, enjoys an incomprehensible tolerance in poetry" (12).[23] Even the first sentence of the preface to *Totality and Infinity*, written almost two decades after "Reality and Its Shadow," announces its bold statement in the language of trickery and deception: "Everyone will readily agree that it is of the highest importance to know whether we are not duped . . ." (*On conviendra aisément qu'il importe au plus haut point de savoir si l'on n'est pas le dupe . . .*) (21).

How, by this reckoning, does experiencing the artwork endorse the *ingénieur* John Cutter's contention that we really do not wish to know magic's secret, that we want to be fooled (if only to repress our suspicion that its method is not harmless)?[24] Phenomenologically considered, art can be compared to a "waking dream": it "disincarnates" reality; it "stops time" (10); it eludes and evades; most of all, it locates the spectator "among things as a thing, as part of the spectacle" because, perceptually speaking, one's trust and confidence have been encouraged only to be exploited. Thus, surfaces of objects—their *Pledge*—can readily be transformed into interiors—their *Turn*: as Levinas puts it, "the hidden becomes open and the open becomes hidden" (*TI*, 192).

As for any *Prestige* in the Levinasian account, it is at best anticlimactic: objects, through the play of form, are never really "brought back"; instead, "reality remains foreign to the world, inasmuch as it is given" (*Existence and Existents*, 53). Through the work of materialization, art already "extracts" things from the world, rendering them exotic in the etymological sense, *on the outside*, exterior to themselves—which is where they remain. "Finally after he hangs it on the wall, he understands," say the final lines of Dan Pagis's prose poem "The Art of Contraction": "this painted blade of grass, which implies the entire meadow, also denies the entire meadow."[25] Mimesis re-presents;

it brings back, but at a cost. This is art's shadow-work: for what *is* a bird-in-the-hand worth, after all, if prey to the vicissitudes of *pledge* and *prestige*?

Beyond the play of surfaces, Levinas helps us think additionally of material form as a problem of obverse and reverse—which is not just simply the difference between the front and back of, say, a painting on canvas. "The obverse would be the essence of the thing whose servitudes [meaning its dependence on form of some sort] are supported by the reverse, where the strings are invisible."

> Proust admired the reverse of the sleeves of a lady's gown, like those dark corners of cathedrals, nonetheless worked with the same art as the façade. It is art that endows things with something like a façade—that by which objects are not only seen but are as objects on exhibition. . . . The notion of façade borrowed from building suggests to us perhaps that architecture is the first of the fine arts. But in it is constituted the beautiful, whose essence is indifference, cold splendor, and silence. By the façade the thing which keeps its secret is exposed, enclosed in its monumental essence and in its myth, in which it gleams like a splendor but does not deliver itself. It captivates by its grace as by magic, but does not reveal itself."
> (*Totality and Infinity*, 192)

Although the prepositional object I intentionally omitted from the end of the famous first sentence of *Totality and Infinity* I quoted above is, in fact, the word, "morality" (that is, "si l'on n'est pas le dupe de la *morale*") art—or, in this formulation, material aesthetics—becomes its own troubled vehicle for illusionism in Levinas's earlier writing.[26] Art's trustworthiness is called into question by both its "holiday" aspect—"We distrust the poetry that scans and bewitches our faces, and all that which, in our lucid life, plays [*sejoue*] in spite of us"[27]—and our compromised agency as its uninnocent bystanders.[28]

Criticism's obligation to undo art's magic by rendering it intelligible, by putting it in motion and making it speak "in the language which makes us leave our dreams" coincides with the tenor of some of Levinas's essays on Judaism and his Talmudic readings, where the ethical is played off against the ensorcelled. In "A Religion for Adults" from *Difficult Freedom,* for example, Levinas writes, "myth, albeit sublime, introduces into the soul that troubled element, that impure element of magic and sorcery and that drunkenness of the Sacred" (48). The very title of Levinas's reading of *bSanhedrin* 67a–68b, "Désacralisation et désensorcellement," pits magic as sorcery against holiness, which for a post-Talmudic age sounds the cautionary note, "That is what sorcery is: the modern world; nothing is identical to itself . . . all speech is a magical whisper" (152).[29]

In Levinas's later philosophical writings, however, such as the essay "Language and Proximity" in *Otherwise Than Being*, we find a more positive and much less severe depiction of art, an *intrigue*, even an *adventure* (Levinas's terms for ethical involvement). For a calculus of loss, we are given a poetics of proximity instead, for which "sensibility must be interpreted first of all as touch."

The proximity of things is poetry; in themselves the things are revealed before being approached. In stroking an animal already the hide hardens in the skin. But over the hands that have touched things, places trampled by beings, the things they have held, the images of those things, the fragments of those things, the contexts in which those fragments enter, the inflexions of the voice and the words that are articulated in them, the ever sensible signs of language, the letters traced, the vestiges, the relics—over all things, beginning with the human face and skin, tenderness spreads. Cognition turns into proximity, into the purely sensible. (*Otherwise Than Being*, 118–119)

Sustaining the Introduction's emphases on the tactile drawn from Nancy, Derrida, and Chrétien, I call attention in these exquisite sentences to the emphasis on hands and on touching and the way these metonymies fan out, as in Aristotle's *De Anima,* to all the other senses. What distinguished touch as the *sensus universalis* for Aristotle was not only its sensitivity and pervasiveness—"the most bodily of sensory organs"— but also its coextensiveness with animal life and the synonymy of the tangible and the sensible *tout court.*

Aristotle made the sense of touch "indispensible" because he tied it directly to mortality; through its many and varied surfaces, flesh is in a perpetual state of lived vulnerability, and thus touch is the bodily sense "by which we live" (*De Anima* 435b17) and, if excessive, the surest path to death (435b14).[30] Unique among the senses, touch "implicates itself in what it perceives," as Chrétien puts it in *The Call and the Response* (99), in contradistinction to the other organs of sense which are not "immersed in the very realm in which they serve as instruments of measure and discrimination" (100). Touch is consequently a mean, with qualities of hot, cold, dry moist always being a matter of something hotter, colder, drier, or moister than we are. That is to say, "we only feel what exceeds us" (99).[31]

Tactile immanence and corporeal sensibility happen to be basic to Levinas's rethinking of ethics (and aesthetics) in his late masterwork *Otherwise Than Being* as well as in shorter essays from the same vintage like "Without Identity."[32] Crucial to these is the notion of *proximity*, a preliminary statement of which in the essay "Substitution" (1968, revised as the central chapter for *Otherwise Than Being* in 1971) explains it as "a relationship with what cannot be resolved into 'images': "In starting with touching, interpreted not as palpitation but as caress, and language, interpreted not as the traffic of information but as contact, we have tried to describe proximity as irreducible." Perceptually, proximity is experienced first as touch and tactility—as such, an "otherwise than" the economy of being and essence, commonly figured as the grasping hand of self-interest.[33]

Relationally, it also names a mode of human encounter, "the relationship with the neighbor in the moral sense of the term," which also has a temporal aspect as *diachrony*: a "difference, a non-coinciding, an arrhythmia in time" (*OTB*, 166). Interpretively, proximity—to a textual tradition, for instance—signifies a closeness that does not accomplish coincidence, an approach that stops short of arrival. In all these senses, proximity describes the condition of catching up and therefore being late or behind, drawn from ahead (Levinas will say, "assigned"), by some Other, who, paradoxically, "has come, to be sure, but left *before* having come,"[34] at once near and infinitely remote. Not exclusively a human neighbor, that Other, in my understanding, can refer to another order of drawing from ahead and making near—say, a textual corpus or tradition (religious or secular), and even a self-standing work.

To retrieve Nolan's film at this juncture, both magic and art teach belatedness: John Cutter's patter tells us this much. Both allegorize loss, balancing mimetic gain against expenditure. As Walter Benjamin has suggested, they also hold out the possibility of moving from a world of authoritative or habitual ritual to a more plastic horizon of democratic politics. Viewers, listeners, readers do not merely stand by during *Pledge*, *Turn*, *Prestige* but rather actively intervene in the artwork's transmission; our willed credulity (and repressed accountability) make the illusion possible.[35] Hands and touching in connection with the trope of proximity thus bring us back to the machinery of close-up magic, to its fundamentally manipulative logic and misdirection, but also to its staging of "an experiment in empathy" (as Adam Gopnik quotes the magician Jamy Ian Swiss). "The magician awakens us from the dogmatic slumbers of our daily life, our interactions with cards and hoops and things. He opens a door by pointing to a window." If the magician does so, we sanction that passage in the first place—even if the magician appears to get there before we do.[36]

As the title certainly intimates, hands, together with the objects they hold—in this case, books—figure centrally in *To Make the Hands Impure*. So does the trope of proximity (which we can now see working implicitly for Nancy and Derrida's analysis of touch) as an impinging condition upon the event of reading, a mobile hinge between religious and secular, between the literary and the scriptural, between ethics and the aesthetic. While much more can and will be said about these ideas as organizing categories for reading, already nicely anticipated by Levinas, I make a transition from them here to a rather different perspective on art and its criticism, drawn from writings by Edward Said.

The resulting interreading of Said and Levinas will set the stage for the first of several pointed rapprochements between "religious" and "secular" in this book. In the present chapter, a brief digression by Said on the eleventh-century exegete Ibn Ḥazm in his famous essay, "The World, the Text, and the Critic," affords an opportunity for a lateral connection to the rabbinic figure of Ibn Ezra (Ibn Ḥazm's rough contemporary), which will lead us thence into the domain of Levinas's Talmudic readings. Beyond the instructive use of the examples themselves, however, the layers of interplay here further evince the workings of proximity: reader to reader, worldly touch to consecrated reading, difficult to holy.

THE WILL TO WORLDLINESS: EDWARD SAID

John Cutter has no monopoly on three-part exposition. In his famous essay "Secular Criticism" (1983) from *The World, the Text, and the Critic*, Edward Said expounds his own formula for a triadic pattern that rehearses "the passage from nature to culture," and consists of an exchange or "cooperation" between two modes of belonging, *filiation* and *affiliation*, "located at the heart of critical consciousness."

> [I]f a filial relationship is held together by natural bonds and natural forms of authority—involving obedience, fear, love, respect and instinctual conflict—the new affiliative relationship changes these bonds into what seem to be transpersonal forms—such as guild consciousness, consensus, collegiality, professional respect, class and the hegemony of a dominant culture (20).

Said identifies the pattern in its third transposition as "an instance of how easily affiliation can become a system of thought no less orthodox and dominant than culture itself." Not inappositely described under the rubric of "prestige," then, the third act in this cultural drama "becomes in effect a literal form of" *re-presentation:* "the deliberately explicit goal of using that new order to reinstate vestiges of that kind of authority associated in the past with filiative order." Through a selective account of modern cultural history and literary modernism that includes Arnold, Eliot, Eric Auerbach, György Lukács, and Raymond Williams, Said arrives at "the structure of literary knowledge" as an institutional practice or artifact "heavily imprinted with the three-part pattern I have illustrated here."

Admittedly, "Filiation, affiliation, representation" only very loosely correspond to *Pledge, Turn, Prestige*. Yet as with Georges Poulet's essay previously, the forced analogy is edifying. Both patterns model acts of staging—art and magic alike as self-stagings beyond whatever particular scenes or tableaux they may enframe. Both patterns pivot on the role of re-presentation such that the third part or act of each marks the seam where the parallel between them becomes most pronounced. Of the dominant system of humanistic scholarship, for example, Said says,

> Thus we find the university experience more or less officially consecrating the pact between a canon of works, a band of initiate instructors, a group of younger affiliates; in a socially validated manner, all this reproduces the filiative discipline supposedly transcended by the educational process.

The guild structure of magic, with its initiates, affiliates, and own canon of works, does not operate much differently; magicians are both each other's rivals and sibling-parents. The symbolic capital of *prestige* lies at the very heart of the scholastic enterprise, too, whether in the form of a *trahison des clercs* (as Said often cites French philosopher Julian Benda), or just a *tour d'ivoire*. As with the preceding section on Levinas, then, the utility of John Cutter's account of magic's *technē* as a foil for "the passage from nature to culture" is rhetorical—a stage-setting device. By contrast, any juxtaposition between Said and Emmanuel Levinas like the one I want to suggest now needs some buttressing.[37] Let me do so then by adducing some telling similarities in the midst of obvious difference.

However widely the two thinkers may differ on their respectively metaphysical and worldly understandings of art, Levinas and Said understood themselves fundamentally as intellectuals—both culturally relocated humanists, both philologically inclined and influenced by phenomenology, both exemplary readers who ascribe enormous consequentiality to authorship and the contrapuntal character of criticism.[38] Their common difference from Poulet in this respect is the shared pressure each places on *interiority* and the correlative obligation for a reader to sustain an exterior critical vantage.

Where Levinas locates the (philosophical) critic outside the hermetic world of artistic creation as a kind of deartificer, a spokesperson for the necessary work of mediation and communication, Said awards him or her the privilege of oppositionality, disaffection, and "counter-memory," the willingness to become "unhomed" (like Auerbach or Swift) which is the privilege of *secularity*.[39] Perfectus vero cui mundus exilium est: "He is perfect to whom the entire world is as a foreign land," repeatedly cites Said, quoting Auerbach from "Philologie der Weltliteratur," himself quoting from Hugh of St. Victor's *Didascalion*. And whereas worldliness connotes distinctly political responsibilities for Said, the necessity of the critic's or author's being grounded in circumstantial and situational reality, for Levinas the concept signifies the nontotalizable property of any single book, text, discourse, or utterance, as I have already had occasion to cite in the prologue: "[Books] belong to a world that they do not enclose. . . . They interrupt themselves and call to other books and are interpreted in the final analysis in a saying distinct from the said" (*Otherwise Than Being*, 171).[40]

If writing opens a space for intervention in Said's criticism, it marks the trace of its interruptions, in Levinas's thinking. In neither case, however, do we find the falling away of barriers, the neutralizing of inside-and-outside, extolled by the solitary reading of Pouletian phenomenology, poised, as it appears, between the quasi-mythical and quasi-magical. Not so remarkably, for all their self-evident differences—political, philosophical, ideological—both Levinas and Said converge at this point of criticism as a stand against the mythical.

Thus, "The principal feature of mythic discourse is that it conceals its own origins as well as those of what it describes" (Said); "Philosophical criticism will measure the distance that separates myth from real being, and will become conscious of the creative event itself, an event that eludes cognition" (Levinas).[41] Levinas could even be endorsing Said's own self-image as muscular, situated, worldly critic, admiring a writer like Joseph Conrad as precisely not a *novelist*—the stuff of art-magic, in Levinas's phrase—but an *essayist*, when he writes,

The most lucid writer finds himself in the world bewitched by its images. He speaks in enigmas, by allusions, by suggestion, in equivocations, as though he moved in a world of shadows, as though he lacked the force to arouse realities, as though he could not go to them without wavering, as though, bloodless and awkward, he always committed himself further than he had decided to do, as though he spills half the water he is bringing us. The most forewarned, the most lucid writer nonetheless plays the fool. The interpretation of criticism speaks in full self-possession, frankly, through concepts, which are like the muscles of the mind.

The passage resonates powerfully with Said's critiques of Foucault and Derrida in chapters of *The World, The Text, and the Critic*, along with those whom he derides as purveyors of a "religious criticism" (like René Girard or Harold Bloom)[42] that substitutes the private and hermetic for the social and political. In other, more ideological respects, as exegetes and textual commentators, one primarily historicist, the other idiosyncratically "counterhistoricist,"[43] Levinas and Said stand at a quite a distance from each other despite any accidental, or imposed, proximity.

By now, of course, a superabundance of critique for each figure crowds the academic landscape. Pairings of them, however, remain uncommon. Levinas, as far as I am aware, did not ever refer to Said in writing. In an issue of *The London Review of Books* from 2000, Said published a "Diary" recounting his meeting with Jean-Paul Sartre. "There was talk of Emmanuel Levinas being involved," he writes, "but, like the Egyptian intellectuals whom we'd been promised, he never showed up." That missed encounter may serve to capture the gap between them in print.[44] Nevertheless, their intellectual and cultural locations as a religious and a secular *critic* (whatever their respective religiosity or secularity) demand a reckoning; as a pairing, moreover, *in proximity*, the very "question of location"—already "permanently complicated" in respect to Levinas, says Judith Butler,[45] but just as apposite for Said—becomes even sharper.

For Said, the three acts of *filiation* (biological, national, or otherwise predetermined relationality) *affiliation* (free, individual choice) and *representation* ("by which filiation is reproduced in the affiliative structure and made to stand for what belongs to us") represent modes of both cultural transposition, particularly in modernism, and critical consciousness. As to the latter, secular individual agency has the option of either playing "midwife," enabling, transacting the transfer of legitimacy from filiation to affiliation, or of becoming the agent, to coin a phrase, of "mobilized proximity": "To stand between culture and system is therefore to stand *close to*—closeness having a particular value for me—a concrete reality about which political, moral, and social judgments have to be made, and, if not only made, then exposed and demystified."

Saidian proximity is situatedness, a nearness to the world that informs both a text in its circumstantial reality and the critic's interpretive agency. It is a responsibility and responsiveness to the world. In the lovely formulation Said introduces, proximity describes how "the closeness of the world's body to the text's body forces readers to take both into consideration" (39). Finally, proximity is *affiliation*—a decision made from within one of two governing dispositions, that of "secular human history," in willed independence from the other, "the realm of nature" (a difference, also, between "beginnings" and "origins").[46]

Levinasian proximity—even if Levinas himself consistently performed acts of willed affiliation[47]—is just the fact—or better, the affective event—of otherness and its material claim on me: something that happens to me or which I undergo, not something I elect or will—a "dedicated spirit" on the order of Wordsworth's verses, "I made no vows, but vows/Were then made for me."[48] Through that fundamental, ineluctable orientation *toward the other*, through that "denucleation" and exposure of self, I become invested as an ethical human subject.

Reading, however, as the expression of "critical consciousness," imposes its own obligations. Oscillating between claims outside the self and from within, positioned at the "sensitive nodal point" between acts or attitudes of distanciation and appropriation,[49] lies the moral and political agency Said designates *criticism*.

> On the one hand, the individual mind registers and is very much aware of the collective whole, context, or situation in which it finds itself. On the other hand, precisely because of this awareness—a worldly self-situating, a sensitive response to the dominant culture—that the individual consciousness is not naturally and easily a mere child of the culture, but a historical and social actor in it.

If, as I have glossed Levinas, the experience of art resembles the magician's formula of "pledge, turn, and prestige"—its auditors and spectators being at once complicit witness and empathetic participant—then it is the critical reader—noncomplicit, worldly, undeceived—who is the *Bildungsheld* of Said's three-act drama of secular exegesis. For Said and Levinas alike, however, criticism disenchants: it dispels magic and myth. It prefers sobriety to sentimental education or the lures and snares of the picaresque.

EXCURSUS ON ASCESIS: IBN ḤAZM

But what does a conjunction of such figures do for an inquiry into reading as the book in hand—an ethical practice of making contact, a staging of proximity—which is this book's central theme? Let Said's self-acknowledged digression from the larger argument of his essay, "The World, the Text, and the Critic," suggest a tentative answer, and my own digression on it, a reframing of the question. A composite and complex essay, Said's concerns the way texts and critics are alike "enmeshed in circumstance, time, place, and society—in short, they are in the world, and thus worldly." Beyond the cul-de-sac represented by the notion of a self-sufficient text (a notion, we might add, that also correlates with Levinas's critique of the autonomous ego), Said asks how literary language and everyday language can be thought together, how we can responsibly account for the interplay between text and "worldliness."

Curiously enough, he draws his example from the domain of religious exegesis—specifically, an approach to علم الكلام *'Ilm al-Kalām* (the Islamic interpretive tradition) by the eleventh-century Andalusian grammarian, jurist, theologian (and polemicist), Abū Muḥammad ʿAlī ibn Aḥmad ibn Saʿīd Ibn Ḥazm (al-Andalusī az-Zāhirī, 994–1064). What I outline in this section by spending some time with Said's excursus on Ibn Ḥazm is an interplay between secular and religious energies that, while it is difficult for Said's own critical commitments to entertain ultimately, I try to sustain throughout this chapter and subsequently. From the example of Ibn Ḥazm, therefore, I turn to the case of a near-contemporary, Ibn Ezra, whom I use as a stepping stone to the rabbinic concept of "defilement of the hands" to arrive, finally, at Levinas's Talmudic readings. Any dissonance that may emerge between Saidian and Levinasian critical postures is really subsidiary to a larger claim I want to make about bridging different *kinds* of reading, scriptural and literary, as I move finally to Levinas's and Said's own *readings* of texts in parallel.

Following Roger Arnaldez's summary in his *Grammaire et théologie chez Ibn Hazm de Cordoue*, Said explains that Ibn Ḥazm was an exponent of the Zahiri school of linguists who attended to the "phenomenal words themselves, in what might be considered their once-and-for-all sense uttered for and during a specific occasion, not on hidden meanings they might later be supposed to contain." Said's take on Zahiri grammaticality here might be called quasi-Wittgensteinian, since he intends their exegetical approach as betokening not only the plain sense and surface particularity of words—their "verbal form"—but also in the direction of their normative and conventional use. Said puts this as carefully as he can (he says), in the following summing-up:

> worldliness, circumstantiality, the text's status as an event having sensuous particularity as well as historical contingency, are considered as being incorporated in the text, an infrangible part of its capacity for conveying and producing meaning. This means that a text has a specific situation, placing restraints upon the interpreter and his interpretation not because the situation is hidden within the text as a mystery, but rather because the situation exists at the same level of surface particularity as the textual object itself (39).

The textual point of reference here is the *Qur'an*. Moreover, it is the *Qur'an*'s "uniqueness" as an event," its "pure contingency," that justifies the Zahirite linguistic proposition, as captured by Said, that "Each utterance is its own occasion and as such is firmly anchored in the worldly context in which it is applied" (38). What is curious about Said's choice of Ibn Ḥazm's analytic in his essay is *not* the seeming inconsistency of a devoted secularist adducing an instance of religious criticism in the service of a larger argument about *situation-constraining interpretation*. Said had already devoted several paragraphs to the *Qur'an* in his superb (and contemporaneous) study

Beginnings: Intention and Method, specifically to its status as a uniquely integral and "inimitable" scriptural text, for which all secondary textual or editorial traditions are "essentially supportive, not restorative."[50]

Qur'anic univocity thus contrasts with the heterogeneity of discourse, style, genre, and redaction common to the foundational scriptures of Vico's "Christian Europe." And as should be obvious from Said's ultimately purposeful digression on medieval Islamic exegesis within an essay that begins by discussing Glenn Gould and culminates in brief readings of Hopkins, Wilde, Conrad (and Marx), he is performing the conscientiously *affiliative* move of expanding, by contesting, the Eurocentric limits of the canon. Indeed, the Sunni Ibn Ḥazm (also known as al-Andalusī aẓ-Ẓāhirī) is strategically positioned by Said as instructive counter-theorist to no less a hegemonic Continental philosopher than Paul Ricoeur, providing a complement to the critical tradition of romantic philology, the advent of linguistics, "and the whole rich phenomenon of what Michel Foucault has called the discovery of language" (36).

No, the more curious thing is the deference Said pays to an account of textual meaning for sacred text that, in the particular slant he gives it, suggests a medieval version of linguistic positivism. In his compendious book on Said's oeuvre, Abdirahman Hussein has characterized it as an epistemological empiricism committed to an untroubled referential correspondence between word and object. Hussein frames a pointed question about the gap such a choice opens up between Said's appreciation of Conradian "negativism" (the fourth chapter in Said's book)—"Each sentence drives a sharper wedge between intention (wanting to speak) and communication"—and his apparent endorsement of Ibn Ḥazm's exoteric positivism—that "words had only a surface meaning"—this way: "Why has the dialectical operation produced a profound negativity in one case [Conrad] and lucid knowledge [the Zahirite stance] in the other? Above all, isn't Said in the latter case peddling a version of knowledge which is remarkably similar to the ideological currencies he has denounced elsewhere?"[51]

Hussein belongs to a minority of Said's readers in wondering aloud about the foray into Qur'anic exegesis at all. Another academic from much farther afield, James Dougal Fleming, is equally sharp in his critique of the logic of the Ibn Ḥazm section. Fleming concludes his study of John Milton's hermeneutics of recognition by showing the foray to be wise in its own terms, as consistent with this particular author's own theoretical predilection for the redemptive difficulty of surface reading, but also a dead-end for Said's larger purposes—and thus producing its own cul-de-sac.

> Said himself serves as an example of how hard a fight this is: having introduced, with his usual erudition, the amazing phenomenon of Zahiritism—this utter confound to the ideological claim of continuity between reading and esoteric reading—Said doesn't know what to do with it. All he retains from his 12th-century [*sic*] exotericists, all he applies to his wider argument, is a vague standard of

literary "worldliness." Said's failure to *grasp* his own discussion is all the more striking given his construction of the Zahirites as anti-Orientalists, true Koranists.[52]

My purposes in this book, obviously, are different from both Hussein's and Fleming's. Yet, each of these commentators testifies to a certain awkward logic in Said's excursus on the Zahirites, which for me is also visible. The whole digression has an odd feel to it, which I see as driven by two lapses, one in method and the other in argument. First, the decision to make the *Qur'an* a singular instance of textual and editorial unity makes it difficult for Said—and I use this word pointedly—to *affiliate* parallel religious traditions or religious and secular texts in such a way as to complicate any putative opposition between them or their respective horizons of reception.[53] Second, Said—both in the Zahirite excursus in the "World, the Text, and the Critic" and the two pages on the *Qur'an*'s *Wirkungsgeschichte* in *Beginnings*—seems to sustain a restrictive sense of the variegated kinds and uses of scriptural commentary, both medieval and modern, and of its own possibilities for "critical consciousness."

One reason may be the lamentably un-nuanced opposition between the terms, Islamic and "Judeo-Christian," which occurs with some frequency in Said's writings. Sounding eerily akin to Franz Rosenzweig (notwithstanding Rosenzweig's unfortunate deployment of the same dichotomy but with the polarity reversed)[54], Said declares the *Qur'an*, "unlike the Bible," to be "an event," which, "at its most radical verbal level [is] a text controlled by two paradigmatic imperatives, *iqra* (read and recite) and *qul* (tell)." The *Qur'an* is "the delivery of an utterance" or *khabar* (Allah's allocution to his Prophet), "which is the verbal realization of a signifying intention" or *niyah*.[55] Continuous with the Scripture's eventful imperatives, reading is therefore transacted according to a juridical guideline of limit and "logico-grammatical" definition (*hudd*).[56]

As Fleming observes, the ultimate warrant for this surprising turn in the essay's main argument is its tendentious connection to "worldliness," for it is not immediately clear from Said's summary why Zahirite "ascesis of the imagination" in the service of interpretive parsimony should correlate with the worldly, the situated, the circumstantial in the sense *Said* intends here and elsewhere, specifically for modernist literary fiction and poetry. In one of his late essays, "The Changing Bases of Humanistic Study and Practice," Said places "worldliness" in apposition to the entailments of "power, position, and interests," and connects it to "contamination" by history and "involvement" in material conditions. But surely the utility of the Zahirite example for Said works otherwise, since it concerns semantic norms rather than ideological praxis.

In short, something seems to have been lost in translation. The same might be said for the gap within just a few sentences between identifying a text *as an event* and *as an object*—a distinction that will be fundamental for my own analysis. Admittedly, Said does not see a contradiction between these two notions, but I am not certain he would ascribe the status of "event" to writings by Wilde, Hopkins, and Conrad. And yet, the transition from scriptural exegesis to literary commentary makes the gap between event and object stand out particularly. As Said pivots from Zahirite grammarians to his three differently tormented male literary modernists, he supplies the ostensible transition, which I cite as part of this chapter's second epigraph:

> Here is an ambition (which the Zahirites have to an intense degree) on the part of readers and writers to grasp texts as objects whose interpretation—by virtue of the exactness of their situation in the world—*has already commenced* and are objects already constrained by, and constraining, their interpretation. (39)[57]

The three brief readings of Hopkins, Wilde, and Conrad illustrate two features shared among them: a reflexivity about their own historical writing situations (Said calls this now a "will to worldliness") and a discursive privileging of speech as if the written text were an interchange between speaker and hearer. By way of introducing his examples, Said observes that, "the designed interplay between speech and reception, between verbality and textuality, *is* the text's situation, its placing itself in the world" (40). (This proposition would seem to override any question of historical, bio-graphical situatedness.)

The examples are then followed—again somewhat uncannily—by a reversion to the status of a sacred text, here specifically ideological. Like the third potentially aggrandizing part of the pattern traced in "Secular Criticism"—and "The World, The Text, and the Critic" is the very type of such criticism—by appealing to a mutuality or co-presence of speaker and hearer, literary texts (the Novel, in particular) mask the fundamental discursive inequality on which they depend: that is, in making us attend to them at great length, they "compel attention away from the world."

Moreover, their pretense of equality can very well be considered "an act of bad faith"—a sleight of hand to which, Said notes parenthetically, Zahirite theory has already pointed the way, through its scrupulous fidelity to surface meaning and its innate difficulties. Standing behind such acts of displacement, Said says, is the dis-placing power of foundational scriptures like the Bible, "whose centrality, potency, and dominating anteriority inform all Western literature." Once again, the distin-guishing feature of Holy Writ for Said is a uniqueness "that is theologically and hu-manly circumstantial," a phrase Said intends in the restrictive, though still ambiguous sense indicated above. As clarified in "Religious Criticism," Said's final, cursory and polemical essay in *The World, The Text, and the Critic*, religiously inflected criticism is oxymoronic. And yet, it does not mark too much of a concession to admit, with Mi-chael Fishbane, that in a fully saturated intertextual economy, "the Bible does not address us in its entirety, but as a canon-within-a-canon—as a selected cluster of texts or fragments which live within us amid many other, nonbiblical clusters."[58]

We have ventured far from eleventh-century Islamic linguistic theory in the ten pages that follow Said's digression on the Zahirites, only, it seems, to have circled back; and yet it is not clear to me how far we have actually traveled theoretically. When, at the end of *his* essay, Said speaks of the "essential formal incompleteness" that marks essay form generally and the "ironic disparity" between it and the formal text(s) it treats, he has perhaps generated more irony than he knows. According to his essay's logic, texts are *events*, and they are also *objects*. A hermeneutic system developed by the medieval *interpreters* of the *Qur'an* grounds it circumstantially; but this only the prelude to a fugue in which three modernist *authors* wield "the inherent authoritarianism of their authorial authority": their sovereign *prestige*, if one likes.

The discursive *fiction* of a speech situation on the surface of a literary text seamlessly transposes into the necessary *friction* between authors (or their works) and readers. And most tellingly, the example of Quranic exegesis that stages a discussion of literary modernism is itself staged oppositionally: the Zahirite phenomenalists vs. the Batinist school of esotericism—as if such an antinomy, even if polemically urgent in eleventh-century Córdoba, exhausted the possibilities for critical consciousness when it comes to the practice of reading, of claiming and being claimed by, revering and wrestling with, the "elusive sacred."[59]

I admire this essay, but I am not sure I am fully persuaded by its affiliative tactics or modulating logic. Therein, perhaps, resides an implicit caution against any self-consciously affiliative project, including my own. Bakhtin notwithstanding, one must guard against the centrifugal force of polyphony. In Dana Polan's estimation of Said's essay from her 1985 book review,[60] its purposes can perhaps be best summed up by the twofold meaning of the locution, "[writing] takes place" (537), which unifies the worldly tasks of literature and criticism: writing is an event that affects and effects, and writing happens somewhere particular in time and in space. Said's own essay certainly satisfies both criteria and stands thus as exemplary secular criticism. Yet, its whole feels less than the sum of its parts. And the atomistic part in it I find particularly instructive is its most unpredictable *clinamen*: the swerve into Scripture and medieval exegesis.

Said is a Vichian by affiliation with a post-Enlightenment sensibility. Despite the recurrence of Hugh St. Victor in his writing (a citation that comes to him second-hand), he comes late to medieval texts; they do not particularly draw him. Furthermore, and to italicize the obvious, the interpolated scene of Zahirite semanticism Said constructs does not quite approximate a *scene of reading*. "How to do things with words" for medievals is as textual as it is philosophical, unquestionably. Nevertheless, "reading" (*reciting, telling*) the *Qur'an* as Ibn Ḥazm performs that act cannot really serve as the ostensible vehicle for, indeed raison d'être of, a secular criticism. Yet, it is a bridge *between* the conditions of scriptural and literary reading that my book attempts, in part, to traverse. The next section suggests one model for it.

CLOSE TO MIDRASH: IBN EZRA

In an essay entitled "Placing Reading: Ancient Israel and Medieval Europe," Jonathan Boyarin explains why such bridging calls for some courageous engineering. Playing off another critic's distinction between the biblical corpus denoted as "writing" (Holy Writ, *Scriptura*) on the one hand, and, as construed according to the Hebrew word for that same aggregation of text—*miqra* or "reading"—on the other, Boyarin contrasts biblical and rabbinic scenes of reading with those of medieval Christian Europe as prefiguring the modern. Any sociocultural and historical differences here, substantial though they may be, are better referred not to the metaphysics of writing v. reading, but, more limitedly, to questions of pragmatics and ethnography. Scenes of reading in the Bible and Talmud *take place* in social spaces like the Synagogue, Court, or House of Study; they depict reading as a ritualized speech-act performed in public: preaching, lecturing, telling, and reciting. Scenes of reading in late antiquity and medieval and early modern Europe are privatized, often solitary; they *take place* in interior, domestic space: study and bedroom.[61]

I will return to the critical "engineering" problem such differences raise, which stated forthrightly by Boyarin at the end of his essay, amounts to this: "[literary] reading and indeed literature are the historically generated practices of a particular culture, and not the one in which the Bible [or rabbinic discourse, for that matter] were produced" (88). For the moment, let it be said that once "reading" is introduced as an organizing concept—rather than "interpretation" or "exegesis" or "the construal of meaning"—we have altered the energy field that seeks to place texts in the world. The same, of course, would apply also to the thrust of Levinas's essay, "Reality and its Shadow" and to the act we moderns call "criticism."[62]

דיברה תורה כלשון בני אדם or, *Scriptura humane loquitur*. "The Torah speaks in the language of human beings," says a famous dictum from the school of R. Ishmael (first and second centuries CE) in the biblical *midrash halakhah* known as *Sifre Bamidbar*; it is a statement repeated eighteen times in the Talmud.[63] Unlike the contemporaneous school of R. Akiva's more maximalist approach to *midrash* for deriving or clarifying legal import, drawing meaning from the smallest of particulars (like an apparently superfluous letter), R. Ishmael interpreted such features of style as illustrating a commonality between holy text and human speech: *lashon bnei adam* may be a pitted or corrugated surface, yet we still successfully traverse it.[64] This paragraph marks my own swerve into a region, time, and critical activity roughly *proximate* to—although, in the Levinasian sense, also separate from—Ibn Ḥazm's Muslim linguistics.

Avraham ben Meir ibn Ezra (1092–1167) was born in Tudela in the province of Navarre, 335 miles from Córdoba. A true polymath, he was the last of the Golden Age Iberian poets and perhaps the most accomplished—and worldly-situated—Jewish intellectual of his day. The *Stanford Encyclopedia of Philosophy* calls him perhaps "the most important cultural broker of the medieval period."[65] He is best known for his grammatical writings, *Moznayim* (1140), *Tzakhot* and *Sefer ha-Yesod* or *Yesod Diqduq* (both 1145), which (unlike Ibn Ḥazm's school) emphasize morphological transposition back to trilateral roots when textual meaning is at issue, and his Torah commentary, which aside from its prominent inclusion in most great postmedieval editions of the Hebrew Bible with commentary, itself became the object of multiple supercommentaries.[66]

Now, in his commentary on the Book of Genesis, Ibn Ezra makes somewhat subversive use of R. Ishmael's midrashic dictum by suggesting that the surface particularity of the biblical text shows its author (Moses himself, perhaps) to be limited in both human perspective and human language.[67] In other words, the problem of divine authorship, the Sinaitic revelation notwithstanding, has been neatly resolved with reference to a Talmudic precept about exegesis. This is by no means the only instance of Ibn Ezra's idiosyncratic approach, and would seem to roundly qualify Said's conflation of "Judeo-Christian" exegesis with its basis in "revealed" scripture.

When Said writes, for example, that "texts within the Judeo-Christian tradition, at whose center is Revelation, cannot be reduced to a specific moment of divine intervention as a result of which the Word of God entered the World; rather the Word enters human history continually, during and as a part of that history," one rather suspects he has in mind the Gospel of St. John and the Pauline epistles.[68] A genealogy for Christian *allegoresis* that begins with rabbinic *midrash*, conversely, might well have figured as part of his calculus, and its absence is unfortunate considering the counterweight it offers to the logic of textual supercessionism (this, despite Said's proximity to Eric Auerbach's essay on the "Figura").[69] Similarly, the Saidian analysis of Zahiri hermeneutics actually benefits from a lateral conjunction with its specifically medieval Jewish counterpart—hence, the virtue here of introducing the example of Ibn Ezra.[70]

When, for example, Edith Wyschogrod speaks of "the mark or trace of rabbinism [that] must be incised across the history of philosophy as *critique*,"[71] a contextualizing space is opened for us to consider, briefly, the exegetical tradition Ibn Ezra inherits. As is by now fairly familiar in the wake of the 1986 Budick-Hartman volume, *Midrash and Literature*, medieval rabbinic hermeneutics conventionally distinguishes four interpretive layers indicated by the acronym, *PaRDeS*:[72] (1) *Peshat* פשט, plain or surface sense, from a verb meaning "to flatten out"; (2) *Remez* רמז, a word meaning "hints," and thus indicating allegorical or other extrinsic connections; (3) *Derash* דרש, "search" or "inquire," lending itself to a method that works midrashically, with comparative reference to other instances or morphological transpositions of the same word in the biblical corpus; and (4) *Sod* סוד, secret or hermetic sense. While the *peshat/derash* binary can be found in the Talmud employed by rabbinic sages,[73] the opposition between "literal" and "nonliteral" is really a medieval practice, commonly utilized, for example, by Ibn Ḥazm's contemporary, the preeminent exegete from northern France, Rashi (Rabbi Shlomo ben Yitzḥak, 1040–1105). Ibn Ezra based his understanding of it as it was refined by the Babylonian *Geonim*, the presidents of the two great Talmudic academies of Sura and Pumbedita (seventh–eleventh centuries); he himself approached the two terms dialectically.

And while the fourfold schema of *PaRDeS* does share an obvious resemblance to the post-Patristic methodology of literal, allegoric, tropologic, and anagogic levels,[74] any hyphen here between "Judeo" and "Christian" risks misconceiving the parallel, whose historical relation is real but something less than a congruence. Indeed, the matter of medieval hermeneutics for Jewish, Christian, and Muslim traditions, and the place in it of what Said would call "travelling theory" is an immensely complex one. It suffices to say, perhaps, that the antinomy between literal and allegorical stances, or plain and hidden senses, that Said locates in a debate about language in eleventh-century Andalusia is but a strand of a much richer and variegated tapestry. We are dealing with a set of scriptural texts that, in Fishbane's pertinent formulation, are at once "glyph and hieroglyph, sense and transcendence,"[75]

So, despite Spinoza's distortion of his innovations in the seventeenth century and the still-common characterization of him as merely a grammarian, Ibn Ezra's example here is salutary and I enlist it for two reasons. The first is methodological; I want to push off of what I see as Said's partial miscue by outlining an instructively dissimilar interplay between religious and secular practices and material phenomenologies of reading. One of Said's concluding gestures in "The World, The Text, and the Critic" is apropos: quoting Lukács, he confesses, "The essayist is a pure instance of the precursor" (52).

Before I conduct that move in earnest, however, let me explain the second reason by availing myself of a contemporary study on Ibn Ezra that states the case for, if not the "worldliness" of a theory about how scripture can and should be read, then a much fuller, less polarized dimensionality for it. The comparison I am drawing has less to do with the local and specific examples of Ibn Ezra and Ibn Ḥazm themselves within the highly charged field of medieval theories of reading, than with one critical consciousness about how to "think proximity": in contraposition to another.

In her intellectual biography and translation-commentary of his *Introduction to the Torah* in the *Sefer ha-Yashar*, Irene Lancaster makes the following claim for Ibn Ezra as an innovator in philosophical grammar as Wittgenstein intended the term, and an advocate for a more supple and dialectical approach to *peshat* (textual meaning as "sensuous particularity"):

> In his view, the correct *pshat* interpretation represents a deepening understanding on the part of the reading audience, enabling them to grasp the symbolic meaning of a text without sacrificing the surface meaning. In this way, the ordinary becomes symbolic: *pshat* [surface] becomes *sod* [anagogic]. . . . Because *pshat* is directly linked to *sod* in Ibn Ezra's system, it is no longer merely an interpretive device, but is imbued with divinity. Once could even argue that just as engaging in midrashic interpretations had been a religious act for the rabbis of the Mishna and the Talmud, so engaging in *pshat* interpretations became a religious act for Ibn Ezra.[76]

Certainly, other recent recuperations of Ibn Ezra's intellectual importance—for both the Middle Ages and beyond—propose differently ambitious estimations. In "Abraham ibn Ezra and the Twelfth-Century European Renaissance," for example, Ángel Sáenz-Badillos suggests intellectual "agreement or harmony" (albeit it short of "real, demonstrable, historical connections") between Ibn Ezra and the likes of Abelard of Bath, John of Salisbury, and last but not least, the medieval affiliative precursor figure for Edward Said, Hugh of St. Victor. In other words, Ibn Ezra was not just a great medieval Jewish philosopher, commentator, grammarian, and poet, but a culture hero of the Little Renaissance whose worldliness, circumstantiality, and situatedness (while not exactly ventilating the same air as Theodor Adorno or Giambattista Vico), might well have appealed to Said.[77]

But I find Lancaster's account of Ibn Ezra particularly suggestive because it situates Ibn Ezra (if we export Said's phrase) *close to* midrash: hence, the analogy she draws between midrashic interpretation (roughly, third to ninth centuries CE) and medieval exegesis focused on *peshat*—which, to recall, is the counterpart and contemporary to Zahiri phenomenalism. "Midrash," writes Daniel Boyarin, "is best understood as a continuation of the literary activity which engendered the Scriptures themselves."[78] Proximity to *midrash* implicitly looks forward as well, if not to markedly different kinds of texts (for example, literary), than to a sensibility that may adapt itself to another hermeneutic situation (though Lancaster does not advance this particular claim).[79]

At the same time, it should be granted, *pace* Wyschogrod's stringent criterion above, that the term or category of *midrash* "fails to depict Levinas's philosophical work even in a stretched sense."[80] This, I think, is indisputable, and marks a fault-line between Levinas's two bodies of work (Judaistic and philosophical) that is fairly easy to blur, with imprecise definitional or descriptive consequences for both. But the particular question that Lancaster assigns to Ibn Ezra and a life spent with text can thus be reformulated this way: how do I *situate* myself relative to the respective demands placed upon me by the Hebrew language (grammar), by the interpretive practices that have preceded me (tradition), and by my own critical consciousness (philosophy)? These anticipate Edward Said's acknowledged constraints, as they also do, Emmanuel Levinas's.

Levinas's own midrashic sensibility—as a programmatic statement of the sort of critical consciousness on display in his *lectures Talmudique*—can be gleaned from the following passage in "On the Jewish Reading of Scriptures," from *Beyond the Verse*:

> The reading processes that we have just seen at work suggest, first, that the statement commented upon exceeds what it originally wants to say; that what it is capable of saying goes beyond what it wants to say; that it contains more than it contains; that perhaps an inexhaustible surplus of meaning remains locked in the syntactic structures of the sentence, in its word-groups, its actual words, phonemes

and letters, in all this materiality of the saying which is potentially signifying all the time. Exegesis would come to see, in these signs, a bewitched significance that smolders beneath the characters or coils up in all this literature of letters. (109)[81]

This is how Levinas understands R. Ishmael's dictum about human language: the Torah's contraction of the Infinite into the finite, its surplus of meaning. Furthermore, precisely because its interpretive excess links individual commentators to each other and binds different periods and styles of commentary, scripture is holy through its ethical "coordination" of self to neighbor: "the Word of God which commands and vows me to the other, a holy writing before being a sacred text" (xii). In other words, the holiness of the scriptures lies in their capacity to make me a *neighbor* to others and to reorient me as such to them.

"*Miqra*," the rabbinic term for a scripture that is really a reading-as-reciting, also means "calling out." Torah is *miqra* both because it summons and solicits its reader-interlocutors, all its commandments bound up in regard for the neighbor, and because, as in the commentator Rashi's daring act of ventriloquy that Levinas will often cite, *ein ha'miqra hazeh omer elah darsheini*, "this text says nothing other than 'expound me'." Six hundred years later in Geneva, Rousseau would speculate that language originated by means of the jussive commands, "love me" (*aimez-moi*) and "help me" (*aidez-moi*).[82] In eleventh-century Troyes, Rashi threw the Torah's voice, making it speak even more performatively *k'lashon beni adam*, "in the language of men." And what it says demandingly is, "gloss me."

In a footnote to the essay from *Beyond the Verse* quoted above, Levinas remarks,

> In the texts invoked, well-defined situations and beings-equal to themselves,
> holding themselves in definitions and frontiers that integrate them in an order and
> make them rest in the world—are traversed by a breath that arouses and ignites
> their drowsiness or their identity as beings or things, dragging them away from
> their order without alienating them, taking away their contours—as in paintings
> by Dufy.[83]

Levinas's essay was published in 1979, more than three decades after "Reality and Its Shadow" and *Existence and Existants*, and only a few years after "The World, the Text, and the Critic" was published in its journal version by Said. In the interim, which includes all of the Talmudic readings and the publication of *Otherwise Than Being*, Levinas's understanding of the textual and the aesthetic had evolved. One notes, for instance, the bleed between those matters and the midrashic practice he brings to reading rabbinic texts, in the two passages above. The language of enchantment ("magic") now seems to inhere productively in a text: "a bewitched significance that smolders beneath the characters or coils up in all this literature of letters."

For another, in the footnote, rabbinic texts now appear to be thought together with the formal features of modern art that were the object of so much dubiety in "Reality and its Shadow." By retrieving both Levinas and Said in this way after the excursus on Ibn Ezra, I wish to emphasize that a midrashic/aggadic sensibility not only participates in, rather than merely supplement (or as Said would have it, "complement") the act of invention that brings the text into the world, but also attunes itself to situation, circumstantial reality, and worldliness (albeit not quite in Said's sense of these terms) *après la lettre*.[84] The practitioner of *midrash*, the *darshan*, is someone who explicates text, and also homileticizes or preaches—roles or signifying practices that Levinas adapts to the entirely modern conditions of his Talmudic readings given at the Colloque des Intellectuels Juifs de Langue Francaise.[85]

A distant cousin to Cutter's magician, we could say, the *darshan* manipulates the textual object at hand, which becomes both what it was ("pledge") and also what has now been made of it ("turn-prestige"). In other words, *drisha* (inquiring, seeking, demanding—from *l'drosh*) is *hashava* (bringing back—from *l'hashiv*).[86] As Levinas says, capturing what I earlier called "the risk of mimesis," "It seems essential to me, then, that the Jewish reading of Scripture was pursued in the uneasiness, but also in the expectation, of *midrash*."[87]

Michael Fishbane's "What is the Meaning of a Sacred Text?" narrates the transition from ancient to classical Judaism as the reopening of a closed, written text (the biblical corpus) by a set of hermeneutic procedures instituted by the rabbinic Sages such that "the very sanctity of the biblical text was hermeneutically established" (123). Intracanonical boundaries were overcome into the bargain, just as thresholds between sacred text and the hermeneutic system that had been developed (and legislated) to expound it were blurred. But something else also occurred.

> And further, this very same Pharisaic hermeneutical tradition reciprocally established new criteria for the sanctity of the biblical text—transferring to its physical state hermeneutically established notions of priestly contagion. Thus the Pharisaic expression "to defile the hands" is the technical phrase for an inspired, sacred text. Arguably, this designation also served polemical, exclusionary purposes—specifically against the Sadducees (123).

This marks the point in the argument where my book's title, after a brief outline in prologue and introduction, gets its fuller due. What Levinas identifies as the bifold of uneasiness and expectation also aptly describes a pair of hands in their aspect of seizing a text. The next chapter begins with the rabbinic proscription against defilement as, strangely, a textual property, restaged then by Levinas in some of his Talmudic readings, which set the stage in turn for a final juxtaposition of Levinasian and Saidian fingerprints for exegesis.

CHAPTER 2

Sollicitation and Rubbing the Text

Reading Said and Levinas Reading

You asked me what is the good of reading the Gospels in Greek.
I answer that it is proper we move our finger
Along letters more enduring than those carved in stone,
And that, slowly pronouncing each syllable,
We discover the true dignity of speech.

—Czeslaw Milosz

[One who] was reading [a sacred] book [in scroll form on Shabbat while sitting]
on an elevated [threshold] and one end of the book rolled from his hand [outside
and into the public domain below] he may roll] it [back] to himself [since one
of its ends is still in his hand. However, if] one was reading on top of a roof
[which is a private domain] and [one end of] the scroll rolled from his hand
[into the public domain below], as long as [the edge of the book] did not reach
to [within] ten handbreadths above the public domain, the book is still in its
own area, and] he may roll it [in] to himself. But once the book has reached to
[within] ten handbreadths [above the ground, he is prohibited from rolling it
back to himself. In that case] he [may only] turn it over onto the side with
writing [so that the lettering of the book should face down and not be exposed
and degraded].

—Tractate *Shabbat* 5a

I have read and re-read [the Bible] until in many parts the pages have faded
out—I mean, my fingers have rubbed off the dots, and I must supply whole
verses from memory.

—Helen Keller

TO MAKE THE HANDS IMPURE

Tum'at yadayim, as we saw, signifies a special halakhic category within the vast apparatus of cultic observance during the First and Second Temple periods by which objects (vessels, clothes, and houses, for example) and persons were distinguished as either ritually clean or unclean: *tahor/tamei*. In Judaism, the concept of *tum'ah* (from the Hebrew for "sealed" or "blocked"), as the marked term of the binary, applies not only to animal sacrifice and vicissitudes of the human body (childbirth and death, emissions and exudates) or food and liquid, but also to questions of propriety regarding ritual intent or location (while making a Temple offering, for example), and— surprisingly enough—the material status of scripture.[1] Primarily, however, persons, houses, vessels, sacred food, and drink are *meqabel tum'ah*, "susceptible to impurity."[2]

Tum'at ha'met (corpse) is the severest (*avi avot ha'tum'ah*) contaminant among the eleven *avot* or "fathers" of *tum'ah*.[3] There are degrees of *tum'ah*, first, second, third, and so on, with diminishing levels for each successive *v'lad* ("offspring") *ha'tum'ah*. "Defilement of the hands" signifies a *sheni l'tum'ah* or second-level "descendant"; hands cease to be *tamei* not through recourse to *tevilah* (immersion) in a *mikveh*, but more simply through washing with a vessel (*netilat yadayim*). Finally, *sifrei haqodesh*, sacred books (but, *pace* Martin Goodman, better translated, "writings of the holy"[4]), *themselves* correspond to a *sheni l'tum'ah* and make the hands of the person touching them *tamei* (as could *tefillin*, and in some sources, their housings and straps).[5] As the Mishnah states the principle in *Yadayim* 3:5, "all holy scriptures defile the hands":
כל כתבי הקדש מטמאין את הידים.

We learned briefly—and the rabbinic sages of the first to third centuries register a certain confusion about its etiology—holiness (of scripture) became attached to a strictly cultic concern for purity (of object), with touch accordingly figured as transference and hands being the medium of conduction. There is thus no halakhic category of *tum'at einayim*, *tum'at oznayim*, *tum'at af*, or *tum'at lashon*—defilement by sight, hearing, smell, or voice, although Jewish law leaves no bodily orifice unlegislated when it comes to godly conduct. (In ancient Judaism, holiness was apparently regarded as possessing a substance-like quality [*sancta contagion*], which gradually ceded in the rabbinic period to strictly halakhic determinations.)[6]

And yet, *tum'at yadayim*—defilement of and by the hands, a secondary degree of impurity that leaves the rest of the body clean—became linked in a logical but still not entirely self-evident way to holy books.[7] And even though it became common practice outside the Temple to wash one's hands before Torah study, the connection between scripture and ritual purification was never exclusively functional—for example, hygienic (Heb. *neqiah*). The question, as both historian Martin Goodman and philosopher Emmanuel Levinas have each asked from within their respective disciplinary predilections, remains open. "But why would a text that is the work of the Holy Spirit make the hands impure?" (EL). "But what exactly did they mean by ascribing sanctity to a book? Did they refer to the ideas spoken within the book, or to the words of the book when spoken, or to the book itself as a physical object, or to all of these?" (MG).

Goodman's answer calls attention to the special status of sacred scrolls in ancient Judaism, for which "no parallel can be found in Greek and Roman paganism" (103.) The rabbis retroactively tied such sacrality to the Hebrew Bible's inspired content as well as to the more pragmatic matter of which books in it were to be regarded as canonical. In the Talmudic tractate *Megillah*, for example, a question surrounds which of the *Ketuvim*, Song of Songs, Esther, and Ecclesiastes, none of which actually contains the *shem ha'meforash* or Tetragrammaton, are to considered part of the canon, the criterion being whether they transmit uncleanness or not. The mishnaic tractate *Yadayim* includes a similar dispute between Sadducees and Pharisees about the writings of the epic poet Homer.

> The Sadducees say: We have a quarrel to pick with you, O Pharisees, for according to you the Holy Scriptures defile the hands where as the writings of Homer would not defile the hands. Rabban Yoḥanan ben Zakkai replied: Have we naught against the Pharisees save this: According to them the bones of an ass are clean while the bones of the Yoḥanan the High Priest are unclean! They answered him: Their uncleanness corresponds to their preciousness, so that no man would make spoons out of the bones of his father and mother. He said to them: So too the Holy Scriptures, their uncleanness corresponds to their preciousness. The writings of Homer, which are not precious, do not defile the hands. (4:6)

The paradoxical equation for holy books, then, is between impurity and valuation— "precious," therefore "unclean."

But Scripture's materiality—its object-status as parchment the Talmud names "our [or their] body" (*bMegillah* 9a)—would seem to stand behind all later correlations with the human form, and specifically hands, as susceptible to "defilement."[8] In his two Talmudic readings, "The Translation of Scripture" (on *bMegillah* 8b–9b) and "For a Place in the Bible" (on *bMegillah* 7a) from colloquia devoted to the theme of "the seventy nations" and collected in *In the Time of Nations*, Levinas translates the latter formulation—which, halakhically, denotes something other than *physical* contamination—as "stripping the text of its religious eminence"—that is, interpretive maculation, a willful or careless, and thus *sullying* disposition to read, but also an impatience with the mediating frame of Talmudic discourse, as if the Torah's membrane could be "touched" bare (or empty)- handedly—without, that is, the scrim of commentary. He tells us that his purpose is to distill the "singular meaning" of the rabbinic principle, "whatever its true origin may be." Thus, from "The Translation of Scripture,"

> the reading of the Book of books presupposes not only the current procedures of understanding, which make it possible to grasp a thought in the letters as a hand seizes an object. The reading is enveloped in an older wisdom. A wisdom older

than the patent presence of a meaning in the writing. A wisdom without which the message buried deep within the enigma of the text cannot be grasped. It does not let itself be touched by hands that remain bare: as if it might make them dirty. Only books that have lost their inspired message can pass for books that no longer make the hands that touch them unclean. They can without danger fall into the hands of anyone. (38–49)[9]

This is no Levinasian critique of the light-handed and manipulative mimesis that he finds in the close-up magic of the aesthetic. Instead, the human touch in relation to a *saintly* text is a heavy-handed one: it seizes, it grasps, it sullies, it misappropriates. In "For a Place in the Bible," hands are "'*asqaniot*—always busy, taking hold of everything.[10] Indeed nothing is more mobile, more impertinent, more restless than the hand" (24).

The touch of immodest hands on text, then, signifies the stuff of both impiety and impropriety. And so, Levinas, too, knowledgably extends the Sages' conflation of *qedushah* and *tum'ah*, sanctity of scripture and purity of object, which we see from "Desacralization and Disenchantment," his Talmudic reading from 1971, elaborated outside the strict bounds of the halakhic formulation for defiled hands: "holiness [*sainteté*]: that is separation or purity, the essence without admixture that can be called Spirit and which animates the Jewish tradition." Its opposite in that essay is not "impurity" per se but rather a more atavistic or totemic notion of "the sacred" (*le sacré*) such as we might find expounded in Durkheim, Levy-Bruhl, or Eliade: that which blurs boundaries and which, in its impersonality, calls up the notion of the *il-y-a*, the brute "there is," explored by Levinas in early work like *De l'existence à l'existent* and *Le temps et l'autre* (1947).[11]

Even before those works, however, and three decades before the Talmudic readings given at the Colloque des Intellectuels Juifs de Langue Francaise, Levinas is thinking about the sacred somewhat differently in a way that anticipates a theory of reading and hermeneutic sensibility that may allow us to bridge the worlds—for criticism's sake—of religious and secular textuality. In the short essay, "The Meaning of Religious Practice" from 1937, he declares,

> The ritual is precisely the behavior of one who, amid the racket of our everyday action, perceives the mystical resonance of things. If it stops us at the threshold of the natural world, it is because it introduces us into the mystery of the world. It touches the sacred face of things. . . . It is efficacious and transitive, it is work, it accomplishes—it is an event.[12]

Such an analysis, even if it appears to swerve from the direction of Levinas's anti-aesthetic rhetoric if not his thought from the 1940s onward, invites us to consider the act of reading along the lines of such an "event": that is, the *ritual* character of literary reading alongside circumscribed liturgical and scriptural practices, which is the intimation of this book. If "to write" is an intransitive verb (Roland Barthes),[13] then "to read" shares with religious practice, properties both efficacious and transitive, and touches the sacred face of things.

> My condition—or my un-condition—is my relation to books. It is the very movement-towards-God [*l'à-Dieu*]. Language and the book that arises and is already read in language is phenomenology, the 'staging' in which the abstract is made concrete. . . . This coming and going [*ce va-et-vient*] from text to reader and from reader to text, and this renewal of meaning, are perhaps the distinctive feature of all written work, of all literature, even when it does not claim to be Holy Writing. (*Beyond the Verse*, 171)

Holy Writings may possess some other secret supplementary essence, but "it is because all literature is inspired that religious revelation can become text and show itself to hermeneutics" (171), a rather remarkable claim that would appear to give priority to (worldly) text over (divine) revelation.

TO BLOODY THE HANDS

But for the moment, and to return to the effectual properties of hands: a more famous instance of their *force majeure* in Levinas's Talmudic readings is the story of the Amoraic sage Rava (Abba ben Yosef bar Ḥama, ca. 270–350 CE) in tractate *bShabbat* 88a— "A Sadducee [sectarian—other editions of the text have מין *min*, a variant for "heretic"] saw Rava buried in study holding his fingers beneath his foot and rubbing it so hard that blood spurted from it"—that gets turned into an allegory of hermeneutic practice. Robustly applying his own friction, Levinas comments as follows:

> *Le geste de Raba est bizarre: il frotte son pied si fort que le sang en jaillit: à force de s'oublier dans l'étude! Comme par hasard, frotter pour que le sang en jaillisse est peut-être la manière dont il faut frotter le texte pour arriver à la vie qu'il dissimule. Beaucoup d'entre vous penseront avec raison qu'en ce moment même je suis en train de frotter le texte pour en faire jaillir du sang. Je relève le défi! A-t-on jamais vu lecture qui soit autre chose que cet effort exercé sur un texte? Dans la mesure où elle repose sur la confiance accordée à l'auteur, elle ne peut consister qu'en cette violence faite aux mots pour leur arracher le secret que le temps et les conventions recouvrent de leurs sédimentations dès que ces mots s'exposent à l'air libre de l'histoire. Il faut en frottant enlever cette couche qui les altère. Je pense que vous trouverez cette méthode de travail naturelle. Raba en se frottant le pied donnait une expression plastique au travail intellectuel auquel il se livrait.*

Raba's gesture is odd: he rubs his foot so hard that blood spurts out. That was the degree to which he forgot himself in study. As if by chance, to rub in such a way that blood spurts out is perhaps the way one must "rub" the text to arrive at the life it conceals. Many of you are undoubtedly thinking, with good reason, that at this very moment, I am in the process of rubbing the text to make it spurt blood—I rise to the challenge. Has anyone ever seen a reading that was anything other than this effort carried out on a text? To the extent that a reading rests on the trust granted the author, it can consist only in this violence done to words to tear from them the secret that time and conventions cover over with their sedimentations as soon as those words are exposed to the open air of history. One must, by rubbing, remove this layer which corrodes them. I think you would find this way of proceeding natural. Raba, in rubbing his foot, was giving plastic expression to the intellectual work he was involved in. ("The Temptation of Temptation," *Nine Talmudic Readings*, 46–47)

Is this legerdemain? If not, then by rubbing that word a little as Latin *legere* (reading) plus French *demain* (hand), an interlinguistic pun reveals some freely exercised readerly manipulation.[14] "Rubbing" the text in this sense would mean exposing its corrugations and irregularities; as Annette Aronowicz has cited French commentator David Banon, it complements Levinas's usage of *sollicitation* to connote a singularly agitated mode of reading.[15] Where the Helen Keller example I cite again as an epigraph to this chapter suggests mimetic loss—the wear endured by the pages—the Levinas example figures interpretive gain: *il faut en frottant enlever cette couche qui les altère*, accreted layers of received meaning abraded and removed.

The distinction has a distant cousin in the disparity between a work's embedded "truth content" and, in its afterlife, the increased protrusion of "material content" that Walter Benjamin ventured in his essay on Goethe's *Die Wahlverwandtschaften*.[16] It certainly seems quite far removed from Poulet's astonished "critical consciousness" with its various modalities ("nuances of identification and non-identification") of criticizing subject-and-criticized object relations.[17] Can we even draw a correspondence between the literary critic's vocation as outlined by Poulet (or Edward Said, for that matter), and the practice of Talmudic reading—mobile, abrading, appropriative— reengineered by Levinas?

Levinas appears to suggest as much himself when he generalizes that practice to intensive reading of all kinds in the passage above. His own literary criticism takes the form of allusions to a host of authors (mostly novelistic) that includes Dickens, Poe, Shakespeare, Zola, Racine, Gogol, Dostoevsky, Grossman, other Russians, highly idiosyncratic reflections on Proust, LaPorte, Leiris, Blanchot, and Celan, unattributed revoicings of Rimbaud and Baudelaire, and, in particular, an essay on S. Y. Agnon, which, as Jill Robbins has keenly observed, finds both affinity and affiliation with Agnon's own midrashic sensibility (although, this may simply be another example of Levinas's discovering himself in what he reads).[18] As Robbins also suggests, the technique of classical midrashic commentary, and certainly reproduced in Levinas's own commentary on the Talmud, involves a close cousin to *frottage*: "midrash reads until it finds a knot, like a hard place, or node, or bump in the smooth text of readings" (139).

Sandor Goodhart prefers "gap, tear, hole, discontinuity, wound, silence, lack"[19] to Robbins's "knot, node, or bump," but in either case the hermeneutics of *midrash*, as a secondary textual intervention, engages the prior text in its need to be manipulated, even altered, but more prosaically: *manhandled*.

Levinas has written elsewhere that "language is a battering ram"[20] so he surely knew the Talmudic commentary in *bShabbat* 88b that continues *directly* after the story of Rava (and also appears in Tractate *bSanhedrin* 34a):

תני דבי ר' ישמעאל (ירמיהו כג) וכפטיש יפוצץ סלע מה פטיש זה נחלק לכמה ניצוצות

כל דיבור ודיבור שיצא מפי הקב"ה נחלק לשבעים לשונות/

אף מקרא אחד יוצא לכמה טעמים

> "In R. Ishmael's School it was taught: *And like a hammer that breaks the rock in pieces* (Jeremiah 23:29), i.e., just as [the rock] is split into many splinters, "just as a hammer is divided into many sparks, so every single word that went forth from the Holy One, blessed be He, split up into seventy languages" (*bShabbat* 88b) / "so also may one Biblical verse convey many teachings." (*bSanhedrin* 34a)[21]

But the notion of working upon by "rubbing" the (Talmudic) text is not particularly remarkable in the light of other rabbinical formulations by the Sages themselves, like *yegiah v'ameil* (the work of toil and taking pains in study), the second component of which is a verb that means not only "delve" but also "knead" or "work through"—as by massage.

It also bears comparison with a related metaphor Levinas uses when he reads a portion of the *mishnah* from tractate *Pirqei Avot* 2:15, "The words of the sages are like glowing coals" this way: "Why not fire instead of embers? Because one must blow on them to revive them."[22] Strenuous reading requires not only excoriation by hand, but patient insufflation, a trope Levinas says he has borrowed from R. Ḥayyim of Volozhin. Pertinently, this image of the reader respiring in the face of the Mishnaic text, in two late Talmudic Readings from 1973 and 1989, is inflected by the adverb, "tenderly" (itself echoing the trope of "a further deep breathing even in the breath cut short by the wind of alterity" at the end of *Otherwise Than Being* [180], where the ethical subject is pronounced "a lung at the bottom of his substance").[23]

No, what is singular is the audacious simile itself: comparing the work of reading to an exposure and wounding of the body that appears as compulsive as it does an act of displacement.[24] Levinas is correct: it is an odd gesture. But his translation of the Aramaic text is (one assumes, knowingly) a loose one. For the *gemara* says this:

ויתבה אצבעתא דידיה תותי כרעא וקא מייץ בהו וקא מבען אצבעתיה דמא. /*v'yatvah etzba'atah diyadei totei qra'ah v'kah mayetz bahu mab'an etzbe'atei damah* ("He was sitting with his fingers squeezed under his feet, and his fingers were gushing blood").

The grammar is somewhat ambiguous, since the word *etzba'atah* can mean both fingers and toes in Aramaic lexicon. But evidently, what the text is trying to convey is that Rava was sitting with fingers under his feet, with such grinding pressure that it inadvertently caused blood to flow from them. Rashi's commentary assumes "fingers" and Hebraicizes the Aramaic action verb as *ma'akh*, "to crush, dissolve by rubbing"; and most commentators have taken their cue accordingly.[25]

What does *not* appear to be the case, however, is a hand exfoliating a foot so violently as to make it bleed. Instead, digits seem to have been mashed under the pressure of sitting (or even perhaps by one foot grinding against its fellow, although as I said, "fingers" not "toes," tends to be the standard glossing of *etzb'atah*).

Moreover, the odd detail of the spurting blood may well be construed as giving "plastic expression" to *something*, since the gnomic aggadic text does call for comment; but perhaps not quite as Levinas has parsed it. Thus, the larger context of the *sugya*[26] (pericope) Levinas chose to expound centers on *kabbalat- hatorah*, the covenantal moment in Exodus 24 when the Israelites—with famously inverse chronologic—utter *na'aseh v'nishmah*, "we will do and we will hear," after witnessing God's law pronounced at Sinai. *This* is the topic Rava is so engrossed in. As Levinas elaborates at length, the Talmudic discussion centers on that seemingly counterintuitive "doing before hearing"—hence the Sadducee's upbraiding of Rava: by his reckoning, the impetuousness which causes blood to spurt while "buried" in Torah study is the same impetuousness that (foolishly) underwrites "we will do and we will hear" in the first place—as if to say, "these carelessly bloodied fingers are your just deserts for doing before hearing." From later in the *sugya*:

> The Sadducee said to Rava, "Oh impulsive one, who puts the mouth before the ears. You still persevere in your impulsiveness. First you should have heard the commandments so you would know whether you are able to accept them. And if you did not hear them first, you should never have accepted them!

As we have seen, Levinas exports the blood-spurting incident from the plane of *peshat* to serve as a vivid allegory for reading—that is, not merely engrossment of attention but purposeful *abrasion* as hermeneutic method. It is his own super-aggadic demonstration of the eisegesis at work in the rabbinical tradition, the way a *darshan* characteristically "reads into" (*aller solliciter*) scripture. But a stricter, perhaps more disinterested account of the Talmudic text shows fingers as the *object* rather than the agent of rubbing—even if the skin's exposure is crucial to both scenarios.

If hands customarily *hold* texts, *trace* them with index finger, and even *incise* them— all figures for responsive reading as *rubbing*—then Levinas's simile does not quite work. It may rub the Talmudic text to make it spurt blood, as Levinas freely confesses, thus penetrating its essence, its secret scent; but the applied friction may also amount to an agitation the text's body does not manifestly incite (although this would be the import of Levinasian *sollicitation*: to "shake up" or agitate the text at hand).

Of such friction as a property solely of the scriptural, and thus its putative difference from a hermeneutic associated with other textual cultures, Geoffrey Hartman writes,

I would like to assert that Scripture can be distinguished from fiction by its frictionality: not only its respect for friction, which exists also in literary texts, but its capacity to leave traces, which incite and even demand interpretation of what it has incorporated. Yet . . . contemporary theories . . . which derive partly from biblical scholarship, make such a distinction more difficult. There may be more cryptomnesia in fiction than in the Bible.[27]

An alternate reading of Rava's spilt blood, however—one that Levinas does not consider—might connect it more directly to the *lemma,* the biblical source chapter for the pericope, Exodus 24: 4–8:

And Moses wrote all the words of the LORD. And he rose early in the morning, and built an altar at the foot of the mountain, and twelve pillars according to the twelve tribes of Israel. Then he sent young men of the children of Israel, who offered burnt offerings and sacrificed peace offerings of oxen to the LORD. And Moses took half the blood and put it in basins, and half the blood he sprinkled on the altar. Then he took the Book of the Covenant and read in the hearing of the people. And they said, "All that the LORD has said we will do, and be obedient." And Moses took the blood, sprinkled it on the people, and said, "This is the blood of the covenant which the LORD has made with you according to all these words."

If we were to try to connect the surface meaning of the anecdote with the *sugya* that incorporates it—after the fashion of Ibn Ezra, say—we might speculate that whatever the plastic expression of Raba's bleeding fingers means, it figurally recalls *the sprinkled blood of the covenant.* The Talmud records Rava's *démarche* to the Sadducee as follows:

For those of us who go in the ways of complete faith, it is written about us "The perfect faith of the upright shall lead them" (Proverbs 11:3). For those people who go in the way of perverseness, it is written about them, "and the perverseness of the faithless shall destroy them."

But Rava's action of single-minded Torah study, even or especially with its bloody effects, may represent the decisive forestalling of the Sadducee's censure before it was even uttered—as if to say, "*This is* how I identify myself with the covenant of *naaseh v'nishmah*: by personalizing it corporeally; what my bloodied fingers recapitulate metonymically is the blood of the covenant as sprinkled on the people."[28]

This happens to be my own gloss, not Levinas's—although I am trying to tread a middle path between his and Rava's footsteps. Instead, he offers a powerful *metaphor*—potent enough to be recited by many of his commentators as the quintessential expression of a Levinasian hermeneutic for reading,[29] sacrificing metonymic fidelity for the (magical-seeming!) effects of allegory. What might this alternate construal of the Talmudic passage do to the various implications of *frottage* that follow from Levinas's own idiosyncratic reading? Or differently put, which interpretation better exemplifies his own trope of kinetic exegesis: Levinas's, which puts its own creative stamp on the passage about Rava and productively misreads it, but does not takes pains to embed it entirely within its ambient Talmudic context, a technique we might call, after Levinas's famous dialectic of Hebrew and Greek), "making Aramaic speak Hebrew?"[30] Or, an exegesis that reads the French *frotter* more "faithfully" by returning to the linguistic original, and connects the textual detail of blood to the other implicit signifier in the text that most obviously coincides with it? This, we would call simply, "making Aramaic speak Aramaic."

Following trends in Bible Studies that are now many decades old, rabbinics scholars have been opening the Talmud to principles of textual source criticism that both refine the hermeneutical situation (David Weiss Halivni and Shamma Friedman) and reconceive its discursive particulars along the lines of a *poetics*, in consequent dialogue with other kinds of literary genres and rhetorics (e.g., Daniel Boyarin, Aryeh Cohen, Sergey Dolgopolski, Yonah Fraenkel, Jeffrey Rubenstein, B. S. Wimpfheimer, Judith Baskin, and Dina Stein).[31] Among a number of innovations that shift the ground of traditional Talmud study, the role of the *stam* (the scribal compositor or redactor) is retrieved from the textual background as a critical intelligence analogous to editorial author—a layer of internal interpretation.

Likewise, the "sea of the Talmud" can now be understood in terms of currents and cross-currents, gradients, regions and zones—discursive vertical layers and horizontal rhetorical seams in complex, dialogic relation beyond the simple binary of *halakhah/aggadah*. In his *Narrating the Law: A Poetics of Talmudic Legal Stories*, for example, Barry Wimpfheimer looks at a short aggadic portion within a pericope about drunkenness on the festival of Purim featuring the same Rava of the bloodied fingers in *bShabbat* 88a.[32] His conclusion about the pragmatics of reading is especially relevant to our concerns here:

> The *Megilla* 7b example illustrates the disjunction between the content of talmudic legal narrative and the typical frame for reading such narratives. The monological frame is motivated by its own interests—the creation of a single precedent through a process of dialectical resolution—to read legal narratives as if they were statutes. Such a reading practice consistently finds the rule of law in a story that may or may not contain it. Invariably, there is content in the complex narrative that resists the simplification inherent in flattening the story into a statute. In order to account for such residue, the reader must work within a *nomos* that recognizes the extent to which the cultural world consists of semiotic systems beyond legal rules, and that these systems, in crucial and nondoctrinal ways, also determine behavior, even to the point of making competing normative claims on legal subjects. (29–30)

Mutatis mutandis, one could say that Levinas reads the Rava anecdote in "The Temptation of Temptation" motivated by *his* interests, ironically enough producing an account of the story more monological (in terms of his philosophical predilections) than dialogically embedded according to the text's own (inter)textual affinities.[33] It is a striking account of the remarkable impress of intense study on readerly hand because, through a handy chiasmus, it *reverses* the thematic polarity of the localized story to arrive at *the impress of intense readerly hand on study*. To adapt the analysis above, *Levinas* consistently finds ethical adventure and intrigue in aggadic stories that may or may not contain them—especially when we consider that neither the Talmud's rabbinic sages nor its redactors identified the "philosophical" thrust of *aggadah* in quite the same way Levinas prefers.

Not unlike the political and sociological unconscious in literary narrative excavated by Fredric Jameson and Pierre Bourdieu, or the homoerotic unconscious in novels and the sexual unconscious in Talmudic narrative as teased out, respectively, by Eve Kosofsky Sedgwick and Daniel Boyarin, Levinas's readings could be said to distill the Talmud's *ethical or metaphysical unconsciousness*, what he calls in "Promised or Permitted Land," its "secret scent,"[34] through its most concentrated fragrance, the *aggadah*. Wimpfheimer and others rightly maintain that *aggadah* is less accurately defined formalistically as a particular textual genre than as a reading practice dictated or overseen by hermeneutic convention—one that, certainly by the Geonic period, was even exclusionary, relative to the prioritization of its halakhic complement.[35]

Levinas's aggadic readings are unconventional, but they powerfully attest to reading *as a hermeneutic practice*. In addition, they are performative in the extreme; as *explications de texte*, they elucidate their chosen passages before an audience by teaching and unpacking them as if they were specimens of literary modernism. If the Talmud can be read analytically for its structural poetics, what Levinas's readings offer supplementarily is their own *poesis*. He finds his own license in the Talmud's already pronounced freedom of expression. In "Promised Land or Permitted Land," which I discuss in the final section of this chapter, he remarks of an instance of *frottage within* the text at hand: "What an odd method of exegesis! A forced reading [solicitation] of the text, if ever there was one. But also an attempt to animate the text through correspondences and echoes" (*NTR*, 55). Moreover, while he does occasionally contextualize his reading within *sugya* or tractate-chapter, as in the magnificent exegesis of *bSota* 37a–37b in *Beyond the Verse*, most are *cuttings*, a secretly scented extract plucked from the surrounding whole, which they customarily do not identify, eschewing chapter reference within a given tractate or leaving undocumented the discursive halakhic flow.[36] (They also do not appear in English translation accompanied by the discussions that preceded and followed them.)[37]

They are correctly named: they are *lectures Talmudique*, Talmudic readings, not Talmudic *learnings*, a point I emphasize in order to capture the customary locution for the way classical Jewish sources are traditionally studied in the Yeshiva—they are "learned" as opposed to "read" or "studied."[38] And although he never says as much (preferring a categorization like "metaphysics and philosophical anthropology"), and though he confesses to lacking the "intellectual muscle" for a commentary that also includes the *halahkah*, it is quite possible that Levinas is drawn to aggadic discourse in the *Bavli* in part because, proportionately speaking, it is nonnormative, "outside the subject" of rabbinic legalistics (so to speak) and thus a kind of intratextual Talmudic "alien" or "stranger," even "widow and orphan."[39]

Earlier, I referred to Levinas's "literary criticism," but that is something of a misnomer. Although he was more than passingly familiar with trends in structuralist and poststructuralist thought, he almost never practiced exegesis on literary texts; at best, he quoted from them or wrote appreciations of their authors.[40] He was not even the closest or painstaking reader of philosophical texts, on the model of say, Derrida's or Cavell's scrupled commentaries. Conversely, his labor-intensive readings of rabbinic texts were brilliant, supersubtle, audacious in their translation of Talmudic knowledge into philosophy's wisdom of love, risky wagers of commentary oscillating with critique.[41]

But in accord with the dictum, *il faut en frottant enlever cette couche qui les altère* ("one must, by rubbing, remove this layer that corrodes them"), they often appear to *participate* in that deterioration or corrosion which rubbing is supposed to undo by, as it were, substituting a Levinasian layer of meaning for a strictly textual one. This willed effacement recalls Rashi's deployment of the Hebrew *ma'akh*[42] ("to crush, dissolve by rubbing, rub off"), a verb that possesses a family resemblance to similar trilaterals, for example, *makhak*, that are concerned with "blotting out" and "erasing." (The irony is piquant, considering the baseline significance to Levinas, in his philosophical anthropology, of *le visage* or "facing"[43]). That is, the logic of Levinas's readings is propelled as much by *appliquez* or *superposez* (imposition) as by *frotter* (exfoliation). For it is certainly true in regard to hermeneutically prehensile, reading hands, too, that "nothing is more mobile, more impertinent, more restless." Derrida's paradox of tact and tactility acquires perhaps unexpected force here, and as Jill Robbins has remarked, while Levinas may "say" Abraham (the figure of departure and otherness), he often "does" Odysseus (the figure of return to origin).[44]

But that is just to say perhaps that Levinas was a midrashist not a Zahirite when it comes to critical consciousness, a weaver and knotter of new or previously hidden threads in the original fabric—in part a reflection of the discursive situation of the Colloque des Intellectuels Juifs that typically included more philosophers than Talmudists, in part the consequence of Levinas's principled selection of aggadic (narrative) portions over halakhic (statutory) ones.[45] It is also to say that for Levinas, texts share with faces the property of "enigma" over "phenomenon," and are to be encountered and solicited rather than deciphered. (The same can be said of Levinas's own writing, which Derrida famously described as making us "tremble"—*soliciter*.)

Although not cognate with the sort of rabbinics scholarship we see in Stephen Fraade's multitiered approach to Tannaitic texts, Levinas, I think would agree with Fraade's valuable distinction between interpretive *mastery* of the sources (text-criticism) on the one hand, and a *manner* of reading them (performativity) on the other.[46] Even if Levinas authorizes rubbing by tying it to "the trust granted the author," he understands that a text is not simply *given* and thus appropriable.[47] It solicits interlocutors and puts them and its latent, as yet unexpressed, meanings on call. In Robert Gibbs's words (embroidering a thread that knots both Levinas and Derrida): "To be legible is not the same as to be visible. . . . Because a text is imperceptible [a fabric of traces, itself a trace][48] it must always risk being lost—even should the book be kept, even transmitted."[49] Indeed when Levinas distinguishes between "holy writing" and "sacred text"—the one a prerequisite for the other—he is capturing this risk structure or vulnerability that exposes—vouchsafes—a text to a set of hands.

> Therein lies the impurity of these inspired texts, their latent impurity. It was not absurd to warn readers of the dangers brought about by the very holiness of the Torah, and to declare it impure in advance. Hands off. Contagion, or something of the sort. The impurity returns to and strikes at the indiscreet hand from which it came. (*In the Time of Nations*, 24)

For our purposes, after the pivot to hands that rub (albeit a feature of Levinas's own midrashic fable), I want now to retrieve the rabbinic connection between hands and defilement from earlier in this chapter and the Introduction, in counterpoint with Edward Said's concern with literary language in dialogue with the world. It will be recalled that Said explicates worldliness as "assured contamination" by "numerous heterogeneous realities."[50] A text is *in* the world. But Levinas also speaks of Talmudic discourse not only as wisdom and philosophy, but also as a *vernacular*. It always exerts pressure on the abstract or the ideal by grounding its discussions of worldly acts (even if referred to a halakhic *nomos*)[51] in material conditions. To use Saidian terms, its authority must have truck with "molestation," a provocative term, to say the least, but signifying, as in the Zahirite example, the maculate nature of interpreting texts "as objects whose interpretation—by virtue of the exactness of their situation in the world—*has already commenced*."

But the fate of "worldliness" in Said's usage, notwithstanding the endorsement of Zahirite parsimony, is polysemy. For it also connotes "philological." In the late essay "The Return to Philology," Said describes the abiding basis of humanistic practice as just that: "a detailed, patient scrutiny of and a lifelong attentiveness to the words and rhetorics by which language as used by human beings who exist in history: hence the word 'secular,' as I use it, as well as the word 'worldliness'" (61). Moreover, this also demarcates the province of art, the category of the aesthetic defined by Said as a resistance to both the givenness of reading and "the leveling pressures of everyday experience from which, however, art paradoxically derives" (63). And yet, again in this late essay, Said also gestures briefly to Islamic hermeneutic induction, which, like the close reading of literary texts, balances reception (appropriation) and resistance (distantiation), *isnad*, *usul*, and *ijitihad*.

The analogue to *midrash*, whether rabbinic or Levinasian, is patent, I think. The main differences from Said's criteria are two: (1) the philological impulse obviously belongs to hermeneutic practices not only secular *but also* religious, and (2) the patient scrutiny of and attentiveness to words and rhetorics exercised through *solicitation* or *frottage* conforms not to "critique" (Said's favored term), but rather to the "craftwork captured in the base meaning of *lectio*" (from Valerie Allen's formulation cited earlier), "namely, the sheer ability to distinguish and enunciate letters on a page." Or, in a (Hebrew) word, *miqra*.[52] Both Levinas and Said apply pressure (Aramaic *mayetz*) to the Pouletian scene of reading as a wholly private affair of quasi-sprit possession. Squeezing it, Said calls it the antinomian "worldly practice of humanism" with "its widening circles of awareness" (75). Rubbing it, Levinas calls it the "beyond" of the scriptural verse—"the 'staging' in which the abstract is made concrete."

Needless to say, the latter is not a textual world with which Said affiliated himself intellectually. When, for instance, in "The Return to Philology," Said supplies a paradigm for critical consciousness—the "non-humanist humanist"—in the form of Isaac Deutscher's *The Non-Jewish Jew*, wherein Spinoza, Heine, Freud, and Deutscher himself serve as exemplars of being "in, and at the same time [having] renounced, their tradition, preserving the original tie by submitting it to the *corrosive* questioning that took them well beyond it" (77), he diverges by orders of magnitude from the Levinasian trope of reading-as-causticity: *Il faut en frottant enlever cette couche qui les altère* ("One must, by rubbing, remove this layer which corrodes them").

By a similar token, Levinas's definition of humanism as a "humanism of the other man" lies quite on the oblique to Said's more conventional usage.[53] But I think the appellation "non-humanist humanist" can be applied to Levinas in the final analysis, as well.[54] And while it might have surprised him at first, Said, I think, would likely have discerned lineaments of affiliation with Levinas's choice of the word "secularism" to describe a necessary *rapprochement* between modernity and the Jewish critical tradition: "The interpretation of the Torah is not a sacerdotal function: clerics, in Judaism, are not ecclesiastics. Jewish clericalism is secular."[55] On the other side of the ledger, when Levinas invokes his reading audience as "we Occidentals, from California to the Urals, nourished as much by the Bible as by the pre-Socratics"[56]—Said's critique of the presumptions undergirding intellectual history in the West kicks in sharply.

Yet, my aim in these first two chapters has not been simply to array Levinas and Said on either side of a positional divide since that merely mimes a binary opposition between religious and secular, scriptural and worldly, that I am at pains to undo.[57] On the contrary, as I say, despite the obvious differences (which could be rehearsed easily and almost interminably), Levinas and Said *do* affiliate, albeit adventitiously, as critical intelligences situated along a seam that connects self-surpassing reading and study to ethical agency and moral commitment.

In "For a Place in the Bible," Levinas distinguishes hermeneutic scrupulosity informed by tradition from a Bible criticism (higher or lower) that grasps and analyzes texts as if they were laboratory specimens, "approaching the verse as a thing or an allusion to history in the instrumental nakedness of its vocables, without regard for the new possibilities of their semantics, patiently opened up by the religious life of tradition" (24).

The key word for me here is not religious but rather "patient." It is the doctrinaire irreverence and impulsivity of positivistic approaches that Levinas rebukes, not the doggedness of their detective work:

> Touched by the impatient, busy hand that is supposedly objective and scientific, the Scriptures, cut off from the breath that lives within them, become unctuous, false or mediocre words, matter for doxographers, for linguists and philologists . . . It may sometimes be necessary in today's world to "get one's hands dirty" and the specific merits of "objective research" applied to the Holy Scriptures must not be belittled. But the Torah eludes the hand that would hold it unveiled. (24–25)

No doubt, Said would wince at the contempt for "philologists" but Levinas intends it in a *mere* sense that I suspect Said would probably endorse: clerical Bartlebys, sub-sublibrarians of the biblical text. In one of his signature lyrical moments, when Levinas writes, "The text is pulled tight over what tradition expands, like the strings on a violin's wood" (*Beyond the Verse*, 137), he articulates a deep accord with Said, for whom, I believe, not only the musical metaphor would have resonated profoundly. To conclude this chapter on that note, Levinas's subtle commentary on *bSota 34b–35a*, "Promised Land or Permitted Land" will be revoiced contrapuntally with Said's complex reading of Joseph Conrad's *Nostromo* in order to help us to clarify that commonality and cast an altering light on each.

DEVOURING LANDS, AND BEGINNINGS;
OR, HOW TO DO THINGS WITH PROXIMITY

At one point in *Narrating the Law*, his book on the poetics of Talmudic legal stories, Wimpfheimer asserts in passing, "The novel and the *sugya* are dissimilar genres of writing" (123). Here, however, I want exactly to coordinate them, through the filter of critical consciousness, and read Levinas's and Said's essays rhetorically. I will not read them in any depth, however. The commentary on "Promised Land and Permitted Land" by Sandor Goodhart, "'A Land That Devours Its Inhabitants': Midrashic Reading, Emmanuel Levinas, and Prophetic Exegesis," is difficult to surpass, frankly, and Said's long and brilliant analysis of *Nostromo* in *Beginnings* would be arduous to recapitulate. Instead, I will select out just a few concurrences for annotation. My aim, once again, is a rhetorical reading of the critic's exposition of his vocation in direct connection with the text for which he is supplying commentary. Contiguities among such exercises of vocation as such are also what I wish to discover.

Levinas's "Promised Land or Permitted Land" was composed for a 1965 colloquium entitled *Israel dans la conscience juive: Données et débats* (the discussion that followed his exposition has not been translated, as is the case, sadly, for all of Levinas's *lectures Talmudique*). The *sugya* from Tractate *Sotah*, which treats the law of "the wayward wife" (Numbers 5:12–29), is embedded in Chapter 7, *Eilu Ne'emarin*; the immediate context for which is a *mishnah* about which languages can be used for the imprecation in the *Sotah's* trial by ordeal (Numbers 5:23), as well as for other halakhic performatives. The blessings and curses (Numbers 6:23) to be recited when the Israelites cross the Jordan is the pretext for a digression about the incident of the spies narrated in both Numbers 13–14 and Deuteronomy 1:19–34,[58] which forms the substance of Levinas's reading. As is typical, he does not thus contextualize the portion he has selected. (The passage is reproduced at the end of this chapter, in part to give a sense of how stylistically sophisticated and imaginative is Levinas's secularization of it.)

What he does offer, however, besides compelling argument, is a keen and at various points quite barbed reflection on Jewish possession of the Land of Israel as commanded and enacted in the Bible, with pointed implications for the territorial conflict between Arabs and Israelis that, at the time of the essay's writing, had not yet come to a head in the 1967 war. His mordant chronological inconsistencies hit home: the twelve explorer-spies plan to shame the land in order to "confound the Zionists": "Please excuse the anachronisms, these excesses of language. We are among ourselves, we are among intellectuals, that is, among people to whom one tells the whole truth. The intellectual has been defined as the one who misses the mark but who, at least aims very far" (56).

Later in the reading, he exclaims, "Oh the forewarned intelligence of realists" in response to the profound moment of mimetic projection when the spies announce, "And we were in our own sight as grasshoppers, as so we were in their sight" (Numbers 13:33). Levinas makes this move frequently in the Talmudic readings, as when, in "Judaism and Revolution," a third-century CE tavern (*pundak*) is rendered as a café, only to prompt a severe Levinasian critique of the café-world as a "non-place for a non-society."[59]

The *trompes l'oreille* we hear in these readings—Levinas's rhetorical "excesses"—bring home the critical consciousness at work in "secularizing" the religious texts in this fashion. An ardent Zionist, Levinas knows full well that the contestation of Bible lands now customarily called "Middle Eastern" is fully present on the contemporary landscape of competing national rights. If the land's original denizens, Canaanites, are Heideggerians, "farmers as spontaneous as the forces of nature and yet capable of organization . . . builders of cities"—"To build, to dwell, to be—a Heideggerian order" (60)—the Israelites have compunctions about their own covetousness, as they are about to become the usurpers of an indigenous population.

> The right of the native population to live is stronger than the moral right of the
> universal God . . . one cannot take away from them the land on which they live,
> even if they are immoral, violent, and unworthy and even if the land were meant
> for a better destiny (67).

Does this make the scrupled explorers Levinasian, then? Actually, no, as Sandor Goodhart explains.

Whether animated by *realpolitik,* might over right (as was the smaller, "deist" faction of the explorers, Caleb and Joshua) or idealism, right over might (as were the "atheist" other ten), the same transferential quality haunts their actions. This same mirror-effect is what the dialogue among rabbis in the *Sotah* passage reveals: each fears other men over and above fearing God (the rabbinic phrase for what Sandor Goodhart calls prophetic thinking). "All the explorers are identified as shameful; the majority report is not singled out for condemnation" (243). A deficit in or a rejection of the halakhic precept *yirat shamayim* (fear of God) motivates each and every actor in the drama, in the Talmud's understanding as reproduced by Levinas's secularizing commentary on it.

In Levinas's view, *yirat shamayim* is most certainly *not* a cover for ideological or national self-interest, but rather a fundamental religious posture of *droiture,* "upright-ness": human elevation and rectitude. The logic (and rhetoric) of his reading hinges upon this assumption; "the invocation of rights due to the moral superiority of Israel is improper" (63). And here is his ringing peroration:

> Only those who are always ready to accept the consequences of their actions and to
> accept exile when they are no longer worthy of a homeland have the right to enter
> this homeland. You see, this country is extraordinary. It is like heaven. It is a
> country which vomits up its inhabitants when they are not just. There is no other
> country like it; the resolution to accept a country under such conditions confers a
> right to that country. (69)

It is doubtful that the nonsecular fidelity expressed here—to a people's deity and that people's consequent election, albeit construed by Levinas as a "surplus of duties," not the stuff of privilege—would win Said's approbation. But such a position identifies Levinas's stake in both "Holy history" (his term) and philosophical messianism, and it obviously cannot be part of a calculus as steeped in Vico's *Scienza Nuova* as Edward Said's.[60]

But having mentioned Said, I turn now to his analysis of Conrad's masterly *Nostromo*, which begins by identifying two "inner affinities" that bind the 1904 novel together: (1) Costaguana itself (the fictional South American locale of the plot) as a kind of promised or permitted land for the creation of the new state of Sulaco, for which almost all the protagonists demonstrate varying degrees of concupiscence, and (2) the tendency for those characters to keep records—much as the biblical story of the explorers' *report* is recapitulated by Moses's Deuteronomic narration, which then becomes a template for the Talmud's and all subsequent rabbinical renditions.

This point of tangency alone would make a hinge with Levinas's exegesis facile at best. Said's point, however, is that the records in *Nostromo* are the product of *anxiety*, much like Conrad's own composition of the novel, whose painful saga Said sedulously rehearses. "In each case, the individual has performed or witnessed problematic, jumbled action from which a descriptive record is distilled and then authorized for public consumption" (106). That is, action (fact) and record ("history"), personified in the novel by the characters of Nostromo and Martin Decoud, are in uneasy suspension and more frequently than not, at variance. As Said goes on to explain, that friction is intensified by the conflict *among* the many records or acts of recording: "The result of this myopia in Costaguana gives *Nostromo* one of its principal subjects" (107).

The novel's title signifies merely a personal designation, one of several that Nostromo—Gian Battista Fidanza, "the Magnificent Capataz de Cargadores," "the indispensable man"—boasts or is given. It's also a joke: connoting both "our man" and "boatswain," it names him relative to others he either represents or serves—he is only arguably the novel's central personality—and in fact until far along in the text's discourse, he is glimpsed peripherally by the various embedded rhetorical performances within the overarching discursive schema of narration. Costaguana itself may actually deserve pride of place as the novel's central presence, and in particular, its majestic, white mountain, Higuerota, which towers over the Golfo Placido.

As Said reads it, Conrad's complex prologue which threads together topography and mythic precolonial history, reveals a hesitation of the novel to begin, "induced by the 'cool purity' of Higuerota, 'which seemed to hold itself aloof from a hot earth' and from Sulaco at its foot, and which shames and humbles the weak and inconsistent humanity below" (122). In *Nostromo*, that is, at least from the perspective of its massif, all humans are grasshoppers—although even the prologue reads like a report: "it is said," "tradition has it," "the story also goes." (Moses's recapitulation in Deuteronomy of the story of the spies shares this affinity.)

Like the biblical narrative about the explorers who, inversely, shame the topography they survey, Conrad's book is about a land—with an indigenous population, various colonial immigrants or corporate powers (French, Italian, American), and most important, what magnate Charles Gould (one of several tragic heroes in the text) compulsively calls "material interests" in the form of a silver mine.[61] All the novel's various subplots are ultimately referred to its opening plot-survey of the land, which remarks, of the middle of the gulf at midday and the surrounding cloudbank, "the sun—as the sailors say—is eating it up."

Said makes a correspondence with Levinas's reading of the *Sotah* passage particularly inviting when he argues, "Thus, *Nostromo* is a novel about political history that is reduced, over the course of several hundred pages, to a condition of mind, an inner state. It is like a *trompe-l'oeil* painting of a city that upon close examination turns out to be an anatomical portrait of the brain" (110). For, this analysis (adjusted for length and genre) resembles the import of Levinas's reading, as brought into relief by Sandor Goodhart. In the *Sotah* pericope, Caleb, when defending Moses, is imagined by Levinas as saying, "He brought us out of Egypt, split the sea for us, and fed us manna. Shouldn't we listen to him, even if he were to tell us to build ladders and ascend to heaven?" Levinas comments:

> Where does the idea of a ladder and of heaven, which are missing in the biblical text, come from? Does the text say; "We shall go up and gain possession of it" (Numbers 13:30)? It is this "we shall go up" which the Midrash uses as a pretext to introduce the idea of a "ladder to ascend to heaven" (65).

"Do you think we will appropriate *a plot of land* for ourselves so that we can use or abuse it?" he continues, this time miming the Talmudic text's stammaitic voice.

And this is the point where Levinas makes an implicit connection to the *sulam Yaakov,* the episode in Genesis 28: 10–19 describing Jacob's ladder, the top of which "reached heaven": "and behold, the messengers of God were ascending and descending on it!" Levinas suggests we gloss it as a trope for reading, that is, the ladder of hermeneutic verticality, transiting above and back down to the text. Thus, Israel, the collective "we" of "we shall go up" is also *Israel*, the name given to Jacob by another messenger in Genesis 32 (retold in Hosea 12). And as he says so unabashedly in *Beyond the Verse*, "The Talmud is the struggle with the Angel."

> The great power of Talmudic casuistry is to be the special discipline which seeks in the particular the precise moment in which the general principle runs the risk of becoming its opposite, which watches over the general from the basis of the particular. This protects us from ideology. Ideology is the generosity and clarity of a principle which did not take into account the inversion stalking this general principle when it is applied. (79)

This is more or less the lesson Levinas draws from the *Sotah* pericope. It is also the particular tragicomedy of *Nostromo*, wherein the purity of generous principles runs afoul of staining—*impure*, and in Said's lexicon, *contaminating*—particulars.

What Goodhart even more dramatically captures is that the "plot of land" (italicized in the passage above) allegorizes the topographic materiality of the Talmudic text itself. Or, rather, between land and text, a mirroring relation makes each reciprocal of the other. Like land, so text: either it vomits up and devours its inhabitants for their instrumentalizing and appropriative desires (like the doxographic "dirty hands" Levinas laments in "For a Place in the Bible"); or it remains at a far distance because of an unwillingness of explorer-interpreters to "go up."[62]

In Goodhart's tidy formulation, "theodicy or atheism in interpretation" (248). On the biblical verse, "It is a land which uses up its inhabitants," Rava (the same sage of the bloodied fingers, yet once more) "taught: The Holy One, Blessed be He said: I had a good intention, but they interpreted it for the worst." Goodhart rubs it this way:

> Perhaps, Raba suggests, we should give up a reading out of fear and start taking possession of the text, of the land differently. Perhaps, in other words, taking possession of the text is like taking possession of the land. Maybe the talmudic text is performing in the text by (or through) the text the very drama being described outside of it. In that case, the way we enter Israel, the way we ascend to heaven, is by reading talmudically [midrashically], by building ladders (251).

"Beyond the verse," Levinas's trope for exegetical plenitude and exertion, then, means something extraterritorial or supraterritorial.[63] Reading is a modality of transcendence. In his most important literary essay, "Poetry and Resurrection" on S. Y. Agnon (which we will encounter again in Chapter 7), Levinas alludes to *melitsah*, an elaborate tessellation of biblical turns of phrase in medieval prose, and the syncopating rhythms it thus sets up between past and present. Likewise, a resuscitated Hebrew language echoes and fore-echoes as a wholly "enigmatic modality . . . beginning with its own trace." This is true, as well, for a "Jewish life" established through daily ritual and remembrance, "the community of Israel and the things pertaining to its exile, and the land regained—these do not have any beginning in the being they spell out" (9). Levinas means something nonworldly here, "a life, properly speaking that does not make up a world," up to and including the land itself: "as if the land meant nothing but the promise of land" (9).

Religion, as rite, "desubstantiates" and "denucleates" being. Like it, Agnon's Hebrew exceeds or contests the merely ontological, in the same way that the land has meaning beyond the brute fact of its territoriality—"as if the body and organs had been created to carry out the commandments, as if fruit ripened on the trees only to give benedictions" (9). One recalls Moses's directive to the explorers in the Torah narrative: "And be of good courage, and bring of the fruit of the land. Now the time was the time of the first ripe grapes" (Numbers 13: 20), which produces the expected consequence a few verses later: "and they showed them the fruit of the land." Levinas's reading of the Talmud's commentary on this episode corresponds to his lofty aspirations for Hebrew in the essay on Agnon: whether promised or permitted, the fundamental truth about the land is that it is to be *consecrated*.

Said's critical predilections will not allow him to follow such a reading or such a philosophy. Human history is made by men, and art shares that artificing intelligence: this is one essential meaning of "worldliness." Yet, another parallel suggests itself between hermeneutic sensibilities here, since Levinas (as glossed by Goodhart) is really talking about a necessary friction between intention and interpretation, or as Said would express it, authority and molestation. That push-pull, alternately receptive and resistant, but always *willed*, is the *cantus firmus* of all Said's literary commentary. And this is how he expresses it in relation to *Nostromo*, almost as if in oblique commentary to Levinas's reading of *bSota 34b–35a*:

> Take for your beginning the most chaotic place on earth, believe something strongly enough, apply it to that place, and you are able to author a new beginning whose intention is to make order out of chaos, because underneath everything, there is a benign continuity. The discernment of that order, however, is subject to the burdens—indeed to the molestations—of all individually authored schemes (114).

Canaan is not Costaguana, of course. The founding of a nation state in the latter, and the question of its governability, speaks in the vocabulary and syntax of nineteenth-century nationalism, not biblical theocracy.[64] And yet, as Said's analysis illuminates, "Nostromo aspires to no authority on matters of history and sociology, and neither does it create a normative world that resembles our own" (11)—which is, of course, one of the historical novel's generic imperatives. Rather, structurally analogous to the manner in which the Talmudic text, as it were, remaps the biblical narrative of territorial possession, few other modern texts allegorize the condition of its author and his own compositional politics of founding, inventing, and originating to the extent that *Nostromo* does. Conrad's novel is thus *about* Beginning as both a poetics and a problem: which, through the oppositional pathos of action-or-record "reveals itself to be no more than the *record* of novelistic self-reflection" (137).

Anachronistic as it may be, here I align myself with Levinas's own rhetorical strategy in "Promised Land or Permitted Land" by proposing that what the aggadic excursus on shaming and/or ascending to the Land does—through the translucence of Levinas's commentary—is to *novelize* the Torah text which it mediates. And I mean "novelization" in Mikhail Bakhtin's sense of a "contact-zone" with other genres, a dialogizing process that is also a secularizing one. And I intend "secularize" in Levinas's and Goodhart's senses, where the critical practice of Talmudic commentary maps itself onto "the very spirit of the notion announced by the modern [secular] state."[65] This may well *not* be what Said typically means by "secular" in his criticism: worldly, circumstantially situated. But it does, I think, introduce a space of proximity in which Said and Levinas can be thought together and brought together in the common vocation of critical consciousness.

Let us recall the terms introduced by critics Dana Polin and Gerald Bruns in relation to the respective demands of Said's critical practice and of *midrash*:

> [Polan] Writing "takes place." In this, there seems to be at least two operative meanings. On the one hand, writing functions as an *event* in the world . . . as a material force that affects and effects; on the other hand, Said suggests that, as an event, writing takes place in precisely a place, a historical situation where it bears an affiliation with various institutions (ideological, political, cultural).

[Bruns] The Bible always addresses itself to the time of interpretation; one cannot understand it except by appropriating it anew. . . . Midrash is not only responsive to the Scriptures as a way of coping with the text's wide-ranging formal problems; it is also responsive to the situations in which the Scriptures exert their claim upon human life. Think of Midrash as the medium in which this scriptural claim exerts itself. . . . But in midrash the text is never taken all by itself as an analytical object; the text is always *situated*. Thus, the task of midrash is never really reproductive; it is always productive of new understanding . . . . a way of keeping the Bible open to those who answer its claims.

When Levinas typically finds correlations for his cherished philosophical premises in the aggadic passages from the Talmud he selects for commentary and when Said interprets Nostromo as *performing* the dialectical tension between authority and molestation, the terms that anchor his own critical paradigm, we are witness to the drama I sketched at beginning of the previous chapter.

For *Pledge, Turn, Prestige* not only names the imaginative legerdemain of authors, traditions, and texts, but it also identifies what criticism can transact when it "enters into the artist's games," as Levinas expresses it in "Reality and its Shadow." If that transaction is not to be "parasitic," however, nor substitutive,[66] then the critic must be the agent for situating and situatedness, as Bruns and Polan and Levinas and Said clarify. Although he does not use the word in this connection in that early essay, the task of criticism as Levinas defines it is interruptive in the best sense, an ethical supplement to a work that appears complete and self-saturated; its raison d'être is to mediate inside and outside, and its mechanism is that of tact.[67] The critic, according to this argument, can be defined as the one "who can say about the work something else than the work."

And if the critic's vocation is necessarily secular (though I believe Levinas's commentarial writing countervails that notion, narrowly construed), then "the task of criticism [still] remains essential, even if God was not dead, but only exiled." For the critic is both a reader who "dirties his hands," and an agent of consecration, of *frottage* and exscription, for texts that have the capacity to make the hands impure. Through his or her devices, contamination—whether construed as worldly circumstantiality or hermeneutic (im)propriety—passes back and forth between authorial text and readerly world. The next chapter examines two instances when manhandling a text situated uneasily on the divide between religious and secular sensibilities impinges upon its status both as a *beginning*, a sanctioned intention, and as a *fate*, a surprise legacy inadvertently entrusted to readers' hands.

TEXT OF *BSOTA 34B–35A* (SONCINO TRANSLATION)

Send for yourself men—Resh Lakish said: ['For yourself' means] from your own mind; because does anybody choose a bad position for himself? That is what is written: And the thing pleased me well—Resh Lakish said: It pleased me [Moses] well but not the All-Present.

That they search the land for us—R. Hiyya b. Abba said: The spies aimed at nothing else than discrediting the land of Israel. Here it is written: That they may search [*we-yahperu*] the land for us, and elsewhere it is written: Then the moon shall be confounded [*we-haferah*] and the sun ashamed etc.

And these were their names: of the tribe of Reuben, Shammua the son of Zaccur. R. Isaac said: It is a tradition in our possession from our forefathers that the spies were named after their actions, but only with one has it survived with us: Sethur the son of Michael. [He was named] Sethur because he undermined [*sathar*] the works of the Holy One, blessed be He; and Michael [was so named] because he suggested that God [el] was weak [*mak*]. R. Johanan said: We can also explain [the name] Nahbi the son of Vophsi. [He was named] Nahbi because he hid [*hikbi*] the words of the Holy One, blessed be He; and Vophsi [was so named] because he stepped over [*pasa'*] the attributes of the Holy One, blessed be He.

And they went up by the South and he came unto Hebron—it should have read "and they came"!—Rava said: It teaches that Caleb held aloof from the plan of the spies and went and prostrated himself upon the graves of the patriarchs, saying to them, 'My fathers, pray on my behalf that I may be delivered from the plan of the spies'. (As for Joshua, Moses had already prayed on his behalf; as it is said: And Moses called Hoshea the son of Nun Joshua [meaning], May Yah save thee [*yoshi'aka*] from the plan of the spies.) That is the intention of what is written: But My servant Caleb, because he had another spirit with him.

And there were Ahiman, Sheshai and Talmai—Ahiman [was so named because he was] the strongest [*meyuman*] of them; Sheshai because he made the earth like pits [*shehithoth*]; Talmai because he made the earth like furrows [*telamim*]. Another explanation: Ahiman built 'Anath, Sheshai built Alash, and Talmai built Telbesh. The children of Anak—[they are so called] because they wore the sun as a necklace [*ma'anikin*] owing to their stature.

Now Hebron was built seven years—what means "was built"? If I say that it means actually built, is it possible that a man constructs a house for his younger son before his elder son; as it is written: And the sons of Ham: Kush and Mizraim? But [the intention is], it was seven times more productive than Zoan. There is no worse stony ground in all the land of Israel than Hebron, and that is why they bury the dead there; and there is none among all the countries superior to the land of Egypt, as it is said: Like the garden of the Lord, like the land of Egypt; and there is no place superior to Zoan In all the land Egypt, as it is written: For his princes are at Zoan. Nevertheless

Hebron was seven times more productive than Zoan. But was Hebron stony ground; behold it is written: And it came to pass at the end of forty years, that Absalom said unto the king, I pray thee, let me go [and pay my vow . . . in Hebron]; and R. Iwya—another version is, Rabbah b. Bar Hanan-said: He went to fetch lambs from Hebron; and there is also a teaching: [The best] rams are from Moab and lambs from Hebron!—From that very fact [it is proved that the land was stony]; because the soil is thin it produces pastures and the cattle grow fat there.

And they returned from spying out the land and they went and came. R. Yohanan said in the name of R. Simeon b. Yohai, It compares the going to the coming back; as the coming back was with an evil design, so the going was with an evil design. And they told him and said: We came etc., and it continues, Howbeit the people are strong. R. Yohanan said in the name of R. Meir, Any piece of slander, which has not some truth in the beginning, will not endure in the end.

And Caleb stilled [wa-yahas] the people concerning Moses—Rabbah said, [It means] that he won them over [hissithan] with words. When Joshua began to address them, they said to him, 'Would this person with the lopped-off head speak to us!' [Caleb] said [to himself], If I address them [in the same strain as Joshua], they will answer me in like manner and silence me; so he said to them, 'Is it this alone that Amram's son has done to us!' They thought that he was speaking to censure Moses, so they were silent. Then he said to them, 'He brought us out of Egypt, divided the Red Sea for us and fed us with manna. If he were to tell us, Prepare ladders and ascend to heaven, should we not obey him! Let us go up at once and possess it, etc.'

But the men that went up with him said: We will not be able etc. R. Hanina b. Papa said: A grievous statement did they make at that moment, viz. For they are stronger than we—read not than we but than He; as it were even the master of the house cannot remove his furniture from there.

It is a land that eats up the inhabitants thereof. Rava expounded: The Holy One, blessed be He, said: I intended this for good but they thought it in a bad sense. I intended this for good, because wherever [the spies] came, the chief [of the inhabitants] died, so that they should be occupied [with his burial] and not inquire about them. (Others say that Job died then and the whole world was occupied with mourning for him.) But they thought it in a bad sense: It is a land that eats up the inhabitants thereof.

And we were in our own sight as grasshoppers, and so we were in their sight. R. Mesharsheya said: The spies were liars. As regards 'we were in our own sight as grasshoppers', very well; but how could they know that 'so we were in their sight'? But it is not so; for when [the inhabitants] held their funeral-meal they ate it beneath cedar trees, and when [the spies] saw them they climbed the trees and sat there. Then they heard them say: 'We see men like grasshoppers in the trees'.

And all the congregation lifted up their voice and wept. Rabbah said in the name of R. Yohanan: That day was the ninth of Ab; and the Holy One, blessed be He, said: They are now weeping for nothing, but I will fix [this day] for them as an occasion of weeping for generations.

But all the congregation bade them stone them with stones, and it continues, And the glory of the Lord appeared in the tent of meeting. R. Ḥiyya b. Abba said: It teaches that they took stones and hurled them against Him Who is above.

Even those men that did bring up an evil report of the land died by the plague. R. Simeon b. Lakish said: They died an unnatural death. R. Ḥanina b. Papa said: R. Shila of Kefar Temarthah expounded; It teaches that their tongue was elongated and reached down to their navel, and worms issued from their tongue and penetrated their navel and from their navel they penetrated their tongue. R. Nakhman b. Isaac said: They died of croup.

CHAPTER 3

Blaise Pascal, Henry Darger, and the Book in Hand

The fold is not an accident that happens to the blank. From the moment the blank (is) white or bleaches (itself) out, as soon as there is something (there) to see (or not to see) having to do with a mark (which is the same word as margin or march), whether the white is marked (snow, swan, virginity, paper, etc.) or unmarked, it re-marks itself, marks itself twice. It folds itself around this strange limit. The fold does not come up upon it from outside; it is the blank's outside as well as its inside, the complication according to which the supplementary mark of the blank (the asemic spacing) applies itself to the set of white things (the full semic entries), plus to itself, the fold of the veil, tissue, or text upon itself. By reason of this application that nothing has preceded, there will never be any Blank with a capital B *or any theology of the Text*.

—Jacques Derrida, "The Double Session"

So we might see our model in Emerson's "Divinity School Address" which seeks to free us from our attachment to the one who brings the message, an attachment in effect according to Emerson, of idolatry. So what I am producing here or proposing might be thought of as *a theology of reading*. . . . (I imagine that reading, so motivated, will not easily lend itself to classroom instruction. Would this be because of the nature of reading or because of the nature of classroom instruction?).

—Stanley Cavell, "The Politics of Interpretation"

R. Parnach said in the name of R. Yoḥanan, "Anyone who grasps a Torah scroll with his bare hands will be buried bare [without shrouds]." Why imagine a punishment as severe as being buried bare? Say, rather, that the statement means, He will be buried bare, without *mitzvot*. Why imagine a punishment as severe as being without *mitzvot*? Rather, said Abaye, the statement means that he will be buried bare of **that** *mitzvah* [the one he performed at the time he grasped the scroll with his bare hands].

—Talmud *Bavli*, Tractate *Megillah* 32b and *Shabbat* 14b

FOLIE-À-DEUX: *LE MÉMORIAL* AND *IN THE REALMS OF THE UNREAL*
"With his doublet all unbraced"

Late at night on November 23–24, 1654, in his chambers on the rue des Francs-Bourgeois Saint-Michel, Blaise Pascal experienced something momentous. A spiritual ecstasy, a dream-vision, a psychotic episode, a premonition of his own mortality: one or all these things, Pascal's *Nuit de feu* marked his so-called "second conversion," which was to be dramatic and lasting for his association with the Jansenists of Port Royal. Materially, it impressed itself upon him threefold. First, he transcribed the experience in a single page of fervent and ciphered prose; an elliptical fusion of his own rapturous sentiments and scriptural allusions from the Vulgate and Louvain Bibles, it has come to be known as *Le Mémorial* since its publication in the 1742 edition of the *Pensées*.

Second, he made a fair copy of that paper document on parchment, altering the text slightly by omitting some words, specifying biblical references, and adding six lines at the end. Third and finally, he folded the original testimonial in half, enclosed it within the parchment, and sewed the doubled text (aptly enough) inside his doublet so that, worn upon his body, it would always cover his heart. An interior transformation embodied not once but twice, only to be sequestered and made interior all over again beneath a third external layer, but sheathed or grafted as if it were a second skin. Anticipating Derrida's musings on Stéphane Mallarmé's *Mimique* in the excerpt above, the *Mémorial* was plus to itself, the fold of the veil, *and* text upon itself, with some ecstatic theology added for good measure.

Biographers speculate on the proximate cause or motivation of Pascal's conversion experience, pointing to a possibly apocryphal incident involving a near-fatal carriage accident on the Pont de Neuilly. Whether or not Pascal's "night of fire" on November 24 was brought on by a brush with death shortly before, the added detail of cause-and-effect certainly satisfies the desire for a more dramatic narrative: if we typically read for plot. Had the document not been found in Pascal's clothing by a servant shortly after his death in 1662, it would very likely have remained buried with him, albeit still interposed, the intimate companion to post-mortem memory. For the eight years he carried these papers on his person like an amulet, it is not clear whether he reread them. Evidently, he did transfer them from an older coat to a new one when his clothing became worn out. Having internalized his own writing (making it as much an act of *memorization* as *memorializing*), Pascal could, one assumes, regularly imagine the palimpsest's proximity burning its fire into his heart, its call to spiritual wakefulness ubiquitous yet invisible, wholly concealed yet indelible like a tattoo.

"Although reading may give form to time, it does not count in time; it leaves no trace; its product is invisible. The marks in the margins of the page are the marks of writing not the marks of reading."[1] Thus does critic Susan Stewart asterisk the traditionally solitary and necessarily unmarked nature of the act to which historians like

Roger Chartier, Paul Saenger, or Stephen Roger Fischer refer as "private reading."[2] This is reading's customary condition, even its pathos; we read a book, but we don't really *memorialize* that experience, even if the reading itself, as Proust insisted, happens to have summed up whole days, realms of experience. What Pascal's text does is to interiorize the *writing* of it to an extreme degree while (putatively) making it inaccessible to the later interiority of reading. If "the time that cannot count in the diary is the time of the writing of the diary" (Stewart), then the *Mémorial* is oddly named, and not by Pascal: it was only such in secret, that is, unnamed and unrecorded.

Pascal's sister Gilberte Perier does not mention either the incident or the amulet in her biography, *La vie de Monsieur Pascal.* Personally, I would like to think this testifies to her discretion. But then, I would be reading into *her* text. Gilberte's children, however, informed a priest about the propitious discovery, and we do have his account:

> A few days after M. Pascal's death, a servant happened to notice that one part of the lining of the dead man's doublet appeared thicker than the rest. Having pulled apart the seam, he found a little parchment in M. Pascal's hand and folded. Within this parchment, there was a paper written in the same hand; the one was a faithful copy of the other. Immediately, the two documents were brought to Mme. Perier, who showed them to several friends. All agreed that this parchment, written with such care and in such remarkable script, was doubtless a sort of *Mémorial* that he had guarded very carefully in order to preserve the memory of something ever-present before his eyes and his mind.[3]

Assuredly, this first report of the discovery was meant in the spirit of fidelity. To preserve a memory beyond the limits of Pascal's own as a testament to his piety was motivated by a scrupulosity similar to that which Walter Benjamin ascribes to mimetic truth in *The Origin of German Tragic Drama*: "not a process of exposure which destroys the secret but a revelation which does it justice."[4] But that, of course, is the operative question here: what happens when someone else's revelation falls into my ready hands, and what, then, is meant by doing it justice?

At this point in my text, readers can see a reproduction of the *Mémorial.* Its text translates to English as follows:

> *The year of grace 1654,*
>
> *Monday, 23 November, feast of St. Clement, pope and martyr, and others in the martyrology. Vigil of St. Chrysogonus, martyr, and others. From about half past ten at night until about half past midnight,*
>
> *FIRE.*
> *GOD of Abraham, GOD of Isaac, GOD of Jacob*
> *not of the philosophers and of the learned.*
> *Certitude. Certitude. Feeling. Joy. Peace.*
> *GOD of Jesus Christ.*

My God and your God.

Your GOD will be my God.

Forgetfulness of the world and of everything, except GOD.

He is only found by the ways taught in the Gospel.

Grandeur of the human soul.

Righteous Father, the world has not known you, but I have known you.

Joy, joy, joy, tears of joy.

I have departed from him:

They have forsaken me, the fount of living water.

My God, will you leave me?

Let me not be separated from him forever.

This is eternal life, that they know you, the one true God, and the one that you sent,
   Jesus Christ.

Jesus Christ.

Jesus Christ.

I left him; I fled him, renounced, crucified.

Let me never be separated from him.

He is only kept securely by the ways taught in the Gospel:

Renunciation, total and sweet.

Complete submission to Jesus Christ and to my director.

Eternally in joy for a day's exercise on the earth.

May I not forget your words. Amen.[5]

It is a very brief expostulation, twenty-eight lines long, several at five words or fewer. Now that the *Mémorial* has seen daylight, as a found object and true hieroglyph, it lays itself open to all manner of perusal, residing, as the expression has it, *in the public domain.* No longer simply "Pascal's" *Mémorial,* part and parcel of the proper name, it is also interpretively and projectively "ours," a posthumous legacy of the inventor of the Pascaline, the first mechanical calculator.

But I do not wish either to read it or to comment on its text. This is not a Talmudic reading or any other kind of exegesis; moreover, I prefer to hold citation at bay.[6] For our business here is really neither with Pascal nor with his exposed text, but with his readers. The questions to be considered are not difficult to extrapolate at this juncture of the book, touching as they do on precinct and trespass, propriety and use, consecration and profanation, and last but not least, on touch or tact itself.

Since they are also manifestly sober questions, and recalling Charles Altieri's admonition about ethics-talk from the prologue, I am reminded, improbably enough, of an edifying moment in an episode of *The Simpsons.* In it, Rabbi Hershel Krustofsky is approached by various people for advice: "Reb Krustofsky, should I finish college?" one man asks. "Yes," intones the Rabbi. "No one is poor except he who lacks knowledge." "Rabbi, should I have another child?" asks a woman.

"Yes," says the Rabbi sententiously. "Another child would be a blessing on your house." The final instance (following the rule of three): "Rabbi, should I buy a Chrysler?" to which Rabbi Krustofsky responds, "Could you rephrase that as an *ethical* question?" The inquirer pauses to think for a moment and says, "um . . . is it *right* to buy a Chrysler?"[7] The Talmudic comedy here reminds us how persistent is the deontological swerve in ethics-talk; and while I purposefully defer it, the question of right and rights in regard to reading will continue to importune.

"As a spontaneous utterance of life, a work of art poses tasks for ethics, not the reverse," wrote Bruno Schulz.[8] But as neither Schulz nor, admittedly, from a vastly different cultural register, *The Simpsons* can provide the needed critical scaffold here, let me appeal instead to Geoffrey Harpham's collections of essays on ethics and literature, *Shadows of Ethics*,[9] which defines ethics in a number of helpful ways. "Ethics is locked into a relation with things—discourses, cognitive styles, ways of evaluating—that are alien to it and yet still its own" (x). It is "a hub or matrix from which various discourses, concepts, terms, energies fan out and at which they meet, crossing out of themselves to encounter the other, all the others" (37). This "dynamic engagement with otherness," Harpham writes, "is the key to the kingdom of ethics; where such an engagement is, there is ethics" (x).

As to specifically textual engagements, Harpham advances two important claims: 1) ethics matters because it is the point at which literature intersects with theory, "the point at which literature becomes conceptually interesting and theory becomes humanized" (33), where "theory becomes literary and literature theoretical" (35); and 2) the nature of literary transactions for texts, writers, and readers alike gets disturbed, shadowed from within and without, both clarified and obscured, by ethical interpositions (ix). In a word, ethics and reading "shadow" each other (not a metaphorics Emmanuel Levinas would necessarily endorse, since as we saw in chapter one, these terms for him are mutually exclusive). Yet, the shadowing that Harpham limns feels especially applicable to a singular text like Pascal's, whose naked materiality—what the poet Virgil famously called *lacrimae rerum*, "the tears of things"—therefore marks a limit-case.

This shadowed and shadowing aspect of ethics does not at all, however, correspond to a more conventional ethics of reading geared to content and moral exemplarity. Take, for example, the faculty of discernment flagged by Maimonides in the following excerpts from his commentary on ethics. He is commenting on a *mishnah* from the wisdom-tractate *Pirqei Avot*, which declares, "Shimon the son [of Rabban Gamliel] says: All my days I have been raised among the Sages and I have found nothing better for oneself than silence" (1:17).

I invoke Maimonides here in part because of his commonsensical and highly traditional equation of "literature" and moral content, in the general context of ethical norms and conventions. I turn to him also because he weighs in on "the secular" from the perspective of religious scruple, articulating a seam of meaningful adjacency visible between the two that becomes visible in both limit cases coordinated in this chapter—albeit without the programmatic Maimonidean slant.

> And I say that according to the obligations of our Torah, speech may be divided into five categories: *metzuveh, ne'esar, ma'us, ahuv, mutar* commanded, forbidden, odious, desired [or, laudable], and permissible. The fourth category, which is esteemed, is speech/discourse that praises virtue, intellectual or ethical, and that castigates vice of the same two varieties (intellectual and ethical), and that awakens the soul to these [virtues] through stories and poems, and that uses the same means to help avoid [vice]. And so [such discourse] praises the virtuous according to their virtue, so that their conduct will be admired by others who will emulate it, and to castigate the wicked according to their deficiencies, so that their deeds will be despised by others and they will distance themselves from [the wicked] and not conduct themselves as they do. And there are those who call this category—by which I mean learning virtuous traits and distancing oneself from deficient traits—*derekh eretz* [lit. "the way of the land," but idiomatic for "proper conduct"].
> . . . And know this: that poetry, whatever its language of composition, must have its content investigated, and it follows the rules of other discourse, as we have already categorized them. And indeed I have explained this, even though it should be clear, because I have seen elders and men of virtue from our nation who, when they attend social occasions (lit. "with wine"), such as weddings and the like, and someone wants to poeticize in Arabic—even if the content of the poem praises valor or generosity—and this is from the esteemed *category* [of discourse]—or in praise of the wine, they will criticize it with every kind of criticism and forbid themselves to listen. But if a poet sings any kind of Hebrew poem/song, this will not be criticized, and it will not be taken seriously even if it contains a kind of discourse that is forbidden, or odious *speech*. And this is utter foolishness, for discourse should not be deemed forbidden, permitted, cherished, hated, or commanded according to its language of utterance, but rather according to its content. For if the subject of the poem is virtue, then it should be recited in whatever tongue; however, if its content is unseemly, one ought to restrain himself from reciting it, no matter the tongue.[10]

Here, ethics becomes synonymous with the discourse of didacticism—literary texts whose subject is either virtue, or, concomitantly, the denunciation of vice. (The discussion of linguistic (im)purity is fascinating in its own right, specifically the fact that lascivious content in Hebrew remains unredeemed despite being expressed in the Holy Tongue, which I mention again in this book's final chapter on language and translation.)

Because the ethical agency of readers is reduced by such a definition merely to assessing the moral character of a text as either virtuous or deplorable in content (over and above linguistic or textual form) and then ranking texts accordingly, it won't carry us very far at all for the transactional sense of the ethical as it impinges upon read-ing a text like Pascal's. Esteeming the esteemed, condemning the odious, a stance of "judicious spectatorship" (as that originally Humean conceit as been refined for contemporary ethical criticism), fails to capture the ethical exigency of the *Mémo-rial*—at least as positioned lying in our hands.[11] Let me dwell then for a moment more on the purely inadvertent circumstances of the document's discovery and the accident of its reception, which has meant an unintended availability for comprehensive scru-tiny—in a word, for *reading*.

Following the precedent I quoted earlier, all subsequent biographies and critical appraisals of Pascal take note of the *Mémorial*. It has received its fair share of intensive close readings. In his Freudian psychobiography *Pascal: The Man and His Two Loves*, John Richard Cole, for instance, proceeds decorously, as if entering a holy of holies—"It remains powerfully attractive to other believers," Cole writes, "and I approach this unique document with great respect," (106). That doesn't stop him, however, from analyzing the text at length as a specimen of separation anxiety and attachment dis-order.[12] Another reader, Calin Mihailescu, permits himself freer license:

> The exclusively visual grip on the text has been reinforced not only by its *visionary* character, but also by the contexts in which it has been written, found, and read. Any time one reads it—aware of the secrecy of the *Mémorial*—one probably feels as if one is peeping through the keyhole at a scene not meant for "representation." This exercise in a small yet comforting obscenity leaves the unaware actor unprotected against the eye of the unwelcome spectator. The mystic turns out to be ridiculous, superstitious, evil, insane. How could one explain otherwise the absence of Pascal's wonderful prose? The author seems to have been forsaken by the *génie de la langue française*. He speaks in tongues—the combination of French and Latin is effected under the sign of the Pentecost. He forgets grammar, yet the *Mémorial* is not a-grammatical: the lack of verbs (ll. 1–11, 25–28), the "unhappy" ambiguity of the deictics, and the ruptures harassing the syntax point to the *anagrammatical* shaping of the text. The ear, however, can recover the rhythms beating here.[13]

And in fact, what follows in Mihaliescu's analysis is an energetic account of the *Mémorial*'s prosody, its *anagrammatical* shaping: secret puns, resonances, the whole sonic drama of its sentences. Mihaliescu writes, "Pascal kept the *Mémorial* at his chest, a precious but secret stigmatum, and also a reverse purloined letter posted to his fu-ture selves, not to be stolen by the thieves of time. He knew his text by heart" (15). And yet obviously, now we know it too. It is laid bare before our eyes and ears; we hold it in our hands.

Like any text, then, the *Mémorial* becomes infinitely appropriable, a stimulus for hermeneutic ingenuity: transferred out of Pascal's hands, it ceremonially or unceremo-niously passes through ours. In his book *Masters and Friends*, Paul Valéry, for example, dismissed the document outright: unlike Leonardo's irrepressible genius, Pascal "having changed his new lamp for an old one, wasted hours sewing papers into his pockets at a time when he might have honored France by discovering the infinitesimal calculus" (365). In the eighteenth century, Condorcet disparaged the *Mémorial* as a "mystic amulet," a pietistic fetish. In the twentieth century, Cuban writers like José Lezama Lima, Cintio Vitier, Eliseo Diego, and Fina García Marruz, associated with the *Orígenes* journal, venerated that same piety as a vehicle for their own stylized poetics.[14]

In either case, talisman for metaphysical presence or self-consuming artifact, it represents, one might think, the kind of writing ripe for Derridean exegesis. After all, its compressed lyricism reads almost like Mallarmé; its discovery registers a classic slippage between presence and absence, disclosing the vanishing points of "genre," "law," "religion," "literature" "archive," and other such super-categories through the principle of supplementarity; it is iterated, physically doubled, creased, inserted, enfolded, marked and remarked, the fold being the Derridean trope for the structure of internal difference; as thus both "dissemination" and "hymen," it inscribes death and pronounces the *"toujours déjà."*[15]

Brief treatments of Pascal *do* happen to appear in Derrida's oeuvre, in the prefatory sections of the essays, "Force of Law: The 'Mystical Foundation of Authority'" and "Psyche: Inventions of the Other" on Paul de Man, the crossing point between them (alongside de Man's own formidable essay, "Pascal's Allegory of Persuasion") being the celebrated fragment 298, *"Justice, force,"* from the *Pensées* (Brunschvicg edition). But to my knowledge, Derrida never mentions the *Mémorial*, and we are left to assign any exegesis of it to the library of Derrida's unwritten books or as its own proto-*mémorial*, composed though yet to be unearthed. But whatever Derrida *might* have said about it, Pascal's amulet becomes an unintended ghostly presence behind Borges's famous claim about the general fate of metaphor in "Pascal's Sphere": just another "intonation" in metaphor's ceaseless metonymic slide.[16]

For our purposes here, perhaps the most relevant, though still oblique light might be cast upon it from within Derrida's essay on Kafka, entitled "Before the Law," which anticipates the vocabulary of tact and touching we have already encountered in his book on Nancy:

> Reading a text might indeed reveal that it is untouchable, literally intangible, precisely because it is readable, and for the same reason unreadable to the extent to which the presence within it of a clear and graspable sense remains hidden as its origin. . . . Perhaps man is the man from the country as long as he cannot read; or, if knowing how to read, he is still bound up with the unreadability within that very thing which appears to yield itself to be read. He wants to see or touch the law, he wants to approach and "enter" it, because perhaps he does not know that the law is not to be seen or touched or deciphered. (197)

Derrida's argument here touches on the peculiar paradox of *being before the law*, being present to it, in front of it, as if it were a text, while the law itself remains prior (the other sense of "before") to any point of reference, anarchic, unfounded, and therefore in some crucial way, *not present*, even to itself, an argument he propounds once again in *Archive Fever* in relation to a short text "unearthed" and transcribed by Ḥayyim Yosef Yersuhalmi.

> To be precise. We are before this text [Kafka's] that, saying nothing definite and presenting no identifiable content beyond the story itself, except for an endless *differánce*, till death, nonetheless remains strictly intangible. Intangible: by this I understand inaccessible to contact, impregnable, and ultimately ungraspable, incomprehensible—but also that which we have not the *right* to touch. This is an "original" text, as we say; it is forbidden or illicit to change or disfigure it, or to touch its form. (211)

At second hand, we could also smuggle in the specter of Derrida to haunt the margins of Pascal's *Mémorial* by citing the case of Paul Auster, the American fiction writer, poet, and essayist whose sensibility closely haunts the margins of Derrida's own philosophy. Auster awards prominent mention to Pascal's text in "The Book of Memory" (appropriately enough for a link with Derrida, immediately prior to an anecdote about meeting French essayist/poet Francis Ponge). After briefly describing the document and reproducing the first of its three "movements" or strophes, Auster says that the *Mémorial* testifies to "the moment of illumination that burns across the sky of solitude" (137).[17] It also captures the constraining and liberating power of memory—the fact that like memory itself, in Stephen Fredman's lovely apercu, Pascal's hidden text possesses both an outside and an inside.[18] Auster concludes by suggesting that epigraphs for the book he is writing right now, "The Book of Memory," can be found elsewhere in Pascal's writing, specifically, from the *Pensées*:

> Thoughts come at random and go at random. No device for holding on to them or for having them. A thought has escaped: I was trying to write it down; instead I write that is has escaped me. (370, Brunschvicg)

> As I write down my thought, it sometimes escapes me; but this makes me remember my own weakness, which I am constantly forgetting. This teaches me as much as my forgotten thought, for I strive only to know my own nothingness. (372)

But like the treatment of an ostensibly inviolate, privately remembered document made public in the form of "*Mémorial*," Auster says nothing about how the piously concealed text itself became exposed, thus slip-knotting the question of original intent, of the particular *kind* of work Pascal had composed (is it even a "work?"). Instead, he personalizes it as an analogy for something else entirely, the constraining and liberating power of memory in the space we call literature.

So, the *Mémorial* finally becomes a literary text in the sense we are familiar with—to be puzzled out for style, genre, form, and content.[19] But every single reading that text has prompted, literary or otherwise, is *accidental*, and that is the point I want to stress here. Unlike, say, Rousseau's *Confessions*, which counts on being read and understood, or even Pascal's own *Pensées* which were fragmentary and also written on scraps of paper but never concealed, Pascal's *Mémorial*—as *Mémorial*—displaces itself from inside to outside, private to public, without any intention to do so; like Freud's *Wunderblock* or "mystic writing pad," it *becomes* writing before our eyes, so to speak, with unforeseen horizons. *Habent sua fata libelli*, says a Latin proverb, cited by both Levinas and Walter Benjamin, as it happens: Pascal's text is now a book with a fate—in the hands of literary history and interpretive potency, and as I keep insisting, in the literal hands of others.[20]

The seemingly naïve question I want to pose therefore is: what does the reading we take for granted look like when we bend its light through the prism of a found object like Pascal's *Mémorial*? "One doesn't seek the found object, as Picasso famously remarked. One *finds* it. Even better: it finds you, looking back at you . . ."[21] What, consequently, explains the ethics of literary reading generally as a matter of taking and holding? Intuitively perhaps, one feels one understands the force of such a question. But I prefer to leave it suspended, deferring any categorical answer, by pivoting now from Pascal's *Mémorial* to another tale of fortuitous discovery and unwilled entrance into the public domain: the case of the twentieth-century "outsider artist" Henry Joseph Darger, author of probably the longest extant piece of imaginative fiction in world literature.

"How to Get Out of the Room That Is the Book?"

Henry Darger died on April 13, 1973, and was buried in the paupers' plot of All Saints Cemetery in Des Plaines, Illinois. Without formal education past elementary school, much of his early life was confined to charitable institutions of various kinds, including a five-year stay in the Lincoln Asylum for the Feeble-Minded. His adolescence and adulthood were also spent in institutions, where he made his meager living as a custodial laborer. From 1922 until shortly before his death (in the last of such institutions, the St Augustine Home for the Aged), Darger lived the entirety of his penurious and isolated years in two crabbed apartments on Webster Street in Chicago, by day working as janitor or dishwasher in a series of hospitals on the North Side, and when no longer able to work, attending Mass in a nearby church several times in a single day. By night, indefatigable and prodigious, he was engaged in an altogether different kind of labor, as was discovered shortly before his death.

For, upon entering his small two-room flat to dispose of what was thought to be the debris of an impoverished life—piles of discarded newspapers, books, phonograph records, cheap votive objects, homemade balls of twine, boxes of rubber-bands and broken eyeglass-frames, disposable plastic maple syrup containers and empty bottles of Pepto-Bismol, shoes—Darger's neighbors discovered an entire and astonishing interior life given form through homemade art and seemingly interminable prose. At this point in my text, readers will see (and hold in their hands) photographic reproductions of Darger's room. To reprise Calin Mihailescu's verdict on Pascal, here too, "one probably feels as if one is peeping through the keyhole at a scene not meant for representation.'" Notwithstanding, a book of photographs documenting that room upon its postmortem entries by Darger's fellow tenants has now also been published.[22]

Besides the rubbish, the ephemera of a lifetime's strange archivalism, there was this: 15,145 pages, typed single-space, of an historical chronicle/mythic fiction/religious epic/adventure-story/war correspondence/apocalyptic narrative/secular scripture entitled *The Story of the Vivian Girls in What is Known as the Realms of the Unreal, of the Gland[e]co-Angelinian War Storm, Caused by the Child Slave Rebellion* (1909–1938) distributed over fifteen bulky hand-bound volumes, some eight inches thick;[23] a sequel of almost 11,000 handwritten pages in sixteen volumes, *Further Adventures in Chicago: Crazy House;* a 5,084-page autobiography, *The History of My Life* (1939–1946), of which only the first 206 pages actually narrate Darger's bare and depopulated life, only to be self-interrupted by a permanent swerve into densely apocalyptic and repetitive fabulation; *Book of Weather Reports* (1958–1967), consisting of seven ring-binder volumes of a journal detailing ten years of amateur meteorology; *Diaries* (1911–1917, 1969–1972) and miscellaneous personal ledgers; and last but hardly least, 318 double-sided illustrations (some as large as twelve feet long) collected into three large albums, meant to accompany *In the Realms* as a complementary visual text.

Tacked to the walls or hung on string, were also his own collages of newspaper clippings, magazine illustrations, coloring book pages, and photographic enlargements. The artwork is now to be found in museums from the United States to Japan. The writings, in all, over 30,000 pages of typed and hand-written text, have yet to be read in their entirety by anyone. While much of it is conventionally literary, by turns derivative, amateurish, arresting, grotesque, beautiful, and even sublime, the rest, because of its obsessional, accretive, and encyclopedic character, remains all but unreadable. Like Pascal's *Mémorial*, only retroactively appropriated, Darger's work, in perhaps never being intended for eyes to scan and hands to hold it other than its creator's own, almost defies the very category of literary communication.

Darger is known to have had a single close companion in his lifetime, evidently also something of a social misfit, very possibly disturbed.[24] (Psychologist and art historian John MacGregor speculates that the two of them may have formed a kind of *folie-à-deux*). He eventually moved away and died in 1959; whether he knew of Darger's writing or functioned as their audience cannot be determined, but since he was almost certainly illiterate, he could not have read any of it. In the time Darger lived on Webster Street, his landlord, Nathan Lerner, Lerner's wife, and Darger's fellow tenant David Berglund had each been afforded brief access to Darger's quarters, noting an artwork in progress but nothing else. Yet Darger chose to tell none of them about his writing, an oeuvre that for over sixty years both filled his life and in some essential way substituted for and constituted it.

In the Realms of the Unreal was begun in 1910–11 and was finished sometime in the 1930s; begun in 1939, *Crazy House* was completed by the mid-1940s. Darger continued to work on both texts, putting most of his energies into illustration, and composed his other manuscripts up until 1969, two years before he passed away. When Berglund visited him in the hospital shortly before his death and expressed elation at discovering his astounding feats of authorship and artistry, Darger said simply, "It's too late. . . . Throw it all away." And in a later interview, Berglund observed, "It was like I had punched him in stomach, taken the wind out of him." (19). In summing up his own narrative of discovery as prologue to his critical exercise in Darger-like gigantism, John MacGregor, Darger's dogged commentator, asks the correct and salient question:

> Henry Darger's art was, and remained, a secret life work, hidden from all eyes. Would he have wanted his pictures exhibited around the world? Would he have wanted his writings published; or books such as this one written about his life and work? Or are we invading the privacy of this man—wrongfully entering his secret world? This is a real moral issue. By what right do we enter Darger's life, explore his room, read his books, look at his paintings? (19)[25]

It wasn't just Darger's artwork and writings that lay open to trespass. The cluttered apartment in which he lived, with its collections, some haphazard, others painstakingly catalogued and assembled (cartoons, retouched photographs), lent itself to his recuperative imagination, too, and was in a very concrete way continuous with his prose, collages, and illustrations—the counterpart to Pascal's doublet that both hid and housed the *Mémorial*. Indeed, MacGregor advances the trenchant and deeply insightful explanation of the agglutinative nature of Darger's entire compositional and creative process—the tracings, the collage, the surfeit of documentary detail: *Henry Darger adopted what came to hand.*

> To draw means to bring into existence an image which has not previously existed. . . . Tracing makes no such claim. It is a mode of adopting an image that is already in existence, and of moving it from one environment to another. It is a means of achieving contact and of obtaining possession. (162)

It seems that Darger's lifelong mission was adoption, reclamation: for quotidian loss or lack *in* the world he sought compensation by *inventing* a world, which then needed to be compulsively and ceaselessly filled (even aggressively and sadistically, at times), an intrapsychic fantasy rendered through word and image. His was a life confined, *sentenced* to, but also liberated by, the compulsive properties of invention; his drawing and writing permitted him the satisfactions, mastery, but also the horror of "an endlessly prolonged and elaborated daydream" (MacGregor, 538). Elias Canetti (whom I quote again later), once wrote, "Keeping people alive by means of words—

isn't that almost the same as creating them with words?"[26] Once having made his fictional world, Darger evidently committed himself to sustaining and preserving it—like the Deity invoked by Jewish liturgy who "daily and constantly renews the work of creation." Indeed, he was devoted to it.

Yet, misprising the privacy at stake here was the rather spectacular curatorial decision made by the American Folk Art Museum last year in an exhibition entitled, "The Private Collection of Henry Darger," which proposed the theory that by pasting collages and drawings on his own walls, Darger "the vernacular modernist" was not merely a secret artist but a secret art collector as well. Happily enough for its own *modus vivendi*, a museum would thus find its own sanction in the work of a creator for whom, however, the very notions of exhibition and public display were alien in the extreme. It is also a telling instance of the difference between Darger's brand of adopting objects in order to make contact with or hold on to them, and the academic enterprise of appropriation we call the archive. In *Archive Fever: Freudian Impressions,* Derrida writes of the archive's infinite regress, the way, for instance, the biblical Moses becomes Freud's Moses, only to become Yosef Ḥayyim Yerushalmi's Freud's Moses, where each new sedimented layer is significant less for its content than, as Derrida puts it, "the scene of reading it provokes and in which the reader is inscribed in advance."[27]

> There is no meta-archive, Yerushalmi's book, including its fictive monologue, henceforth belongs to the corpus of Freud (and of Moses, etc.), whose name it also *carries*. The fact that this corpus and this name also remain spectral is perhaps the general structure of every archive. By incorporating the knowledge deployed in reference to it, the archive augments itself, engrosses itself, gains in *auctoritas*. But in the same stroke it loses the absolute and meta-textual authority it might claim to have. One will never be able to objectivize it with no remainder. The archivist produces more archive, and that is why the archive is never closed. It opens out of the future. (67–68)

Listen now to the hopeful exuberance of a very different voice—Henry Darger's own, as it announces entry across the threshold of his fiction, into the Realms of the Unreal:

> —The description of the great war, and its following results, is perhaps the greatest written by an author, on the line of the fabulous war that could ever be entitled with such a name. (Vol. I)

> —The accounts of the numerous stirring scenes here will, we hope, become interesting and attractive as well as fascinating reading to the people of our nation, but also highly important and valuable though unreal. (Vol. II)

> —The poet, the painter and the artists, even if they were to seek this all out under the allurement of fiction or truth, could not have accomplished any more. (Vol. III)

—The author writes the scenes in this volume as if he often had experienced
them himself, as if one time he is on the side of the foe, at another on that of the
Christians. . . . Let the reader follow battle after battle with the others, let him
follow every event and adventure, and then if he can, if he sets his mind and heart
on it, take it on as if he himself was an actual participant. (Vol. IV)

A reader is often identified as such within the work, addressed conventionally,
taken inside as co-experiencer, sympathetic witness. That may well have been only a
stylistic device. It quite possibly indicated Darger himself.[28] While we cannot be sure
that Darger had even the time to reread what he had written, MacGregor suggests,
rightly I think, that the acts of writing and illustrating were absolutely imperative for
him, a necessity as compelled and cumulative as his writing, as grandiose and hyperbolic as his subject, whether or not they lent themselves to acts of meditative reading
or viewing by himself or others. He wrote prodigiously, compulsively, because he *had*
to, which may be a tautology but also the underpinning of Darger's realm of the day-
to-day real. Yet we cannot help but also observe one of the recurrent tropes in Darger's
prose, the protestation of his story's untellability in any complete or ultimate sense—
which is at the same time belied by its seeming interminability, its compulsive
ongoing-ness of narration and depiction:

Indeed, the story of this great tragedy which occurred in Northern Angelinia
and Southern Calverinia can never be written as it would have really been had it
truthfully occurred. Since the world's worse cataclysm of these terrible three
weeks and ten days large forces of war correspondents and newspaper men and the
Gemini and others have been struggling desperately to convey throughout the
nation and even to the whole world itself from time to time as much particulars of
the tragedy as possible. They have written and sent in as much of the reports by
wireless and the like but it was impossible for them to tell all and the whole world
at best can and will never know all of it for the millions of horrible tragedies
written by the flood disaster will forever remain mysteries, and if they had really
happened only Eternity could reveal all. . . . Only God himself would have known,
and therefore for the rest let it remain forever in the boundlessness of his great
omniscience. But if so, the realm of the finity, the weak and staggered senses of
mankind may gather only small fragments of the disaster and may strive with the
most incompleteness to convey what we say is the merest impression of the saddest
and most shocking and astounding story . . . (Vol. IV)

By now, we have ventured into the inner precincts of Henry Darger's writing much
further than we did with Pascal's hidden amulet. Pascal and Darger. From the sublime to, well, to another realm of the sublime altogether, Pascal and Henry Darger repose
unexpectedly and restively in the same, shared space. Coupling them as I do here (and
again in Chapter 5) identifies that space as nothing either man could have envisioned,

since each thought himself alone, unviewed, although they are now together—though my own critical legerdemain—in each other's company.

I have performed this operation in previous books, using juxtaposition itself as an ethical "technique," and we should certainly pause to consider the particular paradox of instrumentalizing two works in such fashion in the service of an ethics of criticism. But for the moment, I merely want to mark the difference here: If Darger's case resembles Pascal's, it is chiefly because both have been accidentally *discovered*, and thus subject not only to text-immanent readings but also to the chordal kind that creates harmonics where none existed before.

In the introduction to his study on Darger, "Henry Darger: Author, Artist, Sorry Saint, Protector of Children" (and we might add, "menial, isolato"), Michael Bonesteel, a counterpart to Cole, says, "He did not do this to make 'art' or 'literature.' He did not do this to gain fame or make money. He did it to save his life. And though he fought with God over it and risked his soul in the process, it worked" (7).[29] To that extent, Pascal does not seem so very distant, and indeed, he isn't. In the foreword to art historian and psychoanalyst John MacGregor's mammoth 720-page treatment, *Henry Darger: In the Realms of the Unreal*, Darger's landlord and posthumous patron, Nathan Lerner, says of him: "He loves God, and manages to stand tremendous physical pain. Yet he is not prepared to accept undeserved suffering. So he suffers, and then he taunts God. It is not much different with Pascal, though Pascal did it very consciously" (6).[30]

On its face, though, despite such unelected affinities, the juxtaposition feels perverse. Scale, form, style, authorship, cultural authority and influence, religious sensibility (though this last one is tricky as both Pascal and Darger were ecstatics of a sort): the vectors of difference only increase as any possible adequation between the two writers opens on to a vanishing point. But as with Pascal, my business is really not with Henry Darger, however tempting a subject he may be. It is with the scene of reading that the discovery and archiving of his work now prompts.

Literary critic Michael Moon's *au courant* and instructive *Darger's Resources* was written, it announces, "to dispel the myth" of Darger's isolation—"almost a parody of the Romantic idea of the solitary, isolated tragically misunderstood artist" (1)—while acknowledging, however, that "he seems to have succeeded in keeping his literary and artistic work to himself." Moon's aim is to retrieve the collaborative, appropriative, intertextual dimensions of Darger's oeuvre, and thus replace the conventional, one-note lament for an "historical and cultural vacuum" with a robust stereophony of "the writer and artist [who] enacted and embodied a new set of possibilities, living as a working adult outside of any family structure" (2). And yet, the question of what Levinas would call "outside the *subject*" retains its force for speculating on the case of Henry Darger anterior to any "reading" of him or of what Moon calls his "sequelating" ambitions.[31]

Let us recall MacGregor's question again. "By what right do we enter Darger's life, explore his room, read his books, look at his paintings?" One of the striking features of MacGregor's own Brobdignagian study of Darger is its insistent motif that such-and-such a feature of Darger's writing or drawing "demands" or "requires" *explanation* (a reflex Moon's book replaces with careful glossings underpinned by queer and cultural studies). Notwithstanding the self-check that introduces his inquiry, MacGregor proceeds to submit every possible detail in sight to relentless scrutiny in the name of *verstehen*, of bringing light to hermeneutic shadow. And while much of the analysis is eye-opening, some seems to reveal more about the Kinbote-like critic than the Shade-like author.[32] As with Darger's work itself, one feels that this particular archival undertaking could never properly cease, resembling as it does the famous map that corresponds in scale and detail to the terrain it represents in Borges's "Partial Magic in the Quixote."[33]

There have, of course, been some famous modern attempts at a total archive of the self, the *Inman Diary* for instance, the 37.5 million-word daily account by Robert Shields, or the ninety-one-year-long effort by Col. Ernest Achey Loftus, CBE.[34] But those journals all aimed outside themselves, the interior externalized, just like more celebrated acts of literary autobiography like Augustine's, Rousseau's, Witold Gombrowicz's, Kafka's. The last one of these, famously, was also never meant to see light, along with its author's notebooks, letters and manuscripts, including the three now-famous novels: all, "without exception . . . to be burned . . . as soon as possible." And certainly, the archive on Kafka is one of the largest augmentations, engrossments of its kind. But Max Brod knew that the artist's proprietary desires in this case had to do not with the privately or intimately sacred but rather with the unappeasable scruples of authorship, for was Brod himself not addressed as Kafka's reader and custodian? To wish away the work out loud is already to pronounce it and conjure its presence.

Darger's work, like Pascal's *Mémorial*, is different. It appears—too late, however—to want no more than to keep its interiority intact, enfolded. Even its innocent *Don Quixote*-like moments of backlit authorship seem to answer to *that* very limit. More than once, MacGregor notes the curious metafictive moment in volume 1 of *In the Realms* in which characters happen upon the very books that narrate their adventures, and proceed to speculate about their author, Henry J. Darger:

> Soon they had them on the table. Evans proceeded to examine them. He took the pictures first. These he examined carefully. "Why this is very extraordinary," he explained. "Every picture seems to look at you straight in the face, as if you had some secret to tell them, or as if you suspected them of knowing your thoughts. And probably he had to use them as company as he was childless." "Maybe that is so, and he wanted them all to look as if they were paying attention to him," said Jennie. "He must have been a very odd man. . . . He certainly did make a good history of the Glandco-Abbeiannian war . . . He has every battle in their correct places, and he predicts that he served in them all, and an account of everything you little girls went through and of my many experiences and rescues. . . . Here's

his full signature, address, and everything, little girls." They all at once crowded around him to see, and sure enough this is what they read:

History of the Glandco-Abbeiannian War
Written by Henry Joseph Darger
St Joseph's Hospital, 2100 Burling st
740 Garfield Avenue, Chicago, Illinois

Yet MacGregor ignores the equally telling hint of (accidental?) self-allegory in a passage he also cites about a "Crazy Quilt" map that the Vivian girls have drawn:

If the time comes when we don't need it any more, we can decide to destroy it. . . . Just the same we must not be overconfident, and must be careful not to give the spies any chance, and those around us who are perfect strangers to us, we must keep the map from their view, and also those who are not fitted to the work we occupy. In other words we must hide the map when it is not in use.

When, we might ask, is writing not meant for reading, that is, to be grasped and taken in, apprehended by hand, comprehended? What if "use" is something wholly private or restrictive, ensuring that the work, when not employed, is kept out of view? Doesn't the fact that a work resides materially in the realm of the publicly real as opposed to privately unreal force it hugger-mugger into the economy of exchange and substitution, of *frottage* and worldliness that it never elected for itself? One of Darger's collage-illustrations of his heroines the Vivian Girls running in advance of a storm, bears the inscription, "Assuming nuded [*sic*] appearance by compulsion . . ." And the girls are indeed unclothed (after Darger's fixated penchant): evidently the impending violence of the storm or else their own haste has compelled such "denuding." But Darger's caption can serve as a warning generally for the twin fates assumed by his and Pascal's *libelli* alike: formerly covered up, they now manifest themselves bare, and answer to compulsions (whichever may motivate them authorially), not their own.

I want to offer these two instances of denuding—publicizing Pascal's and Darger's privileged (or clandestine) work—as limit-cases for this chapter's particular twist on an ethics of reading. I have chosen them deliberately because they are extreme: they presuppose MacGregor's question, "by what right" do we read? Now, before we grapple with an answer, I may need to revisit what I mean by an ethics of reading. Reading, in this case, signifies primarily literary reading, which doesn't mean reading that is confined exclusively to literary texts but rather a certain way we approach a given work. The element of "attitude" was at the heart of C. S. Lewis's now-underread *Experiment in Criticism*. In a more recent version of that experiment, Derek Attridge explains,

To read a literary work responsibly, then, is to read it without placing over it a grid of possible uses, as historical evidence, moral lesson, path to truth, political inspiration, or personal encouragement, and without passing judgment on the work or its author (although in other accounts it may be vital to make such judgments). It is to trust in the unpredictability of reading, its openness to the future. From this reading, of course, a responsible instrumentality may follow, perhaps one with modified methods or goals. The ethics of literary reading is less a matter of the exercise of a certain kind of effort on each reading—though it is that (including the effort of disencumbering the reading self)—than a disposition, a habit, a way of being in the world of words.[35]

Let me put adduce a much more conventional notion of what the role ethics plays for literary reading. It comes from George Eliot's novel *Middlemarch* and is a justly famous allegory of reading. The fact that Eliot's text *is* a novel is significant for me because it is in that genre particularly, albeit not exclusively, through its narrative aspect, its dependence on plot and the representation of character, the peculiar rhetorical function of a narrator's discourse, and the shape of its sentences, that the ethics of literary experience dramatically takes shape.

> Your pier-glass or extensive surface of polished steel made to be rubbed by a housemaid, will be minutely and multitudinously scratched in all directions; but place now against it a lighted candle as a centre of illumination, and lo! The scratches will seem to arrange themselves in a fine series of concentric circles round the little sun. It is demonstrable that the scratches are going everywhere impartially, and it is only your candle which produces the flattering illusion of a concentric arrangement, its light falling with an exclusive optical selection. These things are a parable. The scratches are events, and the candle is the egoism of any person now absent—of Miss Vincy, for example.[36]

Two chapters later, this same morally instructive and authoritative narrator gives voice to one of the great reflexive moments of self-interruption in the modern literary canon or outside of it,

> One morning, some weeks after her arrival at Lowick, Dorothea—but why always Dorothea? Was her point of view the only possible one with regard to this marriage? I protest against all our interest, all our effort at understanding being given to the young skins that look blooming in spite of trouble; for these too will get faded, and will know the older and more eating griefs which we are helping to neglect. In spite of the blinking eyes and white moles objectionable to Celia, and the want of muscular curve which was morally painful to Sir James, Mr Casaubon had an intense consciousness within him, and was spiritually a-hungered like the rest of us. (278)

In these examples from Eliot, *reading*, as a hermeneutic performance, as deciphering or even fleshing out, is the stuff of necessary egoism, of subjective slant. And the lessons are reflexive ones: as the narrator collaborates intimately through metaphor and self-interrogation with her subject and her readers, so her readers re-orient those messages toward the reading of Eliot's novel. Where is my candle positioned in relation to this text? How do my own prejudices and biases determine where my hermeneutic sympathies will go? Yet, Eliot's moralizing might still share a tangency with Attridge's idea. How alert are we, she is asking, to something's or somebody's singular otherness? What is the ethical consequence of as simple an act as looking?

Literary/philosophical criticism like Martha Nussbaum's *Poetic Justice* and *Love's Knowledge* poses such a version of an ethics of reading as one that has to do with attentiveness, acuity, a training in moral and perceptual sensibility. Its dominant move, propositionally as well as methodologically, is toward philosophical reasoning about values: literary texts teach discernment and moral judgment. Textual encounters in their concrete particularity—Nabokov called it "the supremacy of the detail" and the "capacity to wonder at trifles"[37]—are inevitably referred to a set of more general categorical principles. Literary reading becomes a species of *phronesis*.

The examples of Pascal and Darger are meant to invite thinking about the ethics of reading in a different sense. Staying with the correlation between vision and ethical discernment for one more moment: an analogy presents itself with Barbara Kruger's photo collage in which a sculpted face stares impassively in profile while superimposed upon it is a descending series of one-word labels on the left of the image that say, "Your gaze hits the side of my face." In W. J. T. Mitchell's reading,

> The words "belong" alternately to the statue, the photograph, and to the artist. . . .
> This picture sends at least three incompatible messages about its desire (it wants
> to be seen; it doesn't want to be seen; it is indifferent to being seen). Above all, it
> wants to be *heard*—an impossibility for the silent, still image. . . . In the face of
> Kruger's abject/indifferent image, the beholder is simultaneously "caught looking"
> as an exposed voyeur and hailed as a Medusa whose eyes are deadly. (45)

In short, aesthetic looking (as we well see again when we come to Bakhtin and Cavell in Chapters 5 and 6) is never completely innocent.

But to leave the visual for the tactile (and also implicitly aural, as if a book wanted to be heard, too), the governing metaphor for an ethics of reading with which we are now already familiar is that of making contact with a text, grasping it, having it pass through the hands—like the pupils under the tutelage of Mr. Wopsle's great aunt or in Walter Benjamin's childhood classroom in Berlin we saw in the introduction. So, what might be the ethical status of the book-in-our-hands, and where lies the "oversight" for our reading—an amphibolous word, of course, that connotes both an unintentional failure to notice or do something and also the action of overseeing something? On the spectrum of agency between the poles of unhindered personal freedom, and "uncommitted crime," (to paraphrase Adorno's famous epigram from *Minima Moralia*),[38] where do we locate an ethics of reading?

"UNDER A HIGH COMPULSION": THE BOOK IN HAND

One way we might think about the question is sketched in the following aphorism from Elias Canetti's *The Human Province*:

> There are books that one has for twenty years without reading them, that one always keeps at hand, that one takes along from city to city, from country to country, carefully packed, even when there is very little room, and perhaps one leafs through them while removing them from a trunk; yet one carefully refrains from reading even a complete sentence. Then, after twenty years, there comes a moment when suddenly, as though under a high compulsion, one cannot help taking in such a book from beginning to end, at one sitting: it is like a revelation. Now one knows why one made such a fuss about it. It had to be with one for a long time; it had to travel; it had to occupy space; it had to be a burden; and now it has reached the goal of its voyage, now it reveals itself, now it illuminates the twenty bygone years it mutely lived with one. It could not say so much if it had not been there mutely the whole time, and what idiot would dare to assert that the same things had always been in it.[39]

Books are not simply companions or friends, as writers from Petrarch and Francis Bacon to literary critics like C. S. Lewis and Wayne Booth have invoked that hoary theme.[40] Rather, their proximity ("there are books that one always keeps at hand") generates a mysterious, transformative *energia*. In traveling, occupying space, accruing time, remaining near, a book, as it were, "dictates" a reading of itself. This almost personificatory power exceeds Poulet's notion, in chapter one, of a book's passive "appeal," for Canetti imputes an agency or efficacy to books which they exercise on the order of relic, talisman, or votive object.[41]

The force of this was brought home through an experience related to me by my wife, who is a professor of modern Jewish literatures. It is quite common for many books in Yiddish published during the twentieth century, in perhaps ironic echo of the redoubtable trope of Jewish wandering, to suffer an itinerant fate—migrating or exiled from private collections to public libraries to college and university libraries to preservational institutions like the Yiddish Book Center.[42] In a twist on the Benjamin/Dickens classroom scenes, these are books visibly marked by the imprints of their former possessors: ex libris decals, fingerprints, even in the case of a copy of I. J. Singer's 1927 novel *Shtol un ayzn* ("Steel and Iron") purchased by my wife, a rosebud boutonnière, with flower attached to tinfoil pressed between the leaves of pages 88 and 89.

Such affection-cum-*lacrimae rerum* is presaged (but also sweetly ironized) in a poem by Moyshe-Leyb Halpern entitled פֿרעג איך בײַ מײַן ליבער פֿרוי (*Freg ikh bay mayn liber froy*), a sort of secular *hadran* (the valediction for Talmud study):

> Freg ikh bay mayn liber froy
> Vi azoy tsu farendikn dem roman

In mayn bikhele
Zogt zi: dos glik zol avek mit der ban
Un tsurikvinken mit a tikhele,
Zog ikh: tikhele shmikhele
Zog zi: bikhele shmikhele

So I ask my dear wife
How to finish the affair
Of my little booky—
Says she: Let happiness leave on a train
And wave back with a hanky.
Says I: hanky-panky
Says she: Booky shmooky.[43]

Halpern's valediction (whose play with diminutives continues in the same vein for another twenty lines) is a jest, of course, composed in 1934, when Yiddish culture still could claim an intermittently flourishing global life—even in Havana.[44] But that the books in question *here*, so many decades later, are *written* in Yiddish makes their migrancy, *their* waving back, so to speak, even more poignant: once the possession of individual readers, many of them simply await adoption by benefactors that will "conserve" them—much as Darger did with the ephemera he took home with him.

We learn, "Representing the whole of Darger's creative and personal meditations, the manuscripts and images became fetishistic objects, imbued with a value But did *these* books *have* to travel, occupy space, become a burden, even if they now flagrantly advertise their dependency—like Poulet's metaphoric "animals for sale . . . so obviously hoping for a buyer?" Or did they do so inadvertently, without consent, "mutely the whole time (what bookcase housed them originally and where?)?[45] Either way, their material reality exerts a tangible claim. They have become, we might say, negatively enchanted. Their fate is Sebaldian.

Another way to think about the Darger and Pascal examples, thus, would begin with their material aura, which, like Levinas's evocations of human skin, is tied intrinsically to their vulnerability. It not only recalls Levinas's correlation of art and magic but also borders the neighborhood of recent studies on the history and theory of response that emphasize the artwork or artifact as a locus of auratic potency. For example, David Freedberg's compendious *The Power of Images* ends with a chapter that details famous incidents of criminal violence directed against artworks, for example, Rembrandt's *Night Watch*, Michelangelo's *Pietá*, Velázquez's *Rokeby Venus*, and Poussin's *Dance Around the Golden Calf.*[46] Literary analogues that reflexively confirm the book's vulnerability are (just to take nineteenth-century English texts as specimens), plot incidents like the hurled or abandoned volumes that commence *Vanity Fair* and *Jane Eyre* and the distressed schoolroom books we saw earlier from *Great*

Expectations, or on the empirical plane of actual readers' material aggression recorded on the page, William Blake's famously truculent marginalia.[47]

More recent examples in each genre would be the burnt books in Bradbury's science fiction *Fahrenheit 451* or the lacerated codex of David Friedman's mixed media work, *Self-Interpreting Bible* (2004)—although, as James Wood reminds us in a recent essay on personal libraries, while aura may thus attach itself to the individual object, when they are massed together, books no less than other entities gathered *en masse*, offer up a "rather stupid materiality."[48] And yet, surely we have to reckon with the dimension of materialist hermeneutics whenever we think about text that comes to us embodied in some way.

Thus, the title–question of W. J. T. Mitchell's *What Do Pictures Want?* presupposes what we might call auratic thrall as a basic condition for viewing art—if we were to confine ourselves, say, just to portraits of reading, that would be the difference between the classical repose of Jean-Baptiste Siméon Chardin's *Un philosophe occupé de sa lecture* (1757) and the agitated, astonished reader in René Magritte's *La lectrise sourmise* (1928).[49] Reflexive correspondences from literary fiction that come to mind are the title of Manuel Puig's *Maldición eterna a quien lea estas páginas*, "Eternal Curse on the Reader of These Pages," or the drama instigated in the first "stage" of *Pilgrim's Progress* when a Testament so convulses the imagination of its reader that he leaves home and hearth. Many more examples could be adduced, of course, since the phenomenon of scarred-or-scarring books (defilement in a nonrabbinic sense) is both an historical commonplace and a serviceable trope. So let pick up instead where this chapter's final epigraph, the *gemara* from *bMegillah* 32b, leaves off, returning us to the concept of barehandedness (whether interpreted as temerity or sacrilege) as a nonfigural, nonmetaphoric version of aura that is distinctly apotropaic.

As we have learned, the Mishnaic Sages ruled that because of its intrinsic holiness, the parchment of a Torah scroll must not come into direct bodily contact, and that even a ritual hand washing (*netilat yadayim*) will not suffice as prophylaxis; codified by subsequent legal codes like the *Shulḥan 'Arukh* (1563) and *Mishnah Berura* (1884–1907), the edict stipulates that some kind of cloth must interpose between scroll and hand. That interdiction accords with an entire halakhic protocol regulating the proper handling of ritual texts and objects.

The trope of the nakedness (that of both object and person) is consistent;[50] thus, Torah scrolls are mantled when not being read from, are over-wrapped (typically in a prayer shawl) for even casual transport, and in the interludes (*bein gavra l'gavra*) between recited sections (*aliyot*) of the Sabbath or Festival Torah service, are overlaid by a special cover. By extension, *sefarim* (books with religious content) are accorded their own elaborate de jure apparatus of reverential comportment which, not coincidentally, calls precise attention to their *vulnerability*, as can be glimpsed from these illustrative *halakhot*:

—A *sefer* should be handed from one person to another and may not be thrown or tossed.

—A *sefer* should not be placed face down nor stood upside down; if found like this, it must be turned face up, or repositioned; if it falls, it must be reverently kissed upon being picked up.

—A *sefer* may not lie or stand directly on a chair, bench, couch, or bed that one sits upon.

—A *sefer* should not be left open if one is leaving the room for an extended period of time.

—If stacked, *sefarim* are placed in order of rising *qedushah*: Pentateuch on top of Prophets and Writings on top of Talmud volumes, prayer-books, etc.

—It is prohibited to be unclothed in the presence of a *sefer*, to place leaves from one *sefer* inside another, to use a *sefer* for personal protection, e.g., to shield oneself from the sun's rays; to block another person's view.

—When a *sefer* ages and becomes no longer usable, it must be put aside in a safe place or buried in the ground. It may not be burned or discarded.[51]

Of course, such punctilio is not confined to sacred scriptures and holy books—hence Canetti's example and that of orphaned Yiddish books looking for their Brownlow-benefactors. Owners typically prize the books they hold—like any valuable possession—sometimes demonstrating an extreme reverence (although its material connection to bodies other than human through the integral elements of leather and parchment, or the processes of mass-production like pulping that cheapen any fetishizable aura might just as legitimately prompt a purely instrumental and even impertinent *anti*-tact[52]). Walter Benjamin's essay "Unpacking My Library" picks up where Canetti's rhapsody on the appealing "face of things" leaves off:

> Ownership is the most intimate relationship that one can have to objects. Not that they come alive in him [the collector]; it is he who lives in them. So I have erected one of his dwellings, with books as the building stones, before you, and now he is going to disappear inside, as is only fitting.
>
> The most profound enchantment for the collector is the locking of individual items within a magic circle in which they are fixed as the final thrill, the thrill of acquisition, passes over them . . . The period, the region, the craftsmanship, the former ownership—for a true collector the whole background of an item adds up to a magic encyclopedia.[53]

The catch is that we thus depart the realm of proximity (in a loosely Levinasian sense) for an intimacy, as Benjamin calls it, derived exactly from owning and collecting—quintessentially "Ulyssean" predilections.[54] And while extensive personal libraries of *sefarim* presumably distinguish their householders, ownership and the collector's impulse feels somehow secondary to that enterprise. It is quite common in study halls or synagogues, for example, for such books to be inscribed with the acronym לה"ו standing for a verse from Psalm 24: *la'shem ha'aretz u'mloah*, "The earth is the God's and the fullness thereof." In effect, cancelling legal entitlement indicated by the proper name, that inscription gestures to both authority and propertied prerogative as derived elsewhere. One does and does not "own" such books. They have, so to speak, their own "politics."[55] "The double etymology of *liber*," writes Leah Price, "points to the book's Janus-faced potential:

> some medieval commentators traced it to the word for the "bark" on which texts were inscribed, others to the action ("*liberare*") that texts were expected to perform. Grounded in a material substance or linked with a lofty abstraction, the same object bound by its medium is credited with the power to free its users. (*How to Do Things with Books*, 5)

At this point, therefore, one may perhaps wish to ground the argument in the notion that, at least, authors—in the form of intention or proprietary interest—stand over the texts they compose, even if only to the extent that proper name is linked to proper name, e.g., Newton's *Principia*, Eliot's *Middlemarch*, Flaubert's *Madame Bovary*, Wallace's *Infinite Jest*. Is not that the point, one may ask, of troubling so much about the fate of Pascal's and Darger's unaddressed, privatized writing? That neither of them *authorized* that very public fate? And yet, the ethics of first or final say happens to be quite supererogatory to this book's primary concerns. This is what I mean to indicate when I call the Pascal and Darger examples, "limit cases"—which, however, like scrolls and *sefarim* in that other reading practice, *must still be taken up and read* if one wishes to interrupt the potentially *schlecht Unendlichkeit*, the "bad infinity," of overscrupulous tact. And thus, the question I want to pose about an ethics of reading generally in relation to such cases "folds itself around this strange [and very same] limit."

As to authorial prerogative, Milan Kundera treats the ethical problematic it raises in the final essay, "You're Not in Your Own House Here, My Dear Fellow" from his *Testaments Betrayed*. Kundera reminds us that in 1924, Max Brod found two letters from Kafka, "one ink, folded and addressed to Brod, the other more detailed and written in pencil" (in uncanny echo of Pascal's *Mémorial*), in which Kafka wrote, "My last testament will be very simple: a request that you burn everything" (255). ("Everything" actually denoted the private letters and diaries as well as the novels and short fiction Kafka had deemed less than fully successful.[56]) We know, of course, that Brod "betrayed" that testament, and that he also kept for himself a suitcase-full of Kafka's drawings, travel diaries, letters, and drafts that passed into the possession of his secretary Esther Hoffe and subsequently, her daughter Eva.[57] In the spirit of the essay's title (a rebuke by Igor Stravinsky to Ernest Ansement, forbidding editorial cuts to his 1937 composition *Jeu de cartes*), Kundera writes,

> I think of the ending of *The Trial:* the two men bend over K. and one of them thrusts a knife deep into his heart . . . "'Like a dog,' he said. It was as if the shame of it must outlive him." The last noun in *The Trial:* "shame." Its last image: the faces of two strangers, close by his own face, almost touching it, watching K.'s most intimate state, his death throes. In that last noun, in that last image, is concentrated the entire novel's fundamental situation. . . . This transformation of a man from subject to object is experienced at shame." (261)

One might well think of a resonance with Darger on his deathbed telling a visitor to discard all he had produced because it was simply "too late." Later in the same essay, Kundera pronounces on Brod's "model for disobedience to dear friends" this way: "a judicial precedent for those who would circumvent an author's last wish or divulge his most intimate secrets" (274). Yet, I do not see this moral predicament as particularly relevant for the examples of Pascal and Darger—that is, that they have been *shamed*, somehow—for the simple reason that texts *always* exceed their authors' purpose. This is a principle nicely illustrated in the Talmud, of all texts, by the famous *aggadah, tanur shel Akhnai* ("The Oven of Akhnai") in *bBava Metzia* 59b, where the Sages discount a *bat qol* (heavenly voice) in the adjudication of a particular halakhic matter (ritual purity v. impurity, as it happens):

> Whereupon a Heavenly Voice cried out: 'Why do ye dispute with R. Eliezer, seeing that in all matters the *halakhah* agrees with him!' But R. Joshua arose and exclaimed: *lo ba-shamayim hi* (Deut 30:12), "It [the Torah] is not in heaven." What did he mean by this?—Said R. Jeremiah: "That the Torah had already been given at Mount Sinai; we pay no attention to a Heavenly Voice, because Thou hast long since written in the Torah at Mount Sinai, 'After the majority must one incline'." R. Nathan met Elijah and asked him: "What did the Holy One, Blessed be He, do in that hour?"—"He laughed [with joy]," he replied, saying, 'My sons have defeated me [*nitzhuni banai*], my sons have defeated me.'"[58]

In Edward Said's terms, authors abdicate the place of authority for the law of necessity, which is "molestation"—history, circumstance, contingency, world. The historian Michel de Certeau stakes an even more radical claim: in denying their real situation—already historically contingent—authors create and authorize the *fiction* of a place of their own (*une place proper*).[59] And in correcting for the invention Levinas and Said alike accord to the ostensible mastery of readers, de Certeau names them "poachers," and posits this memorable formulation:

> Far from being writers—founders of their own place, heirs of the peasants of earlier ages now working on the soil of language, diggers of wells and builders of

houses—readers are travelers; they move across lands belonging to someone else, like nomads poaching their way across fields they did not write, despoiling the wealth of Egypt to enjoy it themselves. . . . Reading takes no measures against the erosion of time (one forgets oneself and also forgets), it does not keep what it acquires, or it does so poorly, and each of the places through which it passes is a repetition of the lost paradise. (174)

We have been speaking about books in their material, corporeal, handleable aspect, but, as textual scholar Jerome McGann reminds us, this fundamentally erosive or molestable or defeatable condition, is really the "textual condition" itself, a network of symbolic exchanges and material negotiations that simply underwrites the vagaries of textuality. A text's very fate, then—across the grain of Levinas's mistrust of the aesthetic we saw ventured in "Reality and Its Shadow"—is to become a kind of "twilight half-entity."[60]

McGann's unexceptionable argument rests on the conceptual substitution of writing for reading, of textual *making* for some science or correlative practices of interpretation, of the "phenomenal event" of textuality for an "act of the mind" (Paul de Man's phrase), of tractable materialism for the various semblances of romanticism. McGann puns on the Welleck/Warren piety about "the mode of existence of a literary work" by emphasizing, rather, its "Mode of *Resistance*" (11), which refers to wholly internal patterns of self-attention.[61] Continuing the chain of substitution, and to recall both Levinas's trope for the hermeneutic exercise of frictional contact and the Nancy/Derrida paradox of tactility (*hoc est enim corpus meum* v. *noli me tangere*), I want to consider such resistance as the "desire" of the *Mémorial* and *In the Realms of the Unreal* to *hold themselves at remove*, thus forgoing or forbearing the proximity of symbolic exchange.

To complete this tangent before we return to Pascal and Darger, art historian David Freedberg makes a pertinent point about the textual condition as always latently on the border with imagery together with its consequent affective responses. Even in ostensibly aniconic religious traditions like Islam and Judaism, figured representation sometimes overlays (or indwells) graphic expression; his examples are a nineteenth-century Basmala in the form of a parrot and Yosef ibn Ḥayyim's fifteenth-century *Kennicot Bible*, whose colophons contract images of animals and naked humans into the form of letters. "We can say to ourselves that what is on the page is always a text" Freedberg writes; "but," he adds, "it becomes an image" (56). And later in the same chapter, he adds,

What I have been claiming is that we cannot conveniently divorce our responses to religious images from those which are nonreligious, or supposedly "value-free" (i.e., which only are supposed to have purely "aesthetic" value) simply on the basis of an ontological distinction between the two classes. (77)

These are important propositions as we try to come to terms with the Darger and Pascal texts as limit-cases for an ethics of reading attuned to touch and proximity. And so, to transpose Freedberg's first idea to the pragmatics of reading, we can say to ourselves that the book in our hands is certainly always there at our disposal; but with a found text like *Le Mémorial*, that ordinary, prosaic instrumentalist attitude becomes more ethically tinged, if not subject to outright torsion. That is, a certain definable *disenchantment* ensues when it (or Henry Darger's work, for that matter) becomes visible and tangible to anonymous eyes and hands; it has been expelled from what Benjamin calls "the locking of individual items within a magic circle." Benjamin's formulation is particularly apt here for Darger when we consider that the artist's creative and aesthetic labor was deeply rooted in the collecting, or adopting, of images and textual models according to his own ethic of reclamation and reenchantment.

Freedberg's second point about the permeable border between "sacred" and "secular" should be sufficiently familiar by this point in my own argument. But do the Darger/Pascal examples credibly bestride that putative divide? And are they, in fact, paradigmatic (Pascal more obviously, Darger perhaps arguably so)? Freedberg's argument in *The Power of Images* concerns itself less with the intrinsic form or content of images than, as his title indicates, historical accounts of and theoretical postulates for *response*—embodied, affective, cognitive.[62] And it is in this light, that I want to transpose the whole question of propriety or entitlement, keeping in the foreground, as well, McGann's programmatic point about texts—as transactions of writing and reading—that are *produced* beyond the question of what they mean and how to interpret them.

In my prologue, I noted that an ethics of reading in relation to W. G. Sebald's and Michael Arad's artworks suggests a certain *ritual* sensibility or practice, and accordingly I quoted Levinas's assertion of a "religious essence of language . . . which all literature awaits or commemorates." My claim here is rather different. I have purposefully eschewed *reading* Pascal's *Mémorial*, and the passages from Darger's writing, although perhaps needless to say it is not easy to restrain the exegetical impulse, the prehensile, tactile hands of explanatory concepts or illustrative percepts that are '*asqaniot*.

The brief examples of critical writing on Pascal's text cited earlier in the chapter plainly attest to the ease with which such a work, (to export Rashi's famous dictum) cries out, "interpret me!" No less should be true of Darger's singular output. Having previously referred to criticism on Pascal, let me briefly quote here from an essay in the "weather issue" of *Cabinet Magazine* entitled, "The Moral Storm: Henry Darger's *Book of Weather Reports*."[63]

> Darger's notebooks can, in fact, frequently be read as an excruciatingly detailed moral account book of how well the weatherman was doing his job. The implications of this job (and Darger's own self-imposed regulatory relation to it) come to take on a set of complex moral and allegorical senses. Nowhere is this more vivid

than in Darger's 15,000-page illustrated novel, *In the Realms of the Unreal,* where weather and its interpretation are crucial—at once quotidian and allegorical, scientific and divine.

But this commentary does not merely locate Darger's writing in a literary constellation. It identifies its moral-allegorical cast as recognizably—generically—religious:

> In some ways, Darger's endeavor can be imagined within the broadest tradition of Western religious painting: he wanted to make utterly palpable the moral universe he had invented. *Realms* was designed to overwhelm our senses. Narrative incidents were to be situated within complex atmospheres. . . . And it is in this way that Darger's pathological overtones, his obsessions, begin to place him in the elevated company of those painters who failed Western religious painting by allowing the need for palpable particularity, visualization, and atmosphere to overcome and obliterate the appropriate generality more frequently needed for the goals of moralizing narrative. . . . For most readers and viewers, though, it is this very gap between the simplistic moral rhetoric, a rhetoric of pathos and obligation, and the multivalent, pathological detail that makes Darger's work so fascinating, and so disturbing.

Now, such analyses are certainly compelling; moreover, they model a careful, even ethical critical sensibility at work. When, for example, the critic compares Darger's weather diaries to St. Ignatius's *Spiritual Exercises,*[64] or when, as above, he ventures into Freedberg's notional realm by describing the sensuous effect of Darger's work as intentionally "overwhelming," I feel duly inculcated into its formal mysteries (although I might resist the notion that it is *our* senses that the work is "designed" to engulf). Obviously, the sort of exegesis I practiced on Sebald and Arad in the prologue would pay dividends for Darger's writing, which, compared to the pictorial work, has been the object of proportionately less critical scrutiny. But is that what an ethics of reading in this case wants principally to achieve: a reading, an interpretive practice or commentary, what Poulet called that "astonished consciousness [which] is the consciousness of the critic?" *Frottage?* Or, rather, *tact?*

In interviews, Levinas frequently put Hamlet's famous ontic question in quotation marks and supplemented it with what he believed to be a more originary question masked beneath, "is it righteous to be?"—that is, is it enough, simply, to wrestle with my being without wondering about its ethical conditions and consequences, without acknowledging whom else my own "being" impinges upon, or upon which other's claims are laid?[65] Instead of venturing the obvious speculations about Pascal's conversion epiphany or Darger's seemingly ceaseless act of world-making and world-preserving as hermetic texts that need decoding, I want to stay the hand of interpretation and have us remain, rather, at the level of their production and (unintended) reception as *events.*

Earlier, I cited Walter Benjamin's "Epistemo-Critical Prologue" to his *Ursprung des deutschen Trauerspiels* that truth, in its ephemeral aspect, is "not a process of exposure which destroys the secret but a revelation which does it justice" (31). In respect to Pascal and Darger, however, it appears such truth was quite personal; the revelation that did it justice seems to have been meant primarily if not exclusively for themselves. Perhaps a more apposite text from which to have cited, then—surely, in the case of Darger's photo enlargements and his original technique of tracing copies—would be "The Work of Art in the Age of its Technological Reproducibility," specifically the Benjaminian concept of "aura," a cultic quality of free-standing, even "pure" aesthetic value. Thus:

> What withers in the age of mechanical reproduction is the artwork's aura. . . .
> What, then, is the aura? A strange tissue of space and time: the unique apparition
> of a distance, however near it may be . . . . Every day the urge grows stronger to get
> hold of an object at close range in an image [*Bild*], or better, in a facsimile
> [*Abbild*], a reproduction. (22–23)[66]

This gets us closer to what feels at stake in the dual pathos of Pascal's and Darger's repossessed writing as the "twilight half-entities" they remain.[67]

Freedberg has read Benjamin's essay sedulously, and its influence is palpable in his theory of affective/aesthetic response: "Aura," he writes, "is what liberates response from the exigencies of convention" (433), his aim being a program of "reclamation" that seeks to "democratize" response. What captivates it, by contrast, is a set of socially repressive mechanisms and attitudes—museums, the cultured viewer, the general discourse of art criticism (both lay and academic), all thriving on the *denial* of (emotional) response. This does not quite dovetail, however, with Benjamin's particular point about exigencies, which are, in his account, tied entirely to modernity's technological turn to the mass-engendered and mass-circulated copy. Nor does it entirely convey Benjamin's sense that aura also transmits authority, a kind of untouchability: auratic works ward off familiar contact and resist being tampered with (or at least, with impunity).[68] As in Levinas's essay, "Reality and Its Shadow," pictorial or sculpted image becomes the privileged domain here; but, I am venturing a similar claim for the material effect of the situation I have called "the book in hand." For, tact cannot ultimately stay the friction demanded by touch: we *must* read.

"IS ANYTHING SO RIDICULOUS AS MELON COVERS?"

The strictures listed earlier regarding Jewish holy books have their correspondences in other religious or cultural traditions, for example, editions of the *Qur'an* in book-form or مصحف (*mus'haf*), which demand الوضوء (al-wuḍū) purification through hand ablution, or the immersion/cremation rituals for distressed Hindu scriptures as prescribed by the sixteenth-century manual of Gaudiya Vaishnavism, the *Hari-bhakti Vilasa*.[69] Such procedures italicize vulnerability—a variant, perhaps, of Georges Poulet's more generalized notion of any book's "openness," as we saw in chapter one. Auratic or simply exposed, objects like Pascal's *Mémorial* or Darger's writings and art are *encountered* in the most sensuous, bodily sense of the term: "against" or "in front of" us.

If ethics, as Levinasian proximity, just means encounter, than what Freedberg (perhaps too vehemently) suggests is the machinery of human repression when faced with the affectingly visible may be extended to our daily, casual relation to the maculate, molestable book in our hands. Call this the fatality of the real. In an incident recorded in his letters, Gustave Flaubert describes a hailstorm in Rouen.

> *Il y a là un caractère de grande farce qui nous enfonce. Y a-t-il rien de plus bête que des cloches à melon. Aussi ces pauvres cloches à melon en ont vu de belles! On crait un peu trop généralement que le soleil n'a d'autre but ici-bas que de faire pousser les choux.*

> There is something of an immense farce that worsts us. Is anything so ridiculous as melon covers? Well, those poor melon covers really had a time of it! . . . It is rather too generally believed that the sun exists to make cabbages grow.[70]

Flaubert's immediate point is antinomian: "Contingent Evil, which is perhaps not the Necessary Good, but which is Being nonetheless." But it also attests to the merely casual (dis)regard of something so quotidian as the act of reading. Or to put it more pointedly, is anything so ridiculous as book jackets?

I said I would not subject Pascal's text to the assortment of symbolic exchanges and material negotiations which *is* that act of reading, but one line among the ecstatic exclamations of the *Mémorial*, whatever their author may have intended, has always stuck out for me: *Grandeur de l'âme humaine*, "Grandeur of the human soul." I take this gnomic utterance certainly not with reference to Flaubert's mordant, secular, disenchanted, and disabused sensibility. Rather, it touches me because, by "enchanting" the parchment sewn into his doublet, Pascal seems to personify such *grandeur*. But the word suggests other possibilities, too.

Other than "fire" and "Joy, joy, joy, tears of joy" (which are testaments to his *exstasis*), it is the only line in the text not self-evidently addressed to or invocative of God. What can it mean, then? I resist the various line-by-line glosses to be found in the critical literature. Somewhat perversely, I take it instead, as a kind of alert, a flashing train signal to unintended readers: that is to say—and here, I reinvoke Flaubert (who may be not so far from an enchanted sensibility of his own)—it is rather too easily believed that books exist to make my aggrandizement of them "take hold." Reading is not so innocent or unencumbered, so ordinary, as we may think.

In an essay mentioned previously, Valerie Allen substitutes "difficult reading" for "difficult freedom" as her own gloss on a Levinasian solicitude for the book,

> the phenomenological encounter with the book in all its opacity and concrete specificity, its belonging to the world into which we are thrown. It is through this intransigent "being-there" of the book that we can speak of the intentionality also

of limb and organ. It is because we read that we possess nose, hands, cheeks, and feet. We *are* because we read and *as* we read. (26)[71]

An audacious reading, to be sure, but no less so than Pascal's and Darger's extreme fidelity to their own texts, their *difficult authoriality*. One can find in Darger's writings numerous parallels to Pascal's fiery religious faith (along with not infrequent displacements of that faith in the form of denunciations and defiance, triumphs of *his* will).

In his essay on Darger, Lytle Shaw accentuates the curious way in which Darger's descriptive prose will frequently reflect back onto the compositional, graphic elements of its making:

> *Ink-dark* threatening clouds of fantastic colors and shape . . . over the southwestern horizons, with amazing animation. Darker and darker became the ponderous globular avalanches of clouds, which though purple in color at first, became an *inky* hue or exactly looked like smoke, while a strange ominous booming roar was heard along the distant horizon in that direction[:] clouds upon clouds that arose from a treacherous *smudge* along the rubbish under the snow, ignited by the fierce heat of the conflagration in the tree tops.

Perceptively, Shaw points to the words I have italicized as marking—even if only subliminally—Darger's authorial presence in his work, limning a "metaphorics of writing."[72] In other words, the obsessional nature of the work itself is continually bound up with Darger's incessantly resumed acts of willed invention, a creation renewed daily and continually. *In the Realms of the Unreal*, in every sense of the word, *depends* on its author, Henry Darger.

And yet, the work, along with Darger's other books, is now in our hands. And, to reprise Allen's reversal of the customary logic of causation, it is through this intransigent "being-there" of that work that we can speak of the intentionality of those hands. Both Shaw and Freedberg have recourse to Roland Barthes's passionate, verbally munificent understanding of how literary texts can work on us, seizing our imagination, touching us tenderly. Freedberg, for instance, several times cites *Camera Lucida*—less a work on photography than a memorial to Barthes's mother, which, however, Barthes confesses, borrows "something from phenomenology's project and something from its language" (20). Specifically, Freedberg lights on the now-famous bivalence of *studium* and *punctum*:

> What I feel about these photographs derives from an average affect, almost from a certain training. I did not know a French word which might account for this kind of human interest, but I believe this word exists in Latin: it is *studium*, which does not mean, at least not immediately, "study," but application to a thing, taste for someone, a kind of general, enthusiastic commitment, of course, but without special acuity. . . . It is by *studium* that I am interested in so many photographs, whether I receive them as political testimony or enjoy them as good historical

scenes: for it is culturally (this connotation is present in *studium*) that I participate in the figures, the faces, the gestures, the setting, the actions. (26)[73]

On the plane of reading text—and holding books—we would call this a *prosaics*: phenomenologically speaking, Husserl's "natural attitude," or as Barthes expresses it, "that very wide field of unconcerned desire, of various interest, of inconsequential taste" for the general class of photographs that lie, "alas, inert under my gaze. The *studium*'s alter-ego, however, its Dr. Hyde, so to speak, is another matter, entirely:

> The second element will break (or punctuate) the *studium*. This time is it not I who seek it out (as I invest the field of the *studium* with my sovereign consciousness), it is this element which rises from the scene, shoots out of it like an arrow, and pierces me. A Latin word exist to designate this wound, this prick, this mark made by a pointed instrument: the word suits me all the better in that is also refers to the notion of punctuation, and because the photographs I am speaking of are in effect punctuated, sometimes even speckled with these sensitive points; precisely, these marks, these wounds, are so many points. This second element which will disturb the *studium* I shall therefore call *punctum*; for *punctum* is also: sting, speck, cut, little hole—and also the cast of the dice. A photograph's *punctum* is that accident which pricks me (but also bruises me, is poignant to me). (26–27)

My allusion to Stevenson is not merely rhetorical, since, where Barthes distinguishes these two components of photography as belonging to two classes of images, I would prefer to regard them dialectically—as if two aspects of the same physicality—if we extend this phenomenology of viewing to the act of reading. I might therefore put it this way: the *studium* describes the state of affairs for the book-in-hand that we typically take for granted: we read unencumbered. *Punctum* identifies the latent force of *singularity* in literary texts as we saw elucidated in the passage by Derek Attridge quoted earlier, but with one difference: the text/book in our hands, in the phenomenological event of reading, necessarily and concretely *encumbers* the reading self. It is "precise," in Barthes's (and also W. G. Sebald's) sense.[74]

It is also deeply transitive, on the model of Darger's work—if, that is, we acknowledge that the-book-in-our-hands is not necessarily an object of reverence enjoining proper handling etiquette, as in the halakhic stipulations for *sifrei qodesh* (holy books), but rather an encumbrance, an ethical weight which rubs on or against us before we rub it: Canetti's "burden" and Levinas's "contagion." In short, confronted by the limit cases of Darger and Pascal, we read as if *under a high compulsion*. But, when it comes to the difficult and the holy, don't we always?

As we move now to the next chapter where sensibility, in its Levinasian mode, becomes conspicuously encumbered and at issue, and having given Pascal's *Mémorial* a chance to "speak" on its own, let the penultimate, reprised words of readerly "underwriting" in this chapter belong to Henry Darger. What he styles "participation" (so echoic of Levinas's sense of that term in "Reality and Its Shadow"[75]) can serve as a complement to the claims of answerability as proposed here, just as to "set mind and heart" on the textual condition has its bodily correlative in hands that grasp and hold:

> The author writes the scenes in this volume as if he often had experienced them himself, as if one time he is on the side of the foe, at another on that of the Christians. . . . Let the reader follow battle after battle with the others, let him follow every event and adventure, and then if he can, if he sets his mind and heart on it, take it on as if he himself was an actual participant.

The twin matters of authorship and reading-as-event voiced compel our further attention. I return to them as well as to Darger and Pascal in Chapter 5, where we look at the ethics of reading through the lens of Mikhail Bakhtin, and once again consider embodiment and corporeality as anchors of the hermeneutic situation.

PART TWO

Genres

CHAPTER 4

Ethics of Reading I

Levinas and the Talmud

A kind of music, a pensive sonority, a more or less dense play of anagrams.

—Roland Barthes

The proper names in the middle of all those common names and common-places, do they not help us speak?

—Emmanuel Levinas

PART I

Listening on Canine Frequencies

> It would a little better express my sense of Wittgenstein's practice if we translate the idea of bringing words back as leading them back, shepherding them which suggests not only that we have to find them, to go where they have wandered, but that they will return only if we attract and command them, which will require listening to them.[1]

That is the philosopher Stanley Cavell writing about the philosopher Ludwig Wittgenstein. Cavell will himself be shepherded back in Chapters 4 and 5; philosopher-reader Emmanuel Levinas, however, is this chapter's explicit focus. Previous chapters have staged sonorities between Levinas and Said, Henry Darger and Pascal, Sebald and Michael Arad. The dialogism on display in this chapter, by contrast, depends on the way a given text solicits on its own or dialogically affiliates with, another—a proximate shepherding, let us call it.

This describes the manner in which Levinas reads rabbinic texts (indeed, describes the commentarial drive *of* those texts), and my own analyses mimic its allusive design. And while Cavell's work appears again at greater length in this book, I quote his distinctive voice here because his words above speak directly to my concern with proximity, and, as we shall see, a distinctively vocal instance of tactility. "In Cavell's formulation," writes David Suchoff, "Wittgenstein treated words as if they were animals with something to say back to us about their names."[2] I invite us, thus, to hear the quoted passage as if it were talking specifically about dogs, an association that brings me conveniently to Levinas, who penned a short but oft-cited essay on dogs in his collection of essays on Judaism and perhaps his most idiosyncratic book, *Difficult Freedom: Essays on Judaism*.[3]

That essay is titled "Name of a Dog; or Natural Rights," which will be interread in this chapter with (and thus made proximate or adjoining to) the final section and essay of that book, "Signature." The two pieces, written around the same time, have not typically been discussed together.[4] The first, in part, tells a short narrative—an anecdote, really—about a dog. The second supplies a modest intellectual autobiography, preceded by a unique set of epigraphs. In each, I want to train our ears toward a voice—one that we only hear described through reminiscence, another that is quoted to us as a *"conversation surprise"*—"overheard in a conversation on the Metro."

In echo of Cavell, I suggest that we will have to find these expressions of voice, if not the words they speak (or the sounds they bark), by going where they have wandered; concomitantly, they will return only if we attract and command them, which will require listening to them. Cultivated listening like this—the *mishnah* in the tractate on ethics, *Pirqei Avot* 6:6, calls it *shmi'at ha-ozen*, the attentive "listening of the ear"—is another feature for an ethical physiognomy of reading. It does not, however, fall back on sentimental phonocentrism but, rather, depends on a form of that *tact* we have already seen ascribed by Nancy to a writer—"addressing himself, sending himself to the touch of something outside, hidden, displaced, spaced"—yet also, I want to insist, very much the burden of a reader. That "touch" is, again, a contiguous one in this chapter: the seam between multiple texts, voices, narratives.

The point of the various acts of retrieval staged in the first half of this chapter—putting various dog stories through their separate paces and touching upon anonymous subway voices saved from oblivion—is to connect ethics to reading again, this time as a matter of frequencies, of harmonics, of "dogged particulars."[5] The larger connections I wish to draw bring together voice, anecdote, and a hermeneutic of *sollicitation* ("summoning" or "calling," *shepherding*, even). Arpeggiated story tangents form a kind of polyphonic latticework against which the two Levinas recitatives from *Difficult Freedom* are meant to resound (although the role Levinas himself assigns to storytelling in his oeuvre is an ambivalent one at best).[6] And while the concrete facts of the book in hand may recede in this chapter, the Levinas cleavages in each of its two parts function as their own ethical intrigue or adventure inside a *corpus partes extra partes*: "like two vowels in a dieresis, maintaining a hiatus without elision."

Strictly speaking, neither in the first pair of essays corresponds to that genre of Levinas's nonphilosophical writings that orients itself to the Talmud. Yet, insofar as "Name of a Dog" is bordered midrashically and the epigraph for "Signature" favors plurivocity as a mode of instruction, the genre affiliation still feels apposite. I devote the second half to a further exploration of Levinas's exegetical style in his *lectures*

Talmudique—in particular, his very last presentation, entitled "Who is One-Self?" which I will read in close company with both the Hebrew/ Aramaic source texts and a related essay about the eminent Talmudist and student of the Vilna Gaon, R. Ḥayyim ben Isaac of Volozhin (Ḥayyim Volozhiner). If Levinas may be thus adapted, reading contiguously enjoins a *difficult fidelity*: to texts in their individual integrity and to their joinery, to individual words, to their sounds, and to the shapes of their sounds—as if these could be felt, touched, and even aurally caressed.

The section that follows now, however, is designed in sympathetic resonance with the composite structure of "Name of a Dog" and the odd intersection of epigraph and exposition in "Signature." As the bark of one hound in particular—a vocal analogue to the brute materiality of the book in hand—prompts a sequence of dog allusions in Levinas's essay, so I now turn to the first of four modulations on dogs.

I Am Thinking of Bobby

> At the end of the year 1831, I found myself on the left bank of the Mississippi, at a place named Memphis by the Europeans. While I was in this place, a numerous troop of Choctaws (the French of Louisiana call them Chactas) came; these savages left their country and tried to pass to the right bank of the Mississippi where they flattered themselves about finding a refuge that the American government had promised them. It was then the heart of winter, and the cold gripped that year with unaccustomed intensity: snow had hardened on the ground, and the river swept along enormous chunks of ice. The Indians led their families with them; they dragged along behind them the wounded, the sick, the newborn children, the about to die. They had neither tents nor wagons, but only a few provisions and weapons. I saw them embark to cross the great river, and this solemn spectacle will never leave my memory. You heard among this assembled crowd neither sobs nor complaints; they kept quiet. Their misfortunes were old and seemed to them without remedy. All the Indians had already entered the vessel that was to carry them; their dogs still remained on the bank; when these animals saw finally that their masters were going away forever, they let out dreadful howls, and throwing themselves at the same time into the icy waters of the Mississippi, they swam after their masters.[7]

This anecdote is drawn from the chapter "On the Three Races That Inhabit the Territory of the United States" in Alexis-Charles-Henri Clérel de Tocqueville's *De la démocratie en Amérique*. Its pathos is unambiguous, culminating in the sound of dreadful howls (whose dread readers cannot actually "hear," of course), and the melancholy image of the Choctaws' canines desperately swimming in pursuit.

Quoting the anecdote this way may suggest a not-so-subtle reversal of polarity: a famous Frenchman (political thinker and historian) writes an anecdote about Americans, just as I will have occasion shortly to re-narrate an anecdote by a famous Frenchman (philosopher and Talmudic commentator). That would be only trivially true, however. More pointedly, I quote these because both their pathos and anecdotal form put one in mind of Bobby: the dog Levinas says *he* is thinking of in his essay from 1975, "Nom d'un chien; ou, le droit naturel," "Name of a Dog; or Natural Rights," composed in 1975 and included in the second edition of *Difficult Freedom* from 1976.

Je pense à Bobby, Levinas confides. It is one of his most lapidary sentences, and one that a number of his commentators (including myself just now) have revoiced in their own commentaries; in its austerity, the sentence just seems to invite repersonalization. Yet, unlike other commentaries, whether censorious or admiring, I stop just short here of concluding that what Levinas *says* about Bobby in this small essay is coextensive with what he may *think* about him—on the level of recollected sensibility, for example: the feel of Bobby's coat, or his breath and saliva on the hand that caressed it, what was glimpsed in his eyes, the distinctive sound of his bark, the sound of Levinas's own voice calling Bobby by name. I note only that Levinas says he is *thinking of* Bobby, which surely includes remembering him. It may even mean loving him, for, *la pensée est amour.*[8]

And yet, "presumption," cautioned Montaigne in his famous essay on animals, "is our natural and original disease."[9] If, consequently, there are limits to what one, "by the strength of his understanding," should infer from "the secret and internal motions of animals," (those are Montaigne's words), then I rather think we should be willing to extend a certain margin of opacity to such thinking. For whatever else it is, the anecdote about Bobby is a token of reminiscence. And since the true function of an anecdote is often political (according to literary critic Frank Lentricchia, "to trigger a narrative sense of community"), then let us propose that Levinas's essay is nominally about such community.[10]

The essay, composite and self-revising, consists of a series of detours—into midrash, into wordplay, into Levinas's distinctive register of ethical metaphysics—each of which leads to something of a rhetorical cul-de-sac on which Levinas appears to put a delicately mocking pressure. "*Mais, trêve de théologie! Mais, trêve d'allégories! Mais l'exégèse subtile que nous citons ne se fourvoie-t-elle pas dans la rhétorique? Voire.*" ("But enough theology, but enough of these allegories But perhaps this subtle exegesis we are quoting gets lost in rhetoric? Indeed.") Apropos of such rhetorical stratagems by Levinas, Jacques Derrida remarks that a whole book could be written on his use of exclamation points, a punctuation mark "Name of a Dog" exhibits in abundance.

It is, in fact, the textual rhetoric of *Difficult Freedom* that is my real subject here, as it was for the earlier readings of Sebald and Arad.[11] And so the key word for me in all these "but enough ofs" is the word "rhetoric" itself, which customarily carries a negative connotation in Levinas's writing. "Rhetoric approaches the other not to face him but obliquely" (*non pas de face, mais de biais*), Levinas wrote in *Totality and Infinity*, which Jill Robbins has glossed as meaning "having an angle on the other, approaching him with an agenda," versus straight talk (*droiture*) which is rectilinear and unslanted. Writing like the kind I am performing now is "rhetorical" by taking certain permitted liberties with language, as I gladly accept in negotiating a convention-ally determined contract with readers.

But Levinas's own prose is rhetorical too, highly so; to the degree it sometimes over-flows and "overspeaks" itself, says more than it says, it offers us certain interpretive opportunities. To anticipate myself slightly, what the essay on Bobby graces us with *is just* the "name of a dog" and that dog's signature voice even if it is not mimetically present, thus soliciting a more imaginative hearing on our part. Such solicitude echoes the late philosopher Edith Wyschogrod's claim about the "heterological" nature of the name cited in the prologue: that it is an "ethical placeholder" through which we "give [others] countenance."

Notwithstanding Levinas's offhand remark in an interview that animals do not possess a "face" (which has earned the reproach of many critical readings of "Name of a Dog"), such gift of countenance properly becomes a reader's task.[12] In this chapter, therefore, I want to consider a transitive ethics of reading as an interpretive capacity for such grace on the model of Levinas's own scrupulosity as a reader of rabbinic and other kinds of text. Moreover, retrieving a previous formulation, I will continue to style this as an aggadic or midrashic sensibility, in the looser sense I have been em-ploying. The efficacy of that approach will become even clearer in the second half of this chapter, when I shift to another of Levinas's Talmudic readings.

As to our own ethical agency as readers, it will take two forms: (1) By orchestrating some of its sounds, readers of *Difficult Freedom* become its signatories of a sort. "It is the ear of the other that signs," wrote Derrida somewhat enigmatically, putting maxi-mum stress on our acuity as an ethical debt we incur through our acts of reading.[13] In thus "listening" to Levinas, being dogged about particulars, we return his text to him and in his name, while at the same time extending or exceeding its boundaries.[14] (2) Through that attentiveness, a dispassionate or disinterested reading becomes an *altered* and a tact-ful reading.

In respect to the miscellany of texts and their narrative ethics here, one dog story prompting commentary in the form of other dog stories can be understood "midrashi-cally" as not just supplementing but also participating in, by revoicing, the original text. A similar principle applies to partnering "Name of a Dog" with another essay in *Difficult Freedom*, which it neighbors only remotely. Placing them in conversation as I do here mimes the way questions about voice and signature posed by the rhetoric of *Difficult Freedom* necessarily implicate us in their concerns, as if we thereby become "overtaken in the dialogue of the question about itself and with itself."[15]

"Name of a Dog" is slightly over 1,100 words long. Technically, it begins not with "*Je pense à Bobby*" but with an epigraph drawn from Exodus 22:30. Half its time is spent in "high hermeneutics" and "subtle exegesis," in Levinas's phraseology, figura-tions of dogs in the Torah (the epigraph verse along with another from Exodus, 11:7) as connected to each other by the Talmud, together with allusions to La Fontaine and Homer. They follow here, in the Robert Alter translation:

> 22:30 And consecrated men shall you be to Me; flesh in the field torn of beasts you shall not eat; to the dog you shall fling it.

> 11:6–7 And there shall be a great outcry in all the land of Egypt, the like of which there 'has not been and the like of which there will not be again. 7 But against the Israelites no dog will snarl, from man to beast; so that you may know how the LORD sets apart Egypt and Israel.

The essay's second half narrates an anecdote prefigured in the essay's first half by the famous sentence, *Je pense à Bobby*. Here is that anecdote, dog story number two in my series of four; the year is 1944, and the place is Fallingbostel, a Nazi prison camp near Bergen-Belsen:

> There were seventy of us in a in a forestry commando unit for Jewish prisoners of war in Nazi Germany. . . . The French uniform still protected us from Hitlerian violence. But the other men, called free, who had dealings with us and gave us work or work or even a smile—and the children and women who passed by sometimes and sometimes raised their eyes—stripped us of our human skin. We were merely a quasi-humanity, a gang of apes. . . . We were beings trapped in their species, despite all their vocabulary, beings without language . . . no longer part of the world. . . . And then about halfway through our long captivity, for a few short weeks before the sentinels chased him away, a wandering dog entered our lives. One day he came to meet this rabble as we returned under guard from work. He survived in some wild patch in the region of the camp. But we called him Bobby, an exotic name, as one does with a cherished dog. He would appear at morning assembly and was waiting for us as we returned, jumping up and down and barking in delight. For him, there was no doubt that we were men.

According to the less persuaded readings of his essay—and there are several of them—the great flaw in Levinas's thinking is that it is guilty of an excess of ethical humanism.[16] His thinking, culpable for that, stays too close to the philosophical neighborhood of Aristotle, Kant, Heidegger, and others in its anthropocentric complacency. At his best, say these critiques, Bobby bears witness to humanity at the moment of a willed effacement of it, when it has been hollowed from without. As a more or less mute witness, entrapped in the biologics of specieshood, Bobby and his and his animality cannot command us, we are not obligated by him; responsibility and otherness, in Levinas's definition of those terms and the magnetic field of ethical force he engineers for them, are our obsession, not Bobby's.

Although in an interview, Levinas initially grants that, "one cannot entirely refuse the face of an animal," he concludes by wondering, "I don't know whether a snake has a face. I cannot answer that question." And indeed, according to his critics, he has nothing significant to tell us about the ethical status of the "para-" or "infra-human" beyond the definitionally safer perimeter of the interhuman. What is needed, argues

Matthew Calarco (to take one example), is an ethics that is "rigorously and generously agnostic": a humanism, as it were, *of the other organism*. But then, responsibility for countenance, as I have already suggested, may no longer be Levinas's problematic, whatever his position on our proximity to other species and vice versa.

It is worth noting a technical fact here many of such readings that wish to push against the grain of the essay overlook, but which Holocaust memoirs, like Primo Levi's or Alexander Donat's, for instance, record as a commonplace.[17] "The dog" as such (let us picture a German shepherd or Doberman pinscher) was not exactly a figure of hospitality and benevolence in the *Konzentrazion Lager*, where barking and growling meant something besides sociability.[18] The stray, Bobby, is thus remarkable not only because of his innate friendliness but because he must have seemed like a veritable counter-dog, in his lack of ferocity, to the *Gebrauchshunde* which constituted the distinctive animal presence in all Nazi police and military actions. More simply put: "Blondi," Hitler's beloved German shepherd, was also the name of a dog. A more compelling argument about "Nom d'un chien" prefers the concept of the "creaturely" to any supposed impasse between human and animal.[19] Both of these approaches will be roads not taken in my exposition, however.

I prefer instead to read Levinas's essay on the bias, obliquely. Consider, then, the brief text where "*le chien Bobby*" was first identified as such. On the second page of Levinas's *Carnets de Captivité #6* from 1944, we come upon the isolated sentence not unlike the stray dog himself, "The dog Bobby is likeable because he loves us back, thinking outside our distinctions and social rules."[20] Here, Bobby is present and immediate—not yet a *topos* or figure, but an existant, antecedent to Levinasian notions of "the face" or "the other"; he is a "friend of man" before being freighted with transcendence as a human foil as in the essay from 1975. He is also a name: Bobby.

"A dog with a name has a better chance of survival than a stray dog who is just a dog in general," observed Hannah Arendt in passing in *The Origins of Totalitarianism*,[21] and I am certain you will agree that this has been the lucky fate of "the last Kantian in Nazi Germany"—even if the proper name "Kantian" in more recent commentary has tended to siphon much of the attention away from the nickname itself, Bobby's own *nom exotique*.

This was a real dog, more embodied in personal testimony than the "*littéralement un chien*" of Exodus 22:31, the epigraph for this short essay. The dog had a name and was called by it; more significantly, through being given a name, Bobby ceased to be "*un chien errant*," a wandering dog, which "*entre dans notre vie*" (entered our life). Instead, he became "*un chien chéri*" (a treasured dog). The essay's title is not, Wallace Stevens–like, "anecdote of the dog," but rather and very simply, *the name of a dog*: the name by which a dog is called. This is calling in its double sense: christened and summoned. And whether barking precedes calling or the other way around, a colloquy between humans and domesticated animals joins name to voice as the mechanism for creating or sustaining conversation.

Name of a Dog

In her book *Adam's Task: Calling Animals by Name*, the trainer of animals and philosopher of language Vicki Hearne elucidates that mechanism this way:

> It is only when I am saying, "Gunner, Come!" that the dog has a name. His name becomes larger when we proceed to "Gunner, Fetch!" and eventually when he and his name become near enough to being the same size, he is as close to having a proper name as anyone ever gets. When Drummer Girl learned her name, one of the things it meant was that she became able to fit into her name properly; when I said in her story that "her soul was several sizes too large for her," I could as accurately have said that her soul was several sizes too large for the truncated version of a "name" she has so far had, not a name she could answer to. Without a name and someone to call her name, she couldn't enter the moral life.[22]

So let us identify this juncture as the point where the dog as narrated to us by Levinas and the "solemn spectacle" of the Choctaws' dogs in Tocqueville (whose names we do not know, though they surely must have had them) part company. What Bobby gives us is the proper name *and* the bark or friendly growl that answers or elicits it. In Tocqueville, even more starkly than in Levinas, what we register starkly is solely the canine voice—sounded not because an animal has been called, but in creaturely sorrow as that dog's natural right.

Jacques Derrida, reading Levinas's essay in *The Animal Therefore I Am*, parses the moment Genesis 2:19 where the Lord parades all living creatures before Adam, *lirot ma yikra lo*, "in order to see what he could call each one," as marking the very first usurpation: animals were created first—their natural right is one of primogeniture, so to speak—and yet they become subject to human linguistic mastery through being called.[23] For Hearne, by contrast, and in the descendants' version of Adam's task that we glimpse in Levinas's essay, calling animals by name makes them enter the moral life, or as Levinas puts it, *entre[r] dans notre vie*. Moreover, to recall Jean-Louis Chrétien's beautiful formulation, as an act of primordial hospitality, the animals' "first guardian, their first safeguard, is that of speech, which shelters their being and their diversity."[24]

Yet, animals, or rather dogs, may also enter the moral life quite nameless. And they may do so unexpectedly. In the essay, Levinas characterizes the dog as "someone who disrupts society's games" (*celui qui dérange les jeux de société [ou la Société elle-même] et que l'on reçoit, dès lors, comme un chien dans un jeu de quills*), who disrupts and therefore interrupts. At least one critic has noticed how the essay itself, placed at more or less the midpoint of *Difficult Freedom*, has a kind of interruptive effect in relation to the work as a whole. "Name of a dog"—the essay, that is—interrupts. So, in fact does the colloquial phrase in French, as Levinas was fully aware: for in addition to its plain sense, *"Nom d'un chien"* is also a minced oath somewhere on the scale of substituting "son of a gun," or "for crying out loud," as one critic has nicely render it, "doggone," for less polite expletives.[25]

So the essay's title is a pun on the way both dogs and language itself can interrupt. And interruption in Levinas's philosophy happens to be a recurrent trope: ethics interrupts, the affective encounter with another interrupts, poetry interrupts, and last but not least, criticism interrupts. "A book," we have already quoted Levinas, is interrupted discourse catching up with its own breaks." And especially in his shorter texts, Levinasian style itself is often a self-interrupting one, as we have already seen in his expressions of mock disdain: "enough of x/enough of y." But to deepen this point about interruption, I now introduce a third dog story.

In *Lord Jim*, Joseph Conrad's century-marking novel from the year 1900, we are witness to a famous scene of Jim on trial, recalled by our narrator Marlow:

> The devil lets me in for that kind of thing. What kind of thing, you ask? Why, the inquiry thing, the yellow-dog thing—you wouldn't think a mangy, native tyke would be allowed to trip up people in the verandah of a magistrate's court, would you?—the kind of thing that by devious, unexpected, truly diabolical ways causes me to run up against men with soft spots, with hard spots, with hidden plague spots, by Jove! and loosens their tongues at the sight of me for their infernal confidences.[26]

If we paraphrase, "the anecdote I am about to relate concerns an interruption caused by a dog which led directly to my becoming someone's confidante for their own stories and anecdotes." Or in short form, *a dog made me listen.* In the "inquiry thing, the yellow-dog thing," Marlow's companion's stumbles over a dog belonging to native Malays in a courtroom where Jim and his fellow officers are on trial; which in turn prompts the dog to "leap away without a sound," and the companion to point it out to Marlow as "a wretched cur" (a very different sort of *nom de chien*); which then prompts Jim to mistake the companion's voice as Marlow's own and the comment as directed to himself: which then seems to prompt "an oriental voice to whine directly"; which in turn finally seems to prompt the dog "in the very act of trying to sneak in at the door," to be diverted from that action. The passage is typically read as a purely functional, even mechanical hinge—hinted at not-so-subtly by the chime of the dog's own snapping at a fly "like a piece of mechanism" (53)—that serves to bring Jim and Marlow together in a relationship that will define the rest of the novel, the background details providing merely local color.

A reading of the novel by Sanjay Krishnan that I particularly esteem, however, re-directs attention to just these apparently marginal details—the dog's movements, the whining "oriental voice" and the chain of interruptions they initiate.[27] This dog quite literally disrupts one of society's games—in this case, juridical proceedings. But he also interrupts the diegesis of the novel. In other words, just as the yellow dog is described as "weaving himself in and out amongst people's legs," so the superfluous details of the dog and its native owner's whining voice weave themselves into the narrative discourse, respectively bringing one partially into view and making the other quasi-audible. These details then get connected directly to Jim, who, in being momentarily diverted, "sees the animal," as Krishnan pointedly puts it. "The animal is not there to serve his needs. It is not there to consolidate his view of himself; it is turned elsewhere" (153). That elsewhere ultimately takes tangible shape as the fictional country of Patusan in the second half of Conrad's novel, where both Jim and Conrad's readers are given an opportunity to hear something more ethnically substantial than just the "whine" of "oriental" voices.[28]

Now, I want to call Krishnan's intervention an ethical reading of, at least this small moment in, Conrad's work in the sense I have outlined for Levinas's essay. It has selected out a detail for us, finding it, as Cavell would say, by going where it has wandered—a detail that has returned by being attracted, which requires listening to it. In this reading, then, disrupting animals make us aware of otherwise effaceable natives, not to mention a Jim who momentarily escapes being just a theme for Marlow or even for himself. "He existed for me," says Marlow, "and after all it is only through me that he exists for you. I've led him out by the hand; I have paraded him before you" (164).

Levinas's judgment about such parading is severe: such intimacy between persons "cannot give itself out as an example, or be narrated in an edifying discourse."[29] Postcolonialist, modernism- and genre-studies readings of the novel concur: "one might say," says Jed Esty for instance, "that it is Marlow's innocence that is most at stake in *Lord Jim*," a precariously balanced "faux-skepticism" in tandem with the tarnished hero's own romantic self-image and arrested development and the narrative's complexity of framing devices, that serve as so many screens for occlusion.[30]

But if Marlow merely records its peripheral presence, Jim does *see* the animal, if only in momentary relation to both himself and darker-skinned others; likewise and if only for a moment, we *see* Jim and the dog turned toward one another. We also register, if only subliminally, the presence of "Oriental voices." In short, devil or deus-ex-machina, the dog in Conrad's novel produces an interruption, but purely on the plane of textual rhetoric, even to the point of speaking above or behind that text's narrator.[31]

By contrast, Tocqueville has merely recorded an incident; what we do with his anecdote's silent natives offset by their howling dogs is our business, entirely. Something analogous to Conrad's dog story happens in Levinas's, however, which is also the stuff of anecdotal reminiscence. Even his own calculated self-interruptions seem to prepare us for a diversion of our reading attention for which we can subsequently claim a certain ethical agency. And as a result, we *see* and at least figuratively *hear* the animal.

Or at least, that possibility has been created for us. A background story has been brought into view, a delighted barking disports in the foreground for our momentary quasi-acoustic awareness. As the dog in the courtroom scene of *Lord Jim* interrupts, by cutting across, Marlow's representation, so Bobby's name and his playful bark create a kind of rhetorical harmonics in Levinas's essay, a momentary trap for our own attention. For a split second and even if only readers realize it, Marlow's "natural right" as narrator has been superseded. Similarly and even if Levinas is not Joseph Conrad (though he did once think of becoming a novelist.), an anecdote in his essay has created an opportunity for listening, so to speak, on canine frequencies. And like Tocqueville on the Mississippi's *rive gauche* positioned as both onlooker and earwitness, we are, "called here *by the text*" (155) in Krishnan's trenchant phrase, by dogged particulars even if they subserve Levinas's larger and more self-conscious rhetorical purposes.

I want to emphasize the significance for me that this is a *narrative* moment in Levinas's book, just as the thinking of Bobby happens not as philosophy but as memory and as story. Aside from that bark, which if not quite speech, of course, *is* voice, there is, I believe, one other instance in which we "hear voices" in *Difficult Freedom*.[32] Strictly speaking, we *overhear* them. They precede the final essay in the collection entitled "Signature," and I turn to them next. Before I do so, however, I would like to take the liberty of saying another word or two about "Name of a Dog" in connection with theological or allegorical uses of the canine that provide our fourth and final dog story.

Attentive Readiness: Egypt and Ithaca

The concluding paragraph in "Name of a Dog" alludes to the famous moment in Book 17 of the *Odyssey* where Odysseus's faithful dog Argos recognizes him after a twenty-year absence. The personal anecdote Levinas relates is also obviously a scene of *anagnorisis*—of recognition. "*Nous attendait au retour,*" Levinas says of Bobby: he was waiting for us when we returned, that is, with memory and expectation. The non-Homeric element in Levinas's story, of course, is its absence of a hero and, as Levinas points out, a place to come to, which perhaps may capture a difference for Levinas between the Hellenic and the Judaic as cultural schemas with different epic convictions.

Or, perhaps that hero *just is* Bobby, "the last Kantian in Nazi Germany," even if lacking "the brain needed to universalize maxims and drives." But Levinas quickly discards the textual world of Greek heroic return for biblical leave-taking on a grand scale, returning to the verse from Exodus (11:7), to which he had alluded previously: "He was a descendant of the dogs of Egypt. And his growling, his animal faith was born from the silence of his forefathers on the banks of the Nile." And that is how the essay ends.

So, the biblical allusions actually bookend the entire three-page text, enclosing all the other allusions as well as the short narrative about Bobby. Unnoticed by most commentators, the essay is thus primarily exegetical: a *midrash*. But I find myself drawn, as in the extract from Conrad's novel, to two small details in the recognition scene between Argos and Odysseus from Homer that Levinas leaves unstated.[33] This is the passage (ll. 290–310):

While [Odysseus] spoke
an old hound, lying near, pricked up his ears
and lifted up his muzzle. This was Argos,
trained as a puppy by Odysseus,
but never taken on a hunt before
his master sailed for Troy. The young men, afterward,
hunted wild goats with him, and hare, and deer,
but he had grown old in his master's absence.
Treated as rubbish now, he lay at last
upon a mass of dung before the gates –
manure of mules and cows, piled there until
fieldhands could spread it on the king's estate.
Abandoned there, and half destroyed with flies,
old Argos lay.

But when he knew he heard
Odysseus' voice nearby, he did his best
to wag his tail, nose down, with flattened ears,
having no strength to move nearer his master.
And man looked away,
wiping a salt tear from his cheek: but he
hid this from Eumaios, and said to him,

"Eumaios, this is amazing, this dog that lies on the dunghill.
The shape of him is splendid, yet I cannot be certain
whether he had the running speed to go with this beauty."

(Fitzgerald translation)

We notice first that it is actually Odysseus's *voice*, overheard by Argos, which makes the dog "drop his ears and thump his tail, nuzzling low" (Fagles translation) to signal cognizance of his old master, too old and infirm to muster more strength. Odysseus, who is in disguise, responds in kind—indeed, it may be one of the purest depictions of kindness in literary space—by speaking about Argos obliquely as "such a dog, of such quality" (Mitchell translation) without mentioning, let alone calling, Argos by name:[34]

δὴ τότε γ᾽ ὡς ἐνόησεν Ὀδυσσέα ἐγγὺς ἐόντα,
οὐρῇ μέν ῥ᾽ ὅ γ᾽ ἔσηνε καὶ οὔατα κάββαλεν ἄμφω,
ἆσσον δ᾽ οὐκέτ᾽ ἔπειτα δυνήσατο οἷο ἄνακτος
ἐλθέμεν.

Something has passed in the fraternity of man and animal here, in their shared moral life, a silent recognition in the absence of name and voice, not altogether different from the silent recognition of Israelites by Egyptian dogs in the essay's epigraph.[35] It does, however, signally differ from the chain of other, familial recognition scenes involving Telemachus, Penelope, and Laertes in in Books 16, 23, and 24 of *Odyssey* that "keep this narrative from crossing the threshold of mutual recognition," as Paul Ricoeur observes in his book on the philosophy of *anagnorisis*. This is because such "degrees of recognition" are "inextricably entwined" with a history of violence, and thus mark "stages along the path of vengeance that ends with a massacre of pitiless cruelty."[36] If nothing else, Argos's recognition of Odysseus upon expiring precedes this closed circle of recovered mastery. It bespeaks not only noetic capacity in canines, as Jan Söffner explains in a perceptive essay, but also "intercorporeal communication": "Argos and Odysseus recognize each other by *sharing* physical motion."[37] A small drama of tact.

The second element I want to remark, by way of both contrast and similarity, alongside the fact that in Levinas's mid-twentieth-century recognition scene a dog *has* been named in his own hearing, is the feature Levinas identifies about Bobby in particular: neither his size nor his breed but rather the way he barks *gaiement . . . et son aboiement d'ami—foi d'animal*. Fidelity here is expressed by Bobby's voice—his barking and friendly growling. In contradistinction to both Homeric and biblical dogs, he is voluble but respectful, loyal by being expressive. Tocqueville was also struck by a powerful instance of canine fidelity in the midst of human degradation, in more or less the same persecutory neighborhood as the mise en scene for Levinas's story. On the bank of that particular river, however—the Mississippi, not the Nile—the Native Americans' dogs are the only creatures who give voice to grief.

Bobby lacks what Vicki Hearne terms a "vocabulary," the language of training and human intervention, which makes him stand apart from the dogs in Homer, Conrad, and Tocqueville (which are all pets presumably). Odysseus's Argos expires by evincing the lasting influence of that contact. Hearne writes that, "The moral transformation of the dog comes about through stories, stories that provide a form of life within which responding to what is said is a significant possibility."

> The stories, if they are elaborate enough, are frequently about people in confusion who, through the shock that comes from recognizing the reality of the relationship with the dog and then the development or the restoration of that relationship, are enabled to put their own moral and social world in order. The dog may, through an act of devotion or heroism, compel acknowledgment. (25)

This, of course, is Homer's epic gesture. It is not Levinas's, nor is it Tocqueville's or Conrad's, for that matter. But it is the anecdote of the dog in Conrad, marginal though it may be, that points the way to the others, and especially to Bobby. "I can say that I hear a dog but what I hear is his bark," wrote the philosopher Hans Jonas: "For the sensation of hearing to come about, the percipient is entirely dependent on something happening outside his control and in hearing he is exposed to its happening. All he can contribute to the situation is a state of attentive readiness for sounds to occur."[38]

"Attentive readiness for sounds to occur." This is Cavell's point about Wittgenstein. Even if the bark is inaudible on the page, it disposes us, it leans us toward it in a state of attentive readiness, bridging the story of Bobby and Levinas's story about himself in "Signature," as well as positioning us on the edge of a formidable "as if"—Levinas's "extreme attention to the Real."[39]

Clandestine Companions

Let me turn to that essay now. Quite a lot longer than *"Nom d'un chien," "Signature"* also happens to divide into two parts—a short autobiography (Levinas calls it a "disparate inventory") that eschews the first-person pronoun, and a philosophical précis. It is the only essay in the collection that serves as its own major heading (Levinas's book is divided into six such major sections), and the only one with prominent epigraphs just under that heading. These are the three "strophes" in this odd, epigraphic prose poem:

> "The language that tries to be direct and name events fails to be straightforward. Events induce it to be prudent and make compromises. Commitment unknowingly agglomerates men into parties. Their speech is transformed into politics. The language of the committed is encoded."

> "Who can speak in a non-coded way about current events? Who can simply open his heart when talking about people? Who shows them his face?"[40]

> "The person who uses the words 'substance,' 'accident,' 'subject,' 'object,' and other abstractions . . ."

They conclude with the significant parenthesis "(*D'une conversation surprise dans la métro*)" (From a conversation overheard on the subway). Excluding Bobby's inaudible bark, these are really the only voices that we really "hear" in *Difficult Freedom*. If they do not belong to Levinas himself (for it may well be his own conversation, with Levinas the one being overheard by others), how might this conversation be connected to a reading of "Name of a Dog" premised on anecdote, voice, and *solicitation*?

In 1989, Maurice Blanchot composed an essay about Levinas entitled, "Our Clandestine Companion."[41] At first blush, the title suggests a formulation we might possibly take to refer to Levinas himself, the notary public to his personal signature, so to speak. While that may be its subtext, in fact, the title signifies the vocation of philosophy— "our companion, at day, at night . . . giving us to believe there is nothing awake in us, nothing vigilant unto sleep, that is not due to her difficult friendship." ("Difficult friendship": it sounds like "difficult freedom.") Blanchot's idea, a long footnote to Levinas's untimely meditation that the twentieth century "will have witnessed the end of philosophy," is that philosophy-as-vocation will be a constant presence in our lives even if its proper name or face is obscured as our "unavowable friend." Thus, we are in some sense all philosophers.

I confess to being one of those readers of Blanchot's essay who drew an inference from the title that it was going to include some sort of portrait or even biography of Levinas himself. Clandestine yet companionate somehow: did that perhaps describe Blanchot's friendship with Levinas? Even more to the point, could these qualities also be enlisted to describe the general reader's experience of Levinas's work as an openness that is also sometimes furtive, self-concealed in some way perhaps—hence the plural possessive in "our" clandestine companion? It becomes immediately clear, however, that it is *philosophy* Blanchot has in mind here, not Levinas the person or the writer. Because philosophy courts an invincible skepticism, because language is already skepticism, philosophy is vulnerable to being in some way delegitimated as a vocation or a pursuit.[42] We persist in our entanglement with it, as if it were more lover than spouse.

"But philosophy is precisely not an allegory," Blanchot insists. So, if I can mobilize Blanchot's formulation deliberately nearer to Levinas himself, in the direction of his essay, "Signature," structurally speaking, three *compagnes clandestine* keep company in it, three separate but contiguous parts. Working from back to front, (1) a précis of Levinas's ethical philosophy, (2) a compact personal history, and (3) the conversation overheard in the Metro. The first two, certainly, are nonallegorical, even though they appear to have been rhetorically transposed with each other: the biographical inventory is dispassionate and *zero degré* where its philosophical counterpart is, as Novalis might say "dephlegmaticized," vivified, in keeping with Levinas's discursive project, generally, which rouses and startles to life both speculative philosophy and a course of action.[43] Between the précis and the biography is interposed this dramatic pivot-sentence: "It [the biography] is dominated by the presentiment and memory of the Nazi horror" (291). It's a statement that, formally if not rhetorically, suggests an analogy with "*Je pense à . . .*" in "Name of a Dog," since here, too, Levinas's thought is the stuff of presentiment and memory. *This*, the Nazi horror, is what he is thinking of. In the companion essay, of course, it was Bobby.

In fact, what I would invite us to consider now is "Signature" and "Name of a Dog," as each other's own clandestine companion. Each essay contains a narrative kernel, a story, cushioned respectively by philosophical and rhetorical discourses in excess of the strictly biographical—or is it the other way around? Each registers a voice—or rather, *in* each, *we* can construct an acoustics—*aboyant gaiement* in the one, *conversation surprise* in the other. If these suggest an act or event of Saying that overflows the Said (in the terms developed by Levinas's later philosophy)—and I am cautious to suggest as much since I believe, like vulgar Marxism there is such a thing as vulgar Levinasism—the overhearing that happens underground in "Signature" does come to us as a *voice*. For that is how it is rendered on the page, a human cousin to Bobby's *aboiement*. Rhetorically speaking, the essays share an elective affinity, which is given to us to construct as, at these particular moments, the "listeners" of *Difficult Freedom*. What I have been loosely calling midrashic reading just *is* this sort of critically engineered affiliation among textual symbiotes. Lastly, each essay dramatizes an inter-ruption within the context of the book that encompasses it.

But as far as "Signature" itself is concerned, if the philosophy-as-vocation is precisely non-rhetorical, what shall we make of the overheard conversation? Is the voice Delphic? Parodic? Allegoric? A prooftext for Hans Jonas's observation that in hearing, we are exposed to the pure event of someone else's voice? Obviously, the content of the conversation seems tailor-made for Blanchot's point that we are all philosophers now, and the remark probably dearest to Levinas is the second one: "Who can simply open his heart when talking about people? Who shows them his face?" Perhaps, we are all clandestine in some way—a human predisposition we saw so joyfully and transcendently disavowed by Bobby's frankness. At any rate, while each overheard remark dovetails with Levinas's particular philosophical concerns (which does hold out the possibility that the conversation is Levinas's invention, although that bit of legerdemain would be uncharacteristic), the conversational snatches do not necessarily comment on what immediately follows them in the essay proper.

"The language that tries to be direct and name events fails to be straightforward," says the first of these. "Events induce it to be prudent and make compromises. Commitment unknowingly agglomerates men into parties. Their speech is transformed into politics. The language of the committed is encoded." Superficially, this might seem to correspond to the rhetorical choices in Levinas's own prudent exercise in self-identification. But surely the speech of "Signature" is not therefore transformed into a kind of politics, even if it feels obliged by a certain clandestinity. The second epigraph wonders aloud, "Who shows his face . . . when speaking?" yet the transparency and self-presence invoked here are tied to discourse about other men and about current events, not self-evidently to the self that speaks, or in this case, is overheard.

The third epigraph, a fragment and perhaps the most uncanny of them, says, "The person who uses the words 'substance,' 'accident,' 'subject,' 'object,' and other abstractions . . . ." On one hand, this might effectively describe Levinas himself in his vocation as philosopher; several of those words actually appear in the essay. On the other hand, the sense seems to be that such abstractions fail to make language straightforward or direct; they are encoded; they don't disclose a face. I will confess to a certain aural pleasure in catching the way that the content of these epigraphs, whether intentionally or not, folds back on itself in the form of a *conversation surprise*. In "dialogue" with Levinas's own self-effacing disparate inventory, which at best exhibits Levinas's face *dans le profil*, the epigraphs consist solely of disembodied voice—one word for which in a Levinasian lexicon is *trace*. (Whether it is Levinas himself or the readers of his essay, the interlocutor's role gets shifted uncomfortably close to what Elias Canetti assigned the ambiguously tinged term, "earwitness.")

The source for all three conversational fragments is anonymous, possibly fictive—midway between a neighbor and a bare third-person, proximate to oneself on the subway car but politely kept clandestine.[44] And yet as a *troisième personne,* she or he (or

they) do(es) not appear to be an embodiment of the Levinasian *tiers* on a purely textual plane, the third party and other-to-the-Other (*L'autre*) who brings fraternity into
ethical relation and relieves the extreme severity of the face-to-face by connecting it to
a world of justice and politics. It is almost as if the overhearer (in this case, Levinas),
were a Metro King Gyges (as the famous Greek myth's ring of invisibility is invoked
allegorically in *Totality and Infinity*).[45] Perhaps this is what Levinas means when he
says elsewhere in *Difficult Freedom*, "To have an outside, to listen for what comes from
outside, oh, miracle of exteriority" (29). Otherwise put, Levinasian *tact*.

Outside Suggestion

One is also reminded again of Joseph Conrad, a famous overhearer himself—of
English, certainly[46]—specifically, of a moment in the short story "The End of the
Tether," which, among other things, is about the permeable borders between speakers
and earwitnesses: "And our conduct after all is so much a matter of *outside suggestion*."[47] We would thus overhear "the conversation overheard" in suggestive relation to
the compressed account of a life and the philosophical statement that follow it. Judith
Butler, in *Giving an Account of Oneself*, offers a similar parable about the productive
anomaly at the root of any story we tell about ourselves:

> If we require that someone be able to tell in story form the reasons why his or her
> life has taken the path it has, that is, to be a coherent autobiographer, we may be
> preferring the seamlessness of the story to something we might tentatively call the
> truth of the person, a truth that . . . might well become more clear in moments of
> interruption, stoppage, open-endedness—in enigmatic articulations that cannot
> easily be translated into narrative form. . . . What is recognized about a self in the
> course of this exchange is that the self is the sort of being for whom staying inside
> proves impossible. One is compelled and comported outside oneself . . . by virtue
> of a convention or norm that one did not make, in which one cannot discern
> oneself as an author or agent of one's own making.[48]

Read this way, "Signature" suggests a lesson about being forced into some exterior relation to oneself in the act of self-accounting, as if the clandestine companion that is one's
philosophy is actually the discourse through which one is most intimately revealed—
similar to the way the Bobby anecdote in "Name of a Dog," pre-staged rhetorically by
"*Je pense á* Bobby," seems to overflow both the arguments that precede and follow it.
Textually, the short narrative itself "survives" amid that essay's various rhetorical stratagems, as Bobby continually jumps up and down, barking with delight, as if waiting
for our reading. In the case of each essay, a little interruptive story "about" exteriority
thus performs its own exterior rhetorical relation—likes dogs marking their territory.

The voice overheard at the end of *Difficult Freedom* is one that is neither greeted nor
invoked; its citation by the author does not correspond, in the visual terms that we
find in the very first essay in *Difficult Freedom*, to "looking at a look or aiming at a face

in its epiphany, its direct revelation, as language or discourse" (these are tropes familiar from *Totality and Infinity*). But it nevertheless represents, I believe, what that same essay calls "*une sortie de soi*" (a moving out of oneself). And while "Signature" does not express or even dramatize the sort of transfiguring dialogue Levinas endorses at the end of *Otherwise Than Being* as "*vie dangereuse, comme un beau risque à courir*" (a dangerous life, a fine risk to be run), I think the risky dialogue that can be constructed between it and "Name of a Dog" offers a fine lesson in proximity, in shepherding, attracting, commanding, and listening to texts that wander and return. And on lower than-canine-frequencies, perhaps such interference patterns of outside influence in the midst of personal recollection, such gratuitous lessons in exteriority, are what giving an account of oneself must ultimately mean—which is how, finally, I understand the *inside* hinge between these two essays.

"*Mais la liberté n'est pas devenue plus facile*" (but freedom does not become easier), Levinas writes at the end of the preliminary note to *Difficult Freedom*. It can capably serve, I believe, as a sentiment shared as his book's responsible reader, who consequently owes it a certain measure of difficulty, an *exégèse difficile* outside the textual economy of reciprocal exchange—the aspirational alterity, for example, with which Levinas himself performs readings of Proust or Blanchot or Agnon or Spinoza, or the Talmud for that matter, to various degrees or success. At the same time, one feels the tug of the leash, resisting too many freedoms, taking too much *liberté*.

In his book *On the Psychotheology of Everyday Life,* critic Eric Santner footnotes an early essay by Levinas from 1951, "Is Ontology Fundamental?" which explains that grasping the other in the general economy of being, "on the horizon," is not the same as looking him or her in the face.[49] Santner's modification, through his psychoanalytic account of being answerable to the Other's claims, is to suggest that such a face is animated by a kind of psychological tic that excites us in the literal sense of the word: it solicits our attention by calling us out. In my inventory of voices from the rhetorical underground of *Difficult Freedom*—inventory in its etymological sense of *what we come upon*—this tic takes the form of an acoustic perturbation that calls to us—like those high-pitched harmonics produced by Galton's whistle that only dogs, such as Bobby, can hear. We might call ourselves, then—even as we do come upon the text "much later"—signatories of such sounds unheard, "the ear of the other that signs."[50]

Whatever the import of Levinas's "Signature" in its own right and however *le chien Bobby* may serve as a means to a rhetorical end, this section of the chapter has asked us to "hear voices"—to assemble, as it were, into a contrapuntal "speech-ark," the plaintive howl of all-but forgotten Native American dogs, the joyous barking of one German canine that befriended French prisoners in the vicinity of Bergen-Belsen, the faceless and nameless subway passengers that enable both Levinas and the reader of *Difficult Freedom*, as each other's clandestine companion, to "co-sign" his text in attentive readiness for its sounds to occur.

PART 2

Anokhi Afar Va'efer/V'anakhnu Mah?

> To posit subjectivity in this responsibility is to catch sight of a passivity in it, is
> never passive enough, that of being consumed for the other (*autrui*). The very light
> of subjectivity shines and illuminates out of this ardor, although the ashes of this
> consummation are not able to fashion the kernel of a being existing in and for
> itself, and the I does not oppose to the other any form that protects itself or
> provides it with a measure. Such is the consuming of a holocaust. "I am dust and
> ashes" [*anokhi afar va'efer*] says Abraham in interceding for Sodom. "What are
> we?" says Moses more humbly still.
>
> "God and Philosophy" (*CPP*, 168)

> A thing exists in the midst of its wastes. When the kindling wood becomes smoke
> and ashes the identity of my table disappears. The wastes become indiscernible; the
> smoke drifts off anywhere. If my thought follows the transformation of things I
> lose the trace of their identity very quickly.
>
> *Totality and Infinity*, 139–140

Several times in his work, Levinas alludes to the eerily suspended episode in Genesis 18 when Abraham bargains with God.[51] For instance, in the essay on Kierkegaard "Existence and Ethics" collected in *Proper Names*, in the final lecture in his lecture course "Death and Time" collected in *God, Death, and Time*, and as the governing trope of his final (and briefest) Talmudic reading, "Who is One-Self" from 1989, published posthumously in *New Talmudic Readings*.

In this second section of the chapter, I want to link that reading's analysis of self-effacement (*bitul hayesh*) with an essay Levinas wrote from roughly the same period (1985) entitled "Judaism and Kenosis." Together, the *lecture talmudique* and the instance of philosophical criticism, establish an antiphony of voice: they are best read, I believe (as with the two essays treated earlier), contiguously and contrapuntally. With both texts, we are in the discursive realm Edward Said would call "late style," which "has the power to render disenchantment and pleasure without resolving the contradiction between them" (141). One especially feels that interplay in Levinas's final Talmudic reading.

Before commencing, however, I want to underscore the second epigraph to this part of the chapter, a passage from *Totality and Infinity* I quoted previously in a note in Chapter 1. In that book, Levinas's phrase for the evanescence and mutability of material objects in the world is "the return of the thing to its element." While unrelated philosophically to Levinas's more conspicuously *religious* citations of the Abraham episode, there is a precedent in later Jewish (*mitnagdic*) rabbinic literature that effects a hinge between these two respective senses of "ashes." In his *Meshekh Hokhma*

("The Price of Wisdom"), a halakhic Torah commentary, the Lithuanian-Polish Rabbi Meir Simhka ha-Kohen of Dvinsk (1843–1926) explains Abraham's expression of nullity as precisely *the return of the thing to its element*. Moreover, in Abraham's case (albeit not for Levinas's table), this granulation of identity also effectuates purification, "as plants of *terumah* which became impure are replanted and then become pure; and as impure water becomes pure on contact with pure water."

Purity and impurity are once again the tropological concerns of Levinas's Talmudic reading, "Who Is One-Self," an exegesis on a homiletic moment in the tractate *bHullin* (חולין, "Ordinary Things"), which treats the laws of slaughter and meat preparation and consumption according to stipulations by the Mishnah, the Tosefta, other Tannaitic traditions, and the Torah. (The passage Levinas discusses is reproduced at the end of this chapter.) The *Meshekh Hokhma*'s interpretation of "dust and ashes" also comports with its precursor mitnagdic treatise of theological musar, *Nefesh Ha-Hayyim* ("Soul of Life"), by Rabbi Hayyim of Volozhin (1749–1821), which is of seminal importance to Levinas, and the subject of "Judaism and Kenosis" (among other writings in his oeuvre).[52]

I mention these correlations because they happen to provide an especially ambient framework for understanding Levinas's final Talmudic reading in dialogue with the essay on Hayyim Volozhiner. In his own phraseology, Talmudic commentary and the midrashic sensibility of the rabbis is the expression of sonority, as he tropes in "Revelation in the Jewish Tradition": "Just as the strings of a violin are stretched across its wood, so is the text stretched across all the amplifications brought by tradition" (137).[53] And of the period in which Hayyim of Volozhin, a disciple of the Vilna Gaon (1720–1797, wrote, Levinas remarks, "It was a time when that tradition seemed to renew itself from within" ("Judaism and Kenosis," 119).

In a resolutely Levinasian statement (though he intends it with reference to Gadamer), Gerald Bruns suggests that, "the encounter with tradition always brings our desire for totality up short."[54] Tradition—not to be confused with its institutions— is "seamed" with resistances; we confuse it with an allegorical process of smoothly integrated, assimilated samenesses at our peril. Rather, tradition inducts us into the temporal analogue of *frottage*: "not the persistence of the same," Bruns says, but a more frictional encounter with cultural alterity, open to the future, infinite instead of totalizing. Bruns says the following about Petrarch's letters to the illustrious dead:

> One way to summarize this point would be to say that in Petrarch we see a critical turn from allegory to satire as a mode of coping with the historicality of being. Instead of rewriting the discourse of the other in order to remove its strangeness or to fit it into the conceptual framework of the present, Petrarch enters into this discourse in order to shake the present (or his own self) from the dogmatism of self-possession. (202)

I think that this posture, certainly in part, describes Levinas's own self-willed relationship to tradition, which came late in his life, and was mediated by both European philosophical conversation in the interwar years (as Samuel Moyn has claimed), "a secularization of a transconfessional, but originally Protestant, theology of encounter with the divine" (12), and his highly charged personal relationship with Mordechai Shushani (alias R. Hillel Perelman, a student of Rav Abraham Isaac Kook), from whom he first learned to study Talmud.[55]

Not surprisingly, with its emphases on influences like Kierkegaard, Heidegger, and Barth and its genetic argument about the crystallization of Levinasian ethics in the crucible of the early Cold War, Moyn's critical history of Levinas's intellectual development has met with resistance in certain blocs of Levinas scholarship, certainly among his coreligionists and apologists in modern Jewish philosophy. And while I feel this sort of needful revisionism sometimes bears out the Dubner Maggid's philosophy of how to hit a bulls-eye (shoot the hole, then paint the target around it), this is not a debate I can rehearse here.[56]

Rather, in line with Bruns's (in this respect, ironically Levinasian) view of tradition articulated above, I want to affirm Moyn's claim that as regards Levinas's crafted Jewish inheritance, "the rhetoric of finding has to be replaced with the rhetoric of making" (16). But this just means that Levinas's own highly mediated relationship to Jewish texts and tradition exhibits all the traits of what Said calls "affiliation." Similarly, as Moyn cites Levinas himself, from his review of H. A. Wolfson's *Philosophy of Spinoza*, "There is a place for a philological history [that] understands a doctrine as a literary product, bearing the imprint of the influences undergone by the author" (19).

For our purposes here, and to return to the trope of "dust and ashes," Levinas's affiliative coupling of Ḥayyim Volozhiner and Talmudic *aggadah* of the sort he reads in the passage from *bḤullin* 88b–89a offers us a remarkable demonstration of the way he stretches strings over wood, an ethical acoustics that understands reading as attunement in accord with textuality as its own intricate harmonics. Let me attend, now, to the homiletic excerpt Levinas draws from tractate *Ḥullin* by, first, going all the way to the end of the tractate to cite what is known as the *hadran*, a formulaic prayer recited by all students who complete a tractate,[57] whose etymology combines ideas of both adornment and return:

> We shall return to [adorn] you, *Ḥullin*;
> May you return to [adorn] us!
> Our thoughts are with you, *Ḥullin*;
> May your thoughts be with us!
> We shall not forget you, *Ḥullin*;
> May you not forget us—
> Not in this world or the world to come.

Tractate *Hullin* is thus apostrophized and also invoked prosopopoeically: it returns to its readers, it thinks about them, it does not forget them. In a lecture given on completion of this very tractate in 1973, Rabbi Joseph B. Soloveitchik likened the *hadran* formula to a mother's always latent awareness of her children, whatever happens to be distracting her or prompting her to leave their presence temporarily: departure is always the occasion for subsequent return.[58]

While this may seem to resemble Levinas's own trope of maternity by which he expresses the self's bearing the Other without absorbing it (a figure he borrows from Numbers 11:12 in which Moses describes himself as a wet-nurse (*omein*)[59] to the aptly named Children of Israel), I would express the *hadran*'s significance somewhat differently (and less sentimentally).[60] I earlier alluded to Levinas's evocation of Xenakis's cello music in *Otherwise Than Being*, which "bends the quality of the notes emitted into adverbs. Every quiddity becomes a modality, the strings and woods turn into sonority" (41). As a covenantal dialogue between reader and text, the *hadran* could be said to give voice to what Levinas calls the "verbalness of verbs."

It is a linguistic performativity he also locates in poetry, psalmody, and prophecy, and conforms, as Bettina Bergo expresses it, to a "witnessing-as-spectacle"—an "ad-verbialness" which, being neither active verb nor designatory noun, lets the *autrement* or "otherly" character of ethical encounter with another person (or a text) "resonate."[61] This tractate I study *connects* me to do it: not necessarily as infant to parent, but as co-presence, as covenantal partner, just as I am bound to address it—*address it*—through ongoing call and response, what Talmudic discourse itself calls *shakla v'tarya* ("give and take"), or in Levinasian argot, *va-et-vient*.

A version of this same ambience or sonority, of course, is also what underpins the dialogic background to Abraham's negotiations with God that Levinas has chosen to gloss in his reading of *bHullin* 88b–89a. *Afar va'efer*, the Torah's paronomasia on "dust and ashes" is an obvious biblical analogue for Levinasian tropes of self-diminishment, and it makes the ideal counterpart to an analysis of humanity's world-sustaining responsibility so great that even God has need of it, which he conducts in the essay on Hayyim of Volozhin, "Judaism and Kenosis." Indeed, the two texts in tandem, Talmudic reading and essay on eighteenth-century moral treatise, form the perfect complement to a well-known Hasidic teaching by Reb Simkha Bunim of Pershysch (1765–1827) that each person should carry two slips of paper, one in each pocket, on one of which is written *Bishvili nivra ha-olam*—"for my sake the world was created," and on the other, *V'anokhi afar va'efer*—"I am but dust and ashes."[62]

Neither a *lamdan-hasid* nor a *maskill*; neither a kabbalist (like R. Hayyim) nor an halakhist (like R. Soloveitchik); discoursing on neither classical Torah commentaries (such as the sixteenth-century *Mikraot Gedalot* which includes, among others, those of Ibn Ezra and Rashi) or the major texts of medieval Jewish philosophy; neither partial to Jewish legal codes nor an enthusiast of the various collections of post-Talmudic midrash; rarely adducing liturgy or the language of prayer: Emmanuel Levinas locates

himself within the three-thousand-year expanse of textual Jewish tradition at effectively two nodes: the Talmud, through his idiosyncratic aggadic approach to it, and
the early nineteenth-century scholarship-based Lithuanian sensibility of the *Nefesh
ha-Ḥayyim*, a text he mentions repeatedly.

It is a telling assemblage of affiliative choices to have made at mid-life, especially
within the context of his deep background in philosophy (the Greek), his lifelong love
of the *beau langage* of Western humanism (the European), and his quite nontradi-
tional relationship to classical Jewish sources (the Hebrew, or Aramaic). For Levinas,
the Talmud is both prephilosophical (ethically founded) and essentially philosophical
(in its ethical hermeneutics). The *Nefesh ha-Ḥayyim*, an ethico-kabbalistic work treat-
ing both theology and mystical prayer, constitutes, in Alan Nadler's phrase, a "pane-
gyric to the world-sustaining potency of *Talmud Torah* [Torah study] . . . as the central
religious activity and highest spiritual value in Judaism" (162, 151). Between them, we
find the poles of Levinas's Jewish, Hebraic, biblical humanism.

But where the essay on Ḥayyim of Volozhin is more or less self-contained, situating
both author and text historically and unpacking the latter quite carefully, without
tractate *Ḥullin* in hand, a reader of Levinas's "Who Is One-Self?" would not be cogni-
zant of the Talmud's text-immanent background there. For the tractate, in Talmudically
laconic fashion, proposes—but only to dismiss—a possible *third* commandment-as-
reward for Abraham's self-abnegation—that of *kisui hadam* ("covering the blood"),
which putatively supplements the two already merited *mitzvot* indicated there: 1) the
ashes of *parah adumah* ("the red heifer" of Numbers 19:17) and 2) the earth given to be
swallowed by the *sotah* ("the woman suspected of adultery" of Num. 5:17).

In fact, the *mitzvah* of *kisui hadam*[63] forms the comprehensive halakhic framework
within which Levinas's selected periscope briefly digresses in order to expound strictly
homiletic implications of *bitul hayesh* (the concluding *mishnah* that governs this section of the chapter begins, "With what may we cover [blood] and with what may we
not cover [it]?"). Thus, the translation of the Talmudic text that introduces Levinas's
reading says, "Must one also add [*kisui hadam*] 'the earth covering up for blood?' This
bears only on a perfecting of the commandment, but to no one's advantage," on which
Levinas pithily comments "Gratuitous supposition" (118), and moves on.

Yet, the Talmud's question goes directly to the halakhic issue it has just spent an
entire chapter discussing, and its quick negation is a purely technical matter.[64] Levinas's
dismissal leaves the average interlocutor at the 1989 colloquium and the average reader
of this redacted lecture unenlightened about the central significance of that *mitzvah*
to the discussion at hand. And yet, Levinas immediately remarks, "But how forget the
articulations of the thought which this very hypothesis raises in a subtle Talmudic reflection attentive to all that is un-said which resonates in the said" (118)? Is he still speaking about the commandment of *kisui hadam* about which the aggadic homiletics now
fall silent? And if so, what exactly would those articulations be, since halakhically
speaking, the Talmud has already disposed of the query in customary lapidary manner?

As the translator Richard Cohen notes in his preface to *New Talmudic Readings,* *Quant-a-Soi* ("Who Is One-Self?") most certainly represents an underedited and perhaps even unedited composition by Levinas, and thus does not approximate the stylistic standard of the more burnished, if still quite challenging and sometimes even opaque, Talmudic readings Levinas published in the 1960s, 1970s, and 1980s. But I am not sure myself what Levinas intends here, especially since the next sentence says "The link between Abraham's thought and the test of the wife suspected of misconduct seems to me profound," chiming with the excerpt's canceled possibility of a third "ritual as reward."

To step back from the micro-level of the text for a moment, pages 88–89 are the concluding pages of tractate *bHullin*'s Chapter 6, which is indeed titled "*Kisui hadam.*" The chapter is "a large-scale composite that resembles a code of rules rather than an extended discourse on principles."[65] The pericope's main speaker Rava (or Abba ben Yosef bar Ḥama), is the eminent third-century Amoraitic sage of the Pumbedita Academy whom we have already met in the Talmudic readings discussed in Chapter 1. Pertinently enough, it happens there is one other place in Levinas's oeuvre in which he refers to tractate *bHullin*, and we find it in the essay "Judaism and Kenosis" where he discusses the familiar aggadic parable of "The moon that makes itself little" (*bHullin* 60a), which, like Abraham, enters into disputatious parleying with God.

The general topic for the 1989 colloquium of French-speaking Jewish intellectuals at which Levinas delivered his reading was "As-For-Oneself." One suspects that it afforded Levinas an opportunity to inscribe talmudically a theme of enduring philosophical importance to him: the passivity of the ethical subject that is "never passive enough, that of being consumed for the other," a self-offered holocaust that finds its most striking biblical objective correlative in Abraham's "I am but dust and ashes."[66]

The rationale for *afar va'efer* in the aggadic excerpt from *bHullin*, by contrast, is object-related in the extreme: the *stam* (Talmudic scribe) has used the halakhic discussion of the suitability of earthen or ashen sediment for covering blood and more specifically, a small debate between Beit Hillel and Beit Shammai about whether *efer* (ash) and *afar* (earth) are synonymous, to introduce the famous verse from Genesis when Abraham intercedes for Sodom—which serves, however, entirely as an *asmakhta* (Aram. אסמכתא; "support," "reliance"), a biblical citation deployed as to support a halakhic ruling without suggesting that the *halakhah* actually derives from this exegesis.

Levinas' analytical challenge in his reading, then, is to explicate the Talmud's connection of Genesis 18:27 to the two *mitzvot* of the *para adumah* and *sota* according to the his own ethical predilections, which he regards as already articulated by the rabbinic discourse—even if left "unsaid." He does this in two ways: just as the ritual of the "red heifer"—whose paradoxical workings ensure that the water mixed with the ashes of the slaughtered cow differentially purify those who have become impure through *tum'at hamet* (corpse), but defile the priest who performs the ritual—reminds me of my own death and thus orients me toward the other;[67] so, the ritual mixture of *mayim hamarim* (water and earth from the Temple floor), which the *sotah* (the word means "wayward") is compelled to swallow, alerts me to the "amphibology of eros" (119), the equivocal, concupiscent nature of even spousal "loves," and thus once again, oriented, like the paradigm of Abraham, toward an *ethical*—that is, nonequivocal, elevated, holy—order of human relation.[68]

The *peshat* of the Talmudic text does not make such connections overt. In his commentary, Rashi, for instance, regards the presence of dirt and ash in these two ceremonies as signaling the way commandments transfigure the lowliest of substances through Godly service. The *Beis Halevi* (a Torah commentary by Yosef Dov Soloveitchik, 1820–1892) suggests a temporal dimension: if Abraham's "dust and ashes" was an existential confession about both his preterit nullity (possessed, like earth, of no past) and his proleptic insignificance (like ash, lacking any future), then the *mitzvah* of the red heifer compensates by purifying a person's future (serving, too, as a decreed mechanism into futurity for the Jewish people's purification) and the *mitzvah* of the suspected wife's trial by ordeal exculpates her by "sanitizing" her past.

By contrast, Levinas's assertions that "Impurity is the name of an always already sordid egoism" (116) or that conjugal love involves "a call to another purity beyond bourgeois prudence" (118) constitute *frottage* of a rather vehement kind, and, one must admit, a high order of exegetical *liberté*. Where the rabbinic hermeneutic concentrates on this-worldly benefit bestowed in the merit of Abraham's statement by two *mitzvot* of the most terrestrial sort, Levinas's ethical hermeneutic construes an irruption of alterity as the ritual safeguard for the "*as-for-me*"—"some traces of a 'me' which is affirmed in its devotion to the other and which *is* because it is obligated" (121). So far, so Levinasian.

bHullin 89a adds a second aggadic "strophe" about Abraham's "dust and ashes" in the same vein: the two mitzvoth of *tefillin* (Exodus 13:9, 16—in the form of *retzuot* or leather straps) and *tzitzit* (Numbers 15:39—in the form of *teheilet* or blue thread), are given as rewards in this world; the former (in Rashi's explanation), because when worn on the head, *tefillin* display God's presence, the latter (again, following Rashi), because the blue thread in the fringes (after a series of indexical analogies) resembles the celestial Throne of Glory, which reminds God in turn of Jews' performing the *mitzvah* of *tzitzit*, itself pointing to all the other 612 commandments combined. For Levinas, the rituals of "the strap" and "the thread" signify, respectively, "the escalation of disinterestedness in a conflict, the very idea of the battle of the Good" (120), consequent upon Abraham's refusal of plunder in a parley with the King of Sodom (Genesis 14:23), and "blue as blue, essential moment of elevation" ("elevation," in Levinas's vocabulary, is a word connoting ethical rectitude, the "height" that comes with obligation).

Levinas's lyricism just here is quite remarkable. It is one of his most exquisite prose poems.

It is a vision and elevation across the dissimilarities of similarities, a comprehension of spiritual levels across the variations of the sensible. Here meaning is determined as if through the specificity of a blue warm, luminous and of mysterious clarity, different from the forbidden secret of black and from the violent cry of the blazing of read. Blue as blue, essential moment of elevation. (121)

In the last few pages of "Who Is One-Self?" Levinas reflects on the modulation from Abraham to Moses and Aharon in the third "movement" of the aggadic extract, which contains four additional homilies on the subject of humility, encapsulated by identity-statements in the Pentateuch: Abraham's "I am but dust and ashes" and Moses/Aharon's "for what are we?"

In parallel with Rava (or R. Yoḥanan), Levinas accords priority to the latter as betokening "the new and fullest meaning of the 'as-for-oneself'": "to say this in the language of piety: through the merit of he who restrains himself in a quarrel, the wholeness of being subsists" (124). Likewise, the Talmud, through midrashic word-play, connects the word *mah* "what" (but also thus signifying "nothing") in Moses and Aharon's "what are we" (Exodus 16:8) to *blimah* in Job 26:7 (which, construed as two words, *bli mah*, means "without anything") to *bolem*, a word meaning "muzzled." Abraham's elemental nullity modulates to Moses and Aharon's nullity-without-substance which pivots to the notion of world-sustaining self-restraint, a muted oneself.

The final homily of the pericope plugs conspicuously and irresistibly into the argument of Ḥayyim Volozhiner's *Nefesh ha-Ḥayyim* that humanity, in its elevated humility, supports the entire cosmos. Indeed, the *Nefesh ha-Ḥayyim* pointedly explores the nature of Moses's humility ("I am but dust and ashes" revised as "what are we?"), which represents a direct link with *bḤullin* 88b–89a that Levinas was most assuredly aware of (as he indicates without citation in the companion essay, "'In the Image of God' According to Rabbi Hayyim Volozhiner").[69] And yet for some reason, he mutes the connection, leaves it un-said, and "restrains himself."

Similarly, this spiritual concept of nothingness has a counterpart in Levinas's early philosophical reflections on the *il y a* ("there is"), which Michael Fagenblat relates, not to cosmological *kabbalah* in its eighteenth-century Volozhin guise, but rather to the biblical mytheme of chaos preceding creation, *tohu va'vohu*, in Genesis 1:2. Fagenblatt's book takes pain to root Levinas's philosophy in classical Jewish thought, specifically Maimonides.[70] He mentions Moses de Leon and Baḥya Ibn Pakuda as source-analogues for Levinas's theologics of creation, as well as Maimonides's negative theology. But his book, like many of its peers, seeks to establish a determinative *philosophical* grounding for Levinas's multivocal thought.

My concerns are more restrictively dialogical (in the local sense Mikhail Bakhtin intends). Thus, it is directly here, in the crossing point between Talmud and mitnagdic treatise, that I believe we catch site of how Levinas's elective Jewish textual affinities—a harmonics of sentences, motifs, and turns of phrase—help him craft an ethics of reading as an *acoustics*. Latent for Levinas, then, in *bḤullin*'s midrashic excursus on Abraham's *anokhi afar va'efer*, is the trope of (im)purity, which, while the tractate itself is more overtly concerned with the minutiae of *kisui hadam*, discloses the link between defilement and aggrandizement, between impurity and self-possession, which we saw previously animating Levinas's considerations of the rectitude of reading.[71] In "Who Is One-Self?" that trope takes the following form:

> That the consciousness of being "dust and ashes" does not estrange Abraham from
> his disinterestedness, from his care for the other—near or far; that all the true
> values remain true for him, despite the death for which everything is the same, this
> is the purity of the truly human humans of whom Abraham is the father. As if
> henceforth, and by the simple fact of his humanity, the patriarch were the source
> of a water which purifies, promised, to all his descendants, across the mitzvah of
> the 'red heifer,' whatever the place, in the recipe of this water, the red heifer
> deserves. (117)

Although, as we have learned, the halakhic category of *tum'ah* is itself intangible and immaterial, its effects are tightly bound up with the physical world. Abraham's confessed denucleation of self into minute particles suggests that, at bottom, the one-self is, fundamentally, the stuff of dust and ashes, Pascal's *"Le moi est haissable"*[72]—which, nevertheless, as the substrate or distillation of identity in that very form, attain a purified state. Transposed into the chiastic theme of "the conjunction of elevation and descent, of the greatness of humility or the humility of greatness" (117), the ethical burden Levinas reads into and out of *bḤullin* 88b–89a becomes the ethical-philosophical burden of "Judaism and Kenosis," which as Levinas indicates, explores, first, the general ontology of the *Nefesh ha-Ḥayyim*—the "connaturality" of man and divinely re-created worlds—and second, the meaning of prayer.

> Man, by acts in agreement with the Torah, nourishes the association of God
> with the world; or, by his transgression, he exhausts the powers of that divine
> association. The growth of the holiness, the elevation and the being of the worlds
> depend on man, as does their return o nothingness. (125)

> [God] needs prayer, just as he needs those who are faithful to the Torah, in order
> to be able to associate himself with the worlds, for their existence and elevation. . . .
> The worlds cannot continue to be, simply by virtue of the energy of their substance:
> they must be justified in their being, they need the ethical mediation of man,
> they need man and man's prayer, which are for the others. . . . To pray signifies,
> for a "myself," seeing to the salvation of others instead of—or before-saving
> oneself. (129)

This ethical philosophy of kenosis—God's kenosis—expresses the complement to the conclusion of the *sugya* from *bḤullin* 89a about humanity's *bitul hayesh*: "Rava, others say R. Yohanan, also said, 'The world continues to exist because of [the merit of that humble utterance of] Moses and Aaron; for it is written there, "What are we?"' And it is written here [of the world], "He hangs the earth upon nothing."'" The point here is not, however, to rehearse symmetries between Levinas's various bodies of writing (a question about correspondence vigorously debated by Levinas scholars), especially considering that the two texts here are drawn respectively from the *lectures Talmudique* and the so-called confessional writings (essays on Judaism)—that is, already closely aligned. Biblical and rabbinic tropes freely traverse the full landscape of Levinas's oeuvre through their own *va-et-vient*, anyway.

Rather, as with "Signature" and "Name of a Dog" from *Difficult Freedom*, I am interested in a certain attunement to the harmonics of text, which can also be thought of, according to Cavell's prompt from the beginning of this chapter, as bringing words back as if we were shepherding them. To wander where words have gone, and then attract and command them in order to beckon them back, we were told, requires listening to them. They are thus in our care if not our custody—akin to the leaves we turn when we read the book in hand. (And if not the book-object itself in these particular texts of Levinas, then certainly with *afar va'efer*, strap and thread, blood and scroll (from the episode of the *sotah*), we find ourselves still solidly located in a very material world.)

We see this attracting and commanding of words on display *in* both texts Levinas interprets, the Talmudic and the mitnagdic. Levinas's own compositions, which either reinscribe or paraphrase them, transpose that idea to a self-conscious modeling of hermeneutic acuity, a dynamic he expresses with particular force and lyricism in "The Pact" from *Beyond the Verse*:

> Transmission thus involves a teaching which is already outlined in the very receptivity for learning it. Receptivity is prolonged: true learning consists in receiving the lesson so deeply that is becomes a necessity to give oneself to the other. The lesson of truth is not held in one man's consciousness. It exploded towards the other. To study well, to listen well, is already to speak: whether by asking a question and, in so doing, teaching the master who teaches you, or by teaching a third party. (79–80)

To recall his own material metaphor that sonorizes an ethics of reading, Levinas stretches the strings tight over the wood—strings in this case that have been pre-harmonized by Hayyim Volozhiner's explicit citation of the Talmudic passage from *bhullin*.

And as on a stringed instrument, the two texts discover adjacency, despite different purposes, dates of publication, and rhetorical occasions. One's own commentary, in turn, introduces an exterior lamina in the form of an auxiliary acoustic—a slide or capotasto over the strings. Mikhail Bakhtin would call this "проникновенное слово" (the "penetrated word"[73]), a way of both intervening in the other's discourse and being marked in turn. Although Levinas does not use the formulation himself, we might also appeal to the intransitive construction in Yiddish, *zikh arayntrakhtn* "to think oneself into something" which anthropologist Jonathan Boyarin equates with "thinking in Jewish,"[74] to capture the entire resonating process of layered textual voices that, through the dialogical operation of reading, become "notes emitted into adverbs," Levinas's "verbalness of verbs."

As we leave Levinasian precincts now for those of Bakhtin, a certain striation in the otherwise blended surface of Levinas's final Talmudic reading calls attention to itself, offering us an unexpected conduit. When, in relation to the *sotah*, Levinas speaks of the "authentic purity" in marriage that lies "beyond bourgeois prudential consider-ations," he associates the latter with "all the splendor of the Western literature of the novel in which love becomes fable and play . . . the literature of the novel as the pre-rogative of culture, but without doubt at the antipodes of the Torah which is the order of the non-equivocal" (119). And yet, equally if not more striking, to conclude the Talmudic reading collected in *In the Time of Nations* entitled "Beyond Memory" and delivered for the 1985 Colloquium "Memory and History," Levinas devotes its final pages to an admiring description of, and then lengthy quotation from, Vassily Gross-man's 1959 novel Жизнь и Судьба (*Life and Fate*).[75] Grossman's novel became an important source-text for him in the last decade of his life.

Surely, by Levinas's lights, *Madame Bovary* or even *Anna Karenina* (given its Rus-sian provenance) do not correspond to the same class of novel as *Life and Fate*, an often grim saga of historical realism about the defense of Stalingrad. But the latter, like the Talmud or *Nefesh ha-Hayyim* (however wildly divergent in tone and subject matter), has at its core the abiding consciousness of an "invincible humanity." And whether a novel is seen as situated in literary space "at the antipodes of the Torah" or as a ground within which to raise "despair of the human . . . to Jewish consciousness" (89), Levinas has nonetheless located for us the Novel's significance *as genre*. The ques-tion of *its* domain for an ethics of reading, in deliberately oblique connection with our unlikely pairing of Darger and Pascal, is the one to which we turn next.

TEXT OF *BHULLIN 88B–89A* (SONCINO TRANSLATION)

Our Rabbis taught: One may cover up [the blood] only with dust: so Beit Shammai. But Beit Hillel say. We find ashes referred to as dust, for it is written: And for the un-clean they shall take of the dust of the burning [of the purification from sin]. Beit Shammai, however, say. It [ashes] might be referred to as 'the dust of the burning' but it is never referred to as 'dust' simply. A Tanna taught: To these they added coal dust, stibium, stone dust. Some add, even orpiment.

[Levinas's selection begins here:] Rava said: As a reward for our father Abraham having said: I am but dust and ashes, his descendants were worthy to receive two com-mandments: the ashes of the [Red] Cow, and the dust [used in the ceremony] of a woman suspected of adultery. Why does he not reckon also the dust used for the covering up of the blood?—Because that is only the perfection of the commandment but it is of no advantage [to the performer].

I will not take a thread or a shoe-strap his descendants were worthy to receive two commandments: the thread of blue, and the strap of the *tefillin*. Now as for the strap of the *tefillin*, [the blessing bestowed on its account] is clear, for it is written: And all the peoples of the earth shall see that the name of the Lord is called upon thee; and they shall be afraid of thee,' and it has been taught: R. Eliezer the Great says: This refers to the *tefillin* worn upon the head. But what [is the blessing bestowed on account] of the thread of blue?—It has been taught: R. Meir says. Why is blue singled out from all the varieties of colours? Because blue resembles the colour of the sea, and the sea resembles the colour of the sky, and the sky resembles the colour of a sapphire, and a sapphire resembles the colour of the Throne of Glory, as it is said: And they saw the God of Israel and there was under His feet as it were a paved work of sapphire stone; and it is also written: The likeness of a throne as the appearance of a sapphire stone.

R. Abba said: Grave indeed is theft that has been consumed, for even the perfect righteous cannot make amends for it, as it is said: Save only that which the young men have eaten.

R. Yoḥanan said in the name of R. Eleazar son of R. Simeon. Wherever you find the words of R. Eleazar the son of R. Jose the Galilean in an *aggadah* make your ear like a funnel. [For he said: It is written,] It was not because you were greater than any people that the Lord set His love upon you and chose you. The Holy One, blessed be He, said to Israel, I love you because even when I bestow greatness upon you, you humble yourselves before me. I bestowed greatness upon Abraham, yet he said to Me, I am but dust and ashes; Upon Moses and Aaron, yet they said: And we are nothing; upon David, yet he said: But I am a worm and no man. But with the heathens it is not so. I bestowed greatness upon Nimrod, and he said: Come, let us build us a city; upon Pharaoh, and he said: Who is the Lord? Upon Sennacherib, and he said: Who are they among all the gods of the countries? upon Nebuchadnezzar, and he said: I will ascend above the heights of the clouds; upon Hiram king of Tyre, and he said: I sit in the seat of God, in the heart of the seas.

Rava, others say R. Yoḥanan, said: More significant is that which is said of Moses and Aaron than that which is said of Abraham. Of Abraham it is said: I am but dust and ashes, whereas of Moses and Aaron it is said: And we are nothing. Rava, others say R. Yoḥanan, also said: The world exists only on account of [the merit of] Moses and Aaron; for it is written here: And we are nothing, and it is written there [of the world]: He hangs the earth upon nothing. R. Ila'a said: The world exists only on account of [the merit of] him who restrains himself in strife, for it is written: He hangs the earth upon *belimah*. R. Abbahu said: On account of [the merit of] him who abases himself, for it is written: And underneath are the everlasting arms.

CHAPTER 5

Ethics of Reading II

Bakhtin and the Novel

Pure everyday life is a fiction, a product of the intellect. Human life is always
shaped and this shaping is always ritualistic (even if only "aesthetically" so).

—M. M. Bakhtin, "From Notes Made in 1970–71"

An actually pronounced word cannot avoid being intonated, for intonation
follows from the very fact of its being pronounced.

—M. M. Bakhtin, *Toward a Philosophy of the Deed*

Just as the plot or story of my own personal life is created by other people—the
heroes of my life, so the aesthetic vision of the world, its image, is created by
the consummated or consummatable lives of other people who are the heroes of
this world.

—M. M. Bakhtin, "Author and Hero in Aesthetic Activity"

BAKHTINS

Like Levinas, there are more than a few Bakhtins, depending on the prevailing winds
that blow through various academic disciplines and beyond their terrain. A liberal
pluralist Bakhtin, a Western Marxist Bakhtin, a cultural studies Bakhtin, a sociology
of knowledge Bakhtin, a genre studies Bakhtin, a semiotics and linguistics Bakhtin, a
rhetoric and pedagogy Bakhtin, a philology Bakhtin, a Slavics Bakhtin, an Anglo-
American and European Bakhtin, a narratology Bakhtin, a legal studies Bakhtin, a
women studies Bakhtin, a cyber and haptics Bakhtin, a performance and film studies
Bakhtin, a punk Bakhtin, a gender, race, and nation Bakhtin, a postcolonialism
and postapartheid Bakhtin, a visual arts and musicology Bakhtin, a human sciences
Bakhtin, a secular humanism Bakhtin, an Eastern Christianity Bakhtin, a metaphysics
Bakhtin, a transdisciplinary Bakhtin. Add to this incomplete list the multiplier effect
of Bakhtin refracted through his signature terms and concepts, among them heteroglossia, novelization, carnival, chronotope, translinguistics, speech genres, architectonics and

answerability, outsideness/extralocality, and dialogism, and polyphony gives way to plenitude.

Through a combination of mother wit and fortune (some if it an ill wind), Bakhtin matured like a *Bildungsheld* from one period or stage to another—a narrative arc that, despite its terrible setbacks, moved productively both forward and back. His entire intellectual life, biographically considered, appears nothing short of novelistic in its succession as well as recapitulation of forms. His was a one-man genealogy of beginning again, constantly rehearsing a dialectical push-pull of authoritative influences and internally persuasive impulses.[1] If, for example, in one of first published works, к философии поступка, "Toward a Philosophy of the Deed," he identifies as a metaphysician, in his very last essay, к методологии гуманитарных наук, "Toward a Methodology of the Human Sciences," his vocation appears to be something else again: Gary Saul Morson and Caryl Emerson label it a "moral prosaics in the humanities" (98). At the end of his life, "philologist" and "literary theorist" were evidently not his favored self-descriptions.[2] And in the conclusion to his penultimate work, "Notes from 1970–71," he frankly acknowledges, "My love for variations and for a diversity of terms for a single phenomenon. The multiplicity of focuses. Bringing things closer [a bringing close of the distant] without indicating the immediate links" (155).

"Immediate links" are also what underwrite his many critics' affiliative inclinations of one sort or another. We can pinpoint, for example, a Clark/Holquist Bakhtin, an Emerson/Morson Bakhtin, a Kristeva/Todorov/de Man Bakhtin, a Hirschkop/Shepherd/Godzich Bakhtin, a Kozhinov/Isupov/Konkin Bakhtin, and a Bhabha/Gates/Booth Bakhtin, as just some of the second-order Bakhtinian critical permutations, in addition to numerous compounds of Bakhtin hinged to other formative thinkers, including, perhaps not surprisingly and as I will discuss, Emmanuel Levinas.[3] A stockpile of specialized terminology accrues accordingly,[4] of which I confess I must avail myself in some part, following these descriptive preliminaries.

Just as the rabbis allocate seventy faces to Torah, so, in the most optimistic reading, the proliferation of Bakhtins fulfills and extends rather than traduces his meaningfulness, confirming the propensity for any truly generative thinker to become unfinalizable in and through his work. "I am in myself the condition of possibility of my own life," he wrote, "but I am not its valuable hero. . . . Thus the hero of a life may become the narrator of it."[5] This chapter aspires to something less than a narration. But, as its title indicates, it will link Bakhtin to genre and to the Novel, liberally understood. Its focus will be less on Bakhtin proper than the backlighting his ideas provide for the Pascal/Darger cases we have already explored, in conjunction with a continuing attention to materiality and embodiment in the scene of reading.

The novel is Bakhtin's special textual object of critical scrutiny,[6] but it is still metonymic for him of larger notional attitudes about language and literary discourse, indeed about human communicative possibilities. Gary Saul Morson and Caryl Emerson show concisely how Bakhtin's thinking evolves from a concern with the architectonic act to the novelistic or dialogic word, and how the notion of an answerable signature shifts to that of обрашченность ("addressivity") accordingly.[7] Similarly, Alexandar Mihailovich has explored how religious discourse and theological tropes get *novelized* under Bakhtin's hand: christology, a thematics of embodiment, the chronotope of corporeal words, all achieve a new dialogic life in Bakhtin's philosophical and literary criticism.[8] In rough resemblance to Levinas, Bakhtin creates hybrid conversations between philosophy, religion, and the literatures and rhetorics of more secular (worldly) textual traditions, knitting them together with a remarkably plastic vocabulary that creates a weave of contiguities.

I will briefly lay out the Bakhtin/Levinas connection here, but for most of what follows, the Bakhtin I want to enlist is the one whose "theologically inflected aesthetics" (as they have been dubbed)[9] fill out the horizon in which we have already located the limit cases of Henry Darger and Blaise Pascal. I confine myself to early philosophic essays from his *Nevel'-Vitebsk* period (1919–24), together with some final notations by him from 1975 in "Toward a Methodology for the Human Sciences."[10] The difficult (literary) and the holy (scriptural) will once again function as proximate horizons for the scene of reading, as will the question of the book as material object.

I invite us to keep in mind Bakhtin's singularity as a "philosopher of the deed" in echo of his book-long treatise from the 1920s and limned by the vocabulary-cluster, активность ("activeness"), мир поступка ("world of the performed act"), событие бытииа ("ongoing event of being"), акт дэиатэльность ("act/activity"), постлупление ("uninterrupted performing of acts"), from this same period—all of them kinetic terms, all tied to moral imperatives of consequentiality and accountability.

By contrast, however, key Bakhtinian concepts, like незавершенность ("unfinalizability"), or металингвистика ("metalinguistics") установка на чужуиу реч ("orientation toward the speech of another") or ответственность ("answerability") that have generated a substantial commentarial literature in connection with ethics will not receive any direct focus here.[11] Instead of situating Bakhtin disciplinarily (critic? theorist? philosopher? social thinker? author?), I want us, rather, to regard him principally as a *reader* astride the double boundary of ethical/aesthetic and religious/secular sensibilities. That orientation, in turn, asks us to contemplate our burden as *his* readers. Where exactly, in other words, might his earliest and latest writings locate *us*?

LEVINAS AND BAKHTIN

Before bending those questions, and Pascal and Darger, toward the borrowed light of Bakhtin, I want to return momentarily to the question of genre and to Emmanuel Levinas, for whom a Bakhtinian sobriquet, мои ближнии ("my meaningful adjacent fellow"), feels peculiarly apt (as well as channeling this book's Prologue). In connection with what we have already seen of Levinas's sentimental attachment to the novel—in, for instance, its Russian (Goncharov, Grossman, Dostoyevsky), French (Proust), and

English (Dickens) manifestations—and beyond a content-oriented notion of moralized discourse that Bakhtin subordinates to the dialogical possibilities of narrative discourse, what, for Bakhtin, makes the novel itself so emblematic and such a "transgredient" category? This is a question that has already been posed quite eloquently by the scholar Graham Pechey. I quote him here at length:

> The obverse of the better-known Bakhtin who celebrates the novelization of the high genres and the carnivalization of the sacred is the Bakhtin who in effect sacralizes the novel, who makes of it a talisman we may wear against the idolatrous temptations of our late-modern world. The objects of modern irony and parody are not the holy or otherworldly as such, but their worldly simulacra. Bakhtin wishes us to see that challenges to representation within representation do not threaten what is beyond representation. On the contrary: they reinforce its claim upon our attention; the grotesque in art does not work against the sublime any more than incarnation works against transcendence. It is in this sense that the novel is our gospel, and (like the Gospels themselves) it offers at every turn a direct route from the everyday into the most elevated. Every character, thanks to the orchestration of dialogism, can be a "personality," every voice (as he was to put it later) a "social language"; every element is potentially more than itself, everything exceeds its own bounds, speaks to a context that has no earthly limits. The novel is a holy writ of endlessly permutable content: modern writing as epitomized by the novel is perennially postmodern in so far as it turns any story into the means of breaking open the linear continuum of history and admitting the blazing light of the other.[12]

Doubtless, this is *not* an appreciation of what the novel can accomplish as genre—to discover what only the novel can discover[13]—that Levinas would be able to share, despite the philosophical significance he finds in Vasily Grossman or the resuscitation of the Hebrew language and its reverberations he comes upon in fiction by Shai Agnon. But then, that temperamental divergence merely italicizes Bakhtin's potentiality as an uncanny other or neighbor/stranger to Levinas in respect to some of the latter's more pronounced blind spots. If Peachey is right (as I believe him to be), Bakhtin seizes upon a distinctly *secular* textual power, which, insofar as it is anticipated by the prenovelistic thrust of the four Gospels—through their poetics of narrative discourse, plot, characterization, and what we might call the "voice" or language of objects—nonetheless unsettles any easy divide between sacred and non-sacred. (As for the Hebrew Bible, Bakhtin most likely regarded it as an expression of *epic* form and discourse.)[14] In short, the Novel *self-transcends*, which is its raison d'être. In doing so, it dialogizes as a matter of course, turns language into heteroglossia, and makes genre multiform, effectively reversing the thrust of Occam's famous razor: *Numquam ponenda est necessitates sine pluralite.*

By contrast, the Hebrew Bible does not at all aspire novelistically or even proto-novelistically so far as Levinas is concerned.[15] Talmudic *aggadah* is too elliptical a narrative form, *midrash* too unironic a citational strategy, and mishnaic narrative forms too fastened to a legal apparatus to be easily correlated with the robustly "transgredient" (Bakhtin's word) aspects of novelistic discourse. Indeed, these link up with ideologically self-conscious expressions of authoritative discourse like the Bible and the Talmud only by a wide stretch—a stretch Levinas has no particular interest in pursuing, anyway.[16] If Levinas's culture heroes might be said (guardedly) to be Rava, Rabbi Akiva, Ḥayyim of Volozhin, and Agnon, Bakhtin's are the quartet of Dante, Rabelais, Goethe, and Dostoevsky. To my knowledge, Levinas mentions all four of these in various contexts (Rabelais's character Messer Gaster, for instance, appears in a passing allusion in *Totality and Infinity*), in addition to Cervantes, Pushkin, Molière, and many other writers. But performatively reading the secular does not offer Levinas his preferred métier. The aesthetic risks of "participation" (at least, as delineated in "Reality and its Shadow") remain formidable.

The trope of "participation," as in участное инкарнированное сознание ("participatory-incarnated consciousness"), possesses such a vastly different valence in Bakhtin's thought than it does in Levinas's, specifically in relation to textual experience. Ethically or religiously, I may *participate*—that is, take up my place—in tradition's chain of transmission, as a matter of sober hermeneutic practice; otherwise, according to Levinas, as an aesthetic activity, participation courts both dissolution of boundaries and the dissolute risks of "defilement of the hands."

Contrariwise, Bakhtin understands aesthetic participation (in dance, *par excellence*) as a kind of mystical rapture and communion, which the plane of textuality invites while at the same time affirming the necessity of boundary and separation.[17] If—and only if—the sacred ("authoritarian") word is revoiced and placed in dialogue (certainly, the province of commentary and what Levinas knows as *midrash*), then scriptural and literary discourses can cohabit in the same textual universe for Bakhtin because (to adapt Peachey's terms), through the aesthetic activity each inaugurates (albeit differentially), they offer the promise of a "border where art and the holy and the everyday meet" (173).

There have been several juxtapositions of Levinas and Bakhtin in the critical literature.[18] Convergences, affinities, eerie resemblances abound when these two figures share critical space—not least, a shared love for Dostoevsky. Most of the studies stress complementarity over divergence, or, as in Daphna Erdinast-Vulcan's, end up framing Bakhtin's as the more pragmatic model, namely, Bakhtin as a better reader of Dostoevsky than Levinas. In my own case, *Narrative Ethics* inclined more toward thematic and metaphoric correspondence (crossing points) than sustained negative capability. Almost all the critical dialogues tend to eschew the hermeneutic Levinas of the Talmudic readings and the less philosophically ambitious essay collections, which, however, as Colin Davis has strongly insisted, is where we see Levinas's most moving and creative close reading on display.

As I indicated, though, my central focus in this chapter is directed toward Darger and Pascal, through an expressly Bakhtinian optic. Proximity between Levinas and Bakhtin, though a rich area in its own right for exploration in specific connection with their congruent performances as critic-readers, has been confined to this section alone. Indeed, a fuller dialogue between them cedes to a brief but strategic pivot to two of Bakhtin's other Others: Walter Benjamin around the question of aesthetics and Stanley Cavell on the poetics of "acknowledgment," in order to set the stage for the chapter to follow. But let us return now to the role of the reader caught by glimpses in Bakhtin's work.

DOINGS: FROM AUTHORING TO READING

Earlier in the book, I quoted Stanley Cavell on Emerson's "Divinity School Address," which "seeks to free us from our attachment to the one who brings the message," and thus offers us a model of "a theology of reading." How does Cavell mean that phrase, exactly? He expands on it in *Conditions Handsome and Unhandsome* by explaining that writing like Emerson's or Thoreau's teach us, paradoxically, to "leave them." For, mistaking their thoughts for ours risks a kind of idolatry. "The problem is that the text's thoughts are neither exactly mine nor not mine."[19] The theological moment in reading,[20] for Cavell at least, addresses how we understand our proper investments of belief, autonomy, and dependence. But as Bakhtin has formulated a very similar question, this is how we negotiate between "authoritative" and "internally persuasive" purchases on the texts we read.

Earlier in "Discourse in the Novel," Bakhtin writes in an often-quoted passage:

> As a living, socio-ideological concrete thing, as heteroglot opinion, language, for the individual consciousness, lies on the borderline between oneself and the other. . . . The word in language is half someone else's. It becomes "one's own" only when the speaker populates it with his own intention, his own accent, when he appropriates the word, adapting it to his own semantic and expressive intention. Prior to this moment of appropriation, the word does not exist in a neutral and impersonal language . . . but rather it exists in other people's mouths, in other people's contexts, serving other people's intentions: it is from there that one must take the word, and make it one's own. . . . Language is not a neutral medium that passes freely and easily into the private property of the speaker's intentions; it is populated—overpopulated with the intentions of others. Expropriating it, forcing it to submit to one's own intentions and accents, is a difficult and complicated process. (294)

Utterance involves a kind of productive profanation. If making words one's own means crossing further and further thresholds from some mythically sacrosanct precinct, then speaking, to twist our organizing formula just a bit, *makes the words impure*. There are additional lessons here in how Bakhtin's own words get appropriated at the borderline between "one's own" and "someone else's" through explication and redaction;[21] and the same would apply to Levinas and Cavell as evangelists of a sort, bearers of a message.

In his introduction to the essays collected in *Art and Answerability*, Michael Holquist proposes that since many of Bakhtin's early and late works were left unfinished or became fragmented, in order to engage them responsibly, his readers must reciprocally perform the sorts of transgredient and generously consummating acts that Bakhtin ascribes in authors. "The paradox that obsesses Bakhtin here is one that his readers cannot avoid: we must *do* what these essays are *about*," Holquist writes.[22] Thus, in one of his few explicit writings about reading practice, Bakhtin encourages students of a scholarly book: "The greater and more insistent are our demands towards the book, the more will it speak to them. It does not care for indifferent readers and does not respond to them."[23]

But it is fair to inquire whether one can really "do what these essays are about" considering that they are not only fragmented but ambivalent—or at least unresolved—in the context of the Dostoevsky book written only five years later and the general arc and maturation of Bakhtin's thought?[24] My own ambitions here are far more modest than trying to establish a *point d'appui* (as Bakhtin would say) to an admittedly frangible architectonics, a "system" that never quite gets fully systematized, or to refine its contradictions.[25] Rather and more restrictively, I want to learn what Bakhtin can tell us about the ethics of reading, which is not really theorized by him as such.[26] "The provocation of Bakhtin's work, writes Peter Hitchcock, "is usually to be found in his theoretical constructs rather than the readings that he provides to elaborate them."[27] I agree. Our task then becomes the edifying integration of such constructs into readings of our own devising.

Typically, when the proper noun "Bakhtin" is conjoined to "reading," it yields locutions like "Bakhtin's reading of X," "a Bakhtinian reading of Y," or "a Z reading of Bakhtin."[28] Almost all of Bakhtin's writing shows us *Bakhtin reading*, to be sure: reading Pushkin, Rabelais, Dostoevsky, Dickens, and other author-heroes of literary fiction and poetry, reading philosophy and criticism, indeed, reading his own earlier work. Yet, the dominant *energia* in Bakhtinian textual dynamics—what he calls the событие архитектоника ("event-architectonic")—is assigned to the act of *authoring* or to genre and discourse themselves.[29] While the listener and his "apperceptive background" are discussed at length in both "Discourse in the Novel" and "The Problem of Speech Genres," a direct correspondence between those speech-constructs and their counterparts in reading is not one we should unproblematically assume.[30]

Moreover, диалога or "dialogue" and "prosaics" (Morson/Emerson's term) are properly *linguistic, rhetorical* properties in a textual economy, as well as being tied to pragmatics.[31] Bakhtin's final essay on the human sciences thus remains distinctive for its emphasis on hermeneutic roles and attitudes, just as this book's core concern remains the *staging of reading*—for which "the book in hand" serves as metonym—as itself an ethical practice. While Bakhtin does in fact mention "the actual book" (58–59) in *Toward the Philosophy of the Deed* as a specimen of lived-experiential reality, what, again, does he have to tell us about it when it makes contact with our hands? And what, consequently, does reading look like in his thought as an instance or a modality of "aesthetic activity?"

When for example, both in that fragment and the "Author and Hero" treatise, all values, spatial-temporal as well as sense-content-oriented, collect, like filings to a magnet, around an individual subject's or author's "emotion-volition"—the signature that ratifies acknowledgement, the intonation that stamps a unique self upon pronunciation—the act of reading would consequently seem to be as singularized as writing: an eventful, participative, *aesthetic* activity. And not just for Bakhtin's readers, but as regards wholly answerable, uniquely participative, compellingly obliged, concretely individual—"incarnated"—readers *tout court*.

And yet, in both *Philosophy of the Deed* and "Author and Hero,"[32] when Bakhtin performs a reading of Pushkin's famous 1830 poem Разлука ("Parting") apostrophizing Amalia Riznich, the interpretive drama of событие-моменты ("event-moments") seesaws exclusively between authorial values and hero(ine)-centered values. His critical self-positioning—the "turn" and "prestige" after the "pledge"—remains implicit, to be sure. But its valence is not activated in the foreground, and the *critic's answerability*—what Levinas dramatizes as *frottage* and insufflation—does not materialize in front of us. Certainly, Bakhtin *reads* the poem: his is *explication de texte* and close reading of a high and rigorous order. But the exegetical effect is almost as though the poem reads itself.

Pushkin's lyric dramatizes not only the way human mortality anchors all transcendental categories,[33] but also the tension between here and elsewhere, homeland (Russia) and foreign land (Italy), between speaker and absent interlocutor, and implicitly between the *I* and the *other*, the two-plane or biaxial structure of lived experience so essential to Bakhtin's analysis in his early phenomenological essays.[34] The poem, through Bakhtin's reading, *describes* an ethics as the act of boundary crossing (poet-self/beloved-other, life/death). Indeed, it could be said to represent the lyrical compression of Bakhtin's subjective sense of "the ethical," generally: art and life as mediated by a situated личность ("individual personality") through active responsivity.

Bridging his earliest and his late writings, such ethical, quasi-religious sensibility remains more or less consistent in Bakhtin's work. So perhaps we might expect the performative deed of reading to mimic that very tension—the non-alibi, the "here," of my hermeneutic position on the one hand, the book in hand, its "there," on the other. But it is not immediately clear how reading the Pushkin poem *enacts* an ethics—that is, as one might perform a deed. In the course of this chapter, we will see whether other examples drawn from within Bakhtin's work or outside it can help us clarify the problem.

READING FOR THE *PLOT'*

There is no misplaced apostrophe at the end of the preceding subhead. While the phrase appears to recycle Peter Brooks's famous study of plot-driven reading, it is actually a bilingual pun; the Russian Ъ (tvordjznak) or "hard sign," a silent character that depalatalizes the preceding consonant, is represented in Roman characters by the diacritical '. Russian плоть (or *plot'*) means "flesh," which in Bakhtin's usage connotes something beyond a reduction of matter to the merely physical. The root term underpins terms like уплотение ("concretion") and оплотенност ("enfleshment"), and воплошчение ("embodiment"), which Bakhtin will deploy to account for constitutive features of linguistic communication.

Corporeality and contact between bodies at or across a borderline remain consistent themes in Bakhtin's writing from the earliest work on intersubjectivity and ethical/ aesthetic видение ("seeing"), through the Dostoyevsky book of 1929, the "Forms of Time and of the Chronotope in the Novel" essay of 1937, the Rabelais book (first submitted as a dissertation in 1940), up to and including his very last writings. (And just as Levinas is in some sense always hostage to the amputation of family lost in the Shoah, so Bakhtin's own body from childhood through midlife extirpation to death remained a constant reminder of frail mortality and pain.)[35]

For example, воплошчение ("embodiment") in the neo-Kantian writings on aesthetic philosophy and axiology from the 1920s, as Mihailovich carefully unpacks the metaphor, gives off certain christologic and perichoretic reverberations, just as раввоплошченныи дукх ("disembodied spirit") suggests sub-textual echoes of the Fall.[36] Similarly, on the way to crystallizing the concepts of genre and dialogue that would ground the Dostoevsky book of 1929, and mediating the respective pulls of philosophical idealism (*Lebensphilosophie*) on one hand, and scientific materialism on the other, Bakhtin conducted an argument with both Formalist and Marxist schools of thought about the proper analytical approach to verbal "material."[37]

In the famous definition of the chronotope, Bakhtin writes, "Time, in effect, becomes palpable and visible; the chronotope makes narrative events concrete, makes them *take on flesh, cause blood to flow in their veins*" (italics mine).[38] And from the same period, the essays "Discourse and the Novel" (1934–35) makes repeated use of body imagery to depict the way literary style itself takes on flesh, as for example, "a language that has somehow more or less materialized, become objectivized, that [the author] merely ventriloquates,"[39] where materialization means to become оплотненныи ("enfleshed").

In the 1940s, Bakhtin reads for плоть in the gross carnality and carnival laughter he finds in Rabelais. A decade later in "The Problem of Speech Genres" (1952–53), the generic structure and flow of conversation is concretized as a chain-link structure of speech utterances that "touch" each other contiguously. Finally, in late style writings from the 1960s and 1970s, Bakhtin returns to the incarnational and circumcessionist themes of indwelling and various tropes of seeing from the 1920s, as well as to the special vocabulary of spatial relations that recall the 1930s essays on the chronotope, the Bildungsroman, and novelistic discourse: "A person has no internal sovereign territory, he is wholly and always on the boundary; looking inside himself, he looks *into the eyes of another* or *with the eyes of another*.[40]

But where, we could ask, does embodiment in Bakhtin get connected to the act of reading or to hermeneutic agency? Does Bakhtin's thought offer any analogues to Levinas's trope of proximity-as-*sensibility* or to the meditations on touch and tactility by Derrida, Chrétien, and Nancy? Can we, in fact, read Bakhtin for плоть? That Bakhtinian ethics are incarnational in spirit, and that Bakhtin's poetics of the body harken back to a long-superseded medieval tradition of transcendent corporeality only complicates the question (though it also has the virtue of bringing Bakhtin quite close to Levinas in a shared religious commitment to the premodern).[41]

PASCAL, DARGER REVISITED

To explore that question, heeding Cavell's advice about resisting the idolatrous pull of authorship (about which Bakhtin feels so ambivalently himself), I want to orient us to whatever Bakhtinian harmonics we may be able to detect by revisiting now the limit cases of Blaise Pascal and Henry Darger. Aside from its recursive advantages for this book's general argument, that decision derives largely from the fact that Bakhtin is powerfully drawn to borderline problematics and the defining power of гранитса or предел ("the boundary"). Personhood, language, even history—all represent boundary phenomena for him.

The figures of Darger and Pascal and their writings, *Le Mémorial* and *In the Realms of the Unreal* (together with *Further Adventures in Chicago: Crazy House, The History of My Life,* and *Weather Reports*) feel especially pertinent, therefore, since they, like Bakhtin himself, bestride a border between authoring and answerability. Moreover, ailing in body and/or mentally afflicted, Darger and Pascal each speak to a certain "body-language" in Bakhtin that construes aesthetic wholeness in direct relation to mortality and wounded consciousness and thus, implicitly, to tact.

In Pascal's case, the philosophical vocation in tension with событийность ("eventness") or единственный переживание ("once-occurrent lived experience"),[42] and the condition of aesthetic вненачодимость ("outsideness") in Darger's, map almost irresistibly onto Bakhtinian coordinates. That qualifier "almost irresistibly" should give us pause, however, perhaps even prompting some sensible resistance. In addition to naturalizing these texts in a fashion I would still wish to defer, I am not sure what the exercise gains us beyond the intellectual satisfaction of recoding linguistic or literary content as conceptual terminology. And that seems a somewhat paltry answerability.

Pascal suffered from lifelong migraine headaches and possible stomach cancer; Darger's psyche, it appears, was profoundly afflicted if not tormented. Each case offers us not only a singular, and courageous, instance of a creative act pronounced and performed, but also—in the words of this chapter's second epigraph—that same act "signed" under the auspices of its own singular *intonation*. "We use the term, 'emotional-volitional tone,'" writes Bakhtin in *Towards a Philosophy of the Deed*, "to designate precisely the moment constituted by my self-activity in a lived-experience—the experiencing of an experience as mine: *I* think—perform a deed by thinking" (36). And in his very last work: "*Tone*, released from phonetic and semantic elements of the word (and other signs) is important. . . . To a certain degree, one can speak by means of intonations alone, making the verbally expressed part of speech relative and replaceable, almost indifferent" (164, 166).

In the limit-cases of Pascal and Darger—in both the uniqueness of their own "answerable acts" and the space they open for ours in response—we approach, I think, what Bakhtin means when he adds, "The word that would characterize [the unity of the actual and answerably act-performing consciousness] more accurately is *faithfulness*" (*Deed*, 38). In perhaps the most impassioned portion of his otherwise dense and repetitive "first philosophy" of the act, Bakhtin fore-echoes both Derrida's image of "the ear of other" with its exigencies of underwriting and signature, and Stanley Cavell's theme of acknowledgment, which I introduce later on:

> It is not the content of an obligation that obligates me, but my signature below it—the fact that at one time I acknowledged or undersigned the given acknowledgment. . . . What we shall find everywhere is a constant unity of answerability, that is, *not* a constancy in content and *not* constant law of the performed act (all content is only a constituent moment), but a certain actual fact of acknowledgment that is once-occurrent and never-repeatable, emotional-volitional and concretely individual. . . . That which can be done by me can never be done by anyone else. The uniqueness or singularity of present-on-hand Being is compellingly obligatory. (39–40)[43]

Bakhtin calls this нудительность or "compellentness" (that is, as self-derived rather than externally enforced), my *non-alibi in Being*, не-алиби б бытии. Likewise, being an участник ("a participant") and being the agent of участность and причашчение ("participativeness") signals something more than just presence: through my agency, I am *conjoined* with the act I perform, and through its свершение ("completedness"), *united* with its consequences. Author and consummating deed *co-inhere*.[44] In a passage that resonates uncannily with Pascal's *Mémorial*, Bakhtin explains this doctrine of irreplaceability, of unique, embodied self-activity this way:

> Being that is detached from the unique emotional-volitional center of answerability is a rough draft, an unacknowledged possible variant of once-occurrent Being; only through an answerable participation effected by a unique act or deed can one get out of the realm of endless draft versions and rewrite one's life once and for all in the form of a fair copy. (44)

By borrowed light, then, the coupling of "outsider artist" Henry Darger and religious philosopher Blaise Pascal—avatar of the автор-созертсатель ("author-beholder") in one case, dramatic instance of естетицеское событие ("the aesthetic event") in the other—illuminates Bakhtin and vice versa. Neither limit case could really afford the слово с лазеикои ("word with a loophole"), which might otherwise relieve the internal pressure on their own respective architectonics of answerability or the sheer material fact of suffering in body and mind. Each, in his different way, epitomizes the non-alibi, заданны ("the posited") with its horizons open toward futurity, over данныи ("the given," and consequently sealed—what Jack London's fictional protagonist Martin Eden called "work performed"[45]); each prized правда ("the truth of an event") over истина ("apodicticity"). Through their works (our only access to them now), both figures display a life lived in "fair copy."

RITUAL ACTS

When discussing Darger and Pascal, I twice quoted a phrase about the "fleeting image of truth" from Walter Benjamin's *Trauerspiel* book, specified by him as "not a process of exposure which destroys the secret but a revelation which does it justice." I asked how that distinction might apply to *Le Mémorial* and *In the Realms of the Unreal*, and what reading-as-revelation might mean in their cases, considering the fact that the authors were themselves the revealers—as if they each not only performed *Pledge, Turn, Prestige* but were also positioned as that ritual's sole spectator-witnesses. In his book on Bakhtin and Benjamin, Tim Beasley-Murray begins his analysis by emphasizing the importance of *ritual* for both thinkers—Bakhtin as habitual tea-drinker and smoker, Benjamin as compulsive collector and fetishistic scrivener.[46]

At the same time, each expressed great ambivalence about the force of habit. "Author and Hero" oscillates between a theory of the subject and an aesthetic theory about narrative conscience, with a distinctly ritualized account of relationship—self is to other as author is to hero—common to both (Bakhtin never quite leaves the legacy of German Romantic aesthetics behind).[47] In that treatise, rhythm—that aesthetic element so suspect to Levinas—is celebrated by Bakhtin as the generous, consummating bestowal of form upon another, a "shaping" as well as a "singing"; and yet, five years later in "Discourse in the Novel," rhythm is contemned as an engine of demediation, stunting full discursive materialization and dialogic possibility.

Likewise, Benjamin celebrated modern modes of technologized image, like montage, because they interfered with the routine habitualized consciousness of modernity sociologist Georg Simmel called the *blasé attitude*: "an incapacity . . . to react to new sensations with the appropriate energy."[48] Shock, in an odd way, works in concert with aura (or in the case of allegory, *Schein*, "semblance") to preserve the artwork or image from deadening, from etiolation; just as the collector and the "destructive character" (the one dedicated to "making room" and "clearing away"), rehearse a dialectic.[49] But along with those behavioristic rituals of his, which seem crafted in part to compensate for the incessant uprooting he endured, Benjamin also prized lasting, iconic performances that obey the strictures of tradition, like oral storytelling.

Despite their ambivalences (different in each case), then, Bakhtin and Benjamin nevertheless wrestled with what they perceived to be reifying forces of tradition—philosophical, literary, religious/theological—that ever incline toward the monologic, centripetal or Ptolemaic. Gerald Bruns, we recall from Chapter 4, has termed this the "allegoric" as opposed to "satiric" mode. In Проблемы творчества Достоевского (*Problems of Dostoevsky's Poetics*), Bakhtin offers a provocative example of ritualized language made internally kinetic. It is a passage cited by many toilers in the Bakhtin archive:

> "Life is good." "Life is good." Here are two absolutely identical judgments, or in
> fact one singular judgment written (or pronounced) by us twice; but this "twice"
> refers only to its verbal embodiment and not to the judgment itself. We can, to be
> sure, speak here of the logical relationship of identity between two judgments.
> But if this judgment is expressed in two utterances by two different subjects then
> dialogic relationships arise between them (agreement and affirmation). (183–184)

It is the ritual aspect of Darger's and Pascal's acts of authoring that I want to explore in a little more depth here, in tandem with a certain ceremoniousness they invoke on the plane of reception. Their respective intonations—the counterpart to the different vocalizations of "Life is Good," as it were—solicit the under (or counter-) signing ear of the other, or as Bakhtin would express it in the optical terms he develops in "Author and Hero," our избыток видение ("surplus of vision"). In Bakhtin's lexicon, this is заданный ("a task to be accomplished"); in the language of Benjamin's essays, it is *Aufgabe*, as in "Die Aufgabe des Übersetzers." Through the setting of a task, one creates and self-authorizes the conditions for consequent answerability.

"But answerability entails guilt, or liability to blame" (1), Bakhtin writes, somewhat perplexingly, in the short manifesto from 1919, Искусство и Отвественность ("Art and Answerability"). Why? Because art and everyday life each traffic in reciprocal betrayals. Both, in forgetting each other, "make their own tasks easier [and] relieve themselves of their own answerability. For it is certainly easier to create without answering for life, and easier to live without any consideration for art" (2). How *do* Darger and Pascal look under Bakhtin's penetrating and rather melancholy gaze?[50]

The *Mémorial* was not intended as an artwork, of course, and yet reading nonetheless makes it so. "In his confession Pascal does not acknowledge the dull directedness of 'pure experience,'" writes Calin Mihailescu. "It is rather the process of writing up this experience that introduces it in the Pascalian canon (as it fires). Writing heightens experience from *truth* to *verisimilitude*" (14).[51] Contrariwise, *In the Realms of the Unreal* aspires courageously to the sublime, the beautiful, and the grotesque, even if it falls below a certain aesthetic standard Bakhtin would ascribe to those "great works" whose lasting literary value accrues against the horizon of "great time."[52] With its line-gloss of scriptural annotations (the Book of Ruth, the Gospel of John, etc.) that Pascal added to the body of the text and certain words rendered in Latin instead of French, we could claim a certain dialogic sensibility for the *Mémorial*. *In the Realms of the Unreal*, likewise, exhibits a heteroglossia all its own. It expresses at once a liberating enthusiasm and profound guilt about not only the doings it describes but its own *poesis*. Quite similarly, the rapturousness of Pascal's *nuit de feu* includes a healthy dose of guilty Christian conscience. Both works and their authors seem to approach a consciousness of what Bakhtin seems to mean by the guilt that attends answerability, and its liability to blame.

Now, the textual condition of Pascal's and Darger's texts could be readily mapped onto Bakhtin's intricate account of the burden in aesthetic activity assumed by author and assigned to hero—this, despite the enormous cultural, historical, and expressive gulf that separates the two of them as "authors." (If nothing else, the exercise would throw Bakhtin's categories in relief by means of both their congruencies and incongruences with these works, each instructive.) But Bakhtin defines the authorial only in tensile relation to the value-category of the hero; character-to-character relationships, protagonists and subordinates, do not play any vivid role in Bakhtin's analysis, which needed the polyphonic innovations of the Dostoevsky book to open them up.[53] Interrelationally speaking (which is only how these value-categories work), "hero" describes Darger's entire fictional program, where character and plot are entirely subordinate to proliferating detail. The hero of *In the Realms of the Unreal* or *Weather Reports*, very simply, is the narrative's own ongoingness.

This same value-category becomes more elusive in regard to Pascal's devotional testament, which is neither narrative nor hero-centric in any obvious way. "GOD of Abraham, GOD of Isaac, GOD of Jacob/Not of the philosophers and of the learned," "My God and your God," "Righteous Father," Jesus Christ": these appear to be the addressed second-persons of the *Mémorial*; but insofar as the text is both vocative and invocative, they may also seem to point to the third-party authority Bakhtin calls the надаресат (the "superaddressee"), "whose absolutely just understanding is presupposed."[54]

Pascal's text is, by turns, votive, lyrical, and self-annotated; mostly, it is just profoundly *authored*. But one thing it is not is literary fiction. Darger's pastiche of authors as different from each other as L. Frank Baum, Harriet Beecher Stowe, Cervantes, and Dickens, of bygone children's literature, newspaper clippings, and Civil War histories, and last but not least, of his own obsessional fantasy life, falls short of Bakhtinian ethical-aesthetic criteria like "consummation" and оживление ("vivification"). But it, too, is undeniably and intensely *authorial* on the blended planes of art and life through the "unity of its answerability." It is also *novelistic* (in Peachey's sense).

"Authoredness" like this would be one way of conveying the ritual aspect I have proposed for both works. The category of "heroic," however, poses more analytical

challenges for us if we wish to locate it anywhere *in* Darger's and Pascal's works themselves, since it is where or how the aesthetic is made manifest, and through which the
axiological category of "the other" is effected. Bakhtin's innovation, in fact, was to rescue the *hero*'s agency from both the Kantian aesthetic tradition (where it languished)
and Russian formalism (where it was made entirely subordinate to plot), through the
narrative bipolarity of author/hero, which mirrors a phenomenology of self/other. As
Ilya Kriger helpfully explains, if the modality of *self*, open, free, unfinalizable,

> always projects: in space toward the object of its intentionality, in time toward
> goals that recede into a boundless future . . . the *other*'s relation to the world is
> one not of horizontal movement but of location within an environment (*okruzhe-
> nie*). In space, the *other* is externalized as a bounded body among other physical
> objects. In time, the other exists as temporally bound by birth and death, in fact,
> as always already dead and brought to life again as the subject of a biography.
> The bounded space and biographical time of the other is, furthermore, filled with
> a stable meaning, a determinate, unchangeable, fated manner of being in the
> surrounding world. (555–556)

Authors must thus fix, place, and reframe their heroes, gifting them with the finished
structure of a determinate whole, removing them from the "open unitary and unique
event of being," thus converting them (as Kriger says) from the category of *self* (heroic
and prospective) to *other* (authorial and retrospective). Heroes sacrifice the "open, ethical
event of a lived life" for the author's "artistic interestedness" in it and the encompassing
aesthetic objectivity that consequently shapes it into a completed whole. Authors need
heroes to justify their outside position of valuational support; heroes cede autonomy and
even die for that redemptive, sustaining, and as Bakhtin says, *loving, gift-giving* creativity.[55] The operative positionality here is that of being "overshadowed": heroes do not
stand *beside*, *against*, or *inside* authors, but rather are relocated onto a completely new
and different representational plane where they are, in effect, reborn and reembodied.

"After all," writes Bakhtin (now shifting to a philosophical vocabulary of selfhood
and otherness), "it is only the other who can be embraced, clasped all around, it is
only the other's boundaries that can all be touched and felt lovingly" (41). Concomitantly, "the excess of my seeing is the bud in which slumbers form and whence form
unfolds like a blossom" (24). But all this happens on the boundary: *"Form is a boundary* that has been wrought aesthetically [and] it is only on the boundaries of two consciousnesses, on the boundaries of the body, that an encounter is actually realized and
the artistic gift of form is bestowed" (97).

And readers? Their agency, it seems from early sections of the essay, consists in
answering with their own bipolar alignment, a double consciousness, as it were, that
draws upon both authorial-transgredient and heroic-unconsummated imperatives and
energies. Through that synthetic power, readers are thus potentially supra-authorial
and transheroic; or else, in their dual loyalty, they split the difference, borrowing from

Peter to pay Paul.[56] If authors' or selves' bodies represent an "inner body" (as the mode of intentional consciousness), and others' bodies delineate an "outer body" (sculpted by hands not its own),[57] how might we then begin to speak about the book in hand? How do *its* materiality as agitated or insufflated object and *our* materiality as tactile agents factor into the Bakhtinian equation? What room is there, if any, for an ethics[58] of reading in the senses I have proposed for the limit-cases of Darger and Pascal, or for that matter, the scenes of reading in Sebald and Arad, the stagings of the Talmud by Levinas and of Conrad's *Nostromo* by Said? Where does "tact" figure here?

Toward a possible answer, let us return to the problem of the *form* in which Darger's and Pascal's texts come down to us as found objects. If I am to keep faith with that "textual condition," then its only immutable law, as literary theorist Jerome McGann expresses it, is the law of change, which declares that the "life histories" played out by texts—their production and reception history—"will exhibit a ceaseless process of textual development and mutation" (9). We know that such variation obtains semiotically: this is what Paul Ricoeur famously dubbed the "surplus of meaning": since any text exceeds its author's intentions and transcends its compositional circumstances of time, place, and cultural specificity, "what is to be interpreted in the text is a proposed world which I could inhabit and in which I could project my ownmost possibilities."[59] Yet, conversely, in a document's material aspect, as artifact, do we not have a paradigm of stable and dependable form?

Surely, we want to insist, this exactly describes the case of Pascal's *Mémorial* and Darger's *In the Realm of the Unreal* whose textual life is the very stuff of original manuscript. More obviously than other texts, these works subsist *as originals*, their singularity ratified by being archived in museum and national library. Does the fact that Pascal's came into the light of day already doubled as scrawled paper original folded into fine-hand parchment copy alter the fact that it was never intended as the projected space for others' "ownmost possibilities?" And even if Darger's vast thirteen-volume writings, which existed first in longhand and were subsequently copied by him to typescript[60]—does this empirically challenge their essentially invariant palpability? These texts, above all, exits as singularities, and their subsequent compunctious "violation" only accentuates that fact; for, in Mihailescu's words, "one probably feels as if one is peeping through the keyhole at a scene not meant for 'representation.'"

And yet, McGann's point about changefulness actually applies with persuasive force to just these texts, which even in their "original" state attest to authorial variations in the process of composition, and whose textual condition exceeds their linguistic or even bibliographic form; more simply stated, these texts not only vary within and across the socialized contexts they have now acquired after being forced out of their prelapsarian quietude, but they also vary from themselves.[61] And that is a "molecular" friction or self-agitation our contact with them brings out. McGann's epigraph for *The Textual Condition* is drawn from the nineteenth-century writer-artisan William Morris: "You can't have art without resistance in the material"—which, given

Morris's socialist sympathies, almost makes the book's thingness a figure for labor and an inadvertent agent of class struggle.

What McGann means is that the (literary) book in hand does not describe a one-way condition of custodianship and passivity. Rather, books agitate on their own. They exemplify the transposition effected by aura in Walter Benjamin's essay, "On Some Motifs in Baudelaire": *die Aura einer Erscheinung erfahren, heißt, sie mit dem Vermögen belehnen, den Blick aufzuschlagen* ("Experience of the aura . . . rests on the transposition of a response common in human relationships to the relationship between the inanimate or natural object and man. The person we look at, or who feels he is being looked at, looks at us in turn. To perceive the aura of an object we look at means to invest it with the ability to look back.")[62] I would therefore retrieve Valerie Allen's lovely formulation deployed earlier in relation to Pascal and Darger, which effectively reverses the Bakhtinian polarity of inner and outer body, authorial self and heroic other, and asks us to consider the physical effect of books upon those who see, touch, and hold them: "it is through this intransigent 'being-there' of the book that we can speak of the intentionality of limb and organ. It is because we read that we possess nose, hands, cheek, and feet."

Earlier in her essay, Allen embodies ethical reading—as phenomenal event—by suggesting a similitude with biblical manna as glossed by Levinas in "Promised Land or Permitted Land": "By this analogy with manna, one is always reading yet never reading: always reading, because the previous reading must continuously be made present again; never reading, because we are forever in-between readings, because, with no leftover, manna is always absent" (18). McGann's more Christianized version goes like this: "In this world, time, space, and physicality are not the emblems of a fall from grace, but the bounding conditions which turn gracefulness abounding. It is equally a world where the many departures from grace—our damaged orders and beings—appear in correspondingly determinate forms" (9).

In that light, the portrait painted so far of Darger's and Pascal's texts in its quasi-Dickensian lights is actually a partial one. They are more than just orphaned Oliver Twists or homeless Jos,[63] forced into the workhouse-factory and street-sweeping exposure of our reading. Even if their twin fates were authorially unintended, *Le Mémorial* and *In the Realms of the Unreal* have been given another life, heroically speaking. In the hands of not just Brownlow-readers . . .

> The old gentleman was a very respectable-looking personage, with a powdered head and gold spectacles. He was dressed in a bottle-green coat with a black velvet collar; wore white trousers; and carried a smart bamboo cane under his arm. He had taken up a book from the stall, and there he stood, reading away, as hard as if he were in his elbow-chair, in his own study. It is very possible that he fancied himself there, indeed; for it was plain, from his abstraction, that he saw not the book-stall, nor the street, nor the boys, nor, in short, anything but the book

itself: which he was reading straight through: turning over the leaf when he got to the bottom of a page, beginning at the top line of the next one, and going regularly on, with the greatest interest and eagerness.[64]

. . . but also of Benjamin/Canetti-like readers:

> The teacher would call my name, and the book then made its way from bench to bench; one boy passed it on to another, or else it traveled over the heads until it came to rest with me, the student who had raised his hand. Its pages bore traces of the fingers that had turned them.
>
> Now one knows why one made such a fuss about it. It had to be with one for a long time; it had to travel; it had to occupy space; it had to be a burden; and now it has reached the goal of its voyage, now it reveals itself, now it illuminates the twenty bygone years it mutely lived with one. It could not say so much if it had not been there mutely the whole time, and what idiot would dare to assert that the same things had always been in it.[65]

The *material* textual condition of a text in the public domain seems to *need* the alteration that comes from mobility and tactile contact. It seems to *want* to be touched—akin to the first of the three "incompatible messages" W. J. T. Mitchell finds in Barbara Kruger's artwork, "Your gaze hits the side of my face," and which we will discover in relation to cinema when we come to Cavell in the next chapter. This is also the point Leah Price drives home about the use-value publications variously acquired in *How to Do Things with Books in Victorian Britain*. Authorial reclusiveness and seclusion, perhaps not surprisingly, limits this dimension of a text's becoming rather than aesthetically consummating it. Books require nothing less then *breathing* in the open air. And yet, if we may put it this way, Darger's and Pascal's have nevertheless had their coffins forced.

If we can legitimately export some of Bakhtin's insights *outside* the bounds of their formal argumentation (as I anticipated we would in my prologue), *performer-heroism* become a property of reading, and the plane of the *heroic* gets restaged as an ethical-hermeneutic practice. This is something for which Bakhtin prepares the ground in "Author and Hero" when he puts the question pointedly to readers' perception of a particular genre, самоотчетисповедь ("confessional self-accounting"), marking the only explicit place in the essay where the act of reading is highlighted. Bakhtin asks "through whose eyes" it is read, inasmuch as the genre lacks both author and hero and "no position of being axiologically situated outside" that interrelationship. That is to say, not only has the scrim of fiction been removed, but confessional self-accounting also has no need for an object-world or environment, features no plot, includes no constitutive relationship with another.[66] Indeed, it is a discourse of stages: initial incompleteness (reflection), entreaty (address), and only finally, transgredience (faith in some transcendent consciousness).

In the case of the *Mémorial*, what happens very possibly—for readers other than Pascal himself—is an *aestheticization* of the work, compelling it to deviate from its own self-understood and ultimately enactive purposes (this describes Mihailescu's approach, for example, or that of the Cuban *Orígenes* poets). To respond like this *resembles* authorship as Bakhtin has explicated it, since it bestows an "excess" upon a putative hero and thereby performs a "primary act of creation" (albeit a "primitive one"). Yet, such a decision calculatedly misconceives the work's "immanent and extra-aesthetic purpose," (148) since the "performed act" of the accounting itself is entirely self-circumscribed; it fundamentally *lacks a hero.* Very simply, to aestheticize it, to make it literary, risks performing an act of hermeneutic bad faith.

Bakhtin's compunction about genre here looks very different in the lighter-fingered hands of Derrida, who, recall, turns bad faith to analytic advantage when he proclaims, "I will not mix genres," and then proceeds to the "genre-clause," the law of internally deconstituting "participation without membership" by which a particular example of a class of texts—say "confessional self-accounting"—becomes undone in its supposed purity and bounded belonging within a particular genre. All that contamination follows from paratextual headers like "A Novel" or "An Epic in Ten Books," or "Diary." But, as we know, Pascal's text (we'll come to Darger in a moment) is pristine in this respect: *no* contaminants, *no* legend such as "A Talismanic Act of Confessional Self-Accounting by Blaise Pascal" or "My Pietistic Devotion" taints either parchment copy or scrawled paper original. As for its intentionality, the self-understood point of the document Pascal has left us,

> a performed act needs the determinateness of the end to which it is directed and the determinateness of the means for achieving that end, but it has not need for the determinateness of its performer—it does not need a hero. The performed act itself tells us nothing about the performer; it tells us only about the objective state of affairs in which it was performed: it is axiologically generated only by this state of affairs, and not by a hero. . . . That is why any reflection upon an already accomplished act does not illuminate the author (in regard to who he is, what kind of person he is), but represents a merely immanent critique of the act from the standpoint of its own ends and its own "ought." . . . The essential constitutive moment of this form is the fact that it is a self-objectivation, that the others with his special, privileged approach, is excluded; the only principle that organizes the utterance here is the pure relationship of the *I* to itself. (140–141)

Since "pure" self-accounting is effectively impossible, according to Bakhtin (axiological self-address cannot really take place in solitude), the ultimate limit it represents marks a tangency with the ultimate limit that is confession. "Petitionary tones, the tones of prayer, intertwine with repentant or penitential tones" (144). Absent Derrida's deconstructive move, his main point proves salient: genres do blend, almost inevitably. Bakhtin's definitional thrust, however, lies otherwise and makes Derrida's entirely beside the point. Confessional self-accounting is a self-performed act but not a consummating one. Bakhtin describes it as "potentially infinite," a unitary and open-ended event; restlessness and unconsummatedness are its defining features, just as otherness in no way shapes or finishes it. "The petition and the supplication themselves remain open, unconsummated; they break off, as it were, into the unpredetermined future of the event" (143). Confessional self-accounting is a pure, "axiologically solitary" act—in the form of *both* the experience itself of Pascal's "night of fire" *and* his record of it.

> *Who*, then, should the reader of a confessional self-accounting be? And *how* should he perceive it in order to actualize the extra-aesthetic purpose that is immanent to it? What is essential here is that there is no author before us with whom we could co-create, nor is there a hero whom, we could, together with the author, consummate in purely aesthetic terms. The *subiectum* of a confessional self-accounting stands over against me in the vent of being as the performer of his own act, and I must neither reproduce this act (imitatively) nor contemplate it artistically, but must react to it by performing an answering act of my own (just as in the case of a request addressed to me, I must neither reproduce it—imitate, co-experience it—nor apprehend it artistically, but react to it with answering act: either fulfill it or refuse to do so) . . . (148)

So, we arrive at yet another crux. If not aesthetic, if not an authoring or a novelizing, what would such an "answering act" look like? We cannot join the actual performer of the act or "isolate him in that event," for "the yet-to future of the event conjoins both of us and determines our mutual relationship (both of us stand against one another in God's world)" (149). Evidently, what is solicited—agitated—is something, as we have seen, that Bakhtin names ответственност or "answerability"—less an affect or sensibility than *an act*, which we are obliged to perform. Additionally, since "the world of others is axiologically authoritative for me" (154), as Bakhtin explains in the section on autobiography, the question of what should constitute alterity in and for such an act looms large. Before suggesting lineaments to which I think such an act might correspond, I need to bring Darger back into the mix.

"THE AXIOLOGICAL WEIGHT OF MUSIC"

Earlier, I posited a theological—better, religious—moment in reading, one that we enact or confer that chimes with Bakhtin's theologically inflected aesthetics. And although Bakhtinian ethics is not as easily demarcated as say, Kantian ethics or Rawlsian or Spinozan ethics, "the ethical" shares a certain contiguity with both the religious and the aesthetic in the early and late work.[67] But the question to put to Bakhtin is not about ethics or religion but rather about *aesthetic activity* as it may form a dialogical nexus with the other two. Here's how he identifies it:

Aesthetic activity collects the world scattered in meaning and condenses it into a finished and self-contained image. Aesthetic activity finds an emotional equivalent for what is transient in the world (for its past and present, for its present-on-hand being), an emotional equivalent that gives life to this transient being and safeguards it; that is, it finds an axiological position from which the transient in the world acquires the axiological weight of an event, acquires validity and stable determinateness. The aesthetic act gives birth to being on a new axiological plane of the world: a new human being is born and a new axiological context—a new plane of thinking about the human world. (191)

As Peter Hitchcock and others have pointed out, this is a distinctly modernist notion of art's agency and it ascribes an enormous amount of power to the artist-author and his transgredient arsenal of perceptions and devices—verbal style, for instance, being merely an expression of a comprehensive understanding of "the constituent features of the world, the values of the world and of life" (195). For Bakhtin, creative acts, at bottom, are immanent and transcendental in equal degree: where an artist "stands" in the event of being, in the values of the world, in relation to a hero, authorizes all other aesthetic choices and the production of meanings and forms.

We do not find outsider artist Henry Darger in this definition, perhaps needless to say. His oeuvre—though such terminology feels both pretentious and inexact in this case—lacks a hero and it lacks a whole. If we group *In the Realms of the Unreal*, *Crazy House*, *History of My Life*, *The Book of Weather Reports*, *Diaries*, ledgers and artwork and collages (and even perhaps the junk ephemera, too), Darger never really finished the work he evidently staked his life upon, and possibly never really could have. As I have already proposed, any heroic element (in adapted Bakhtinian terms), lay in its compulsive performance, not the aesthetic consummation it only partially effected. Darger evidently went to Mass several times a day, every day. My sense of the work is that it was somehow continuous with that kind of ritualized religious presence and daily performance.

In no way, of course, does it resemble Pascal's singular act of "confessional self-accounting," about which it must also be conceded that it both corresponds and doesn't correspond to that generic classification we find in "Author and Hero in Aesthetic Activity" (for one thing, the *Mémorial* is properly aesthetic only after the fact, only in being found). Yet, as accidentally *dialogic* and *novelized* and *unfinalizable* as Darger's work might be adjudged, as very much its own individualized *speech genre*, I believe that it, too becomes enframed through, lensed by, viewers' and readers' belated and risky contact with it. This is precisely because of its inadvertent appearance in the light of day, in curated public space, and not for any necessary or sufficient textual property it might be said to possess.

"Of course the hero we mean is the possible hero, that is, the one that has not yet become a hero, has not been shaped aesthetically," (199), Bakhtin says. The prototype for the hero in a work is, as he puts it, "the givenness of a human being as another." That is to say, the author-artist does not fabricate or invent a hero: he *finds* him. And the finding is something that author-artist accomplishes prior to exercising a set of artistic determinations. Both author and hero, so to speak, *become* themselves. Not only does art's material resist, in William Morris's formulation, but so also does the sum of extra-aesthetic *realia* from which authors and heroes alike derive.

Bakhtin's phrase for this pre-given, pre-aesthetic "materiality" is *axiological weightiness*, or "the reality of an event" (199).[68] Toward the end of his essay—an essay, one must say, with many unresolved ambiguities and complex crosscurrents—Bakhtin modulates from author-artist to music-listener as an agent of alteration (for which, we know, Bakhtin uses a religious-materialist vocabulary of embodiment and consummation):

> In music, we can feel the resistance, the persistent presence of a possible consciousness, a lived-life consciousness, a consciousness incapable of being consummated from within itself, and it is only insofar as we feel it that we perceive the power, the axiological weight of music, and that we perceive every new step it takes as an act of overcoming and a victory. In feeling this possible cognitive-ethical tension or directedness, which is incapable of being consummated from within itself yet is mortal, we also feel the great privilege qua event of being another, of being situated outside the bounds of another possible consciousness; we feel our own gift-bestowing, resolving, and consummating possibility, our own aesthetically actualized formal power: we create musical form not in an axiological void and not amidst other musical forms [music in the midst of music] but in the event of lived life. And it is only this that renders musical form serious, renders it valid and momentous qua event. (201)

This truly sonorous passage stands out in a treatise of often dense and intricate argument. If I understand him correctly here, Bakhtin has opened a space once again for the recipient as a *custodian* of art, as opposed to specifying the roles and responsibilities of its producer, its creative engine. In the few sentences that follow this rhapsody, he modulates back to literature and verbal art, closing the section on "Content, Form, and Material" with this peroration: "A work of art must feel its way toward and find an axiological reality, the reality of the hero as an event." The essay (excluding the supplementary section, which provides a reading of Pushkin's poem, Разлука) concludes with a tantalizing brief modulation to the figure of "the reader," whose task, evidently, is to defer to the authorial "principle" and eschew any desire to individuate an author as a biographical person.[69] Reading taps into the creative vein responsible for the acts of "seeing and forming" in a work, and makes the author "the unity of the transgredient moments of seeing that are actively referred to the hero and his world" (208).[70]

Personally, I find the passage about an object-less art like music more compelling, in the same way that the section on "confessional self-accounting" also triggers the rare meditation on reading practice as the performing of an answering act of one's own. Graham Pechey has said that, according to Bakhtin's paradigm, "we cannot understand deeds except as (possible) texts; that the deed and the text are figures for each other" (132). Just as texts become "works"[71] in late Bakhtin when they resonate through acts of reception, transmission, or recitation, so answers correlate with both utterances and performances. In a word drawn from a different philosophical rhetoric, they are *speech-acts*.

Answerability, we learned from the short manifesto "Art and Answerability," entails guilt, liability to blame, since the worlds of life and art are so very difficult to integrate in the everyday. From *Toward a Philosophy of the Deed*, we also learned that answerability manifests itself as a signature or a fair copy: authorship, of a sort.[72] Finally, from "Author and Hero," we learned that alterity is the value-category that founds окружение ("environment"), that creates the circumstances and conditions for воплощчение ("embodiment"), that enables оживление ("vivification") and solicits завершить ("consummation").

I conclude that the nature of an answer-word or answer-act of one's own, whatever form it might take, is neither predetermined nor easily determined. Indeed, fifty-five years after writing these essays, speaking of a work's finalized whole in relation to its unfinalized context in his final work, "Toward a Methodology for the Human Sciences," Bakhtin says, "This meaning (in its unfinalized context) cannot be peaceful and cozy (one cannot curl up and die within it" (160). Significantly, this happens to be the same essay in which Bakhtin prominently reflects on hermeneutic agency: the first word of the essay, indeed it stands alone without a predicate, is понимание ("understanding"), and texts (in their aspect Paul Ricoeur had already come to label mimesis3 or "refiguration"), have become "works."[73]

BAKHTIN AND CAVELL

It is time to plait these several strands together. The instrumental questions I posed at the beginning of the chapter were these: (1) What "face" can Bakhtin add to a multi-sided ethics of reading? (2) What does he have to tell us about "the book" when it makes material contact with our hands and what does such corporeal reading look like in his thought as a modality of "aesthetic activity?" (3) How do we understand our proper investments of belief, autonomy, and dependency in reading (the dialectical play of authoritative and internally persuasive purchases on the texts we read), as framing a "theological" or religious moment?[74] (4) In "reading" Henry Darger and Blaise Pascal, what exactly constitutes a performed and answerable deed that might therefore illuminate Bakhtinian constructs about hermeneutic agency?

The first three questions effectively fold into the fourth, so the argument in the remaining pages of this chapter will be led by it. I had suggested previously in the book that In the *Realms of the Unreal* and *Le Mémorial* defy the norms and expectations of literary communication, which is what makes them limit-cases—or "novelized" bound-ary phenomena, in Bakhtinian terms. What these texts *want* now that they are exposed is nothing they could answer for themselves, of course. What we want for them, conversely, matches part of what Levinas calls the reader of Talmud's herme-neutic struggle with the Angel.

Thus, Michael Bernard-Donals concludes his riposte to Gary Saul Morson by suggesting, "consistent with Bakhtin, and running counter, I think, to Morson—is to look at the complexities and different strands in Bakhtin's own work, and to keep from trying to make that work 'our own'" (54).[75] It may be specific to the genre of "confes-sional self-accounting" for its readers "neither [to] reproduce this act (imitatively) nor contemplate it artistically, but [to] react to it by performing an answering act" of their own. And yet, since readers are *not* authors, even perhaps on general principles, respond-ing to a work necessarily exceeds its author's purposes or desires for it, as consonant with Bakhtin's excursus on "creative understanding" in his 1970 interview with *Novy Mir*.

Is it ironic, or merely prescient of Bakhtin, that Bernard-Donals's caution against making a work "our own"—meaning to appropriate it for our own purposes—is an-ticipated and answered in "Discourse in the Novel" by a different semantic horizon for the same phrase: "The authoritative word demands that we acknowledge it, that we make it our own; it binds us, quite independent of any power it might have to per-suade us internally" (374)? Bakhtin's rhetoric of deference here obviously differs from the sense of признавать ("to acknowledge") and признательность ("acknowledg-ment") as undersigning that we saw in *Toward a Philosophy of the Deed*. But however we negotiate the boundaries of a given work, we must still somehow *answer* it, in "compellingly obligatory" fashion. An approach to what that responsibility may in-volve is signaled for us, in advance of the next chapter, by philosopher Stanley Cavell, who uses Bakhtin's rhetoric of acknowledging (in the second sense here) to quite dif-ferent effect.

In *The World Viewed*, Cavell expands slightly on the concept as he developed it in the essays, "Knowing and Acknowledging," "The Avoidance of Love," and "Music Discomposed."[76] In the later book, beyond a proffered speech act that goes beyond knowledge—"It is not enough that I know (am certain) that you suffer—I must do or reveal something (whatever can be done. In a word, I must *acknowledge* it"[77]—to *acknowledge* an artwork means to respond (affirmatively or not) to its *own* claim of acknowledging the conditions of the medium for which it speaks representatively. "Painting, being art, is revelation; it is revelation because it is acknowledgment; being acknowledgment, it is knowledge, of itself and of its world" (110). Such art, specifically modernist, acknowledges its "total thereness as an event of the wholly open," as well as its independence from both its creator and its viewers. Cavell calls this a "candor" that reveals the work is "complete without me, in that sense *closed* to me" (111).

For example, a painting may acknowledge its frontedness, or its finitude, or its specific thereness—that is, its presentness; and your accepting it will accordingly mean acknowledging your frontedness, or directionality, or verticality towards its world, or any world—or your presentness, in its aspect of absolute hereness and of newness. (110)[78]

Later in the same chapter, he expands on this idea:

These works exist as abstracts of intimacy—declaring our common capacity and need for presentness, for clear separateness and singleness and connection, for horizons and uprightness and frontedness, for the simultaneity of a world, for openness and resolution. They represent existence without assertion; authority without authorization; truth without claim, which you can walk in. (118)

If art's acknowledgement, for Cavell, is a matter of self-reference (an artist's self-awareness that confirms our conviction, in turn), it is also "an act of the self (if it is one of recognition, then its is not like recognizing a place but like recognizing a government)" (123). Acknowledgment in both realms, the intersubjective and the artistic, is a declaration or exhibition of limits and autonomy, but also an expression of obligation—either to others or to a given medium. It is "immediately related to issues of presentness and theatricality in aesthetic, epistemological, and theological contexts" (169).

Spanning, also, a putative divide between ethics and aesthetics, it therefore roughly approximates Bakhtin's notion of answerability: art *actively* declares its presentness before us, as we articulate and make present what is separate from us and our desires for it, what we otherwise might be inclined to suppress, leave unarticulated, or fail to face. We do that, also, by taking up a position *outside* what confronts us. Art "faces me, draws my limits, and discovers my scale; it fronts me, with whatever wall at my back, and gives me horizon and gravity. It reasserts that, in whatever locale I find myself, I am to locate myself" (114). "In response to modernist painting, I am concentrated, finitized, incarnate" (117). But if the work of art performs a stringency of acknowledgment in regard to its own procedures, my acknowledgment of that revelation is the necessary and reciprocal response, my exercise of tact.

Art's self-acknowledgment speaks to the medium itself: "One might say that the task is no longer to produce another instance of an art but a new medium within it" (103). Cavell also calls this "establishing a new *automatism*," where that word signifies "artistic discoveries of form and genre and type and technique" (105): by coming to terms with the physical constituents of its medium, "searching out its conditions of existence" (107), an art form risks its warrant, its power, its effects, thereby rediscovering them and making that rediscovery public. It, so to peak, *ontologizes* its self-reference and its exhibited condition.[79] Both the artistic medium and a particular art-object are, as Cavell puts it, thus "free[d] from me" and "give[n] new grounds for autonomy" (108). The work, the tradition, the medium, all become *reinvested*. This, according to Stanley Cavell, is art's "real work."

In an interpersonal realm, such reinvestment as "acknowledging" means taking on—articulating, registering, making present—what *demands* to be acknowledged, what makes a claim upon me, which, at its most profound, is the world itself or another person independent of my fantasies about them. This happens emotional-volitionally, as Bakhtin would say, not epistemologically or categorically. Indeed, to perform acknowledgment, say, of another's pain or of one's own mind, is to register the limits of both knowing and skepticism (which by Cavell's lights, are equally revelatory), to acknowledge separateness, yet still be present somehow and to present oneself, in one's response.

The authoritative word's "demand" that we "acknowledge" it is obviously quite different, for there, in Bakhtin's analysis, we are being asked to become simply reflectors and mimics, to reiterate "Life is good" with exactly the same intonation and verbal embodiment as it was pronounced to us. Cavellian acknowledgement is obviously far closer to Bakhtinin ответственност that to this more authority-driven notion of compulsory concession. But introducing Cavell's vocabulary at this transition point not only lets me pivot on the term *acknowledge*, letting it resonating with both Cavellian and Bakhtinian tonalities. It also prepares the ground for Chapter 6.

"We do not so much look at the world as look *out at* it, from behind the self" (102), Cavell writes in *The World Viewed*. This observation is crucial for the next chapter's turn in argument. Suffice it say here, though, that what it intimates is a certain torque in natural attunement, our routine relationship to the world around us as a kind of thwarted worldliness in which our desires for the world are twisted or obstructed by our fantasies of it. One of art's functions (or virtues or provocations) is to raise that condition to consciousness and create certain conditions for acknowledgement.

One element in such acknowledgment, for Bakhtin and Cavell alike, is separateness. There is a parallel with Levinas here, too—not with the aesthetic moment or experience, however, but with the ethical: the moment of primordial speech. The face, Levinas's trope for ethical relation, speaks and what it says, first, is the "No" of the Decalogue's sixth commandment. לא תרצח ("you shall not shed innocent blood") states, so to speak, the possibility within interdicted possibility. In Jill Robbins's succinct gloss, "The face is delivered up to my powers, and, at the same time, refuses them. These powers, are, at the limit, murderous" (*Altered Reading*, 64). And as we saw previously, while art is also "delivered up to my powers," that is, by inviting them, it also arrests and deflects them at the same time. It does so, first and foremost, through what Cavell calls its autonomy, its separateness from us.[80] The artwork is not one's own—at first, anyway—a "first meaning" entailed, I think, by the adventitious discovery by its accidental readers of Pascal's and Darger's texts.

We cannot be sure what *In The Realms of the Unreal* "wants" from us. We may well choose to follow its author's poignant invitation, "Let the reader follow battle after battle with the others, let him follow every event and adventure, and then if he can, if he sets his mind and heart on it, take it on as if he himself was an actual participant." In doing so, of course, we merge our fantasies with its own. Conversely, we can follow Bakhtin's model for listening to music (something more than what is conventionally called "appreciation"), when we answerably *create musical form*: "we also feel the great privilege qua event of being another, of being situated outside the bounds of another possible consciousness; we feel our own gift-bestowing, resolving, and consummating possibility, our own aesthetically actualized formal power." This is art's "real work," according to Mikhail Bakhtin—it teaches us the creative lesson of outsideness. Unison or homophony is not what voice seeks, but rather novelizing counterpoint—another voice sounded against mine. But in either case, whether we give into Darger's solicitation or maintain Bakhtinian rectitude, these choices *enjoin* us. They ask of us a fair copy and a signature.

A fortiori, this applies to the unsigned and never-in-need-of-signing *Mémorial* of Pascal, addressed *not* to any future readers but either *to* God or *in* God's presence. And with it, we enter precincts of acknowledgment that Cavell's colleague Hillary Putnam, in his subtle introduction to Franz Rosenzweig's *Understanding the Sick and the Healthy*, expands vertically and laterally:

> In ordinary circumstances, circumstances in which neither doubt nor justification is called for, our relation to the familiar things in our environment, the pen in our hand, or the person in pain whom we are consoling, is not one of either "knowing" or "acknowledging." Rather, Cavell suggests, it is one of acknowledging (or, sadly, failing to acknowledge). Our task is not to acquire a "proof" that "there is an external word" or that our friend is in pain, but to acknowledge the world and our friend. I suggest that we read Rosenzweig, the religious thinker, as adding that it is our task to acknowledge God (indeed, as a profoundly religious thinker, albeit also a profoundly humanist thinker, Rosenzweig does not think one can acknowledge any one of the three—God, Man and the World—as they demand to be acknowledged unless one acknowledges the other two). But like Cavell's Wittgenstein, Rosenzweig insists that acknowledging is not a matter of knowledge.[81]

Plainly, we have no choice but to read Pascal's previously secreted text now. Yet I think Mihailescu's conceit is apt: it will always seem to us as glimpsed through a peephole. And even if effectively unreadable in its ponderous length and loosely structured massing of detail, *In the Realms of the Unreal* will have to endure the choice we make to occupy our time with its perusal. In the singular extremity of their "found" state, neither, of course, can be held in hand; their corporeality, any (im)purity that might be transmitted *to* or *by* hands on account of something sacral, does not touch us palpably.

That is why I have insisted on referring to them as limit-cases, a limit we might then work back from, in order to reflect on various ethical—as Bakhtin and Levinas would say, phenomenological, and as Cavell would say, ontological—exigencies presupposed by the act or practice of reading. That is also why, in concluding this chapter, I want to reprise some of the variations on the theme of touching from my introduction. To touch, says Jacques Derrida, is to touch the border; but that is a law of tact that plainly does not obtain for Darger and Pascal. For the limit their texts announce is simply that they elude our grasp, despite the accidental "excsription" they also announce as texts that stand exposed: to themselves and the world. In Jean-Luc Nancy's evocative words, this exposition embodies "the fact that writing indicates its own outside, is decanted and shows things." Even Jean-Louis Chrétien's scruple to "lay bare the fact that touch is never bare" feels beside the point here, because, as I already had occasion to observe, touching never gets us close enough.

It is the auratic rather than tactile element, then, that tempers restless and impertinent, *'asqaniot* hands in their approach to Pascal's and Darger's works. "Doing readings" may therefore be just the wrong phrase to use in this connection, since its instrumental character falls rather wide of the mark set for us by Bakhtin's акт-поступок ("deed") and поступление, a gerund inflection that suggests both the serial aspect of performing acts and its present-tense quality, that is, "something that we haven't quite finished with or that hasn't yet finished with us."

At the end of the first edition of his book, *The World Viewed*, Cavell restates what it is that the art form of the movies acknowledges: "what is always to be acknowledged, its own limits: in this cases, its outsideness to the world and my absence from it" (146). These are daunting concepts; in the second edition, with an added postscript of almost seventy pages, Cavell acknowledges that his book he wrote is difficult and perhaps even incomprehensible. It is certainly oracular. But, in line with the qualifications he introduces in the second edition by opening up the discourse on movies to include the world of animated cartoons, I believe that his "reflections on the ontology of film" can be made to bear relevantly on the comparatively obscure fates of Pascal's lyrically miniature textual world and Darger's novelistically gigantic one: "a world complete without me which is present to me," he writes, "takes my life as my haunting of the world, either because I left it unloved (the Flying Dutchman) or because I left unfinished business (Hamlet)" (160).

While a case could probably be made for even *dual* correspondences, quite unlike the radically exhibitionistic ontology of film, or indeed the communicative economy of most imaginative discourses, *Le Mémorial* and *In the Realms of the Unreal* were never meant to include me or anyone else: as such, they will always reside *outside*. (And if that claim does not ultimately signal consilience, given ambiguities in both stories, their narrative of reception still yields a sustainable and edifying fiction.) Through my appropriation, their words acquire a sort of слово с оглиадько ("sideward glance"), a loophole they did not purpose. My exotopic or "extimate" access to them is thus leased, not owned. But through that tenancy, I believe we come close to Cavell's insight about cinema as the photographing, projecting, screening, exhibiting, and viewing of reality, which is dual: (1) "In screening reality, film screens its givenness from us; it holds reality from us; it holds reality before us, i.e., withholds reality before us" (189);[82] and (2) as the movie camera stands outside the world that it photographs and the movie screen then projects or exhibits, so movies have the capacity to locate their viewers, who are silent and hidden in public, *in* the world: "They permit the self to be wakened, so that we may stop withdrawing our longings further inside ourselves" (102).

This insight can be flanked by some of the insights we have seen proposed by Levinas about the Talmud's "extreme attention to the real," as well as by some of those Bakhtin labored to articulate in *Toward a Philosophy of the Act* and "Author and Hero in Aesthetic Activity." In a wholly singular way, on the plane of verbal art, not philosophizing, Pascal and Darger seem to have arrived at something like these same insights—that is to say, *with our complicity* as their unintended readers. Even if in their cases the self and its longings were their own and not ours; and even if the awakening proved to be an immuring of that self and a sequestering of those longings into an interior world of private expression; the unchosen fate of their texts, nonetheless burdens us with a project—not a given, дан, but rather something *given to us*, задан, something whose tactful undertaking, whose *handling*, we, in turn, "set as a task." And in turning next to two very different worlds, theater and cinema, marking out contours for an ethics of reading becomes, once again, a version of that project and that task.

CHAPTER 6

Ethics of Reading III
Cavell and Theater/Cinema

A staircase went up from the northeastern corner to the northwestern corner, whereby they could go to the roofs of the chambers. . . . And at the entrance to the upper chamber were two cedar posts by which they could mount to the roof of the upper chamber. And in the upper chamber the ends of flagstones marked where was the division between the Sanctuary and the Holy of Holies. And in the upper story were openings [לולין] into the Holy of Holies by which they used to let down the workmen in boxes [תיבות] so that they should not feast their eyes on the Holy of Holies.

—*Mishnah Middot*, Chapter 4:5

I surprise my hearers with their own hearts.

—William Shakespeare (as voiced by Kenneth Gross)

The voice is Jacob's voice, yet the hands are Esau's hands. But he did not recognize him . . . (Robert Alter translation)

—Genesis 27:22–23

TEVOT

Stanley Cavell's memoir *Little Did I Know: Excerpts From Memory* (2010) introduces us to a rather thickly described Jewish upbringing for which his non-autobiographical writings may not quite have prepared us.[1] References to Jewish material culture do not exactly stand out in the body of his work. It is fair to assume that the passage from the mishnaic tractate on Temple measurements that stands as the first epigraph to this chapter is not one with which he would necessarily be familiar. The mechanism it describes, however, can be taken for a somewhat uncanny precedent for two harbingers of the cinematic machinery, the *camera obscura* and the *lanterna magica*, the latter of which Cavell mentions in passing in his book on film, *The World Viewed: Reflections on The Ontology of Film*.

True, it promises something less than a family resemblance. And it does not quite speak to previous rabbinical pronouncements we have seen about holiness as a function of defiling the hands—as a determination about textual *kinds*. But as Cavell himself is no stranger to speculative genealogies or inventive analogies, I let it stand.[2] The point of the admittedly implausible comparison, however, is to stress the paradox of being present in the midst of spectacle—or at least, in the place for spectacle—but somehow hindered, withheld, or unseen. It should call to mind some of Cavell's profoundest insights about what it means to view the screened reality projected by a motion picture, or to witness tragic drama within the space of a theater but not to share the same space as the characters whom one is therefore helpless to defend or assist.

The audience assembled at the performance of a play or the showing of a film can, so to speak, claim an exemption: after all, it is *those* persons onstage or onscreen to whom things happen or whose actions matter, not those who merely occupy paid seats as innocent spectators. To use Cavell's term, there is an ontological difference between character/actor/performer on the one hand, and spectator, on the other. That difference is the question this chapter will consider by sketching another face for an ethics of reading, a face attuned to the special form of reading we execute as dramatic or cinematic watchers, not grasping a book in our hands but, rather, sitting bodily adjacent to others all around us. If the hard currency of the physical book cedes, thus, to the spatiality of theater and the material presences housed within, the adjacency staged here is no less meaningful that that constructed by Michael Arad in the outdoor theater of lower Manhattan.

According to rabbinic commentaries, the "boxes" or crates identified in the *mishnah* quoted above were closed on three sides and attached to pulleys so that the priestly workmen's sights would be confined exclusively to the walls they were to clean without risking an untoward glance at the Holy of Holies.[3] Like the magic lantern zoetrope and darkened chamber, and the viewing conditions of the movie theater each distantly resembles, the boxes artificially constrained and directed vision.[4] Like the various physical separations between stage and its doings on the one hand and an audience and its doings on the other, the boxes lent themselves to distance and separation if not outright avoidance, a word Cavell exploits, rich with significance for an analysis of Shakespearean tragedy and its performative discontents.

Cavell, quite possibly, would be gratified to know that the word תבה in Hebrew denotes not only box (or ark or closet) but also both "word" and "musical bar."[5] There are only two places in the Torah in which that word happens to be used, each an instance of deliverance: God's commandment to Noah to build and measure an ark (Gen. 6–9), and Moses floated in a chest of bulrushes (Ex. 2:3–5); commentaries, especially Hasidic ones, note the collocation. And although the word for ark in the case of *aron ha-edut* ("Ark of the Testimony") is different from *tevah*, a linguistic correlation shadows the object itself there, too, as we can see in the *midrash* from *Exodus Rabbah*, "those who carried the ark that contained the holy words were actually carried by the ark" (36.4). (In its concern with language, that *midrash* also happens to create a sort of off rhyme with the *mishnah* about descending viewing boxes.[6])

Obliging a connection between Stanley Cavell's literary philosophy and *mishnah/ midrash* like this enables me once again to underscore a relationship between the textually difficult and holy as figures for the secular and religious traditions we "carry" and which reciprocally carry us. The condition of the workmen navigating between לולין and תיבות in the בית המקדש (the Holy Temple), insinuates a certain sonority, albeit a distant one, with Cavell's analysis of cinema and theater to which I now want to turn.[7]

"How could film be art," Cavell wonders in *The World Viewed*, "since all the major arts arise in some way out of religion? Now I can answer: because movies arise out of magic; from *below* the world. The better a film, the more it makes contact with this source of its inspiration; it never loses contact with the magic lantern behind it" (39). Like many of the sentences Cavell has committed to prose, these are at once difficult and deceptively simple. Implicit in them, first of all, is a relation between magic and fantasy on one hand and the everyday or ordinary on the other. Among the genres covered in this book—literary fiction, scripture and scriptural commentary, tragedy, criticism—it is film that lays the greatest claim to an instrumental apparatus like *Pledge, Turn, Prestige* from our first chapter.

Parlor magic and illusion essentially found the art—although in his most recent book on film, Cavell allows that the magic is of a peculiarly mechanized sort, "a nineteenth-century set up, a mechanical contraption."[8] Second of all, here at least, Cavell evidently regards magic (in its best sense) and religion coextensively. In *Senses of Walden*, written one year after *The World Viewed*, Cavell takes Thoreau up on his hint that his own book is a sacred text, a scripture: "Writing—heroic writing, the writing of a nation's scripture—must assume the conditions of language as such; re-experience, as it were, the fact that there is such a thing as language at all and assume responsibility for it—find a way to acknowledge it—until the nation is capable of serious speech again" (32).

This is obviously a diacritical sense of the religious—indeed, it bears comparison with Levinas's understanding of the work of exegesis and Bakhtin's theologically inflected aesthetics. And yet in both cases, the magical and the textual, Cavell finds a warrant for his own philosophical criticism as the interrogation of various claims of reason, the search for criteria made by and for the self and community in practiced, principled utterance: meaning what we say, saying what we mean. Film and theater permit us to "spy" on this practice, as it were, to rediscover and perhaps reclaim what we routinely practice outside their spaces.

Cavell's work, across the various genres *it* explores, among them poetry, philosophical prose, film, opera, and psychoanalysis (but, significantly, the novel only rarely, the notable exception being the title essay in *Philosophy the Day After Tomorrow*), pivots on the way everyday life can become screened or otherwise distorted through instrumentalities of reason and knowledge. He traces various manifestations of being thus out of tune with words, the world, and the ethical claim posed to selves by others in his analytic of "skepticism," and in in the writings from the later 1980s through the 2000s, through several accounts of moral perfectionism. In *Pursuits of Happiness: The Hollywood Comedy of Remarriage* (1984), for example, Cavell recasts the problem of skepticism as "the wish to transgress the naturalness of human speech" (74), which speaks to our proximity to or distance from the things and people we invoke through the words we routinely use.

Naturalness, in the form of "reality" and "presence," and invocation, in the form of a projected, enacted, and speech-filled world, lie at the heart of Cavell's examination of cinema and theater as venues where we receive instruction about such things. Film, Cavell tells us, satisfies our wish from the world re-created in its own image. In so doing, it creates a platform for the same wish that animates all other arts, as Cavell construes them, the wish for making self and world present, for "presentness." Theater satisfies the wish by endowing a plot, a scene, a set of characters and their dialogue with presence. The experience of watching a movie or attending a play has something to tell us about living within reasonable limits and the risks of trying to thwart or transcend them, an education that begins in the very moment of our watching.

He rehearses his own much-argued message about cinema's *philosophical* potential in the 1983 essay, "What (Good) Is a Film Museum? What Is Film Culture?":

> The condition of human perception I claim film reveals is our modern fate to live in the world primarily by viewing it, taking views of it. As if something has increasingly been happening to us over the past two or three centuries that has produced a sense of *distance* from the world . . . . I find the issue already full blown in the writings of Emerson and Thoreau, whose dedication to what they call the common, the low, the near, is as something that others feel as threatening the world but that they feel is being lost to the world. I might express the fear of film, along these lines, as one of a sense that we may perish from a nostalgia for the world, from what I have called a nostalgia for the present. (110)

Forms of such "nostalgia" pervade the repertoire of philosophical, cinematic, and literary works Cavell selects for his painstaking and illuminating readings. I said my own task was limited to tying that inquiry to another face of a readerly ethics. That means trying to "step into the middle of someone else's activity of reading," as Timothy Gould has evoked the scenics here when Cavell reads others and his readings are read in turn.[9] But because the involutions of regress can be daunting here, I am less concerned with Cavell's (philosophical) practice as a reader—a modeling that Gould rightly characterizes as a *voice* twinned with, or underwritten by, a *method*—than with the material scenes of reading he establishes for us in a theater or movie house.

Even if such situations necessarily become that of "viewing" or being "co-present" because of the technical nature of film and drama as performance-based media, I feel emboldened to continue using *reading* to describe a particular act or event, and *ethics* as a descriptive category for being held to account for the agency one thus exercises. But I also feel the warrant of what one might call *overstepping*—not orienting the feet exactly in accord with someone else's footsteps, but edging them in a further direction instead. And after all, that rather appositely captures what happens when Cavell (over) reads—by overstepping—others.

CHANNELING CAVELL

This chapter, thus, follows a voice and method already patterned in the chapters on Levinas and Bakhtin. Just as each paused rhetorically to acknowledge the stakes of taking on such formidable figures, this one does as well. Gould, one of Cavell's most perspicuous readers, observes that in being stylistically singular (possessed of an "eloquent" voice) but also systematic about practical "steps to be taken" (method), Cavell's doubleness of voice "seems to be quite hard to get hold of" (47). It is, indeed. Its artfulness shading into mannerism, sometimes the least winning feature of the Cavellian prose style, makes an easy target for critique and imitation alike.[10] Yet, in "The Avoidance of Love," an essay esteemed by Harry Berger but also acknowledged by him as so exceptional "that the danger of falling under its spell made the desire to resist it unavoidable,"[11] Cavell's combination of the profound and the moving in the essay continues to astonish; literary criticism rarely scales such expressively metaphysical heights.

The World Viewed, the book that followed the essays collected in *Must We Mean What We Say?* (1969), contains many moments of profundity, several that are deeply moving, even lofty, and more than a few that are potentially obscurantist in their half-disclosed "promptings." Its particular genius is the determination to make film mysterious again, or to reckon with its intrinsic strangeness, to suggest powerfully that its significance is yet to be discovered; but it does this, ineluctably, by tracking Cavell's own idiosyncratic philosophical and cinematic predilections, which restricts it accordingly as a an account of film's workings. It is by turns a fascinating and occasionally frustrating book, and stands apart from Cavell's later collections of film-readings, *Pursuits of Happiness*, *Contested Tears*, and *Cities of Words*, not least because it now reads in ways it obviously had not anticipated, despite the commanding vantage of contemporary "lateness."[12]

To take one instance, when the book does not draw its examples from American movies (his word for these is "traditional"), its awareness of international cinema is confined to Western Europe: Denmark (Dreyer), France (Bresson, Carné, Cocteau, Goddard, Ophuls, Resnais, Renoir, Truffaut, Vigo), Germany (Weine, Riefenstahl), Italy (Antonioni, De Sica), and Sweden (Bergman), with obligatory single references to Kurosawa, Eisenstein, Lev Kuleshov, and Dziga Vertov. It is part of the book's timing that its restrictive sample of films happened to coincide with the advent of New (or postclassical) Hollywood, as the history of the medium was not just being supplemented but reimagined through newer national cinematic traditions from Asia (China), the Middle East (Iran), South America (Brazil), Africa (Senegal) and Eastern Europe (Poland, Czech Republic, Hungary, post-Yugoslavia, the Baltics).[13] A burgeoning body of contemporaneous third-world literary fiction offers a contemporaneous parallel.[14]

A more serious limitation may inhere in the correlation between philosophical curiosity and the film medium's "aesthetic possibilities of projecting photographic images" (33) as confined to "the *role* reality plays in this art" (165). Cavell draws out one of the book's motivations as the need to think and write about film "with the same seriousness that any work of art deserves" (163). But a distinctly accidental feature of the book, even if some of the analysis speaks directly to the likes of Bazin, Kracauer, or much earlier work like, say, Paul Goodman's "The Proustian Camera Eye," is its concurrence with the advent of serious academic film theory—feminist, Lacanian, structuralist-semiotic, Bakhtinian.[15] And in this regard, Cavell's elective affinities are confined to his critic-contemporaries: "It is generally true of the writing about film which has meant something to me that it has the power of the missing companion. Agee and Robert Warshow and André Bazin manage that mode of conversation all the time; and I have found it in, among others, Manny Farber, Pauline Kael, Parker Tyler, Andrew Sarris" (13).[16]

Indeed, Cavell's special sense of cinematic "language" follows from his own philosophical vocabulary as grafted onto selected aspects of the medium, in particular the automatism of the camera, its cinematography, the structure of montage. Some translation would be needed, however, to arrive at the critical vocabularies of Metz, Baudry, Chion, or Deleuze. But again, is this a fair critique? At any rate, it highlights the idiosyncratic nature of Cavell's film criticism. Michael Wood's fine essay, "The Languages of Cinema," for instance, in considering "how and when national cultures count and don't count" (79) goes to the heart of certain questions Cavell nowhere takes up. Wood's initial queries, "What is the language of a Russian film? Of a Japanese film" sharpen our consideration of Cavell to an ironic point, since the examples that Wood proceeds to analyze happen to be the Russian and Japanese film versions of Shakespeare's *King Lear*—Grigori Kozintsev's Король Лир (*King Lear*, 1971) and Akira Kurosawa's 乱 (*Ran*, 1985).[17]

In the former case, as Wood explains, we hear Boris Pasternak's translation of the play as the film's screen speech, but reading the subtitles (the screen text) gives us back untranslated Shakespeare. In the latter case, the content has been significantly altered in addition to the language—the words that are so essential to Cavell's intimate reading. Lear's daughters have become the Great Lord's sons. Wood's meditations on the double translation involved here—medium and culture—are astute:

> A film world is always remade, put together out of pieces. Both of these films ask
> us to think about the pieces and the putting together. And beyond that, since the
> translation is double (from medium to medium and from culture to culture) they

ask us to think of national origins of two sets of pieces, and of the national styles involved in putting them together—assuming that even the most talented individual directors do not work entirely outside of any tradition. What is a national film style? Is there an international film style? (83)

These are questions Cavell's body of film commentary is not quite poised to answer, for the semantic and semiotic complexities here present us with parallels to the properly ontological frame of a viewed world: that is, "the world heard" and the rendering of its diverse tongues decoded or translated (the *mise-en-scène* of our next chapter).[18]

When Cavell felt the need to append his book with a long postscript in the 1979 enlarged edition, "More of *The World Viewed*," he deployed the full force and authority of his voice in defending his philosophical argument about cinema's "essence," which effectively meant restating its premises rather than entertaining alternate formulae or vocabularies, however.[19] The secondary bibliography of those who have endeavored to get hold of that voice in the two kinds of writing illustrated by the *Lear* essay and the film book grows apace. For the most part, it follows the lead of that appended essay, a restatement or revoicing. As before in this book, I adduce a selection of those commentarial voices, myself. But like the chapters on Levinas and Bakhtin, I do not attempt anything close to a comprehensive account of Cavell's thought, or even a full reading of the single essay and book on which I concentrate in this chapter. A certain familiarity with his body of work is nevertheless presumed. If I am successful myself in "getting hold of" some part of his voice or his method, it is oriented toward refining my own convictions about an ethics of reading, as I clarify in the final section; this chapter makes no larger claim than that.

In that section, I take Cavell's advice in *Conditions Handsome and Unhandsome* and "take leave" of his writing, deferring instead to a immediately contemporary movie whose subject, however nostalgically rendered for mass appeal, just *is* film, and which may have something at least partially Cavellian to tell us about this particular medium's aesthetics of the affects in tandem with its performative *effects*. As with Bakhtin, then, I will be using Cavell's work as a certain kind of optic through which to refract my overarching concerns—a sort of commentarial magic lantern. Cavell's broad philosophical themes of working through skepticism's repudiation of the ordinary or perfectionist writing (e.g., Emerson, Nietzsche, or Rawls), or the recovery of voice, do not, however, receive any prominence here.[20] I am equally restrictive about Cavell scholarship, for the most part eschewing the likes of Arnold Davidson, Stephen Mulhall, Richard Fleming, Richard Eldridge, Andrew Norris, or Ted Cohen.[21]

I acknowledge the consequent loss in not taking up the academic conversation about Cavell's thought. It is counterbalanced, I feel, by the gain of an internally persuasive voice, and is thus consistent with the treatments of Levinas in chapters 1, 2, and 4, and of Bakhtin in chapter 5. To be sure, Bakhtin and Levinas can exert a certain Plotinus Plinlimmon– or Hugh Vereker–like influence on certain of their readers. But as those names drawn from fiction by Melville and James are meant to signal, Cavell's Americanness sets him apart. And what may make him the trickiest of the three and therefore a uniquely mesmerizing influence is not just the eclectic range of his own sources and influences but also the self-conscious model for reading he proposes as the stuff of transference and reversal.

In Gould's diagram of it in *Hearing Things*, we have, in fact, an uncannily close neighbor to the mechanics, and theatrics, of *Pledge, Turn, Prestige*: (1) first, the philosopher-writer becomes a reader of others' philosophical writings; (2) second, that reader of prior texts becomes one who is read *by* them; (3) third and finally, into the footsteps of that philosopher writer/reader is transposed the forward march of his empirical readers, who both follow him but presumably also strike out on their own. This tends to place many of Cavell's commentators in an intriguing rhetorical bind, especially those like Cohen, Gould, Rothman, Affeldt, or Conant, who number among his former students.[22] Will the singular affect of Cavell's voice be channeled, reproducing the gyres of his thought and mirroring its obscurities? Or can the language game of criticism contrive some adverse, "outside" relation to it, instead?

Richard Fleming, for instance, devotes an entire book to "an invitation to a reading" of Cavell's four-part *The Claim of Reason*. Likewise but in more condensed fashion, Stephen Mulhall limits his 1996 essay, "On Refusing to Begin," to that book's first four paragraphs. Rothman and Keane's *Reading Cavell's The World Viewed* presents itself as essentially the Talmud to Cavell's filmic Torah. But the latter's stylized compression, while it may sometimes meet with clarity from its dual commentators, generally yields through its revoicing only additional opacity.[23]

The need to speak both on Cavell and *like* Cavell may bespeak a certain transferential quality of the work that carries over into the commentary. But it may also say something about the profession of academic philosophy, to which Bakhtin and Levinas remained more or less vocationally "exotopic."[24] It speaks as well, one suspects, to certain fence-and-neighbor impingements on the various disciplines and their respective stakeholders that Cavell's work forces into provocative conjunction.[25] Not wholly dissimilar from Cavell's own self-understanding as the practitioner of a certain philosophical method and the vocalizer of a certain stylized voice, *reading* Cavell will always involve negotiating the insistent question of boundaries. And reading Cavell *well*, that is, from outside the spell cast by his language, presents its own challenge.

It is difficult, in short, to escape not only the powerful disciplinary clamp on intellectual allegiance but also the sheer force of authoritative discourse when expounding upon, or even contending with, a writer of such signature tonalities as Stanley Cavell. Between the approach that takes too little liberty (is *too* sedulous and derivative) and the one that may take too much (on the model of Cavell's own adventurous juxtapositions, such as Kant and Frank Capra, *North by Northwest* and *Hamlet*), a potential space exists for the "uninvented third possibility" that permits an alternative critical staging.[26]

Moreover, I endorse Gould's larger point about Cavell's model of reading as a method or practice, "reading is the way of proceeding that transfigures the text of your circumstances into the occasions of your activity" (190), not least because it *exactly* describes the circumstances of Sebald's narrator and the visitor at Michael Arad's September 11 Memorial, the legatee of Pascal's and Darger's *textes trouvé* and the hermeneutic dramas of *frottage* and "outsideness" modeled by Levinas and Bakhtin. But my focus here, even if centered on the theatrical aspect of "Cavell reading," will be deliberately *off*-center.

Rather than explicate Cavell's particular interpretations of a film or a play, then, I want to concentrate our attention on the *material places or situations* that serve as their staging ground. In other words, I am less interested in *doing a reading* of, say, Cavell's "reading *of King Lear*" (which is the subtitle of "The Avoidance of Love") than in following the implications of such readings as they bear on the conditions of sitting in a theater and watching a play or a film. That the same word "cinema" in common English usage denotes both a medium or industry and a place, or that the telling locutions of "filmgoing" or "theatergoing" predicate *attendance* at a movie or a theatrical performance, point me, therefore, to a strand in Cavell's criticism that, while it folds sometimes into warp and sometimes into weft in his general argument, I particularly wish to isolate. Cavell's model of reading, the *method* Gould ascribes to him, is certainly as user-centered as those we saw for Levinas and Bakhtin. But the sometimes fetishistic aspect of Cavell's voice (and here I demur from Gould's position), sets up an interference pattern, in my hearing, at least, when explicated or mimicked *as* a reading.

In an interview with Andrew Klevan, Cavell pauses to consider the vagaries of film-quotation for a "reading" of a movie:

> Discussing a film differs from discussing a painting, where you can stand before an object, or sit with a slide on a screen indefinitely, and *that* is what you're thinking about. With music you can quote a passage, whistling or at the piano. But when the film is gone again it is again gone. But then we should look at quoting more closely. Even with literature, the home of quotation, you're saying words in your voice, in a particular moment, to some point. Professors of English used to be tempted to think of themselves as Shakespearean actors when they read speeches from the plays. Is this quoting or performing?

It is certainly the case that *North by Northwest*, when screened in a theater, is indisputably *not* the same kind of material object as *In the Realms of the Unreal* or a Vilna edition of the Talmud. Cavell's question about quoting versus performing even holds true for each of the latter cases, as well: they can be performed as well as quoted. And yet, the real relevance for me of this passage is very simply the wish to overstep, or step aside from the predicament it describes, and to attend, rather, to Cavell's hints about the motion picture (and theatrical) *event,* which, when it is gone again is again gone— a modality of evanescence and mutability that I want to suggest is exactly *part* of the philosophical strangeness and mystery Cavell takes such pains to reflect upon (even if it remains subsidiary to his primary focus).

A major objection presents itself here, however, which, I recognize applies also to what I have been consistently terming "the-book-in-hand." Technology since Cavell published *The World Viewed* in 1971 or since Bakhtin drafted his notes "Toward a Reworking of the Dostoevsky Book" a decade before, has altered so dramatically that the material objects, "book" and "film," can no longer be casually identified with the models for them Cavell and Bakhtin construed as normative.[27] That is to say, the embodied, spatial conditions of *watching a film* (going to the movies) and *reading a book* in the twenty-first century put maximum pressure on what must consequently seem now a quite unreconstructed account of the tactile.

Not to have to sit in a movie theater with others in order to watch a film (the advent of online movie sites and portable media players, videodisk commerce like *Netflix*, or the television culture of Turner Broadcasting Network's "Classic Movies"[28]); using electronic devices that *bypass* the materiality of a codex with leaves, covers, mass, and volume (despite the fact that e-books might still be colloquially referred to as "page-turners"): these innovations would seem to require substantially modified assumptions about the *ontology* of films and books, and the *phenomenology* of viewing and reading. This is also a point about the standing of Cavell's arguments to which I will return in the conclusion of this chapter, having already addressed it in a preliminary footnote about animated film.

And yet, to the extent that hands still hold *hand*-held devices or operate *touch*-screens, bodies still sit in chairs while head and eye saccades respond to moving images on monitors or descending lines of a text, the corporeal shift is neither absolute nor, indeed, in need of elaborate qualification.[29] For our purposes, then, I will assume that what distinguishes watching a performance of *King Lear* or a screening of *Night of the Hunter* is its virtual communality and sociality: the sheer presence of others in silent, proximate, ritual accord. Moreover, private reading is never wholly private anyway, a latency borne out by the scenes of reading staged by Sebald and Arad (the chances of being the only person present to read the names at Arad's September 11 Memorial are miniscule at best, and Sebald's narrator in *The Emigrants* is only contingently solitary as he walks past the gravestones in the Kissingen cemetery). Reading is always invisibly accompanied.

Watching film or tragic drama materially *intensifies* the ritual dimension I have several times underscored in the preceding chapters as a complement to the act of reading, but it does not represent an entirely different experience. As Cavell might even say in one of his practiced mannerisms, call such embodiment the meaningful adjacency of persons, the proximity of their physical nearness. It is this aspect of Cavell's reflections on cinema and Shakespearean tragedy that I particularly want to bring out here, although he himself registers a consistent ambivalence around terms like "presentness" and "viewing" as properties of both *presentation* and *medium*.

When he defends the value of coming to terms with films through memory alone, what is possible to remember as much as a particular film one has seen is the *seeing* of the film, the occasion and event of it. This, of course, is the Proustian point about individual days remembered because of the revelatory book one happened to be reading at the time; and it applies, certainly, to one's aesthetic education in public, e.g., concert-going, a play or recitation, bookstores, and the intimacies and mysteries of memory thus activated. (Is this phenomenon so categorically different from cherished reminiscence of other public exhibitions like sports?) I suspect this element would factor into Cavell's program for a "humane criticism dealing with whole films" (12), even if relegated to the background. I choose to foreground it here.

THEATERS

But we seem to have left our workmen stranded in the chamber of the Temple that permits only occluded views of the Holy of Holies. So let us return to them now, or to their proxies, by way of proceeding. Obviously, the most patent difference between these functionaries and a filmgoer or theatergoer is the behind-the-scenes aspect of their work, which may therefore suggest closer analogies with a projectionist or theatrical technician (although that analogy is also imprecise, since an audience is still lacking). No, the point of tangency I want to emphasize that makes the comparison heuristic, that makes such workmen resemble spectators, is the artificially contracted space and the obligatory separateness within it, alongside a nearness to (potential) spectacle and ritualized community.

If it may be put it this way, in the Holy Temple's *tevot*, persons are temporarily "housed" something like the way they are in a (movie) theater: they witness—up until a point; and they are prohibited from fully participating in the "action" to which they are proximate. They share a virtual companionship. They are located in a liminal space of intrusion and exposure, but also protected by the cordon of remove and non-participation. It is one of Cavell's principal arguments that cinema and tragedy both leave their audiences exposed, and thus, strange to say, unaccountably accountable. In that reading, they provide at once both safe and risky displacements of "real life."

Shakespeare's play *King Lear*, as Cavell's memoir indicates, is a play that has been with him for a long time; he recalls fondly the UC Berkeley student theater production for which he contributed a score of incidental music. He tells us that, alone among the Shakespeare canon, he knows it from memory, and "from having worked, it seems, with others to weigh every word of it" (218): "no other experience of theater," he maintains, "has made a greater lasting impression" upon him. Working on a theatrical production, moreover, "creates a sheer familiarity with it that exceeds the knowledge gleaned in customary exposure to other objects of literary study" (217).

In particular, the play's language becomes deeply, resonantly *present*: "each line can be delivered then and there, and responded to then and there." It is not surprising, then, that the critical essay on *King Lear* he was to compose twenty years later, "Cavell's magic looking glass onto Shakespeare," in Gerald Bruns's words,[30] exhibits this thoroughgoing intimacy with its words and their possible projections or orientations in the course of investigating the play's peculiar investments, for characters and spectator/readers alike, in presentness.

The argument of the "The Avoidance of Love: A Reading of *King Lear*" clusters around three foci: (1) a meditation on character in tragic drama, which includes the bodily tropes of seeing and being unseen that pervade Shakespeare's text; (2) the blindness lodged in critical insight that fails to account for the thematic implications of such motifs; and (3) the status (function) of an audience at a performance of *King Lear*. The inquiry makes implicit common cause with Aristotle's *Poetics* since both it and Cavell's essay concern themselves with delimiting formal elements of *mythos*, *ethos*, *protagonistes*, *mimesis*, *catharsis*, and *anagnorisis*. As regards the first focus, Cavell explains,

> My purpose is not to urge that in reading Shakespeare's plays one put words back into the characters speaking them, and replace characters back from our possession back into their words. The point is rather to learn something about what prevents these commendable activities from taking place. (41)

One key word here, of course, is "reading," for this inquiry about character and utterance obviously presumes that the text of King Lear corresponds to "the book-in-hand," a function of "literary experience." The "learning something" that happens on the plane of reading—anybody's thoughtful and exposed reading, that is—correlates in turn with the second focus, literary critics' underreading of the particular theme that Cavell's analysis of Shakespeare's play brings out in the first half of his essay, an avoidance or failed recognition that he insists directly follows from the play's own internal dynamic of resisted presence and shame.

Criticism, Cavell says, naturally traffics in immodesty and melodrama (82), a claim with which one imagines many literary critics, from Richard Poirier to Peter Brooks, J. Hillis Miller to Eve Sedgwick, Harry Berger to Stephen Greenblatt, would concur. For Cavell, however, this represents a philosophical problem, as indeed, does the tragedy of *King Lear* itself. The agency of characters inside the play and the lines they speak, shares with critics' pronouncements outside the play a common all-too-human tendency for fantasies of privacy and the risks of shame (Cavell calls these "exhilaration" and "shame" in the economy of gain and loss specific to criticism).

The brand of critical consciousness that Cavell advocates, conversely, is called "philosophical criticism," which "can be thought of as the world of a particular work brought to consciousness of itself" (84). This, then, "the progress from ignorance to exposure," brings us to the third focus, which for my purposes, overshadows the other two, both of which (albeit for different reasons), verge on disembodiment: the characters because they are too far "inside" a work, the epistemologically self-assured (immodest and melodramatic) critic because he or she is *too* far removed from the work's transferential properties and possibilities.[31]

The essay's transition to this third focus is encapsulated in this sentence: "The medium is one which keeps all significance continuously before our senses, so that when it comes over us that we have missed it, this discovery will reveal our ignorance to have been willful, complicitous, a refusal to see" (85). By "medium," Cavell now moves what he has been calling the work (an object of reading) into the realm of its dramatization and performance. Thus, a few pages later,

> Kant tells us that man lives in two worlds, in one of which he is free and in the
> other determined. It is as if in a theater these two worlds are faced off against
> one another, in their intimacy and their mutual inaccessibility. The audience is
> free—of the circumstance and passion of the characters, but that freedom cannot
> reach the arena in which it could become effective. The actors are determined—
> not because their words and actions are dictated and their future sealed, but
> because, if the dramatist has really peopled a world, the characters are exercising
> all the freedom at their command, and specifically failing to. They are, in a word,
> men and women; and our liabilities in responding to them are nothing other than
> our liabilities in responding to any person—rejection, brutality, sentimentality,
> indifference, the relief and the terror in finding courage, the ironies of human
> wishes. (88–89)

This is not a passage, so far as I know, that has received much play from Cavell's commentators, and yet it surely represents one of his profoundest, and transparent, pieces of prose. Tragedy—its torsions, denials, resistances—is not just enacted on a stage; rather, it leaks out past the proscenium into the scene of viewing and reading, the stage of our actions as observers. This tragic play by Shakespeare, at least, solicits a particular "mode of perception" from its viewers (and readers); that is to say, *King Lear* makes exceptional—but not unnatural—demands.

Thus, Cavell anticipates the obvious objection, which he mimics perfectly: "You forget that this is theater; that they are characters up there, not persons; that their existence is fictional; that it is not up to us to confront them morally, actually enter their lives" (90). But we are already confronted by them, is the substance of Cavell's rejoinder, which makes the difference between "character" and "person" recede accordingly. And we are already confronting them, he says, "unless my head or heart is lowered, in fear or boredom" (90). We just cannot "offer" or "share" our presence and/ or intervention.

"Continuous presentness" is the name Cavell gives to the peculiar conditions he isolates for the layered temporal space of performed play and immobilized, silenced— yet nevertheless, *moved*—viewer. It is at this moment in his analysis that Cavell introduces the problem of skepticism, whose definition, very significantly he restricts as follows:

. . . we think skepticism must mean that we cannot know the world exists, and hence that perhaps there isn't one (a conclusion some profess to admire and other to fear). Whereas what skepticism suggests is that since we cannot know the world exists, its presentness to us cannot be a function of knowing. The world is to be *accepted*; as the presentness of other minds is not to be known, but acknowledged. (95)

Shakespeare's *King Lear*, in Cavell's reading, more than thematizes the "plot" of overcoming knowledge. It enacts it. More precisely, author and text exploit the conditions of viewing or witnessing to which the architectural and social space of theater lends itself. It thus opens a world for us in a very particular way.[32] The question, "what is a theater?" asked aloud by Cavell in his essay, lies at its heart, just as its sibling question, "what is a cinema" drives the reflections on the ontology of film in *The World Viewed* (and if we delete the indefinite articles before both nouns, then the subtly altered inquiry, what are theater and cinema, becomes equally relevant for Cavell, and his readers.

Thus, film, as expressed in "More of the World Viewed," Cavell's 1979 postscript to *The World Viewed*, "is a moving image of skepticism" (188). Colin Davis is correct to note the double meaning here (as in Sebald earlier): the machinery of cinema is propelled by images set in motion, but those images also possess affective capacity—we are *moved* by them. I would add that we are moved—oriented—also epistemologically. Movies are like skepticism because both involve *projections* of reality that we have not authored ourselves but manipulate us all the same, a darker implication of the machinery of *Pledge, Turn, Prestige*.[33]

The other side of the coin is that film enables us to *view* that projection at work and consequently to step away from it in order to arrive at empirical, participatory acknowledgments *in the world*. Cavell's 2010 memoir fulfills the first sentence of *The World Viewed*: "Memories of movies are strand over strand with memories of my life" (xix), for anecdotes about filmgoing in Sacramento, New York, Berkeley, Los Angeles, about moving pictures and being moved by pictures, fill its pages.[34]

In a fine statement of the problematic he has tracked through a number of books, Cavell says there, "film brings an unprecedented, if not unanticipated, medium into play that questions the switchpoint between public and private. This makes the medium of film inherently philosophical" (204). That assertion does not differentiate among comedy, melodrama, or suspense (genre categories Cavell's writings on film specifically address), so Cavell is staking a fairly large claim here about the medium itself, the way it shows philosophy to be the "invisible accompaniment of the ordinary lives that film is so apt to capture" (6) as he puts it in *Cities of Words*. What does the term "medium" mean, exactly? The work as materialized on spools of film stock (or flash drives and DVDs, for that matter)? Or the work as materialized before spectators in a darkened theater? Cavell covers both bases in *The World Viewed*, so "viewed" may at times signify "as captured (rendered) on film," and at other times, "shown, exhibited, viewed, that, is by *us*."

King Lear's relevance for Cavell, along with other plays by Shakespeare or Beckett's *Endgame* and Ibsen's *A Doll's House*,[35] suggests a similar slippage, since the first half of it treats formal particulars in the text of the play and the second, the drama's reception by literary critics and theatrical audience. But in the main, "The Avoidance of Love" appears to consolidate a slightly more restrictive claim about Shakespeare's tragic drama as formally linked to the conditions of its presentation in a theater. Genre and medium here mutually illuminate another.

It matters that Cavell will coin the term "genre-as-medium" to articulate what he especially identifies in cinema as one of its defining properties. In fact, in the 1982 essay "The Fact of Television," Cavell spends what he calls "a few dozen paragraphs" explaining his idiosyncratic nesting of the concepts "genre" and "medium" in the composite formulation: "I wish to preserve, and make more explicit—or curious— this double range in order to keep open to investigation the relation between work and medium that I call the revelation, or acknowledgement, of the one in the other" (80).[36]

Here it become quite evident that Cavell means the form of the medium over and above the circumstances whereby it is witnessed, taken in. The tension between these things is one of the aspects of Cavell's early book on film that I wish particularly to "shepherd." But let us for the moment restrict ourselves to the essay on *King Lear*, before we turn to *The World Viewed*, because as different as photography is from painting or film from television for Cavell in that book—all of these arts being poised at the moment of modernism—so do modern cinema and Renaissance theater necessarily and revealingly diverge as artistic media that respectively screen or stage our attunements or misattunements to world, to words, and to each other.

Cavell conducts an excursus on the instructive "case of the [southern] yokel" who goes up on stage to save Desdemona from Othello's strangulating black hands[37]; he also reflects on the difference between Desdemona death and the eighteenth-century tragedienne Sarah Siddon's mimesis of it. Both examples serve as a prompt for considering not only the social conventionality of our presence in a theater but also the larger question of what "witnessing" or "being present" in a theater fundamentally mean.

In previous work, I briefly compare Cavell's account of the southern yokel's ostensibly deluded intervention with Bakhtin's *aesthetic* critique: "the spectator loses his place outside and over against the imaged life of the dramatic personae" (73). But for Cavell—especially since earlier in the essay, he troubles the aesthetic by pointedly resisting its being equated to "a context in which I am to do nothing" (91)—the problem is both philosophical and descriptive, the question, multiple: why are we there? why do I sit there? what, if anything, do I do? Like Bakhtin, Cavell, contests the notion that I merge somehow with the characters in a play or film, that, indeed, these media instruct us in identification and impersonation. If I happened to find myself in Othello's position or as Othello, nevertheless "I would still not know what possibility I am to envision as presented by this play" (102).

Rather, the philosophical *and* descriptive answer to all the questions above is to be found in the peculiar conditions of *King Lear* as *staged* in front of its audience—its listener-spectators. One's presence before characters acting out various denials or failures of recognition *names a problem*—something already designated for us under the rubrics of *tact* and *proximity*:

> The trouble is that we no more merely see these characters than we merely see people involved elsewhere in our lives—or, if we do merely see them, that shows a specific response to the claim they make upon me, a specific form of acknowledgement; for example, rejection. . . . The plain fact, the only plain fact, is that we do not *go up* to them, even that we cannot. (102)

In Cavell's syntax of choices with which the "grammatical entity" of a fictional character presents us, we do not simply register their presence, nor can we properly be said to "be in" their presence (we are unseen and unheard by them). Rather, characters in front of an audience of theatergoers (or behind or alongside it, depending on the ingenuity of a given production) are *in their presence*. That is to say, our presence in a theater, our being present there, both enacts a certain kind acknowledgment of/for the characters up on stage, and "shows what acknowledgement in actuality is" (103)—which may well mean teaching us about the acknowledging acts we routinely underperform in real life when we do not put ourselves in the presence of others or "reveal ourselves to them." Cavell's logic here is acute:

> The conditions of theater literalize [I might say, "materialize" or "embody"] the conditions we take for existence outside—hiddenness, silence, isolation—hence make that existence plain. Theater does not expect us to stop theatricalizing; it knows that we can theatricalize its conventions as we can theatricalize any others. But in giving us a place within which our hiddenness and silence and separation are accounted for, it gives us a chance to stop. (104)

An analytical problem remains, and Cavell is too meticulous to ignore it. "Then what expresses acknowledgment in a theater? What plays the role there that revealing ourselves plays outside?" (105)? In *Narrative Ethics*, I entertained the tantalizing remarks Cavell then introduces about possibly theorizable congruencies and disjunctions between literary genres, in particular between dramaturgy and narrative discourse. After all, readers of novels—and readers of *King Lear*, for that matter—may also be described as hidden, silent, and isolated. Moreover, they can no more "approach" a novelistic character than they can those in performances of tragic drama because "they and we do not occupy the same space; there is no path from my location to his" (105). I feel now, however, that I was thereby loosening Cavell's very strict account of theatrical conditions and "acknowledgment in a theater."

The analytical gain, of course, is that, not only "there they are" (on stage) as Cavell says of those characters in *King Lear*, but *so are we*—in front of them, in the audience.

In other words, we must answer for our presence in the particular space of a theater. We do that by accounting for theirs. Cavell answers his own question about the form acknowledgment there by distinguishing between the structural/imaginative inability to put oneself in the *presence* of fictional characters (or share their space) and the ethical[38] capacity to *make them present* by assuming the burden of their present.

This signifies the fact that they cannot foresee their own ends, and that what happens to them in one's own presence, from one's seat in the audience, is coeval with what is happening to them at that moment.[39] "Catharsis, if that is the question, is a matter of purging attachment from everything but the present, from pity for the past and terror of the future" (109). What is left is only the acknowledgment of separation, which the characters accomplish in isolation and the theatergoers perform in each other's company.

Concomitantly, to the question left hanging, "why am I there?" Cavell answers, "The point of my presence at these events is to join in confirming this separateness" (109). To the question, "why do I do nothing," he answers bluntly,

> . . . if I do nothing because there is nothing to do, where that means that I have given over the time and space in which action is mine and consequently that I am in awe before the fact that I cannot do and suffer what is another's to do and suffer, then I confirm the final fact of our separateness. And that is the unity of our condition. The only essential difference between them and me is that they are there and I am not. And to empty ourselves of all other differences can be confirmed in the presence of an audience, of the community, because every difference established between us, other than separateness, is established by the community—that is, by us—in obedience to the community. It is by responding to his knowledge that the community keeps itself in touch with nature. (110)

This last point offers a crossing point between tragedy and comedy; but even there, "Join hands as we may, one of the hands is mine and the other is yours." Or as we have had it framed for us previously: touch as tact never gets us close enough.

And when we leave the theater? When we become theater-leavers, or theater-goers in the opposite direction, after joining temporarily in the ritual of attendence? "At the close of these successions, we are still in a present: it is another crossroads. . . . Because the actors have stopped, we are freed to act again; but also compelled to. Our hiddenness, our silence, and our placement are now our choices" (113–114). In the coda to the essay, Cavell leaves the theater, too, and reflects upon tragedy as an ongoing national and political event; or, rather, he makes these thematically intrinsic dimensions of it contemporary.

America, Cavell writes sadly, has "become tragic." By 1967, the essay's date of completion (it was begun in 1966, following "Knowing and Acknowledging"), the assassinations of Robert Kennedy and Martin Luther King Jr., the My Lai massacre and the highest single-year number of casualties in the Vietnam War were all one year away, the cessation of US involvement was still six years away. As tragic as the national landscape was then appearing to Cavell—"it is killing itself and killing another country in order not to admit its helplessness in the face of suffering, in order not to acknowledge its separateness" (116)—calamity had yet to expend its full force. And yet, "Tragedy has moved into the world, and with the world has become theatrical" (115).

But what classical tragedy showed—"*why* we (its audience) are helpless"—and thus its justification, were no less relevant: "that pain and death were in our presence when we were not in theirs" (117). Instrumentally, thus,

> a purpose of tragedy remains unchanged: to make us capable of acting. It used to be that by showing us the natural limitations of action. Now its work is not to purge us of pity and terror, but to make us capable of feeling them again, and this means showing us that there is a place to act upon them. . . . One function of tragedy would show . . . that the stakes of action and inaction are what they always were . . . that at every moment there is a present passing me by and that the reason it passes me by is the old reason, that I am not present to it. In *King Lear*, we miss presentness through anticipation, we miss the present moment by sweet knowledge of moments to come or bitter knowledge of moments past. Now we miss presentness through blindness to the fact that the space and time we are in are specific, supposing our space to be infinite and our time void, losing ourselves in space, avoided by time. . . . Our tragic fact is that we find ourselves at the cause of tragedy, but without finding ourselves. (118–120)

Though mourning historical and social realities now sixty years past, these are hardly superseded reflections, if updated to September 11, 2001, and the wars in Iraq and Afghanistan; to Hurricanes Katrina and Sandy, the Gulf Coast oil spill and other environmental disasters; to the various financial debacles of national shame; to the senseless homicide sprees in an elementary school and a darkened cinema, no less. Cavell's somber reckoning of tragedy having moved into the world and the world having becoming theatrical is no less pertinent, no less acute.

CINEMAS

Having left the theater Cavell's philosophical agency was to move on by directly reentering it in its guise as movie house, at the same time as it was to (re)visit Thoreau's theatricalized cabin near Walden Pond. His philosophical criticism of seven plays by Shakespeare in *Disowning Knowledge* (including *Antony and Cleopatra* in the updated edition) attest to tragic drama's hold on Cavell's thinking, just as the reflections on the ontology of film in *The World Viewed* mostly concern that medium of cinema over and above the cinema as *place* or *environment*.[40] In the introduction to *Disowning Knowledge*, Cavell mentions *Antony and Cleopatra*, *The Winter's Tale*, and *Coriolanus* (all post–*King Lear* in the Shakespearean chronology of composition and performance) as other plays for which "the stake . . . is the state of our participation in the ceremony of theater."[41]

On the recurrent skeptical problem of "unknowableness from outside," Cavell also says in specific connection with Cleopatra's "final nested acts of theater" (291), "it is the work of this theater to present itself as an instance of the ceremonies and institutions toward which our relation is in doubt, exists in doubt, is unknowable from outside" (29)—but he seems to intend "theater" here as more medium (dramatic spectacle) than circumstance or environment.[42] The extended analysis of exposure and presentness in the text of *King Lear* as descriptive also of the special circumstances, "the *conditions* of theater"—which include an audience's presence at the play's performance—retains its singularity.

As matters of oeuvre, while "The Avoidance of Love" looks forward to the succession of essays Cavell was to write about Shakespearean tragedy and romance as well as to the genres of remarriage comedies and melodramas in 1930s and '40s Hollywood films, it is probably best classed in the immediate context of its sibling essays in *Must We Mean What We Say?*, like "Ending the Waiting Game: A Reading of Beckett's *Endgame*," "Aesthetic Problems of Modern Philosophy," and "Knowing and Acknowledging," and in company with *The World Viewed* and *Senses of Walden*, which in the new preface to *Must We Mean What We Say?* Cavell calls a "trio."

Common themes link all three, like the staging of and desire for both separation and attunement. Composed within a year of each other, *Senses* and *World* form their own recto and verso. As *Senses* seeks to understand Thoreau's memoir of dispossession that establishes the criteria for repossession, so the book on film (also a memoir), not only crafts philosophical language in a new key (much like *Walden*) but also rehearses its own story of loss—the "break" Cavell says he experienced in his "natural relation to movies"—as a preparation for repair or commemoration through voice, and the writing of the book itself (in echo again of Thoreau) as an experiment in method.

From his early work on J. L. Austin, Wittgenstein, and ordinary language philosophy to his later work on moral perfectionism and opera, the story of repossession of, or reattunement to, the world has been Cavell's archnarrative. Like Thoreau and Emerson, like Shakespeare, like the movies, Cavell populates his writing with avatars of the philosophizing self "in order to wrest the world from our possessions so that we may possess it again" (22). "The Avoidance of Love" and *The World Viewed*, through their respective media of theater and cinema, alike seek to analyze Cavell's metaphysical version of the Fall: "At some point, the unhinging of our consciousness from the world interposed our subjectivity between us and our presentness to the world. Then our subjectivity became what is present to us, individuality became isolation" (22). How theater and cinema point a way out of the impasse is Cavell's correlative philosophical task, the mechanism that springs the lock.

A digression in *The World Viewed* is devoted to Cavell's account of modernist painting (standing for all modernism), which is set up by an assertion early in the book,

"To maintain conviction in our connection with reality, to maintain our presentness, painting accepts the recession of the world" (23). Later, he expands upon that claim:

> If modernism's quest for presentness arises with the growing autonomy of art (from religious and political and class service; from altars and halls and walls), then that quest is set by the increasing nakedness of exhibition as the condition for viewing a work of art. The object itself must account for the viewer's presenting of himself to it and for the artist's authorization of his right to such attendance. (121)

Cavell's idea is that visual arts like painting and sculpture are fundamentally tied to the medium's need to make things present and artist's declaration of his own autonomy. The art of film is different, however, even surpassing photography's particular commerce with theatricality.[43]

> Media based upon successions of automatic world projections do not, for example, have to establish presentness to and of the world: the world is there. They do not have to deny or confront their audiences: they are screened. And they do not have to defeat or declare the artist's presence: the object was always out of his hands. (118)

Cinema manages, almost magically, to overcome the interposition of subjectivity. "How do movies reproduce the world magically? Not by literally presenting us with the world, but by permitting us to view it unseen" (40).[44] Film and photography thus release us—as if we no longer had to worry ontologically about holding anything in our hands or looking through peepholes. Lear's predicament, if it were filmed (screened and projected), is not something we need worry about failing to acknowledge; for the medium *itself* exempts us.

> Film takes our very distance and powerlessness over the world as the condition of the world's natural appearance. It promises the exhibition of the world in itself. This is its promise of candor: that what it reveals is entirely what is revealed to it, that nothing revealed by the world in its presence is lost. (119)[45]

And yet, while it does not exactly offer us "a place to stop" our fantasies, as Cavell attributes to theater, cinema nonetheless also holds us captive, just as "the camera holds the last lanyard of control we would forgo" (119); movies house and place us in their own—one must say—theatrical and theatricalizing, way. Film and photography's philosophical hold on Cavell presents him with the paradox of spectators' excision from the screened and projected world of reality and their desires and fantasies for it, while still being located *somewhere*, in front of it: each "maintains the presentness of the world by accepting our absence from it . . . and a world I know, and see, but to which I am nevertheless not present (through no fault of my subjectivity), is a world past" (23).[46]

Unlike theater where presence may be interrupted but still preserved, where character and actor are decidedly separate, where individuals rather than types and "individualities" prevail, by the specific nature of the film medium (its *automatism*), "movies allow the audience to be mechanically absent" (25). "In viewing a movie my helplessness is mechanically assured" (26),[47] a paradox that sits at the core of *The World Viewed*. The book, like "The Avoidance of Love," meditates on the metaphysical deficits in presence and presentness incurred through the experience of cinema, to be somehow *philosophically* made up: "Philosophy simply puts everything before us, nor deduces anything—since everything lies open to view there is nothing to explain."[48]

Movies resemble philosophy if we allow that they also put things before us, where everything is open to view. And yet they bespeak a deep mystery (or "strangeness," as Cavell expresses it in "What Photography Calls Thinking") about our relationship to them—what we want from them, and consequently what they can do for us: "The idea of and wish for the world re-created in its own image was satisfied at last by cinema" (39).[49] *This* is their ethics of reading us—their "thoughtfulness"[50] about themselves—and our ethical challenge in reading them.

Accordingly, I especially favor Cavell's notion of philosophy as a "responsiveness, of not speaking first."[51] In common with theater, the metaphysics and ontology of the medium educate us about our routine, everyday encounter with epistemological projection and displacement, about screening and separation *in actuality*. As an internal or self-reflexive dimension of art, acknowledgment means that certain films have the capacity to reveal the medium, to tell us something about what cinema *does*, how it *works*.

But unlike the *Lear* essay, the film book often wears the privacy of both its rhetoric and the experiences for which it seeks an account on its sleeve. It commences by announcing mournfully—a side-shadowing of Thoreau—that Cavell's original (or natural) relationship to movies is now broken, and part of what it signified was "companionship": "The audience of a book is essentially solitary, one soul at a time; the audience of music and theater is essentially larger than your immediate acquaintance—a gathering of the city; the crowd at a movie comprises various pools of companions, or scattered souls with someone missing" (10).

During the many years when Cavell was a devoted moviegoer, as he documents from time to time in his memoir, *Little Did I Know*, "When moviegoing was casual and we entered at no matter what point in the proceedings . . . we took our fantasies and companions and anonymity inside and left with them intact" (11).[52] Nowadays, when the conditions of moviegoing have changed (and it should be borne in mind that *The World Viewed* was written at least two decades before *Netflix* and the multiplexe became the fashion), "the old casualness of moviegoing has been replaced by a casualness of movieviewing, which I interpret as an inability to tolerate our own fantasies, let alone those of others—an attitude that equally I cannot share" (11).

Cavell's point seems to be that whereas these days, movie showtimes are scheduled "as at a play," back then, collective arrival and departure at the same time did not comport with the looser aggregate nature of screenings (news, short subject, multiple features). This seems, however, to reflect a highly selective take on the social history of moviegoing, which, in its philosophical investments, risks a set of claims that are not so easily generalized across divisions of class, region, and even country (claims that do, however, chime with the tenor of lament by film historians and critics in the decades after the publication of *The World Viewed* bemoaning the decline of the industry[53]). More immediately, though, it is just not clear how to read the tone in this and other such melancholy judgments about new movieviewing vs. old moviegoing; the memoir's brief mentions of films and theaters, for example, do not sound a comparable note.

What exactly is the relationship between an increased philosophical impatience with "an audience" because of which "a claim is made upon my privacy" now (such that I am forced to renounce it), on one hand, and nostalgia for the days of one's own by-gone filmgoing, on the other? At any rate, sentiments like, "I feel I am present at a cult whose members have nothing in common but their presence in the same place" (which makes moviegoing uncomfortably resemble pornography), autobiographically step away from the book's philosophical concerns and risk isolating Cavell within an elected privacy that would still seem to demand accounting for.

Critiques of Cavell's book, even when they get it more or less right, tend to focus either on its analyses of image, resemblance, the "automatism" of photograph and moving picture, the account of modernist painting, or on the subsidiary importance in it of ideological elements like race.[54] But for the most part, they tend to let stand these inaugural claims about audience and Cavell's perfectionist nostalgia, his Fitzgerald-like threnody for his lost city of the movies.[55] He expresses candor about the anxiety prompted by "new audiences" for movies, "as though I cannot locate or remain together with my companions among them" (11). Of all the gnomic or crystalline sentences in *The World Viewed*, I find these among the most moving—and most unnerving. And so some time is spent on them later on.

But for the moment, Cavell's claim about the different audiences for different kinds of art, and the old and new audiences for cinema, needs to be read alongside the very last footnote (in the first edition) to a sentence in the final pages of the concluding chapter, "The Acknowledgment of Silence" about film's "absolute freedom of narrative" (156) as also "the knowledge which makes acceptable film's absolute control of our attention" (157). Here is that footnote:

> Music also exercises an absolute control of our attention; it justifies this by continuously rewarding it. Painting allows attention an absolute freedom; nothing will happen that is not before your eyes. The novel can neither command absolute control nor afford absolute freedom; it operates in the weave between them, as lives do. Its permanent responsibility is to the act of conversing with us. (174)[56]

The proposed polarity between novels and cinema, I suspect, is reversible, since Cavell does not philosophize much in his work about the novel, as other philosophers and scholars of the genre do.[57] If film neither delimits nor prelimits human experience across the "wide screen" of its range, the novel's ethic, we are told by Kundera and Bakhtin alike, does likewise through its commitment to heteroglossia and to "what only the novel can discover."[58]

But, the purported difference between the world narrated and the world viewed is less significant to me that the intensely private history Cavell implies here about his own experience of moviegoing: "movies, unless they are masterpieces, are not there as they were . . . . If you see them now for the first time, you may be interested and moved, but you can't know what I know" (10). This assertion of singularity is not quite theatrical, but it certainly verges on it; here, criticism does approach the stuff of immodesty and melodrama. Consider, by contrast, "There are perhaps no days of our childhood we lived so fully as those we believe we left without having lived them, those we spent with a favorite book." This is Proust at the beginning of his elegiac preface to Ruskin, "On Reading," quoted previously in this book's introduction as a commentary on Levinas's notion that books constitute "a modality of our being."

Even if we neither write prose nor preside over an extraordinary discourse about the ordinary like Stanley Cavell's or Marcel Proust's (or Emmanuel Levinas's, for that matter), many of us lay claim to personal histories, narratable or not, rooted in the book-reading and moviegoing of our youth and adolescence. Moreover, many of us are still able to have the sort of experience in a movie theater evoked in the following passage from Walker Percy's *The Moviegoer* about seeing one's own familiar environs captured in a film:

> Afterwards in the street, she looks around the neighborhood. "Yes it is certified now." She refers to a phenomenon of moviegoing which I have called certification. Nowadays when a person lives somewhere, in a neighborhood, the place is not certified for him. More than likely he will live there sadly and the emptiness which is inside him will expand until it evacuates the entire neighborhood. But if he sees a movie which shows his very neighborhood, it becomes possible for him to live, for a time at least, as a person who is Somewhere and not Anywhere.[59]

Compare this now to a key passage from Cavell's appended chapter, "More of *The World Viewed*":

> But obviously [reality] is not actually present to us either (anyway, obviously not present with us) when it appears to us on the screen. So I was led to consider that what makes the physical medium of film unlike anything else on earth lies in the absence of what it causes to appear to us; that is to say, in the nature of our absence from it; in its fate to reveal reality and fantasy (not by reality as such, but) by projections of reality, projections in which, as I had occasion to put it, reality is freed to exhibit itself—I cannot say that I was entirely surprised to find that my emphasis on reality has caused a certain amount of unhappiness among readers of my book. (166)

The speaker in Percy's novel is its narrator, Jack "Binx" Bolling, ironic, detached, skeptical, a spectator-observer of life, who, not surprisingly, likes to attend movies. At one point in the novel, set in New Orleans, Bolling notices William Holden coming out of Pirate's alley. A young, couple notices him too, and the narrator is unflinching about what such an encounter between a seemingly unhappy ordinary people and a certified star really means: "the boy can only contrast Holden's resplendent reality with his own shadowy and precarious existence" (16). Holden is offered a match, and for a moment, redemptive film-star magic smiles upon the briefly fortunate couple: "The boy has done it! He has won title to his own existence, as plenary an existence now as Holden's" (16). As for Bolling the narrator, he characterizes himself to us elsewhere as "keep[ing] a Gregory Peckish sort of distance" (68, 70, 71).

Although he is middle-aged, his mordancy recalls another hero of mid-century existentialist American fiction who, by sheer coincidence, happens to share "Holden's" name. J. D. Salinger's Holden Caulfield, as he informs us on the first page of *Catcher in the Rye,* has little use for film: "If there's one thing I hate, it's the movies. Don't even mention them to me." Binx Bolling, by contrast and like Cavell, goes to movies regularly and happily—though he is less tempted to give himself over to the viewing or the views than Cavell. Yet, he also tells us that while other people may remember climbing the Parthenon at sunrise or meeting a girl in Central Park, what he remembers is John Wayne dispatching three gunmen in *Stagecoach* or Orson Welles picking up a kitten in *The Third Man*. Obviously, memories of the movies are interwoven strand over strand with *his* life, too.

So far as I know, Cavell never mentions these fictional moviegoers in his writing on film. Both possessed of ironic temperaments (the one more susceptible to film's power than the other, however), these two literary characters position Cavell's own moviegoing in an intriguing light: not just his wiling suspension of disbelief but his willingness to be taught by what he sees. What makes Cavell such an exceptionalist moviegoer, I wonder, so full of rue for its lost magic? How does his analysis of the screen interposed by subjectivity between self and world reflect back onto his own subjectively conditioned experience of moviegoing—in Atlanta, in Manhattan, in Berkeley, in Cambridge, and in Jerusalem?

In "More of *The World Viewed*," Cavell tellingly refracts that experience through a self-admitted inward turn of voice:

> Whereas in writing about film I felt called upon to voice my responses with their privacy, their argumentativeness, even their intellectual perverseness, on their face; often to avoid voicing a thought awaiting its voice, to refuse that thought, to break into the thought, as if our standing responses to film are themselves standing between us and the responses that film is made to elicit and to satisfy. (163)

The large and defining difference between the essay on *Lear* (with its "hope for conviction from the reader," as Cavell confides), and the book on film lies, I think, in the open representativeness of the one—its repeated reference to the divide between the play's characters and *us*—and the coded particularism of the other. "I want words to happen to me," Cavell says in *The World Viewed*, using the representative first person; "my saying of them makes their meaning private" (127). This does not, however, mean that Cavell the author's reflections on film are either hermetic or unshareable.

Here, I concur with Timothy Gould's reservations about William Rothman's imputation of a wholly idiosyncratic voice to Cavell whose instructive point, then, just *is* its idiosyncrasy: "This uniqueness of Cavell's voice is taken to constitute the uniqueness of Cavell's contribution to philosophy."[60] *The World Viewed* is often labored and opaque. Certainly, some of the "obscure promptings" to which Cavell confesses in his preface remain obscure when one closes the book.[61] To that degree, Cavell preserves some of the mystery of the medium, which he—and it, of course—so powerfully acknowledge. But however stylized, the Cavellian lyricisms and sinuous sentence shapes do not in the end contrive to conceal a learnable method of understanding which amounts to the book's intended scene of instruction.

No, what remains highly personal in his "metaphysical memoir"—unsayably so, it appears—is not Cavell's experience of a film but rather his individual experience of going to the movies, as one member of the "crowd [that] comprises various pools of companions, or scattered souls with someone missing." It appears from the book's preface that Cavell was not to be found among the latter, since he says there that not only are "memories of movies strand over strand with memories of my life" (xi), but that his "experiences [of films] are lined with conversations and responses of friends I have gone to the movies with" (9)—rather like, say, Binx Bolling in the passage quoted above, who brings his fiancée Kate to a showing of *Panic in the Streets* where they see projected the New Orleans neighborhood where the movie theater in which they now sit is located. In any event, one is tempted, even licensed, I think, to infer that "companions" (the chapter is titled "An Autobiography of Companions") includes both the actors on the screen and the onlookers watching them—in proximity.[62]

In "The Fact of Television," distinguishing between the "succession of automatic world projections" he identifies as the defining feature of cinema over against television's technology of "monitoring,"[63] Cavell throws something of an incomplete pass:

> Of course, no one would claim that the experience of a movie is just the same run on television as projected on a screen, and everyone will have some informal theory or other about what the difference consists in—that the television image is smaller, that the room is not otherwise dark, that there is no proper audience, hence that the image is inherently less gripping, and so on. But how much difference do such differences make? A difference, sufficient to give us to think, between the medium of film and that of video is that, in running a film on television, the television set is (interpretable as) a moviola; though unlike a moviola, a monitor may be of as a device for a film without it. A way to begin characterizing the difference, accord-

ingly, is that the experience of a film on television is as of something over whose running you have in principle a control; you are not subjected to it, as you are by film itself or television itself. (93)

Screens many times the size of a human, darkness, an audience of strangers who gaze is fixed upon the same object, that object's capacity to *grip* its viewers: these are some of the conditions Cavell lists for the experience of watching a film. Unlike theaters, "movies do not have to deny or confront their audiences; they are screened" (118). This is not to deny or to fail to confront movies' own special mode of theatricality, the fact that projection or screening of the world inescapably *dramatize* it.

And yet, whether physically present to it in the space of a theater or as a pure function of its special technology,

> We are at the mercy of what the medium captures of us, and of what it chooses, or refuses, to hold for us. This comedy of self-reference satirizes the effort to escape the self by viewing it, the thought that there is a position from which to rest assured once and for all of the truth of your views. (126)

Think of the final shot of Fellini's *Le notti di Cabiria* when a tearful but spontaneously gladdened Giuletta Masina fixes her gaze for an instant directly on the camera and at us, or the famous freeze-frame and zoom shot of Antoine Doinel's (photographed) face that ends Truffaut's *Les quatre cents coups: we* are the ones seen, the *Prestige*—but also the snare—of reenchantment. But Cavell's examples here are all drawn from film comedians, among them the Marx Brothers, W. C. Fields, and Buster Keaton, but most radically, from Ole Olsen and Chic Johnson's *Hellzapoppin'* (1941), which Cavell recalls as

> a moment in which either Olsen or Johnson, finding himself caught, as it were, by an off-sprocket film alignment (the frame separation dividing the top and bottom halves of the screen), hoists himself over the frame separation to rest wholly within the upper half of the screen. (125)[64]

What species of acknowledgment transpires by means of film, and what acknowledgment is asked from its viewers? Or as Cavell puts it, "what is it the movie's turn to acknowledge?"

> Knowing your claim to an acknowledgment from me, I may be baffled by the demand you make for some special voicing of the acknowledgment. Any word of mine should amply make my presence known to you. The experience is not uncommon: I know I am here; you know I am here; you know that I know I owe you the acknowledgment. Why isn't that enough? Why am I called upon to do something, to say specific things that will add up to an explicit revelation? Because what is to be acknowledged is always something specifically done or not done; the exact instance of my denial of you. The particular hurt or crudity or selfishness or

needfulness or hatred or longing that separates us must be given leave to declare
our separateness, hence the possibility of our connection. It is balm, but it must
still touch the wound. (128)

Cavell makes this observation in a chapter about the camera, which in some way not
merely by trick of self-reference must now (that is, at a cultural moment subsequent to
features of the medium that movies in their youthfulness could simply take for
granted), make its presence known, and thereby declare something about what it
captures on film: not "merely declare itself [but] at least give the illusion of saying
something" (129). As he then declares in crescendo, "The questions and concepts I
have been led to admit in the course of my remarks all prepare for an idea that the
camera must now, in candor, acknowledge not its being present in the world but its
being outside its world" (130).

Cavellian outsideness is not quite Bakhtinian outsideness. The latter enables aesthetic consummation and ethical agency; from it, is derived the "excess of seeing"
which is the very "gift of otherness." Nor does Cavellian outsideness exactly correspond to Levinasian exteriority. "To have an outside. To listen to what comes from
outside": Levinas calls this the "miracle of exteriority," a state of being *outside the subject*, separate but therefore ethically available. "The camera is outside its subject as
I am outside my language" (127), says Cavell. But these are both ontological conditions, "conditions of candor," enabling facts of autonomy and separateness, rather
than limiting deficiencies. Cameras and speakers necessarily stand apart from what they
film or express but that does not mean either is structurally alienated or the source of
untruth; neither, in Cavell's terms, is "metaphysically dishonest."

In the book's final chapter, Cavell offers a final restatement of these propositions—
that film "must acknowledge, what is always to be acknowledged, its own limits: in
this case, its outsideness to its world, and my absence from it. For these limits were
always the conditions of its candor, of its fate to reveal all and only what is revealed to
it, and of its fortune in letting the world exhibit itself" (146).

But the propositions being summarized here are also glossed by Cavell in a mourn-
ful first-person passage that echoes his lament for the natural relation with films and
filmgoing now broken; but here, it appears, intended as specific to late-modern film
technique, a change (modernism, finally?) that has overcome cinema in the 1960s:

The world's presence to me is no longer assured by my mechanical absence from it,
for the screen no longer naturally holds a coherent world from which I am absent. I
feel the screen has darkened, as if in fury at its lost power to enclose its content. . . .
I have described this loss of connection, this loss of conviction in the film's
capacity to carry the world's presence as a new theatricalizing of its images,
another exhibiting of them, another replacement of the intensity of mystery with
the intensity of mechanism. I have also suggested that this in turn was a response
to the draining from the original myths of film of their power to hold our convic-

tion in film's characters. The conventions upon which film relied have come to seem conspiracies: close-up, which used to admit the mysteriousness of the human face, now winks a penny-ante explanation at us. (131)

It will be recalled that in the opening chapter of *The World Viewed*, Cavell expresses a very similar nostalgia and regret, but in specific relation *to the audience:* "the old casualness of moviegoing has been replaced by a casualness of movieviewing, which I interpret as an inability to tolerate our own fantasies, let alone those of others—an attitude that equally I cannot share." (A new tactlessness, so to speak.)

It will also be recalled that in "The Avoidance of Love," contrariwise, collective human presence before the stage held redemptive potential: "The audience is free—of the circumstance and passion of the characters, but that freedom cannot reach the arena in which it could become effective." The purging of human differences, Cavell insisted there, can be confirmed only "in the presence of an audience, of the community, because every difference established between us, other than separateness, is established by the community—that is, by us—in obedience to the community."

The basic text of *King Lear*, from its first performance on December 26, 1606, and excluding the 150-year run of Nahum Tate's 1681 de-tragedified version endorsed by Samuel Johnson, through Victorian and ever more modern and ingenious restagings, has remained more or less the same; likewise, the same acts of acknowledgment as illuminated by Cavell's reading have been summoned of its audience, if sometimes only implicitly, throughout the play's now four-century-long stage history.

By contrast, within sixty years of their inception as an art and industry, "traditional" movies have suffered alteration and so has their audience: a loss of conviction, a draining of their mythic power to hold *our* conviction. In both cases, a complicity or complicitousness, between medium and its possibilities, and between medium and witnessed presentation or (exhibition), prevails. Cinema, however—the technology of animated images of the human—is exceptionalized by Cavell, in its belated modernist moment, for a kind of ontological decline or *coup de mal.*

He rehearses again the difference between theater and movie house in the appended "More of *The World Viewed.*" Human beings are "fictionalized," molded, by film because of the nature of the medium itself, whose mode therefore, Cavell says, "is more closely bound to the mythological than the fictional" (210):

> My formal reasons for this intuition revolve around my obsession with the particular
> mode of presence of the figures on the screen and the particular mode of absence
> from them of their audience. I speak of "a world past," and the idea of pastness
> threads through my books, as does the idea of presentness and of futurity. (210)

In theater, the time is always now, even if spectators and characters inhabit different spaces. I am present there, Cavell says, at something that is happening. With film, contrariwise, "I am present . . . at something that has happened" (26, 210).

Furthermore, "I relate that idea most immediately to my passiveness before the exhibition of the world, to the fascination, the uncanniness, in this chance to view the manifestation of the world as a whole" (212). Cavell will speak not only of the fictional, or more accurately mythological, modality of the world viewed but also of the "contingency" of the viewed absent from the filmed world s/he views on screen and the "anarchism . . . contained in the condition of viewing unseen" (215). All this, Cavell says in the concluding paragraph of his book, is something film affirms as the state of its viewers' immortality—"a world complete without me which is present to me" but therefore also one in which "the present judgment upon me is not yet the last" (160).

To view the world is also somehow to "haunt" it. Therein lies film's philosophy, which Cavell ties directly to Kant's, Hegel's, and Nietzsche's toward the end of the supplementary chapter (although he leaves them unnamed). "The myth of film is that nature survives our treatment of it and its loss of enchantment for us, and that community remains possible even when the authority of society is denied us" (214).[65] What I do not understand about this profound articulation of cinema's ontological mystery and strangeness, however, is where it leaves the empirical film audience in the event of its collectivity.[66] For Cavell's book ends as it begins, on a hushed note of privacy and singularity. As problems of tact and ethical proximity—or more prosaically, as the problem of reading—how does the embodied experience of watching a movie then compare, if I have understood him correctly, to Cavell's searching (and searing) account of the assembled witnesses at a stage production of *King Lear*? That is the question with which I wrestle in the next and concluding section.

AN AUTOBIOGRAPHY OF COMPANIONS

At the beginning of this chapter, I call attention to the physical spaces of theater or moviehouse by referencing a relatively arcane and admittedly incongruous architectural feature of the Holy Temple in Jerusalem, first built by Solomon in 957 BCE and reconstructed under the authority of Cyrus in 538 BCE. Cavell's professional connection to that same city in its modern avatar consists of study group and lecture appearances in 1986 (published as part of the edited collection *Languages of the Unsayable: The Play of Negativity in Literature and Literary Theory*, and subsequently, early versions of his Carus Lectures that in published form became the book, *Conditions Handsome and Unhandsome: The Constitution of Emersonian Perfectionism*), and lectures given at Hebrew University in 1992 that became *A Pitch of Philosophy: Autobiographical Exercises*.

In his preface to the latter, Cavell recounts filmgoing experiences at the Jerusalem *Cinematheque*, and in the final essay, "Opera and the Lease of Voice," briefly discusses *Gaslight*, the 1944 film to which his essay in the preceding collection was devoted. Specific to his reading of that movie (whose heroine, Paula Alquist Anton, played by Ingrid Bergman, trains to be an opera star in the footsteps of her murdered aunt) are, "questions fundamental to thinking about opera . . . Who sings, the actor, the character. And even: What is singing? What causes it? [that the film] asks us to ask" (135).

The connection between these two distinct episodes of Cavell's own presentational, solo performances, coincidentally or not, is embodied, takes shape, in theatrical spaces—opera-house and cinema—whose audiences are essential to the artistic medium there on display. Spatially, instrumentally, even materially, the Temple's *tevot* represent vastly different structures and perform vastly different functions. But other than the presentation on *Gaslight* and visits to film showings at the Cinemateque (conceivably, also, to theatrical performances at the Jerusalem Theater which, however, he does not mention), Cavell's presence in Jerusalem might—if one wanted to minimize the ontological, temporal distances or exaggerate the connection—also be affiliated with the uncanny experiences of long-dead workman catching views of a sacred chamber, curtained and totally dark within.

But that would be too much of stretch, even for this overstepping critic. I would, however, like to use Cavell's brief references to filmgoing at the Cinemateque[67] to segue back to his remarks about audience at the beginning of *The World Viewed*. "The movie seems naturally to exist in a state in which its highest and its most ordinary instances attract the same audience" (5), he says there. He then lists a personally significant but otherwise random series of moments and actors' gestures in Hollywood films to whose importance "anyone ought to be able to rise in recognition of," for which "the highest sensibility must thrill," and "merely to think of" which must consequently "provide us with a fair semblance of ecstasy" (6).

It will be remembered how all this wonder is tied by Cavell to the experience of fellowship and sociality: "The events associated with movies are those of companionship or lack of companionship" (10). Yet now (1971), he acknowledges a disorder or break in this natural relation:

> I have mentioned my increasing difficulty over the past several years to get myself
> to go to new movies. This has to do partly with an anxiousness in my response to
> new films I have seen (I don't at all mean I think they are bad), my anxiousness in
> what I feel to be new audiences for movies (not necessarily new people, but people
> with new reasons for being there), as though I cannot locate or remain together
> with my companions among them. I take this as something of more than clinical
> interest. (11)

Speaking personally, I am not quite sure what to do with such passages, but they seem to me as obscure as, if not more so than, those sentences in *The World Viewed* where Cavell's pitch of philosophy is articulated at such a rarified a level (Galton's whistle again), that perhaps only other ordinary language philosophers of a similarly fastidious bent can sound them out accurately.

Few aspects of Cavell's book now appear more dated than these. I now suggest more pointedly than my previous hints in this direction: approximately the same length of time now separates the original publication of Cavell's book from the early years of (bona fide) "talkies," to some of which he alludes in the course of his reflections on the ontology of film. Dramatic developments in medium technology (digital photography, THX audio reproduction, nonlinear editing, 70mm format, computer graphics imaging, motion capture, 3D); the asymptotic rise in the sheer number of people now routinely assembled to produce a big-budget Hollywood film (end credits now list literally hundreds of them); a mammoth shift in the kinds (genres) of movies now made (fantasy, epic adventure, film-versions of television series, cartoon shows, comic books, animated films, sequel franchises, horror, documentary); wholesale corporate restructuring of the industry and media conglomerate tie-ins; remarkable transformations in the ways movies are now watched (multiplex and IMAX screens, television commercials and elaborately produced trailers before the feature, DVDs, internet and cable-viewing options): these, it seems to me, put potentially more pressure on Cavell's philosophical account of cinema than the latest Žižekian film theory.

I do not have his individual readings of (mostly) Hollywood films in mind. Rather, I mean his *account* of the phenomenon and event itself, his "autobiography of companions." Let me then, as promised, shift my attention from his book and venture onto a new plane, with my readers' indulgence: the author's own autobiography of companions. There was a time in my life (late adolescence), just around the time Cavell was writing *The World Viewed,* when I regularly frequented repertory movie-houses in New York City, thereby receiving a highly compressed education in film, consisting of both American and "foreign," sound and silent. This schooling continued once I left the East Coast for San Francisco, and continued for several years thereafter in the various repertory theaters devoted to retrospectives. I confess I share Cavell's special fondness for traditional motion pictures: and like him (it appears from the concluding pages of his memoir), I continue to see new movies regularly and avidly. My preference, however, continues to be seeing them projected many times larger than my height and with powerful sound systems in cavernous movie theaters (the smaller the screen or theater, the less ritualized it feels). I like, in other words, to be *subjected* to the movies and the experience of viewing them.

Back in 1970s New York and 1980s San Francisco, however, I suppose I would have had to number myself in the movie houses of both cities among the "scattered souls with someone missing" (10). Seeing a film unaccompanied is probably not a generally popular preference, it is safe to say, judging from the many internet websites that debate the social and psychological rectitude of solitary moviegoing. It is not clear to me, however, that it differs appreciably from accompanied moviegoing, since the movie audience like the theater audience for *King Lear*—notwithstanding Cavell's distinction between screen and stage—is collected in the same space and time.

While it may capture or alter the experience of one's own viewing (like the concert hall or opera experience), sitting next to, behind, in front of a companion, merely adds another member to the audience, collectively considered and defined by mutual ano-

nymity. Moreover, as I have already suggested, if one takes the meaning of companions in *The World Viewed* to be double, referring also to the figures populating the film
projected and screened in front of one, then companionship may just as legitimately
be imaginative and virtual, a potentially meaningful adjacency.

But the same may be accurately said for many kinds of liturgical prayer and worship, too. One example from Jewish tradition is a silent service called the *Shemoneh
Esrei* a series of eighteen (plus-one) benedictions recited normatively in a quorum of at
least ten, ideally in a synagogue containing a Torah scroll, following an invariant text
written in the first person plural. (This is the speech-act situation described in the
opening pages of the introduction, where a deficiency of persons in a Havana synagogue, however, is made up for by the substitution of scrolls.)

In two of his most beautifully written essays collected in In *Quest of the Ordinary,*
"Recounting Gains, Showing Losses (A Reading of *The Winter's Tale*)" and "Being
Odd, Getting Even (Descartes, Emerson, Poe)," as well as in some poignant remarks
in his memoir about his father's pawnbroker business, Cavell stresses the significance
of counting, being counted, or counting for in relation to telling, being accounted for
or giving an account. These inflections, of course, also go to the question of what constitutes an audience, and what its meaning, purpose, and responsibilities might be.

When one ponders the aesthetic question of onlooker-witnesses, and of being
counted among them, a number of textual sources come to mind, many of them fairly
obvious. Let one more obscure prompting be Robert Frost's 1915 lyric "The Tuft of
Flowers," with its quoted adage in the end (that like others in the Frost canon, does
not necessarily speak for or encapsulate it, and in fact restates an earlier line in it). The
poem ends with these six verses:

> But glad with him, I worked as with his aid,
> And weary, sought at noon with him the shade;
> And dreaming, as it were, held brotherly speech
> With one whose thought I had not hoped to reach.
> "Men work together," I told him from the heart,
> "Whether they work together or apart."[68]

The designated other in these lines, the speaker's immediate companion and audience, is a butterfly, not another man, who, however, points to the visible signs of that
man's previous presence on the same landscape and of his manifest labor.

> But he turned first, and led my eye to look
> At a tall tuft of flowers beside a brook,
> A leaping tongue of bloom the scythe had spared
> Beside a reedy brook the scythe had bared.

A worker takes up a place in a space vacated by another laborer who has worked it
before: this is a piece of the poem's essential argument—work as a kind of tact.

> I went to turn the grass once after one
> Who mowed it in the dew before the sun.
> The dew was gone that made his blade so keen.
> Before I came to view the leveled scene.

Philosophers do this; so do filmmakers, painters, novelists, poets; so does a religious commentarial tradition like the Talmud. So, in a *wholly* absent sense, does a movie audience.

Frost's sense of craft ensures that poems about labor almost invariably dramatize the making of the poem itself, aesthetic activity in general. Aesthetic activity in this poem might be embodied by the act of mowing; but it can also take the form of "sheer morning gladness," the mystery of leaving a mark by not leaving a mark, working around something and thus italicizing its presence, in the case of this lyric, a tuft of flowers.

> I left my place to know them by their name,
> Finding them butterfly weed when I came.
> The mower in the dew had loved them thus,
> By leaving them to flourish, not for us,
> Nor yet to draw one thought of ours to him.
> But from sheer morning gladness at the brim.

Through his unexpected glimpse at another's vacated presence, the speaker finds that he himself is an audience, just as he feels the companionate presence of another, albeit nonhuman, watcher. The poem stages companionship for us, certainly. But it also stages the commerce of presence and absence, or being privy to something beheld, into whose ontological threshold we cannot quite cross over.[69]

Curiously enough, work and spectacle are also coordinated for us by the image of workmen in the *tevot* of the Holy Temple, as well—where even if they are not co-present, other laborers have left signs that they have been there before in the same exact place. What they have beheld (or not beheld), their successors unfailingly track onto, too. Each one of them is both inside but left outside: together, they share this dilemma in common. Public prayer is similarly structured insofar as ritual and spiritual labor are performed among others and declared in the plural, even though one may be communing primarily with an invisible and inaudible presence or with oneself.

Cavell has already shown us how tragic theater may also produce such effects. But it remains unclear how watching a movie, notwithstanding all its potential resemblance to religious ritual—ceremonial darkness, concentrated time and space, affective transport, multiple gazes focused on the same object, with awe, wonder, joy, sadness, or confusion—participates in the same economy of representation. Cavell even recapitulates certain propositions from "The Avoidance of Love" in *The World Viewed*, while drawing differences between the media of dramatic plays and movies. But the virtue of the lines quoted above from Frost seem to me to apply to the condition of the film-audience, too, whether its members happen to sit in their seats accompanied by companions or not. And as sketched in the first pages of Chapter 1, religion, art, and magic all map onto potentially shared Venn diagrammatic spaces.

A link between the latter two, art and magic, stands behind (or as he will express it, "below"), Cavell's analysis of the ontology of film in *The World Viewed*. In the concluding pages, I want to play off it, by returning not to Christopher Nolan's *Prestige* but rather to another film that happened to see release while I was in the midst of thinking through further implications of the texts by Cavell I have treated in some depth here. The claims I make about it will not be as generalized as those in *The World Viewed*. Rather, I restrict them to certain observations that follow from particulars of content and form—"*this film* viewed"—that give me some leverage for the question I have posing all along in this chapter about audience. The nature of the movie as such also has the virtue of allowing me one further pass at the metaphor of viewing boxes that constrain and direct vision while they secure distance and separation.

That movie is Martin Scorsese's 2011 *Hugo*, based on Brian Selznick's 2007 picture-novel, *The Invention of Hugo Cabret*, intimately concerned with the origins and machinery of moviemaking, its magic and material culture.[70] So far as I know, Cavell never mentions Scorsese or his movies in his writing and film; and if the two figures have been brought together, as in the essay, "The Shows of Violence," by Irving Schneider,"[71] it is only around a theme peripheral to Cavell's chief concerns. Scorsese's film certainly contains enough intertexts (Hitchcock, Welles, Lang, Vigo), to serve as a crossing point between director and philosopher, but I turn to it here principally because of its value as supplement to Cavell's account of the medium and its "automatism."

Hugo is "about" many things: filiation and affiliation, movie history (especially silent pictures),[72] magic, cinema and literature as twin imaginative media, cultivation and aesthetic appreciation, plots of the ordinary and intervention by the extraordinary, art and mechanics, dreams and illusion, time, technology, objects and automatism, collecting, brokenness and repair, effects—special and otherwise, patrimony, companionship, the necessary loneliness of the spectator. Its main plot also centrally revolves around the "cinemagician" Georges Méliès, the obscurity that became his fate for a time and his belated rediscovery, and the founding moment of film he embodies—its quintessential *Pledge, Turn, Prestige*. But Scorsese's movie asks an additional question throughout, on the model of Cavell's philosophical inquiries about tragic drama, film, and opera, but much more explicitly than they. And that is: What is an audience? What does it mean to watch mutely?

This, it seems to me, is the organizing question *The World Viewed* appears to pose at first only to let recede. For one thing, what one misses in Cavell's account are reflections on the special kind of mimesis, the effects, that cinema brings about in an audience that has already passed the test of presentness, namely, its "passiveness before the exhibition of the world." But this is, properly speaking, not an ontological property of movies but rather their phenomenal or epiphenomenal *effect*.[73] The sympathetic weeping, laughter, or dread done in accord with the weeping and laughter and dread seen on the screen, the marvel felt in synch with the enraptured look of filmed amazement (what, for films of more recent vintage, has been dubbed "the Spielberg face"):[74] this is the stuff of sensibility, and what earlier centuries, in the arts or philosophy, designated as the cultural province of "sympathy," "sentiment," and "sensation" (e.g., Marivaux, De Quincey, Mary Shelley, Mary Elizabeth Braddon).[75]

Consider this example from our Jansenist friend Blaise Pascal, who here condemns the mimetic contagion loosed and licensed by theatrical experience:

> All great amusements are dangerous to the Christian life; but among all those which the world has invented there is none more to be feared than the theatre. . . . For the more innocent it appears to innocent souls, the more they are likely to be touched by it. Its violence pleases our self-love, which immediately forms a desire to produce the same effects which are seen so well represented. . . . So we depart from the theatre with our heart so filled with all the beauty and tenderness of love, the soul and the mind so persuaded of its innocence, that we are quite ready to receive its first impressions, or rather to seek an opportunity of awakening them in the heart of another, in order that we may receive the same pleasures and the same sacrifices which we have seen so well represented in the theatre. (*Pensées* 1.11)

Pascal's thought, of course, became a sustained polemic in Rousseau's great 1758 *Lettre a d'Alembert sur les spectacles* (whose decisive influence on his thinking Cavell in fact acknowledges in the preface to *The World Viewed*). The *Letter* is probably the most impassioned critique of performance art's exhibitionism and its effects, *les manières de vivre qu'on y verra dépeintes et qu'on s'empressera d'imiter*, "the ways of life that [theatergoers] will see depicted which they will be eager to imitate" (111).[76] In a wholly secularized sense, we might just call this film's allegorical capacity to defile the hands—what Salinger's Holden Caulfield kept at a safe distance with his perfectly apotropaic phrase, "goddam movies."[77] "*Cinéma pur*"?—only a filmmaker's term.

Cavell himself marks this capacity in his treatment of the "Hale's Tour" scene in Max Ophuls's *Letter to an Unknown Woman*:

> It shows the audience of the film (represented by the pair in the compartment) to endow the passing scenes presented to them (some rather obvious travel poster paintings) with incomparably more emotion than those painted panoramas can be expected to call for in themselves—as if this allegorized response to film reveals the response to film as inherently excessive, say inherently melodramatic. But then, where in response to the arts, can one's response be said not to be excessive?[78]

Hale's Tours (a late nineteenth-century amusement ride that, as a cinema designed to resemble a railway carriage, simulated the motions of train travel along with a phantom landscape) were contemporary with the moment in the history of cinema that Scorsese's own film documents. As for the effect Cavell calls "excess emotion," a function (as he acknowledges) of both mechanized pseudo-magic and unalloyed nostalgia—*Hugo* virtually depends on it. When Cavell says further that an "overtly magical response" and a reciprocal sense that "the actual world is in itself quite boring" are attitudes that "seem called for by each other," he seems almost to have anticipated Scorsese's intent for *Hugo* and its pendulum-swing of cinema's "excessiveness" and "disillusionment."[79]

In *Hugo,* we see the audience thrice depicted, and in two of those instances, the figure of Méliès is positioned either in front or behind it. In the first, a flashback, at an amusement park, Méliès and his wife duck into a Théâtre du Cinématographe run by the brothers Lumiere just in time to witness the first public exhibition of a motion picture *L'arrivée d'un train en gare de La Ciotat* (1895). According to popular legend, the fifty-second film had such a startling effect on its first audiences that there was a collective rearing back as if the train were to continue its forward motion past the proscenium and into their seats.[80]

While not actually violating the separateness between medium and viewers so essential to Cavell's analysis, this myth attests to the palpable transfer of mimesis, which we see actually *observed* by Méliès in Scorsese's movie. A train station is in fact the staging area for almost all of the film's plot: Hugo lives in secret clock-chambers above the Montparnasse station, where Méliès, neglected in later years, became a toy salesman, watching its goings-on through small apertures as if the scenes played out below—all cinematic clichés of quotidian romance, constabulary patrol, shop commerce, and spectatorship—*were* a movie.

And the image of the violently propulsive train becomes a dream-motif in the story when Hugo fantasizes that he drops something into the tracks as a train, unable to brake in time, crashes horrifically over him and into the station and streets below, literalizing the mythic fear of perilous mimesis activated for *L'arrivée d'un train*'s initial viewers.[81] This image in turn, is reenacted in "real life" toward the movie's end as Hugo is rescued in the nick of time from an oncoming train (identical details of the train crew attempting to stop it and identical shocked onlookers), as an automaton he is carrying (a major engine for the movie's storyline) caroms onto the tracks.

The condensation of imagery and symbol here is incredibly rich: trains and technology, viewing, automatism, fear and suspense, the individual and the crowd, movies and dreaming, and last but certainly not least, rampant mimesis. The second instance of an audience pictured in the film occurs at its end, as Méliès, toward the end of his life, is publically recognized. *Hugo*'s audience, through an implied fading effect, becomes continuous (contiguous?) with the audience applauding Méliès (we watch them in their seats from behind in ours), as Méliès walks onto the stage, faces them, speaks briefly, lights a cigarettes, and performs the stage-magic of "jump-cutting" into an image of his much younger actor-self lighting a cigarette in *Le roi du maquillage* from 1904.

The third glimpse of an audience in *Hugo* appears when Hugo Cabret and his companion Isabelle, the goddaughter of Méliès, steal into a movie theater which Méliès had forbidden her to frequent, in order to watch the famous death-defying clocktower scene from Harold Lloyd's 1923 picture *Safety Last*—a scene that is, once again, reenacted later in Scorsese's film, as Hugo eludes his mock-Javert police inspector by climbing outside the clocktower at Montparnasse station and perching himself on its giant hands.[82]

Here, Cavell's program in *The World Viewed*, a philosophy of film but also film *as* philosophy, meets Scorsese's film head on. The first two passages below from Cavell's book evince its wide distance from what I think is at stake in *Hugo*; the third draws them quite close to each other.

> I suppose that the old casualness harbored the value of illicitness that from the beginning was part of moviegoing. But the strictures of the new audience do not dispel illicitness or make it unnecessary; the audience is not a gathering of citizens for honest confession and acceptance of one another. The new need for the gathering is as mysterious as the old need for privacy; so the demand that I forgo privacy is as illicit as my requirement to preserve it. (11–12)

> It is as though the world's projection explains our forms of unknownness and of our inability to know. The explanation is not so much that the world is passing us by, as that we are displaced from our natural habitation within it, placed at a distance from it. The screen overcomes our fixed distance; it makes displacement appear as our natural condition. (41)

> Film returns to us and extends our first fascination with objects, with their inner and fixed lives; and it studies what is done in and with them, which Baudelaire also mentions. What is done in and with one of these contrivances, where they are placed and why—this is something with a drama of its own, its unique logic of beginning, middle, and end; and they create the kind of creature who may use them. These are forms that effect cinematic possibilities. (43–44)

If they do speak to the particulars and the sensibilities of Scorsese's film, I believe the first two passages are challenged and get recast by *Hugo*'s secular devotion to the magic of the medium and the power of effect. In other words, I see such a film as directly invoking the *audience's* presence. Call it "the viewer viewed." Many, many movies (including some to which Cavell alludes), depict movie audiences. In "The Acknowledgment of Silence," for instance, Cavell offers this insight:

> The movie's power to reach this level must have to do with the gigantism of its figures, making me small again. (For all the times the motif of a character watching a movie has been used, that is a possibility of the medium I remember acknowledged only once: when in *Saboteur* a man chased through Radio City Music Hall runs across the stage in front of the screen, his human size in comparison

with the size of the screen character seems that of an entirely other race—about the size of Fay Wray wriggling in the sky-blown hand.) It must also have to do with the world it screens being literally of my world. (154–155)

And yet, it seems to me, both *Hugo*'s form and content take the audience's significance *exactly* for granted. Hence, together, they propose something that refines Cavell's large but undifferentiated claim that the impact of movies its "too massive, too out of proportion . . . to speak politely of involvement" (154). If it is true that "we involve the movies in us," then we are also answerable for the (im)polite involvement. And this is a matter neither licit nor illicit. It is one of the claims made on us by the fact of our presence: say, when we watch a man chased through Radio City Music Hall who runs across the stage in front of the screen. *He* is being pursued, certainly. But our own detachment—as, and experienced in, an audience—is not scot-free; rather, it should serve as a place to begin.

The "natural condition" imagined by Scorsese's film, like the Victorian novel (which it palpably references) and the Harry Potter books, is displacement—orphanhood, as I will explain—rectified and redeemed. There is thus nothing casual about either the audience internal to the plot of *Hugo* or the one outside that has paid to see it; once, the fact of it has been granted, certain responsibilities (yet to be specified) ensue. Nor does it stretch the point to suggest, as I did for Darger's picture-books—which in some sense, do work like an extended film—that acts of reclamation and adoption freight the horizon of reception with the ethicized ontology, if you will, of orphaned existence. To that extent, *Hugo*'s empirical audience, in the state of susceptibility that fairly defines filmgoing, plays the double role of both Oliver Twist and Mr. Brownlow, Cordelia and Lear: the moviehouse becomes, as it were, an orphanage and at the same time, a place of rescue, a topos where we are denied but also where we acknowledge. Such acts of acknowledgment, in the sense of Cavell's *Lear* essay, place pressure upon a privileged self-separation as embodied by Cavell's attested break in his natural relation to the movies. *Hugo*, in short, questions Cavell's cavils.

Yet, the third and last passage above about objects (from the brilliant chapter, "Baudelaire and the Myths of Film"), and quite by accident, seems to get at the film's very heart. It sometimes may seem that movies are more about objects than people: a child's sled, a black falcon statuette, a red dress, a femur bone, an intercostal clavicle, a stolen bicycle, a harmonica, a baby carriage, the Empire State Building, a bouncing globe, Zuzu's petals, a helicoptered statue of Jesus, torn sacks emptied of gold dust, a crop duster, a ring, a necklace, earrings, a red balloon, guns, telephones, hats, cars, trains, a prosthetic hand, a pair of crutches, eyeglasses. *Hugo* fully exploits the physicality and object world of the film medium itself, such as cameras, screens, celluloid stock, but also its mechanical cousins: clocks, toys, trains, automated contrivances. It is one of the truly great films about what Heidegger called *das Zeug*, or "gear," "equipment."[83] Such object relations not only engineer cinematic possibilities, it seems to me. They also, and theatrically, activate mimetic desire. The automaton that belongs to Hugo Cabret in the film and the heart-shaped key that triggers its mechanism for which he searches become objects of the audience's desire, too. They are things to be reached for, with the mind's hand.[84]

One of the features making *Hugo* stand out in Scorsese's work, even among the more genre-conscious homage films he has directed (e.g., *The Color of Money*, *Cape Fear*, *The Age of Innocence*, *The Departed*, *Shutter Island*), is the very contemporary film category in which it was classed in 2011, that is, MPAA rated PG "children's film" or, in the more market-driven phrase, "family entertainment." *Hugo* was released for the Thanksgiving holiday, 2011, along with several other movies tailored especially for youth but with that sophisticated edge of reference and knowing quality that pulls in an already established adult audience for such films. To that degree, it does exemplify a trend in filmmaking that postdates *The World Viewed*, spurred by mutually rein-forcing demographic shifts and the fabrication of the Hollywood product, a trend piquantly analyzed by a *New Yorker* article from 1997 by Kurt Anderson entitled "Kids 'R' Us."

Not surprisingly in that short piece, Anderson looks first to film, identifying Steven Spielberg as the chief cultural arbiter for the consequent "demographic blur" whereby adult sensibilities become juvenilized and the immaturity of youth is not only vali-dated but capitalized upon, because Spielberg (along with George Lucas) "invented the signal modern Hollywood hybrid—high-end Saturday matinées for grownups, chil-dren's movies that adults unashamedly want to see."[85]

The result, over the last two decades, has been another blur among media and dis-tinct expressions of the play instinct as films have more and more elected to (re)tell children's stories and comic books, to address an audience that takes its bearings from children's sensibilities, to develop a look and sound that diminishes the distance between cinema and sibling technologies like comics and video games. It is no acci-dent that *Toy Story*, across three films, names the conflation of narrative and knick-knack that now prevails in so many mainstream movies across a range of genres (science fiction, adventure, horror, fantasy).

If *Hugo*, shot mostly from a child's point of view, participates in this market, it pos-sesses even stronger affinities with the kind of object-oriented sensibility cultivated by decidedly anti-mainstream animators like the Quay Brothers—*Street of Crocodiles*, *The Cabinet of Jan Švankmajer*, *The Calligrapher*, *The Comb (From the Museums of Sleep)*—as well as the long-standing literary tradition of automata associated with works like Hoffman's "Automata" and "Der Sandmann" (a text Cavell happens to read at length in *In Quest of the Ordinary*), Melville's "The Bell Tower," or Collodi's *Pinoc-chio*.[86] As in a Quay Brothers film or Hoffmann's short story, the objects it reveals to us are allowed to retain their mystery.[87] That is just to say that Scorsese, building on Selznick's template, has created a web of generic and textual associations, all of which conspire to give form and shape to the desire to cross over thresholds between animate and inanimate, private and shared, filmed (viewed, exhibited, screened) and *touched* or longed for with tactile intensity.

The verses from Genesis in the third epigraph to this chapter are ones Cavell has commented on in several places to the effect that it is evidently possible (for Isaac, at least) to be assured by the sense of touch over and above hearing. "Between the two forms of signature, by hand and by voice," Cavell says in *A Pitch of Philosophy*, a father can apparently "trust the hand more than the voice," as Cavell had ventured the dilemma previously in *Philosophical Passages,* even if it is unlikely that a son's voice has not been recognized, after all.[88] In these instances, Cavell says he is "reading the child," as exemplified for him by Wittgenstein's scene of instruction that commences *Philosophical Investigations*, on Augustine's theory of language acquisition—an "isolated child divining the words of others" (174). This prompts him to consider the displaced blessing in the Jacob and Esau narrative, and the way voice (as originary consent and the right to speak), inheritance, and theft are fatefully entwined—though we should add touch as well.

Hugo is most definitely a film devoted to *reading the child*, with its thematics of theft and inheritance, voice and touch (as signatures of the self), at center stage—even if they do not involve fraternal discord or competition. But the thought-world it really inhabits is that of literary fiction and the novel, not philosophy. Earlier, I quoted Cavell from *Little Did I Know* that questioning the hinge between public and private is what makes cinema "inherently philosophical." In the immediately preceding sentence, Cavell writes, "I might say of novels that they are meant to make private what is public and private business, make them mine" (204). The Bakhtinian in me disputes the claim. Novels are also where the private decisively becomes public, where singular meets, and gives itself over to, plural.

Nowhere is this is this more apparent, dialogically, ideologically, and as a condition for emplotment than around orphanhood. As Kazuo Ishiguro's narrator says at the end of his novel *When We Were Orphans* (2000), "to try and see our missions through to the end"[89] is the unfinished and sometimes unfinalizable condition that opens the world's possibilities through the figure of the orphan. The mimetic tradition of the orphan is where *Hugo*'s affective and representational allegiances lie most demonstrably anchored, along with the consequent role assigned to foster parents or godparents, and the reclamation that is adoption.

And here, I believe, is chiefly where Cavell's reflections on the ontology of film stop short of accounting for some of cinema's *own* "natural relations." Much like Henry Darger and his unintended readers, even if the film's audience ineluctably identifies with Hugo's fortunes and desires, it is perhaps even more powerfully oriented with respect to those persons—or those realms of magic—through which he gets *adopted*.

Watching Méliès take in the audience's reaction, behind their backs, to the Lumiere brothers' film, and watching him again behold spectators that now, more properly, are seated in front of him in his honor; watching Hugo as he watches the "filmic" plots performed under his gaze in Gare Montparnasse, and watching him view *Safety Last* in a moviehouse as he gets seized by the manager for illicit entry and ejected from the bosom of the audience: by the example of these scenes, Scorsese's audience is asked a more consequential question than the definitional or categorical one that asks, what is an audience? And that harder, ethical inquiry is: what does an audience *do,* what does it "make happen," what is it responsible for or obligated to, when it isn't identified merely with its "passiveness before the exhibition of the world," and thus given over to the safe clandestinity of its own world as unseen (unviewed).

In the most provocative way I can think of framing that question, what are the risks of an inheritance thus "stolen" through the cover of blindness? What *doesn't* get acknowledged by, as it were, an audience's failing to adopt the world exhibited before it, or more locally, by its failing to adopt a single boy—together with a neglected progenitor fallen on hard times—through each of whom, magic, the wonder of machinery, and the art of filmmaking have been spliced together?

This, I suggest, is the third act of *Pledge, Return, Prestige* that belongs entirely to an audience in its modality as host for the duration of a film like *Hugo.* We have seen in a previous chapter how adopting images serves as a means to achieve contact with them, an expression of custodianship and hospitality. If tragic drama like *King Lear* offers us a place to stop, as Cavell writes in "The Avoidance of Love," and return to the world purged of everything but our separateness, newly capable of the wisdom needed to reveal ourselves, to cease theatricalizing others, then a moviegoing experience like *Hugo* suggests, I think a stage consequent—or additional—to being allowed a mechanically engineered absent, as Cavell formulates the problem in *The World Viewed,* having "our helplessness mechanically assured" (25). If we truly are helpless in front of and absent from the world screened before/from us, which lets us be read by it accordingly, then we are also situated exotopically (in Bakhtin's sense): advantaged by dint of separation to offer the generative, gift-giving creativity that is "surplus of vision."

The obvious objection here is that no one really does this while watching a movie; no one fosters or shepherds the world viewed, no one plays an adoptive role in relation to it. All one does is sit and *view,* and as Cavell puts it, "accept" what one views. We are too busy being thus instructed by film or else given over to the longing of mimetic desire, to do much more than resist skepticism's pull and its "nostalgia for the present": "to be willing to let the world appear as such" and to be willing to allow the self to exhibit itself without the self's intervention" (159). Audiences *are* tactless.

I would say this in response. Cavell, in *The World Viewed* and elsewhere in his writing, attests to the way in which philosophy discovers its voice or arrogates it as its inheritance: it can thus be said to come into its own, a function of both that voice's birthright and (perfect) pitch, which consequently makes representative claims "I brag for humanity," as Cavell likes to quote Thoreau.

Cavell's reflections on the ontology of film in *The World Viewed* are not meant to be private musings, despite the privileged and rueful note one detects when it comes to the question of audience—especially since, philosophically considered, film questions the distinction between public and private in the first place, according to Cavell. His reflections are intended to reveal "the essence of the medium," *grammatically* as Wittgenstein would say, and thus to rehearse the move from metaphysical to everyday use already modeled for us by our relationship to ordinary language. If some of its promptings as well as some of its discursive turns remain obscure, *The World Viewed* is intended not as hermetic or esoteric but, quite the contrary, as revelatory. Its account, ultimately, is meant to jibe with, by speaking for, *anyone's*.

But in response, we can perfectly well object, "no one experiences movies the way Cavell insists we do; everyday moviegoing and filmwatching are just not that philosophical." Oneself as the "haunting of the world?" "A world complete without me which is present to me is the world of my immortality?" That immortality as commensurate with "nature's survival of me" such that "the present judgment upon me is not yet the last?" These last gnomic pronouncements of *The World Viewed* ask much of a quotidian audience, which, like a Samuel Johnson in the face of Berkeleyan sublimations, might simply conclude, "I refute it thus!"[90] If, however, Cavell's account does capture something fundamental about the stakes of cinematic art as restricted to certain aspects of the medium, then the specifically ethical, tactful picture of viewing that I have sketched here does find and justly "arrogate" its own voice. And besides: where in response to the arts, can one's response be said not to be excessive?

John Logan's script for *Hugo* specifies the following details for its opening sequence:

> A huge clock suspended from the ceiling of the station . . .
> Behind the ironwork dial we see a face peering out . . .
> Hugo Cabret looks at us . . .
> Hugo turns away from the dial and moves through the tunnels behind the clock.
> A serpentine maze of passageways. . . .
> We move with him as he goes quickly up and down spiral staircases . . . ducking through tiny openings . . . swerving in and out of dark passages . . . . up and down, back and forth.

That a movie audience is made to identify with an orphan protagonist is nothing new: Griffith's *Orphans of the Storm* and Chaplin's *The Kid* (both from 1921), various adaptations of Dickens novels, the *Harry Potter* movies, Victor in Truffaut's *L'enfant sauvage* (1970), Ofelia in Guillermo del Toro's *El laberinto del fauno* (2006) are just a few examples. A few pages earlier, I said that Scorsese's film "reads the child." Its utility for me here is that it also *reads the audience*. When I said that there are three scenes depicting the audience in *Hugo,* I undercounted. There are actually four. The one I omitted does not take place in a moviehouse but rather in a music hall in which Méliès performs the stage illusion of the levitating woman. We see Méliès and his magician's assistant-wife from the back so that we see the entire audience, orchestra and mezzanine, in rapt attention, whom we see once again closer, filling the screen as they applaud wildly.

And if one wished to push the trope to its limits, there is also a fifth and a sixth scene, reciprocal chimes. In the first iteration Hugo's father has him put his hands over his eyes and then open them, to reveal the automaton perched on a table, "a wind-up figure, like a music box" the father has found, who surmises that it was built "by a magician." The scene's double has Hugo perform the same "trick" for Isabelle, Méliès's goddaughter; this time, even more like a stage illusion performed for an audience, the automaton is revealed perched on the same desk to similarly astonished eyes, as a canvas covering is whisked away.

Even more spectacularly, when the machine is engaged, its writing hand dips pen in ink and proceeds to draw the iconic image of the man-in-the-moon with the space capsule puncturing its eye from Méliès's 1902 film, *Le Voyage dans la lune*. As I have suggested, though, the "Prestige" to any "Pledge, Turn" belongs not only to the magician's skill whereby the levitated woman is "brought back" to earth, or the automaton "brought back" to working perfection. Exceeding its given state of "mechanical helplessness," the way in which an audience takes up its part in what magician Jamy Ian Swiss, we recall, identifies as an "experiment in empathy," is how it more than accepts the world it views. In preceding chapters, I also characterized such participatory consciousness on the horizon of reception as the stuff of countersigning. I reaffirm it here.

And if we note that Cavell's book culminates with the chapter, "The Acknowledgment of Silence," we are dealing here with silence as Bakhtinian pause rather than as gap, "the beginning of a word," an open, unfinalized, and continuous structure.[91] In connection with Darger, I had suggested that adoption serves a redeeming function: "for quotidian loss or lack *in* the world he sought compensation by *inventing* a world, which then needed to be compulsively and ceaselessly filled, an intrapsychic fantasy rendered through word and image." The audience for Scorsese's *Hugo* (as but one example of a film's "adoptability") cannot be said to invent it, of course, since its absence from that world, as Cavell insists, is a given. But the space opened for its imaginative fosterage of that world, "bringing it back, so to speak," as a permutation of Cavellian acknowledgment, is the prestige that distinguishes it ethically.

PART THREE

Languages

CHAPTER 7

Abyss, Volcano, and the Frozen Swirl of Words

The Difficult and the Holy in Agnon, Bialik, and Scholem

> Bear up under my greetings, old scrolls
> and tolerate the kisses of my mouth, ancients of dust.
> From wandering the foreign isles, my soul's returned
> and like a homing pigeon, with tired wings and scared,
> it beats again upon the gates of its youth's nest.
> Do you still know me? I'm so-and so! . . .   6
> And now, after the change of time,   47
> and I am furrow browed and furrow souled,
> so the wheel of my life has brought me back
> and stood me once again before you, hidden ones of the bookcase,   50
> offspring of Lvov, Slavita, Amsterdam and Frankfurt,
> and once more my hand leafs through your scrolls
> and my eye gropes, tired, among verses
> and seeks silently between the curled tails of the letters
> struggling there to catch the footprints of my soul . . .
> I look, I see—and I do not recognize you, old folk,   60
> from within your letters now won't gaze
> any longer into the depths of my soul opened eyes,
> sad eyes of the ancients of old,
> and I no longer hear from there the whisper of their lips,
> that stir in a forgotten grave, untouched by human foot.
> Like black pearls, whose string is broke
> your columns of text are to me; your pages widowed
> and every letter by letter separately orphaned—   68
> has my eye dimmed and my ear grown faint?
>
> —Ḥayyim N. Bialik, לפני ארון הספרים "Before the Bookcase" (1915)

In a sense, we are guests at our own table, we ourselves, I Myself. So long as we speak German (or even if we speak Hebrew, Modern Hebrew, the Hebrew of

1921!) we cannot avoid this detour that again and again leads us the hard way from what is alien back to our own.

—Franz Rosenzweig to Gershom Scholem, March 10, 1921:
On Rosenzweig's *Tischdank* (ברכת המזון or "Grace After Meals")

. . . Like this consent of Language / This loved Philology.

—Emily Dickinson, "A Word Made Flesh"

VOCABLES: BIALIK, MAIMONIDES, (BENJAMIN)

The excerpt from Bialik's poem as the first epigraph begins with a contact between scroll and person far more intimate than any proscribed by the Talmud. It terminates, at least as I have reproduced it here, with the poem's title—transliterated as *"Lifnei aron ha-sefarim"*—rendered in Hebrew characters. Part of what Levinas calls the Gemara's "secret scent" lies in its orthography and graphemes, the characters that make up the Hebrew-Aramaic alphabet. So, indeed, does the secret scent of Bialik's poetry. If the classic books of Jewish religious instruction no longer exert their pull on the poem's speaker, if their columns of text are like black pearls whose string is broke, their pages widowed, and every letter by letter separately orphaned: still, the alphabet itself, the endoskeleton that supports the content, figuration, and music of the verse he writes remains wholly available to him, indeed essential.

Frequently in this book, albeit not entirely consistently, I have rendered non-English words in their proper characters, like the Hebrew of the Levinas chapters, the Cyrillic spelling of Bakhtinian terms in Chapter 5, the several instances of Arabic, the Homeric Greek of the recognition scene between Odysseus and Argos in Chapter 4, even the Japanese characters for Kurosawa's film *Ran* in a note to Chapter 6. I have also sometimes left Levinas's and Derrida's French to speak for itself, or at least to accompany the English translations of certain passages or phrases (as I have left Levinas's Lithuanian surname to speak for itself without the acute diacritical commonly used when rendered in French). Preferring to use non-Roman alphabets means eschewing transliteration (maintaining the approximate sound) for preserving the "look" of signifiers in the original tongue; similarly, retaining moments in the Romance original more closely preserves the "original" voice that wrote in it.

To what end, though, one might well ask, when there are certainly many readers who do not recognize the characters as *sounds*—as I, for instance, cannot knowledgably grasp the relation between the characters for "chaos" in Japanese and the phoneme, *"ra,"* that they spell. The decision may appear punctilious to a fault. After all, do the four lines from the Odyssey reproduced in the original Greek bestow a more meaningful silent recognition *upon* the scene they describe, even if, as we have been reminded, the scene is all *about* a silent recognition? Certainly, where this book's dedication page is concerned, the choice to "speak" in Yiddish was motivated by the desire for *those* words and *that* sound to be expressed by characters that convey an instantly recognizable materiality.

The thrust of such questions is the burden of this final chapter. When previous chapters of *To Make the Hands Impure* have quoted Russian and Hebrew, Aramaic and Greek, a minor fidelity problem insinuates itself that, in paraphrase of Benjamin, we could call "the task of the transliterator": which is the more faithful rendering of the target language? Whether it is relevant or not that *Aufgabe*, Benjamin's word in German for the translator's "task," can also evidently mean "defeat,"[1] still transliteration, at least in some cases, raises its own issues of fidelity. Take the Bialik poem, for example. To make it scan correctly as Bialik intended, the words should be given a stress on the penultimate syllable, and certain letters like ת (*tav*), given their Ashkenazi Hebrew articulation.[2] Indeed, this is how scansion *and* recitation of his poetry have been canonized for Israeli speakers who happen to accentuate the language quite differently in the standard, Sephardi phonology of 'Ivrit (Modern Israeli Hebrew).

At the turn of the twentieth century, Bialik (1873–1934), already known as Israel's *ha-meshorer ha-le'umi* (national poet) since the publication of his lyric "El Ha-Tzipur" in 1892, together with his fellow poet Saul Tchernichovsky (1875–1943), translator of Homer's *Odyssey*, among his many other accomplishments, became innovators in composing accentual-syllabic poems that used Ashkenazi accentuation. The subjects of their poetry and sense of themselves as poet-legislators revolutionized Hebrew letters. But their meticulous attention to formal particulars, that is, Hebrew letters in their basic sense, captures their particular contribution to the תְּחִיָּה (*tehiyah*, "revival") of Modern Hebrew.[3] Their poetics—and the politics of that poetics—was thus a function, in part, of their poems' pronunciation, their sound over and above their sense.

If we transliterate just the first two lines of Bialik's poem, for example, to vocalize it this way: "*Es peQUdas shLOmi Se'u, a'TIqei g'VIlim/URtzu et-neSHIkas pi, y'SHEnei Avaq*" remains more faithful to the verses' integral prosody and phonology than vocalizing it "*Et pequDAT shloMI se'U, a'tiQEI g'viLIM/urTZU et-neshiKAT pi, y'shenEI aVAQ*, which is how it should sound in conventional modern Hebrew pronunciation—failing, thus, to do the music of Bialik's verse full poetic justice. Transliterating it according to Sephardi phonology alters what Franz Rosenzweig would call the particular *Sprachdenken* or "speech thinking" at work in Bialik's language world. It defers or distances what should be proximate, adding perhaps one degree of exile too many for this self-consciously exilic poet, whom we thereby leave partially stranded, or as his poem expresses it, still "wandering the foreign isles."

If, further, we sustain fidelity to Bialik's poem in its aspect of *ars poetica*, we observe that the rueful alienation its speaker feels for the holy books and religious tradition that once nurtured him are *materially embodied* by the sound of the words to which he remains nevertheless connected, situating him thus on that same plane of venerable textuality as the "old scrolls" and "ancients of dust." For it is Ashkenazi phonology, dating back to medieval Europe or, as some scholars believe, even earlier to the Geonic or Mishnaic eras,[4] whose phonemes bridge the gap between the scrolls and the poem, and which also happens to embody the vocables recited in a yeshiva like Volozhin, where Bialik spent his youth learning Talmud and Mishna. There, to add yet one last layer, Bialik would discuss those source-texts with fellow pupils and teachers in the European Jewish vernacular of Yiddish, Hebrew's increasingly vexing neighbor-stranger at this crux of rising Jewish nationalist consciousness.[5]

In a fine essay, Barbara Mann brings out the stresses at play in "Before the Bookcase," stresses that are more than just metrical:

> Thus lurking within the deep structure of Bialik's scene is the Yiddish distinction between two kinds of books: the Germanic *bikher*, a more general usage indicating secular books, and the Hebraic *sforim*, meaning religious texts only. . . . The terms also refer to two distinct but related semiotic realms within Eastern European Jewish life, itself composed of low and high cultures marked by linguistic difference. Each language, and each set of texts, demanded a different kind of reading. Thus, the activity of *lernen* or *leynen torah* (to study or read Jewish law) constituted a particular kind of Jewish self, a male subject who was immersed and enmeshed in the text he studied. In contradistinction, the idea of *araynkukn in a bukh* (to browse or look at a secular book) implied another kind of self, one whose physical distance or separation from the text was indicated in the Yiddish verb *kukn* (to look). Bialik's speaker addresses *sforim* in "Before the Bookcase," but the poem effectively collapses the distinction between the two kinds of books; he looks at the *sforim* which no longer carry meaning for him, and they break apart, characterized only by their own pure, unintelligible materiality—"like strands of black pearls, whose string was cut."[6]

The Bialik-speaker kisses them reverently in the first line, with its deliberate echo of *Song of Songs* 1:2, "Let him kiss me with the kisses of his mouth." He even takes them out of the bookcase, holds them in his hand, in order to leaf through them. What he does not do, however, is "immerse" again. He remains estranged—the unceasingly diasporic Bialik, displaced from within, unhomed at that pole of Jewish cultural metaphysics in permanent tension with its binary complement, a creature of Bavel as much as a citizen of Yerushalayim.[7]

Does the situation of estrangement inside Bialik's poem bear at all on this book's concern with the book in hand? Can we plug its occasional intimations of touch into the matrix we have been constructing in six prior chapters? What does it have to tell us about proximity, about tact, about the difficult and holy? Can one speak a sacred language as a foreign language, and is a sacred language more one's own or more foreign in general (as Derrida has voiced these questions in *Monolingualism of the Other*)? What alternative is there to being "a guest at one's own table," in Rosenzweig's piquant phrase; or to add the voice of Gershom Scholem, how to find one's footing in a holy language spoken anew? Where "touch" now means the impingement of one language upon each other, how does their adjacency (to recall our introduction) both mark a limit and set a tripwire?

Since these questions will take shape gradually in the sections to follow, I defer a direct answer for the moment. At this juncture, I would invite us simply to observe that the poem's recognition scene, unlike the one we saw staged by Sebald's narrator in the Jewish cemetery of Kissingen, is a failed one. *Hataqiruni od?* ("Will you still know, recognize me") the speaker asks sadly in line 6. *Ani ploni* ("I am so-and-so")— using the Talmudic placeholder for proper name familiar to any rabbinical student, underscoring the affectionate jest of sign (wished-for recognition) answered by equivocal countersign (avowed anonymity).

These *gevilim* and *sforim* (in Ashkenazi pronunciation) represent the classical Judaic texts, Alan Mintz reminds us, from which Bialik, in collaboration with Yehoshua Hone Ravnitzky, compiled the legends which make up his famous *Sefer ha'aggadah*, published four years earlier.[8] (Like Levinas, Bialik was impelled more by aggadic than halakhic sensibilities.) Line 50 tells us that the *'atiqei gevilim*[9] (ancient scrolls) of line 1 are *genuzei aron* (hidden ones of the bookcase), from the same root as for *genizah*, the storage room for books fallen into disuse and waiting for burial. The poem's diction conjures a bygone language world, even as the speaker within the poem bids it valediction.

Yet, if the biblical metaphors of diminished sight and hearing and the Talmudic allusions are drawn from the very books he faces, so their estrangement from him is marked in the identical register (widow, orphan): *they* are estranged from him. If he cannot find his way toward them or the textual life of traditional learning with which they formerly nourished him, so they no longer gaze at or speak to him. At the end of the poem, the speaker turns instead to the natural world outside, which had already expelled him from the study hall (or welcomed his flight from it), spreads his arms upward and addresses the stars. "Faithful translators of my heart," he calls them, as he wonders aloud whether they, too, have also grown quiet or whether it is, in fact, he who has "forgot your tongue and do not know any longer your speech."

The final, plaintive verse, *'anuni kokhvei-el, ki 'atzev ani* ("Answer me, stars of God, for I grow sad"), sounds the poem's minor key of pathos, at the same time, however, as its phonetic harmonics takes us back once again into the world of ancient scrolls and the liturgy of Jewish prayer. In critic Dan Miron's words, "The poem describes the poet's tragic situation as a kind of linguistic calamity or semantic catastrophe: a once adept translator had forgotten the languages [both religious tradition *and* nature] he used to translate from."[10] And yet, as we see, those languages—and in particular, their intonation and accent—reside still in his speech. The sound of Bialik's Hebrew poem still chimes with the voice of the ancient scrolls. Its letters are the same as those to which Talmudic discourse ascribed the word "body" so as to capture the proximity of their materiality to the human—in Said's fine phrase we recall from Chapter 1, "the closeness of the world's body to the text's body."

Among the various intertexts this chapter will trace for it, Bialik's poem may thus also be heard in ironic tension with the passage from Maimonides on poetry quoted in Chapter 3: "And know this: that poetry, whatever its language of composition, must have its content investigated. . . . For if the subject of the poem is virtue, then it should be recited in whatever tongue; however, if its content is unseemly, one ought to restrain himself from reciting it, no matter the tongue." Maimonides conjures a secure linguistic world whose boundaries are unmistakable, not fungible. Bialik's speaker—an avatar of Maimonides's משורר ("poet") the philosopher could not have anticipated— must nevertheless confront a void or chasm unforeseen by twelfth-century religious ideology. Like black pearls, whose string is broke, so those (possibly Maimonidean?) columns of text are to him, now. The tradition itself has lost both its voice and generational continuity for him. *Proximity*, perhaps, is all one can contrive.

TOHU תהו (CHAOS): BIALIK, LEVINAS, AGNON (ROSENZWEIG)

Linguistic calamities like these, but also countervailing advantages and strokes of fortune, will form the topics of this final chapter of the book. The impingement of what is called the sacred on what is called the secular will continue to be our focus, retrieved from earlier chapters and positioned once again in the foreground. Here, I postulate again: how might we imagine that impingement as tangency or contiguity instead of opposition? I asked but did not directly answer how Bialik's psalm of estrangement might bear upon an ethics of reading. I also left hanging the question of orthographic scruple: why it should matter ethically, perhaps—which alphabet is deployed when discussing texts in need of translation for English readers. An obvious example for this book would be the transcriptions of Talmudic discussions *not* in their original Aramaic and Hebrew at the ends of Chapters 2 and 4.[11]

That scruple is joined to a complementary anxiety about translation. The primary texts to be covered here were originally composed in Hebrew, German, and French, just as Chapter 3 was devoted, in part, to a brief seventeenth-century text in French, which even if not analyzed in any detail, was still rendered by an English approximation that fails to do real justice—poetic justice—to its singularity of sound and syntax. "Ethics is locked into a relation with things," Geoffrey Harpham has told us before, "discourses, cognitive styles, ways of evaluating—that are alien to it and yet still its own." While I use the various multilingual texts to scaffold this problematic in a new way, a first approach may be ventured if we notice that Bialik's poem has broken language down to its granular level: *ḥol os VAos l'NAFsha hi yeSOmah* (every letter by letter separately orphaned).

The estrangement pictured here is a singular one: a modern speaking Hebrew estranged from a traditional Hebrew dimly seen and faintly heard. The poem's question is thus elemental, notwithstanding its modernist scenario of the stricken artist-creator: how to speak Hebrew, how, rather, to keep speaking and thus *revive* it? If this were the scene of language instruction crafted for us by Bialik's famous essay, "Revealment and Concealment in Language"—which we come to in the next section—then "language broken down to its granular level" might suffice as an explanation. For, that essay laments the state of language spoken in a fallen world generally. The linguistic imaginary in "Before the Bookcase," however, is a religious and literary one. A decade has passed between poem and essay, and in that time, Bialik's own sense of poetic mission has etiolated. In the meantime, Hebrew as a national language and cultural birthright, has triumphantly been revived, or as Levinas preferred to say, "resurrected."

Yet, Miron's formulation of "linguistic calamity or semantic catastrophe" has implications well beyond Bialik's own personal sense of mission, as we shall see. A tension between *qodesh v'ḥol* (sacred and secular) may have defined Bialik's maturation as a poet, one who left behind the House of Study in the Volozhin yeshiva for an intellectual journey that saw him eventually settled another kind of house to become nationally known as Beit Bialik (House of Bialik), on the street named for him in Tel Aviv.[12] But it also inheres within cultural anxieties felt by many Jewish philosophers, critics, and writers in the early decades of the twentieth century for whom the modernist revival of Hebrew posed basic questions about linguistic patrimony and homeland, and about the capacity of one's secular tongue to translate another, more ancient (and originally religious) one. In this sense, the ethics of reading ancient scrolls, widowed pages, and orphaned letters[13] folds into an ethics of writing about them, of finding perhaps some continued relationship to them while nevertheless feeling answerable to the claims of modernity, or of meditating and polemicizing on the propriety, the efficacy, even the necessity, of translation.

This chapter explores such tension in earnest, looking first at Bialik's 1915 essay, "Revealment and Concealment in Language," written five years after his great collaboration with Yehoshua H. Ravnizsky on the *Sefer ha'aggadah*, "The Book of Legends"), the compendium of non-halakhic material from the Talmud, that in its aggregate was the same force that was to draw Levinas into a world of Jewish textual tradition both novel to him and yet somehow deeply familiar.[14] Complementing Bialik's essay but also refracting it through the prism of a later and much different stage of Jewish intellectual history, therefore, will be Levinas's essay from 1975, "Poetry and Resurrection: Notes on Agnon."

Bialik called the essay of 1915 *Gilui v'khisui balashon*, "Revealment and Concealment in Language"). He holds a special place among the many writers who contributed to the new and burgeoning tradition of Modern Hebrew prose, as that essay, the jewel among a total of twenty-six such pieces demonstrates. In a somewhat likeminded essay from the same year as "Before the Bookcase," entitled *Ḥevlei Lashon* ("Birth Pangs of Language"), Bialik spoke of his own mandate to act as a conduit for poetic currency and its "linguistic assets," as he named them. Only poets could mediate between a revived Hebrew and a new Hebrew-speaking and reading public, Bialik insisted. And yet even for them, language could still become barrier, one of his prime metaphors in the 1915 essay, instead of bridge. In fact, the national poet himself fell famously silent after 1908, ceasing to produce poetry with any regularity in the last eleven years of his life.[15]

Whatever its internal doubts about language's mediating capacity, Bialik's essay will, for the section that follows it, serve as a bridge to a famous confessional letter that Gershom Scholem wrote to Franz Rosenzweig in 1926 on the subject of the revival of Hebrew, entitled *"Bekenntnis über unsere Sprache."* After being largely forgotten for many years after its composition but experiencing a kind of revival itself through being reissued in the 1970s, Scholem's letter prompted Jacque Derrida to produce one of his most meticulous close readings, "The Eyes of Language: The Abyss and the Volcano." Each of those works, the modernist and the postmodern, take us back to Bialik, as they lead, in turn, to a third section that focuses on "Scripture and Luther," Rosenzweig's essay on translation from 1926 together with a review essay on the "New Hebrew" from 1925 and his "Afterword" to his translation of Yehudah Halevi's poetry from 1927. As it concludes, this section pause to gather together elements from the readings of Bialik, Levinas, Scholem, and Derrida that precede it, along with Derrida's long footnote on Rosenzweig in *Monolingualism of the Other* and Benjamin's essay, "The Translator's Task."

The presence of Levinas and Derrida alongside Bialik, Scholem, Benjamin, and Rosenzweig adds a new dimension to the contrapuntal and dialogic criticism that has characterized the rest of the book so far. Unlike previous chapters, however, the effect is rather like that of Bialik's black pearls, except on a knotted rather than a broken string. The writings gathered here under the rubric "languages" are made to speak to each other (sometimes improbably, other times more reasonably) as do the Sages on a randomly chosen page of Talmud: across time and geographical locale. I want thus to propose a sort of veined or tessellated intellectual history, a constellar,[16] interessayistic set of relations both modernist and postmodern. Or, to construe them visually, the silhouettes for the roughly contemporaneous documents by Bialik, Scholem, Rosenzweig, and Benjamin cast each other in side shadow, at the same time as they are backshadowed by much later writing of Levinas and Derrida.[17]

My own critical discourse follows suit, side- and back-shadowing accordingly as it moves among the various essays, through moments of tangency or meaningful adjacency. That said, maybe it is the category of the uncanny (a word that haunts Scholem and Rosenzweig in particular) with its shimmy and shimmer between familiar and unfamiliar that suits the structure of this chapter best. Bialik's "Before the Bookcase" sets the stage, and the chapter concludes antiphonally with an ode to the Hebrew language by Abraham Regelson, who first met Bialik in Cleveland and memorialized his passing in 1934 with the elegy *"Al ish hakokhavim"* (On the Man of Stars).

Let me return to Bialik, now, by way of an idiosyncratic usage of *"la poésie"* that Levinas's essay, "Poetry and Resurrection," chooses in regard to Agnon. As we saw previously, "poetry" eventually became a catchall when Levinas wished to evoke literary discourse generally, not just the restrictive genre of versifying. Thus, the "poetry" in the title of Levinas's essay actually refers to the prose fiction of S. Y. Agnon, Bialik's counterpart in literary modernism, outliving him by fifty years, however. Similarly, when Levinas refers to "the poetic word" and "the poetic web" in Blanchot's writing or when he titles his other essay on Blanchot in *Noms Propres*, "Le regard du poète," poetry is made coterminous with literary language and experience, generally.

Bialik, too, distinguishes between poetic and nonpoetic discourses, but he intends it to signify the gulf that separates literary expression from that of logic—efferent, instrumental, systematic language. His striking metaphor of walking on ice to describe these two methods represents the high-water mark, so to speak, of "Revealment and Concealment in Language":

> The masters of exposition, find their sanction in the principle of analogy, and in the elements common to images and words, in that which is established and constant in language, in the accepted version of things—consequently, they walk confidently through language. To what may they be compared? To one who crosses a river walking on hard ice frozen into a solid block. Such a man may and can divert his attention completely from the covered depths flowing underneath his feet. But their opposites, the masters of allegory, of interpretation and mystery . . . the masters of poetry, are forced to flee all that is fixed and inert in language, all that is opposed to their goal of the vital and mobile in language. On the contrary, using their unique keys, they are obliged to introduce into language at every opportunity—never-ending motion, new combinations and associations. The words writhe in their hands, they are extinguished and lit again, flash on and off like the engravings of the signet in the stones of the High Priest's breastplate, grow empty and become full, put off a soul and put on a soul. By this process there takes place, in the material of language, exchanges of posts and locations: one mark, a change in the point of one iota,[18] and the old word shines with a new light. The profane turns sacred, the scared profane. . . . And to what may those writers be compared? To one who crosses a river when it is breaking up, by stepping across floating, moving blocks of ice. He dare not set his foot on any one block for longer than a moment, longer than it takes him to leap from one block to the next, and so on. Between the breaches the void looms, the foot slips, danger is close . . . (24–26)

"Revealment and Concealment in Language" means what its title straightforwardly designates.[19] Unlike "The Sacred and Secular in Language," a lecture written twelve years later in 1927, the substantive, "language," in the earlier work stakes no nationalist claim; it does not explicitly or exclusively signify Hebrew. As has been pointed out by many of its commentators, the essay reveals multiple influences, among them Ahad Ha'am, Nietzsche, *kabbalah*, literary modernism, perhaps even Spinoza.[20] Pretty clearly, however, whether read in Hebrew or in translation, its spirit is also patently *midrashic*. "To what may they be compared?" Bialik says, conspicuously referencing the rhetoric of rabbinic parable. "Poetry," as a discursive practice for Bialik, thus bridges the modernist innovations he brought to a revived Hebrew, *and* the imaginative linguistic play already staged in this book for us by the aggadists and midrashists of the rabbinic tradition.[21] Does he not have an ally in Levinas in this regard?

After wondering aloud whether Agnon's work belongs to an unbroken chain of Jewish textual tradition or bears witness to its rupture, Levinas's essay considers the duality of poetry (imaginative fiction), which is an "art," that also necessarily evinces the signs of a "document" or "discourse." Such discourse is what Wittgenstein terms *alltäglich*, or "everyday" language, and what Gershom Scholem will shortly call *tagtäglich* ("day by day"). But while its objects may sometimes thus be quotidian—that is, "spoken of in the newspapers, posters, memoirs, and letters of every passing age," its essence, Levinas says, is fundamentally allusive and metaphorical, an "interlinear trace"—"like a footprint that would precede the step, or an echo preceding the sound of a voice" (7).

This would be poetry's essential signification, its "real work," a claim we have previously seen ventured by Levinas in his later philosophical work. But he takes a further step beyond Bialik's argument to suggest that while a poem—say for argument's sake, Bialik's "Lifnei aron ha-sefarim"—might illuminate a critical argument—like, say, the one Bialik himself propounds in his essays on language—we thus run headlong into an ethical dilemma about so *utilizing* "pure poetry" for instrumental purposes.

Poetry corresponds to or instances Saying (*le dire*). Drafting it into the service of clarification or commentary, even in the very name of "exegesis," reduces it to the level of Said (*le dit*), and thus would seem to constitute but another means of severing the *sounded* or *sung* string of black pearls. For Levinas, this problem goes even deeper in a way Bialik does not quite entertain, although the differences here are instructive. "There is an ambiguity or an enigma about the *Hebrew* word" (9, italics mine), Levinas writes. It surfaces when the language itself is resuscitated, made modern, since beneath it resides a "semantic homeland" of biblical scripture whose tonalities and "turns of phrase" reverberate upward.

When we come to Scholem's letter in a moment, we will be introduced to a more violent image of underground movement—"*ein Vulkan*," a volcano, which by "housing" the Hebrew language ensures that it *ist zum Bersten voll* ("full to bursting"). Levinas's idea here does not address sanctity as such in any specifically linguistic capacity—on the order, say, of rabbinical stipulations regarding *tum'at yadayim*, defilement of the hands. He does not specify a biblical or rabbinic nomenclature for Jewish law and religious practice. His sole example of Hebrew language or discourse is restricted to Agnon's fiction. But he does insist that the "Holy tongue" does not inhabit the same locutionary and acoustic space as ordinary language.

Levinas directly ties enigma on the plane of utterance (the ethical counterpart, we recall, to mere cognizable "phenomena") to the *religious* sensibility of Jewish texts and to "the symbolism of rite" (10). We have seen how these connote for him the category of "*beyond*." They, as it were, make ethics *textual*. Or rather, the Jewish textual tradition, in both its content and the rhetorical demands it makes on its readers, discloses another horizon for ethical relation. Thus, in the essay on Agnon, Levinas speaks of a "desubstantialization of being," a stratum of Saying beneath the Said, of trace below and beyond being, as part and parcel of "the Hebraic mode of expression [which] denucleates ultimate solidity beneath the plasticity of forms, as taught by Western ontology." And reciprocally, "the Jewish way of life" lived as practice and in ritual mirrors "the sonority of the language in which it is expressed" (10): "In Agnon, what is at stake is resurrection. Closer to us than any present, the Unrepresentable will not be represented in the poem. It will be the poetry of the poem. Poetry *signifies* poetically the resurrection that sustains it: not in the fable it sings, but in its very singing" (12).

But evidently, the "Jewish way of life" (so construed), participates in this resurrection *itself*, even in the midst of unthinkable cultural depredation and national calamity— as for example, the extermination of all one's fellow Jews in the Polish town of one's birth, as he finds detailed in Agnon's story הסימן ("The Sign") from his final collection of stories, *The Fire and the Wood*. Or, we might legitimately add, the murder of Levinas's own parents and siblings during these same awful years. "Life, sustaining its allegiances to the confines of death, thus goes beyond its being, its limits reaching beyond those limits; and, beyond being, it tastes the taste of Resurrection" (16). Poetry—especially in the hands of those, like Agnon, who "keep the Torah of life"— tastes that taste, as well. The turn that Levinas's own intellectual development after the war takes in the direction of the classical Talmudic sources might also be said to exemplify it.

I want to emphasize that we do not find this sort of backshadowing in Bialik's essay. For one thing, hardly trivial, Bialik was saved from knowledge of the fate of European Jewry operationalized by the Nazi death machine a decade after his death. Moreover, "resurrection" and "the rite" as a "substratum of being" are neither Bialik's ideological, *nor even his poetic* concerns: this, despite the common terrain of *aggadah* for both Galician poet (Bialik) and Lithuanian-born philosopher (Levinas).[22] Levinas's concerns, by contrast, are obviously *belated* and *freighted* well beyond Bialik's strictly modernist, *Tehiyah Ha-'Ivrit* (revivalist) sympathies. He testifies to this overtly in the phrase from "Signature" in *Difficult Freedom* that we have previously encountered as effectively locating his entire *oeuvre*: "dominated by the presentiment and the memory of the Nazi horror" (291).

Bialik was also not Berdyczewski.[23] He did not subscribe to the belief that "the waters of *Ha-Shiloah* [the Hebrew monthly edited in Odessa and Warsaw from 1896– 1926 and founded by Ahad Ha'am] will tear the heart of every Jewish man in Israel into two separate parts, a Jewish part and a humanist part."[24] While a committed משכל (*maskil*, heir to the Jewish Enlightenment), Bialik never repudiated his origins in Radi and Zhitomir in the Ukraine, his adolescent years in the Volozhin yeshiva, and even the Yiddish of his upbringing; they suffuse his poetry and his thought. If no longer religious to the same degree, once his career took him from Odessa to Berlin and finally Tel Aviv, he, too, was sustained, poetically in his sense (aggadically), by "the Torah of life."[25] Jewish dualism, as he styles it in the essay of the same name, is a Jewish given. Shepherds and farmers, *halakhah* and *aggadah*, exile and return, expansion and contraction, the real and the ideal: such contraries form a caduceus in Bialik's synthetic imagination.

"Poetry and prose" suggest another such proto-synthesis, putatively opposed but essentially complementary. Primordial humankind for Bialik was poetic (though not quite in Levinas's religiously inflected sense of the term).[26]

> So, for example, it was for the first man when taken aback by the sound of thunder ("The voice (sound) of the Lord is in the power, the power of Lord is in the glory"), overcome by amazement and terror-stricken, he fell on his face before the divinity. Then a kind of savage sound burst spontaneously from his lips—let us assume, in imitation of the nature—resembling a beast's roar, a sound close to the *r . . . r* to be found in the words for thunder in many languages. Did not this wild cry vastly free his confounded soul? Did not this meager syllable, this seed of the future word, embrace a complete volume of future emotions, powerful in their novelty and vigorous in their savagery, resembling terror, fear, amazement, submission, astonishment, preparedness for self- defense? And if it was true, was not the first man himself at that moment an artist and lofty seer, an intuitive creator of an expression pointing to a deep and complicated inner disturbance? (12–13)

Without recourse to the traditional Babel narrative (an intriguing omission), but rather with allusions to the rabbinic-halakhic concepts of *dalet amot, reshut hayahid,* and *reshut ha-rabbim* (individual space, private and public domains), kabbalistic tropes of *klippot* and *nitzotzot* (husks and sparks), and to creation narrative images of *tohu* (chaos) and its reinscription as *blimah* (void) in Job 26:7 (which we last saw in Levinas's commentary to *bHullin* 89), Bialik records the fate of postlapsarian language from its sublime origins to its inevitable decline as mundane and *alltäglich/tagtäglich*.[27]

"How shaky is their bridge of mere words, how deep and dark the void that opens at their feet, and how much every step partakes of the miraculous," says Bialik of the Talmud's *lashon bnei adam* (the language of men). Repeatedly, Bialik appeals to biblical narrative (Lot's wife in Gen. 19:16–26; God's revelation to Moses at the burning bush in Ex. 3:6 and later in Ex. 33:20 and Ex. 33:11) or rabbinic *midrash* (the four who enter *Pardes* in *bHagigah* 14b) in order to italicize and backshadow the source tradition with linguistic negative theology, the barrier or void that is language itself. "*No word contains the complete dissolution of any question. What does it contain? The question's concealment*" (16).

> With our very lips we construct barriers, words upon words and systems upon systems, and place them in front of the darkness to conceal it; words upon words

and systems upon systems, and place them in front of the darkness to conceal it; but then our nails begin immediately to dig at those barriers, in an attempt to open the smallest of windows, the tiniest of cracks, through which we may gaze at that which is on the other side. But alas, vain is the labor of man! At the very moment when the crack is apparently opened—another barrier, in the shape of a new word or system, suddenly stands in place of the old, shutting off the view again. (20)

At this point, Bialik's register shifts even more somberly to an echo of the *Book of Kohelet* (Ecclesiastes). Words and systems (*kameot* or "talismans") succeed each other in ceaseless oscillations of revelation and concealment. Yet, "The most dangerous moment—both in speech and in life—is that between concealments, when the void looms" (23).

The idea of כיסוי (*khisui*, "concealment," a term we recall from the Torah's proscription of *kisui ha'dam*) here is intriguing since, as Gurevitch suggests, it connotes not only rupture or blockage/collapse,[28] but also dialogic possibility, the motion permitted by traversing blocks of ice, which implicitly (although Bialik never quite gets to social conversation), mimes the openings or pauses we know as breaks in everyday dialogue. Likewise, the distinctively poetic ability to perceive language's true form as קורים של תהו ("web of chaos")—as actually *blocks* of ice exposing the water surrounding and underlying them rather than a frozen surface that only *feels* like *terra firm* but merely hides the "depths flowing underneath"—suggests a danger ultimately worth courting.

Any laurels that poets might deserve are owing to their conscious swerve toward the linguistically vital and mobile and away from the fixed and inert—although we should note how Bialik's metaphors get (purposefully?) mixed, as the vital and mobile share the same figural space with the frozen and floe-like. "Masters of poetry" make language writhe and shine; their "concealments" are actually revelations, seen aright: brief flashes, which postpone the Void that *all* speakers of language ineluctably face. For we all cross the same river, expositors and poets alike, whatever our allegiances to either *naḥiyut* ("stasis, fixity") or *tenuatiut* ("kinesis").

To retrieve now the comparison between Bialik and Levinas, this is *not*, however, what the latter intends in the essay on Agnon by "the frozen swirl of words" from "the depths of the Scriptures," which "fix oral discussions and traditions." "Beneath the froth, like an intricate lace," Levinas writes there, "stands the minute script of commentaries on commentaries" (8). And what is that commentarial work that links the Jewish generations if not the stuff of *ritual*, as we saw it explicated in the essay from 1937 (only three years after Bialik's death), "The Meaning of Religious Practice?" Again,

The ritual is precisely the behavior of one who, amid the racket of our everyday action, perceives the mystical resonance of things. If it stops us at the threshold of the natural world, it is because it introduces us into the mystery of the world. It touches the sacred face of things. . . . It is efficacious and transitive, it is work, it accomplishes—it is an event.

Entirely consistent with that same attitude as expressed by the Agnon essay, a seemingly "static movement of the signs that go toward the 'deep past'" does not ultimately signify what we might therefore perceive to be the "dead language" of Holy Scripture, "in which each expression stands in its final inviolable space" (8). Rather, what only *appears* immobile or "frozen" (precisely because of its immemorial origins in that "deep past"), is capable of being turned and turned "this way and that" through the agitation of "superimposed texts" that thus consistently breathe life into it and sustain its life.[29] Its life lies in its dialogicity; and thus, paradoxically, it becomes the lingua franca of the House of Study where reading *itself* is ritual, work, event.

We will soon see how favorably this compares to Franz Rosenzweig's analysis of the eternality of "holy language" which *"immer lebendig geblieben"* (always remained alive). For what frees up the "frozen swirl of words" is precisely their capacity for renewal. Rosenzweig will use the growth metaphor of treasure as opposed to organism: *"die Sprache wird immer reicher"* (the language grows richer and richer). Strictly speaking, whereas linguistic "death" is reserved solely for the vernaculars, the languages of the world, the Holy Tongue alone, as Rosenzweig had put it in his 1925 essay on the "New Hebrew," signifies an *"Unfähigkeit zu sterben"* (inability to die).[30]

Moreover, like Levinas's categories of *le saint* (the holy) as opposed to *le sacré* (the sacred), Rosenzweig's sense of Hebrew's intrinsic *qedushah* correlates it with both its "demand to be understood, word for word" and its fundamentally dialogic, midrashic life, the fact that it "swarms with quotations": this is Hebrew's archetypal and anti-idealist *Sprach-denken*.[31] *All* language for Bialik, conversely—sacred *or* secular, Hebrew *and* otherwise—is *blimah*; it hangs on nothing, and in its recesses one finds a Void. The metaphor of frozenness, whether as vast sheet or broken up into blocks, merely provides the illusion of security as its speakers vainly attempt to make it cohere; it is solid *enough*, that is to say, since it can be walked upon, but its structural vulnerability is bound up with its ultimate mutability.

Nor, in similar fashion, do Bialik's antinomies of poetry/logic and revealment/concealment conveniently align, since poets are subject to the same linguistic forces as everyone else, given the origin of language in chaos. At best, poets like Bialik are awake to the reality beneath them; all others sleepwalk. Significantly, poets are called *ba'alei aggadah* in Bialik's Hebrew. Like their predecessors in *midrash*, their special knack, we could say, creates a *poeticization* of the religious. In the opposite direction, just as in "Before the Bookcase," a discourse in modern Hebrew cannot help but avail itself of the source lexicon associated with the *beit midrash* (house of study).

We will see momentarily that Gershom Scholem uses extraordinarily similar imagery to Bialik's to describe the uncanny (re)actualization of Hebrew as an everyday language. "We do live inside this language, above an abyss," writes Scholem, "all of us with the certainty of the blind. But when our sight is restored, we or those who come after us, must we not fall to the bottom of this abyss?" It should not surprise us, however, since Scholem certainly knew Bialik's essay and had it in mind when he wrote his address to Rosenzweig.[32] Like Levinas, Scholem is profoundly transfixed by a drama in which the secular and the holy are superimposed on one another. But to tarry with Bialik, we see that "the profane turns sacred, the sacred profane," more or less prosaically, as a matter of diurnal course.

It is not that secular and sacred uses of language don't differ, often by a wide margin. But as noted acutely by Arnold Band, Bialik's true subject in "Revealment and Concealment" (just as it was to be for the essay "Halakhah v'aggadah," published one year later in 1916) has really been "literature—not religious behavior—all along."[33]

> When Bialik states that in this world of "tenuatiut" of the constant shifting and seething of figural language, "hol" (profane) becomes "kodesh," (sacred) and "kodesh," "hol," and that these categories are no longer distinguishable or meaningful, he speaks with the experience of the master of figural language. . . . In his own idiosyncratic way, the way of an innovative poet constantly working with the language of traditional Hebrew texts, Bialik sacralizes the languages [sic] and through it his own literary projects. (294, 296)

This generative and *kinetic* potential of imaginative language for writers and readers alike—"*la poésie*" for Levinas, "гетероглоссиа" (heteroglossia) for Bakhtin, "worldliness" for Said, and what Cavell (in *Senses of Walden*) calls "words, sentences, and portions"—is what this book has evoked as "the difficult," in dialectical relation to "the holy." And it may be said to bestride the rabbinical binary of pure and impure texts, books, or dispensations of language that we have seen unpacked in earlier chapters.

When it comes to Bialik's short talk "*Al qodesh v'hol balashon*" (The Sacred and Secular in Language), delivered in 1927 before the Legion for the Protection of the Language in Tel Aviv, that dialectic has become rigidified and even suspended, as the focus has shifted noticeably to exclusively national considerations. The lecture's date signifies nineteen years since the famous Czernowitz Conference declared Yiddish to be the national Jewish language and fourteen years since the Conference of Hebrew Language and Culture in Vienna responded by making the opposing case for Hebrew.

In the same year that Bialik gave his lecture, PEN International created a Jewish PEN Club for Hebrew and Yiddish writers alike in Wilno-Vilnius-Vilna, only to become the Yiddish PEN two years later once Hebrew writers lobbied for their own autonomous PEN chapter in Palestine. In other words, the generic status of "Jewish language" (as if it were monolingual) at the time Bialik was parsing the sacred and secular was deeply riven by competing territorial and nationalist interests.[34] Bialik's tone is also quite different in this later piece, as befits the rhetorical occasion and departure from a literary essay that it represents. Indeed, the title of that address might have been more accurately rendered as the Hebrew equivalent to what Scholem, just one year before in the title of *his* address to Franz Rosenzweig, called unsere *Sprache*: that is, "*our* language." For in it, Bialik concedes the utility of having "turned the sacred into the profane"(89) once and for all by secularizing the holy tongue.

And yet, Bialik insists, "the ideal of Hebrew speech should not be secular speech, but sacred" 91). "A language," it appears, is neither sacred nor secular; or rather, they are codependent, for "every nation has a holy and a secular language" (89). Along with the "foundation of sanctity" in the language—"books and literature," that is, traditional Jewish practices of reading—what Bialik wants to preserve is the dialectical pull within the linguistic "instinct" that consecrates whatever words it assembles for utterance: the "urge" to "create and produce from the language and raise it to be a sacred tongue" (91). "Without the sacred," Bialik insists, "there can be no secularity. Just as without the Sabbath, the days of labor are pointless" (94).[35] Gershom Scholem will subject such pronouncements to the refiner's fire. His somewhat censorious view of Bialik the poet was bound up with his sense that the *literary* loss—a sort of poetic סטרא אחרא (*sitra aḥra*, "other side")—incurred by inscribing the sacred within the secular was a forced and estranging element of anachronism.[36] By the time he came to deliver the lecture on the sacred and secular, sadly and significantly enough, Bialik's bardic voice has ceased.

I unpack the crossing point between Bialik and Scholem in the next section. Here, however, another comparison with Levinas's celebration of Agnon retains its pertinence. As we saw, poetry for Levinas both embodies—poeticizes—resurrection and serves as its linguistic vehicle. In Agnon's Modern Hebrew, with its tessellations of *melitsah* (a pattern of interpolated biblical and rabbinic phraseology), we "hear the rustle of that surreality" (11).[37] When Bialik speaks for himself, by contrast (for Levinas has, in effect, *ventriloquized* Agnon), he claims only that poetry embodies a more self-conscious (ethical?) awareness of the disunity integral to both language and self. An Edmond Jabès or Jacques Lacan *avant la lettre*, so to speak, H. N. Bialik provides us with a sketch of language—all language—as sustained and conditioned by internal exile. The pathos of *his* "poet's vision" (in Levinas's phrase) is that language, even and perhaps especially *resurrected* language, is a pretense of tangibility. Zali Gurevitch is quite right to characterize this essay, notwithstanding its playful metaphoricity, allusiveness and synthetic imagination, as "gothic."[38]

Additional questions accumulate, along the lines of those I proposed earlier.

1. What is the state of the language—let us now call it "Hebrew," since that is the particular tongue in which this essay speaks—that this celebrated *Ostjüde* bequeaths to his German-Jewish coreligionists and fellow skirmishers in the politics of language, Gershom (born "Gerhard") Scholem and Franz Rosenzweig, one of whom wrote poetry and the other performed the task of its translation?[39]

2. Does Bialik's principled skepticism about the ontic emptiness of language speak to Scholem's localized fears about the lava roiling beneath Eliezer Ben Yehudah's vision of an everyday Hebrew spoken by shopkeepers and children?[40] More dramatically, on the plane of imagery: does *tohu* ("chaos") speak to *Abgrund* ("abyss")?

3. Is there, as Gurevitch puts it, a specific "Hebrew revealment, a revelation of Hebrew" to be glimpsed in that transposition from universal *language* to local *langue*?[41]

4. And can we extrapolate somehow from Bialik's essay to Rosenzweig's ethico-philosophical investment in translation, especially in regard to לשון הקודש *lashon haqodesh* ("the holy tongue") of the Hebrew Scriptures, at whose resurrection Levinas marvels and Scholem confesses prophetic alarm?

Let us see how they take shape in hands of two of Bialik's contemporaries, divided exactly by their respective ambivalent allegiances to one language and land over another, where ethics is "locked into a relation" with contiguities.

ABGRUND: SCHOLEM, BIALIK, DERRIDA (LEVINAS)

I turn to Scholem in this section. The fullest historical and cultural contextualization of Scholem's text to date still belongs to William Cutter's 1990 article in the journal *Prooftexts*, which introduced English readers to it after it had been presented by Jacques Derrida at the School of Criticism and Theory in 1987 in a French translation by Stéphane Mosès.[42] Literary critic Gil Anidjar has justly underscored the Babelian accents gathered here for this German-French-English-Hebrew (sacred/secular, written/spoken) *mélange*. As Scholem narrated the story in *From Berlin to Jerusalem* reproduced by Derrida in "The Eyes of Language," he had corresponded with Franz Rosenzweig in 1921–1922 about translation and the efficacy of Zionism, in its lived expression, by emigrating to Palestine as a solution to the problem of the Jewish Diaspora, and specifically, the cultural situation of German Jews. Rosenzweig's loyalty to *Deutschjudentum* and Scholem's to Zionism were deeply at odds.

Hebrew, Rosenzweig insisted, was a holy over and above a "Jewish" language; a Jew's relationship to it, curiously enough, is that of a kind of *Übersetzer/Übertrager*[43] because it must always remain at a certain distance from the everyday. Yet nonetheless, Modern Hebrew (or *Neuhebräisch*, as Rosenzweig called it in his 1925 essay "Anläßlich der Übersetzung von Spinozas Kritik"), even if foolishly secularized into something merely *bodenwüchsige* (territorial), must still make dialogic contact with its sacred "deep past"—just as Levinas argued for Agnon's fiction and Bialik maintained in "Al qodesh v'ḥol balashon."[44] As is turns out, a linkage among Agnon and Bialik, Scholem, and Rosenzweig, precedes (foreshadows) my own orchestration of their voices. Agnon submitted a fragment of what was to become his novella *Bilvav yamim*

(*In the Heart of the Seas*) to the same fortieth birthday presentation for Rosenzweig in 1926 for which Scholem wrote his *Bekenntnis*. Agnon's story won the first Bialik Prize in 1934, and was included in the *Sefer Bialik festschrift* the same year, after receiving Bialik's particular approbation shortly before he died.

But to continue with Rosenzweig's essay: mediation by way of translation was part and parcel of Jews' condition after Babel. Foreignness was a given wherever they resided; any language they speak is not one they could be accurately said to possess: *Sein Sprachleben fühlt sich stets in der Fremde* ("their linguistic life always feels itself to be in a strange land").[45] An "open tradition" (Galili Shahar's term) like that espoused by German Jewish culture, however, kept all channels open, sustaining the link to ancient sources that is essential to the transcendental and fundamentally deterritorialized— meaning of the Hebrew language.[46] Hebrew, in this prophetic, messianic, but also productively diasporic sense, was both immemorial and always *to come*. Exchanging Jerusalem for Berlin, Rosenzweig cautioned Scholem, will not substitute a supposedly more authentic, reanimated life for a Jewish diaspora that, in his view, was still very much alive, and indeed crucial to Jewish cultural survival. It was the "periphery" on which the orientation of a circle's center depended.[47]

Having been attenuated by Scholem's own move to Jerusalem that year to take up a position at Hebrew University, the conversation with Rosenzweig was reactualized four years later. By that time Rosenzweig was already severely compromised by symptoms of degenerative motor neuron disease, when Scholem was asked to contribute to a volume of handwritten texts in Rosenzweig's honor.[48] That invitation became his text *"Bekenntnis über unsere Sprache"* ("Confession on the Subject of Our Language"). (The text is reproduced in full at the end of this chapter in German and English translation.) In a number of respects, it seemed to come around to Rosenzweig's skepticism about the necessarily self-alienated character of a *verweltlicht* ("secularized") Hebrew vernacular as spoken by its Zionist practitioners, with their "sureness of the blind."

If Bialik's essay on linguistic *blimah* and *tohu* can aptly be characterized as gothic, then Scholem's document earns the similarly apposite labels of "esoteric" and "uncanny"—and not only because Scholem had established his renown as the foremost scholar of Jewish mysticism in his time.[49] The import of his letter is as politically charged as it is (theo)-philologically:

> Aber unheimlicher als das arabische Volk steht eine andere Drohung vor uns, die das zionistische Unterfangen mit Notwendigkeit heraufbeschworen hat: Was ist es mit der „Aktualisierung" des Hebräischen?

> But much more uncanny than the Arab problem is another threat, a threat which the Zionist enterprise unavoidably has had to face: the "actualization" of Hebrew.

Scholem, with Martin Buber, was a founder of ברית שלום/تحالف ألسلام (*Brit Shalom/ Tahalof Essalam*, Jewish-Palestinian Peace Alliance). His intellectual Zionism was of the liberal democratic, binational sort.[50] As premature as those sympathies may have been, given the politico-national circumstances that underpinned the founding of Israel (and condition it still), so, obviously, were Scholem's exaggerated fears of which "threat" portended the greater *Unheimlichkeit*.

The idea was that even if Arab-Jewish relations within the future State of Israel were to be normalized some day, the volcanic and abyssal qualities of Hebrew as a "national language" would defer this people's normalization indefinitely.[51] Scholem's cultural sympathies were an odd amalgam of *maskilic* and esoteric: he subscribed to *Die Öffentlichkeit*, the concept of a new Jewish public sphere, critiqued *Die Wissenschaft des Judentums*, the new Jewish critical scholarship, and initially embraced but later undercut *Die Neuhebräisch*, a new Hebrew. Both German Jewish European and a beneficiary of *aliyah* to Palestine, Scholem surely felt his own metaphysical predicament to be uncanny.

Scholem's choice of *Bekenntnis* rather than, say, *Bericht* (as in Kafka's "Ein Bericht für eine Akademie"), is sufficiently intriguing to throw Derrida back on a paradox of the confessional speech-act: the contradiction of a confessor who acknowledges that he is as blind as those whose unconscious use of the language he decries, thus implicating them as well, but who nevertheless also somehow holds himself aloof from them, "a kind of singular, solitary Zionist" (197).[52] Dana Hollander adds to this idea of a singularizing speech act that nevertheless conscripts others the insight that Scholem also "draws Rosenzweig into the horizon of that desire" (154). I myself am thrown back on Bakhtin's analysis of the forward-looking (and driven) nature of confessional discourse in "Author and Hero in Aesthetic Activity."

Such discourse, Bakhtin speculated, if stalled before its final stage of transgredient "faith" in an Other. It is hindered by "the purity of self-awareness" (141), never really progressing *outside* itself or its own internal restiveness. (Scholem's letter obviously shares in common with Pascal's *Mémorial* the fact that it was found after its author's death.) But Hollander is quite right: the text certainly has a human addressee, and that is Rosenzweig, who played the role of antagonist in relation to Scholem's Zionism, linguistic and otherwise. It is dated "26 Dezember 1926," with Rosenzweig's name as recipient above the body of the text in the letter's title ("An Franz Rosenzweig"), and with Scholem's as signatory (first name, "Gerhard") at the bottom, dated "Jerusalem, den. 7 Teweth, 5687."

There is no Hebrew *in* the letter, and I am not the first to note the profound irony of *unsere sprache* as the chosen signifier instead of *leshonenu* ("our language"). Indeed, the ethical-semantic field "charged" by a choice such as this elucidates precisely why I began this chapter by foregrounding the question of orthography and transliteration. As Derrida acutely puts it, Hebrew "is a language in the name of which, in view of which, out of which they speak together, they have been corresponding for a long time. And this language then, is in several senses of the word, the *subject of the letter*" (200). What Derrida does not note, however, is that the letter *is* framed, conventionally enough for a German Jew who has emigrated to Palestine, by the same date rendered in Gregorian and Hebrew calendars, which captures something of its implicit linguistic double consciousness.

In a late lecture, "My Way to Kabbalah" (1974), collected in *On the Possibility of Jewish Mysticism in Our Time*, Scholem describes his impressions of *unsere Sprache* in Palestinian climes as an "extremely vital language, characterized by an anarchistic lack of rules." He had learned Hebrew in 1911 after studying it "diligently, with warm effort" after the fashion of Goethe's *Faust* which he quotes. The process by which new and old Hebrews were to encounter each other in the future, as he could thus attest through his own linguistic *Bildung* would be both "fruitful and dangerous."[53]

By contrast, German, certainly in correspondence with Rosenzweig, had to have provided a safer and more contained choice in which to formulate an argument about the intrinsic volatility of Modern Hebrew. *Das gespenstische Volapük* ("the gho[a]stly gibberish") and *ausdrucklose Sprachwelt* ("faceless lingo"), is how Scholem startlingly conjures it. For, "conjuring" is deeply at issue in Scholem's fiery rhetoric.

> Es steht nicht mehr in unserer Hand, die alten Namen tagtäglich zu beschwören, ohne ihre Potenzen wachzurufen. Sie werden erscheinen, denn wir haben sie ja freilich mit großer Gewalt beschworen.
>
> We have no right to conjure up the old names day by day without calling forward their hidden power. They will appear, since we have called upon them, and undoubtedly they will appear with vehemence!

Derrida refers to these conjuring secularizers as "*les sorciers ensorcelés*" (spellbound sorcerers, 215) and "demonic sorcerers' apprentices" (198), picking up on Scholem's rhetoric of "*dämonischen Mut*" (demonic courage) and "*die Wunderkraft der Sprache*" (the miraculous power of the language).[54] With Galili Shahar, I want to tease out (as Derrida does not), the affinity here with the gnostic element identified by Scholem in his essay from 1970, "The Name of God and the Linguistic Theory of the Kabbalah," as the stuff of "practical magic."[55] But however the letter is refracted, or whichever companion texts are brought to bear on it, it's hard to imagine a more concentrated demonstration of the Uncanny at work at the levels of both Saying and Said.

Scholem's letter to Rosenzweig is rife with the language of profanation. Imagery of volcano and abyss, imputations of spectrality, revenants, conjuration, mesmerism, demonism, and not least two references to "*apokalyptischen—Stachel, Weg*" (thorn, road)— stand over the piece, and function as the most memorable figuration in this most electrically charged of confessions, whose rhetoric no less than its axiomatics, as Derrida rightly says, is "*tout autre*" (wholly other). In other words, Scholem's text, while it may seem to counterweigh the sacred and secular (alongside the binary oppositions Derrida and others note: concealed and revealed, private and collective, mystical and political, eruption and fall), can be read as staging a genuinely uncanny drama of *supernaturalism.* To speak Hebrew, in effect, is to "conjure" divinity, which, one notes, is not the same linguistic operation—albeit using some of the identical signifiers and vocables—as prayer, benediction, or reciting Torah and learning Talmud.

Derrida's "internal" reading is characteristically sharp and attuned, and two analytic moments particularly stand out for identifying the text's double-voiced *Unheimichkeit:*

1. [Scholem] insists simply on the verge of the abyss—this is his desert, his place without place—he insists and sojourns at this improbable border. And one shall never know—this at least will be the question guiding my reading, but, for essential reasons, it will also remain unanswered—whether at this limit where no settlement is possible Scholem asks for a *shibboleth* in order to get out of the abyss, or, finally, in order to rush into it and be engulfed by it. There will be some difficulty in identifying his desire here. (197)

2. What is it that anguishes Scholem and gives his letter its properly apocalyptic tone? Is it the fact that we, the majority of us, almost all of us, are walking as blind men on the surface of sacred language? Or is it the fact that this language will fatally come back, or rather that it will open itself upon its own abyss, upon itself, upon its essence, inasmuch as this essence remains abyssal? Does Scholem wish that the abyss remain open, or does he hope that it will close one day since the vigilant and immediate experience of an abyssal language risks becoming properly unlivable? This equivocation cannot, I believe, be resolved in this letter. It is the letter's entire power of fascination—and the fascination always relates to Scholem's indecision, one that he neither can nor wants to master. Thus is what gives the envoi its apocalyptic tone. (203)

Language—Hebrew language, specifically—as both a "dead" language and a more living language than the term customarily indicates is revolutionary and apocalyptic upon being reawakened; and it will wreak a kind of vengeance on its speakers by turning against them (*gegen ihre Sprecher wenden wird*). It extracts sacrality from sacred text, repurposing it for *la parole.* A kind of *Pledge, Turn, Prestige* as profanation, such sorcery risks linguistic effects it can't control. (And thus does Scholem's letter also haunt the precincts of a neighboring text about the uncanny power of language: Bialik's "Gilui v'khisui balashon")

For me, the most powerful moment in Derrida's reading is an interpretation ventured only to be abandoned. By positing a third possibility that would function as "a kind of metaphysical referee" (200), the form of the question it postulates, i.e., "transcendental and dialectical," effectively compromises the deconstructive method of the analysis. And yet, I will conjure it back to interpretive life here. This is the insight Derrida posits and then retracts:

One might let oneself be tempted here by what I take the risk of calling the hypothesis of the third language. . . . The expression third language would rather name a differentiated and differentiating element, a medium that would not be *stricto sensu* linguistic but the middle/milieu of an experience of language that, being neither sacred nor profane, permits the passage from one to the other, translating one into the other, appealing from one to the other. In other words, according to the logic of this hypothesis . . . one would really have to suppose, precisely, that signatory and addressee locate themselves between the two languages, and that the former [the sacred], the one who warns, presents himself as ferryman [*passeur*], as translator, as mediator. Partaking of the two languages, the intercessor only speaks them out of the experience of a third . . . not yet or no longer sacred or secular, or *already still* both at once, permits one to take this step on the edge of the abyss. What, then, would this language be in general, this third language that lets surge within itself the adversity—sacred/nonsacred? holy/not-holy? (Levinas)

Elsewhere in the essay (205), Derrida mentions the related antinomy of "pure/impure" in specific relation to apocalyptic discourse and *kabbalah*.[57] (He does *not*, of course, pursue the textual transposition of defilement by/of hands we have seen Levinas explore talmudically.) Yet, the parenthesis enclosing Levinas's name in the passage above reminds us at least of the Levinasian contrast between "*le sacré*" (the sacred) and "*sainteté*" (the holy). Both Scholem and presumably Derrida (even more intriguing, given the Levinas connection) take these terms to be synonymous. "Holy" and "sacred" locate the same referent. Annabel Herzog pinpoints exactly Scholem's conflation of these categories when she writes of his "nostalgia for the holy and quasi-magical power of the ancient divine Hebrew" (229).[58]

Of course, here, between a mitnagdic (French-)Lithuanian sensibility cocooned within a philosophical vocation and a German Jewish kabbalistic bent that infuses the vocations of philology and Jewish history, yawns a divide perhaps as great as that between sacred and secular uses of language or the many other oppositions that surface, both programmatically and so uncannily, in Scholem's *Berkenntnis*. As we recall from a previous treatment, Levinas defines *holiness* in terms of "purity, the essence without admixture that can be called Spirit and which animates the Jewish tradition." Contrariwise, "the sacred is in fact the half light in which the sorcery the Jewish tradition abhors flourishes"—which, in the modern world, signifies a condition where "nothing is identical to itself [and] all speech is a magical whisper."[59] (I come back to this point in connection with Scholem and again when we come to Rosenzweig, for it will prove to be of critical importance.)

Herzog helps us by reinserting a missing supplement or hypogram in Derrida's analysis, a verse from Psalms 36:7 that explains Scholem's choice of *Vulkan* and *Abgr-*

und as his organizing metaphor: צדקתך כהררי אל משפטיך תהום ברה אדם ובהמה תושיע ה', "Your justice like unending mountains, Your judgment the great abyss [*tehom*]."[60] "Justice" and "judgment" add a biblical subtext to the kabbalistic and Bialik overlays (Bialik, in fact, uses the identical verse from Psalms at the beginning of "Gilui v'khisui balashon"),[61] which returns Scholem's text to the historical Palestinian context of debates on the *Tehiya Ha-'Ivrit* by Ahad Ha'Am, Berdyczewski, Yosef Hayyim Brenner, and, of course, Bialik himself. These are not nuances Derrida is able to discern.

But, as Herzog points out, they bring out the locally and historically *political* subtext of the confession: Scholem's increasing anxiety about the costs of political Zionism, political sovereignty and the "'foreign' choice of secular politics" (233). "Foreign" chimes with the rhetorical question Derrida poses in *Monolingualism*: "Can one speak a sacred language as a foreign language? Is a sacred language more one's own or more foreign in general" (199, Herzog's modified translation)? She rejoins it by affirming Derrida's discarded hypothesis about three languages, but modified itself by a Bakhtinian intuition of her own:

> To my mind, Derrida has the right intuition of a conflict or contrast between three languages. However, these languages are not the secular, the sacred, and the in-between (neither sacred nor secular or "already still both at once"). They are rather: one's own language, one's foreign language, and one's sacred language. The problem revealed by the writing in *German* of a letter about the conflict between *secular Hebrew* and *sacred Hebrew* is that of foreignness in every language and of the vain desire to find authenticity on a land that will host you as it hosts language. . . . I wish therefore to argue that Scholem's concern is not the relationship between holiness and alienation but more precisely the relationship between holiness and *foreignness*. (232)

"Sacred," I think, is the correct choice, since so much of Scholem's sense of it is tied to numinous and, yes, quasi-magical properties. The third option of "one's sacred language," in other words, holds open the possibility of a fourth and distinct modality, that is, one's *holy language*—or rather, a language that in Levinasian patois is on the way, from the sacred to the holy.

Does such a passage describe the linguistic situation Scholem configured for himself, given all his deep learning in *kabbalah*? Did the New Hebrew represent a desacralized language (albeit an illusion thereof)? Or merely one that—again only purportedly—aspired to disenchantment, disencumbered of the "apocalyptic thorn," but whose reenchanted obverse, according to Levinas, denotes a world of "bad secrets"? Herzog describes Scholem's anxieties as deriving from "loss of proximity" to the linguistic sacred. And while Scholem's rhetoric speaks of *religiöse Gewalt*, *heiligen Sprache*, and *heilige Tradition*, these all seem to connote the numinous. And thus neither his text nor Herzog's commentary entertains a distinction like Levinas's. In

"Desacralization and Disenchantment," Levinas tells us twice that he has "asked himself" whether holiness "can dwell in a world that has not be desacralized" and "whether the world is sufficiently desacralized to receive such purity" (141).

These are not Scholem's questions. Rather—and here I have to speculate with Herzog—that it was the *foreignness* of the Hebrew Scholem heard and spoke, especially in tension with his German *Muttersprache* that, in the guise of what he wished to conjure—*die Sprache der alten Bücher* ("the language of the ancient books") whose "*jedes Wort . . . aus dem 'guten alten' Schatz entnommen wird*" ("every word . . . taken from the good old treasures"), gave him present-tense political reality instead of the mystified Sacred of *Antiquität*. And thus, I find it peculiarly apt that Scholem's *Berkenntnis* ends with the Hebrew date, 7 *Teweth* (in Roman characters) and its author's name rendered as *Gerhard* Scholem, not *Gershom* . . . or even, גרשם שלום.

ÜBERSETZEN: ROSENZWEIG, BENJAMIN, SCHOLEM (DERRIDA)

Franz Rosenzweig concludes his review-essay of Klatzkin's translation of Spinoza and the "New Hebrew" with a cautionary lesson about a picture book he has there in front of him "*mit Landschaftern aus Palästina und zweisprächigen Text*" (scenes of Palestine and a bilingual text). He quotes the German Orientalist preface with its *ersatz* shades of Tagore and "*Aus diesem mit allen Wassern neudeutschen Universitätidealismus ge- und verwaschenen*" (its peroration washed [and washed out!] with all the waters of the idealism of modern German universities; 271). Then he quotes the Hebrew version (but rendered in German), noting its explicit, dialogic echo of Micah 6:8. "*Aus gebildetem Gewäsch ist in der Übersetzung, die nicht ihrem allfälligen Können, sondern dem gesetzesmäßigen Müssen der Sprache folgte, das einfache Wort der Wahrheit geworden*" (The translation has converted educated balderdash into the simplicity of truth, and its success is not due to any degree of ability but to submission to the laws of language; 271). His essay's own wry colophon then pronounces the Latin formula *Quod erat demonstrandum* (at which he had earlier poked fun when translated into Hebrew from Spinoza), which he follows with the Talmudic formula, *shema miney* ("hear/conclude it from this")—once again, rendered in German: *Hören von diesem!*

This small trilingual episode (quadrilingual, if one counts the Latin), writes small the larger issue that we saw teased out for Gerhard/Gershom Scholem, a conflict or contrast between three languages: one's own language, one's foreign language, and one's sacred language. Rosenzweig's native German corresponds to the first, the Germanicized Hebrew that corresponds to Klatzkin's Hebraicized Latin to the second, and the Talmudic soundbite (more or less) to the third. Rosenzweig, more wisely than Scholem, it would appear, understood the parasite in the host, which is the inescapable foreignness lodged in one's "own" language. This is something that Slavoj Žižek and Eric Santner have both stressed in their books dealing with implications of what they call, after Freud and Lacan, the "Neighbor Thing":

Every language, by definition, contains an aspect of openness to enigma, to what eludes its grasp, to the dimension where "words fail". This minimal openness of the meaning of its words and propositions is what makes a language "alive." We effectively "understand" a foreign culture when we are able to identify with its point of failure: when we are able to discern not its hidden positive meaning but rather its blind spot, the deadlock the proliferation of meaning endeavors to cover up.[62]

Nearness in this sense—the desire for "one's own"—necessarily traffics with otherness, something also basic to Mikhail Bakhtin's argument about "the necessity of having to choose a language," the fact that "with each literary-verbal performance, consciousness must actively orient itself amidst heteroglossia, it must move in and occupy a position for itself," and that consequently, "one must take the word and make it one's own" (*Dialogic Imagination*, 294–295). Indeed, it would probably be more helpful (even without Derridean or Lacanian-inspired theories of self-difference), to speak here in terms of language*s*, even when attempting to parse the meaning of *unsere Sprache*. The *currently* heteroglossial state of spoken Hebrew as *our language*— with all its many diversified strata depending on who speaks it and how its words, according to the Bakhtinian model, are "expropriated"—would seem to make that point all by itself, something neither Scholem *nor* Rosenzweig could not have anticipated.

Derrida ventured his own *rapprochement* with Rosenzweig in his book *Monolingualism of the Other; or, The Prosthesis of Origin*, a text that concerns, among other things, the givenness of a language or national discourse and one's stake in being said thus to "possess" it, and the self-difference which marks any ostensibly proprietary, sovereign, or "monolingual" tongue. Derrida proposes three recursive theses: (1) "We only ever speak one language—or rather one idiom only," (2) "We never speak only one language—or rather there is no pure idiom," and finally "I only speak one language (and, but, yet), it is not mine."[63] But while the book's creolized politics of language stops far short of making such a claim, what if we align these three premises with Annabel Herzog's triad for Scholem's letter? That system of correspondence would then give us (1) the language we speak is *one's own*; (2) the language we never speak is *the foreign*; (3) the language I only speak that yet is not mine is *the sacred*.

Rosenzweig's philosophy of translation was not far removed from the notion of grammatical "speech-thinking" in his *Neue Denken*, that is, time-bound, addressed to some Other: "the difference between the old and the new, logical and the grammatical thinking, does not lie in sound and silence, but in the need of an other, and what is the same thing, in the taking of time seriously."[64] In the "Afterword" to his translation of Yehudah Halevi's poetry, Rosenzweig claims not just the possibility but the indispensability of asking the target language to "reproduce an alien tone in all its alienness" from the source text: "the creative aspect of translating can only manifest itself in the region of then creative aspect of speech itself" (Galli translation, 170): *nicht das Fremde einzudeutschen, sondern das Deutsche umzufremden* ("not to Germanize what is foreign but to make foreign what is German"). But "the sacred," as we have been speculating, in thus the *more-than-foreign*.

Although the "Afterword" differs in some crucial respects from Benjamin's "The Translator's Task," his now-famous foreword to his Baudelaire translation from three years previous, by positing the "renewal of one language through another—through an alien language" (171), Rosenzweig's thought approximates the Benjaminian idea that translation's transformative potential *includes* the mother tongue. As Derrida re-formulated it, that can only mean that mother tongues, like mothers, can simply go mad.[65] As the original language "matures" under the translator's hand, according to Benjamin—its *"Richtung"* (direction) oriented toward the articulation (or release) of a *"reine Sprache"* (pure language)—so the "alien voice" transmitted through translation, says Rosenzweig, makes the original "different from what it was before" (253).

As what Benjamin calls *"eine Form"* (a mode), that is, something other than a vehicle of transmissibility of content, the act of translation communicates *"Übersetz-barkeit"* (translatability) above all:[66]

> The task of the translator consists in finding that intended effect [intention] upon the language into which he is translating which produces in it the echo of the original. . . . Unlike a work of literature, translation does not find itself in the center of the language forest but on the outside facing the wooded ridge; it calls into it without entering, aiming at the single spot where the echo is able to give, in its own language, the reverberation of the work in the alien one.[67]

Last, both Benjamin's and Rosenzweig's translation credos preserve a space for an unas-similable foreign element amid the kinship of languages promised by that "translat-ability," and both see translation of the Scriptures as paradigmatic for all translation.[68]

In the earlier essay from 1916, "On Language as Such and the Language of Man," however, Benjamin makes Scripture exceptional rather than paradigmatic: "Language attains its full meaning in the realization that every evolved language (with the excep-tion of the word of God), can be considered as a translation of all the others" (69–70). And this takes us back to the Scholem-Rosenzweig debate. One could say that the position that regards one's own language as hovering between the native and the alien—from the modified triad I proposed—already presides over both these philoso-phies of translation, which also track laterally to Bialik, Scholem, Agnon, and the singular condition of the "Hebrew of 1921!" But where for Scholem Biblical Hebrew haunts and demonizes the modern revival of the language, *Neuhebräisch* for Rosen-zweig connotes something both very old and brand-new, ancient and modern, sacred and vernacular: the linguistic perturbation of *umzufremden*.

In "Die Schrift und Luther," Rosenzweig implicitly addresses the status of the third element in the Herzog/Derrida triad of correspondences, the one that Benjamin ex-ceptionalizes in his essay of 1916: "the language I only speak that yet is not mine, or *the sacred*" (and that Derrida also captured in his "Des Tours de Babel" essay as a "*pas de sens*," as that which "would give *at the limit* the ideal measure for all translation").[69] He does so by staking a claim for productively "alienating" the Hebrew Bible through translation and thus "releasing" it from the constrictive hold exercised upon the text in German by Luther's sixteenth-century *Die Bibel*,[70] which was largely founded on the Latin of the Vulgate:

> If somewhere it has become familiar, customary possession, it must again and anew, as a foreign and unfamiliar sound, stir up the complacent satedness of its alleged possessor from outside. This book and this book alone among all the books of humankind must not find its end in the treasure house of human culture—because, precisely, it must not find an end in the first place. . . . It is borrowed more often than is any other book, and yet there are always more copies available. Then some reader approaches the desk and requests the book. The attendant comes back: no copies left. The librarians are appalled, desperate, bewildered; just now, when Frau Professor Day-Before-Yesterday picked up a copy for her husband, all the shelves were full. The Bible is written for the sake of the reader who has been denied it.

The collaborative Buber-Rosenzweig translation of Scripture was midrashic in sensibility, carefully attuned to form (*Gestalt*) as the vehicle for restored revelation, or as the essay on Luther has it, "the totality of human speech" (Rosenwald translation, 66). The Bible's "foreignness" is thus intended to be recognized by *all* its readers, hence Rosenzweig's incentive to retranslate—or rather, detranslate—Scripture for German Jews and Germans alike.[71] It also bespoke his own aesthetic sensibility in *The Star of Redemption* regarding the peculiar affinity between, on one hand, the Jewish imaginary as a diasporic "community of fate," and, on the other, the autonomous (orphaned?) work of art: "*unheimlichen lebensvollen und doch lebensfremden Lebendigkeit*" (uncanny in its vitality which is full of life and yet alien to life).[72]

Jewish religiosity bound to traditional text and commentary (or in Rosenzweig's vision, to a *Lehrhaus*) expresses itself as *ganz Kuntswerk* as opposed to mostly secular *Gesamtkunstwerk*. Yet, it also constitutes "*Mehralkunstwerk*" (more-than-a work of art), which, as Zachary Braiterman reminds us, signifies a simultaneous fusion with and detachment from the aesthetic.[73] In terms I have had recourse to before in this book, the relationship between the difficult and the holy for Rosenzweig signifies is no less uncanny than dialogical. Art and ethical adventure expressed as the task of translation share a proximity that means something more than co-presence along parallel lines and also something less than a twinning of duplicate features. Or, to use the alternate vocabulary that Rosenzweig's *Star of Redemption* deploys, visible and invisible, physical and metaphysical, profane and sacred, immanent and transcendent forge interpenetrating alliances; each component of every pair not only implies but also dialogically *requires* its correspondent.

Where Rosenzweig's translation of Yehudah Halevi's poetry aimed for a hybrid register that would "speak Jewishly" (*es sehr jüdisch spricht*) while transvaluing German, the Buber-Rosenzweig Bible had to achieve the same end while working through and against previous translations (Luther's but also Mendelsohn's 1783 and Hirsch's 1867–1878 editions);[74] neither of them, in Rosenzweig's estimation, passed the test of *Unheimlichkeit* by successfully returning the text to its "*undichterisch-überdichterisch*" (unpoetic-superpoetic) origins.[75] Rosenzweig configured this twentieth-century German-Jewish innovation as translation by means of self-estrangement. Oona Eisenstadt has called it "detranslation," and reminds us of Scholem's observation in his commemorative address of 1961 that far from its utopian vision of a German-Jewish open tradition, *Die Schrift* (*Buber-Rosenzweig*) marked "the tombstone of a relationship that was extinguished in unspeakable horror."[76]

To conclude this brief treatment of Rosenzweig's essays and circle back to Scholem, one of translation's virtues, indeed its very obligation, is to relieve the pressure introduced by *Schrift* over the enunciative power of *Sprache* that is any language's motor and wellspring. As speech is time-bound, so translation is not confined to a one-time affair but rather, and necessarily, becomes continually reperformed and renegotiated. To that extent, the performative dimension of the translator's agency resembles the *miqra* of the biblical text, as we saw it explained in Chapter 1: a reading that is a reciting that is also a calling-out. As he wrote in a 1927 letter, "The Unity of the Bible": "The unity of the written Torah and the unity of the oral Torah—or, as we might say, of the read Torah—together creates the translator's task" (Rosenwald translation, 24). German *Schrift* is encouraged to "learn Hebrew," so to speak, by becoming the vehicle for *miqra*.[77]

This cuts obliquely across Benjamin's valedictory image in "The Translator's Task" of an interlinear Scriptural translation as being "the prototype or ideal of all translation": "For to some degree all great writings, but above all holy scripture, contain their virtual translation between the lines" (Rendall translation, 165). For Rosenzweig, this bias toward the written as visual would still sidestep the scrupulosity needed for *hearing the text speak* in translation: "Die schöpferische Leistung des Übersetzens kann nirgends anders liegen als da, wo die schöpferische Leistung des Sprechens selber liegt" / The creative achievement of translation must coincide with none other than the creative achievement of speaking (Galli translation, 170).

It is not clear that Scholem's letter was picking up on Rosenzweig's use of "abyss" or whether he was hewing to a motif to which he often had recourse, but this is what Rosenzweig says about *Sprache/Schrift* and *Abgrund* in his "Afterword" to the Halevi translation: "Der Übersetzer macht sich zum Sprachrohr der fremden Stimme, die er über den Abgrund des Raums oder der Zeit vernehmlich macht" / The translator makes himself the mouthpiece for the foreign voice which he makes audible above the abyss of Space or Time (Galli translation, 171).[78] Since this brings us back to the figuration of a resuscitated Hebrew as *Abgrund* or *Vulkan*, with their cross-echoes of Bialik's *tehom* (abyss) and Levinas's "frozen swirl," I would like now to tie these already individually twisted threads together.

CROSSOVER AND SIDE ROAD: SCHOLEM, ROSENZWEIG, BIALIK (WITTGENSTEIN)

In the *Berkenntnis*, Scholem writes, Wir leben ja in dieser Sprache über einem Abgrund, fast alle mit der Sicherheit des Blinden, aber werden wir nicht, wir oder die nach uns kommen, hineinstürzen, wenn wir sehen werden ("We live with/in this language over an abyss, nearly all of us with the confidence of the blind, but must not we or those who came after us stumble into it when we see again?") For Rosenzweig, this living with/in a language as being suspended over its abyss does not refer to *Neuhebräisch* as a product of the "*Säkularisierung*" the language has newly "actualized." Rather, any "*Aktualisierung des Hebräischen*" represents in Rosenzweig's opposing view the "*Umfremdisch*" (estranging) and "*Zuwanderisch*" (migrational) qualities latent in the holy tongue to begin with.

Through the actualizations of reading-recitation and especially *translating*, the *Abgrund* of Hebrew reveals itself to be an eternal property of the language and of the Jews who serve as its vehicle wherever they may happen to find themselves. By Rosenzweig's reckoning, the Hebraic and Judaic are fundamentally translational categories anyway—as is only apt since etymologically, the word "Hebrew" stems from a root *'I,V,R*, e.g., עברי and עברית ("a Hebrew" and "the Hebrew language"), which captures the basic sense of "transfer" intrinsic to both Latin *translatio* and Greek ερμηνεύω.[79]

> The Hebrew, in his etymological meaning, is a passer-through (*la'avor*), a breaker-off (*'avera),* a transgressor (*'avera*), a passer-on, a producer and a creator (*ubar, me'uberet, ibur hahodesh*); he is also someone who takes into account that which is outside of himself (*Ba'avur she . . .*)[80]

So, the sacred will necessarily impinge upon what is called the secular.

As a poetry that signifies "between the lines," to recall Levinas's example, Agnon's language illuminates the "continual fission" in which "the signifying of the Scripture resonates within the inmost reaches of the living word" (12). Bialik's similar premise, in his late lecture (almost exactly contemporary with Scholem's letter to Rosenzweig), "Al qodesh v'ḥol balashon," emphasizes the sacred in language as the realm of "transmigration," what textual theorists of the contemporary moment know as "polysemy," "plurivocity," "multivocality."

"Gilui v'khisui balashon" throws a more skeptical light on the diasporic nature of utterance, there imagined biblically as void and barrier, and kabbalistically as the tension between husk and core: "Long established words are constantly being pulled out of their settings, as it were, and exchanging places with one another" (25). But I think the essay's ultimate equanimity, its faith, finally, in enlivening nonverbal languages like "songs, tears, and laughter" (26), finds common cause with Rosenzweig's convictions of linguistic renewal, and his belief that human speech itself—dialogue—performs the act of translation:

> If the spoken word were to remain throughout history at the height of its glowing power, if the same original complex of emotion and thought which became attached to it in its prime were to accompany it always, perhaps no speaking person would ever attain to its self-revealment and particular illumination. In the final analysis, an empty vessel can hold matter, while a full vessel cannot; if the empty word enslaves, how much more is this true of the full word. (14–15)

The drama being played out in Scholem's letter (so construed by Derrida), of secularization's flattening effect and its "'politcolinguistic' profanation" vs. "the revenge or return of the sacred" (194), is just what languages do (Bialik). Benjamin and Bakhtin would probably concur. In the special case of Hebrew (put perhaps only historically singular not intrinsically so), if the language is *zum Bersten voll* ("full to bursting"), that is merely owing to its cumulative dialogism, the way it "swarms with quotations" (Rosenzweig). Derrida's Scholem, Rosenzweig, Bialik, and Levinas's Agnon all converge around this central understanding of the Hebrew language, in Rosenzweig's phrase, as "tied up with the past" (269). But for Rosenzweig and Bialik alike, this chiefly means that "it does have obligations to the rest of the world, even when spoken by the youngest child in the most recently founded settlement" (Glatzer translation, 269). The language, in effect, is neither an abyss nor a volcano. It is a shifting ground.

We have seen this basic poetics of transfer either ramped up to the intensity of melodrama or italicized in each of the readings that make up this chapter. Reiterating Annabel Herzog's corrective once again, I would accentuate the way in which a relationship between holiness and some experience of alienation—whether internal to language (Bialik, Rosenzweig) or contingently imposed upon it (Derrida's Scholem and Levinas's Agnon)—can be mistaken for an interaction between holiness and *foreignness*. Jews, according to Rosenzweig, must continually grapple with the vagaries of being "*in der Fremde*" (in a strange land), on at least two fronts: linguistically as well as topographically, through vagaries of communication and national belonging. But that condition does more than just model the pathos of a "foreignness in every language and of the vain desire to find authenticity on a land that will host you as it hosts language" (Herzog, 232), that is, the "politicolinguistic" bifold of (1) the language we speak is *one's own* and (2) the language we never speak is *the foreign*.

It also teaches Bialik's lesson about walking on blocks of ice, which, we should note, departs from the sea of the Talmud entirely. Call such traversal both *translatability* and *transmissibility*. Call such a crosser of tongues, an *'Ivri*. "Language," wrote Ludwig Wittgenstein in the *Investigations*, "is a labyrinth of paths. You approach from *one* side and know your way about; you approach the same place from another side and no longer know your way about" (§203). And again, in §426, "In the actual use of expressions we make detours, we go by side-roads. We see the straight highway before us, but of course, we cannot use it, because it is permanently closed." This must count also as a confession about the state of our language.[81]

An allusion to Wittgenstein should remind us here that all this talk of homelessness and peril in language is a thoroughly modernist preoccupation. Bialik, Scholem, Rosenzweig, and Agnon[82] were all afflicted with it; Benjamin's messianism was, in part, an expression of it, as well. If we recall the epigraph to Chapter 4, Stanley Cavell speaks of the gain in nuanced understanding "if we *translate* the idea of bringing words back as leading them back" (italics mine). The passage actually terminates a paragraph that contains a sentence in the very same vein, but one that I previously omitted: "But the translation is only a little better, because the behavior of words is not something separate from our lives, those of us who are native to them, in mastery of them. The lives themselves have to return."[83]

The resonance of *all* those sentence with the six authors assembled here who treat the fate of Hebrew should be self-evident. Certainly, Rosenzweig, Scholem, Bialik, Derrida, and Levinas/Agnon *all* have in mind the return of Jewish lives—or "Jewish life"—as exemplified by the return of Hebrew. But Cavell's admittedly incidental use of "translate" and "translation" should also invite us to contemplate what acts of translation can and cannot do. Even granting the Benjaminian premise that "translation ultimately has as its purpose the expression of the most intimate relationships among languages" (154)—a relationship he later figures as interlinearity—its corollary remains just as salient: "translation is merely a preliminary way of coming to terms with the foreignness of languages to each other," (157), or in the more famous image, the glue that joins together "*Scherben eines Gefässes*" (fragments of a vessel).

Wittgenstein's sentence in the German original that Cavell translates reads, "*Wir führen die Wörter von ihrer metaphysischen wieder auf ihre alltägliche Verwendung zurück.*"[84] "Leading words back" instrumentally improves upon "bringing words back," according to Cavell, chiefly because the idea of shepherding is implicitly connectable to shepherds' own agency: one should realize that they, too (or their lives), also "have to return." In making the suggestion of a more felicitous English rendering, Cavell underscores the reciprocal foreignness of *zurückführen* and "to bring back." This training in proximity is what translation can effectuate. What it cannot do, accordingly, is overcome the foreignness, the *Umfremdung* and *Unheimlichkeit* internal to a given language itself. (We may be reminded of the pledged bird "brought back" in John Cutter's vanishing birdcage and the price paid for it.)

This is also what Bialik laments in his poem that began our chapter:

> I look, I see—and I do not recognize you, old folk,
> from within your letters now won't gaze
> any longer into the depths of my soul opened eyes,
> sad eyes of the ancients of old,

and I no longer hear from there the whisper of their lips,
that stir in a forgotten grave, untouched by human foot.
Like black pearls, whose string is broke
your columns of text are to me; your pages widowed
and every letter by letter separately orphaned—

I translated that title "Before the Bookcase," but on Cavell's model (and Benjamin's, not to mention Rosenzweig's and Scholem's) a more delicate and palpable rendering would be "Facing the Bookcase," since so much of the poem's imagery is physiognomic, as in, for example, eyes no longer staring into eyes. This is also why I sounded the early note of punctilio in regard to orthography and transliteration. For how do we lay claim to such (linguistic, lexical, alphabetic) foreignness if we simply ignore the question, blithely moving on to the communicative work that both Rosenzweig and Benjamin tell us is only secondary to what we can now call an ethics of translation?

This, incidentally, is the question Levinas takes up in his Talmudic reading of *bMegillah* 8b–9b, "The Translation of the Scripture," glossing a *baraita* (Aramaic ברייתא, meaning "external" or "outside"), that insists on the materiality of "the body, i.e., the letters used in translated texts, the ink and the construction, the form of the book itself" (42).[85] The language we take from granted and our comfortable home in it are brought up sharply—Derrida's and Levinas's *soliciter* or "tremble"—by the visions of living in a language or walking upon its surface we have seen, where its very cratered, volatile nature *undermines* any uncritical or somnambulant attitude toward conjuring it into speech. Presumably, this is how we remain tact-ful.

In the beginning of this chapter, I also asked how "impingement" could be construed as tangency instead of opposition? If the question *über unsere Sprache* ("about our language") is framed, after the fashion espoused by Rosenzweig, in terms of speech itself—*Übersetzen/Übertragen/Übersetzbarkeit*—then tangency really does become the operative term, as Benjamin conjures as a task for translators:

> Just as a tangent touches a circle fleetingly and at only a single point, and just as this contact, not the point, prescribes the law in accord with which the tangent pursues its path into the infinite, in the same way a translation touches the original fleetingly and only at the infinitely small point of meaning . . . (Rendell translation, 163)

And so finally, to consider a last iteration of the element in the Derrida/Herzog triad left hanging, how pertinently can this chapter's readings be brought to bear on the assumption that "the language I only speak that yet is not mine is *the sacred*?" It is Rosenzweig who suggests an answer, from his essay "The Secret of Biblical Narrative Form." Glossing a passage from Goethe about the use of the Luther *Bibel* by Protestant institutions which praise it for delivering religious content without the barrier of aesthetic form (as if this pair formed an inevitable dichotomy), Rosenzweig writes,

Religious discourse ["the speech of faith"] does not then sink into the prose of bare "content"; rather it must—for it cannot do otherwise—avail itself of all means of expression, must sound all tones, must possess all its apparently fixed and prefabricated, independently transmittable "content" only by grace of the transient moment of oral expression. (Rosenwald translation, 130)

Abyss, void, volcano, gate, denucleation, polyvocal swarm, core and husk, portage and ferryman, fragments of a vessel: the cumulative record of such figuration attests to the unmistakable overlap between the respective claims of religiously infused content and of aesthetic form. The point, for Rosenzweig, and indeed all the essayists tethered here, concerns "the means by which the Bible can rescue the immediacy of the word for the mediated and mediable Scripture" (130). In its union of stimulus and point, says Rosenzweig, biblical *Schriftsprache*[86] seeks above all to *address* its reader/listeners; this is its twinning of "revelatory message and commanding instruction" (134). To the extent that Holy Scripture permeates discourse across the dividing lines of poetic and prosaic, secular and scared, pure and impure, it can be said to be "the language I only speak." This disseminating effect is uniquely the case for biblical discourse in the estimation of Rosenzweig, but, to varying degrees, the idea is also variously reflected by Bialik, Scholem, Agnon, Levinas, and Derrida.

And to the extent that Holy Scripture aspires to be "the language I only speak *that yet is not mine*," a translation of it, as characterized by Scholem in his commemorative address to Buber in 1961, may be simply utopian. Scholem called the Buber-Rosenzweig Bible "a kind of *Gastgeschenk* which German Jewry gave to the German people,"[87] his mood darkening a few sentences later when, its messianism betrayed, that *Gastgeschenk* is refigured as a "tombstone." But if it is true, as he wrote thirty-five years earlier and twenty years before that tombstone retroactively marked a grave, that "the secularization of the language is only a *façon de parler*," then the language itself retains its *"Unheilsschwer"* power, its *"religiöse Gewalt,"* its essential *"Unheimlichkeit"*—its compositing of layers foreign, sacred, and one's own. Hebrew, in this prophetic sense but also productively diasporic sense advocated by Scholem's sometime contender Franz Rosenzweig, is revealed, once again, as both immemorial and always *to come*: the sensibility, also, with which Bialik's speaker stands before his bookcase.

BOOKCASES: LEVINAS, BIALIK, AGNON (DE QUINCEY)

As I noted earlier, Levinas dignified the poetic in his later philosophical writings, even when he invokes ethics as situated on a plane higher than or oblique to aesthetics. "Language spoken by embodied minds," language as expression, "is above all the creative language of poetry" ("Signification and Sense," *CPP* 16–17). "Being as a whole—signification—glows in the works of poets and artists" (18). In his Talmudic Readings, however, while engrossed in ancient texts of a deep religious past, he sounds a more cautious note. To take a last example, "The Translation of Scripture," a reading of *bMegillah* 8b–9b, concludes with apparent disdain for the liberties of poetic language as compared with the more sober and restrained discourse of philosophy:

> I say it again a bit differently—and, for me, this is the beauty of Greece that must dwell in the tents of Shem: the language of deciphering. It demystifies. It demythicizes. It depoeticizes as well. Greek is prose, the prose of commentary, of exegesis, of hermeneutics. A hermeneutic interpretation that often uses metaphors, but also the language that "demetaphoricizes" metaphors, conceptualizes them, even if it must always begin anew. One must always demetaphorize the very metaphors by which one has just demetaphorized the metaphors, and wring eloquence's neck. (53–54)[88]

And yet, after taking some rhetorical liberties of its own, the peroration ends with a wink at Verlaine (just as *Totality and Infinity* begins with an unsubmerged allusion to Rimbaud).[89] One is thus left unsurprised that Bialik's poems and essays, Scholem's confession, Rosenzweig's speech-thinking, Derrida's essay on Scholem, and even Levinas's essay on poetry and resurrection in Agnon all thrive so much on their capacity for *re*metaphorization. They would be so many instances of what Gianni Vattimo called "art's claim to truth,"[90] its wager on both proximity and (im) purity.

But is this figural vivacity, what Bialik imaged as a vital and mobile force over and above the fixed and inert, a function of language's surface or of its abyssal interior? This question (with its implications for the task of translation, we should add) was ventured in different ways by Levinas and Bialik at the beginning of our chapter. And implicitly, it poses an ethical corollary, beyond speculating on the nature or structure of language, about its *uses*. Moreover, in specific regard to Hebrew, the question of linguistic surface and depth for all the essayists we have looked at folds into a set of intricately entwined concerns about a "semantic homeland" in the "deep past" and a "symbolism of the rite" which devolves from it (Levinas), on one hand, and energies of revealment and concealment (Bialik) tied to national or collective meanings, on the other. If there are ethical obligations to be extrapolated for disinterested *readers* of these several texts—or more accurately put, in these texts' imbrication—they are captured for me in two moments, one I draw from Bialik and the other from Levinas.

Although we had passed over it initially, the title of Bialik's poem, "Lifnei aron ha-sefarim," discloses a not-so-hidden intertext, in which we can hear the old scrolls, the hidden ones of the bookcase, speaking. In 1 Kings 8:5, we read

והמלך שלמה וכל־עדת ישראל הַנּוֹעָדִים עליו אתו

לִפְנֵי הָאָרוֹן מזבחים צאן ובקר אשר לא־יספרו ולא ימנו מרב:

Vehamelech Shlomo vechol-adat Yisrael hano'adim alav ito lifnei ha'aron mezabechim tson uvakar asher lo-yisafru velo yimanu merov

Also King Solomon, and all the congregation of Israel who were assembled with him, were with him before the ark, sacrificing sheep and oxen that could not be counted or numbered for multitude.

Maimonides's commentary to the *Mishna* explains that when blood was sprinkled onto the Holy of Holies on the Day of Atonement, it was done in a manner *lifnei ha'aron*, in the area that fronted the Ark's covering or lid (rendered in most Christian Bible translations as "mercy seat," itself a usage based, as it happens, on Martin Luther's coinage, *gnadenstuhl*). In Bialik's hand, all that hieratic and ceremonial drama now contracts itself to the dimensions of a humble bookcase—albeit one containing holy books and scrolls. The two tangents, holy and difficult, touch.

This would seem to be a highly localized instance of how the revealed and concealed, the holy and the quotidian, become *themselves* imbricated and entwined, notwithstanding a critical desideratum (like Said's) to tease them apart and maintain their separation. Their form, as Baudelaire remarked of Thomas De Quincey's writing, is "naturally spiral," or as De Quincey himself might have said, palimpsistic.[91] They already come down to us in compound form, whether we are estranged from them, or they from us. In Levinas's reading of Agnon's story "The Sign," survival of the poet as he contemplates his hometown's exterminated community is attached to the void left behind in the heretofore dependably transmitted tradition. Levinas encapsulates the existential dilemma bluntly: "Who will be able to read the Scriptures?"

> The mortality of the tradition reveals the rhetoric concealed by poetry—that last refuge of transcendence in Western humanism. Agnon's anguish—that is its focal point. It is not anguish over the end of traditional Jewish life, but over the possible end of the literature that could bring it back to life, before the crisis of Western humanism. (15)

This chimes with Scholem's bitter judgment about the Buber-Rosenzweig Bible, as well: who is now left to read it? What I want to suggest, provocatively, is that such questions position *all of us* before the bookcase where readers become ritualizers.

TANGENCY: AGNON, REGELSON

I turn last and very briefly to Agnon, this time standing outside Levinasian gloss. Indeed, it now bears mention that Levinas's evocation of Agnon is a highly selective one—the fabulist, folkloric, aggadic storyteller of the short fiction, at once subversive and sentimental. While some of the early stories from the 1930s do in fact feature a strange motif of tactile alterity between man and book,[92] Levinas does not appear to have in mind the later, modernist Agnon—the Agnon of the long, deeply complicated, sometimes agonized novels about unhappily transplanted life in pre-state Palestine,

T'mol Shilshom (1945) and the unfinished, posthumously published *Shira*. The protagonist of the latter, Manfred Herbst, a German-Jewish history professor in midlife crisis, spends much of his time "before the bookcase," both his own and those in the Jerusalem bookstores he frequents, preoccupied with the physicality of books.

> He began to sort through familiar and unfamiliar books, with his eyes and with his hands. Some were books he had been looking for; some, he began to covet as soon as he saw them. If he had had seven eyes and ten hands at each of his fingertips, he would not have been able to satisfy his desires.[93]

Herbst's bibliophilic moments of libidinal touch depicted here echo the Talmud's observation about hands that are *'asqaniot*, busy, indiscriminate, furtive. Agnon's novel is partly a satire of academic life at Hebrew University in the 1930s, and Herbst's eager, unreserved (Levinas would say "voluptuous") tactility is obviously quite different from the encumbered but tender sensibility of Bialik's speaker. We last left him kissing and leafing through his *'atikei gevilim* (just like some of the Agnonian protagonists in the *Sefer Ha'Ma'asim* collection whose commerce with holy books and manuscripts is shot through with reverence and trepidation). Bialik's poem is depopulated; by contrast, Herbst's professional life compels him to rub shoulders with a parade of fellow academicians.

One of these he encounters by chance while out walking in Rehavia (Jerusalem's "professors' neighborhood"). He is a scientist about whom Herbst had already heard a rumor that made him weep: "He wanted to study a particularly deadly tropical disease. But, in all the Land of Israel, he couldn't find anyone suffering from it. He exposed his own body to the disease and tried to cure himself with the drug he had invented."[94] As they converge upon each other, the narrator remains close to Herbst's point of view and says, "He and Herbst were not closely connected. One of them worked in the humanities; the other worked in science. But, since they worked in the same institution, they did know each other. When Herbst saw him, he bowed, kissed his hand, and went on his way" (533).

Herbst's gesture of bodily reverence—kissing the hand of the man who has infected his own body for the good of science—is striking. Thereafter, he laments the state of things in his own field, where no one would so heroically risk his life for the common good. But he soon collects himself and recollects the example of the esteemed humanities professor and mentor Alfred Neu, who is none other than a fictionalized version of Gershom Scholem. The moment is captured by Agnon like this:

> Because of his wrinkled soul, because of his need to deprecate himself and his profession, Herbst forgot about all the true scholars, even Neu, whose entire lives, their entire whole lives, are devoted, truly devoted, to their work. If need be, they would no doubt take risks in order to achieve their end—their sole end being true scholarship. (534)

And with that homage to the likes of Scholem, and Rosenzweig, and Benjamin—and by extension, of Bialik, and I believe Levinas and the late Jacques Derrida, too—we, ourselves face the bookcase. Herbst's reverential but sorrowful kiss of the scientist's hand is not, after all, so utterly removed from the sorrowful but reverential kisses the sorrowful speaker in Bialik's poem bestows upon his sacred texts.

And thus, in its "naturally spiral" way, does this chapter glance off the analogy between person and scroll that we recognize from the introduction. Obviously, the material question this book has heretofore pursued mostly takes the form of what Dan Miron aptly calls "contiguity," the marginal overlapping, intersection, or actual abutment of texts and traditions, where tangency and impingement describe the organizing principle of the "interessayistic set of relations" I outlined in the first section.[95] Bialik, Scholem, Rosenzweig, Benjamin, Derrida, Levinas, and, finally, Agnon "touch upon" each other within the constellating framework of a revived Hebrew and modernism's post-Maskilic pressure on a traditional Jewish text-culture.

The scrolls that make the lips (im)pure in Bialik's poem and the hand capable of producing a similar effect in the passage from Agnon's *Shira* are the closest this chapter comes to the some of the tropes and emblems of embodiment we have seen previously. They also, obviously, illustrate an order of proximity and adjacency that runs parallel to a strictly textual or rhetorical one. But there is another emblem of embodiment on display here, recognized by Levinas, Bialik, Rosenzweig, and Scholem all, and that is the Hebrew alphabet, whose letters embody "the tangible and tactile atomic units out of which all meaning is constructed."[96] When I spoke earlier of a "charged" ethical-semantic field determined by choices of orthography and transliteration, I had just such atomic units in mind.

However, there is also this:

חֲקוּקוֹת אוֹתִיּוֹתַיִךְ בְּתַבְנִית עוֹלָמִי, רְחִימָה בַּלְּשׁוֹנוֹת
,חַרְצָן בְּזַג, עִנְבָּל בְּזוֹג, רָזֵךְ רָחַשְׁתִּי, הוֹ עִבְרִית
בַּכֹּל אֲגַשֵּׁשֵׁךְ אוֹר מִתְגַּשֵּׁם
בַּכֹּל אַשִּׂיגֵךְ שֵׂכֶל מִתְנוֹצֵץ

Ḥaquqot otiyyotayikh b'tavnit 'olami rchimah balshonot!
hartsan b'zag, inbal b'zog, razekh rhashti, ho 'ivrit . . .
baqol agashesheikh or mitgashem
baqol asigeikh sekhel mitnosets

Engraved are your letters in the structure of my world, beloved among languages.
The seed in the grape, the clapper in the bell, your secret I have expressed, O
    Hebrew. . . . In all things I will seek you, light that has become embodied,
In all things I will grasp you, sparkling reason.

So read the first two lines of Abraham Regelson's (1896–1981) matchless extravagant twenty-stanza dithyramb to the Hebrew tongue published in 1946, "*Ḥaquqot*

otiyyotayikh." In its almost too fond attachment to what the Hebrew language represents and can accomplish (ironically enough for an American Hebraist more diaspori-
cally minded than Bialik[97]), it is a world away from "Before the Bookcase." Alternately
pantheist and Heracleitan, its paean to Hebrew as divine logos also situates it on the
oblique compared to the "shaky bridge of words" in "Revealment and Concealment in
Language."[98] Regelson's poem is also, in some entirely necessary but quite untragic
sense, largely untranslatable, with its hermetic diction, stylized syntax, dense and
complex wordplay.

In stanza three, in keeping with its unembarrassed consciousness of its lavishly
worshipful stance, effectively deifying Hebrew as a goddess, the poem knowingly trips
itself up with rhetorical *occupatio* in bodying forth what it says it should not:

הֵן הַבּוֹלְטוֹת וְהַשִּׁלְדִּיּוֹת בְּגֵוֵךְ אֲרַמֵּז,
וְאֶדֹּם מִן הַקְּמָטִיּוֹת וְהַבֵּין-פִּרְקִיּוֹת,
הַדָּם וְהַלֵּחַ וְהַמֵּחַ עַל תַּעֲלוֹת-זְרִימוֹתֵיהֶם

Hen haboltot v'hashilyyot bgevekh aramez,
v'adom min haqimtiyyot v'haben-pirqiyyot
hadam v'haleakh v'hameakh al ta'a lot-zrimotehem

Therefore I will allude only to the protruding and skeletal qualities of your body
and I will remain silent about those creases and between the joints, the blood, the
marrow, and the rich tissue in all their oozing channels.[99]

This celebration of intimacy, of grasp and feel, is the more remarkable, considering
its author's understanding of what his "forced banishment" (as he calls it) in the diaspora has earned him: "It was because of that same distance that the Hebrew language
could reveal itself to me in its allure as a complete phenomenon in a way that allowed
me to see what could be seen by no one who lives within it and feels as if he swims in
the blood of its veins."[100] Regelson's lines also serve as the enfleshed rejoinder to the
stark figure Bialik used in "Ḥevlei Lashon," his 1905 essay anatomizing the revived
speech life (or else, death) of Hebrew, "a language that is not alive, its digestion
weakened . . . begins to show the dry bone of its philological skeleton."[101] But what we
previously glimpsed as Bialik's tortured estrangement, in Regelson's bardic achievement becomes the fructifying consequence of the "outsideness" conferred by living in
the diaspora.

Not only does the poem indulge an all but religious passion for the language, its
structure, forms, and lexico-semantic possibilities, along with an erudition that discloses the vast world of classical Jewish learning, of biblical and rabbinic reference,
just behind its baroque and lofty proscenium. It also, in Alan Mintz's words, "makes
us feel that the words of the Hebrew language are tangible and animate objects in
themselves" (92). To that end, Regelson's speaker is even more sensorily driven than
Bialik's and Agnon's Herbst: all three converge in needing to touch what they read.

All three also attest to a complexly tensed ethical poetics, facing or standing before books, words, and letters—whether these last are imprinted onto one's DNA or experienced as painfully orphaned *disjecta membra* at that same atomic level.

Even if only implicitly, the other essayists given voice here, Scholem, Rosenzweig, Levinas, and Derrida, conduct their respective hymns, threnodies or jeremiads about language and translation within same charged acoustic particle-field. Concatenating the metaphors: together, they comprise a knotted string, with *unsere sprache / notre langue* at one end and לשונינו *leshonenu* at the other. Beneath might be an abyss or volcano or frozen swirl or treasure house; above may be the *mazzalot*, as both "constellations" and, at the "heights of [Hebrew's] vowels," the "signs that guide the letters," descried by Regelson in his ode. Whatever and wherever it is, that is where we find the difficult and holy in close proximity. That is where they touch.

GERSHOM SCHOLEM: BEKENNTNIS ÜBER UNSERE SPRACHE

An Franz Rosenzweig

Dies Land ist ein Vulkan: Es beherbergt die Sprache. Man spricht hier von vielen Dingen, an denen wir scheitern können, man spricht heute mehr als je von den Arabern. Aber unheimlicher als das arabische Volk steht eine andere Drohung vor uns, die das zionistische Unterfangen mit Notwendigkeit heraufbeschworen hat: Was ist es mit der „Aktualisierung" des Hebräischen? Muß nicht dieser Abgrund einer heiligen Sprache, die in unsere Kinder gesenkt wird, wieder aufbrechen? Freilich, man weiß nicht, was man tut. Man glaubt die Sprache verweltlicht zu haben, ihr den apokalyptischen Stachel ausgezogen zu haben. Aber das ist ja nicht wahr, die Verweltlichung der Sprache ist ja nur eine façon de parler, eine Phrase. Es ist schlechthin unmöglich, die zum Bersten erfüllten Worte zu entleeren, es sei denn um den Preis der Sprache selbst. Das gespenstische Volapük, das wir hier auf der Gasse sprechen, bezeichnet genau jene ausdruckslose Sprachwelt, in der die „Säkularisierung" der Sprache möglich, allein möglich werden konnte. Überliefern wir aber unseren Kindern die Sprache, die uns überliefert worden ist, machen wir, das Geschlecht des Übergangs, die Sprache der alten Bücher lebendig in ihnen, so daß sie sich an ihnen neu offenbaren kann—muß denn dann nicht die religiöse Gewalt dieser Sprache eines Tages ausbrechen? Und welches Geschlecht wird dieser Ausbruch finden? Wir leben ja in dieser Sprache über einem Abgrund, fast alle mit der Sicherheit des Blinden, aber werden wir nicht, wir oder die nach uns kommen, hineinstürzen, wenn wir sehen werden. Und niemand weiß, ob das Opfer Einzelner, die in diesem Abgrund zugrunde gehen werden, genügen wird, um ihn zu schließen.

Die Schöpfer der neuen Sprachbewegung glaubten blind, bis zur Verbohrtheit, an die Wunderkraft der Sprache, und das war ihr Glück. Kein Sehender hätte den dämonischen Mut aufgebracht, eine Sprache da zu beleben, wo nur ein Esperanto entstehen konnte. Jene gingen, und gehen noch heute, gebannt über den Abgrund, er schwieg, und sie haben ihn, die alten Namen und Sigel, weitergegeben an die Jugend. Nun graust es uns manchmal, wenn aus einer gedankenlosen Rede des Sprechers ein Wort der Religion uns erschrickt. Unheilsschwer ist dies Hebräisch: in seinem jetzigen Zustand kann und wird es nicht bleiben, unsere Kinder haben keine andere Sprache mehr und es [ist] nur wahr zu sagen, daß sie und allein sie die Begegnung werden bezahlen müssen, die wir ihnen, ohne zufragen, ohne uns selbst zu fragen, verschafft haben werden. Wenn die Sprache sich gegen ihre Sprecher wenden wird—auf Minuten tut sie es schon in unserem Leben, und das sind schwer vergeßliche Minuten, in denen sich die Vermessenheit unseres Unterfangens uns offenbart—werden wir dann eine Jugend haben, die im Aufstand einer heiligen Sprache bestehen können wird?

Sprache ist Namen. Im Namen ist die Macht der Sprache beschlossen, ist ihr Abgrund versiegelt. Es steht nicht mehr in unserer Hand, die alten Namen tagtäglich zu beschwören, ohne ihre Potenzen wachzurufen. Sie werden erscheinen, denn wir haben sie ja freilich mit großer Gewalt beschworen. Wir freilich sprechen in Rudimenten, wir freilich sprechen

eine gespenstische Sprache: in unseren Sätzen gehen die Namen um, in Schriften und Zei-
tungen spielt der oder jener mit ihnen, und lügt sich oder Gott vor, es habe nichts zu
bedeuten und oft springt aus der gespenstischen Schande unserer Sprache die Kraft des
Heiligen hervor. Denn die Namen haben ihr Leben und hätten sie es nicht, wehe unseren
Kindern, die hoffnungslos der Leere ausgeliefert werden. Jedes Wort, das nicht eben neu
geschaffen wird, sondern aus dem „guten alten" Schatz entnommen wird, ist zum Bersten
voll. Ein Geschlecht, das die fruchtbarste unserer heutigen Traditionen: unsere Sprache,
übernimmt, kann nicht und mag es auch tausendfach wollen, ohne Tradition leben. Jener
Moment, wo sich die in der Sprache gelagerte Macht entfalten wird, wo das „Gesprochene"
der Inhalt der Sprache, wieder Gestalt annehmen wird, wird jene heilige Tradition wieder
als entscheidendes Zeichen vor unser Volk stellen, vor dem es nur die Wahl haben wird:
sich zu beugen oder unterzugehen. Gott wird in einer Sprache, in der er tausendfach in
unser Leben zurückbeschworen wird, nicht stumm bleiben. Diese unausbleibliche Revo-
lution der Sprache aber, in der die Stimme vernommen wird, ist der einzige Gegenstand,
von dem in diesem Lande nicht gesprochen wird, denn die, die die hebräische Sprache zum
Leben wieder aufriefen, glaubten nicht an das Gericht, das sie damit über uns beschworen.
Möge uns dann nicht der Leichtsinn, der uns auf diesem apokalyptischen Weg geleitet, zum
Verderb werden.

Jerusalem, den 7. Teweth 5687
Gerhard Scholem

Confession on the Subject of Our Language

This country is a volcano! It harbors the language! One speaks here of many matters that may make us fail. More than of anything else we are concerned today about the Arab. But much more sinister [uncanny] than the Arab problem is another threat, a threat which the Zionist enterprise unavoidably has had to face: the "actualization" of Hebrew. Must not the conundrum of a holy language break open again now, when the language is to be handed down to our children? Granted, one does not know how it will all turn out. Many believe that the language has been secularized, and the apocalyptic thorn has been pulled out. But this is not true at all. The secularization of the language is only a *façon de parler,* a phrase! It is impossible to empty out words which are filled to the breaking point with specific meanings—lest it be done at the sacrifice of the language itself! The ghastly gibberish which we hear spoken in the streets is exactly the faceless lingo that "secularization" of the language will bring about; of this there cannot be any doubt! If we could transmit to our children that language which was transmitted to us, and if we could revitalize the language of the ancient books in this transitional generation, would it not then reveal itself to them? And then, would not the religious power of this language perforce break open again one day? But which generation will bring this about? Is it not true that almost all of us live with this language over a volcano with the false security of the blind. Must not we or those who came after us stumble into the abyss when we fail to see again? And nobody can know whether the sacrifice of those who perish will suffice to close the hole and avoid the plunge into the abyss.

Those who initiated the rejuvenation of the language believed blindly and almost obstinately in its miraculous power. That was their good fortune! Nobody with clear foresight would have mustered the demonic courage to try to revitalize a language in a situation where only an Esperanto could have been created. They walked and still walk [spellbound] above this abyss, which remained hidden, and have transmitted this language to our youth together with all the ancient names and seals. Today it seems weird to us and at times we are scared and frightened to hear a religious phrase quite out of place, in a totally unrelated context. *Fraught with danger is the Hebrew language!* It cannot remain and will not remain in its present state! Since our children no longer have any other language, they and they alone will have to pay for this predicament, which none other than we have imposed upon them without forethought and without question. If and when the language turns against its speakers—and this has occurred already on bitter and unforgettable occasions when the arrogance of this undertaking has become apparent—will we then have a youth which can exist in and survive the revolution of a holy language?

Language is Name. In the name rests the power of language, its abyss is sealed with the name. We have no right to conjure up the old names day by day without calling forward their hidden power. They will appear, since we have called upon them, and undoubtedly they will appear with vehemence! We speak in rudiments, we speak a ghastly language: the names go in circles in our sentences, one plays with them in publications and newspapers. It is a lie that that is not important, even if a holy force may erupt suddenly out of the shame of our language! Names have their own life! If it were not so then woe to our children, who would be pushed into the void and emptiness without any hope! Each word which is not newly created, but taken from the good old treasures, is ready to burst. A generation which accepts the most fruitful of our holy tradition—our language—cannot simply live without tradition even if it would fervently wish to. The moment when the power stored in the language unfolds again, when the spoken word, the reality of our language, gets form and reality again, that moment will place this holy tradition as a decisive token before our people. God will not remain silent in the language in which He has affirmed our life a thousand times and more. This unavoidable revolution of the language, in which His voice will be heard again, is the only issue that is not spoken about today in this country. Those who called the Hebrew language back to life did not believe in this trial yet they created it. May it not come to pass that the imprudence which has led us on this apocalyptic road ends in ruin.

Jerusalem, 7 *Tevet* 5687 Gerhard Scholem

The Book in Hand, Again

The Talmud asks the following question: "What should be done on the Shabbat day when a fire breaks out, given that it is forbidden to put the fire out." One is not allowed to put the fire out, but it is permissible to save certain objects by taking them out of the blaze. Among the objects to be saved from the fire, holy books have absolute priority. So the books should be saved, but not all the books . . . There are holy books and then there are the others, "real books" and "false books." So the question underlying the whole text is: "What is a book? What is a book that makes it worth saving from the fire?" The relationship between the book and the fire, we shall see, is extremely important, so important that the expression "it may be saved from the fire (book)" is, in the text, equivalent to "it is a book." The saving reveals the book. (We may add that the root S.F.R means both "book" and "border," among other meanings.)

—Marc-Alain Ouaknin, *The Burnt Book: Reading the Talmud*

This is a question, *the* question, about whether reading a printed work of writing is first of all the reading, say of literature, philosophy, history, art criticism, your choice, or instead, and more tangibly yet, the *reading of a book*—or of course (though by what interchange and equilibration?) both.

—Garrett Stewart, *Bookwork*

A first rate artisan in skill told me that he had been so reduced in the world . . . that though in his youth he could take in the *News* and *Examiner* papers . . . he could afford, and enjoyed, no reading, when I saw him last autumn, beyond the book-leaves in which he received his quarter of cheese, his small piece of bacon or fresh meat, or his savelovs; and his wife schemed to go to the shops who "wrapped their things from books," in order that he might have something to read after his day's work.

—Henry Mayhew, *London Labor and the London Poor* 2:114

"THE BOOK"

> This solid rectangular opacity becomes a book only in carrying my thought
> towards other givens, still or already *absent*: the author who writes, the readers who
> read, the bookshelves that hold, etc. All these terms are announced without being
> given in the solid rectangular opacity imposed on my sight and hands. These
> absent contents confer signification on the given . . . . [and yet,] . . . this solid
> rectangular opacity does not subsequently take the sense of *book*; it is already
> signifying in its supposedly sensible elements. It cuts into the lamplight, the
> daylight, it reflects the sun that rose or the lamp that was lit and also reflects in my
> eyes, as the solidity reflects—not simply to organs that apprehend it in a subject
> and thereby are somehow opposed to the apprehended object but also to beings
> who are *beside* that opacity, in the *heart* of a world, common both to that opacity,
> that solidity, those eyes, those hands, and myself as body. There never was a
> moment in which meaning *first came to birth out of a meaningless being* and outside
> a historical position where language is spoken. This is doubtless what was meant
> when we were taught that language is the habitation of being. (Emmanuel Levinas,
> *Humanism of the Other*, 10–13)

This book, fittingly, concludes with "the book." The voice immediately preceding
belongs to Levinas, excerpted from "Signification and Sense" (also translated as
"Meaning and Sense"). In the first section of this rather difficult essay from 1964,
Levinas wants to think through receptivity as the means by which he have access to
meaning, and also the role of metaphor (as that which "carries something away") in
describing, but therefore also seeming to falsify or "overload" the date empirically
given to our senses. Aslant Husserlian theories of intuition, and other intellectualist
models of consciousness from Plato through Hume to the logical positivists, and
alongside Heidegger's alternate model of *Dasein*'s "horizon," the chief claim Levinas
ventures here speaks to the givenness of objects in the world.[1]

"The book," in his example, suggests neither some signification to be referred to
absences that consequently orient or ground it, since "signification does not console a
disappointed perception, *it just makes perception possible*" (11). Nor, as Levinas will
eventually resituate his analysis, should it be understood as wholly a function of contingent placement in a world, against a horizon. Things may indeed manifest *as* this or
that, as signification, he tells us, before they are worked on by perception. Just so,
meaning calls forth an embodied cultural world, a world "that resembles the order
of language," whose totality is not objectively constituted, but the product of a "free
creative arrangement" (14) instead. Meaning also takes shape through culturally
bound, discrete acts of "gathering," within a horizon of "subjective gesture." "Experience," as Levinas sums up the phenomenology of language and perception (albeit
sounding very much like Cavell's Emerson), "is a reading, an understanding of sense,
an exegesis, a hermeneutic, and not an intuition" (13).

In a quasi-Bakhtinian move, Levinas further suggests that words do not lie congealed in dictionaries, with reference solely to the things they designate but rather, refer "laterally, to other words." Priority is thus assigned to the "figurative sense"; language makes being "glow." But since language refers to the contingent positions of its users, such illumination, however primordial, requires the active participation of those who "receive" and not merely reflect it. "It is the embodied subject who, in collecting being, will raise the curtain," say Levinas, as if in echo of Rousseau's *Letter to D'Alembert*. "The spectator is the actor" (15). Both "the world" as an enclosure and the contingent positions of perceiver-receivers in it consequently give us something more that a strictly Euclidean picture of signification, and it is *language* that supplies this added dimension.[2]

Yet, this initial picture of signification with its example of "the book" is analytically deficient, Levinas will ultimately argue. Later in the essay, he decisively contrasts the opening exposition of meaning/signification (linguistic, symbolic, cultural, and "economic") with what he calls *le sens*, whose structure, he insists, is *particulier:* "a unique sense," which also maps onto a uniquely one-way orientation. Since meaning, as rendered in our picture above, becomes either immanent (Heidegger) or relative (Merleau-Ponty), we are left with no unified or "eternal" perspective on the things of the world. Such creeping pluralism (or multiculturalism—a term, however, that Levinas does not employ), needs an overriding principle if is not to be either incoherent or "atheist," that is, as indicating radical apartness.

The dialectical construct needed here Levinas calls "sense," which in French also means "direction" or "orientation." It specifies the category of what is Other (*Autrui*), and therefore exceeds both contingent meaning and cultural difference or relativity. The "primordial event" of *le sens* in a Levinasian vocabulary signifies *the otherwise*; it exchanges the givenness of things with the "trace" of *Illeity* in them—neither sign nor effect (collectable into some whole, gathered into an economy of signification), but rather the uncompensated, gratuitous, one-way "Work" of ethical agency, an "absolute, *liturgical* orientation of the Same to the Other" (29).[3] *Le sens* correlates with an "elevation," a "rectitude" and a "rectilinear movement" (35) toward ethical Infinity, toward the "Entry and Visitation" manifested through the Other's face: the non-Euclidian space "beyond" essence and "otherwise than" Being.[4]

Yet, however important it may be for an integrative understanding of Levinas's enterprise, the philosophical argument about "sense" over "signification" goes much further than my immediate concerns in this epilogue. Moreover, its strictly *philosophical* argument also exceeds the selective utility reflected by the Talmudic readings and essays in previous chapters. I have recapitulated its argument up until a point simply to let it speak in its own terms, without commentary of my own. I want now simply to return to the picture in Levinas's example of the "solid, rectangular opacity" we call a book, and tarry with it, whatever Levinas's later argument about alterity may propound.

I am too transfixed by the object itself. Since the essay is really an engagement with Merleau-Ponty, "the book" in Levinas's example does not quite approximate the same object from which Georges Poulet extrapolated a phenomenology of reading in Chapter 1. The solid, rectangular opacity before us now is not being proposed as a vehicle by which "I think the thoughts of another" or through which its physicality is replaced by "a congeries of mental objects" (55) that hover somewhere between the boundaries of my own and another's consciousness. Poulet's analysis, we recall, revolves around "what happens to me" while reading a book. By contrast, Levinas confines himself to the book in hand. Notably, though, its exemplarity is short-lived; Levinas never returns to it in the course of the essay's exposition once he makes his characteristic *clinamen* "towards the Other."

And so, there it still remains before us, solid, opaque, and rectangular: imposed on sight and hands, cutting into the lamplight and the daylight, reflecting the sun that rose or the lamp that was lit, reflecting further in my eyes, which, as their own objects, are positioned *beside* that opacity, in the *heart* of a world.[5] Analogous to the book itself, the means by which I look at or grasp it are common to that opacity, that solidity: those eyes, those hands, and myself as body. As Levinas writes in "Transcendence and Intelligibility" (written twenty years after "Meaning and Sense") "Presence . . . in its concreteness, it is the offering of itself to the hand which takes and, consequently, through the muscular contraction of the grasp . . . it refers to a solid which the hand encompasses or which the finger of the hand indicates" (152).

When Levinas disinters the buried metaphors of *Begriff* and con*cept*, he says in italics, "*these metaphors are to be taken seriously and literally*" (152). Yet, unlike Poulet's "Phenomenology of Reading"—or Sartre's *What Is Literature?* for that matter[6]—Levinas's essay from 1964, "Meaning and Sense," never quite gets to what happens when "*un solide*" that is a rectangular opacity gets read, that is, when the covers get opened and the leaves inside are fingered and turned, and thus marked by that contact. By contrast and once again, let me cite from Bruno Schulz: a scene of *frottage* and a reprise of "the book":

> The Book . . . Somewhere at the dawn of childhood, the very first daybreak of life, the horizon shone with its gentle light. It lay in its full glory on Father's desk, whilst he, silently engrossed in it, patiently rubbed with a licked finger its ridge of decals until the blank paper began to mist, blur, to loom with blissful anticipation. Shreds of tissue paper began suddenly to peel away to disclose a mascared, peacock-eye rim, and my swooning gaze fell into a virgin dawn of godly colours, into wonderful dampness of the purest azures. Oh, the wearing away of that film! Oh, that invasion of splendour.[7]

While not quite what Levinas has in mind for his rhapsodic turn on "rubbing the text," the Schulz passage still drives the point home, following directly, as it does, upon a fantasy of unmediated proximity: "For under the imaginary table that separates me from my readers, don't we secretly clasp each other's hands?"[8] Poulet almost instantly dissolves this same felt contiguity, "the sensible elements" that Levinas considers (and that Schulz mythifies), in order to get "inside" the phenomenology of reading. Even Igitur, the child in Mallarmé's eponymous text (without ever having taken it in hand), *ferme le livre—souffle la bougie* ["closes the book and snuffs out the candle"]).[9] Yet, between those two thought philosophical experiments, Levinas's fore-shortened one and Poulet's dematerializing other, oblique to the literary invocation of a depersonalized codex, this book and its aggregate chapters lie suspended—while all the time, however, also cradled in readers' hands—its tactileness in sync with readers' tact.

An ordinary book is a like a meteor, continues Schulz, with only "one moment when it soars screaming like the phoenix, its pages aflame"; those pages "soon turn to ashes," however, or become "congealed" or "extinct," their fiery fullness is reduced to the "wooden clattering, like a rosary," of "stone dead messages." Schulz also refers this transitoriness to the "borrowed life" lived by all books when they "aim at being Authentic" and thus become subject to its gravitational or magnetic force, absorbed as so many tributaries flowing into some "ancient source." Nevertheless, what is a finite in a book is redeemed through infinition in the present moment, for a fragment of a book—as if it were a Torah scroll—can "unfold while being read"; it "grows in the reading, its borders open on all sides to all fluctuations and currents."[10]

The epigraph from Garrett Stewart above poses the question I have explored in less rhapsodic form: how to anchor the light, innocent yes of reading.[11] The mooring I have used throughout has gone by the name, "ethics," and I have appealed to various discourses, Levinasian and otherwise, outside the mechanics of reading to ground and specify the term. But despite multiple studies on the subject, what I have investigated does not really have a technical term of its own: *ethi-tactics*? *ethilexia*? *éthique de toucher*? *das Buch-ethik*?[12] And it probably shouldn't. I make the point only to put a little pressure on what has been my own preferred critical phraseology—like *tact* or *pledge*.

For "the ethics *of* reading" already exports its first substantive into the realm of the second; properly speaking, though, it still represents a kind of incursion. Reading *may* be ethical, just as it may be politically, mechanically, socially, economically, erotically, and otherwise conditioned. Yet, the act itself resists such adjectival and adverbial imposition. (The genitive formulation so common in academic discourse today, that is, "the *X* of *a*, or of *b*, or of *c*" almost asks to be subverted, anyway, or else consigned to the fate of a phrase like "politics of meaning," popular for a short stretch in the 1990s and now sounding like so much deflated, uncirculated coinage.)

Perhaps by default, "the book in hand" is the expression to which I have had most recourse. It reminds us of where the book *lies* at any given time in its use, the fact that we take it and hold it and that it literally depends on such tangency as the shared border between its agency and ours. Because it is doing philosophical work, Levinas's example of the book *at hand* does not quite find its way toward the sorts of considerations about always-busy hands that he contemplated in several of his Talmudic readings. Nor does it take on ethical weight and density the way he ascribes to the unique, one-way orientation that tacks beyond signs in order to align with the epiphanic "wind" of the absolutely Other. The solid, rectangular opacity we call a "book" merely illustrates the givenness of signification, both horizontal and horizonal.

And yet there it is still positioned in front of us, "already signifying in its supposedly sensible elements." Which particular book could it be? one wonders. Among many instances of book as object in literary space, perhaps it corresponds to a volume in Catherine Earnshaw's "select library," as discovered by Lockwood at the beginning of Emily Brontë's *Wuthering Heights,* its books (including a Testament) inscribed in their margins by the young Cathy's pen-and-ink commentary ("some were detached sentences; others took the form of a regular diary").

Such books represent one of the most compelling mimetic emblems in all literature of the would-be materialization of the act of reading; the effect of a book's tactile "thereness" on its reader and that reader's mark on it of a whole other realm of signification, the almost magical process by which books are made "one's own." Or perhaps it identifies with the book that John Reed throws at Jane Eyre or the book that Becky Sharp tosses out of the carriage window in *Vanity Fair,* mimetic emblems of the book as blunt force.[13]

When, by contrast, prompted by the book-friendliness of Victorian literature, I try to think of an image correspondent to the *sens* with which Levinas underwrites ethical alterity, that happens vertically and breaks through the contingency of meanings to orient us *otherwise and beyond,* a 1918 poem by Thomas Hardy, "The Whitewashed Wall," comes to mind:

> Why does she turn in that shy soft way
> Whenever she stirs the fire,
> And kiss to the chimney-corner wall,
> As if entranced to admire
> Its whitewashed bareness more than the sight
> Of a rose in richest green?
> I have known her long, but this raptured rite
> I never before have seen.
>
> —Well, once when her son cast his shadow there,
> A friend took a pencil and drew him
> Upon that flame-lit wall. And the lines
> Had a lifelike semblance to him.
> And there long stayed his familiar look;
> But one day, ere she knew,
> The whitener came to cleanse the nook,
> And covered the face from view.

"Yes," he said: "My brush goes on with a rush,
And the draught is buried under;
When you have to whiten old cots and brighten,
What else can you do, I wonder?"
But she knows he's there. And when she yearns
For him, deep in the labouring night,
She sees him as close at hand, and turns
To him under his sheet of white.[14]

Levinas would call this concealed mark of anterior presence, the "trace."[15] And yet the tactile immediacy of the caressed wall where a mutable shadow had been cast[16] stays with one, just like Levinas's almost offhand image of the physical book in equipoise with the "beings who are *beside* that opacity, in the *heart* of a world, common both to that opacity, that solidity, those eyes, those hands, and myself as body." In Elaine Scarry's beautiful (and Arendtian) formulation, "all states of being—not just overt, physical activity but even what appear to be forms of physical inactivity like reading or perceiving or feeling-inevitably entail reciprocal jostling with the world."[17]

THIS BOOK

If we therefore place Levinas's solid, rectangular opacity on the shelf of an imaginary bookcase that also contains "the book" from Bruno Schulz; the books fingered in Benjamin's recollection of his Berlin childhood and Mr. Wopsle's great-aunt's improvised classroom in Dickens's *Great Expectations*; the book Canetti transported for twenty years and then read under a high compulsion; Stéphane Mallarmé's *Igitur* with its empty room and *un livre ouvert que présente la table* in Georges Poulet's lyricized evocation of it; Henry Darger's *In The Realms of the Unreal* and Pascal's *Mémorial*, as if the one were still at 851 Webster Street and the other still sewn into a doublet; the books that both do and do not make the hands impure as prescribed in the Talmudic tractates discussed by Levinas; Catherine Earnshaw's library; the Yiddish books from a synagogue library in Cuba "airlifted" to safety in Amherst, Mass.; the books Herbst fingers in Jerusalem bookstores in *Shira*; and finally all the books, offspring of Lvov, Slavita, Amsterdam, and Frankfurt, no longer recognized by Bialik's speaker, their columns of text like black pearls, whose string is broke, every letter, widowed and orphaned: imagine such an assemblage.

If all these codices are allowed to materialize in front of us, and if we supplement them with the inscribed granite and bronze surfaces pictured by Sebald and engineered by Arad, and even the piece of paper wondrously inscribed by Scorsese's celluloid automaton (and seen by us ensconced within the modern *tevot* of playhouse or Cineplex), we confront *the* question, about whether reading a printed work of writing is the reading of its content and genre; or instead, and more tangibly yet, the *reading of a book*—or of course (though by what interchange and equilibration?) both.

This book, which its readers now hold in *their* hands, has sought to stage that interchange and equilibration through the lenses of philosophical criticism and literary criticism, but also by means of texts unintended for a readership other than their authors, alongside essays, poems, and a film—nearly all of them in the form of rectangular opacities that this author has held in *his* hands. The book he has written has endeavored, if only as a pledge, to make that reading materialize through the turn and prestige of other pairs of hands and under other pairs of eyes.

A reader may legitimately cavil. How does this stylized example of "the book" from Levinas, or any of the others, bear on this or that sort of everyday reading done in the world: this law textbook, that civil war history or introduction to morphology, this magazine containing a short story, that tattered play script for a performance of *King Lear*, this piece of erotica, that comic novel or thriller?[18] Even with Franz Kafka's famous insistence that *Wenn das Buch, das wir lesen, uns nicht mit einem Faustschlag auf den Schädel weckt, wozu lesen wir dann das Buch?* ("If the book we are reading does not wake us, as with a fist hammering on our skulls, then why do we read it?")[19]: we still take our bearings from the ordinary, where such contact feels exorbitant enough that we might wish our reading to be freed of touch altogether—certainly, if maculation shades into molestation. Isn't that where the ethics of reading should give us some quarter?

Yet, consider three quite vernacular examples, from the text-image work of cartoonist and urban elegist Ben Katchor, whose inimitable style concerns among other plangent themes the poetics of ephemera. In the first of these "picture stories," Katchor's protagonist, Julius Knipl, sits next to a young man on the subway, "reading a battered paperback." In panel two, Knipl hands him a scrap and says, "Here, the top of page 218." Accepting it, the youth replies, "Thank you, thank you. Most people don't understand." Across the next six panels, his speech balloons explain the book as an inadvertent legacy:

> But, you see, this copy is an heirloom, purchased by my grandmother at the Port Authority Bus Terminal. . . . She got only halfway through it but considered it her favorite book. It sat for many years on the bottom shelf of her telephone table and then, when she died in 1964, passed into the possession of my mother, who read it four times while on jury duty in the early 70s. My older sister preferred it to her high school reading assignments; the beginning of chapter thirty-two was already missing. . . . But now that I'm finished with school, I feel that it's time for me to take the plunge and see for myself what made this one book endure over the years while the others were lost and forgotten.[20]

In the final panel, Knipl reaches down to retrieve another unbound page, with the caption, "Here, page 378."

A related strip in the same volume imagines a "Misspent Youth Center," where people who have squandered some portion of their past (including "books bought but not read") line up in front of teller's window where, pages or leaves of a sort, "crisp new ten-and twenty-dollar bills are, for a small fee, exchanged for the worn and tattered currency of the past." The speech bubbles in two adjacent panels read,

> A 1958 Federal Reserve banknote from Washington, D.C. For twenty dollars—that's close enough! I never thought I'd see that one again. All the things we purchased are long gone—broken or irretrievably lost—but the money itself, which passed through our hands, can be relocated by date and serial number (55).

For the most ephemeral book in hand of all, a third strip from one of Katchor's earlier collections bemoans the fate of a particularly utilitarian print genre as it approaches its expiration date:

> At this time of year, telephone books all over the city . . . begin to buckle and collapse under their own weight. The distinction between the white and yellow pages becomes unclear. The advertisements suddenly look out of date. One man finds the page he needs has been ripped out. Other people are tempted to perform a strong man's stunt. Mr. Knipl has unconsciously spared one page from the annual harvesting of last year's phone books.[21]

All three of these little fables (in line with much of Katchor's comic art) instance Virgil's *lacrimae rerum*, which in this case distill the pathos of materiality as *gripped by or passing through human hands*: the one page spared, the 1958 banknote in place of some irretrievable purchase of the same vintage, "the top of page 218."

But when literature and scripture *as event* mark the limit, how do we then define other commonplace, vernacular acts of reading "up"? To take a very different and the starkest kind of example, consider the grease-stained *bletl* (page) of Talmud that had been used as sandwich wrapper by a Nazi guard at the Wolfsburg subcamp, now improbably salvaged by Jewish hands and studied with maximal devotion and "extreme attention to the real."[22] When confronted with a text as starkly embodied as a Civil War letter stained with the unstaunched blood of the dying man who has written it, how do we then imagine that an impersonal book, a mere object, can ever earn the right to the same immediacy, the same exsanguined "impurity" of touch?[23]

Moreover, when we discover that our own reading may well miss the mark of the author's writing (in an interview, Katchor invokes the "Jewish suspicion of the unexplained image," which another interviewer extends to the "suspicion of the unannotated word"),[24] how *tactfully* have we made contact anyway? In his *Paris Review* interview from 2002, novelist Ian McEwan remarks that while "every sentence contains a ghostly commentary on its own processes" (57), which would seem to suggest at least the possibility of narratographic ghost-busting, "literary criticism, which is bound to pursue meaning, can never really encompass the fact that some things are on the page because they gave the writer pleasure."[25] But it is not just the vagaries of composition—the fact of some things being on the page, as differentially experienced by author and reader.

Part of Michael Fried's ingenious argument on impressionist fiction by Stephen Crane and Joseph Conrad is devoted to a recovery on the textual surface of *impression* as such: that materially essential feature of composition which publication necessarily obliterates but which makes itself visible, according to Fried, through a peculiarly displaced metaphorics of displaced, upturned, or blank faces. All such tropes, says Fried, refer to the scene of writing itself, either when pen inscribes paper or when the page simply remains bare, beckoning (or deflecting) an initial stroke:

> the materiality of writing [is] simultaneously elicited and repressed: elicited because, under ordinary circumstances, the materiality precisely doesn't call attention to itself . . . in the intimately connected acts of writing and reading; and repressed because, were that materiality allowed to come unimpededly to the surface, not only would the very possibility of narrative continuity be lost, the writing in question would cease to be writing and would become mere mark.[26]

Even apart from Fried's cunning readings, why would speculations along such lines impinge upon one's reading in the first place unless one became more than customarily conscious of the physicality of the book in one's hands, the fingered page and cradled spine? And thus, the cover-image for this book now in *your* grasp: the separately carved left hand of a seventeenth-century polychrome sculpture, the tenon of its connecting armature exposed, the book in hand inverted from its customarily obscured position, hand on book thus revealing an almost supernaturally vivid tactility.[27]

It seems to me the very "book in hand" rendering of the uncanny intuition from Michel Serres quoted in the introduction: "When I lift these bricks, stones, concrete blocks, I exist entirely in my hands and arms and my soul in its density is at home there but, at the same time, my hand is lost in the grainy body of the pebbles." Or, to take another example, the orphaned volumes of Henry Darger found after his death, their thousands of pages wired or glued together between cardboard and wallpaper covers, all of it assembled by one pair of hands, all that desperate tactility is now exposed to, dependent on, the touch of others.[28]

Conjectures such as these or variants of them compose the ghostly commentary on all the sentences of this book. "But, what would your inquiry say about *this* particular case, *this* genre, *these* reading conditions?" I could imagine myself reasonably queried. That would be one counterthrust of the Levinasian *interrompu*, the obligatory fate whereby this book calls for other books in turn, to be interpreted in a saying distinct from the said. Parrying the question could mean reprising a passage I cited previously in Chapter 3: "the ethics of literary reading is less a matter of the exercise of a certain kind of effort on each reading—though it is that (including the effort of disencumbering the reading self)—than a disposition, a habit, a way of being in the world of words." I spoke there of the *necessarily* encumbered reading self, partly a matter of disposition, habit, and of being, as it were, *chosen* by words. In his interview cited above, McEwan speaks about being a novelist "helpless before" his subject matter: "It chooses you, is the useful cliché" (49).

This resembles the Levinasian counter-force of exteriority originating from "outside the subject"—of *finding* oneself enucleated, de-posed, or as *Otherwise Than Being* expresses it, of being "chosen without assuming the choice"(56). *Metamei yadayim*, the material capacity to make the hands impure, signifies an alteration worked upon *them* through tactile commerce with a text. But *altered reading* possesses another sense, fundamentally bound up with the choice we *exert* as readers (or as spectators in the microspheric "shared inside" of playhouse and movie theater).[29] When Cavell defines acknowledgment as declaring or showing the self; when Bakhtin's grammar of enactment specifies поступление ("the ongoingness of act") as something we persist in undertaking, that we haven't quite finished with (or, to give it its Levinasian twist, that hasn't yet finished with us), the effect becomes chordal.

The term "choice," however smacks of a Kantian or Aristotelian vocabulary for analysis or critique or method that at this concluding moment I do not wish to fall back on. And so I defer once again and finally to the image of the hand as the vehicle for technics and poetics alike. On one hand, manipulation; on the other, the "caress," which in *Totality and Infinity* signifies longing or seeking or aiming, "not situated in a perspective and in light of the graspable" (258). At its most culpable, as "anticipation [that] grasps possibles" (258), the image of the hand for Levinas permits seizure and acquisition, grasping, tearing up, crushing, kneading.[30] "The hand accomplishes its proper function prior to every execution of a plan, every projection of a project, every finality that would lead out of being at home with oneself" (158).

But at the same time, "the forms of objects call for the hand and the grasp. By the hand, the object is in the end comprehended, touched, taken, borne and *related* to other objects, assumes a signification in *relation* to other objects" (191). In this economy, we discern the hand's conspiracy with the eye, as "vision moves into grasp . . . and invites the hand into movement and contact." And yet, the one image Levinas's work assumes only implicitly is one that is deeply present in art and iconography: the book in hand.

If we were imagine this pictorially, drawing a line from the reader's mastery imaged by Chardin's *Le philosophe lisant* (1734) to the reader's shock imaged by Magritte's *La lectrice soumise* (1928) or transfixity imaged by Picasso's *Femme couchée lisant* (1939) to the studied, almost empty introspection of Giacomo Santiago Rogado's *Weiss & Prosa* (2008), or, finally, to the photographic series *On Reading* by André Kertész, with its snapshots of ordinary people perusing books: we discern reading's look.[31] And yet here too, vision more-than-moves into grasp: it effectively controls, overrides, even displaces it.

Obviously, my concern in this book has been, rather, with the *feel* or *touch* of reading, book-to-hand and hand-to-book,[32] which amounts less to the exercise of grasp than to what Levinas calls a "rite" and what I have termed a "staging"—a traversal between the sacred and profane as co-implicated realms or uses. Here, I differ from both Levinas's notion of a "one-way orientation" that elevates mere signification into sense, and Giorgio Agamben's analysis of profanation as the one-way redirection of the sacred by returning it to "the free use of men."[33] "To profane," writes Agamben, "means to open the possibility of a special form of negligence, which ignores separation, or rather, puts it to a particular use" (74). The *repurposing* of tact, then.

But a special scrupulosity may just as well work in the opposite direction, widening, opening up "the sacred." This is the import of the epigraph from Ouaknin above: as the holiness of books is ratified though rescue, so the book itself is revealed *by hand*. If "religious," as Agamben rightly notes, derives not from the verb *religare* ("to bind") but rather, *relegere* ("to gather or bring together, in order to go through—or read—again"[34]), then the "re-reading" modeled in this book's chapters—between the orders of *difficult* and *holy*—is the very mark of that traversal.

This returns me to the question I posed in the prologue about the reading of gravestones: into what meaningful adjacency are we ourselves drawn, reading in others' footsteps and traces, and how, in being "joined" to its project, could we be said, ethically, to "have made something happen?" My speculative limit-case for that inquiry was the scene in the Kissingen Jewish cemetery from Sebald's *The Emigrants*. Many pages later, hoping that the initial claim about ethics fastened to the event of reading has acquired the promised mass and density, I reprise the limit-case here, redeeming pledge through prestige, in the form of a quite different but also strangely similar scene in a Jewish cemetery.

SCENES OF READING, AGAIN

This one, located near the Jersey shore, is taken from Philip Roth's *Sabbath's Theater*—a novel published, as it turns out, a year before the English translation of Sebald's book. Like the character of Mickey Sabbath himself, the scene is exorbitant (cemeteries are otherwise treated irreverently with Shakespearean ribaldry in the novel). But it is its very *textual* prodigality that could be said to enlist readers' agency in its project.

Sabbath is searching for his grandparents' graves: "he saw that only if he travelled methodically up and down, reading every headstone from one end of each row to the other, could he hope to locate Clara and Mordechai Sabbath" (363). One might regard such "reading" as purely utilitarian, a laborious means to an end. And yet, "the hundreds of hundreds of headstones required his concentration, an immersion in them so complete that there would be nothing inside him but these names" (364). At exactly that juncture in the narrative, Roth ensures that our act of reading undergo a smaller mimetic version of that immersive labor: an entire page devoted to a litany of epitaphs, which I reproduce in its entirety here.

Our beloved mother Minnie. Our beloved husband and father Sidney. Beloved mother and grandmother Frieda. Beloved husband and father Jacob. Beloved husband, father, and grandfather Samuel. Beloved husband and father Joseph. Beloved mother Sarah. Beloved wife Rebecca. Beloved husband and father Benjamin. Beloved mother and grandmother Tessa. Beloved mother and grand-mother Sophie. Beloved mother Bertha. Beloved husband Hyman. Beloved husband Morris. Beloved husband and father William. Beloved wife and mother Rebecca. Beloved daughter and sister Hannah Sarah. Our beloved mother Klara. Beloved husband Max. Our beloved daughter Sadie. Beloved wife Tillie. Beloved husband Bernard. Beloved husband and father Fred. Beloved husband and father Frank. My beloved wife our dear mother Lena. Our dear father Marcus. On and on and on. Nobody beloved gets out alive. Only the very oldest recorded all in Hebrew. Our son and brother Nathan. Our clear father Edward. Husband and father Louis. Beloved wife and mother Fannie. Beloved mother and wife Rose. Beloved husband and father Solomon. Beloved son and brother Harry. In memory of my beloved husband and our dear father Lewis. Beloved son Sidney. Beloved wife of Louis and mother of George Lucille. Beloved mother Tillie. Beloved father Abraham. Beloved mother and grandmother Leah. Beloved husband and father Emmanuel. Beloved mother Sarah. Beloved father Samuel. And on mine, beloved what? Just that: Beloved What. David Schwartz, beloved son and brother died in service of his country 1894–1918. 15 Cheshvan. In memory of Gertie, a true wife and loyal friend. Our beloved father Sam. Our son, nineteen years old, 1903–1922. No name, merely "Our son." Beloved wife and dear mother Florence. Beloved brother Dr. Boris. Beloved husband and father Samuel. Beloved father Saul. Beloved wife and mother Celia. Beloved mother Chasa. Beloved husband and father Isadore. Beloved wife and mother Esther. Beloved mother Jennie. Beloved husband and father David. Our beloved mother Gertrude. Beloved husband, father, brother, Jekyl. Beloved aunt Sima. Beloved daughter Ethel. Beloved wife and mother Annie. Beloved wife and mother Frima. Beloved father and husband Hersch. And here we are. Clara Sabbath 1872–1941. Mordecai Sabbath 1871–1923. There they are. Simple stone. And a pebble on top. (364–365)

Sabbath's "material" labor becomes briefly ours, as our hand, so to speak, is forced. And as in Sebald, the episode sorts proper names with the material facts of weighty stone and pebble, the "production of presence" behind any take-away "meaning."[35] Roth's novel banks on *our* proximity, our willingness to go through all sixty-five names (and one "son" unnamed), to reiterate each "beloved"—where such reading-as-incanting *just means* the work of *relegere*: "to gather or bring together, in order to go through—or *read*—again."[36]

   And so, one last time, I return also to Arad's *Reflecting Absence,* where both "concussiveness" and "largesse"—Elaine Scarry's dialectical terms for the "interaction between the material creature and the material world"—so conspicuously converge upon each other. What invites the hand into movement and contact with the bronze parapets at the September 11 memorial is the regress of name to person to material surface—each element, both explicably and inexplicably, standing for the other.

The 2,977 names have not been incised by a pen or "writer's quill," the headstone-image that so moved Sebald's narrator, but rather by precision-calibrated machines that use Hermann Zapf's graceful Optima typeface, backlit so as to produce a "typographic tour de force."[37] But the magic process by which writing becomes altered reading, and the way it both marks and invites marking, is what explains the transformative move from eye to hand, and the turning of its pledge into an always-receding prestige. This is art's ethical adventure.

It is an adventure announced at one of literary inscription's inaugural, epic moments. As this book began with ritual acts of remembrance, so it ends now in mirror fashion with a ritual act of invocation—the ceremonial beginning from *Gilgamesh*, with its detailed instructions about brute materiality and its commandment to read, composed thirteen centuries before the biblical scriptures came alive in Augustine's hands by a fig tree in a Milanese garden:

> He who saw the depths the wellspring the foundation
> Who experienced all things went everywhere
> Saw the hidden secret Returned with word from before the flood
> Who made a distant journey exhausted in peace
> Left his story in stone
> He built the walls of Uruk-the-Sheepfold
> Sacred Eanna the storehouse the sanctuary
> [Regard] the upper wall gleam, the inner wall unequaled
> [Touch the threshold, ancient] Scale the ancient stone stairs to Eanna house of
> Ishtar unmatched by later kings
> Study the foundations, the bricks kiln fired laid by seven sages
> A square sar each of city, garden, and quarry
> Find the copper tablet box
> Release its bronze lock
> Raise the lid of secrets
> Take and read the tablet of lapis lazuli
> The travails of Gilgamesh.[38]

Regard, find, release, raise; and finally, take and read: this is the book in hand.

POSTSCRIPT (A DIFFERENT FLOOD NARRATIVE)

If one wrote a parchment [for a Sefer Torah] and wants to leave it to dry, he may not turn it *al panav* (on its face) even though he intends to prevent dust from gathering on the writing. Rather, the writing must face up, and he spreads a garment over it.

Shulḥan 'Arukh (*Yoreh De'ah* 277:1)

Mar Zutra said: Wrappings of scrolls which are worn out may be used for making shrouds for a *met mizvah* (one who dies without mourners) and this act constitutes their being "stored away."

bMegillah 26b

In addition to 253 deaths across seven countries and 380,000 housing units damaged or wrecked on the eastern seaboard alone, an estimated eighty tons of sacred writings—thirty thousand *sefarim*, pairs of *tefillin*, and several Torah scrolls—were ruined, rendered unfit for use, by Hurricane Sandy in October 2012. *Sheimot* ("names," because God's name is written thereon) is the halakhic status assigned to such items; while they can no longer be ritually used, they cannot be discarded but rather require burial in accordance with the *qedushah* they still possess. Three tractor-trailers (ritually escorted by a crowd as would attend a casket leaving a funeral home) were required to transport the mass of reading matter to its final resting place, a pit twelve feet wide, one-hundred and twenty feet long, and fifteen feet deep: not quite the dimensions of the open area bounded by the Uruk wall and Eanna Temple, but still imposing.

A newspaper account recorded these two particulars: (1) "Because respect for the books demanded that they could not simply be thrown into the pit, the volunteers at first made a line and passed the books to each other as they took them from the trucks." Although the books' sheer number ultimately mandated another, less hands-on (or hand-to-hand) method of deposal, the scene plays a variation on Walter Benjamin's Berlin schoolroom where the tactile also becomes the affiliative, with the book as the very medium of transmission.

(2) In the midst of an otherwise doleful, hortatory sermon for yeshiva pupils about the *mitzvah* of burying sacred objects, the presiding rabbi "reached into a truck and pulled out a book"—preserving, rescuing it spontaneously. *And as if gripped by the very physical contact itself*—for "in touching things, we touch ourselves to them, as it were; we are simultaneously touching and touched"[39]—he kisses the *sefer* three times and restores its unbound covers. In eerie echo of Agnon's story "A Book that was Lost" whose Galician narrator resists letting go of a recovered manuscript destined for shipment to Eretz Yisrael because "for as long as it was in my hand, it bound me to Jerusalem,"[40] the rabbi proclaims feelingly: "We take these *sforim*; we make them holy; this one is mine. I'm not letting it go."[41]

It is always a matter of unbinding the tie that holds the volume together and of letting it breathe, puff for a second, a matter also of having it lose its sufficiency and consistency enough so that it can be found only in the zealousness or nonchalance of the fingers that turn its pages.

Jean-Luc Nancy

NOTES

Prologue: Meaningful Adjacencies

1. The section epigraph is from the Michael Hulse translation (New York: New Directions, 1992), 225.

Four pertinent book-length explorations of the concept of recognition first outlined for us in the *Poetics* and subsequently the subject of many Renaissance, neoclassical, and modern commentaries are Piero Boitani, *The Bible and Its Rewritings*, trans. Anita Weston (New York: Oxford University Press, 1999); Terence Cave, *Recognitions: A Study in Poetics* (Oxford: Clarendon Press, 1988); Patchen Markell, *Bound Recognition* (Princeton: Princeton University Press, 2003); and Paul Ricoeur, *The Course of Recognition,* trans. David Pellauer (Cambridge, Mass.: Harvard University Press, 2005). See also the edited volume by Teresa G. Russo, *Recognition and Modes of Knowledge: Anagnorisis from Antiquity to Contemporary Theory* (Edmonton: University of Alberta Press, 2013).

2. Although not explicitly correlated with the Peircian triad, the scene is explained in Peter Brooks, *Reading for the Plot: Design and Intention in Narrative* (Cambridge, Mass.: Harvard University Press, 1984), as "a misguided attempt to remotivate the graphic symbol, to make it directly mimetic, mimetic specifically of origin" (114). Brooks locates the realm of the symbolic "in transference, in language—where the affects and figures of the past in symbolic form." The ritual of reading in Dickens's novel as *materially* configured is revisited in the Introduction.

3. *The Ark of Speech*, trans. Andrew Brown (New York: Routledge, 2004).

4. *Biographia Literaria: Or, Biographical Sketches of My Literary Life & Opinions*, ed. James Engell and Walter Jackson Bate (Princeton: Princeton University Press, 1985), 7:168.

5. Ai's sound piece also accompanies a site-specific installation, "Untitled" (2011), which consists of nine massive cube-shaped frames covered with identical children's backpacks. A retrospective of his work is described in *Smithsonian Newsdesk*, September 27, 2012 at http://newsdesk.si.edu/releases/hirshhorn-presents-ai-weiwei-according-what.

6. Quoted in "America Remembers," *National Geographic* 167, no. 5 (May 1985). See Robert Pogue Harrison's superb evocation of this intention and its place in a genealogy of epic poetry in "The Names of the Dead," *Critical Inquiry* 24, no. 1 (1997): 176–190,

republished included in his book *The Dominion of the Dead* (Chicago: University of Chicago Press, 2003).

7. See Peter S. Hawkins, "Naming Names: The Art of Memory and the NAMES Project AIDS," *Critical Inquiry* 19, no. 4 (Summer 1993): 752–780.

8. In 2009, Arad laid out his original concept for the memorial in the essay "Reflecting Absence," which appeared in *Places: Forum of Design for the Public Realm* 21, no. 1 (Spring 2009): 42–52. That design was the subject of early critique in advance of subsequent modifications Arad made, specifically in regard to name placement; see, for example, Joel McKim, "Agamben at Ground Zero: A Memorial without Content," *Theory Culture Society* 25, no. 5 (2008): 83–103; Marita Sturken, "The Aesthetics of Absence: Rebuilding Ground Zero," *American Ethnologist* 31, no. 3 (2004): 311–325; and Linda Watts, "Reflecting Absence or Presence? Public Space and Historical Memory at Ground Zero," *Space and Culture* 12 (November 2009): 412–418. More recently, Erika Doss assesses the memorial's aesthetics unfavorably in connection with Douwe Blumberg's "Horse Solder" statue in "*De Oppresso Liber* and *Reflecting Absence*: Ground Zero Memorials and the War on Terror," *American Quarterly* 65, no. 1 (March 2013), 203–214; Adam Gopnik laments both form and function in "Stones and Bones," *The New Yorker* (July 7/14, 2014), 38–44. Neither essay describes or evokes a scene of reading, however.

9. See the September 11 Memorial website, http://names.911memorial.org, and the article "Commemorative Calculus" by John Matson in *Scientific American*, September 7, 2011. See also Allison Blais and Lynn Rasic, *A Place of Remembrance: Official Book of the National September 11 Memorial* (Washington D.C.: National Geographic Society, 2011); David Dunlap, "Constructing a Story, With 2,982 Names," *New York Times*, May 4, 2011; Michael Kimmelman, "The New Ground Zero: Finding Comfort in the Safety of Names," *New York Times*, August 31, 2003; and Nick Paumgarten, "The Names," *The New Yorker*, May 16, 2011.

10. "Promised Land or Permitted Land," *Nine Talmudic Readings*, trans. Annette Aronowicz (Bloomington: Indiana University Press, 1990), 56.

11. Stone rubbing on gravestones or petroglyphs or the rubbing of monumental brasses is a long-standing tradition of recording textures, preserving genealogical information, and, of course, memorializing. On September 11 and 12, 2011, when *Reflecting Absences* was first opened to surviving family members and the general public, pencil-and-paper rubbings were ubiquitous (something any such incised marble slab might invite, of course, but not typically). *Frottage* is also the common technique used by visitors to the VVM. See Kristin Ann Hass, *Carried to the Wall: American Memory and the Vietnam Veterans Memorial* (Berkeley: University of California Press, 1998); Charles L. Griswold, "The Vietnam Veterans Memorial and the Washington Mall: Philosophical Thoughts on Political Iconography," *Critical Inquiry* 12, no. 4 (Summer 1986): 688–719; Kim Servart Theriault, "Re-membering Vietnam: War, Trauma, and 'Scarring Over' After 'The Wall,'" *Journal of American Culture* 26, no. 4 (December 2003): 421–431; and more critically, Marita Sturken, "The Wall, the Screen, and the Image: The Vietnam Veterans Memorial," *Representations* 35 (Summer 1991): 118–142.

12. *Nine Talmudic Readings*, 4. Another moving evocation of this human need for touch is the conclusion to the episode "Knowledge or Certainty" from Jacob Bronowski's *The Ascent of Man* (London: BBC Books, 2011). Walking toward a grassy marsh on the confines of Auschwitz, Bronowski declaims, "Into this pond were flushed the ashes of some four million people. . . . I owe it as a human being to the many members of my family who died here, to stand here as a survivor and a witness. We have to cure ourselves of the itch for absolute knowledge and power. We have to close the distance between the push-button order and the human act. *We have to touch people*" (285). He then bends down, reaches into the pond, and pulls up some of the ash-infused sediment within.

13. In *Pattern Language: Towns, Buildings, Construction* (New York: Oxford University Press, 1977), architect Christopher Alexander expounds the concept as the systematic approach to design problems in the construction of public architecture and civil engineering. Arad's memorial may also be said to accommodate the model of "affective mapping" and some of the questions it seeks to work out—"with whom do I share these losses or losses like them? how to embed my loss within larger historical processes and social forces?"—developed by Jonathan Flatley in *Affective Mapping: Melancholia and the Politics of Modernism* (Cambridge, Mass.: Harvard University Press, 2008), as well as the account of emergent bodily movement and sensation in respect to sociocultural "positional grids" in Brian Massumi, *Parables for the Virtual: Movement, Affect, Sensation* (Durham, N.C.: Duke University Press, 2002).

14. Likewise, in Carole Blair, Marsha S. Jeppeson, and Enrico Pucci, "Public Memorializing in Postmodernity: The Vietnam Veterans Memorial as Prototype," *Quarterly Journal of Speech* 77, no. 3 (August 1991): 263–289, the authors consistently speak of the Memorial's legibility, pointing to the paradox posed by the sequence of names and the symmetry of structure that produces both reading and counterreading (274).

15. "Ethics and Politics Today," in Jacques Derrida, *Negotiations* (Stanford: Stanford University Press, 2002), 297. In *Adieu to Emmanuel Levinas*, trans. Pascale-Anne Brault and Michael Naas (Stanford: Stanford University Press, 1990), Derrida relates the conversation on the rue Michel-Ange again, quoting thus: "what really interests me in the end is not ethics, not ethics alone, but the holy, the holiness of the holy" (4). See also the article by John Caruana, "'Not Ethics, Not Ethics Alone, but the Holy': Levinas on Ethics and Holiness," *Journal of Religious Ethics* 34, no. 4 (2006): 561–583.

16. "'Apres Vous, Monsieur!'" and "Interview with François Poirié," *Is It Righteous to Be? Interviews with Emmanuel Levinas*, ed. Jill Robbins (Stanford: Stanford University Press, 2001), 23–48. In the essay "On the Jewish Reading of Scriptures" from *Beyond The Verse*, Levinas writes, "Ethics is not simply the corollary of the religious, but is, of itself, the element in which religious transcendence receives its original meaning" (107).

17. See Charles Taylor, *A Secular Age* (Cambridge, Mass.: Harvard University Press, 2007), 26–29, and *Modern Social Imaginaries* (Durham, N.C.: Duke University Press, 2003), 18–19. I borrow "secular-and-*other*" from Mark Cauchi's article, "The Secular to Come: Interrogating the Derridean Secular," *Journal for Cultural and Religious Theory* 10,

no. 1 (Winter 2009): 1–25, which both references Taylor's formulation in concert with the Weberian notion of disenchantment, and interrogates Derrida's default undecidability between religious and secular modalities, in readings of *The Gift of Death* and "The Eyes of Language." Ronald Dworkin's Einstein lectures, published posthumously as *Religion Without God* (Cambridge, Mass.: Harvard University Press, 2013), mount a compelling argument for a "religious atheism" that reaches around the secular/religious divide to dignify what we might call the immanently holy. In his review of Dworkin's book, "Beyond Naturalism," *The New Republic* (October 21, 2013), 60–63, philosopher of law Moshe Halbertal remarks pertinently, "If, as I believe, what distinguishes the religious sensibility from the strictly secular is not the concept of God but the category of the holy [then] works of art are like the sacred" (62).

18. The etymology of the word—from the Latin *contaminatus*, past participle of *contaminare*, "to defile," from *contamen* "contact, pollution," from *com-* "together" + *tag-*, base of *tangere*, "to touch"—figures prominently in the Introduction and Chapter 1.

19. Sylvia Benso, *The Face of Things: A Different Side of Ethics* (Albany: State University Press, 2000), 130. (In *Das Ding* from 1951, Heidegger makes a similar move when he notes that *ding* connotes not only "material object" but also "gathering place.") Benso is quoting from the *Brief über den Humanismus* (1947), discussed also by Derrida on Levinas in *Alterites: Derrida et Pierre-Jean Labarriere* (Paris: Osiris, 1986). Hence also perhaps, the thrust of Levinas's preface to *Otherwise Than Being*, a shortened version of Pascal's *Pensée* 295, to which Levinas often alluded in his writing: "'that is my *place* in the sun.' Here is the beginning and the image of the usurpation of all the earth." For a very different, post-Heideggerian (and non-Levinasian) analysis of the thing-world, see Peter-Paul Verbeek, *What Things Do: Philosophical Reflections on Technology, Agency, and Design* (Philadelphia: University of Pennsylvania Press, 2005).

20. Benso, *The Face of Things*, 131. Compare Theodor Adorno, from *Minima Moralia: Reflections on a Damaged Life*, trans. E. F. N. Jephcott (New York: Verso, 2005): "Only by the recognition of distance in our neighbor is strangeness alleviated, accepted into consciousness." On Levinas's use of Pascal, see his dialogue with Richard Kearney, "Dialogue with Emmanuel Levinas," *Face to Face with Levinas* (Albany: State University of New York Press, 1986), 13–34.

21. Intersubjective space is "curved" for Levinas because it is not symmetrical. Just as the one who faces me approaches or stands at a height, creating a spatial difference, so, too, time between differential, not synchronous—what Levinas will term "diachrony" because the Other is both ahead and behind of the subjective self. See César A. Moreno Márquez, "The Curvature of Intersubjective Space: Sociality and Responsibility in the Thought of Emmanuel Levinas," *Analecta Husserliana* 22 (1987): 343–352.

22. *The Elsewhere, On Belonging at a Near Distance: Reading Literary Memoir from East Central Europe and the Levant* (Madison: University of Wisconsin Press, 2002).

23. "There is proximity, but only to the extent that extreme closeness emphasizes the distancing it opens up [;] the law of touching is separation: moreover, it is the hetero-

geneity of surfaces that touch each other." Jean-Luc Nancy, *Being Singular Plural*, trans. Robert Richardson and Anne O'Byrne (Stanford: Stanford University Press, 2000), 5.

24. We could style this an Arnoldian model of aesthetic appreciation. Indeed, in the famous 1853 "Author's Preface" to his poems, Matthew Arnold specifically singles out as anti- or nonpoetical an artwork that merely subjects its readers to something painful without some aesthetically redemptive compensation: "What then are the situations, from the representation of which, though accurate, no poetical enjoyment can be derived? They are those in which the suffering finds no vent in action; in which a continuous state of mental distress is prolonged, unrelieved by incident, hope, or resistance; in which there is everything to be endured, nothing to be done. In such situations there is inevitably something morbid, in the description of them something monotonous. When they occur in actual life, they are painful, not tragic; the representation of them in poetry is painful also" (2–3). *The Poems of Matthew Arnold 1840–1867* (London: Oxford University Press, 1940).

25. In *On Creaturely Life: Rilke, Benjamin, Sebald* (Chicago: University of Chicago Press, 2006), Eric Santner notes the propinquity of an object world where materiality is the stuff of ruin or decay and earthly things' "participation in the violent rhythms of human history . . . the 'mythic violence' that attends the foundation, preservation, and augmentation of institutions in the human world" (114). Thus the gravestones and incised names possess a dual function: (1) a material remainder of the living *as* stone and (2) signifiers that connect family histories and religious life, e.g., the name "Lanzberg," with monumental trauma and unnatural destruction, i.e., the name "Theresienstadt." Daniel J. Sherman's "Naming and the Violence of Place," *Terror, Culture, Politics: Rethinking 9/11*, ed. Daniel J. Sherman and Terry Nardin (Bloomington: Indiana University Press, 2006), 121–148, mounts a very different argument about commemorative naming as inextricably bound up with the politics of master narratives (137) and the appropriation of individual life stories (133).

26. For a treatment of haptics in connection with the politics of recognition, see Kevin Hetherington, "The Unsightly: Touching the Parthenon Frieze," *Theory, Culture & Society* 19 (December 2002): 187–205. See also Avivah Zornberg's beautiful reading of a *midrash* from *Tanḥuma Yashan* on Ex. 25:40 that imagines a *ḥakika*—an engraving by God of the *menorah* on Moses's palm to be used as a blueprint—which she calls a "tactile archive" and "a 'manual,' in the true sense," in *The Particulars of Rapture: Reflections on Exodus* (New York: Schocken Books, 2001), 326–328.

27. "The Meaning of Religious Practice," *Modern Judaism* 25, no. 3 (October 2005): 288.

28. *Economy of the Unlost: Reading Simonides of Keos with Paul Celan* (Princeton: Princeton University Press, 2002), 72. "Epitaphic transaction," as Carson call it, instances one of a set of related exchanges, linguistic, monetary, spatial, and moral, that underpin her profound analysis of two poets widely separated by time and culture. As another species of exchange, compare the epigraph to Levinas's *Difficult Freedom: Essays on Judaism*, trans. Seán Hand (Baltimore: Johns Hopkins University Press, 1990):

"Freedom on tablets of stone (*Tractate of Principles*, 6.2)," a formulation that appears in the Talmud (*b'Eruvin* 54a) as a commentary on the biblical verse (Ex. 32:16), "The *luḥot* were God's handiwork, and the writing was God's writing, engraved on the *luḥot*." "Rabbi Elazar says, why does it say 'engraved?' If the first *luḥot* were not broken, Torah would never be forgotten by Yisrael. [Text that is engraved cannot be erased.] R. Aḥa Bar Ya'akov says, 'no nation would be able to rule over Yisrael, as the verse says *ḥarut* [engraved]. Do not read '*ḥarut*' but rather read '*ḥeirut*' [freedom]."

29. "Celebrated Epitaphs Considered," *The Prose Works of William Wordsworth*, ed. W. J. B. Owen and Jane Worthington Smyser (Oxford: Clarendon, 1974), vol. 2, 189. On the zero-degree quality of such inscription, Jonathan Roberts comments, "Writing is at its best here for the poet because its meanings are sustained by the non-linguistic: the grave, the churchyard, the community within which that inscription makes sense. Such meanings cannot be transcribed, no dictionary could contain those numbers and fix them to the emotions that they evoke for Wordsworth; such meanings can only be established and maintained through community, shared experience, shared affections, a shared world" (370). "Wordsworth's Apocalypse," *Literature and Theology* 20, no. 4 (December 2006): 361–378. See also Dewey W. Hall, "Signs of the Dead: Epitaphs, Inscriptions, and the Discourse of the Self," *ELH* 68, no. 3 (Fall 2001): 655–677. The gibbet scene from the "spots of time" section in the 1805 *Prelude* bears comparison: "but on the turf / Hard by, soon after that fell deed was wrought, / Some unknown hand had carved the murderer's name. / The monumental writing was engraven / In times long past, and still from year to year / By superstition of the neighbourhood / The grass is cleared away; and to this hour / The letters are fresh and visible" (11.293–98).

30. As an integral part of Levinas's later philosophy, "Saying and Said" are the focus of much of the scholarship and commentarial literature. In Levinas's work itself, the pairing is found in *Otherwise Than Being; Or Beyond Essence*, trans. Alphonso Lingis (The Hague: Martinus Nijhoff, 1981), 56; "Language and Proximity" (1986), in *Collected Philosophical Papers,* trans. Alphonso Lingis (Pittsburgh: Duquesne University Press, 1998), 125, and the more politicized analysis in "Peace and Proximity" (1984), in *Emmanuel Levinas: Basic Philosophical Writings*, ed. Adriaan T. Peperzak, Simon Critchley, and Robert Bernasconi (Bloomington: Indiana University Press), 161–170.

31. "*Ce va-et-vient*" is Levinas's figure from *Beyond the Verse*. It chimes with "to and fro shuttling," a locution from Ross Chambers's *Room for Maneuver: Reading (The) Oppositional (In) Narrative* (Chicago: University of Chicago Press, 1991) that identifies the *art de faire* of reading. If the latter names "the practice that activates the mediated quality of all discourse" (Chambers, xvi), in this book the term has so far designated a range of acts and practices, e.g., "literary reading" and "scriptural reading," "scenes of reading" and "stagings of reading," "event of reading" and "ethics of reading." It, too, will acquire contour and shape in the pages to follow.

32. As of this writing, the remains of 1,121 known victims at Ground Zero have not yet been identified. Families of undocumented casual workers, mostly Mexican, were afraid to come forward initially. Henry Fernandez from Ecuador was the only such

worker officially listed in the death toll whose name therefore appears on the parapet of the North Memorial Pool. The Asociación Tepeyac de New York subsequently ascertained as much case-by-case information as possible, publishing several lists of names, the most recent of which has a total of 72 (36 of whom were eventually included on the official New York City count): www.docstoc.com/docs/15719866/list-of-wtc-missing -victims-reported-at-asociación-tepeyac and http://static.911digitalarchive.org/repository/ other_objects/379object.pdf.

33. For critical work on the phenomenon, see Jenny Edkins, *Missing: Persons and Politics* (Ithaca, N.Y.: Cornell University Press, 2011); Benigno Aguirre and E. L. Quarantelli, "The Phenomenology of Death Counts in Disasters: The Invisible Dead in the 9/11 WTC Attacks," *International Journal of Mass Emergencies and Disasters* 26, no. 1 (March 2008): 19–39. See also the following related newspaper articles: Miriam Ching Louie, "The 9/11 Disappeareds," in *The Nation*, December 3, 2001; Sasha Polakow-Suransky, "The Invisible Victims: Undocumented Workers at the World Trade Center," *The American Prospect, Online Edition* 12, no. 21 (December 3, 2001), http://prospect.org/ article/invisible-victims; and Albor Ruiz, "Giving a voice to immigrant victims of 9/11 and aiding families," *New York Daily News*, September 11, 2011.

34. *Otherwise Than Being*, 47, 40.

35. The term "counter-monument" was coined by James E. Young in "The Counter-Monument: Memory against Itself in Germany Today," *Critical Inquiry* 18, no. 2 (Winter 1992): 267–296; see *The Texture of Memory: Holocaust Memorials and Meaning* (New Haven: Yale University Press, 1994) and *At Memory's Edge: After-Images of the Holocaust in Contemporary Art and Architecture* (New York: Littauer Foundation, 2000), especially 140–144.

36. *Otherwise Than Being*, 88. Levinas is quoting from *The Song of Songs* 5:6. He explains the allusion thus: "Beyond the disclosure and exhibition of the known alternate, surprised and surprising, an enormous presence and the withdrawal of this presence. The withdrawal is not a negation of presence, nor its pure latency, recuperable in memory or actualization. It is alterity, without common measure with a presence or a past assembling into a synthesis in the synchrony of the correlative" (90).

37. The relevant texts for Levinas's concepts of trace, illeity, the future anterior of responsibility (*il aura obligé*, "he will have obligated," as Derrida expresses it), are "The Trace of the Other," trans. Alphonso Lingis, in *Deconstruction in Context*, ed. Mark Taylor (Chicago: University of Chicago Press, 1986), 345–359, and "Signification and Sense" (translated by Alphonso Lingis as "Meaning and Sense" in *Basic Philosophical Writings* and *Collected Philosophical Papers*), in *Humanism of the Other*, trans. Nidra Poller (Chicago: University of Illinois Press, 2003). In explaining the trace, Levinas writes, "He who left traces in effacing his traces did not mean to say or do anything by the traces he left. He has disturbed the order in an irreparable way. He has passed absolutely" (357). See also the essay "Language and Proximity" in *Collected Philosophical Papers*, 109–126.

38. In *Otherwise Than Being*, Levinas employs the phrase "dehiscence [or rupture] of proximity" (84), which has both a positive and a negative connotation: (1) the natural

bursting open at maturity of a fruit or other reproductive body to release seeds or spores, and (2) the bursting open of a surgically closed wound.

39. From Edith Wyschogrod's *An Ethics of Remembering: History, Heterology, and the Nameless Others* (Chicago: University of Chicago Press, 1998), 13. The quoted sentence belongs to Roland Barthes, from his essay "The Discourse of History," trans. Stephen Bann, *Comparative Criticism* 3 (1981): 9. See also, in Wyschogrod, the sections "The necessity of naming" and "That which cannot be named" in the first chapter of that book. "Naming the historical object is a response to the other's mortality: to name is to make us forget the fact of death, to write over it. . . . The name is empty: its logical form suggests that its primary function is heterological, that of an ethical placeholder, an appeal to the historian to make manifest that which was" (13). Another term for such ongoingness is "postmemory" (coined by Marianne Hirsch), to describe the tangency of personal memory and impersonal history by means of which memorialization does not merely record the traumatic past but is inhabited, addressed by, and exposed to, it. See Hirsch's *Family Frames: Photography, Narrative, and Postmemory* (Cambridge, Mass.: Harvard University Press, 1997) and *The Generation of Postmemory: Writing and Visual Culture After the Holocaust* (New York: Columbia University Press, 2012).

40. *Narrative Ethics* (Cambridge, Mass.: Harvard University Press, 1995), a pairing of nineteenth- and the twentieth-century English and American texts of prose fiction, with a theoretical apparatus that triangulates Levinas, Bakhtin, and Cavell; *Facing Black and Jew: Literature as Public Space in 20th Century America* (Cambridge: Cambridge University Press, 1998), a pairing of African American and Jewish American authors, with an apparatus that couples Levinas and Walter Benjamin; *The Fence and the Neighbor: Yeshayahu Leibowitz, Emmanuel Levinas and Israel Among the Nations* (Albany: State University of New York Press, 2001), a pairing of post-Shoah twentieth-century Jewish philosophers, Levinas and Yeshayahu Leibowitz (born, respectively, in the Baltic cities of Kovno/Kaunas, Lithuania, and Riga, Latvia, and eventually making their homes in Paris and Jerusalem), with a critical apparatus drawn from their writings; and *The Elsewhere: On Belonging at a Near Distance*, a pairing of twentieth-century émigré or *dépaysé* memoirists from Eastern and Central Europe and the Levant, with a critical apparatus that draws, once again, from Levinas.

41. For example, Charles Altieri, *The Particulars of Rapture: An Aesthetics of the Affects* (Ithaca, N.Y.: Cornell University Press, 2004); David Parker, *Ethics, Theory and the Novel* (Cambridge: Cambridge University Press, 1994); James Phelan, *Living to Tell about It: A Rhetoric and Ethics of Character Narration* (Ithaca, N.Y.: Cornell University Press, 2004) and *Experiencing Fiction: Judgments, Progressions, and the Rhetorical Theory of Narrative* (Columbus: Ohio State University Press, 2007). Cutting against that grain is a group of post-traditional approaches like Georgiana Banita, *Plotting Justice: Narrative Ethics and Literary Culture After 9/11* (Lincoln: University of Nebraska Press, 2012), Robert Eaglestone, *Ethical Criticism: Reading After Levinas* (Edinburgh: Edinburgh University Press, 1997), Andrew Gibson, *Postmodernity, Ethics and the Novel: From Leavis to Levinas* (London: Routledge, 1999), David Palumbo-Liu's model of "deliverary systems" for mimetic

encounters between self and otherness in *The Deliverance of Others: Reading Literature in the Global Age* (Durham, N.C.: Duke University Press, 2012), and C. Namwali Serpell, *Seven Modes of Uncertainty* (Cambridge, Mass.: Harvard University Press, 2014)—distinguished from the others, however, by its imaginative debt to Empson. While allowing that such a listing of titles risks obscuring a discernible genealogy of concepts and formulations for recent work on the ethics of reading that includes my own project, I would differentiate its method and timbre from this countertradition, as well. But see also Dorothy J. Hale, "Fiction as Restriction: Self-Binding in New Ethical Theories of the Novel," *Narrative* 15, no. 2 (May 2007): 187–206, and *On the Turn The Ethics of Fiction in Contemporary Narrative in English*, ed. Bárbara Arizti and Silvia Martínez-Falquina (Newcastle: Cambridge Scholars Publishing, 2007).

42. That agenda becomes an explicit inquiry in Andrew Bush, *Jewish Studies: A Theoretical Introduction* (New Brunswick, N.J.: Rutgers University Press, 2011) and Ra'anan S. Boustan, Oren Kosansky, and Marina Rustow, eds., *Jewish Studies at the Crossroads of Anthropology and History: Authority, Diaspora, Tradition* (Philadelphia: University of Pennsylvania Press, 2011), as well as for a planned project of my own that construes the data field question for Jewish Studies within an ecology of "neighboring." *The Elsewhere* established a precedent for my inter-reading of classical Jewish sources and non-scriptural literary discourse by exporting a Talmudic mnemonic from Tractate *b'Eruvin*, folio 51a, about Sabbath boundaries and Levitical cities of refuge—"Rav Ḥisda said, 'We learn place from place, place from flight, flight from flight, flight from border, border from border, border from beyond, beyond from beyond'"—and applying it to literary memoir by writers from East Central Europe and the Levant as a sequence of organizing tropes: *place, flight, border, beyond.*

43. Anthony Cascardi, as quoted by Charles Altieri in "Lyrical Ethics and Literary Experience," in *Mapping the Ethical Turn: A Reader in Ethics, Culture, and Literary Theory*, ed. Todd F. Davis and Kenneth Womack (Charlottesville: University of Virginia Press, 2001), 30–58.

44. A good example of ethics talk-as-values talk is Elaine Scarry's "Poetry Changed the World: Injury and the Ethics of Reading," which frames a volume of essays and responses, *The Humanities and Public Life*, ed. Peter Brooks with Hilary Jewett (New York: Fordham University Press, 2014). Her focus on literature's ethical power to (1) invite empathy, (2) rely on deliberative thought, and (3) manifest beauty is something my more limited claim assigns to the reading act itself as *tact*—more closely aligned, thus, with Scarry's earlier and fascinating work on the body and touch in Thomas Hardy.

45. This is the analytical problem that Bakhtin faces in "Author and Hero in Aesthetic Activity," one he never completely resolves.

46. These are some of the definitional and programmatic questions Michael Morgan raises at the beginning of his book, *Discovering Levinas* (Cambridge: Cambridge University Press, 2010), with reference to Levinas scholars Robert Bernasconi and Theodor de Boer and to essays by Jonathan Lear on Wittgenstein. Morgan comes to

terms with various dimensions of Levinas's work with respect to Anglo-American rather than Continental or specifically Jewish philosophical traditions.

47. To these, one can also add Maimonidian, as explored by Michael Fagenblat in *A Covenant of Creatures: Levinas's Philosophy of Judaism* (Stanford: Stanford University Press, 2011), and Lurianic, as ventured by Jacob Meskin in "The Role of Lurianic Kabbalah in the Early Philosophy of Emmanuel Levinas," *Levinas Studies* 2 (2007): 49–77.

48. As Edith Wyschogrod explains, such proximity, as a nonspatial formulation, cannot be gathered up or explicated into a Kantian synthesis: "This relation of terms is non-viciously circular, suggesting, rather, that alterity and approach are reciprocally constituted" (*An Ethics of Remembering*, 9).

49. On this question, see Colin Davis, "Levinas and the Phenomenology of Reading," in *A Century with Levinas: Notes on the Margins of His Legacy*, ed. Cristian Ciocan, Adina Bozga, and Attila Szigeti (Bucharest: Romanian Society for Phenomenology, 2006), 275–292.

50. In *Being Singular Plural*, Jean-Luc Nancy defines "staging" as a *praxis* (*scénographique*) and an *ethos* (69, 71) and literature as "language stretched out (*en tension*)" (90) in address and as discourse.

51. I say more about the critical tradeoff of this posture at the beginning of Chapter 5 on Bakhtin and Chapter 6 on Cavell.

52. *Emmanuel Levinas: His Life and Legacy*, trans. Michael Krigel (Pittsburgh: Duquesne University Press, 2006), 187. The term *kivyakhol* (for which Malka's anecdotal usage is unusual) is given special attention by Michael Fishbane in an exhaustive appendix to *Biblical Myth and Rabbinic Mythmaking* (New York: Oxford University Press, 2003), 325–404, and Peter Ochs in *The Return to Scripture in Judaism and Christianity: Essays in Postcritical Scriptural Interpretation* (Mahwah, N.J.: Paulist Press, 1993), 179–182 and 186–188.

53. From her essay, "Levinas, Allegory, and Chaucer's *Clerk's Tale*," in *Levinas and Medieval Literature: The "Difficult Reading" of English and Rabbinic Texts*, ed. Ann W. Astell and J. A. Jackson (Pittsburgh: Duquesne University Press, 2009), 45.

54. This crucial formulation belongs to Jill Robbins, elaborated in *Altered Reading: Levinas and Literature* (Chicago: University of Chicago Press, 1999). Robbins rightly cautions that any attempted rapprochement between Levinas's philosophy and literature must "deal with the incommensurability between Levinas's ethics and the discourse of literary criticism" since the former "cannot function as an extrinsic approach to the literary work of art, that is, it cannot give rise to an application" (xx). And even if "an intrinsic approach . . . one that will take into account what Levinas says about literature and how he says it" (39) stands a better chance of coherence, my own concern here is not the categorical status of literature (or scripture, for that matter), but rather practices of reading, one of which Levinas already models. A number of secondary works have sought to match Levinas's ethics to a certain kind of literary criticism. Despite the promising title, for example, *The Ethics of Reading According to Emmanuel Lévinas* by Roland A. Champagne (Amsterdam: Editions Rodopi, 1998)—published one year before

Robbins's book, in fact—uses the critical lens of male feminism and serves mostly as that application about which Robbins expresses so much dubiety. On this general topic, see my review essay, "The *SARL* of Criticism: Sonority, Arrogation, Letting-Be," *American Literary History* 13, no. 4 (Winter 2001): 603–637.

55. "Virginia Woolf's Mysticism," *The Broken Estate: Essays on Literature and Belief* (New York: Picador, 2010), 109. "If the artwork describes itself, then criticism's purpose is to redescribe the artwork in its own, different language. . . . To describe literature critically is to describe it again, but as it were for the first time. It is to describe it as if literature were music or art, and as if one could sing or paint criticism. Again, but for the first time: the critic shares the language of her subject, but then changes every word, makes it her own tilted subjection. All critics do this, but the writer-critic, wanting to be both faithful critic and original writer, does it acutely, in a flurry of trapped loyalties. The writer-critic's relationship to the writer she reviews may be likened to hearing, in the next room, a sibling playing something on the piano that you yourself know well but have not yet played yourself."

56. *Collected Fictions*, trans. Andrew Hurley (New York: Penguin Books, 1998), 84.

57. Quoted by Manderson in *Proximity, Levinas, and the Soul of Law* (Montreal: McGill-Queen's University Press, 2006), 53.

58. Another example of this tactic can be seen in Jill Robbins's brief reading of "Knots Upon Knots," a short story by S. Y. Agnon (*Altered Reading*, 136–142), less an exercise in exegesis than an outline of adjacency.

59. Cavell uses the phrase to suggest an analogy between the development of *King Lear* and certain "theatrical" structures of classical music. See *Disowning Knowledge: In Seven Plays of Shakespeare* (Cambridge: Cambridge University Press, 2003), 93.

60. As Roland Barthes's explains his notion of text-as-musical score in "Textual Analysis of a Tale by Edgar Allan Poe," *The Semiotic Challenge*, trans. Richard Howard (Oxford: Blackwell, 1988): "to represent the text as a tissue (moreover this is its etymological meaning), as a skein of different voices, [for] a narrative is not a tabular space, a plane structure, it is a volume, a stereophony (Eisenstein repeatedly insisted on the *counterpoint* of his stagings)," 292. Following Paul Ricoeur's *Interpretation Theory*, Nicholas Wolterstorff elaborates the analogy between interpretative practice and realizing scores in *Divine Discourse: Philosophical Reflections on the Claim That God Speaks* (Cambridge: Cambridge University Press, 1995). Compare also the model of diachronic resonance (the distracting accretion over time of ambient "noise" around free-standing art objects) in Stephen Greenblatt, "Resonance and Wonder," *Exhibiting Cultures: The Poetics and Politics of Museum Display*, ed. Ivan Karp and Steven D. Lavine (Washington, D.C.: Smithsonian Institution Press, 1991), 42–56, and revisited by Wai Chee Dimock in a more affirmative vein as a matrix for sensing the emergent "traveling frequencies of literary texts" (1061) in "A Theory of Resonance," *PMLA* 112, no. 5 (October 1997): 1060–1071.

61. *Introduction to Levinas* (South Bend, Ind.: University of Notre Dame Press, 1997), 140–141. A recent derivative study, *Levinas, the Frankfurt School, and Psychoanalysis*

(Middletown, Conn.: Wesleyan University Press, 2003) by C. Fred Alford, begins by paraphrasing this very passage from Davis as a cautionary note ("so that Levinas becomes a deconstructionist, theologian, proto-feminist, or even the reconciler of postmodern ethics and Rabbinic Judaism"), but still manages to mislocate both Levinas and his philosophy.

62. Jeffrey Thomas Nealon, *Alterity Politics: Ethics and Performative Subjectivity* (Durham, N.C.: Duke University Press, 1998), 64.

63. In *From Continuity to Contiguity: Toward a New Jewish Literary Thinking* (Stanford: Stanford University Press, 2010), Dan Miron proposes the concept of "contiguity" for understanding specifically literary relationships among traditions and texts: "The new thinking should leave continuities behind it (not that they do not exist, at least as helpful ancillary syntagms; but they are of secondary importance and have been overly studied and focused on) and focus instead on contiguities or tangentialities" (305). I think the concept also has an import for scholarship that either isolates various strands in Levinas's thought ("*noeuds d'un fil renoué*" knots of a retied thread, to use his own image), or else mobilizes it in relation to diverse intellectual projects by others. Compare, thus, Nancy: "From one singularity to another, there is contiguity but not continuity. There is proximity, but only to the extent that extreme closeness emphasizes the distancing it opens up . . . the law of touching is separation" (*Being Singular Plural*, 5).

64. In this book, for instance, despite his catholicity of tastes (film, opera, continental and analytic philosophy, American literature, British Romanticism, Shakespeare) Stanley Cavell does not invite such manifold conjunctions; Bakhtin almost rivals Levinas in this respect, as I suggest at the beginning of Chapter 5.

65. On the idea of books' "call" for one other in Levinas, see Catherine Chalier, "The Voice and the Book," in *Making a Difference: Essays on the Bible and Judaism in Honor of Tamara Cohn Eskenazi*, ed. David J. A. Clines, Kent Harold Richards, and Jacob L. Wright (Sheffield: Sheffield Phoenix Press, 2012), 60–72.

66. In *Levinas, Storytelling and Anti-Storytelling* (London: Bloomsbury Academic, 2013), Will Buckingham directly takes up the place of "story" in philosophical writing, as Levinas either performs or (sometimes skeptically) thematizes it.

67. "Space Is Not One-Dimensional," *Difficult Freedom*, 263.

68. Franz Rosenzweig's phrase from *Understanding the Sick and the Healthy: A View of World, Man, and God*, trans. Nahum Glatzer (Cambridge, Mass.: Harvard University Press, 1999).

Introduction: Laws of Tact and Genre

1. As was reported to me in July 2012 by Alberto Zilberstein Toruncha, president of Adath Israel de Cuba. On contemporary Cuban Jewry, see Abel R. Castro Figueroa, *Las religiones en Cuba: Un recorrido por la Revolución* (Guadalajara, 2009) and *Quo vadis, Cuba? Religión y revolución* (Bloomington, Ind.: Palibrio, 2010), and Ruth Behar, *An Island Called Home: Returning to Jewish Cuba* (New Brunswick, N.J.: Rutgers University Press, 2009).

2. Kenneth Brandler citing Dr. Jose Miller, late leader of the Cuban Jewish community, in "Jewish Youth Lead the Way in a Long Isolated Community," *Jewish Telegraph
Agency*, January 7, 1996. There is a difference of opinion among rabbinic authorities about
whether minors can make up the deficit in a minyan; it is the practice among some
communities, for example, to allow children over the age of six to count by holding a
ḥumash (Pentateuch) or *Sefer Torah*. See R. Moshe Feinstein, "Including a Minor in
Extraneous Circumstances," (Hebrew) *Iggrot Moshe* (*Oraḥ Ḥayyim* 2:18) (New York:
Noble Press Book Corp, 1982), 188–189, and Aharon Ziegler, "Counting a Minor in a
Minyan," *Halakhic Positions of Rabbi Joseph B. Soloveitchik: Volume III* (Lanham, Md.:
Rowman & Littlefield, 2004), 26–28. See also R. Saul Berman, "The Status of Women
in Halakhic Judaism," *Tradition* (Fall 1973): 5–8. Finally, anthropologist Jonathan
Boyarin relates an anecdote about the custom in the chapter "Death and the Minyan"
from *Thinking in Jewish* (Chicago: University of Chicago Press, 1996), 70.

3. In *Brisker derekh lamdut*, the Lithuanian methodology of Talmud study associated
with the Soloveitchik family dynasty beginning with R. Ḥayyim of Brisk (1853–1918)
and dominant in most modern *yeshivot*, binary distinctions known as *tsvei dinim* help
conceptualize the vast corpus of laws and topics, abstracting from its myriad discussions
certain a priori categories and principles that clarify positions. One of the most important of these is *heftza/gavra* or "object/person," which can be discerned in the background of the lecture by R. Joseph Soloveitchik discussed below. See R. Aharon
Lichtenstein, "The Conceptual Approach to Torah Learning: The Method and Its
Prospects," *Lomdut: The Conceptual Approach to Jewish Learning*, ed. R. Yosef Blau,
(Jersey City, N.J.: Ktav, 2006), 1–44, and R. Mosheh Lichtenstein, "'What Hath Brisk
Wrought: The Brisker *Derekh* Revisited," in the same volume, 167–188.

4. One notable lacuna in various recent studies of Jewish embodiment of late, e.g.,
Sander Gilman, *The Jew's Body* (New York: Routledge, 1991), Howard Eilberg-Schwartz,
People of the Body: Jews and Judaism from an Embodied Perspective (Albany: State
University of New York Press, 1992) Melvin Konner, *The Jewish Body* (New York:
Random House, 2009), Ken Koltun-Fromm, *Material Culture and Jewish Thought in
America* (Bloomington: Indiana University Press, 2010), would be an attention to these
specifically tactile varieties of religious experience. For this book's purposes, it becomes
rather acute in Eilberg-Schwartz's introduction, which consistently tropes on the
suspended relation between "people of the book" and "people of the body." For an
alternate approach, see, for example, Barbara Kirshenblatt-Gimblett, "The Cut That
Binds: The Western Ashkenazic Torah Binder as Nexus between Circumcision and
Torah," in *Celebration, Studies in Festivity and Ritual*, ed. Victor Witter Turner
(Washington, D.C. Smithsonian Institution Press, 1982), 136–146.

5. *Mishnah Berurah* 134–149, *Aruḥ Ha Shulkhan, Yoreh De'ah* 282, *Sh'arei Efraim* 10,
Iggrot Moshe (*Oraḥ Ḥayyim*) 1:38.

6. "A Yid iz Geglaykhn tzu a Seyfer Toyre," with the first (halakhic) half printed in
R. Joseph B. Soloveitchik, *Shiurim le-Zekher Abba Mari Zal, vol. 1* (Jerusalem: Mekhon
Yerushalayim, 1982/3), 240 ff., and the entire *shiur* transcribed by Hillel Zeidman,

published in *Di Yiddishe Voch* (1959), and republished in *Beit Yosef Shaul, vol. 4,* ed.
R. Elchanan Asher Adler (New York: Rabbi Isaac Elchanan Theological Seminary, 1994),
17–67. A Hebrew translation by R. Shalom Carmy appeared in the same volume
(68–103), and a more recent English translated by Shaul Seidler-Feller appears in seven
installments in *Kol Hamevaser* III:1–8 (2009–2010), www.kolhamevaser.com. There is a
powerful and famous aggadic demonstration of this "axiomatic analogy" in the Palestinian
Talmud: *pHagiga* 77b–c, in which R. Meir covers R. Elisha's burning grave with his
tallit (like Boaz covering and thus redeeming Ruth), and defends his action: ולא כן
תנינן מצילין תיק הספר עם הספר תיק תפילין עם התפילין מצילין לאלישע אחר בזכות תורתו ("Did we
not learn, They save the casing of the scroll with the scroll, the casing of the *tefillin* with
the *tefillin* [*mShabbat* 16:1]? They save Elisha-Aḥer for the merit of his Torah"). By
analogy, the license to save holy writing from fire on Shabbat justifies the compassion R.
Elisha shows to R. Meir by saving his "container" (inasmuch as Torah was embodied in
him) from incineration.

7. "A Person is Compared to a Sefer Torah," *Kol Hamevaser* III, no. 1 (September 2009): 25.

8. "The primitive hide stands in opposition to the scribe's desire to fill its surface with
letters. The skin wants to remain empty and blank; it does not want to bear the burden
of writing. Therefore, one may not write any letters of the Torah on unprocessed hide.
One must first prepare the rolls of parchment so that they should be able to absorb the
letters, the words, and the paragraphs of the Torah," *Kol Hamevaser* III, no. 4 (February
2010): 19. A further distinction inheres in the two-sided nature of the parchment itself,
which adds another layer to the analogy between scroll and person: "Just as the Halakhah
differentiates between the two surfaces of 'external' [animal] hide, the hair side (*tsad
ha-se'ar*) and the flesh side (*tsad ha-basar*), which, in processed form, are called '*kelaf*' and
'*dukhsustos*,' [respectively], so does it see in the 'internal' [human] skin both surfaces, the
tsad ha-se'ar and the *tsad ha-basar*. When the human personality is developed, the *tsad
ha-se'ar* is transformed into 'internal' *kelaf* and the *tsad ha-basar* into 'internal' *dukhsustos*." *Kol Hamevaser* III, no. 6 (March 2010): 21.

9. "The *sofer* must have another Sefer Torah (or its text) in front of him to copy from
for it is forbidden to write a single letter by heart and he must recite each word orally
before writing." *Shulḥan 'Arukh, Yoreh De'ah* 274:2. The developing relationship between
scroll and codex in the early Middle Ages around the question of sacrality is traced in
Albert I. Baumgarten and Marina Rustow, "Judaism and Tradition: Continuity, Change,
and Innovation," in *Jewish Studies at the Crossroads of Anthropology and History: Authority,
Diaspora, Tradition*, ed. Ra'anan S. Boustan, Oren Kosansky, and Marina Rustow
(Philadelphia: University of Pennsylvania Press, 2011), 207–237.

10. *Kol Hamevaser* III, no. 1 (September 2009): 25.

11. *Kol Hamevaser* III, no. 2 (November 2009): 22. An even more blatant analogy can
be found in the late medieval Christian devotional practice of representing the body of
Christ as parchment, his blood accordingly construed as ink, the weapons that pierce
him, as writing implements. This trope receives extended treatment by Sarah Noonan
in "Bodies of Parchment: Representing the Passion and Reading Manuscripts in Late

Medieval England," Ph.D. diss., Washington University, 2010. See also Michael Camille, "The Book as Flesh and Fetish in Richard de Bury's *Philobiblion*," in *The Book and the Body*, ed. Dolores Warwick Frese and Katherine O'Brien O'Keeffe (Notre Dame, Ind.: University of Notre Dame Press, 1997), 34–77.

12. With the Torah's anxiety about *kil'ayim* (the Levitical prohibition against grafting, crossbreeding, or otherwise confusing disparate products, and the subject of its own tractate in Mishnah and Talmud) in mind, adjacency signifies a significantly different order of relation than admixture or *mélange*. My use of contiguity here parallels a formulation by Carla Namwali Serpell that she calls *the join* or *the ethics of the adjoining*—"a word, like 'cleave,' that implies both connection and separation—as in the place or line where two things meet, like the joins of a ship's planks" (292). See "The Ethics of Uncertainty: Reading Twentieth-Century American Literature," Ph.D. diss., Harvard University, 2008.

13. These particulars, in specific relation to consecrated food (*terumah*), hallowed things (*qadoshim*), and sacred objects (*klei hamikdash*), are covered in Tractate *Hagigah* in the *Bavli*, folios 18b–27a. See also Tractate *Pesahim*, folios 15b–20a. The latter becomes the point of departure for a nontechnical excursus on *tum'ah* in Adam Kirsch, "Appreciating the Talmud's Sublime Devotion to Torah for Its Own Sake," *Tablet Magazine* (July 26, 2013) http://www.tabletmag.com/jewish-life-and-religion/137870/kirsch-daf-yomi-42/2.

14. The *loci classici* in the *Bavli* are the chapter "*yetziot ha'shabbat*" in *bShabbat* (13b–14a) and "*megillah nikreit*" in *bMegillah* (7a), codified in the *Shulhan 'Arukh* in *Orah Hayim* 147:1. The discussion in Tractate *Shabbat* is known as the *sugya* of *shemonah 'asar davar* (Eighteen Decrees), enacted by Beit Hillel and Beit Shammai in the first century BCE. Twelve of the eighteen measures specify particular sources of ritual contamination; ten derive from the final *mishnah* (5:12) of tractate *Zavim* of which numbers six, *ha'sefer* [scroll] and seven, *ha'yadayim* [hands] are the relevant pair here. *Tractate Shabbos Shottenstein Edition* (New York: Mesorah Publications, 2002) contains a lucid introduction to the laws of *tum'ah* in the context of the Eighteen Decrees. There is a substantial secondary literature on the question of rabbinic authority generally, whether confined to the relationship between Tannaim and Amoraim, or concerned with post-Talmudic perspectives. As example of the former, see Abraham Joshua Heschel, *Heavenly Torah: As Refracted Through the Generations,* trans. Gordon Tucker (New York: Continuum, 2006); of the latter, see the Maimonidean account in Menachem Kellner, *Maimonides on the "Decline of the Generations" and the Nature of Rabbinic Authority* (Albany: State University of New York Press, 1996).

15. The focus on hands in particular is significant since according to rabbinic law both impurity and purification typically affect the entire person rather than being confined to a single body-part. The exceptions are *tum'at yadayim* and *netilat* (washing, but lit. "raising") *yadayim*, respectively, and the rabbinic enactment for the latter was called *stam yadayim* (ordinary hands) because all unrinsed hands were decreed to have the status of *sheni letum'ah*. "This is rooted in a unique characteristic that sets hands apart from the

rest of the body: 'hands are active' . . . operating as if on their own, unfettered by the restraints of the mind's conscious supervision. The hands' tendency for free movement gives them an independent status that other limbs of the body do not have. This distinction allowed the Sages to declare that the hands become impure independently of the rest of the body." See R. Elyakim Krumbein, *Daf Kesher* 136 (Sivan 5748), 2:68–70, trans. R. Eliezer Kwass as *"Netillat Yadayim*—Washing Hands Before Eating Bread," www.vbmtorah.org/archive/ halak56/13halak.htm, and *Talmud Bavli Tractate Chagigah Schottenstein Edition* (New York: Mesorah Publications, 2002), folio 18b.

16. A baraita in *bBerakhot* 22a quotes R. Judah ben Bathyra: אין דברי תורה מקבלין טומאה (the words of Torah are not susceptible to *tum'ah*). It is a principle codified by Maimonides in the *Mishneh Torah* and the Rama in the *Shulhan 'Arukh*. See also Avraham Weiss, "Women and *Sifrei Torah*," *Tradition* 20, no. 2 (Summer 1982): 106–118.

17. Two canonical instances of forbidden touch as related to *qedushah* are: Num. 4:15–17 in which the *bnei kehat* (Kohat clan) are delegated the responsibility of poterage for the sacred objects of the Tabernacle, wrapped in cloth and dolphin skin lest they make contact (*v'lo yigu*) with the hands; and 2 Sam. 6:7 in which Uzza, fatally, reaches for (*vayishlakh*) and grasps (*vayohez*) the *aron haqodesh*. The command *not to touch* is already there, of course, at the Bible's inaugural social moment, in Gen. 3:3. The concept of *negiah* receives intriguing philosophical/rabbinic consideration by Asher Crispe in "A Phenomenology of Involvement without Interference in the Rabbinic and Philosophic Traditions," www.interinclusion.org/inspirations/out-of-touch.

18. "Bringing near" is also a concept treated in the *Bavli*'s discussion of Temple sacrifices, specifically regarding the ritual of *hagashah* (from Lev. 2:8) in which the Kohen's utensil containing the daily *minhah* flour offering is mandated as having to *touch* the southwest corner of the altar (*bMenahot* 60a-b and *bZevahim* 63a–b). Also relevant are the related hand-object rituals of *hanahah* (placement) *semikhah* (laying on of hands) and *tenufah* (waving) that accompany cultic offerings, including "first fruits" or *bikkurim* (Deut. 26).

19. "And why did the rabbis impose uncleanness upon Scriptural books? Rabbi Mesharshiya said: Because originally Terumah foods were stored near Torah scrolls, for they argued: This is holy and that is holy. When it was seen that the books came to harm the rabbis imposed uncleanness upon them" (*bShabbat* 14a). The original collocation of scroll and heave offering is logical but also circumstantial. Thus, "the intimate connection between sacred food and the written scroll" (370) that Edith Wyschogrod proposes as a link between this rabbinic proscription and various instances in the Torah of ingested writing (*het ha'egel* in Ex. 32:20, *sotah* in Nu. 5:11–31, *megilat hasefer* in Ezekiel 2:8–3:3) and the related danger of what she calls "tactile miscegenation" (371) misconceive that purely contingent relationship. See "Eating the Text, Defiling the Hands," in *Crossover Queries: Dwelling with Negatives, Embodying Philosophy's Others* (New York: Fordham University Press, 2006), 360–374.

20. A related question concerns whether the sacred text is prophetically inspired [*ruah haqodesh*] or whether it deserves to be withdrawn [*lignoz*] and only privately circulated

because it might mislead the naïve reader (*bShabbat* 30b and 13b and *Vayikra Rabbah* 28:1). These distinctions are elaborated by Sid Z. Leiman in *The Canonization of Hebrew Scripture: The Talmudic and Midrashic Evidence* (New Haven: Connecticut Academy of Arts and Sciences, 1991). The critical literature on canonicity is extensive, but see especially Moshe Halbertal, *People of the Book: Canon, Meaning, and Authority* (Cambridge, Mass.: Harvard University Press, 1997) and Lee Martin McDonald, *The Biblical Canon: Its Origin, Transmission, and Authority* (Grand Rapids, Mich.: Baker Academic, 2011). As the title indicates, Robert Alter's more syncretic *Canon and Creativity: Modern Writing and the Authority of Scripture* (New Haven: Yale University Press, 2000) calculatedly aligns the two modes I am calling "the difficult and the holy."

21. The word may also denote books of wisdom in Greek (designated *homeros*) or those that are heretical because "changeful" (from Heb. מור). On the general rabbinical significance of Homer, see Ahuvia Kahane, "Homer and the Jews in Antiquity," *Textus: Studies of the Hebrew Bible Project Vol. 25*, ed. Michael Segal and Noam Mizrahi (Jerusalem: Hebrew University Press, 2010), 75–114, and the essay collection *Homer and the Bible in the Eyes of Ancient Interpreters*, ed. Maren R. Niehoff (Leiden: Brill, 2012), especially Yair Furstenberg, "The Agon with Moses and Homer: Rabbinic Midrash and the Second Sophistic," 299–328.

22. This question is pursued, for example, in the chapter "*Kol kitvei*" in *bShabbat* (115a–117b) in a discussion about saving Holy Scriptures from a fire on the Sabbath. At one point (116a) the *gemara* asks whether, in addition to the writing (*ha'ketav*), the blank portions of a Torah scroll (*ha'gilonin*) above and below the writing or between one column and the next or one section and the next can also "make the hands the impure."

23. An analogy can be found within the Torah itself in the Levitical chapters on *tzara'at* (a blemishing affliction of the skin often mistranslated as "leprosy"), which renders persons, clothing, and even houses unclean. As construed by Rashi and glossed by subsequent medieval commentators, the import of Lev. 13: 2 and similar verses in which the high priest "looks at" the blemish and "pronounces" the person or garment or house unclean, is that the *tum'ah* exists, as it were, *only when or because* it is seen and so pronounced. Seeing and speaking (in Rashi's expression, *al pi hakohen* ["by the mouth of the priest"]) not only verify the phenomenon; they *confer* the status of cleanliness or uncleanliness upon it.

24. *Ethics and Infinity: Conversations with Philippe Nemo*, trans. Richard A. Cohen (Pittsburgh: Duquesne University Press, 1985), 117; *Beyond the Verse: Talmudic Readings and Lectures*, trans. Gary D. Mole (Bloomington: Indiana University Press, 1994), xii.

25. Cf. Marcel Proust's preface to *Sésame et le lys*, his translation of Ruskin, also published as the essay *Sur la Lecture* (1905) and translated by Jean Autret and William Burford as *On Reading Ruskin* (New Haven: Yale University, 1971), which expounds upon "le rôle à la fois essentiel et limité que la lecture peut jouer dans notre vie spirituelle" (the simultaneously essential and limited role that reading can play in our spiritual life) (23), with the important qualification that "La lecture est au seuil de la vie spirituelle; elle peut nous y introduire: elle ne la constitue pas"—Reading is the beginning of our spiritual

life; it introduces us to it: it does not constitute it (34). In the specifically modern Jewish philosophical context close to Levinas, see also Franz Rosenzweig's excursus on *lernen* as denoting "the old form of maintaining the relationship between life and the Book" in his "Upon Opening the Jüdische Lehrhaus" address, *On Jewish Learning*, ed. N. N. Glatzer (Madison: University of Wisconsin Press, 2002), 95, the treatment of Levinas's relationship to Jewish Education in Claire Elise Katz, *Levinas and the Crisis of Humanism* (Bloomington: Indiana University Press, 2013), and the essays collected in *Jewishness and the Human Dimension* by Jonathan Boyarin (New York: Fordham University Press, 2008).

26. In public cantillation of the Torah (three times per week including Sabbaths, and on holidays), the same contact point between hand and scroll virtually links each person called up for a recited section: in Ashkenazic custom, the two handles or shafts called *atzei ḥayim* (trees of life) are taken in both hands initially, with one hand holding onto one roller for the duration of the reading; Sephardim (in particular, Mizrahi communities) grasp the *tiq*, a case of either metal or wood that houses the scroll and that is kept vertical. See the general discussion of customs by Simcha Fishbane, "The Symbolic Representation of the Sefer Torah," *Maqom Journal for Studies in Rabbinic Literature* 22 (Spring 2012), www.maqom.com/journal/paper35.pdf.

27. Cf. the analyses of touch and "the hand" in Edmund Husserl, *Ideas Pertaining to a Pure Phenomenology and to a Phenomenological Philosophy—Second Book: Studies in the Phenomenology of Constitution*, trans. R. Rojcewicz and A. Schuwer (Dordrecht: Kluwer, 1989), and Maurice Merleau-Ponty, *Phenomenology of Perception*, trans. Colin Smith (London: Routledge, 2002), both referenced by Derrida in *On Longing*. Merleau-Ponty, for example, speaks—beyond embodiment as a predicate or substantive fact—of its ongoingness as a series of acts, "a body which rises toward the world" (87), opening "to an infinite set of possibilities" (527). The latter dimension is refined briefly but importantly by Judith Butler as indicating a fundamentally *dramatic* situation, for which the proper descriptive vocabulary would rely on "an ontology of present participles," e.g., *a mode of embodying,* rather than "the substance metaphysics of subject-verb formations." See "Performative Acts and Gender Constitution: An Essay in Phenomenology and Feminist Theory," *Theatre Journal* 40, no. 4 (December 1988): 519–531.

28. If this project thus freely translates the phrase "digital humanities," the fate of the bound book in the electronic age will nevertheless not constitute a particular concern of mine here—for which, among similar titles, see *The Future of the Book*, ed. Geoffrey Nunberg (Berkeley: University of California Press, 1996), Nancy's *On the Commerce of Thinking*, and Alan Liu, "The End of the End of the Book: Dead Books, Lively Margins, and Social Computing," *Michigan Quarterly Review* 48 (2009): 499–520. It bears noting, though, that such dramatic shift in technology is not exclusive to the twenty-first century. Elaborating on the difference between "unhandled and handled commodities," for example, Lisa Gitelman writes that, "Records are played while films are shown, a distinction that measures the umbilical distance from producer to product in strangely tactile terms, and one that has blurred with time, challenged by radio broadcasting and

video cassettes. The radio un-handed phonograph records, while the VCR let the audience touch the film." *Scripts, Grooves, and Writing Machines: Representing Technology in the Edison Era* (Stanford: Stanford University Press, 1999), 159–160.

29. As noted by Edward Said in *Beginnings: Intention and Method*, J. Hillis Miller in *Charles Dickens: The World of His Novels*, Walter Reed in *An Exemplary History of the Novel*, and in particular, by both Peter J. Capuano, "Handling The Perceptual Politics of Identity in *Great Expectations*," *Dickens Quarterly* 27, no. 3 (September 2010), 185–208 and William A. Cohen, "Manual Conduct in Great Expectations." *ELH* 60 (1993): 217–259.

30. *Great Expectations* (Oxford: Oxford University Press), 2008, 66.

31. *Berlin Childhood around 1900*, trans Howard Eiland (Cambridge, Mass.: Belknap Press of Harvard University Press, 2006), 56.

32. *Post-Global Network and Everyday Life*, ed. Marina Levina and Grant Kien (New York: Peter Lang, 2010), 27.

33. *Eight Tales from the Major Phase: In the Cage and Others* (New York: Norton, 1958), 183. Interiority and social knowledge are grand Jamesian themes, of course, but while this story is more proximate by date of composition to *What Maisie Knew* (1897), its explicit focus on physical medium also warrants comparison with two short novels from the previous decade, *The Reverberator* and *The Aspern Papers*, both published in 1888. For an extremely sharp treatment of surface and touch in James's work, see Thomas J. Otten, *A Superficial Reading of Henry James: Preoccupations with the Material World* (Columbus: Ohio State University Press, 2006).

34. Quoted in Marta L. Werner, "Helen Keller and Anne Sullivan: Writing Other-wise," *Interval(le)s* II, no. 2–III, no. 1 (Fall 2008–Winter 2009): 958–996. Werner explores this most transparently fused relationship between reading/writing and touching ("a poetics of Braille") as both a limit case and a crossing point between theories of embodi-ment, inscription, and disability. "Paper," she explains, "even the heavy paper used in Braille books, is fragile and tends to warp under the weight of the embossing. It is highly vulnerable to wear and destruction because the indentations are fragile. Indeed, it is a system of writing constantly threatened by erasure. The very act of reading is simultane-ously an act of rubbing out, a passage from the seen to the unseen." Gary Frost's "Reading by Hand: How Hands Prompt the Mind," http://futureofthebook.com/hand.

35. Werner, "Helen Keller and Anne Sullivan," 968.

36. *How to Do Things with Books in Victorian Britain* (Princeton: Princeton University Press, 2012), 9. Valentine Cunningham's *Reading After Theory* (Cambridge: Blackwell, 2002) contains a chapter, "Touching Reading," that specifically addresses the question of how to handle such texts about hands tactfully. Echoing Sebald here and anticipating Nancy, Cunningham writes, "Tact: proper tactility; the gentle touch of the right-minded communicant. Tact as proper behaviours before the tended, the offered sacrament; tact as due attention, a proper attending to: a tenderness of touch; tender attention" (156). David Ayers reviews various approaches to textual "matter," including Benjamin, Butler, Chartier, and Derrida in "Materialism and the Book," *Poetics Today* 24, no. 4 (Winter

2003): 759–780. This issue and the following one (24, no. 5) are both devoted to the question of "Between Thing and Theory."

37. Compare this extreme instance from the mid-twentieth century: "For [my mother], *Mein Kampf* was an object of pure repulsion. . . . But what added to her anxiety was her belief that the book was a contagion, that its gold-leafed pages would defile her should her fingers brush against it by accident when she was searching for another book on the shelf. She didn't want to come into contact with the German soldier's hair or skin particles—which she believed were still clinging to the book. If she touched it, she'd douse her hands with rubbing alcohol to obliterate any trace of it on her skin." Hinda Mandell, "In Curious Pursuit of the Original Owners of 'Mein Kampf,'" *The Forward*, September 12, 2012.

38. Price treats the novel again in her chapter on "It-Narrative and the Book as Agent" (107–135). Not only is it possible, as in the *Copperfield* example, for literary fiction to "reduce narrating subjects to grammatical objects" (126) or to equate "the debasement of a human being with the process of being assimilated to a book" (129). But, on the other side of the coin, it is just as possible to invest books with the properties of speech, human feeling, and personal history, the it-narrative being thus mapped onto the *Bildungsroman*. This is especially case for a subgenre of nineteenth-century English "it-narrative" inventoried by Price: a series of titles from 1806 to 1893 which self-narrate the fortunes of bibles, prayer books, religious tracts, and the like. Of these (even though it sounds the death knell of the genre), *Handed-On; Or, The Story of a Hymn Book* from 1893 replaces a book's ostensible own but thrown voice with a third-person account that takes up the narrative burden on the book's behalf: for "no book can tell the story of its ups and downs in the world or describe how and why it began to pass from hand to hand" (quoted on 120).

39. Levinas is scrupulous in noting that while the Mishnah is a textual production of "Antiquity," the Talmud, properly speaking, belongs to an early medieval period in which "many of the fine traditions of Antiquity were still alive" (*Nine Talmudic Readings*, 97).

40. See the essays in *Levinas and Medieval Literature: The "Difficult Reading" of English and Rabbinic Texts*, in particular, the editors' introduction, "Before the Face of the Book: A Levinasian Pre-face" (1–14); Valerie Allen, "Difficult Reading" (15–34); Cynthia Kraman, "The Wound of the Infinite: Rereading Levinas through Rashi's Commentary on the *Song of Songs*" (207–226); and Moshe Gold, "Those Evil Goslings, Those Evil Stories: Letting the Boys Out of Their Caves" (281–304), all quite rich in their thoughtful *va-et-vient* between Levinasian tropes and literary texts.

41. *Anthropology from a Pragmatic Point of View*, ed. and trans. Robert B. Louden (Cambridge: Cambridge University Press (2006), 29ff and 53ff.

42. For example, Didier Franck's *Flesh and Body: On the Phenomenology of Husserl*, trans. Joseph Rivera and Scott Davidson (London: Bloomsbury Academic, 2014), Butler's *Bodies That Matter: On the Discursive Limits of Sex* (New York: Routledge, 1993), and Foucault's *The Government of Self and Others: Lectures at the College de France, 1982–1983*, trans. Graham Burchell (New York: Palgrave Macmillan, 2010).

43. "Sensitivity is given to itself only in the profusion of the world; it receives itself through the other and by means of the other . . . . Transitivity is thus, radically, first. To live, as Rilke says in his last poem, is truly to be outside—*Draussensein*." Jean-Louis Chrétien, *The Call and The Response,* trans. Anne A. Davenport (New York: Fordham University Press, 2004), 122–123.

44. Nancy extends these ideas directly to the idea ("character," "voice") of the book in *On the Commerce of Thinking: On Books and Bookstores*, trans. David Wills (New York: Fordham University Press, 2009). One of Nancy's shortest and most vivid works, and almost too close to this book's own concerns, it offers a compressed meditation on the commerce and *mêlée*, community and communicability, that books represent, their constant interface between inside and outside, "imprint" and "reprint," closure and opening, rolled *volumen* and stitched codex, at the same time as they each individually aspire to a kind of "exercise in sainthood" (14), a givenness that is also a giving (the "ceaseless refolding upon itself" that constitutes any act of reading) in which Nancy will locate the book's modalized "sacredness" (18).

45. In addition to its juridical aspect of compilation, "corpus" for Nancy connotes a loose assemblage—neither discourse nor narrative but "*clinamen*, a fragile, fractal prose, (53)—*extension* and *exposition,* but in the particular sense of a "self-positing" and a "being exposed" (35). J. Hillis Miller devotes a chapter to Nancy *The Conflagration of Community: Fiction Before and After Auschwitz* (Chicago: University of Chicago Press, 2011).

46. "'Writing' indicates *the very thing that swerves from signification* and which, therefore, is *exscribed. . . .* A word, so long as it's not absorbed without remainder into sense, *remains* essentially extended *between* other words, stretching to touch them, though not merging with them: and that's language as *body*" (71).

47. In another strategic parenthesis, Nancy says, "(the true question of *touching* and, in general, of literary and artistic *sensibility*, the true question of an *aesthetics*, is yet to be posed, or very nearly so, so long as bodies are signifiers above all)" (71).

48. To be touched, of course, is also to be susceptible. For the title of his first book, Sebald chose the portmanteau *Schwindelgefühl,* or "dizzyfeeling" (translated in the English edition as *Vertigo*), divided it in two, and pluralized it to *Schwindel. Gefühle* (a title that hints at an alternate meaning, however: "feelings of swindle"). See, for instance, Brian Castro, "Blue Max: A Tribute," in *Heat* 3 (2002): 119–29: "Beneath a street lamp in the Zeltnergasse, I opened the book to read its title: *Schwindel. Gefühl.* Two words. Vertigo. Feelings. Just a moment. Even with a limited grasp of German, I became instantly suspicious. *Schwindel* of course can also mean swindle, fraud or trick. Have I just been deceived by giddiness, by feelings?" (120).

49. Levinas makes this connection, too, as we will see, for a vocabulary of *tact* and *touche* is essential to his concept of interhuman sensibility. In "God and Philosophy" and "A God 'Transcendent to the Point of Absence,'" for example, he anticipates such metaphors when he describes the paradox of *une mise sans prise* ("a placing without grasp") in relation to a Desire for the Infinite as "an ignition of the skin that touches and [yet] does not touch that which burns beyond the graspable."

50. *Being Singular Plural,* 6.

51. On this essential idea of shared, common space, see "*La comparution*/The Comparance: From the Existence of 'Communism' to the Community of 'Existence',", *Political Theory* 20, no. 3, trans. Tracy B. Strong (August, 1992): 371–398, and *Being Singular Plural*.

52. For alternate genealogies for the hand, touch, and tact, see the chapters on Benjamin, Merleau-Ponty, and Heidegger in David Michael Kleinberg-Levin, *Gestures of Ethical Life: Reading Hölderlin's Question of Measure After Heidegger* (Stanford: Stanford University Press, 2005), and Daniel M. Price, *Touching Difficulty: Sacred Form from Plato to Derrida* (Aurora, Colo.: Davies Group, 2009). See also the postphenomenological topographies of touch by Michel Serres in the first chapter of *The Five Senses: A Philosophy of Mingled Bodies*, trans. Margaret Sankey and Peter Cowley (New York: Continuum, 2008) and Didier Anzieu, *The Skin Ego: A Psychoanalytic Approach to the Self*, trans. Chris Turner (New Haven: Yale University Press, 1989), Constance Classen's *The Deepest Sense: A Cultural History of Touch* (Champaign: University of Illinois, 2012), and her anthology of essays, *The Book of Touch* (New York: Berg, 2005).

53. J. Hillis Miller's *For Derrida* (New York: Fordham University Press, 2009), has a long chapter on the intersection, "Touching Derrida Touching Nancy." Two articles that discuss Nancy and Derrida on touch (the latter, in connection with Levinas) are Donald A. Landes, "*Le Toucher* and the Corpus of Tact: Exploring Touch and Technicity with Jacques Derrida and Jean-Luc Nancy," *L'Esprit Créateur* 47, no. 3 (2007), 80–92, and Dave Boothroyd, "Time and Technics: Levinas and the Ethics of Haptic Communications," *Theory, Culture & Society* 26, nos. 2–3 (2009): 330–345.

54. The essay was first published in *Critical Inquiry* 7 (1980): 55–81 and in *Acts of Literature*, ed. Derek Attridge (London: Routledge, 1992), 221–252, and later included in *Parages* (Stanford: Stanford University Press, 2010). Important related treatments of the concept by Derrida are "Before the Law," trans. Avital Ronell, *Acts of Literature*, 181–220, "Force of Law: The 'Mystical Foundation of Authority,'" *Acts of Religion*, ed. Gil Anidjar (London: Routledge, 2002), 228–298, and *Geneses, Genealogies, Genres, and Genius: The Secrets of the Archive*, trans. Beverley Bie Brahic (New York: Columbia University Press, 2008). See also Pierre Legrand's *Derrida and Law* (London: Ashgate, 2009) and the chapter "Pulsations of Respect, or Winged Impossibility: Poetic Deconstruction," *Around the Book: Systems and Literacy*, ed. Henry Sussman (New York: Fordham University Press, 2010).

55. A famous example is philosopher John Searle's surly response to "Signature, Event, Context," "Reiterating the Differences: A Reply to Derrida," *Glyph* 2 (1977): 198–208, together with Derrida's own reply, *Limited Inc*, trans. Samuel Weber and Jeffrey Mehlman (Evanston, Ill.: Northwestern University Press, 1988). Jonathan Kendall's disdainful obituary for Derrida in *The New York Times* (October 14, 2004) is another instance, one that provoked a raft of outraged responses from Derrida's colleagues and admirers.

56. Margaret Davies, "Derrida and Law: Legitimate Fictions," in *Jacques Derrida and the Humanities: A Critical Reader*, ed. Tom Cohen (Cambridge: Cambridge University Press, 2001), 213–237. See John Llewellyn's explanation of Derrida's essay as an exercise in

"the paradox of quasi-analysis" in "Responsibility with Undecidability," *Appositions of Jacques Derrida and Emmanuel Levinas* (Bloomington: Indiana University Press, 2002), 17–36.

57. Bakhtin, as his oeuvre demonstrates, devoted enormous thought to the question of genre. But Cavell, too, takes it on in quite explicit fashion in both his books on film and tragic drama but also in an essay I will be looking at in Chapter 5, "The Fact of Television," *Daedalus* 111, no. 4, "Print Culture and Video Culture" (Fall 1982): 75–96. As for Levinas, it is worth noting that he typically uses the word "genre" in a quite restrictive sense, for example, "Now, when there are two unique beings, then genre reappears. From this moment on, I think of the other in the genre. . . . The thought of comparison, of judgment, the attributes of the subject, in short, the entire terminology of Greek logic and Greek politics appears" ("The Paradox of Morality: an Interview with Emmanuel Levinas," conducted by Tamra Wright, Peter Hughes, and Alison Ainley, *The Provocation of Levinas: Rethinking the Other*, ed. Robert Bernasconi and David Wood [London and New York: Routledge & Kegan Paul, 1988], 174–175).

58. Peter Mallios, "An Interview with Edward Said," in *Conrad in the Twenty-First Century: Contemporary Approaches and Perspectives*, ed. Carola M. Kaplan, Peter Mallios, and Andrea White (New York: Routledge, 2005), 296.

59. Versatile treatments of the novel can be found in Mark M. Anderson, "The Edge of Darkness: On W. G. Sebald," *October* 106 (Autumn 2003): 102–121; James K. Chandler, "About Loss: W. G. Sebald's Romantic Art of Memory," *The South Atlantic Quarterly* 102, no. 1 (Winter 2003): 235–262; Jonathan James Long, *W. G. Sebald: Image, Archive, Modernity* (New York: Columbia University Press, 2007); and several of the essays collected in *W. G. Sebald: History, Memory, Trauma*, ed. Scott Denham, Mark McCulloh (Berlin: Walter de Gruyter, 2006). On the salient matter of Sebald and translation, see Michael Hulse, "Englishing Max" and Anthea Bell, "Translating W. G. Sebald—With and Without the Author," in *Saturn's Moons: W. G. Sebald—A Handbook*, ed. Jo Catling and Richard Hibbitt (Oxford: Legenda, 2011) 195–215; see also Jo Catling, Anthony Vivis, Christine Wilson, and Stefan Tobler, "Among Translators: W. G. Sebald and Translation," *In Other Words: The Journal for Literary Translators* 38 (Winter 2011): 11–122.

60. "A tangent touches a line or a surface but without crossing it, without a true intersection, thus in a kind of impertinent pertinence. It touches only one point, but a point is nothing, that is, a limit without dimension or surface, untouchable even by way of a finger" (131). See also Derrida's *Paper Machine*, trans. Rachel Bowlby (Stanford: Stanford University Press, 2005), which consists of occasional pieces about the book in print and digital form against the general background of mechanicity in various communicative contexts.

61. *Espacement* becomes a crucial concept for Derrida: "a syncope, a *technē* of bodies, and first of all and everywhere an irreducible spacing (the first word of any deconstruction, valid for space as well as time)" (181). This approximates Nancy's own formulation, "the distancing and strangeness that make up place." In the conclusion to "On the Soul,"

for example, Nancy writes, "But touching upon the self is the experience of touching on what is untouchable in a certain way, since 'self-touching' is not, as such, something that can be touched. The body is the experience of indefinitely touching on the untouchable, but in the sense that the untouchable is not anything that would be back behind, anything interior or inside, or a mass, or a God. The untouchable is the fact that it touches" (135).

62. "One would have to display this logic of the limit, what lets itself be touched does so on its border and thus does not let itself be reached or attained even as it exposes the untouchable itself, the other border of the border, to touch" (299).

63. "Le partage, l'infini et le jardin," *Libération* (February 17, 2000). See also Nancy's article "Exscription," *Yale French Studies* 78 (1990): 47–64, later included in *Birth to Presence*. Compare Derrida: "It [the law] thus inscribes the uninscribable in inscription itself, it exscribes. The law of exscribing, of exscription as "the last truth of inscription" finds here at least one of its essential demonstrations" (309).

64. For an especially creative application of Nancy's and Derrida's work in light of my brief discussion of Arad's *Reflecting Absences* that also cites some of these same passages, see also Stanislaus Fung and Mark Jackson, "Dualism and Polarism: Structures of Architectural and Landscape Architectural Discourse in China and the West," *Interstices: A Journal of Architecture and Related Arts* 4 (1997): 84–91.

65. See Ian James, "Incarnation and Infinity," *Re-treating Religion: Deconstructing Christianity with Jean-Luc Nancy*, ed. Alena Alexandrova, Ignaas Devisch, Laurens ten Kate, and Aukje van Rooden (New York: Fordham University Press, 2012), 246–260, and Claire Colebrook "Derrida, Deleuze and Haptic Aesthetics," *Derrida Today* 2 (2009): 22–43.

66. See Nancy: "To touch is to be at the limit," says Nancy (*The Birth to Presence*, 30). Compare Maurice Blanchot's idea in *L'Amitié* (Paris: Gallimard, 1971) that "what separates becomes relation" (326), his term for which—a sibling to *tact*—is "*la discrétion.*"

67. See the treatment of the hand in the chapter "Body and Touch," in Chrétien's *The Call and the Response*, 94–95.

68. Compare the essay "Passions: An Oblique Offering," first published separately in 1992 and subsequently as the first section of *On the Name,* trans. David Wood (Stanford: Stanford University Press, 1995), 1–31. There, Derrida proposes his own dutiful nonresponse, a "duplicitous" responsibility, to a volume of critical essays on his own work as the stuff of eucharistic ritual and oblique offering—that is to say, what presumably any text that is called to account for itself authorially cannot ultimately lay bare or deliver to frontality, to objective analysis and interpretation. "There is in literature," Derrida says, "in the exemplary secret of literature, a chance of saying everything without *touching upon* the secret" (29); this "secret that impassions" Derrida also describes as a "call [*appel*]," a performative that not only anticipates Chrétien but also cycles back to the essay's initial pages about critical reading as *the ritual unfolding of a ceremony* or *liturgy*.

69. André Kertész, *On Reading* (New York: Norton, 2008); see also Garrett Stewart, *The Look of Reading: Book, Painting, Text* (Chicago: University of Chicago Press, 2006).

Although Kertész was too tactful to penetrate that far, perhaps nothing emblematizes this relation as dramatically as the bathroom as a kind of library and the toilet as reading chair.

70. In *The Fullness of Being: A New Paradigm for Existence* (Notre Dame, Ind.: University of Notre Dame Press, 2002), Barry Miller distinguishes between "limit *simpliciter*" (which differs in degree, as in an upper limit) and the "limit-case" (which stands outside the relevant category absolutely). I do not press the distinction in my own argument, but more often than not, I use "limit-case" in the sense of "distal."

71. "It sometimes seems that one may in one's mind lay a hand on an image or perform mental operations that are handlike—stretching, tilting, folding," from *Dreaming by the Book* (Princeton: Princeton University Press, 2001), 240.

72. Scarry offers this related elegant observation in a companion essay: "But verbal art, especially narrative, is almost bereft of any sensuous content. Its visual features, as has often been observed, consist of monotonous small black marks on a white page. It has *no* acoustical features. Its tactile features are limited to the weight of its pages, their smooth surfaces, and their exquisitely thin edges" (3)—the latter, nevertheless, a constant and companionate presence for the duration of the reading act. See "On Vivacity: The Difference between Daydreaming and Imagining-Under-Authorial-Instruction," *Representations* 52 (Autumn 1995): 1–26.

73. "Laborers and Voyagers: From the Text to the Reader," *Diacritics* 22, no. 2 (Summer 1992): 51. In rejoinder to the Pouletian model, he insists, "Far from the phenomenology of reading, which erases the concrete modality of the act of reading and characterizes it by its effects, postulated as universals, a history of modes of reading must identify the specific dispositions that distinguish communities of readers and traditions of reading." See also Chartier's *Inscription and Erasure: Literature and Written Culture from the Eleventh to the Eighteenth Century*, trans. Arthur Goldhammer (Philadelphia: University of Pennsylvania Press, 2007).

74. The manipular trope in Levinas is given an especially subtle treatment in Dominic Mastroianni, "Astonishing Politics: Levinas, Emerson, and Thinking Beyond Virility," *Comparative Literature* 65, no. 3 (Summer 2013).

1. Pledge, Turn, Prestige: Worldliness and Sanctity in Edward Said and Emmanuel Levinas

1. "It is a different nature which speaks to the camera than speaks to the eye: so different that in place of a space consciously woven together by a man on the spot there enters a space held together unconsciously." Walter Benjamin, "A Little History of Photography" (1931), in *Selected Writings 1927–1934, Volume 2, Part 2*, ed. Michael William Jennings, Howard Eiland, and Gary Smith (Cambridge, Mass.: Harvard University Press, 2005), 507–530.

2. A direct connection between Méliès's *The Vanishing Lady* and Nolan's *Prestige* is the subject of an article by Rachel Joseph, "Disappearing in Plain Sight: The Magic Trick and the Missed Event," *Octopus Journal* 5 (2011): 1–14.

3. In Christopher Priest's novel of the same name on which the film is based, the stages are specified (not by Cutter but by Alfred Borden, one of the magicians) as *set-up, performance or display*, and *effect or prestige*. See Priest, *The Prestige* (New York: Tom Doherty Associates, 1995), 73–74. Nolan's film is the subject of numerous reviews and webpages; the most extended discussion of the film belongs to Todd McGowan, *The Fictional Christopher Nolan* (Austin: University of Texas Press, 2012).

4. Adam Gopnik, "The Real Work: Modern Magic and the Meaning of Life," *The New Yorker*, March 17, 2008.

5. "You're a magician, not a wizard—you have to get your hands dirty to achieve the impossible," says Cutter. Mimetic duplication (and duplicity) as a kind of way station between science and magic is a linchpin of the plot. Earlier in the screenplay, referring to a machine for teleportation designed by Nikola Tesla, Cutter explains, "This wasn't built by a magician . . . it was built by a wizard. A man who can actually do the things a magician pretends to." (This is a lesson taught far more gothically by a precursor film to Nolan's, David Cronenberg's 1986 horror-science fiction, *The Fly*, which also features the plot conceit of teleportation.)

6. Said discusses Poulet, along with R. P. Blackmur and E. D. Hirsch, in his essay "Sense and Sensibility," collected in *Reflections on Exile and Other Essays* (Cambridge, Mass.: Harvard University Press, 2000). Levinas and Poulet are discussed together by Robert Lumsden in *Reading Literature After Deconstruction* (Amherst, N.Y.: Cambria Press, 2009), 85. Poulet's essay first appeared in *New Literary History* 1, no. 1 "New and Old History" (October 1969): 53–68.

7. "The Phenomenology of Reading," *The Languages of Criticism and the Sciences of Man*, ed. Richard Macksey and Eugenio Donato (Baltimore: Johns Hopkins University Press, 2007). See also the chapter on Poulet in J. Hillis Miller, *Theory Now and Then* (Durham, N.C.: Duke University Press, 1991); the chapter "Reading the Human Figure" in Michael Fischer, *Stanley Cavell and Literary Skepticism* (Chicago: University of Chicago Press, 1989); and the introduction to Doris Sommer, *Proceed with Caution, When Engaged by Minority: Writing in the Americas* (Cambridge, Mass.: Harvard University Press, 1999), which discusses the first of the passages from Poulet reproduced previously.

8. The vase (or vessel), in its "dual nature"—aesthetic and utilitarian—is analyzed to quite different effect in Georg Simmel, "Two Essays (The Handle and the Ruin)," trans. Rudolph H. Weingartner, *Hudson Review* 11, no. 3 (Autumn 1958): 371–385. To these analogies of Poulet's could be added the related role played by puppets, mannequins, and dolls, in writings, for example, by Bruno Schulz, E. T. A. Hoffman, or Rilke. Barbara Johnson's *Persons and Things* (Cambridge, Mass.: Harvard University Press, 2008) analyzes the various mimetic issues here, but see also Victoria Nelson, *The Secret Life of Puppets* (Cambridge, Mass.: Harvard University Press, 2001). In her summary of transitional object theory in the essay "Using People: Kant With Winnecott," Johnson says, for example, that "the properly used object is one that survives destruction" (101) which thereby "makes it real" and thereafter invites a "structure of address" (103),

"creating a space of play and risk that does not depend on maintaining intactness and separation" (105). While the book conjured by Poulet conjures would seems to share some such properties—a quasi-fetish object—Cutter's instruction about legerdemain, by contrast, eschews the "transitional" for what I would call the "staged" object, where destructiveness retains its dark mystery and the created space of play and risk dictates a different set of boundaries and their mimetic meanings.

9. *Leonardo Poe Mallarmé*, trans. M. Cowley and J.R. Lawler (Princeton: Princeton University Press, 1972), 20. Alain Finkielkraut quotes the same sentence in reference to Levinasian philosophy's claim that "awakens us from perception itself" (12) in *The Wisdom of Love*, trans. Kevin O'Neill and David Suchoff (Lincoln: University of Nebraska Press, 1997. Derek Attridge employs the concept of self-staging to comprehend the dimensions of performance, invention, and alterity he ascribes to the artistic experience. See "On Knowing Works of Art," *Inside Knowledge: (Un)doing Ways of Knowing in the Humanities*, ed. Carolyn Birdsall, Maria Boletsi, Itay Sapir, and Pieter Verstraete (Cambridge: Cambridge University Press, 2009), 17–34.

10. See Meir Sternberg, *The Poetics of Biblical Narrative: Ideological Literature and the Drama of Reading* (Bloomington: Indiana University Press, 1987) and Frank Kermode, "Novels: Recognition and Deception," *Critical Inquiry* 1, no. 1 (September 1974): 103–121.

11. "Resonance and Wonder," 49. "Looking may be called enchanted when the act of attention draws a circle around itself from which everything but the object is excluded."

12. Michael Taussig's appositive for "mimesis" in *Mimesis and Alterity: A Particular History of the Senses* (New York: Routledge, 1992), 43, which, in direct relation to magic, he also explains as "this notion of the copy . . . affecting the original to such a degree that the representation shares in or acquires the properties of the represented" (47–48).

13. "Ulica Krokodyli" (The Street of Crocodiles), trans. John Curran Davis, www .schulzian.net/translation/shops/krokodyli.htm. It should, however, be noted that the general allegorical thrust of the story concerns what we might call the "bad infinity" of the aesthetic imagination. The "street of crocodiles"—in contradistinction, say, to the provincial locale in its companion piece, the "cinnamon shops"—lies in a "parasitical quarter" of Schulz's Drohobycz, a district of "pseudo-Americanism," "self-parody," "empty theater," and "sham comedy." If the art and magic exemplify something less than pure, still, the localized image of a maculate book, like so many of Schulz's figurations, takes on a life of its own, which is why I cite it here. See, in this connection, Jerzy Speina, "Bankructwo realnosci: Proza Brunona Schulza" (The Bankruptcy of Reality: The Prose of Bruno Schulz)," in *Towarzystwo Naukowe w Toruniu: Prace Wydzialu Filologicznego-Filozoficznego* 24, no. 1 (1974) and Michal Paweł Markowski, "Text and Theater: The Ironic Imagination of Bruno Schulz," in *(Un) Masking Bruno Schulz: New Combinations, Further Fragmentations, Ultimate Reintegrations*, ed. Dieter de Bruyn and Kris Van Heuckelom (Amsterdam: Editions Rodopi, 2009), 435–450. Schulz's place within Jewish modernity and a constellation of figures like Benjamin and Buber (as discussed in Chapter 7 of this book) are traced in "Ecstasy and Heresy: Buber, Schulz, and Jewish Modernity" by Karen Underhill in the same volume, 27–47.

14. Bruno Schulz, "Mannequins," www.schulzian.net/translation/shops/mannequins .htm. Compare this passage from "Spring" in *Sanatorium Under the Sign of the Hourglass*: "I once saw a stage magician. He was standing on the stage, slim and visible from all sides, flourishing his top hat and disclosing its white and totally empty bottom. Having thus—above all doubt—indemnified his art against any suspicion of a trickster's manipulation, he traced his tangled magical sign in the air with a wand and at once, with a downstroke, with exaggerated precision and vigor, he began to pull ribbons of paper from the hat, colorful ribbons by the cubit, by the yard, and finally by the mile. Soon, the room became filled with the rustling mass of color, illuminated by that hundredfold propagation, that shining accumulation of light and and foaming tissue-paper, but he would not desist from pulling out that never-ending stream while the artist still pulled at the endless weft, despite the terrified voices full of rapturous protest, the ecstatic shouts and fitful shrieks until at last it was as plain as day that none of this was costing him any effort, that its was not from his own reserves that he was drawing that abundance, but clearly celestial wellsprings had opened up to him, not in accordance with human measures or reckonings." www.schulzian.net/translation/sanatorium.htm.

15. From the "Conclusion" to *The Renaissance: Studies in Art and Poetry* (1873). Compare Levinas in *Existence and Existents*, trans. Alphonso Lingis (Pittsburgh: Duquesne University Press, 2001): "for in music this way a quality can divest of all objectivity—and consequently of all subjectivity—seems completely natural" (53).

16. As treated in more depth in chapter six, Stanley Cavell's extremely rich philosophical analysis of cinema, *The World Viewed: Reflections on the Ontology of Film*, makes a set of claims about image and resemblance (e.g., photograph and screen, actor and star) that bear comparison with those I quote from Levinas. "To accept film as an art will require a modification of the concept of art," he writes, for example. The title of Cavell's book cuts to its heart: film does not represent a falsification of the real but rather a pointing to or italicization of it. Cinema—not the representation of reality but rather the projection of it—is "a moving image of skepticism," because its technical rendering of reality brings home the problem of skepticism as something internal to the conditions of human knowledge (an epistemological perspective Cavell shares with Levinas): we may not be able to "know" reality apodictically but we can still acknowledge it and thus locate ourselves and others in it. Another conjunction between the two philosophers is (cinematic) art's proximity to myth and magic. "The image is not a likeness: it is not exactly a replica, or a relic, or a shadow, or an apparition either, though all of these natural candidates share a striking feature with photographs—an aura or history of magic surrounding them" (18) and "I have found myself asking: How could film be art, since all the major arts arise out of religion? Now I can answer: because movies arise out of magic; from below the world" (39).

17. "Reality and Its Shadow," in *Collected Philosophical Papers*, 12. The essay is treated at length in David Gritz, *Lévinas face au beau* (Paris: Editions de l'eclat: 2004). In an essay written twelve years before Levinas, "Mityzacja Rzeczywistości" (The Mythologizing of Reality), Schulz writes, "We usually regard the word as the shadow of reality, its

symbol. The reverse of the statement would be more correct: reality is the shadow of the word. Philosophy is actually philology, the deep, creative exploration of the word." *Letters and Drawings of Bruno Schulz,* trans. Walter Arndt (New York: Harper & Row, 1988), 116–117. Schulz's short text is perhaps better compared, however, to H. N. Bialik's 1915 essay, "Revealment and Concealment in Language," which I discuss in Chapter 7. But see also the compelling critique of Schulz's mythifying by Jaroslav Anders in "Bruno Schulz: The Prisoner of Myth," in *Between Fire and Sleep: Essays on Modern Polish Poetry and Prose* (New Haven: Yale University Press, 2009), 1–27.

18. Levinas makes a distinctive "swerve" here in his treatment of "Enjoyment and Representation" from a fixity and stability things evidently possess ("things have a name and identity") to their transformational possibilities, "the return of the thing to its element": "A thing exists in the midst of its wastes. When the kindling wood becomes smoke and ashes the identity of my table disappears. The wastes become indiscernible; the smoke drifts off anywhere. If my thought follows the transformation of things I lose the trace of their identity very quickly" (139–140). I quote this passage again in part two of chapter four.

19. See Gary Peters, "The Rhythm of Alterity: Levinas and Aesthetics," *Radical Philosophy* 82 (March–April 1997): 9–16.

20. "The Poet's Vision," *Proper Names,* trans. Michael B. Smith (Stanford: Stanford University Press, 1996), 127–139. See also, in this respect, Michael J. Brogan, "Judaism and Alterity in Blanchot and Levinas," *Journal for Cultural and Religious Theory* 6, no. 1 (December 2004): 28–44.

21. In *Vibrant Matter: A Political Ecology of Things* (Durham, N.C.: Duke University Press, 2012), Jane Bennett coins the phrase "thing power" to describe the *conatus essendi* latent in all materiality. That work, in turn, provide the point of a departure for Julia Fiedorczuk's reading of the thingly character of the Schulzian world, "'Thing Power': Bruno Schulz's 'Ecological' Poetics," UC Berkeley Conference on Ecopoetics (February 24, 2013), unpublished conference paper. See also the essay by Michael Mack, "Spinoza's Non-Humanist Humanism" in *Spinoza Beyond Philosophy,* ed. Beth Lord (Edinburgh: Edinburgh University Press, 2012), 28–47, and Gilles Deleuze, *Expressionism in Philosophy: Spinoza,* trans. Martin Joughin (New York: Zone Books, 1990). On the Levinas/Spinoza connection, see Michel Juffé, "Lévinas as (mis)Reader of Spinoza" (trans. Beatriz Bugni), *Levinas Studies* 2 (2007): 153–173, and Edith Wyschogrod, "Ethics as First Philosophy: Levinas Reads Spinoza," *The Eighteenth Century* 40, no. 3 (Fall 1999): 195–205.

22. www.schulzian.net/translation/uncollected/comet1.htm. Imagery of "the hand" also raises a curtain on Levinas's complicated quarrel with Heidegger, for whom the self-secluded and revelatory world of artifacts (*Zeug*) and of artworks, disclosed either instrumentally or mimetically, has primordial significance. Things are "ready-to-hand" and "present-at hand" as equipment, and this phenomenal horizon is what prompts human *Verlässichkeit* and *Sorge,* reliability and concerned handling, through which an object, as Heidegger puts it in "What is Thinking?" invites a fitting response, a "fitting" of hand to thing. (In the later essays from the 1950s, however, Heidegger distinguishes

thing from object, insofar as the former, according to its etymology, signifies the event of "gathering," bringing together the primal oneness of *das Geviert*, "the Fourfold"—the corporeal, the spiritual, the rooted, and the displaced—in relation to which the proper human attitude is one of *Gelassenheit* or "letting be.") See chapters five through nine in Sylvia Benso's *The Face of Things* and part one of Peter-Paul Verbeek's *What Things Do*.

23. Compare Derrida's observation in *On Touching* on the opening pages of Nancy's *Corpus*: "The magician's finger, which makes the tangible untouchable—this is a painter's paintbrush. He must know how to put the finishing 'touch' to his simulacrum so as to make the body vanish in producing it, and so as to reduce it in affecting its production" (61).

24. What Levinas would say about a film like Nolan's or how his early aesthetic theory might be oriented toward cinema or photography as quintessentially modern arts requires a later discussion. To my knowledge, Levinas makes reference to two Chaplin films in *De l'évasion* and *Entre nous* and otherwise remains silent about movies, filmgoing, or what Cavell has called the ontology of film. A special issue of *Film Philosophy* (August 2007), "The Occluded Relations: Levinas and Cinema," is devoted to this connection, with an introduction by Sheila Cooper, i–vii. See also Sam B. Girgus, *Levinas and the Cinema of Redemption: Time, Ethics, and the Feminine* (New York: Columbia University Press, 2010).

25. Israeli poet and Holocaust survivor Pagis (1930–1986) grew up in Rădăuţi, Bukovina, in Romania and became a professor of Medieval Hebrew literature after learning Hebrew as an adult. See *The Selected Poetry of Dan Pagis*, trans. Stephen Mitchell (Berkeley: University of California Press, 1989), 87.

26. Gerald Bruns reads even this early moment in Levinas's aesthetics more positively: consistent with Mallarme's materialist poetics and Maurice Blanchot's recuperative essay, "Le mythe de Mallarmé," art for Levinas, as "pure exteriority, uncorrelated with any interior, constitutes a kind of transcendence." Construing it no longer as a vehicle of or for the visible or an object for passive contemplation, he propounds "an aesthetics of darkness, rather than light, of materiality as against spirit" that leaves one's composure disturbed and one's senses deranged. In a word, one is left "exposed" to art just as, through it, reality is rendered "beside itself, *en deçà*." In line with the turn in thought marked by Levinas's essay from 1965 about ethical alterity, the artwork is better understood as "enigma" than as "phenomenon." One encounters it. It comes upon one, unbidden. Like the neighbor, its mode is *approach:* in so doing, it disturbs and disorders. In this analysis, "Levinasian aesthetics assigns the work of art to the order of the sublime, not to the beautiful." Accordingly, see also Thomas Weiskel, *The Romantic Sublime: Studies in the Structure and Psychology of Transcendence* (Baltimore: Johns Hopkins University Press, 1976), and Stephen Watson, "Levinas, the Ethics of Deconstruction, and the Remainder of the Sublime," *Man and World* 21 (1988): 35–64.

27. "Persons and Figures," *Difficult Freedom*, 121–122.

28. For dependable accounts of Levinas and the aesthetic, see Françoise Armengaud, "Ethique et esthétique: de l'ombre à l'oblitération," in *Cahiers de l'Herne: Emmanuel*

Levinas, ed. Catherine Chalier and Miguel Abensour (Paris: Herne, 1991), 499–507 and "Faire ou ne pas faire d'images. Emmanuel Levinas et l'art d'oblitération," *Noesis* 3 (2000); Gerald Bruns, "The Concepts of Art and Poetry in Emmanuel Levinas's writings," *The Cambridge Companion to Levinas*, ed. Simon Critchley and Robert Bernasconi (Cambridge University Press, 2002), 206–233; Jill Robbins, *Altered Reading: Levinas and Literature*; Richard Kearney, "Levinas and the Ethics of Imagining," in *Between Ethics and Aesthetics: Crossing the Boundaries*, ed. Dorota Glowacka and Stephen Boos (Albany: State University of New York Press, 2002), 85–96; Annelise Schulte Nordholt, "Tentation esthétique et exigence éthique: Lévinas et l'oeuvre littéraire," in *Études littéraires* 31, no. 3 (1999): 69–85; and Edith Wyschogrod, "The Art in Ethics: Aesthetics, Objectivity, and Alterity in the Philosophy of Levinas," in *Ethics as First Philosophy: The Significance of Emmanuel Levinas for Philosophy, Literature, and Religion*, ed. Adriaan Theodoor Peperzak (London: Routledge, 1995), 137–149. See also Thomas Claviez, *Aesthetics and Ethics: Otherness and Moral Imagination from Aristotle to Levinas and from* Uncle Tom's Cabin *to* House Made of Dawn (Heidelberg: Universitätsverlag Winter, 2008); Robert Hughes, *Ethics, Aesthetics, and the Beyond of Language*; Henry McDonald, "Aesthetics as First Ethics: Levinas and the Alterity of Literary Discourse," *Diacritics* 38, no. 4 (Winter 2008): 15–41, Peter Schmiedgen, "Art and Idolatry: Aesthetics and Alterity in Levinas," *Contretemps* 3 (July 2002): 148–160; Matthew Sharpe, "Aesthet(h)ics: On Levinas' Shadow," *Colloquy: Text Theory Critique* 9 (2005): 29–47; and Alain P. Toumayan, *Encountering the Other: The Artwork and the Problem of Difference in Blanchot and Levinas* (Pittsburgh: Duquesne University Press, 2004).

29. Compare from *Beyond the Verse*, "All sorcery, in any case, is the power of words. Is it possible to forget the danger of rhetoric?" (28), and the conclusion to *Otherwise Than Being* (181, 185) where Levinas hints at such danger in his own writing (in the neighborhood of what he calls Heidegger's "theater machinery," 182) by underscoring its thrust toward *étonnement* (astonishment) and its dependence on *formules* (incantations). This is something noted by Derrida in his early essay on Levinas, "Violence and Metaphysics," where *la vague* and *le charme*, wave and spell, come to characterize the shape and effect of Levinas's prose. David Freedberg's observation on the "elements of response" that are stimulated by art from *The Power of Images: Studies in the History and Theory of Response* (Chicago: University of Chicago Press, 1989) is also apposite here: "We dimply recognize them, or suppress the, or sublimate them: we talk about them in terms of the topos and commonplace; but we will not acknowledge that they are the same as those we also conveniently describe as magical or superstitious" (510).

30. Aristotle, *De Anima/ Perì Psūchēs Books II and III* (Oxford: Clarendon Press, 1968), and Ronald Polansky, *Commentary on Aristotle's De Anima* (Cambridge: Cambridge University Press, 2008) Book 2, Chapter 11 (423–435). See also Chrétien, *The Call and the Response*, 97ff.

31. This aspects of bodily sensation that record position and movement of neighboring body parts and the body's overall physiological condition are called "proprioception" and "interception," respectively. The former is discussed at length in the essay "The Disembodied

Woman," an essay in *The Man Who Mistook His Wife for a Hat* (New York: Touchstone, 1985) by Oliver Sacks, as well as in Sacks's autobiography, *A Leg to Stand On* (New York: Touchstone, 1984).

32. He also refigures his metaphor of musicality in terms of reverberance and sonority. See, for example, the passage in *Otherwise Than Being* on *Nomos Alpha for Cello Solo* by Iannis Xenakis where "the *essence* of the cello, a modality of *essence,* is thus temporalized in the work" (40–41), a passage expanded on by Robert Hughes in *Ethics, Aesthetics, and the Beyond of Language* (Albany: State University of New York Press, 2001), 155ff.

33. See, for example, the analyses of manipular power in "Transcendence and Intelligibility," *Basic Philosophical Writings*, 152 and *Totality and Infinity*, 159–162.

34. "Enigma and Phenomenon" in *Collected Philosophical Papers*, 68. In "Language and Proximity," Levinas asserts, "Consciousness is always late for the rendezvous with the neighbor" (119).

35. In addition to the famous analogy around the criterion of perceptual distance, "magician is to surgeon as painter is to cinematographer," consider this observation from Benjamin's essay *Das Kunstwerk im Zeitalter seiner technischen Reproduzierbarkeit*: "Originally the embeddedness of an artwork in the context of tradition found its expression in the cult. As we know, the earliest art works originated in the service of a ritual—first magical, then the religious. And it is highly significant that the artwork's auratic mode of existence is never entirely severed from its ritual function. In other words: the unique value of the 'authentic' work of art has its basis in ritual, the source of its original use value. This ritualistic basis, however mediated it may be, is still recognizable as secularized ritual even in the most profane forms of the cult of beauty." *The Work of Art in the Age of Its Technological Reproducibility, and Other Writings on Media*, ed. Brigid Doherty, Michael W. Jennings, Thomas Y. Levin (Cambridge, Mass.: Harvard University Press, 2008), 24.

36. Gopnik, "The Real Work." Swiss's essays are published in *Shattering Illusions* (Seattle: Hermetic Press, 2002) and *Devious Standards* (Seattle: Hermetic Press, 2011). Ricky Jay's *The Magic Magic Book* (New York: Whitney Museum Library Associates, 1994) brings this idea immediately home in the form of a history of the "blow book" (a conjuring apparatus that works like a flipbook, or *Daumenkino*) which doubles reflexively as the device itself—on which, see also the article by Colin Williamson, "The Blow Book, Performance Magic, and Early Animation: Mediating the Living," *Animation* 6 (2011): 111–126.

37. The most obvious points of difference between them, their respective allegiances to Israel/Palestine, are not a relevant matter here. John E. Drabinski's *Levinas and the Postcolonial* (Edinburgh: Edinburgh University Press, 2011), though it mentions Said minimally (surprisingly enough), would seem to make such rapprochement beside the point, especially if centered on the dialectic of secular and religious criticisms as it is here. While a thoughtful book that politicizes Levinas reception in valuable directions, it does not know how to do much with categories of the literary or aesthetic, and certainly not the Jewish or the Judaic in any engaged sense; nor is it particularly interested in

Levinas (or potentially, Said) as *reader or critic.* If Levinas needs to be decolonized, as Drabinski argues, it would perhaps have made a better case if his critique evinced more curiosity about the "colonial," i.e., subordinate but also aggrandized, intellectual and textual traditions in the Occident, from which Levinas draws so copiously. This is a paramount question for the reception of Levinas, as indeed analogously for Edward Said. A different orientation can be glimpsed in Andrew Bush's essay, "Teaching Continually: Beginning with Lévinas," in *Europe and Its Boundaries: Words and Worlds, Within and Beyond*, ed. Andrew Davison, Himadeep Muppidi (Lanham, Md.: Lexington Books, 2009), 5–24.

38. See the chapter "The Return to Philology" in *Humanism and Democratic Criticism* (New York: Columbia University Press, 2004, and the chapter, "Influences," in Conor McCarthy, *The Cambridge Introduction to Edward Said* (Cambridge: Cambridge University Press, 2010). "Contrapuntal criticism" is a term developed by Said in *Culture and Imperialism* derived from the compositional tradition of classical music as a practical exercise in "organized [thematic] interplay." Using Paul Gilroy's *The Black Atlantic: Modernity and Double Consciousness* as an example, Simon Critchley explains the practice as "a critical historical, genealogical, or deconstructive reflection that would bring us to the recognition of the hybridity, culture, and tradition" (134), in the chapter "Black Socrates? Questioning the Philosophical Tradition," *Ethics, Politics, Subjectivity: Essays on Derrida, Levinas & Contemporary French Thought* (London: Verso, 1990), 122–142. In contrasting it to oppositionality, Jonathan Arac expresses the distinction this way: "Oppositional criticism is aggressive; it cuts. Contrapuntal criticism is loving; it joins." See "Criticism between Opposition and Counterpoint," *boundary 2* Vol. 25: 2 (Summer, 1998), 55–69, reprinted in the volume of essays edited by Paul A. Bové, *Edward Said and the Work of the Critic: Speaking Truth to Power* (Durham, N.C.: Duke University Press, 2000).

39. See "The Changing Bases of Humanistic Study and Practice," in *Humanism and Democratic Criticism*, and "The Public Role of Writers and Intellectuals," 135, 142.

40. Both Derrida's essay "At This Very Moment in This Work Here I Am," *Re-Reading Levinas*, ed. Robert Bernasconi, Simon Critchley, and Robert Gibbs (Bloomington: Indiana University Press, 1991), 11–50, and the chapter "Why Read" in *Why Ethics: Signs of Responsibilities* (Princeton: Princeton University Press, 2000) attend closely to this passage and its "poetics of interruption."

41. *Orientalism* (New York; Vintage, 1978), 321; *Collected Philosophical Papers*, 13. For studies of Levinas, at least, a distinction is often made between "criticism" and "exegesis," echoing a contrast we find in Walter Benjamin between *critique* and *commentary*. The philosopher Richard Cohen, for instance, subordinates the former to the latter, deriving the valence from Levinas himself: "exegesis makes the text speak; while critical philology speaks of this text. The one takes the text to be a source of teaching, the other treats it as a thing" (23). Criticism, in this sense of course, is defined highly restrictively and does not really describe the textual and literary criticism practiced by either Levinas or Said. Samuel Moyn, an historian, would probably regard Cohen's own discipular

relationship to Levinas as an example of "exegetical interpretation rather than critical analysis," reifying a thinker's place in intellectual history as a kind of fashion or fetish, "less like a philosophical position and more like a religious one characterized by articles of faith and ritualistic phraseology" (6). The question then becomes: what sort of exegetical or critical position does Levinas himself take up with regard not only to figures like Heidegger, Husserl, Kierkegaard, or Buber, but to rabbinic discourse and Ḥayyim of Volozhin—a question I examine in the second part of chapter four. See Cohen's introduction to Levinas's *New Talmudic Readings* (Pittsburgh: Duquesne University Press, 1999) and Moyn's *Origins of the Other: Emmanuel Levinas Between Ethics and Revelation* (Ithaca, N.Y.: Cornell University Press, 2005).

42. Geoffrey Hartman offers a trenchant comparison of Bloom's *soi-disant* religious criticism and the RaSHaB (the fifth Lubavitcher Rebbe) in "Who Is an Educated Jew?" in *The Third Pillar: Essays in Judaic Studies* (Philadelphia: University of Pennsylvania Press, 2011), 149–161. For an eloquent demythification of Bloom's version of critical vocation, see William Deresiewicz, "The Shaman," *The New Republic*, September 14, 2011. For affinities between Girard and Said (despite the latter's expressed sentiment), see William D. Hart, *Edward Said and the Religious Effects of Culture* (Cambridge: Cambridge University Press, 2000), 12. Incidentally, the question of whether magic, as a shortcut to the aesthetic, extracts something from the world, or *disenchants* that same object or person instead by calling attention to its enmeshment and corrigibility, goes directly to Said's and Levinas's constructions of the *worldly* in relation to both the secular and religious.

43. As Moyn explains it, "the main thesis of counterhistoricism is that meaning transcends time; and as the label suggests, it is asserted in opposition to historical tendencies in interpretation that reached their apogee in the twentieth century in the discipline of hermeneutics" (344). See "Emmanuel Levinas's Talmudic Readings: Between Tradition and Invention," *Prooftexts* 23 (2003): 338–364.

44. "Diary," *The London Review of Books* 22, no. 11 (June 1, 2000), 42–43. The most prominent exception is Judith Butler's essay, "On Edward Said, Emmanuel Levinas and the Idea of the Binational State" in the Hebrew journal *Mita'am* 10 (2007), expanded in the chapter "Said, Levinas, and the Ethical Demand," in *Parting Ways: Jewishness and the Critique of Zionism* (New York: Columbia University Press, 2012). Said is mentioned briefly as another example of an "ethically committed intellectual" by Roland A. Champagne in *The Ethics of Reading According to Emmanuel Lévinas*. Both happen to be mentioned in a Wikipedia entry on "the Other." And there is Gil Z. Hochberg's article "Edward Said: 'The Last Jewish Intellectual': On Identity, Alterity, and the Politics of Memory," *Social Text* 24, no. 2 (Summer 2006): 47–65, which tropes on Said's comment to *Ha'aretz* shortly before his death, "I am the last Jewish intellectual," in censorious juxtaposition with Levinas's famous interview with Salomon Malka where he resists identifying Palestinians as (Israeli) Jews' paradigmatic Other, giving credence to Butler's critique of what appears to be "the Ashkenazi presumption that underwrites the Levinasian ethical scene" (48). And yet, compare the following observation from Levinas's interview, "The Paradox of Morality," in *The Provocation of Levinas: Rethinking the Other*:

"For example, when we sit down at the table in the morning and drink coffee, we kill an Ethiopian who doesn't have any coffee" (173).

45. *Parting Ways*, 38. Butler's own conjunction of Said and Levinas choreographs a relationship suspended, as she argues for binationalism, between "proximity and aversion" (55).

46. The distinction stands over all of Said's work, but is spelled out explicitly in "Timeliness and Lateness" from *On Late Style: Music and Literature Against the Grain* (New York: Random House, 2006), the essay "Adorno as Lateness Itself," *Adorno: A Critical Reader*, ed. Nigel Gibson and Andrew Rubin (Oxford: Blackwell, 2002), 193–208, and *Freud and the Non-European* (London: Verso, 2003).

47. His belated induction, when he was forty, into the textual confraternity of the "Doctors of the Talmud" is perhaps the most obvious example. No less is his affiliative bond to Russian literature. See Moyn; see also Judith Friedlander, *Vilna on the Seine: Jewish Intellectuals in France* (New Haven: Yale University Press, 1990) and Val Vinokur, *The Trace of Judaism: Dostoevsky, Babel, Mandelstam, Levinas* (Evanston, Ill.: Northwestern University Press, 2009). Levinas discusses the importance of both in the interview with Phillip Nemo, *Ethics and Infinity* (Pittsburgh: Duquesne University Press, 1985).

48. IV: 333–334 of *The Prelude: The Four Texts (1798, 1799, 1805, 1850)*, ed. Jonathan Wordsworth (New York: Penguin, 1995), 159.

49. Here I borrow Paul Ricoeur's dialectical terminology as applied to the general project of hermeneutics. Ricoeur was an interlocutor for Levinas in *Oneself as Another*, trans. Kathleen Blamey (Chicago: University of Chicago Press 1995), and a foil for Said in "The World, The Text, and the Critic."

50. *Beginnings: Intention and Method* (Baltimore: Johns Hopkins University Press, 1975), 199–200.

51. *Edward Said: Criticism and Society* (London: Verso, 2002), 192–193. For a consideration of Said's intellectual trajectory and the recurrent question of method it poses, see Andrew Rubin, "Techniques of Trouble: Edward Said and the Dialectics of Cultural Philology," *South Atlantic Quarterly* 102, no. 4 (Fall 2003): 861–876.

52. *Milton's Secrecy: And Philosophical Hermeneutics* (London: Ashgate, 2008), 192.

53. To revert to Levinas momentarily: in his interview with Phillipe Nemo recorded in *Ethics and Infinity,* not only does he relegate "the dogmatic story of [the Holy Scriptures'] supernatural and sacred origin" to subsidiary significance at best. More importantly, he offers up a necessary dialogic between sacred and secular: "The national literatures, Homer, Plato, Racine, Hugo partake in Holy Scripture, just as Pushkin, Dostoevsky, or Goethe, and of course, Tolstoy and Agnon" (115, 117).

54. Rosenzweig's discussion of Islam in *The Star of Redemption* is, by turns, dismissive and contemptuous, and assigns its belief system, interestingly enough, to the realm of "magic." See Gil Anidjar, *The Jew, the Arab: A History of the Enemy* (Stanford: Stanford University Press, 2003), and the chapter "Speech and Scripture: The Grammatical Thinking and Theology of Franz Rosenzweig" in Michael Fishbane's *The Garments of Torah: Essays in Biblical Hermeneutics* (Bloomington: Indiana University Press, 1992).

55. And yet, "Qur'anic exegesis (تفسير tafsir/طويل ta'wil), is quintessentially an exegesis of the ear, since the eye alone cannot know what it is reading" (130). This observation is drawn from Gerald Bruns's essay "Sufiya: The Mystical Hermeneutics of al-Ghazzālī," *Hermeneutics Ancient and Modern* (New Haven: Yale University Press, 1992), 124–136, which supplies a really vital complement to Said's very quick summary of Zahiri hermeneutics. Born in Iran, Abu Hamid al-Ghazālī, Sufi philosopher who introduced *falsafa* (Aristotelian Avicennism) into Muslim theology and author of *The Revival of the Religious Sciences (Ihyā' 'ulūm al-dīn),* was an exact contemporary of Ibn Ḥazm. Pointedly, Bruns explains that for al-Ghazālī, the text (*mus'haf*) was not a textual object but rather a vehicle of sensibility through which nearness to divine inspiration is established quite literally through the breath—both aurally and orally. In contradistinction to Said's use of Ibn Ḥazm's sense of textual "surface," the Sufi hermeneutics at work here positions readers of the *Qur'an* spiritually as *internal* to it ("included in the verse," Bruns quotes al-Ghazālī), such that situatedness and circumstantiality take on whole new possibilities of significance. This is not a species of esotericism, however, since as Bruns notes, it "remains within the horizon defined by the public, liturgical reading of the Qur'anic text—on the contrary, the text internalizes the one who recites it, so to speak" (136).

56. Ibn Ḥazm first introduced the concept of *zahir*, the "apparent" or literal meaning of words, in his treatise on the affections, *Tawq al-hamamah (The Dove's Neck-Ring).* But since Said's account of Zahirite hermeneutic and Ibn Ḥazm should be placed in the context of general scholarship on Muslim hermeneutics, in addition to Arnaldez's *Grammaire et theologie chez Ibn Hazm de Cordoue: Essai sur la structure et les conditions de la pens a musulmane* (Paris: J. Vrin, 1956), see therefore, Majid Fakhry, *A History of Islamic Philosophy* (New York: Columbia University Press, 2004) and Ignaz Goldziher, *The Zahiris, Their Doctrine and Their History: A Contribution to the History of Islamic Theology,* trans. Wolfgang Behn (Leiden: Brill, 1971).

57. Compare Gerald Bruns on the situatedness of *midrash*: "The Bible always addresses itself to the time of interpretation; one cannot understand it except by appropriating it anew . . . Midrash is not only responsive to the Scriptures as a way of coping with the text's wide-ranging formal problems; it is also responsive to the situations in which the Scriptures exert their claim upon human life. Think of Midrash as the medium in which this scriptural claim exerts itself. . . . But in midrash the text is never taken all by itself as an analytical object; the text is always *situated.* Thus, the task of midrash is never really reproductive; it is always productive of new understanding. It is a way of keeping the Bible open to those who answer its claims." "Midrash and Allegory: The Beginnings of Scriptural Interpretation," *The Literary Guide to the Bible,* ed. Robert Alter and Frank Kermode (Cambridge, Mass.: Harvard University Press, 1987), 625–646.

58. "The Notion of a Sacred Text," *The Garments of Torah,* 128. That essay takes desacralization of the Bible as a *point d'appui.* Even if it is true that we—intellectuals like Edward Said and Emmanuel Levinas alike—are no longer "sustained within a biblical matrix" (and thus delivered over to some version or another of secular criticism), can we not still inquire "whether this notion of a scared text is at all retrievable at this historical

hour"—especially for "those of us who do not unreflectingly talk the language of religious tradition" (121).

59. I borrow this phrase from Danièle Hervieu-Léger's important contribution to the sociology of religion, *Religion As a Chain of Memory*, trans. Simon Lee (New Brunswick, N.J.: Rutgers University Press, 2000).

60. *Poetics Today* 6, no. 3 (1985): 537–538.

61. In "Difficult Reading," Valerie Allen compares rabbinic and monastic (as opposed to scholastic) reading, and contrasts *lectio* with *critique*. "Reading," also Germanic, means "council" or "advice," foregrounds the critical, rational aspect of encountering the text at the expense of the craftwork captured in the base meaning of *lectio*, namely the sheer ability to distinguish and enunciate letters on a page. "Reading too hastily gathers up square letters into *sententiae* that translate into any language. It does not roll sounds on the tongue" (*Levinas and Medieval Literature*, 25).

62. In two illuminating essays, "The Biblical Dialogue of Martin Buber" and "Speech and Scripture: the Grammatical Thinking and Theology of Franz Rosenzweig" from *The Garments of Torah*, Michael Fishbane underscores both thinkers' stress on the Hebrew Bible as a dialogical "event" of spokenness (*Gesprochenheit*), which thus *dictates* a reciprocal interpretive attunement. Especially in Rosenzweig's case, "One becomes a hearer of Scriptures only by reading, but one truly reads this text only by hearing its graphic sounds. . . . For biblical Scriptures is no mere book, but the written traces of speech. For this reason it is not a *Schrift* for the eyes but a *Miqra* (Reading) for the ears. In reciting its words, the reader arouses the inscription from its monologic silence so that the voice of the text becomes his own call for dialogue with the eternal partner" (106).

63. Because halakhic *midrashim* on Numbers and Deuteronomy often accompanied each other, they were known collectively as *Sifre* [books]. The *Sifre* on *Bamidbar* (also known as *Sifra de-vei rav*), redacted in 300–400 CE, is attributed to R. Shimon and shares characteristics with the *Mekhilta de-Rabbi Ishmael* on the Book of Exodus, from the same period. See the modern critical edition by Menah?em Kahana, *Sifre Ba-midbar: mahadurah mevo'eret* (Jerusalem: Magnes, 2011). Rabbinical literature divides into three major categories: *Mishnah-Tosefta, Talmud, and Midrash*. The first of these is fully code-oriented, as established by the *Tanna'im* (70–200 CE): the second is a complex commentary on and amplification of the first by several generations of rabbinical scholars, the *Amora'im* ("sayers") from 200–500 CE, in Palestine and Israel, complied and redacted by the *Stamma'im* ("scribes") just before the Geonic period (650–1050 CE). The Talmud consists of both legal (halakhic) and non-legal (aggadic) material, the latter being a catch-all term for smaller and larger biographical stories, folklore, and homilies: both categories constitute Torah *she'bal peh*, the Oral Law. Midrash, contrastively, is an interpretive apparatus or practice, which can be either aggadic or halakhic in approach, and which forms the basis of various compilations previous to, contemporary with, and also posterior to the Talmudic literature. In the Talmud proper, *midrash* may be cited that deploy aggadic content, but at the same time, interpolated or descriptive *aggadot* will not necessarily perform a midrashic function. "Midrashic" and "aggadic" are therefore

being used loosely in reference to Levinas's exegetical style and sensibility. General introductions can be found in Moshe Halbertal, *People of the Book*; David Charles Kraemer, *The Mind of the Talmud: An Intellectual History of the Bavli* (New York: Oxford University Press, 1990), David Weiss Halivni, *The Formation of the Babylonian Talmud*, trans. Jeffrey L. Rubenstein (New York: Oxford University Press, 2013), Avi Sagi, *The Open Canon: On the Meaning of Halakhic Discourse*, trans. Batya Stein (New York: Continuum Books, 2007), and Hermann Strack and Gunter Stemberger, *Introduction to the Talmud and Midrash* (Minneapolis: Fortress Press, 1996).

64. In the halakhic *midrash Sifra* on Leviticus 13:47, R. Ishmael famously rebuked R. Eliezer, "You are saying to Scripture (*ha-katuv*), 'Be silent until I expound midrashically?'" That is, instead of listening to the text first to hear what it says, interpretive hubris has spoken not only prematurely but, as it were, over and above "the language of men." See Azzan Yadin, *Scripture as Logos: Rabbi Ishmael and the Origins of Midrash* (Philadelphia: University of Pennsylvania Press, 2004), 45–46.

65. *Stanford Encyclopedia of Philosophy*, online edition, http://plato.stanford.edu/entries/ibn-ezra.

66. A little uncannily for our purposes here, Ibn Ezra may well also have had Ibn Ḥazm specifically in mind, for his anti-Jewish polemic, *Refutation of Ibn Naghrila* (eleventh-century Córdoban philologist, grammarian, and poet Sh'muel HaNagid), in various corrective readings from his Torah commentary. See the introduction to *Twilight of a Golden Age: Selected Poems of Abraham Ibn Ezra*, trans. Leon J. Weinberger (Tuscaloosa: University of Alabama Press, 1997), although this speculation has been pointedly challenged. See also, therefore, the review of Weinberger's book by Susan Einbinder in *AJS Review* 24, no. 2 (1999): 389–391.

67. See Irene E. Zwiep's discussion of Ibn Ezra in connection with the idea of authorship in "From *Perush* to *Be'ur*: Authenticity and Authority in Eighteenth-Century Jewish Interpretation," in *Hebrew Language and Jewish Culture*, ed. Martin F. J. Baasten and Reiner Munk (Amsterdam: Springer, 2007), 256–270, and also "Abraham ibn Ezra and the Twelfth-Century European Renaissance," 1–20, by Ángel Sáenz-Badillo in the same volume. Isidore Twersky and J. M. Harris, ed., *Rabbi Abraham ibn Ezra: Studies in the Writings of a Twelfth-Century Jewish Polymath* (Cambridge, Mass.: Harvard University Press, 1993) and the more recent *The Texture of the Divine: Imagination in Medieval Islamic and Jewish Thought* by Aaron W. Hughes (Bloomington: Indiana University Press, 2003) provide general introductions.

68. Levinas sometimes has recourse to the familiar hyphenate formulation but to different effect. On the politics of its usage for Levinas, see the exchange between Annette Aronowicz and Michael Fagenblat in the *AJS Review* 35, no. 1 (April 2011): 105–124. Fagenblat's *A Covenant of Creatures* is explicit in arguing for Levinas's philosophy as a secularized Judaism "addressed to the Gentiles."

69. Paul Reiter's "Comparative Literature in Exile: Said and Auerbach," *Exile and Otherness: New Approaches to the Experience of the Nazi Refugees*, ed. Alexander Stephan (Bern: Peter Lang, 2005), 21–30, offers a corrective to the many constructions of Auer-

bach (including Said's own) as a secular critic and thus precursor figure for Said's intellectual oppositions. "The Text, The World, and the Critic" was originally published under that title in 1975, and should be compared with Said's introduction to the fiftieth-anniversary edition of *Mimesis* (Princeton: Princeton University Press, 2003).

70. The following all supply helpful correctives: Gerald Bruns, "Midrash and Allegory: The Beginnings of Scriptural Interpretation"; Sandor Goodhart, "'A Land That Devours Its Inhabitants': Midrashic Reading, Emmanuel Levinas, and Medieval Literary Exegesis," in *Levinas and Medieval Literature: The "Difficult Reading" of English and Rabbinic Texts*, ed. Ann Astell and Justin Jackson (Pittsburgh: Duquesne University Press, 2009), 227–254; Jill Robbins, *Prodigal Son/Elder Brother: Interpretation and Alterity in Augustine, Petrarch, Kafka, Levinas* (Chicago: University of Chicago Press, 1991); Henri de Lubac, S.J. *Éxégése Médiévale,* 4 vols. (Paris: Aubier, 1959–64), English translation, *Medieval Exegesis: The Four Senses of Scripture Volumes 1 and 2*, trans. M. Sebanc (Grand Rapids: Eerdmans, 1998) and E. M. Macierowski (Grand Rapids, Mich.: Eerdmans, 2000).

71. "Emmanuel Levinas and Hillel's Questions," *Crossover Queries: Dwelling with Negatives, Embodying Philosophy's Others* (New York: Fordham University Press, 2006), 61–75, which first appeared in *Postmodern Philosophy and Christian Thought*, ed. Merold Westphal (Bloomington: University of Indiana Press, 1999), 229–245. I return to Wyschogrod's general argument below.

72. The word itself, פרדס, denotes "orchard" and is derived from the same Persian term from which English gets "paradise." It is associated with a *baraita* that appears in variant forms in both Babylonian (*bḤagiga* 14b) and Palestinian (*Ḥagiga* 2:1, 77b) Talmuds and the Tosefta (*Ḥagiga* 2:3–4): "Four entered *pardes*—Ben Azzai, Ben Zoma, Aḥer (Elisha ben Abuyah), and Akiva. Ben Azzai glimpsed and died; Ben Zoma glimpsed and went mad; Aḥer cut the young plants; Akiva ascended and descended safely." The fates of the four Mishnaic sages have been interpreted as connoting four interpretive postures or approaches, which Sandor Goodhart, for instance reads as (1) idolatrous gazing, (2) specularity fueled by desire; (3) unwarranted appropriation; (4) verticality that is both mobile and reverent. A lucid account of the emergence of the fourfold scaffold for exegesis among thirteenth-century kabbalists can be found in Moshe Idel, *Absorbing Perfections: Kabbalah and Interpretation* (New Haven: Yale University Press, 2002). See also Michael D. Swartz, "Jewish Visionary Tradition in Rabbinic Literature," in *Cambridge Companion to the Talmud and Rabbinic Literature*, ed. Charlotte E. Fonrobert and Martin S. Jaffee (Cambridge: Cambridge University Press, 2007), 198–221; Jeffrey L. Rubenstein, *Talmudic Stories: Narrative Art, Composition, and Culture* (Baltimore: Johns Hopkins University Press, 1999); David Joel Halperin, *The Faces of the Chariot: Early Jewish Responses to Ezekiel's Vision* (Tübingen: C. B. Mohr, 1988); and Gershom Scholem, *Origins of the Kabbalah,* trans. A. Arkush (Princeton: Princeton University Press, 1987).

73. See David Weiss Halivni, *Peshat and Derash: Plain and Applied Meaning in Rabbinic Exegesis* (New York: Oxford University Press, 1991) and Robert Harris, "Medieval

Jewish Exegesis," in *A History of Biblical Interpretation, Vol. 2*, ed. A. Hauser and D. Watson (Grand Rapids, Mich.: Eerdmans, 2009).

74. This interpretive schema builds on Philo, Origen, Jerome, and St. Augustine, and was given wider prominence through Dante's famous letter to Can Grande della Scala. See, in this context, David Shatz, "The Biblical and Rabbinic Background to Medieval Jewish Philosophy," in *The Cambridge Companion to Medieval Jewish Philosophy*, ed. Daniel H. Frank and Oliver Leaman (Cambridge: Cambridge University Press, 2003), 16–37.

75. "The Garments of Torah: Or, To What May Scripture be Compared," *The Garments of Torah*, 44. Two other essays in the same volume, The Teacher and the Hermeneutical Task" and "The Notion of a Sacred Text" speculate on the meaning of the fourfold schema of PaRDeS for pedagogical and intellectual situations of modernity.

76. *Deconstructing the Bible: Abraham ibn Ezra's Introduction to the Torah* (New York: Routledge, 2007), 177, 179.

77. On the model of Amir Mufti's suggestion in "Auerbach in Istanbul: Edward Said, Secular Criticism, and the Question of Minority Culture," *Critical Inquiry* 25, no. 1 (Autumn 1998): 95–125, that *minority* lays central claim to inflecting Saidian "secular criticism," we might word this imagined affinity, "Ibn Ezra in Rome: Edward Said, Religious Criticism, and the Question of Affiliation." Another recent treatment argues for Ibn Ezra's place as a harbinger of a "Jewish Secular" intellectual tradition. See David Biale, *Not in the Heavens: The Tradition of Jewish Secular Thought* (Princeton: Princeton University Press, 2011), 62–69.

78. *Intertextuality and the Reading of Midrash* (Bloomington: University of Indiana Press, 1990), 128. An important companion piece is the later essay, "Take the Bible as Example: Midrash as Literary Theory" in *Sparks of the Logos: Essays in Rabbinic Hermeneutics* (Leiden: Brill, 2003), 89–113. See also the edited volume by Carol Bakhos, *Current Trends in the Study of Midrash* (Leiden: Brill, 2006) and James Kugel, "Two Introductions to Midrash," *Prooftexts* 3, no. 3 (1983): 131–155.

79. Bruns again: "It would be more true to say that midrash gives us an insight into whatever interpretation always is (whatever the method) when interpretation matters to human life. In hermeneutical terms, midrash shows the historicality of understanding." Annette Aronowicz suggests the applicability of Levinas's approach beyond the borders of biblical or rabbinic hermeneutics in "The Little Man with the Burned Thighs: Levinas's Biblical Hermeneutic," in *Levinas and Biblical Studies* (Atlanta: Society for Biblical Literature, 2003), 33–48.

80. Wyschogrod, however, uses certain maxims by Hillel in *mishnayot* from tractate *Pirqei Avot* along with its oldest commentary, the *Avot de Rabbi Natan,* in order to illuminate Levinas's philosophical project. Her methodology, the use of "the miniature," anticipates Michael Fagenblat's "coding" of *Totality and Infinity* and *Otherwise Than Being* according to elemental tropes taken from the Torah, although he seems unfamiliar with her essay. "Miniatures are neither diagrams nor blueprints. They are not, as Lévi-Strauss contends, 'passive homologues' of objects, but rather, they 'constitute a real experiment with the object.' The miniature is seen as a solution to a particular problem,

NOTES TO PAGES 67–69 333

one in which the interpreter is not a passive observer; instead, her act of observation is, even if only subliminally, already one in which passive permutations are envisaged" (64).

81. See also the important essay in the same volume, "Revelation in the Jewish Tradition," in which Levinas says, 'But this invitation to seek and decipher, to *Midrash* [sic], already constitutes the reader's participation in the Revelation, in Scripture. The reader, in his own fashion, is a scribe" (133).

82. *On the Origin of Language*, trans. John H. Moran, Alexander Gode (Chicago: University of Chicago Press, 1986).

83. Raoul Dufy (1877–1953) was a French painter associated with Les Fauves. In the early pages of *Otherwise Than Being*, Levinas treats in passing the question of the "image" again in relation to being, and repeats this formulation about Dufy's paintings, "where the colors spread out from their contours and do not rub up against them" (29), as a hint of a world of materiality and sensibility that has not yet been rendered transparent by philosophy. Dufy's colors thus remain on the "hither side," retaining their opacity as "things." Gerald Bruns reads this moment suggestively in the chapter "Against Poetry: Heidegger, Ricoeur, and the Originary Scene of Hermeneutics" in his *Hermeneutics Ancient and Modern*, 243.

84. I have already referred to *Levinas and Medieval Literature: The "Difficult Reading" of English and Rabbinic Texts* as a volume that makes a strong case for an organic, mutually revealing rapprochement between Levinas's critical consciousness and specifically literary texts. Others are *In Proximity: Levinas and the Eighteenth Century*, ed. Melvyn New (Lubbock: Texas Tech University Press, 2001); *Levinas and Nineteenth-Century Literature: Ethics and Otherness from Romanticism Through Realism*, ed. David P. Haney and Donald R. Wehrs (Newark: University of Delaware Press, 2009); and *Levinas and the Ancients*, ed. Silvia Benso and Brian Schroeder (Bloomington: Indiana University Press, 2008).

85. In "A Land that Devours Its Inhabitants," Sandor Goodhart writes, "What, to date, to my knowledge has never been fully argued, however, is that Levinas is reading midrashically: that midrash is not just one among other modes of rabbinic exegesis but co-terminous with the activity itself; that Levinas recognizes and practices that rabbinic exegetical midrashic mode even when he is 'translating Hebrew into Greek'; and that for Levinas, as for the rabbis, midrashic reading remains above all literary reading." On the history of the *darshan*, see Marc Bregman, "The Darshan: Preacher and Teacher of Talmudic Times," *The Melton Journal* 14 (1982): 3–10. Both Shmuel Wygoda and Michael Fagenblat have coined the phrase, "phenomenological midrash" to describe Levinas's unique approach to rabbinic texts. See Shmuel Wygoda, "A Phenomenological Outlook at the Talmud: Levinas as Reader of the Talmud," http://ghansel.free.fr/wygoda.html, and Fagenblat, *A Covenant of Creatures: Levinas's Philosophy of Judaism*.

86. See the beginning of Chapter 4 and end of Chapter 7, which quote Stanley Cavell on Wittgenstein's notion of "bringing words back" to their everyday uses.

87. "On Jewish Philosophy," *In the Time of Nations*, 169. Also, "Perhaps Jewish texts have always been understood as constantly accompanied by a layer of symbolic meaning,

apologues, new interpretations to be discovered: in short, always lined with *midrash*" (168).

2. Sollicitation *and "Rubbing the Text": Reading Said and Levinas Reading*

1. The following all address the peculiar paradox of scripture as a "source" of ritual impurity: Michael J. Broyde, "Defilement of the Hands, Canonization of the Bible, and the Special Status of Esther," *Judaism* 44, no. 1 (Winter 1995): 65–80; Sergey Dolgopolski, *What Is Talmud? The Art of Disagreement* (New York: Fordham University Press, 2003); Shamma Friedman, "The Holy Scriptures Defile the Hands—The Transformation of a Biblical Concept in Rabbinic Theology," in *Minḥah le-Naḥum—Biblical and Other Studies Presented to Nahum M. Sarna in Honour of his 70th Birthday*, ed. M. Brettler and M. Fishbane (Sheffield: JSOT Press, 1993), 117–132; José Faur, *The Horizontal Society: Understanding the Covenant and Alphabetic Judaism Vol. 2* (Brighton: Academic Studies Press, 2008); Martin Goodman, "Sacred Scripture and 'Defiling the Hands,'" *Jewish Theological Studies* 41, no. 1 (1990): 99–107; Menachem Haran, *The Biblical Collection: Its Consolidation to the End of the Second Temple Times and Changes of Form to the End of the Middle Ages* (Jerusalem: Bialik Institute and Magnes Press, 1996); Timothy H. Lim, "The Defilement of the Hands as a Principle Determining the Holiness of Scriptures," *Journal of Theological Studies* 61, no. 2: 501–515; Jodi Magness, "Scrolls and Hand Impurity," in *The Dead Sea Scrolls: Texts and Contexts*, ed. Charlotte Hempel (Leiden: Brill, 2010), 89–98; Chaim Milikowsky, "Reflections on Hand-Washing, Hand-Purity and Holy Scripture in Rabbinic Literature," in *Purity and Holiness: The Heritage of Leviticus*, ed. M. J. H. M. Poorthuis and J. Schwartz (Leiden: Brill, 2000), 149–162; John C. Poirier, "Why Did the Pharisees Wash Their Hands?" *Journal of Jewish Studies* 47 (1996): 217–233.

2. The cognate concept in Islam is *najasa/tahara*, and the purifying ablutions are *wudu* (partial wash), and *ghusl* (full-body wash). Most Islamic authorities stipulate that *wudu* (including hand washing and teeth brushing) must precede any recitation or reading from the codex form of the *Qur'an*. Barbara A. Holdrege's *Veda and Torah: Transcending the Textuality of Scripture* (Albany: State University of New York Press, 1996) contains a fascinating juxtaposition of scribal, recitative, and transmission traditions in Judaism and Hinduism.

3. *Tum'at hamet* has nine subcategories of its own: (1) A corpse (or even a fraction of the corpse, whether the person was or was not Jewish) (2) A grave (3) A Jew who became *tamei* by contact with a corpse (4) Vessels that touched a Jew who became *tamei* by contact with a corpse (5) Vessels that touched a corpse (6) A Jew who touched vessels that touched a corpse (7) Vessels that touched a Jew who touched vessels that touched a corpse (8) Vessels that touched vessels that touched a corpse (9) *Ohel*: when a corpse overlies something or someone without touching it, or something or someone overlies a corpse without touching it, or when something or someone is within a contiguous space under the same roof. See Maimonides, Introduction to *Seder Taharot* in *Peirush haMishnayot*.

4. The contrast would be with *ketuvim qedoshim* (holy writings) as in *mYad.* 4:6, writes Goodman in "Sacred Scripture and 'Defiling the Hands,'" *Jewish Theological Studies* 41, no. 1 (1990): 99–107.

5. See Yehudah Cohn, *Tangled up in Text: Tefillin and the Ancient World* (Providence, R.I.: Brown University Press, 2008), 140–141.

6. See the articles by Shamma Friedman and Timothy H. Lim; the chapter "Stains of Impurity" in Chaya T. Halberstam, *Law and Truth in Biblical and Rabbinic Literature* (Bloomington: Indiana University Press, 2010); Jonathan Klawans, *Impurity and Sin in Ancient Judaism* (Oxford: Oxford University Press, 2000); *Perspectives on Purity and Purification in the Bible*, ed. Baruch J. Schwartz, David P. Wright, Jeffrey Stackert, and Naphtali S. Meschel (New York: T&T Clark, 2008); and Christine Hayes, "The 'Other' in Rabbinic Literature," in *The Cambridge Companion to the Talmud and Rabbinic Literature*, ed. Charlotte Fonrobert and Martin Jaffee (Cambridge: Cambridge University Press, 2007), 243–278; and the work of Yair Furstenberg on the social role of purity in 2nd Temple and early Christian communities, e.g., *Hand Purity and Eating in a State of Purity: A Chapter in the Development of Halakhah*, diss., Jerusalem: Hebrew University, 2005 [Hebrew].

7. The mishnaic sources for the various rabbinic discussions are *Mishnah Yadayim*, Chapters 3 and 4, *bShabbat* 14a, and *bMegillah* 7a. Tractate *Shabbat* itself begins with a chapter, *Yetziot Ha'Shabbat* ("carryings on Shabbat"), that discusses the various prohibitions for the transfer of objects from one domain to another, the initial examples being those where the hand is assigned agency. Whether it initiates movement (*akira*) or causes an object to be at rest (*hanahah*), the *hand* is thus identified as a basic locus of measureable space: *arba'a al arba'a tefahim* ("four-by-four handbreadths"), or three inches on a side. The second epigraph to this chapter derives from that discussion. The tractate on "hands" in the Oral Torah is translated and contextualized by Jacob Neusner in *Part 19: Tebul Yom and Yadayim*, in his twenty-two volume series *A History of the Mishnaic Law of Purities* (Eugene, Ore.: Wipf & Stock, 2007). A translation of the parallel tractate from the *Talmud Yerushalmi* can be found in *Tractates Šabbat and 'Eruvin*, ed. Heinrich W. Guggenheimer (Berlin: Walter de Gruyter, 2012).

8. No less speculatively but with more attention to the surface particulars of *Mishnah Yadayim* 3:5, which refers to Numbers 10:35–36, Timothy Lim proposes that the connection between sacrality of scripture and *tum'at yadayim* can be traced to biblical narratives about prohibited touch, specifically the story of the Ark of the Covenant and Uzzah's death in 2 Samuel 6:2–7. See "The Defilement of the Hands as a Principle Determining the Holiness of Scriptures." Louis Finkelstein, "The Pharisees: Their Origin and Their Philosophy," *Harvard Theological Review* 22, no. 3 (July 1929): 185–261, explains the principle with reference to cultural and ideological differences between Sadducee and Pharisee. In *The Horizontal Society*, José Faur maintains the rabbinic enactment was designed to detotemize scripture as a possible fetish for veneration and to prevent the "bonding together" of two sacred objects (scroll and *terumah*) in the belief that "their respective sacrality would be augmented" (14). Martin Sicker rehearses the prevalent

theories in *An Introduction to Judaic Thought and Rabbinic Literature* (New York: Praeger, 2007), 10–13.

9. Levinas has an obviously fluid understanding of "scrolls" on the way to becoming "books," but the historical relevance of the *Megillat* (Scroll of) *Esther* as a material text is not insignificant here. According to custom and in keeping with the spirit of the Biblical story, when recited publically on the festival of Purim, a *megillah* is read purposely not as a scroll (like a *sefer Torah*) but as a letter—folded over itself several times in order to simulate pages, as stipulated by the *Geonim*: "spread out like a letter" (פושטה כאיגרת *poshetah-ke-iggeret*). Although it is now almost universally the custom in Jewish communities across the globe thus to read the *megillah* from an unrolled scroll, in previous generations, *megillot* were sometimes interleaved (without being bound), and folded accordion-style on the model of a codex. As such, they mark, we might say, a midpoint between a scroll on one hand and a book on the other, making Levinas's point even more apropos. Michael Broyde explains these details in "Like a Scroll or Like a Letter: A Pictorial Note about *Hilchot Sefer Torah* in contrast to *Hilchot Megilla*" (privately circulated). See also R. Moshe Taragin, "Is Megillat Esther Patterned after a Sefer Torah?" *Yeshivat Har Etzion Israel Koschitzky Virtual Beit Midrash* www.vbmtorah.org/archive/metho67/13metho.htm.

10. The trilateral root עסק signifies "trade, business." Marcus Jastrow's *Sefer Ha-Milim* (New York: Judaica Press, 1992) defines the verb as meaning, "to work, be engaged in, occupy oneself with"; an *'asqan* is an "experimenter: busy, moving automatically" (1099).

11. In *Altered Reading: Levinas and Literature* (Chicago: University of Chicago Press, 1999), Jill Robbins draws out the close parallel in Levinas between the *il y a* and the aesthetic event (91–101). Michael Fagenblat's *A Covenant of Creatures: Levinas's Philosophy of Judaism* (Stanford: Stanford University Press, 2011) connects the *il y a* to Levinas's midrashic reading of Genesis. I say more about this connection at the end of Chapter 4.

12. Peter Atterton, Peter, Matthew Calarco, and Joëlle Hansel, "'The Meaning of Religious Practice' by Emmanuel Levinas: An Introduction and Translation," *Modern Judaism* 25, no. 3 (October 2005): 288. See also Joëlle Hansel, "Beyond Phenomenology: Levinas's Early Jewish Writings," *Levinas Studies: An Annual Review* 5 (Pittsburgh: Duquesne University Press, 2010), 5–17. Compare Levinas's essay "Exigeant Judaïsme" (Demanding Judaism) in *Beyond the Verse: Talmudic Readings and Discourses*, trans. Gary Mole (New York: Continuum, 2007): "It is as if the ritual acts prolonged the states of mind expressing and incarnating their interior plenitude, and were to the piety of obedience what the smile is to benevolence, the handshake to friendship, and the caress to affection" (7).

13. This is the title of a 1970 essay first published in *The Language of Criticism and the Sciences of Man* (which also includes the Poulet essay on the phenomenology of reading), and subsequently collected in *The Rustle of Language*, trans. Richard Howard (New York: Farrar, Straus, and Giroux, 1986), 11–21.

14. An additional liberty derived from such rubbing reminds us that making texts "spurt" blood inadvertently connects Levinas to the otherwise distant figure of country-

man Antonin Artaud, whose 1925 play *Jet de Sang*, or "Spurt of Blood," features a scene in which a bawd bites God's wrist and "an immense spurt of blood lacerates the Stage" (perhaps the least of numerous grotesque moments in the play's four short pages). Coincidentally enough, 1925 was the same year that the Surrealist Max Ernst developed a drawing technique he called *frottage*—the very metaphor for interpretive friction coined by Levinas in his essay—that involved applying sheets of paper or canvas to textured surfaces and rubbing over them with a pencil or crayon. See Max Ernst, *Malningar, Collage, Frottage, Teckningar, Grafik, Bocker, Skulpturer, 1917–1969* (Stockholm: Moderna Museet, Stockholm, 1969), and Tobias Percival Zur Loye, "History of a Natural History: Max Ernst's Histoire Naturelle, Frottage, and Surrealist Automatism," Ph.D. diss., University of Oregon, 2010.

15. Aronowicz, preface to *Nine Talmudic Readings*, xvii and David Banon, *La lecture infinie. Les voies de l'interprétation midrachique. Préface d'Emmanuel Lévinas* (Paris: Éditions du Seuil, 1987), 25. See also "Une hermeneutique de la sollicitation," in *Emmanuel Levinas (Les Cahiers de la Nuit Surveillee, 3)*, 99–115. In his *Paris Review* interview with Edward Hirsch, "The Art of Fiction 133" (1993), novelist James Salter confesses, "I'm a *frotteur*, someone who likes to rub words in his hand, to turn them around and feel them, to wonder if that really is the best word possible. Does that word in this sentence have any electric potential? Does it do anything? Too much electricity will make your reader's hair frizzy." Likewise, the rubboard used in Zydeco music is a " *frottoir.*"

The other common meaning of *frottage* (*frotter, frotteur*) happens to be erotic. For instance, in the chapter "Dawn at the Pyramids," the narrator of Julian Barnes's *Flaubert's Parrot* (New York: Vintage, 1990) remarks of Humbert Humbert, "He is a *frotteur.* Literally, a French polisher; but also, the sort of sexual deviant who loves the rub of the crowd" (69).

16. "Goethe's Elective Affinities," trans. Stanley Corngold, *Selected Writings, 1913–1926*, ed. Marcus Paul Bullock, Michael William Jennings, Howard Eiland, and Gary Smith (Cambridge, Mass.: Belknap Press of Harvard University Press, 1996), 297. Benjamin's terms are *Wahrheitsgehalt* and *Sachegehalt* ("matter"), with each corresponding to a scholarly agency imposed from outside: either *Die Kritik* (critique) or *Der Kommentar* (commentary). Of the former, Benjamin adds this pertinent image: "To an ever-increasing extent, therefore, the interpretation of the striking and the odd, that is, of the subject matter, becomes a prerequisite for any later critic. One may liken him to a paleographer in front of a parchment whose faded text is covered by the stronger outlines of a script referring to that text. Just as the paleographer would have to start with reading the script, the critic must start with commenting on the text. And with one stroke, an invaluable criterion of judgment springs out for him; only now can he raise the basic critical question of whether the semblance/luster [*Schein*] of the truth content is due to the material content, or the life of the material content to the truth content" (298).

17. In the second part of his essay, Poulet compares the methods of five literary critics: Jacques Riviere, Jean-Pierre Richard, Maurice Blanchot, Jean Starobinski, Marcel Raymond, and Jean Rousset.

18. "Agnon's writing, especially in its quasi-biblical or midrashic diction, has a trace-structure, that is, it has the distinctive form of signification in retreat, which is, in the idiom of Levinas's later work, precisely the way the other signifies. That is, it is ethical in precisely Levinas's sense" (*Altered Reading*, 139). Such trace-structure has especial relevance for our purposes in stories from the 1930s like "A Book That Was Lost" or "Knots Upon Knots," where it is *the physical book* itself that can be said to "signify in retreat." I look at the Agnon essay more closely in Chapter 7. In the chapter, "After Ethics: Levinas Without Stories," from *After Poststructuralism: Reading, Stories and Theory* (New York: Routledge, 2004), Colin Davis offers a quite stinging critique of Levinas as a "bad" or "failed" reader of literary works. (See also Davis, "Levinas and the Phenomenology of Reading.") Indeed, this analysis, which I partly endorse, paves the way for Mikhail Bakhtin as the *confrere* and good angel that Levinasian hermeneutics could well have benefited from—the rationale at the core of Chapter 5 in this book.

19. "A Land That Devours Its Inhabitants," 234. Robbins is also troping on Levinas's figure for interrupted discourse, *les noeuds d'un fil renoué* "knots of a retied thread" from *Otherwise Than Being*, 170. The figures of both "tear" and "knot" are explored at length by Derrida in "At This Very Moment in the Work, Here I Am," in *Rereading Levinas*, ed. Robert Bernasconi and Simon Critchley (Bloomington: Indiana University Press, 1991), 11–50, and tracked in turn by Robert Gibbs in Chapter 4 of *Why Ethics? Signs of Responsibilities* (Princeton: Princeton University Press, 2000).

20. "Language and Proximity," in *Collected Philosophical Papers*, 122, 125.

21. The pericope is discussed in detail by David Stern and Susan Handelman in their heated debate in *Prooftexts* 5, no. 1 (January 1985): "Fragments of the Rock: Contemporary Literary Theory and the Study of Rabbinic Texts—A Response to David Stern," 75–95, and "Literary Criticism or Literary Homilies? Susan Handelman and the Contemporary Study of Midrash," 96–103.

22. "Interview with Myriam Anissimov," *Is It Righteous to Be?* 87. It is a figure to which he has recourse in other writings, with especial suitability for his posthumously published *lecture talmudique* "Who is One-Self?" (121), whose dominant motif is "ashes."

23. A subtle article on this trope is Sylvia Benso, "The Breathing of the Air: Presocratic Echoes in Levinas," in *Levinas and the Ancients*, ed. Sylvia Benso and Brian Schroeder (Bloomington: Indiana University Press, 2008), 9–23. See also Michael Marder, "Breathing 'to' the Other: Levinas and Ethical Breathlessness," *Levinas Studies* 4 (2009): 91–110.

24. In *Critical Excess: Overreading in Derrida, Deleuze, Levinas, Žižek, and Cavell* (Stanford: Stanford University Press, 2010), Colin Davis calls attention to the obvious: "the reader cause himself pain in the act of reading," a "self-inflicted wound [that] also entails an act of violence against the work he is studying" (89). In "'Extreme Attention to the Real': Levinas and Religious Hermeneutics," *Shofar* 26, no. 4 (Summer 2008), 36–53, Laurence L. Edwards nicely suggests a similarity with Walter Benjamin's well-known passage on the "historical materialist" in the "Theses on the Philosophy of History," which ends, "He regards it as his task to *brush history against the grain*" (52).

25. See, for instance, *Talmud Bavli Masekhet Shabbat*, ed. and trans. Adin Steinsaltz (Jerusalem: Ha-Makhon Ha-Yiśre'eli Le-firsumim Talmudiyim) and *Koren Talmud Bavli Vols. 2 and 3: Tractate Shabbat* (Hebrew/English), ed. Adin Even-Israel Steinsaltz (Jerusalem: Koren, 2012). The '*Ein Yaaqov* and *Aggadot Hatalmud*, sixteenth-century commentaries on the aggadic portions of the Talmud, and the twentieth-century compilation by Bialik and Ravnitsky, *Sefer Ha'Aggadah*, both record the sense of "fingers bloodied by sitting." The verb מייץ suggests the idea of squeezing, and Rashi elsewhere (on Prov. 33:3) translates it as *empreindre* (Old French for "to press" or "stamp").

26. A *sugya* forms a bounded unit of Talmudic discourse elaborating Tannaitic *mishnah* as debated by later sages (*Amoraim*); but since it is not demarcated as such on the page, "marking" it properly (as redacted by the Talmud's anonymous editorial voice), represents one of many hermeneutic tasks in this highly specialized brand of textual reasoning. In Aryeh Cohen's definition, a *sugya* is "the primary context of all its parts—attributed and unattributed statements, *aggadot, maasim*, proof texts, et al. Its parameters are established both structurally or intratextually, and thematically." *Rereading Talmud: Gender, Law and the Poetics of Sugyot* (Providence, R.I.: Brown University Series in Jewish Studies, Scholars Press, 1988), 148. See also Judith Hauptman, *Development of the Talmudic Sugya: Relationship Between Tannaitic and Amoraic Sources* (Lanham, Md.: University Press of America, 1987) and Louis Jacobs, *Structure and Form in the Babylonian Talmud* (Cambridge: Cambridge University Press, 1991).

27. "The Struggle for the Text," in *The Third Pillar*, 28. Hartman's point of departure in this essay is Auerbach, whose claim for the Bible's quality of lexical "*deutungsbedürftig*" (demanding interpretation) rubs shoulders with Rashi's *hamikra hazeh omer darsheni* (this text says "interrogate me").

28. Aryeh Cohen reads it somewhat differently, as an echo of the story in the same *sugya* of God's holding Mt. Sinai over the Israelites' heads lest they not accept the Torah: "The verb for studying comes from the same root as the noun for eye: *ayayn* is study and *ayin* is eye. Whilst the sectarian was eyeing Rava, Rava was 'eyeing' the text. However, Rava's struggle with the text or the tradition that he was studying was played out as a struggle with himself. He was injured and bleeding from the study. Rava's body was made porous by the intense study of Torah—while his 'prooftext' lauds the 'wholeness' or the 'integrity' of the 'righteous' . . . The ground of understanding [personally accepting the Torah] is even the puncturing of the integrity of the human body. The blood of Rava's struggle is an embodied practice of study—it is an extreme performance of the Divine knowledge overwhelming the human ability to grasp and understand." "Shabbat Parashat Be'Hukotai—17 Iyar 5771—Halfway to Sinai," http://ziegler.aju.edu/Default.aspx?id=7144.

29. See Aronowicz's preface to *Nine Talmudic Readings*; Valerie Allen, "Difficult Reading," *Levinas and Medieval Literature*; and the chapter on Levinas in Colin Davis, *Critical Excess*.

30. Aside from Derrida's famous conclusion to his 1964 essay on Levinas, "Violence and Metaphysics," "Jewgreek is Greekjew. Extremes Meet," see the valuable discussion by

Oona Ajzenstat (Eisenstadt) "Levinas versus Levinas: Hebrew, Greek, and Linguistic Justice," *Philosophy & Rhetoric* 38, no. 2 (2005): 145–158; the final chapter of Tamra Wright, *The Twilight of Jewish Philosophy: Emmanuel Lévinas' Ethical Hermeneutics* (Amsterdam: Harwood Academic Publishers, 1999); Robert Gibbs, *Correlations in Rosenzweig and Levinas* (Princeton: Princeton University Press, 1992); and Robert Eaglestone, "Levinas, Ethics, and Translation," in *Nation, Language, and the Ethics of Translation*, ed. Sandra Bermann and Michael Wood (Princeton: Princeton University Press, 2005).

31. Jonathan Boyarin, *Carnal Israel: Reading Sex in Talmudic Culture* (Berkeley: University of California Press, 1995), *Ha-Iyun ha-Sefaradi: Le-farshanut ha-Talmud shel megorshe Sefarad* (Jerusalem: Makhon Ben Zvi, 1989), and *Socrates and the Fat Rabbis* (Chicago: University Of Chicago Press, 2009); Aryeh Cohen, *Rereading Talmud: Gender, Law and the Poetics of Sugyot* and *Beginning/Again: Towards a Hermeneutics of Jewish Texts* (New York: Seven Bridges Press, 2002); Yonah Fraenkel, *Darkhei ha-Agadah ve-ha-Midrash* (Givatayim: Yad latalmud, 1991); Shamma Friedman, "Literary Development and History in the Aggadic Narrative of the Babylonian Talmud: A Study Based Upon B.M. 83b–86a," *Community and Culture Essays in Jewish Studies In Honor of the 90th Anniversary of the Founding of Gratz College* (Philadelphia: Jewish Publication Society, 1987), 67–80, and *Five Sugyot From the Babylonian Talmud* (Jerusalem: Society for the Interpretation of the Talmud, 2002); David Weiss Halivni, *Mekorot Umasorot* (Sources and Traditions) (Jerusalem: Magnes Press, 1968), *Iyunim Behithavot Hatalmud* (Jerusalem: Magnes Press, 2008), and *The Formation of the Babylonian Talmud*; Mandel, "Between Byzantium and Islam: The Transmission of a Jewish Book in the Byzantine and Early Islamic Periods," *Transmitting Jewish Traditions: Orality, Textuality and Cultural Diffusion*, ed. Yaakov Elman and Israel Gershoni (New Haven: Yale University Press, 2000), 74–106; Jeffrey Rubenstein; *Talmudic Stories: Narrative Art, Composition, and Culture* and *The Culture of the Babylonian Talmud* (Baltimore: Johns Hopkins University Press, 2003); Zvi Septimus, "Trigger Words and Simultexts: The Experience of Reading the *Bavli*," in *Wisdom of Bat Sheva: In Memory of Beth Samuels*, ed. Barry Scott Wimpfheimer (Jersey City, N.J.: Ktav, 2009), 163–185; Moshe Simon-Shoshan, *Stories of the Law: Narrative Discourse and the Construction of Authority in the Mishnah* (New York: Oxford University Press, 2012); Shai Secunda, *The Iranian Talmud: Reading the Bavli in Its Sassanian Context* (Philadelphia: University of Pennsylvania Press, 2013); Barry Wimpfheimer, *Narrating the Law: A Poetics of Talmudic Legal Stories* (Philadelphia: University of Pennsylvania Press, 2011); Judith Baskin, *Midrashic Women: Formations of the Feminine in Rabbinic Literatur* (Hanover, N.H.: Brandeis University Press, 2002); and Dina Stein, *Textual Mirrors: Reflexivity, Midrash, and the Rabbinic Self* (Philadelphia: University of Pennsylvania Press, 2012).

32. For biographies of Rava, other sages, and Talmudic masters, Ephraim Urbach's compendious *The Sages: Their Concepts and Beliefs*, trans. Israel Abrahams (Cambridge, Mass.: Harvard University Press, 1987) remains authoritative.

33. We would still need to defer to Levinas's express methodology as he outlines it, for instance, in his reading "Model of the West" in *Beyond the Verse*. Thus, Jacob Meskin

argues that the typical Levinasian commentary is itself dialogic, since one can also hear reverberating "recognizable rhythms: those of *mussar*, of the Lithuanian yeshiva, and of what one might call mitnagdic mysticism" (91–92). See "Critique, Tradition, and the Religious Imagination: An Essay on Levinas' Talmudic Readings," *Judaism* (Winter 1998): 91–106, and "Toward a New Understanding of the Work of Emmanuel Levinas," *Modern Judaism* 20, no. 1 (February 2000): 78–102.

34. *Nine Talmudic Readings*, 55. Bourdieu, *Rules of Art: Genesis and Structure of the Literary Field*, trans. Susan Emanuel (Stanford: Stanford University Press, 1996); Boyarin, *Carnal Israel*; Jameson, *The Political Unconscious: Narrative as a Socially Symbolic Act* (Ithaca, N.Y.: Cornell University Press, 1981); Sedgwick, *Epistemology of the Closet* (Berkeley: University of California Press, 1990).

35. See the chapter, "Deconstructing Halakhah and Aggadah," 31–62, and also Yair Lorberbaum, "Reflections of the Halakhic Status of Aggadah," *Dine Yisrael* 24 (2007), 29–64, and *Tzelem Elohim: Halakha v'Aggadah* (Jerusalem: Schocken Press, 2004).

36. Yet, this method is admitted and deliberate. For instance, Levinas begins In "The Nations and the Presence of Israel" from *In the Time of Nations* with this disclaimer: "To excerpt from a Talmudic treatise a passage that lends itself to a study on the problems addressed in these meetings is a hazardous enterprise. The very idea of excerpting from the Talmud is a difficult one. The limits of the excerpt always remain uncertain. It is uncertain whether the different sequences of each treatise, apparently connected to one another in many cases by the accidents of compilation, may not have a deeper coherence not visible at first" (94).

37. Notwithstanding the surfeit of books that continue to anatomize Levinas's oeuvre, one that remains to be written is a reading-by-reading dissection of the *lectures Talmudique* that compares them meticulously to the Hebrew/Aramaic original. Although unexceptionable, this is the common lacuna illustrated, to take one instance, by the section on "Interpreting Levinas on Interpretation" in Michael Morgan's *Discovering Levinas* (Cambridge: Cambridge University Press, 2010), 390–394, which mentions some of Levinas's interpreters (David, Gibbs, Cohen, Wright, Wyschogrod), but thereby enlists the textual originals at two or three removes. Similarly, Cohen's explanation of Levinas's hermeneutic speaks at length *about* Levinas's method but does not undertake close readings.

38. See "Studying or Learning?" by the columnist "Philologos" in *The Forward*, March 30, 2007, and the same distinction as elaborated by Andrew Bush in the introduction to *Jewish Studies: A Theoretical Introduction*, 1–10.

39. Certainly, this is how it is viewed in modern *yeshivot*, where it is rarely studied in a curriculum devoted almost entirely to halakhic analysis. R. Yitzchak Blau's *Fresh Fruit and Vintage Wine: The Ethics and Wisdom of the Aggada* (Hoboken, N.J.: Ktav, 2009) is an exception, but its thrust, unlike Levinas's, flattens and simplifies the textual foreground.

40. The most important collections of these writings are: *Proper Names* and *Outside the Subject*, trans. Michael B. Smith (Stanford: Stanford University Press, 1993).

41. Compare the beautiful image in Benjamin's essay on *Die Wahlverwandtschaften*: "If, to use a simile, one views the growing work as a funeral pyre, its commentator can be likened to the chemist, its critic to an alchemist. While the former is left with wood and ashes as the sole objects of his analysis, the latter is concerned only with the enigma of the flame itself: the enigma of being alive. Thus the critic inquires about the truth whose living flame goes on burning over the heavy logs of the past and the light ashes of life gone by" (298).

42. But like the French *frotter,* this verb also had certain sexual connotations. *The Dictionary of the Talmud,* compiled by Martin Jastrow, for instance, cites Tractates *Niddah* 22b ("a fetus which can be squashed by rubbing"), *Yevamot* 34b ("Tamar destroyed her virginity by friction with her finger"), and the various biblical verses that denote "crushed" testicles.

43. Actually, the irony is double. As Adriana Cavarero has noted of the Levinasian figure of "Do no murder" inscribed on the facing person: "Writing—not voice, therefore, but writing; divine revelation, word of God, in the face of the other as text, or rather, the word of God in the face of the one next to me—who is, symptomatically, trace." See *For More Than One Voice: Toward a Philosophy of Vocal Expression* (Stanford: Stanford University Press, 2005), 24, and Chapter 4, "Visage, Figure: Speech and Murder in Totality and Infinity," in Jill Robbins's *Levinas and Literature.*

44. Betty Rojtman's *Black Fire on White Fire: An Essay on Jewish Hermeneutics from Midrash to Kabbalah,* trans. Steven Randall (Berkeley: University of California Press, 1998) proceeds analytically according to a very different concrete image of text: the midrashic trope of *eish shahor al gabei eish lavan* (black fire on white fire) from *Midrash Tanhuma,* Genesis 1, which positions the interpreter in vertical relation to the text (the fourfold model of *PaRDeS*) rather than what we might call the manifestly horizontal one of a book or scroll *in hand.* For Rojtman, whose approach is semiotic and linguistic, the specifically interpretive problematic becomes "the dialectic of incarnation, understood as the inscription of the spiritual in matter," which she expresses as "the intersection of curved and straight lines, the experience of a limit that religious consciousness calls *qedushah,* "sanctification," and whose fulcrum language designates as the demonstrative *zeh*: "this" of "that" which is revealed to me *through this world*" (12–13). By contrast, as I explain later in this chapter, Levinas identifies Talmudic discourse specifically as a *vernacular*: it reads out worldliness because its arguments are rooted in worldly act and practice, and thus exegesis is a worldly or "hands-on" affair as well.

45. Levinas gave twenty-five such readings almost yearly, from 1959 to 1989, brought out in five volumes from 1968 and 1996 by Éditions de Minuit. Of these, two are from *seder* (Talmudic order) *Zera'im* ("seeds"), six are from *seder Mo'ed* ("appointed seasons"), two are from *Seder Nashim* ("women"), eight are from *seder Nezikin* ("damages'), two are from *seder Qodashim* ("holy things"). The sixth order of the Mishnah, *Seder Taharot* ("clean matters"), is not represented in the Talmud *Bavli* except for tractate *Niddah,* on which Levinas did not comment. Most are represented by those in *Nezikin* (torts), which is apposite given Levinas's essential interest in the metaphysics of infringement and

impingement. The individual readings and their dates are listed in Robert Gibbs's *Correlations*, 175.

46. *Legal Fictions: Studies of Law and Narrative in the Discursive Worlds of Ancient Jewish Sectarians and Sages* (Leiden: Brill, 2011), 8. Fraade cites Auerbach's notion of "a transfer of confidence," which chimes with Levinas's stated commitment to a "trust" granted to an author or textual tradition. See also Fraade's introduction to his *From Tradition to Commentary: Torah and Its Interpretation in the Midrash Sifre to Deuteronomy* (Albany: State University of New York Press, 1998). On the distinction between deciphering a text and the more "special case" of "performance interpretation," see also Nicholas Wolterstorff's *Divine Discourse: Philosophical Reflections on the Claim That God Speaks* (Cambridge: Cambridge University Press, 1995), 171–182.

47. "Author" here means organizing consciousness, and it is thus not far removed from Meir Sternberg's construct of "embodied intention" in *The Poetics of Biblical Narrative: Ideological Literature and the Drama of Reading*. At the same time, Levinas takes pains to respect the Talmudic tradition of citing in *the commentator's name* as betokening the inarguable particularity of at least oral authorship: "When he is quoted, an effort is made to respect jealously that uniqueness. When he transmits the saying of someone else, it is meticulously noted, and often a few lines of the text are devoted to going back to the one who said it first, mentioning all the intermediaries" (*In the Time of Nations*, 177).

48. Albeit the residue "of a presencing, never of an absence," in Benso's wording from *The Face of Things*, 137. See also the explanation of Levinas's trace concept in Oona Ajzenstat, *Driven Back to the Text: The Premodern Sources of Levinas's Postmodernism* (Pittsburgh: Duquesne University Press, 2001). In *Radical Atheism: Derrida and the Time of Life* (Stanford: Stanford University Press, 2008), Martin Hägglund mounts a compelling counterargument to those critics (Bernasconi, Critchley, Caputo) who too easily theologize Derrida with Levinas, coordinating the two of them, for example, around ultimately divergent conceptualizations of the trace. Thus, Hägglund quotes Derrida on the *khora* in the 1996 essay "Faith and Knowledge": "[the alterity of spacing] will never have entered religion and will never permit itself to be sacralized, sanctified . . . Radically heterogeneous to the safe and sound, the holy and the sacred, it never admits of any *indemnification*" (85).

49. *Why Ethics? Signs of Responsibilities* (Princeton: Princeton University Press, 2000), 87. Gibbs also cites this important passage from *Otherwise Than Being*, which is elided by Derrida's reading of it in "At This Very Moment Here In the Text I Am": "But clearly, this story itself is without end and without continuity, which is to say, it goes from one to the other—it is tradition. But thereby, it renews itself. The new meanings arise in its meaning, whose exegesis is the unfolding or the history before all historiography" (169). Parenthetically, I might note that Gibb's analysis tracks the Levinasian text that has been both clarified and somewhat obscured (stitched together, made to reiterate itself) by Derrida's annotation similar to the way I have let the Talmudic texts in "The Temptation of Temptation" speak in its own voice *beneath* Levinas's exegetical "oversound."

50. *Humanism and Democratic Criticism* (New York: Columbia University Press, 2004), 49. Both analytically and genealogically, more can be said about the concept of *world* inside "worldliness," given its importance in Said's vernacular. Much recent theorization has accreted around the "global" and "worldly" in respect to canons of literature. One example is Hayot's *Literary Worlds* (Oxford: Oxford University Press, 2012), whose chapter, "Aspects of Worldedness" (indeed, the rhetorical choice of the term "worldedness" itself), is probably the most pertinent here, given its re-reading of Auerbach.

51. See R. M. Cover, *The Supreme Court 1982 Term Foreword: Nomos and Narrative Harvard Law Review Association* (1983): 4–68; Steven D. Fraade, "Nomos and Narrative Before *Nomos and Narrative, Yale Journal of Law and the Humanities* 17, no. 1 (2005): 81–96, and Samuel J. Levine, "*Halacha* and *Aggada*: Translating Robert Cover's *Nomos and Narrative*," *Utah Law Review* 465 (1998): 465–504.

52. The analogy with the hermeneutical *sufiya* of al-Ghazzālī, noted earlier, is just as pertinent.

53. See Levinas, *Humanism of the Other*, trans. Nidra Poller (Chicago: University of Chicago Press, 2005), and Augusto Ponzio, *Signs, Dialogue, and Ideology*, trans. Susan Petrilli (Philadelphia: John Benjamins Publishing, 1993), 107–117. In two essays from *Difficult Freedom*, "For a Jewish Humanism" and "Anti-Humanism and Education," Levinas identifies the Jewish people as the first to recognize a "crisis of the human ideal" and distinguishes Jewish practice and thought from the mythical (as he also does in the essay, "The Strings and the Wood" from *Outside the Subject*). "Hebraic" or "Biblical Humanism," likewise, is another phrase Levinas deploys with specific textual implications, a comprehensive treatment of which can be found in Richard A. Cohen, *Ethics, Exegesis and Philosophy: Interpretation after Levinas* (Cambridge: Cambridge University Press, 2001), some of which is reproduced as the introduction to his translation of Levinas's *New Talmudic Readings*. See also Tamra Wright's *The Twilight of Jewish Philosophy* and Levinas's essay, "The Contemporary Criticism of the Idea of Value and the Prospects for Humanism," *Value and Values In Evolution*, ed. Edward A. Maziarz (New York: Gordon and Breach, 1979), 179–187.

54. Or "alter humanist," to inflect the term coined by John Llewellyn in *Emmanuel Levinas: The Genealogy of Ethics* (London: Routledge Press, 1995), 148.

55. "Secularism and the Thought of Israel" in *Unforeseen History*, trans. Nidra Poller (Chicago: University of Illinois Press, 2004), 117. Levinas's definition differs from secularism as a political doctrine in the genealogy and "grammar of concept" introduced by Talal Asad in *Formations of the Secular: Christianity, Islam, Modernity* (Stanford: Stanford University Press, 2003), from which "the Jewish political tradition" as such is conspicuously lacking anyway. Interestingly, an essay in *Powers of the Secular Modern: Talal Asad and His Interlocutors* (Stanford: Stanford University Press, 2006) by Hent de Vries, "On General and Divine Economy: Talal Asad's Genealogy of the Secular and Emmanuel Levinas's Critique of Capitalism, Colonialism, and Money" (113–133), forges something of a missing link, but the primary focus is on what de Vries calls "global

religion" toward a coimplication of the religious and secular. Marcel Gauchet's *The Disenchantment of the World: A Political History of Religion,* trans. Oscar Burge (Princeton: Princeton University Press, 1997) argues for the derivation of secularism *from* Abrahamic religious traditions, but again the descriptive lacunae in regard to post-Sinaitic, i.e., *rabbinic* Judaism, are conspicuous. For an intellectual counter-tradition of sorts, see the series *The Jewish Political Tradition: Volumes 1 and 2 (Authority* and *Membership),* ed. Michael Walzer, Menachem Lorberbaum, Noam J. Zohar, and Yair Lorberbaum (New Haven: Yale University Press, 2000, 2003).

56. "Without Identity," *Humanism of the Other,* 65.

57. On the general viability of this concept for Said's work, see by Bruce Robbins, "Said and Secularism," *Edward Said and Jacques Derrida: Reconstellating Humanism and the Global Hybrid,* ed. Mina Karavantas and Nina Morgan (Cambridge: CSP, 2008), 140–157, "Secularism, Elitism, Progress, and Other Transgressions: On Edward Said's 'Voyage In,'" *Social Text* 40 (1994): 25–37, and the chapter "The East is a Career: Edward Said" in *Secular Vocations: Intellectuals, Professionalism, Culture* (London: Verso, 1993), 152–179; Colin Jager, "Romanticism/Secularization/Secularism" *Literature Compass* 5/4 (2008), 791–806; and David Damrosch, "Secular Criticism Meets the World," *Al-Ahram Weekly* 769 (November 2005): 17–23. Gil Anidjar, "Secularism," *Critical Inquiry* 33, no. 1 (Autumn 2006), 52–57; Mathieu E. Courville, *Edward Said's Rhetoric of the Secular* (New York: Continuum, 2010); finally, the superb Sydney Lectures in Philosophy and Society by Stathis Gourgouris, *Lessons in Secular Criticism* (New York: Fordham University Press, 2012) and *Edward Said's Translocations: Essays in Secular Criticism,* ed. Tobias Döring and Mark Stein (New York: Routledge, 2012), should also be consulted.

58. Actually, the men sent to explore are *tarim* (from *tur,* "to survey") in the Numbers account and *meraglim* (from *va-yeraglu,* "they spied"—correspondent with the verb *veyashperu* whose meaning Levinas focuses upon in the reading) in Moses's recapitulated narrative from Deuteronomy. The difference matters greatly since internal to the Torah, the exact moral character of their scouting mission is problematized for its readers. See Rav Elchanan Samet, "The Sin of the 'Spies,'" *The Israel Koschitzky Virtual Beit Midrash,* www.vbm-torah.org/parsha.60/37shelah.htm. I discuss the episode in both *The Fence and the Neighbor: Emmanuel Levinas, Yeshayahu Leibowitz, and Israel Among the Nations,* 159ff, and *The Elsewhere,* 14–16.

59. Simon Critchley takes particular issue with Levinas's censorious (and, one must say, rather Lithuanian-Jewish) critique of cafés in his essay, "Persecution Before Exploitation—A Non-Jewish Israel?" *Theory and Event* 3, no. 4 (2000): 30–36. In the autobiographical *John Barleycorn, or, Alcoholic Memoirs* (New York: Century, 1913), Jack London provides the counter-Levinasian perspective on the American saloon, which introduces socioeconomic and class realities Levinas entirely omits: "In the saloons life was different. Men talked with great voices, laughed great laughs, and there was an atmosphere of greatness. Here was something more than common every-day where nothing happened. . . . But in the saloons, even the sots, stupefied, sprawling across the tables or in

the sawdust, were objects of mystery and wonder. And more, the saloons were right. . . . They were not the terrible places I heard boys deem them who lacked my opportunities to know. Terrible they might be, but then that only meant they were terribly wonderful, and it is the terribly wonderful that a boy desires to know. In the same way pirates, and shipwrecks, and battles were terrible; and what healthy boy wouldn't give his immortal soul to participate in such affairs?"

60. However, Adorno's messianic strategy of "negative theology" in, for example, *Minima Moralia*, a text Said frequently cites, suggests a more nuanced possibility for this otherwise clear contrast. See, for example, Thomas Crombez and Katrien Vloeberghs, eds., *On the Outlook: Figures of the Messianic* (Cambridge: Cambridge University Press, 2007). In addition to Levinas's own essays and Talmudic readings on messianism in *Difficult Freedom, Beyond the Verse, New Talmudic Readings,* and *Nine Talmudic Readings,* see Robert Bernasconi, "Different Styles of Eschatology: Derrida's Take on Levinas' Political Messianism," in *Research in Phenomenology* 28, no. 1 (1998): 3–19; Bettina Bergo, *Levinas Between Ethics and Politics: For the Beauty That Adorns the Earth* (Dordrecht: Kluwer Publishers, 1999) and "Levinas's Weak Messianism in Time and Flesh, or The Insistence of Messiah Ben David," *Journal for Cultural Research* 13, nos. 3–4 (2009): 225–248; Jacques Derrida, "Faith and Knowledge: The Two Sources of 'Religion' and the Limits of Reason Alone," trans. Samuel Weber, in *Religion*, ed. Jacques Derrida and Gianni Vattimo (Stanford: Stanford University Press, 1998), 1–78; Martin Kavka, *Jewish Messianism and the History of Philosophy* (Cambridge: Cambridge University Press, 2004); Michael Morgan, *Discovering Levinas*; Bettina Bergo, "The Time and Language of Messianism: Levinas and Saint Paul," in *Levinas and the Ancients*, 178–195; Edith Wyschogrod, *Emmanuel Levinas: The Problem of Ethical Metaphysics*; Terence Holden, *Levinas, Messianism and Parody* (New York: Continuum, 2011). Gershom Scholem's *The Messianic Idea in Judaism and Other Essays on Jewish Spirituality* (New York: Schocken, 1995) remains an important critical source.

61. Silver as a secondary or "dependent" currency in nineteenth-century markets, as sharply brought out in an unsurpassed reading of the text by Aaron Fogel, "Silver and Silence: Dependent Currencies in *Nostromo*," in *Coercion to Speak: Conrad's Poetics of Dialogue* (Cambridge, Mass.: Harvard University Press, 1985), 94–145.

62. Compare, from "The Strings and the Wood" in *Outside the Subject*: "The Bible—a volume inhabited by a people. But also a volume that has nourished that people, almost in the literal sense of the term, like the prophet who, in Ezekiel 3, swallows a scroll. A singular digestion of celestial food" (129).

63. On Levinas's coinage of "extraterritorial," see Robert Bernasconi, "Extraterritoriality," *Lévinas Studies: An Annual Review 3* (Pittsburgh: Duquesne University Press, 2008), 61–77.

64. Benedict Anderson, *Imagined Communities: Reflections on the Origin and Spread of Nationalism* (London: Verso, 1991); Timothy Brennan, "The National Longing for Form," in *Nation and Narration*, ed. Homi Bhabha (New York: Routledge, 1990), 44–70; and Ilana Pardes, *The Biography of Ancient Israel: National Narratives in the Bible* (Berkeley: University of California Press, 2002).

65. "The State of Israel and the Religion of Israel," in *Difficult Freedom*, 217. For further elaborations on the ideological ramifications of this logic, see the excellent book by Howard Caygill, *Levinas and the Political* (London: Routledge, 2002), the chapters on secularism and state and utopia in Ze'ev Levy, *From Spinoza to Lévinas: Hermeneutical, Ethical, and Political Issues in Contemporary Jewish Philosophy* (New York: Peter Lang, 2009). and *Levinas, Law, and Politics,* ed. M. Diamantides (Routledge-Cavendish, 2007).

66. The terms here anticipate J. Hillis Miller's manifesto for criticism as stage magic and more, "The Critic as Host," *Critical Inquiry* 3, no. 3 (Spring 1977): 439–447.

67. On domains "outside" traditional study practice that call it to account for them, see the essay by Aryeh Cohen, "Why Textual Reasoning?" in *The Journal of Textual Reasoning* 1, no. 1, http://etext.virginia.edu/journals/tr/volume1/aryehTR1.html, and his book *Beginning/Again: Towards a Hermeneutics of Jewish Texts.*

3. Blaise Pascal, Henry Darger, and the Book in Hand

1. *On Longing: Narratives of the Miniature, the Gigantic, the Souvenir, the Collection* (Durham, N.C.: Duke University Press, 2003), 14.

2. Roger Chartier, *Forms and Meanings: Texts, Performances, and Audiences from Codex to Computer* (Philadelphia: University of Pennsylvania Press, 1995); Paul Saenger, *Space Between Words: The Origins of Silent Reading* (Stanford: Stanford University Press, 1997); Steven Roger Fischer, *A History of Reading* (London: Reaktion Books, 2003). See also Alberto Manguel, *A History of Reading* (New York: Viking, 1996).

3. Quoted in J. R. Cole, *Pascal: The Man and His Two Loves* (New York: New York University Press, 1995), 105.

4. Walter Benjamin, *The Origin of German Tragic Drama*, trans. John Osborne (London: Verso, 1998), 31.

5. Translation by Elizabeth T. Knuth; edited by Olivier Joseph (August 2, 1999), www .users.csbsju.edu/~eknuth/pascal.html. See also *The Memorial*, trans. A. J. Krailsheimer (London: Penguin Classics, 1966).

6. At least two specifically Judaic connections are worth mentioning in a footnote, however. First, three centuries after Pascal, Martin Buber commented on the *Mémorial*'s now-famous invocation of a God of the Patriarchs rather than of the philosophers: "Overwhelmed by faith, [Pascal] no longer knew what to do with the God of the philosophers; that is, with the God who occupies a definite position in a definite system of thought. The God of Abraham . . . is not susceptible of introduction into a system of thought precisely because He is God." *Eclipse of God: Studies in the Relation Between Religion and Philosophy* (Amherst, N.Y.: Humanity Books, 1952), 49. The same categorical move that distinguishes an Aristotelian God from the God of Abraham, Isaac, and Jacob lies also at the heart of the twelfth-century Kuzari, written by Pascal's rationalist-cum-fideist precursor Yehudah Halevi (1075–1141). Whether Pascal himself was aware of the parallel between Halevi and himself is unknown, but a Latin translation of the Kuzari,

translated and annotated by Joahannes Buxtorf, was published in Basel in 1660, four years before the composition of the *Mémorial*. Yet, the connection is explicitly drawn by none other than Levinas in his seminal essay, "God and Philosophy": "To ask, as we are trying to, whether God can be expressed in a rational discourse which would be neither ontology nor faith is implicitly to doubt the formal opposition, established by Yehouda Halevy and taken up by Pascal, between the God of Abraham, Isaac, and Jacob, invoked in faith without philosophy, and the god of the philosophers" (*Basic Philosophical Writings*, 131). On that connection, see Theodore de Boer, *The Rationality of Transcendence: Studies in the Philosophy of Emmanuel Levinas* (Leiden: Brill, 1997), and also chapter eleven in David T. Runia's, *Philo and the Church Fathers: A Collection of Papers* (Leiden: Brill, 1995), which traces a Jewish antecedent for Pascal's formulation all the back to Philo of Alexandria. That said, an interpretation of the *Mémorial* along such lines, including an account of its author as either philosopher or fideist, would already have committed itself to a reading—that is, a naturalization—of the artifact itself.

7. "Like Father, Like Clown," episode 1991, Jay Kogen and Wallace Wolodarsky, co-writers (airdate: October 24, 1991).

8. "An Essay for S. I. Witkiewicz," *Letters and Drawings of Bruno Schulz*, 113.

9. *Shadows of Ethics: Criticism and the Just Society* (Durham, N.C.: Duke University Press, 1999).

10. *Pirkei Avot/Shemoneh Perakim of the Rambam/The Thirteen Principles of Faith*, trans. R. Elihayu Touger (New York: Moznaim Publishing Corp., 1994), 74–75, and Isidore Twersky, ed., *A Maimonides Reader* (Springfield, N.J.: Behrman House, 1972), 390–394. Raymond L. Weiss's Maimonides' Ethics: The Encounter of Philosophic and Religious Morality (Chicago: University of Chicago Press, 1991), expatiates on these speech categories at length. Maimonides's attitude toward *aggadah* as a "negatively loaded intellectual exercise" (poetic conceit as a spur to reason) is discussed by Marjorie Lehman in *The En Yaaqov: Jacob ibn Habib's Search for Faith in the Talmudic Corpus* (Detroit: Wayne State University Press, 2012). See also Eliezer Segal, "Midrash and Literature: Some Medieval Views," *Prooftexts* 11, no. 1 (January 1991): 57–65.

11. Hume's formulation can be found in *Enquiries Concerning Human Understanding and Concerning the Principles of Morals*, ed. L. A. Selby-Bigge (Oxford: Clarendon Press, 1902), as adapted by Adam Smith as the "impartial spectator" in his *Theory of Moral Sentiments* (1759), and has been embedded in various works on ethics and literature by Martha Nussbaum, e.g., *Love's Knowledge: Essays on Philosophy and Literature* (New York: Oxford University Press, 1990) and *Poetic Justice: The Literary Imagination and Public Life* (Boston: Beacon Press, 1995). Nussbaum's use of the concept provides a point of departure for many subsequent critiques; see, for instance, Stow, *Republic of Readers? The Literary Turn in Political Thought and Analysis* (Albany: State University of New York Press, 2007). In *The Sovereignty of Good* (London: Routledge and Kegan Paul, 1970), Iris Murdoch develops the concept of "attention" (borrowed from Simone Weil and only superficially similar to Nussbaum's formulation) "to express the idea of a just and loving gaze directed upon an individual reality" as "the characteristic and proper mark of the

active moral agent" (34). All these various models (Nussbaum's, Murdoch's, even Maimonides's) might also be referred to the current state of ethical theory, most recently exemplified by the carefully constructed argument of pragmatic naturalism in Philip Kitcher, *The Ethical Project* (Cambridge, Mass.: Harvard University Press, 2011) and contrasted with a very different ethic of attention as sketched by Richard Rorty in his *Contingency, Irony, and Solidarity* (Cambridge: Cambridge University Press, 1989), 141–168.

12. Other biographical treatments of Pascal that discuss the *Mémorial* include Jean Mesnard, "La maison où Pascal écrivit le 'Mémorial'," *Revue d'Histoire littéraire de la France* 55, no. 1 (January–March 1955): 51–55; Marvin Richard O'Connell, *Blaise Pascal: Reasons of the Heart* (Grand Rapids, Mich.: Eerdmans, 1997) and Ben Rogers, "Pascal's Life and Times," *The Cambridge Companion to Pascal*, ed. Nicholas Hammond (Cambridge: Cambridge University Press, 2003), 4–19. Theologian Jean-Luc Marion uses Pascal's text as his point of departure in "Metaphysics and Phenomenology: A Relief for Theology," trans. Thomas A. Carlson, *Critical Inquiry* 20, no. 4 (Summer 1994): 572–591; but perhaps the definitive study in French belongs to Henri Gouhier's theological critique, "Le mémorial est-il un texte mystique?" reprinted in his *Blaise Pascal: Commentaires* (Paris: J. Vrin, 1984), 48–57, and briefly discussed by Leszek Kolakowski in *God Owes Us Nothing: A Brief Remark on Pascal's Religion and on the Spirit* (Chicago: University of Chicago Press, 1995).

13. "Corpus Epochalis: Mysticism, Body, History," in *Surfaces* 1 (1991): 4–34. "To many," Mihaliescu observes pointedly, "this seemed to be the most un-Pascalian of his writings, an apparently ruleless combination of French sentences lacking verbs, Latin inserts, abundant in unwritten exclamation marks, breaking the bonds of syntax; in all, an unstructured chain of words praising God and exhibiting both the frenzied happiness of an accomplished union with the absolute and the despair of being separated from God" (7–8). In *Thinking about God in an Age of Technology* (Oxford: Oxford University Press, 2005), George Pattison foregrounds the text's "syntactical inadequacy" (137) as an interpretive crux for recognizing "the depth of our own responsibility in, so to speak, supplying the missing the grammar that makes sense it. . . . The interpretation of the text becomes self-interrogation, driving us to reflect on what we ourselves really think it would be to experience 'FIRE,' if 'experience' is indeed the matter of the Memorial" (137). Whether it is or not, obviously, my concern with "the matter of the *Mémorial*" goes to the finding of it in the first place, and the handling that ensues.

14. The Condorcet reference is recorded by Robert J Nelson in *Pascal: Adversary and Advocate* (Cambridge, Mass.: Harvard University Press, 1982), 119. On the *Orígenes* poets, see, for instance, Lezama Lima's 1956 essay "Pascal y la Poesía," *Obras Completas: Tratados en La Habana. Ensayos* (Havana: Editorial Letras Cubanas, 2009), 563–565, in which he writes, memorably, "Hay inclusive como la obligación de devolver la naturaleza perdida. De fabricar naturaleza, no de recibirla como algo dado. 'Corno la verdadera naturaleza se ha perdido—dice Pascal—todo puede ser naturaleza'" (564).

15. All these terms are taken from Derrida's essay, "The Double Session," from *Dissemination*, trans. Barbara Johnson (Chicago: University of Chicago Press, 1981), 187–316. "Fold" is also a central concept in Gilles Deleuze's book on Gottfried Wilhelm von Leibniz (who, among other accomplishments, improved upon Pascal's mechanical calculator, the pascaline), *The Fold: Leibnitz and the Baroque*, trans. Tom Conley (Minneapolis: University of Minnesota Press, 1992).

16. *Other Inquisitions: 1937–1952* (Austin: University of Texas Press, 2000), 9.

17. Paul Auster, *The Red Notebook: True Stories* (New York: New Directions, 2002).

18. Stephen Fredman, "'How to Get Out of the Room That Is the Book?' Paul Auster and the Consequences of Confinement," *Postmodern Culture* 6, no. 3 (May 1996).

19. See, for example, Tim Kendall "'Joy, Fire, Joy': Blaise Pascal's 'Memorial' and the Visionary Explorations of T. S. Eliot, Aldous Huxley and William Golding," *Literature and Theology* 11, no. 3 (1997): 299–212.

20. Pascal and Levinas have been discussed together in John McDade, SJ., "Divine Disclosure and Concealment in Bach, Pascal and Levinas," *New Blackfriars* 85 (2004): 121–132. The Latin proverb is cited by Levinas in the preface to *Totality and Infinity* and by Benjamin in his essay "Unpacking my Library."

21. W. J. T. Mitchell, *What Do Pictures Want? The Lives and Loves of Images* (Chicago: University of Chicago Press, 2005), 104. By contrast, I would offer Marianne Hirsch's ten-page decoding in *The Generation of Postmemory* (187–199) of the "testimonial object" bequeathed to a survivor of the Vapniarka concentration camp, a small book of woodcuts and drawings to be cradled "in the palm of a hand" and read "with an insistent gaze," its miniature size almost an calculated goad to painstaking exegesis. Pascal's found text makes no such intentional claim on either hand or eye.

22. *Henry Darger's Room*, with photographs by Kiyoko Lerner, Nathan Lerner, and David Berglund (Tokyo: Imperial Press [2007]). The room has also been recreated in an installation at Studio Chicago, http://studiochicago.blogspot.com/2010/05/henry-darger-room-collection.html, and also the account by Darby Penney and Peter Stastny of salvaged belongings known as "the Willard suitcases" in *The Lives They Left Behind: Suitcases from a State Hospital Attic* (New York: Bellevue Literary Press, 2009), as well as the online exhibit devoted to them, http://www.suitcaseexhibit.org/indexhasflash.html.

23. The work seems to have been begun in 1909 and took eleven years to write out in longhand before being transferred to typescript, beginning in 1912. The actual loss of a 1911 newspaper clipping-photo of Elsie Paroubek, a kidnapped and murdered girl, was transposed by Darger into the plot-engine for the entire fiction, in the form of the "Annie Aronburg Mystery."

24. His name was William Schloeder, and according to Darger's memoir, their friendship lasted fifty years until Schloeder's death in 1969. Like aliases of Darger himself, he makes appearances as a character in the writings. In *History of My* Life, Darger describes the loss: "When in San Antonio three years my friend Whillie died on the 5 of May. (I forgot the year) of the Asian Flu and since that happened I am all alone.

I never palled with anyone since. Where I worked I could not get off to go to his funeral" (125–126). In *Not Even Wrong: Adventures in Autism* (New York: Bloomsbury, 2004), Paul Collins maintains that Darger, along with assemblage artist Joseph Cornell and possibly Schloeder too, were autistic.

25. *Henry Darger: In the Realms of the Unreal* (New York: Delano Greenidge Editions, 2002). A shorter, more analytically nuanced, and less totalizing study of Darger's art and writing is the dissertation by Leisa Rundquist, "Pyre: A Poetics of Fire and Childhood in the Art of Henry Darger," Ph.D. diss., University of North Carolina, 2007. Michael Moon's somewhat misleadingly titled *Darger's Resources* (Durham, N.C.: Duke University Press, 2012) embeds him in the discursive company of Agamben and Aby Warburg on twentieth-century mass culture and the tradition of Arcadian romance. Darger is the subject of a long poem by John Ashberry, a popular song by Natalie Merchant, documentary films by Jessica Yu (2004) and Mark Stokes (2012), and numerous websites, blogs, online articles, and gallery showings.

26. *The Human Province*, trans. Joachim Neugroschel (New York: Seabury Press, 1978), 70.

27. Derrida is referring to Yerushalmi's book *Freud's Moses: Judaism Terminable and Interminable* (New Haven: Yale University Press, 1993).

28. Of course, this is a vexed question, and certainly, an argument can be made that Darger's writing (if not his art) was implicitly addressed to an audience outside it. Even if we grant that possibility, his recorded remarks while he lay dying in the hospital suggest no interest in having his work enter public space.

29. *Henry Darger: Art and Selected Writings* (New York: Rizzoli, 2001). See also Brooke Davis Anderson, *The Henry Darger Collection at the American Folk Art Museum* (New York: American Folk Art Museum, 2001); Klaus Biesenbach, *Henry Darger* (New York: Prestel Verlag, 2009), including essays by Anderson, Bonesteel, and Carl Watson; John D'Agata, "Collage History of Art, by Henry Darger," in *Halls of Fame: Essays* (Minneapolis: Graywolf Press, 2005), 159–168; the two book reviews in *Intuit Outside* Magazine: www.interestingideas.com/out/darger.htm and www.interestingideas.com/out/darger2.htm; Nathaniel Rich, "Storm of Creativity," *The New Republic*, January 5, 2005; and Leo Segedin, "Henry Darger: The Inside Of An Outsider," (January 11, 2006), www.leopoldsegedin.com/essay_detail_darger.cfm.

30. A second instance of uncanny repetition: at the end of MacGregor's book, in its careful appendix, "On the Problem of Diagnosis," Darger is briefly compared with the case of Daniel Paul Schreber, whose own permeable boundaries between life and fiction (the famous "fleetingly-improvised men" that so captivated Freud and Jung), had already occurred to me in connection with Darger.

31. Moon's book is indebted to the chapter on Darger in Saitō Tamaki's *Sentō bishō jo no seishin bunseki* (Tokyo: Ōta shuppan, 2000) on the Japanese tradition of the "otaku," translated by J. Keith Vincent and Dawn Lawson as *Beautiful Fighting Girl* (Minneapolis: University of Minnesota Press, 2011). Something like companion volumes to Moon's book, Jim Elledge's *Henry Darger, Throw-Away Boy: The Tragic Life of an Outsider Artist*

(New York: Overlook Press, 2013) recuperates Darger's biography for queer history, while *H* (Maple Shade, N.J.: Lethe Press, 2012) retells that recuperated life through a series of alphabetically arranged prose poems.

32. An article by Ed Park in the *Village Voice* (April 16, 2002) about MacGregor's controversial specialization in Darger's life and work, "The Outsiders: John MacGregor Unlocks Henry Darger's Unreal Realms," is worth consulting in this respect.

33. *Other Inquisitions*, 46.

34. For Shields and Loftus, see the obituary by Douglas Martin, "Robert Shields, Wordy Diarist, Dies at 89," *New York Times*, October 29, 2007. For Inman, see *The Inman Diary: A Public and Private Confession*, vols. 1–2, ed. Daniel Aaron (Cambridge, Mass.: Harvard University Press, 1985).

35. *The Singularity of Literature* (New York: Routledge), 2009, 109. Attridge's premise is roundly critiqued by Franco Moretti, who writes, "the trouble with close reading (in all its incarnations, from the new criticism to deconstruction) is that it necessarily depends on an extremely small canon. . . . You invest so much in individual texts only if you think that very few of them really matter" (54) "Conjectures on World Literature," *New Left Review* 1 (January–February 2000): 54–68. However, the investment, as Attridge outlines it, would seem to lie more in the reading than in the individual text. If reading is unpredictable, then it is also uncanny. And if it is uncanny, then close and distant, like Freud's famous interlacing of familiar and unfamiliar, fold in upon each other as the modality of "being in the world of words." Attridge's platform might also be compared to the issue of *Representations* 108, no. 1 (Fall 2009), "The Way We Read Now," in particular, the introductory essay by Stephen Best and Sharon Marcus, "Surface Reading: An Introduction," 1–21. That essay, in turn, has been subtly analyzed by Ellen Rooney with reference to Louis Althusser's notion of reading as guilty practice in "Live Free or Describe: The Reading Effect and the Persistence of Form," *differences* 21, no. 3 (2010): 112–139.

36. *Middlemarch* (New York: Penguin, 2003), 264. The metaphor has become a critical commonplace, but J. Hillis Miller's essay, "Optic and Semiotic in Middlemarch," in *The Worlds of Victorian Fiction*, ed. Jerome H. Buckley (Cambridge, Mass.: Harvard University Press, 1975), 125–145, captures its peculiar quality of reversibility. See also Miller's more recent *Reading for Our Time: Adam Bede and Middlemarch Revisited* (Edinburgh: Edinburgh University Press, 2012) and Matthew Beaumont, "Aleatory Realism: Reflections on the Parable of the Pier-Glass," *Synthesis* 3 (Winter 2011): 11–21.

37. *Lectures on Literature* (New York: Harcourt Brace Jovanovich, 1980), 373–374. Nabokov's essay, "Literature and Commonsense" forms the nodal point of the chapter "The Barber of Kasbeam: Nabokov on Cruelty" in the Rorty volume cited previously.

38. "Every work of art is an uncommitted crime." *Minima Moralia*, 111.

39. *The Human Province*, 23. Compare the following passage from Italo Calvino's *Mr. Palomar*, trans. William Weaver (New York: Harcourt, Brace & Company, 1985): A person's life consists of a collection of events, the last of which could also change the meaning of the whole, not because it counts more than the previous ones but because

once they are included in a life, events are arranged in an order that is not chronological but, rather, corresponds to an inner architecture. A person, for example, reads in adulthood a book that is important for him, and it makes him say, 'How could I have lived without having read it!,' and also, 'What a pity I did not read it in my youth!' Well, these statements do not have much meaning, especially the second, because after he has read that book, his whole life becomes the life of a person who has read that book, and it is of little importance whether he read it early or late, because now his life before that reading also assumes a form shaped by that reading" (124).

40. For example, Wayne Booth, *The Company We Keep: An Ethics of Fiction* (Berkeley: University of California Press, 1989).

41. Compare Susan Stewart on the miniature book as talisman in *On Longing*: "The social space of the miniature book might be seen as the social space, in miniature, of all books: the book as talisman to the body and emblem of the self; the book as microcosm and macrocosm; the book as commodity and knowledge, fact and fiction" (41).

42. As their website expresses its mandate, "The Yiddish Book Center works to rescue Yiddish and other modern Jewish books and open up their content to the world. . . . Originally, scholars estimated there were 70,000 Yiddish books extant and recoverable. The Center saved that number in six months and has gone on to recover one million volumes; the achievement has been hailed as the 'the greatest cultural rescue effort in Jewish history,'" www.yiddishbookcenter.org.

43. Halpern's poem is translated and discussed in Benjamin Harshav, *The Meaning of Yiddish* (Berkeley: University or California Press, 1990), 45–46.

44. For a contrary perspective on the possible cultural imperialism that may color the ethics of recovery and retrieval at the Yiddish Book Center, see Rosa Perelmuter, "Yiddish in Cuba: A Love Story," *Hispanófila: Ensayos de Literatura* 157 (2009): 117–132. On the account eventually published in Aaron Lanksy, *Outwitting History: The Amazing Adventures of a Man Who Rescued a Million Yiddish Books* (Chapel Hill, N.C.: Algonquin Books, 2005), 235–40) that proudly relates the export-recue mission of hundreds of books from the library in Havana's Patronato to Massachusetts, Perelmuter thus remarks, "As I finished reading . . . this triumphant veni, vidi, vici left me with an overwhelming sense of embarrassment (Columbus? Caesar? Ugly American? take your pick) and sadness for what I felt was the end of an important connection." As Lansky himself sums up his deed of reclamation—although much of the library seems to have gone missing when Castro "confiscated Havana's Zionist Center and turned it over to the local Arab league" (237)—"within a month of our return every one of Cuba's known Yiddish books was safe and sound in Amherst, ready to be digitized and shared with the world" (240).

45. That "original" home of ownership is a conceit I revisit in the epilogue when I look at the poem, "Before the Bookcase," by Ḥayyim Nakhman Bialik. As Barbara Mann has indicated, that poem should also be compared with Osip Mandelstam's pungent reminiscence about "the bookcase of early childhood" in *The Noise of Time: Selected Prose*, trans. Clarence Brown (Evanston, Ill.: Northwestern University Press, 2002), 78–79.

46. See also "Offending Images" in Mitchell, *What Do Pictures Want?*, 125–144, Anthony Julius, *Transgressions: The Offenses of Art* (London: Thames and Hudson, 2002), and the various examples of demediated bookwork in the chapter, "Politics and the Bibliojet" in Garrett Stewart, *Bookwork: Medium to Object to Concept to Art* (Chicago: University of Chicago Press, 2011), 184–217.

47. See Leah Price's *How to Do Things With Books in Victorian Britain* and *Unpacking My Library: Writers and Their Books* (New Haven: Yale University Press, 2011); and also Jason Allen Snart, *The Torn Book: Unreading William Blake's Marginalia* (Cranbury, N.J.: Rosemont Publishing, 2006). In a recent interview in NPR Books, Price observes, "'Among all the gifts of the electronic age, one of the most paradoxical might be to illuminate something we are beginning to trade away: the particular history, visible and invisible, that can be passed down through the vessel of an old book, inscribed by the hands and the minds of readers who are gone," www.npr.org/2012/06/21/155360197/will -your-children-inherit-your-e-books. Snart quotes Barthes's *S/Z*: "the work of commentary . . . consists precisely in manhandling the text, interrupting it." Obviously, this history of affect corresponds to the history of the book as artifact. Stephen Greenblatt's *The Swerve: How the World Became Modern* (New York: Norton, 2011) provides a prehistory of these considerations in detailed accounts of the production of papyri in antiquity and codices in the Middle Ages, and Peter Stallybrass's "Books and Scrolls: Navigating the Bible," in *Books and Readers in Early Modern England: Material Studies*, ed. Jennifer Andersen and Elizabeth Sauer (Philadelphia: University of Pennsylvania Press, 2004), 42–79, considers rival early modern reading technologies through which "the manuscript book or codex emerged . . . as an alternative to, and sometimes in antagonistic relation to the scroll" (46).

48. Friedman's work can be seen on the cover of Jonathan Boyarin's *The Unconverted Self: Jews, Indians, and the Identity of Christian Europe* (Chicago: University of Chicago Press, 2010). James Wood, "Shelf Life," *The New Yorker*, November 7, 2011.

49. See also Hans Belting, *Likeness and Presence: A History of the Image Before the Era of Art* (Chicago: University of Chicago Press, 1994); Garret Stewart, *The Look of Reading: Book, Painting, Text* (Chicago: University of Chicago Press, 2006); "The Book as Material Instrument: London Literary Publishing, 1885–1900," by Kenneth Clay Smith, Ph.D. diss., Indiana University, 2006; *Cultural Artifacts and the Production of Meaning: The Page, the Image, and the Body*, ed. Margaret J. M. Ezell, Katherine O'Brien O'Keefe (Ann Arbor: University of Michigan Press, 1994); and the chapters, "On Description and the Book" and "The Miniature" in Susan Stewart, *On Longing*.

50. On the sensibility of objects, compare this well-known Rashi gloss on the Torah verse Exodus 20:23, And you shall not go up by steps upon My altar, that you may exposes your nakedness upon it: "Now these matters are an a fortiori conclusion that if [concerning] these stones that have no sense (feeling) to be particular about being shamed, the Torah said that because they are necessary, you shall not behave toward them in a humiliating manner. [In contrast,] your friend, who is made in the image of your Creator and who does object to being humiliated, how much more

must you be careful not to embarrass him" [from *Mechilta* and also discussed in Tractate *bNazir* 45a].

51. Sources: Tractates *b'Eruvin* 97b, *bMenaḥot* 32a, *bMegillah* 26b-27a; *Mishneh Torah* vol. 7 (12 CE), *'Shulḥan Arukh, Beit Yosef,* and *Ha-Mapah* (16 CE), *Ginzei HaQodesh* (20 CE), *Mishnah Berurah* (20 CE), *Arukh ha-Shulḥan* (19 CE), *Igrot Moshe* (20 CE), *Ḥazon Ish* (20 CE), *Ḥelkat Yaakov* (20 CE). A comprehensive guide (in Hebrew) can be found in Yeḥezkel Fainhandler, *Ginze ha-ḳodesh 'al hilkhot genizah u-khevod sefarim* (Laws of Respect and Reverence for Religious Books and Articles) (Jerusalem: Agudat Genizah Kelalit, 2002). *SFR*, the trilateral root for "book," underlies related words that connote "narrating, counting, writing and sending a message." In *An Exalted Evening: The Seder Night* (New York: Ktav, 2009), R. Joseph B. Soloveitchik identifies permanency or the capacity to endure transgnerationally as the distinguishing characteristic of a *sefer*. Compare Leah Price's related observation that "like religious relics, books link us not just to an author but to those who have touched them before" (How to Do Things With Books, 15) and Ilana M. Blumberg's observations about the respect due to holy books in *Jewish Law in Houses of Study: A Jewish Woman Among Books* (Lincoln: University of Nebraska Press, 2007), 75–76. Finally, see the two essays, "The Sacred Book" by Carl Olson (11–23), "The Book as Symbol" (63–65) by Brian Cummings in *The Oxford Companion to the Book*, ed. Michael F. Suarez and H.R. Woudhuysen (Oxford: Oxford University Press, 2010).

52. See, on this subject, part one of Leah Price's *How to Do Things With Books*.

53. *Selected Writings: 1931–1934*, vol. 2, part 2, 487, 492. In his update of Benjamin's essay, "Unpacking My Library Again," *Journal of the Midwest Modern Language Association* 28, no. 1 "Identities" (Spring 1995): 5–18, Homi Bhabha outlines a "contingent dis-ordered historical 'dwelling'" in the anti-systematic collecting of books that embodies what he calls a vernacular, "revisionary cosmopolitanism" (5).

54. See in this connection Benjamin's essay, "Old Forgotten Children's Books," *Selected Writings: 1913–1926*, 1:406–413, and Laurence Roth's trenchant twist on Benjamin, "Unpacking My Father's Bookstore," in *Modern Jewish Literatures: Intersections and Boundaries*, ed. Sheila E. Jelen, Michael P. Kramer, and L. Scott Lerner (Philadelphia: University of Pennsylvania Press, 2011), 280–302. Finally, the phenomenon of inside-the-book talismans in Jewish or Jewish-owned books is recorded by Michael Popek in *Forgotten Bookmarks: A Bookseller's Collection of Odd Things Lost Between the Pages* (New York: Perigee Books, 2011), as is the "privileged, elevating function" of the *ex libris* in Zbigniew Maszewski, "Bianca Looks from above the Book: Readings on the Margin of Bruno Schulz's Ex-Libris for Stanisław Weingarten," *Text Matters* 2, no. 2 (2012): 130–143.

55. The question of the political for object-relations is developed by Langdon Winner in the chapter, "Do Artifacts Have Politics?" in *The Whale and the Reactor: A Search for Limits in an Age of High Technology* (Chicago: University of Chicago Press, 1986), 19–39. See also Garret Stewart's Bookwork and Michael Taussig's Benjamin-inspired discussion of "image politics" in the chapters, "The Talking Machine" and "His Master's Voice," in *Mimesis and Alterity*, 193–235.

56. In the second letter, Kafka was more explicit: "Of all my writings, only the books are worthwhile [*gelten*]: Judgment, Stroker, Metamorphosis, Penal Colony, Country Doctor, and a story: 'Hunger Artist' [which included 'First Sorrow,' 'A Little Woman,' and 'Josephine the Singer, or the Mouse Folk']. (The few copies of Meditations can stay, I don't want to put anyone to the trouble of pulping them, but nothing from that book is to be reprinted.)" The testament and its aftermath are also the subject of Rodger Kamenetz, *Burnt Books: Rabbi Nachman of Bratslav and Franz Kafka* (New York: Schocken, 2010), 59–66 and 108–113.

57. The estate remained in probate until October 2012 when a ruling by the Tel Aviv Family Court favored the National Library of Israel as the proper home for the portfolio of Kafka manuscripts, which will be scanned and made available to the public online. See the articles by Elif Batuman, "Kafka's Last Trial," *New York Times Magazine*, September 22, 2010, and Judith Butler, "Who Owns Kafka?" *London Review of Books* 33, no. 5 (March 3, 2011): 3–8, and the particularly acute essay about the materiality of Kafka's writing for an ethics of reading, C. Namwali Serpell, "Of Being Bridge," *The Comparatist* 36 (May 2012): 4–23.

58. Compare the similar *midrash* of the *yeshivah shel ma'ala* (the Heavenly Academy) in *bBava Metzia* 86a. Of the many critical accounts of "Akhnai's Oven," see the literary text analyses in Daniel Boyarin, "Old Wine in New Bottles: Intertextuality and Midrash," *Poetics Today* 8, nos. 3–4 (1987): 539–556, Rubenstein's *Talmudic Stories*, 34–63, and Nachman Levine, "'The Oven of Achnai' Re-Deconstructed," *Hebrew Studies* (November 2004): 1–11; the theological approaches in David Hartman, *A Living Covenant: The Innovative Spirit in Traditional Judaism* (New York: Jewish Lights Publications, 1998), 33–36, and Eliezer Berkovits, *Not in Heaven: The Nature and Function of Halakhah* (New York, 1983): the legal and rhetorical models by Daniel J. H. Greenwood, "Akhnai: Legal Responsibility in the World of the Silent God," *Utah Law Review* (1997): 309–358, and David A. Frank, "Arguing with God, Talmudic Discourse, and the Jewish Countermodel: Implications for the Study of Argumentation," *Argumentation and Advocacy* 41 (Fall 2004): 71–86; and finally the historical study by Jacob Neusner, *Eliezer ben Hyrcanus: The Tradition and the Man* (Leiden: Brill, 1973), 2:206, 284.

59. *The Practice of Everyday Life*, trans. Steven Rendall (Berkeley: University of California Press, 1984), 44.

60. *The Textual Condition* (Princeton: Princeton University Press, 1991), 3. "Twilight half-entity" is a phrase coined by W. V. Quine to describe to hard-to-locate mathematical abstractions "to which the identity concept is not to apply," and applied to the status of literary objects by Wai Chee Dimock in "A Theory of Resonance," 1064.

61. See René Wellek and Austin Warren *Theory Of Literature: New Revised Edition* (New York: Harcourt Brace, 1984), 174.

62. For example, "The issue is not just how perception may make the images alive, but rather the kinds of response that follow on the perception of the image as lifelike" (159).

63. Lytle Shaw, "The Moral Storm," *Cabinet Magazine* 3 (Summer 2001), www. cabinet magazine.org/issues/3/henrydarger.php. See also by Cal Watson, "The Metaphysics of

Wreckage: An Introduction to the Autobiography of Henry Darger," in the Biesenbach volume, 277–281, and "Recollecting Turbulence: Catastrophe and Sacrifice in the 'History of My Life' by Henry Darger," Ph.D. diss., CUNY, 2012.

64. He quotes from Roland Barthes's essay in *Sade, Fourier, Loyola* (Baltimore: Johns Hopkins University Press, 1997): "The immediate force of this desire [in the *Spiritual Exercises*] is to be read in the very materiality of the objects whose representation Ignatius calls for: places in their precise, complete dimensions, characters in their costumes, their attitudes, their actions, their actual words" (62).

65. Since the various interviews Levinas gave in his lifetime are less challenging to nonspecialized readers than his philosophical writings, in addition to the already cited, volume, *Is It Righteous to Be?*, see the interviews collected in Michaël de Saint-Cheron, *Conversations with Emmanuel Lévinas, 1983–1994* (Pittsburgh: Duquesne University Press 2010).

66. As a "formulation of revolutionary demands in the politics of art," this essay shares with several others by Benjamin from the late 1930s, i.e., "Edward Fuchs: Collector and Historian" (1937), "On Some Motifs in Baudelaire" (1939), and "The Storyteller," a direct connection between aura and evanescence. See *Selected Writings, Volume Three 1935–1938* and *Selected Writings, Volume Four 1938–1940*, trans. Marcus Paul Bullock and Michael William Jennings (Cambridge, Mass.: Harvard University Press, 2002–2003). For instructive treatments of Benjamin's concept, see Carolin Duttlinger, "Imaginary Encounters: Walter Benjamin and the Aura of Photography," *Poetics Today* 29, no. 1 (2008): 79–101; Miriam Bratu Hansen, "Benjamin's Aura," *Critical Inquiry* 34 (Winter 2008): 336–375; Joel Snyder, "Benjamin on Reproducibility and Aura: A Reading of 'The Work of Art in the Age of Its Technical Reproducibility," in *Benjamin: Philosophy, Aesthetics, History*, ed. Gary Smith (Chicago: University of Chicago Press, 1989), 158–174; Samuel Weber, "Mass Mediauras, or: Art, Aura and Media in the Work of Walter Benjamin," in *Mass Mediauras: Form, Technics, Media*, ed. Samuel Weber and Alan Cholodenko (Stanford: Stanford University Press, 1996), 75–207; and Richard Wolin, *Walter Benjamin: An Aesthetic of Redemption* (Berkeley: University of California Press, 1994).

67. In "A Short History of Photography" and "On Some Motifs in Baudelaire," aura is assigned a certain mediating or reciprocal quality, a returned gaze by which objects (or humans) look back at us. It is a concept also deeply, if ambivalently, connected with tradition, for "the aura of the object thus harbors and guarantees the transmissibility of its history" (7), as John McCole shows in *Walter Benjamin and the Antinomies of Tradition* (Ithaca, N.Y.: Cornell University Press, 1993).

68. Contrast here two formulations by Stephen Greenblatt, first, the notion of "resonance" in respect to museum art: "wounded artifacts may be compelling not only as witnesses to the violence of history but also as signs of use, marks of the human touch, and thus links to the openness of touch that was the condition of their creation" ("Resonance and Wonder," 44). Second, a displaced (or hollowed) version of aura— specifically, early Protestant holy books like Tyndale's *Obedience of a Christian Man* from

1527, whose distinguishing features are a certain "abstractness" and "absoluteness" on account of their increased distance from the intimacies of medieval manuals of confession, palpably marked as they are by a scribal hand and other personalizing indices of "ritualized verbal transaction" (86). See "The Word of God in the Age of Mechanical Reproduction," in *Renaissance Self-Fashioning: From More to Shakespeare* (Chicago: University of Chicago Press, 1980), 74–114.

69. For medieval Christian parallels, see Vincent Gillespie, *Looking in Holy Books: Essays on Late Medieval Religious Writing in England* (Turnhout: Brepols Publishers, 2012), and Caroline Walker Bynum, *Christian Materiality: An Essay on Religion in Late Medieval Europe* (Cambridge, Mass.: Zone Books, 2011).

70. *The Letters of Gustave Flaubert: 1857–1880*, trans. Francis Steegmuller (Cambridge, Mass.: Harvard University Press, 1980), 194.

71. Compare Levinas in "Contempt for Torah as Idolatry": "To base one's Jewishness on the teaching of a book is to see oneself above all as a reader, i.e., as a student of Torah" (*In the Time of Nations*, 59). This passage is treated by Robert Gibbs in "The Disincarnation of the Word: The Trace of God in Reading Scripture," in *The Exorbitant: Emmanuel Levinas Between Jews and Christians*, ed. Kevin Hart and Michael A. Signer (New York: Fordham University Press, 2010), 41. Compare also, from a notably different context, *jews and words* by Amos Oz and Fania Oz-Salzberger (New Haven: Yale University Press, 2012): "In Jewish tradition, every reader is a proof reader" (x).

72. The term belongs to Michael Fried, as developed in *Realism, Writing, Disfiguration: On Thomas Eakins and Stephen Crane* (Chicago: University of Chicago Press, 1987) and "Almayer's Face: On 'Impressionism' in Conrad, Crane, and Norris," *Critical Inquiry* 17, no. 1 (Autumn 1990): 193–236.

73. *Camera Lucida: Notes on Photography*, trans. Richard Howard (New York, 1981), 26–27. Barthes's book has acquired a wealth of commentary. I cite, in particular, Margaret Olin, "Touching Photographs: Roland Barthes's 'Mistaken' Identification," *Representations* 80 (Fall 2002): 99–118, in part, because of the double valence of touching, i.e., "The photograph, then, is a trace, a remnant, of the person who was there. The trace is tactile, like a footprint" (100); in part, because of its close attention to the question of viewers' perceptual slippage and capacity for displacement, the fact "that not only do we misidentify [people and things], we misidentify with them" (114). Such a risk, certainly, attaches itself to the circulation of Darger's and Pascal's texts through an economy of reception.

74. Sebald's poetics of the photographic image both extends and puts delicate pressure on Barthes's formulation by merging the personal with the historico-cultural, as can be seen in Austerlitz, for example, where the protagonist's pursuit for an image of his lost mother echoes Barthes's own search in *Camera Lucida*. See Lise Patt, ed., *Searching for Sebald: Photography after W. G. Sebald* (Los Angeles: Institute of Cultural Inquiry Press, 2007) and Jonathan James Long, *W. G. Sebald: Image, Archive, Modernity*. Also pertinent in this connection are Marianne Hirsch's volumes on "postmemory," Michael Fried's *Courbet's Realism* (Chicago: University of Chicago Press, 1997), and the chapters "Melancholy Objects" and "The Image World" in Susan Sontag's *On Photography* (New York:

Farrar, Straus and Giroux, 1977), 51–84 and 153–182. Finally, compare this observation—so different from Nussbaum's Humean paradigm of "judicious
spectatorship"—by Janet Malcolm about the German photographer couple Hilla and
Bernd Becher in "Depth of Field: Thomas Struth's Way of Seeing," *The New Yorker*,
September 26, 2011: "The Bechers' precise looking was a model of ethical rigor" (99).

75. Actually, it is more accurate to say that Levinas works with two, competing
definitions of "participation," one more negatively tinged the other Platonic and positive.
See Philip Lawton, "Levinas' Notion of the 'There is,'" in *Emmanuel Levinas: Critical
Assessments of Leading Philosophers*, ed. Claire Katz (New York: Routledge, 2004),
249–159, and Francisco J. Gonzalez, "Levinas Questioning Plato on Eros and Maieutics,"
in *Levinas and the Ancients*, 40–61.

4. Ethics of Reading I: Levinas and the Talmud

1. "Declining Decline," in *This New Yet Unapproachable America: Lectures after
Emerson after Wittgenstein* (Albuquerque: Living Batch Press, 1989), 35.

2. "Family Resemblances: Ludwig Wittgenstein as a Jewish Philosopher," *Bamidbar:
Journal for Jewish Thought and Philosophy* 1 (2012): 88. In that same issue, also see the
introduction (8–11) by Agata Bielik-Robson, along with her essay "The Promise of the
Name: 'Jewish Nominalism' as the Critique of Idealist Tradition," 12–35.

3. Translated by Seán Hand (Baltimore: Johns Hopkins University Press, 1997),
the volume has been discussed as a whole by Michael F. Bernard-Donals, "'Difficult
Freedom': Levinas, Language, and Politics," *Diacritics* 35, no. 3 (Fall 2005): 62–77; Seán
Hand, "Taking Liberties: Re-situating *Difficile liberté*," *Modern Judaism* 31, no. 1 (2011):
1–22; and Jill Robbins, "An Inscribed Responsibility: Levinas's *Difficult Freedom*,"
Modern Language Notes 106 (1991): 1052–1062. "Readings of Difficult Freedom, "a
conference organized by SIREL (Société Internationale de Recherche Emmanuel
Levinas) in Toulouse in 2010, was devoted entirely to this book.

4. Almost all readings isolate "Name of a Dog" from the larger work encompassing it.
Thus, while it is true that "this brief, rich, playful, moving text" (Derrida's description)
was published separately in 1975 in the company of essays by Beckett, Blanchot, Starobinski, and others in the homage to artist Bram van Velde, *Celui qui nepeut se servir de
mots: à Bram Van Velde* (He Who Cannot Use Words) (Paris: Éditions Fata Morgana,
1975), it takes up space in *Difficult Freedom* in the immediate company of two pieces on
either side, "The Struthof Case," from 1954 and "The Virtues of Patience" from 1963, with
which it shares a number of themes in common. Linking the three consecutive essays—
the judgment of history, the ability to wait and suffer, captivity and human freedom,
natural rights, Jewish singularity—they attest, I would like to think, to Levinas's care in
grouping and ordering the seven sections and forty-seven separate essays that comprise
the later editions of *Difficult Freedom*. Indeed, in its composite structure and thematic
citations from the Torah and allusions to rabbinic commentary, its recollection of the
Shoah that is at once personalized and historical, its concerns with human community in
the face of mass identity and anti-Semitism as the archetype of all internment, its

governing trope of witness as "the debt that is always open": in these respects, "Name of a Dog" is almost paradigmatic for the entire book, and really deserves a deeper contextualization that most critics have given it.

5. In "Hitchcock's Hidden Pictures," *Critical Inquiry* 37, no. 1 (Autumn 2010): 106–130, D. A. Miller explains a readerly disposition he dubs "Too Close Reading," not aimed at a comprehensive interpretation but rather "drawn to details that, while undeniably intricate, are not noticeably important—little particulars that, though demonstrably meant, never strike us as deeply meaningful[;] it does not 'illuminate' the text, but only brings out its shadowy and even shady quality" (126). At the same time, it has the capacity to get "too close" to a text, and "it is through consenting to this undue intimacy, with its blurred boundaries and invaded spaces, that Too Close Reading acquires its weird psychic density" (127). *Difficult Freedom*, of course, doesn't invite such undue intimacy *as a text*; but "Name of a Dog" and the epigraph to "Signature"—expressly when harmonized—seem to *read out* both blurred boundaries and invaded spaces that unexpectedly catch our attention, attaching us to them.

6. This is the burden of Will Buckingham's *Levinas, Storytelling and Anti-Storytelling*, the title's last element signifying how Levinas "tries to undo the telling of stories" (2). Buckingham's book focuses solely on *Totality and Infinity* and *Otherwise Than Being*, the manifest loss being any philosophical attention to the plethora of *aggadah* and *midrash* in Levinas's other writings.

7. *Democracy in America and Two Essays on America*, trans. Gerald Bevan (New York: Penguin Books, 2003), 380. The scene is place in context by Harry Liebersohn in "Discovering Indigenous Nobility: Tocqueville, Chamisso, and Romantic Travel Writing," *The American Historical Review* 99, no. 3 (June 1994): 746–766, and sets the stage for the comprehensive critique by Jodi A. Byrd, *The Transit of Empire: Indigenous Critiques of Colonialism* (Minneapolis: University of Minnesota Press, 2011). The Choctaw nation diaspora followed the treaty at Dancing River Creek of 1830, and is narrated in LeAnne Howe's novel *Shell Shakers* (San Francisco: Aunt Lute Books, 2001) and Jesse O. McKee and Jon A. Schlenker, *The Choctaws: Cultural Evolution of a Native American Tribe* (Jackson: University Press of Mississippi, 1980).

8. The phrase belongs to Nancy, from the freestanding chapter "Shattered Love," in *The Inoperative Community*, trans. Peter Connor (Minneapolis: University of Minnesota Press, 1991), 84.

9. "The Language of Animals: An Apology of Raymond Sebond," in *Selected Essays*, trans. Charles Cotton (New York: Modern Library, 1949).

10. "How to Do Things With Wallace Stevens," in *Close Reading: The Reader*, ed. Andrew DuBois and Frank Lentricchia (Durham, N.C.: Duke University Press Books, 2002), 136–156. For a more general approach, see Joel Fineman, "The History of the Anecdote: Fiction and Fiction," in *The New Historicism*, ed. Harold Aram Veeser (New York: Routledge, 1989), 49–76.

11. Rhetoric, in this restrictive sense, should be distinguished from both Levinas's own use of the term as I explain below and the sort of discursive analysis *on* Levinas's

prose that Jean-Francois Lyotard conducts in his essay, "Levinas's Logic," in *Face to Face with Levinas*, ed. Richard Cohen (Albany: State University of New York Press, 1986), 117–158.

12. "The Paradox of Morality: Interview with Tamra Wright, Peter Hughes, Alison Ainley," in *The Provocation of Levinas: Rethinking the Other*, ed. Robert Bernasconi and David Wood (New York: Routledge & Kegan Paul, 1988), 172.

13. "Roundtable on Autobiography," in *The Ear of the Other: Otobiography, Transference, Translation: Texts Discussions with Jacques Derrida*, trans. Avital Ronnel and Peggy Kamuf, ed. Christie McDonald (New York: Schocken, 1985), 51.

14. In "Derrida and the Question of the Ear," Diane Michelfelder makes a very similar point when she writes about the commanding priority of the authorial Other whose signature readers provide: "The imperative to sign the text demands that we respond to the text not be *answering* it but by *returning the text* to its author through our reading of it in such a way that we recognize his or her irreducible particularity" (52). The philosophical background for the Derrida essay is Kierkegaard's *Either/Or*, which Michelfelder invokes in order to tease out the importance of aesthetics for a "'beyond' of ethics that would still remain ethical in its dimensions" (49), an ethical (for or purposes, read: midrashic) sensibility Michelfelder calls "an ethics of the ear." See *The Question of the Other: Essays In Contemporary Continental Philosophy*, ed. Arleen B. Dallery and Charles E. Scott (Albany: State University of New York Press, 1989), 47–54.

15. As quoted by Michelfelder, Derrida's phrase from his early essay on Levinas, "Violence and Metaphysics," in *Writing and Difference*, trans. Alan Bass (Chicago: University of Chicago Press, 1978), 81. Michelfelder expresses it this way, in relation to philosophy's self-questioning: "To be concerned with this question is basically '*to be read into a conversation*'" (50).

16. In addition to Derrida's *The Animal I Therefore Am* and "And Say the Animal Responded?" in *Zoontologies: The Question of the Animal*, ed. Cary Wolfe (Minneapolis: University of Minnesota Press, 2003), see Matthew Calarco, "Faced By Animals," in *Radicalizing Levinas*, ed. Peter Atterton and Matthew Calarco (Albany: State University of New York, 2010), 113–128; David L. Clark, "On Being 'the Last Kantian in Nazi Germany:' Dwelling with Animals after Levinas," in *Animal Acts: Configuring the Human in Western History,* ed. Jennifer Ham and Matthew Senior (New York: Routledge, 1997), 165–198; Diane Davis, "Greetings: On Levinas and the Wagging Tail" *JAC: A Journal of Composition Theory* 29, no. 1 (2009): 711–774, the response by David D. Metzger, "Bobby Who?" *JAC* 3, nos. 1–2 (2011): 273–283, and the chapter "P.S. on Humanism" from *Inessential Solidarity: Rhetoric and Foreigner Relations* (Pittsburgh: University of Pittsburgh Press, 2010), 144–166; John Llewelyn, "Am I Obsessed by Bobby? (Humanism of the Other Animal)," in *Rereading Levinas*, ed. Robert Bernasconi and Simon Critchley (Bloomington: Indiana University Press, 1991), 234–246, and his *The Middle Voice of Ecological Conscience: A Chiasmic Reading of Responsibility in the Neighbourhood of Levinas, Heidegger, and Others* (London: Macmillan, 1991); and Claudia Welz, "A Wandering Dog as the 'Last Kantian in Nazi Germany': Revisiting the Debate

on Levinas' Supposed Antinaturalistic Humanism," *Levinas Studies* 6 (2011), 65–88. Finally, the more playful lessons in "crittercism" on talking dogs and literary dogs' lives in Ross Chambers, *Loiterature* (Lincoln: University of Nebraska Press, 1999) ask us to think about the gains and losses of ventriloquized speech.

17. Donat, *The Holocaust Kingdom: A Memoir* (New York: Holt, Rinehart, and Winston), 1965; Levi, *If This is a Man*, trans. Stuart Woolf (London: Orion Press, 1959).

18. A larger context for a traditionally Jewish opprobrium attaching to dogs (and indeed, the selective cultural collocation of "dog" and "Jew") is traced in Kenneth Stow, *Jewish Dogs: An Image and Its Interpreters* (Stanford: Stanford University Press, 2006) and *A Jew's Best Friend? The Image of the Dog Throughout Jewish History*, ed. Phillip Ackerman-Lieberman and Rakefet Zalashik (Brighton: Sussex Academic Press, 2012).

19. Eric Santner, Giorgio Agamben, and Beatrice Hanssen all favor this terminology, with common reference to Rilke's concept of *das Offene*, "the Open," or to Walter Benjamin. See Santner, *On Creaturely Life: Rilke, Benjamin, Sebald* (Chicago: University of Chicago Press, 2006); Agamben, *The Open: Man and Animal*, trans. Kevin Attell (Stanford: Stanford University Press, 2002), *Homo Sacer: Sovereign Power and Bare Life*, trans. Daniel Heller-Roazen (Stanford: Stanford University Press, 1998), and *The State of Exception*, trans. Kevin Attell (Chicago: University of Chicago Press, 2005); and Hanssen, *Walter Benjamin's Other History: Of Stones, Animals, Human Beings, and Angels* (Berkeley: University of California Press, 2000). Along similar lines, Lisa Guenther, in an essay on the sensible animality of the human and the compassionate friendship this sensibility makes possible, points to a passage from *Otherwise Than Being* exactly contemporary with the publication of the essay and in uncanny relation to it where Levinas renders the innate human desire for enjoyment as "a dog that recognizes as its own Ulysses coming to take possession of his goods" (226). "*Le flair animal*: Levinas and the Possibility of Friendship," *PhaenEx: Journal of Existential and Phenomenological Theory and Culture* 2, no. 2 (Fall–Winter 2007): 216–238. See also Barbara Davy, "An Other Face of Ethics in Levinas," *Ethics & the Environment* 12, no. 1 (Spring 2007): 39–65. The Benjamin/Levinas connections are traced in Susan A. Handelman, *Fragments of Redemption: Jewish Thought and Literary Theory in Benjamin, Scholem, and Levinas* (Bloomington: Indiana University Press, 1991), Benjamin Andes Wurgaft, "Language and Its Core: Ethical and Religious Subjects in Levinas and Benjamin," *Literature and Theology* 16, no. 4 (2002): 377–395, and Asher Horowitz, "How Levinas Taught Me to Read Benjamin," *PhaenEx* 1, no. 1 (Spring–Summer 2006): 140–174.

20. If the entry is to be read through the lens of Levinas's philosophical writing, with Joelle Hansel, I would look not toward the later works but rather the early analytical essays from the 1930s and 1940s like *On Evasion* (1935) and *From Existence to Existents* and *Time and the Other* (both from 1947) that imagine some of the more nightmarish aspects of being. See also the interview in *Is It Righteous to Be?*, 90.

21. *The Origins of Totalitarianism* (New York: Harcourt, Brace, Jovanovich, 1973), 287.

22. *Adam's Task: Calling Animals by Name* (New York: Skyhorse Publishing, 2007), 167. See also the collection of colloquies among Stanley Cavell, Cora Diamond, John

McDowell, Ian Hacking, and Cary Wolfe, *Philosophy and Animal Life* (New York: Columbia University Press, 2008).

23. *The Animal That Therefore I Am*, trans. David Wills (New York: Fordham University Press, 2008), 17. Derrida's remarks on naming should be compared with Walter Benjamin's reading of the same biblical moment in his 1916 essay, "On Language as Such and on the Language of Man" (*"Über Sprache überhaupt und über die Sprache des Menschen"*), e.g., "The name, in the realm of language, has as its sole purpose and its incomparably high meaning that it is the innermost nature of language itself. The name is that *through* which, and *in* which, language itself communicates itself in absolute." *Selected Writings 1913–1926*, 65. Benjamin's essay, originally composed as a letter to Gershom Scholem, had a decisive influence of Scholem's 1926 "letter" to Franz Rosenzweig, *"Bekenntnis über unsere Sprache,"* which I discuss in the final chapter.

24. Jean-Louis Chrétien, *The Ark of Speech*, trans. Andrew Brown (New York: Taylor & Francis, 2003), 4.

25. Barbara Jane Davy, "An Other Face of Ethics in Levinas," *Ethics & the Environment* 12, no. 1 (Spring 2007): 41.

26. *Lord Jim and Nostromo*, ed. Robert D. Kaplan (New York: Modern Library, 2000), 23.

27. "Animality and the Global Subject in Conrad's *Lord Jim*," in *Reading the Global: Troubling Perspectives on Britain's Empire in Asia* (New York: Columbia University Press, 2007), 133–164.

28. Colonialist soundscapes and the question of voice have received particular attention in Conrad studies of late. See, among others, Gail Fincham, "The Dialogism of *Lord Jim*," in *Conrad and Theory*, ed. Andrew Gibson and Robert Hampson (Atlanta: Rodopi, 1998), 58–74; Michael Greaney's account of "slips of the ear" in *Conrad, Language, and Narrative* (Cambridge: Cambridge University Press, 2002); Robert Hampson, *Cross-Cultural Encounters in Joseph Conrad's Malay Fiction* (New York: Palgrave, 2000); Bruce Henricksen, *Nomadic Voices: Conrad and the Subject of Narrative* (Urbana: University of Illinois Press, 1992); Ivan Kreilkamp, *Voice and the Victorian Storyteller* (Cambridge: Cambridge University Press, 2005); and Jakob Lothe, Jeremy Hawthorn, and James Phelan, eds., *Joseph Conrad: Voice, Sequence, History, Genre* (Columbus: Ohio State University Press, 2008).

29. From the essay "Useless Suffering," in *Entre Nous: Thinking-of-the-Other*, trans. Michael Bradley Smith and Barbara Harshav (New York: Columbia University Press, 2000), 99.

30. Jed Esty, *Unseasonable Youth: Modernism, Colonialism, and the Fiction of Development* (Oxford: Oxford University Press, 2010), 96ff. See also the related essay by Michael Valdez Moses, ""Disorientalism: Conrad and the Imperial Origins of Modernist Aesthetics," in *Modernism and Colonialism: British and Irish Literature, 1899–1939*, ed. Richard Begam and Michael Valdez Moses (Durham, N.C.: Duke University Press, 2007), 43–69, and Brian Artese's commentary on the novel's tribunal science in Chapter 4 along with Conrad's essays on public inquiries into the sinking of *Titanic*, in *Testimony*

on Trial: Conrad, James and the Contest of Modernism (Toronto: University of Toronto Press, 2012), 14–47. Artese's discussion is particularly valuable for its analysis of tendencies in poststructuralist, narratological, and postcolonialist readings of *Lord Jim* alike to project onto its workings a set of theoretical presuppositions that do not fully or accurately account for the novel's formal features of mediated perception.

31. "Devil" exemplifies Marlow's screening propensities; "deus-ex-machina" is Artese's term (128) for Conrad's "antinaturalist" contrivance.

32. On one of its lowest frequencies, *Difficult Freedom* contains a thematic of *voice*, but except for "Signature" and "Name of a Dog," its instances resound discursively in rather dead air. For example, an essay from 1951 is titled (after Claudel), "A Voice on Israel," but no conversation or speech is recorded in it. In the Talmudic readings of messianic *aggadot* transcribed from Colloquium meetings in 1960 and 1961, we hear Levinas himself speak since, as he acknowledges, the form of the essays remains that of spoken texts. In them, as well, we hear the various voices of Tannaim and Amoraim, in the distinctive idiolect of Talmudic discourse, *"amar Rabbi Yosei"* (Rabbi Yosei said) or *Rabbi Yoḥanan mishum Rabbi Shimon Bar Yoḥai omer* (Sage X said in the name of Sage Y); this is the Talmud's persistent staging of *le Dire* as the guarantor of *le Dit*. But these are really only formal markers of vocalization: Levinas's is the dominant voice in these pieces. Spinoza is quoted in *Difficult Freedom*; so are Leon Brunschwig, Simone Weil, Paul Claudel, Franz Rosenzweig, and Yossel Rakover (actually Tzvi Kolitz); but these are all citations. We hear *of* a young Pole who cries "Mummy" at the beginning of the letter Levinas wrote to *Le Monde* in 1954, "À propos du Struthof"; but it is a rhetorical figure of pathos, if I understand it correctly, to ensure we keep the recent past present. Voice itself, as embodied expression, remains quasi-mummified in all of these examples.

33. Lisa Guenther also supplies a beautiful reading of this scene in her *"Le flair animal*: Levinas and the Possibility of Friendship," *PhaenEx: Journal of Existential and Phenomenological Theory and Culture* 2, no. 2 (Fall–Winter 2007), e.g., "We do not know the secret of Ulysses' wiped-away tear or the motivation behind Argos' flattened ears. But the very ambiguity of these wordless gestures, their opacity to us and to each other (and possibly even to themselves), suggests a double asymmetry which at least opens the possibility of friendship, and destabilizes the opposition between ethical men and non-ethical animals, which Levinas explicitly maintains" (231).

34. Similar literary evocations pepper the canonical landscape, of course. Compare the very different description of a dog and a very different Ulysses, from the "Cyclops" chapter of James Joyce's novel (which happens to have generated its own Levinasian reading by Ann Katrin Jonsson in *Ethics and the Modernist Subject in James Joyce's Ulysses, Virginia Woolf's The Waves and Djuna Barnes's Nightwood* (New York: Peter Lang, 2006): "a savage animal of the canine tribe . . . which his master repressed from time to time by tranquilising blows of a mighty cudgel" (244).

35. In a midrash on the Torah Portion *Bo* from the thirteenth-century aggadic compilation *Yalqut Shimoni*, on the verse from Exodus that Levinas cites, various earthly and celestial entities are given voice in a long list ending with a series of animals: "The

dog says: 'Come, let us prostrate ourselves and bow, let us kneel before Hashem our Maker' (Psalms 95:6). Rabbi Yeshaya, the student of Rabbi Ḥanina ben Dosa, fasted eighty-five fasts; he said, Dogs, about which is written, 'And the dogs are brazen of spirit that do not know satiation' (Isaiah 56:11)—shall they merit to recite song? An angel responded from Heaven and said to him, 'Yeshaya, until when will you fast on this matter? It is an oath from The Holy One, blessed be He: From the day He revealed His secret to the prophet Ḥabakkuk, He has not revealed this matter to anyone in the world. But, since you are the pupil of a great man, I have been sent from Heaven to assist you, to tell you that the dogs have merited to recite song by virtue of that what is written about them, 'But against the Children of Israel, no dog shall whet its tongue' (Exodus 11:7).' It continues (in an especially pertinent vein for this book), "Furthermore, they merited that hides tanned with their excrement are made into parchment upon which Torahs, *tefillin*, and *mezuzot* are written. Therefore, they merited to recite song. And regarding your question that you asked, go back on your way and don't continue in this matter, for it is written, 'He who guards his mouth and tongue, guards from afflictions of his soul" (Proverbs 21:23) (*Yalqut Shimoni*, on *Parashat Bo*, 187). A comprehensive list of midrashic and Talmudic references to dogs can be found in Fred Rosner, *Encyclopedia of Medicine in the Bible and the Talmud* (Northvale, N.J.: Jason Aronson, 2000), 101–102.

36. Paul Ricoeur, *The Course of Recognition*, trans. David Pellauer, 73. Bruce Louden, *Homer's Odyssey and the Near East* (Cambridge: Cambridge University Press, 2011) suggests a pertinent comparison of the scene of "immediate recognition" with Argos to the biblical story of Joseph when recognized by his father shortly before Jacob's death, 94–95.

37. "On Nostalgia (and Homer)," *Habitus in Habitat I: Emotion and Motion*, ed. Sabine Flach, Daniel Margulies, and Jan Söffner (Bern: Peter Lang, 2011), 81–91. The essay is also particularly relevant in light of Levinas's distinctly *nostalgic* recollection of Bobby, in which Söffner's analysis can help us locate "a background orientation producing a difference between a habitus experienced as one's "own," and a habitat experienced as inadequate and therefore other" (88).

38. *The Phenomenon of Life: Toward a Philosophical Biology* (Evanston, Ill.: Northwestern University Press, 2001), 139.

39. The antiphenomenalist counter to such a claim is probably most rigorously spelled out by Paul de Man in *The Resistance to Theory* (Minneapolis: University of Minnesota Press, 1986): "It would be unfortunate, for example, to confuse the materiality of the signifier with the materiality of what it signifies. This may seem obvious enough on the level of light and sound, but it is less so with regard to the more general phenomenality of space, time or especially of the self; no one in his right mind will try to grow grapes by the luminosity of the word 'day,' but it is very difficult not to conceive the pattern of one's past and future existence as in accordance with temporal and spatial schemes that belong to fictional narratives and not to the world. This does not mean that fictional narratives are not part of the world and of reality; their impact upon the world may well be all too strong for comfort. What we call ideology is precisely the confusion of

linguistic with natural reality, of reference with phenomenalism" (11). Although de Man's point advocates an implacable ethics of reading both astringent and intellectually compelling, I feel a bargain struck with "attentive readiness for sounds to occur" does not therefore violate the necessary pact we make with linguistic reference. Reading counterreads, but it may nevertheless also incline us *beyond*.

40. Cf. this passage in Julian Barnes's *Flaubert's Parrot* about François Mauriac's *Mémoires intérieurs*: "Reading his 'memoirs' is like meeting a man on a train who says, 'Don't look at me, that's misleading. If you want to know what I'm like, wait until we're in a tunnel, and then study my reflection in the window'" (96).

41. Included in *Face to Face with Levinas*, 41–51.

42. This marks a significant crossing point between Levinas's philosophy and Stanley Cavell's. In addition to Cavell's own *Philosophy the Day After Tomorrow* (Cambridge, Mass.: Harvard University Press, 2005), which devotes part of a chapter, "What Is the Scandal of Skepticism?" to Levinas, see Gerald L. Bruns, "Dialogue and the Truth of Skepticism," *Religion & Literature* 22, nos. 2–3 (Summer–Autumn, 1990): 85–91; Simon Critchley, *Very Little . . . Almost Nothing: Death, Philosophy and Literature* (London: Routledge, 2004); Espen Hammer, *Stanley Cavell: Skepticism, Subjectivity, and the Ordinary* (Cambridge: Blackwell, 2002); Michael Morgan, *Discovering Levinas* (Cambridge: Cambridge University Press, 2010); Paul Standish, "Education for Grown-Ups, a Religion for Adults: Skepticism and Alterity in Cavell and Levinas," in *Ethics and Education* 2, no. 1 (2007), 73–91; and Ewa Płonowska Ziarek, *The Rhetoric of Failure: Deconstruction of Skepticism, Reinvention of Modernism* (Albany: State University of New York Press, 1996).

43. *"Philosophieren ist dephlegmatisieren vivificieren,"* as quoted (and translated) by Walter Pater in his famous conclusion to *The Renaissance: Studies in Art and Poetry* (Oxford: Oxford World Classics, 1998): "The service of philosophy, of speculative culture, towards the human spirit, is to rouse, to startle it to a life of constant and eager observation" (152).

44. Few moments in Levinas's writing open themselves to being ventriloquized as much as this one: it is as plausibly read as a window onto tangent concepts in French philosophy like Jean-Luc Nancy's "singular plural," Blanchot's and Nancy's respective accounts of "community," Derrida on "Hospitality," Badiou on Pauline Love, or finally, as a staging of Levinas's great, late concept of "proximity." In this chapter, however, I am confining myself to a very local and restrictive field of acoustics.

45. Levinas refers to it on pages 90 and 173. See the essays, "Getting Under the Skin: Platonic Myths" by Tanja Stähler and "Lending Assistance Always to Itself: Levinas' Infinite Conversation With Platonic Dialogue," in *Levinas and the Ancients*, ed. Sylvia Benso and Brian Schroeder (Bloomington: Indiana University Press, 2008), 62–102.

46. In Aaron Fogel's ingenious formulation, Conrad "worked as what I call an 'overhearer' of English in several senses. . . . He was interested dramatically in scenes of overhearing and he also presented English diction at times as 'overheard.' Conrad approached English, as he had to, with a studied alertness to its terms and polysemy; but it was also one of his gifts to be able to 'dramatize' polysemy and polyglossia unsentimen-

tally" (*Coercion to Speak: Conrad's Poetics of Dialogue*, 41). See also Geoffrey Galt Harpham's analysis of the same gift in the chapter "To Write in English" in *One of Us: The Mastery of Joseph Conrad* (Chicago: University of Chicago Press, 1996), especially 150ff.

47. *Youth/Heart of Darkness/The End of the Tether* (Cambridge: Cambridge University Press, 2010), 158. Fogel spends some time on this phrase in his reading of the story in *Coercion to Speak*.

48. *Giving an Account of Oneself* (New York: Fordham University Press, 2005), 27–28.

49. *On the Psychotheology of Everyday Life: Reflections on Freud and Rosenzweig* (Chicago: University of Chicago Press, 2006), 88.

50. Derrida, from *The Ear of the Other*: "It is rather paradoxical to think of an autobiography whose signature is entrusted to the other, one who comes along so late and is so unknown. But it is not Nietzsche's originality that has put us in this situation. Every text answers to this structure. It is the structure of textuality in general. A text is signed only much later by the other. And this testamentary structure doesn't befall a text as if by accident, but constructs it. This is how a text always comes about" (51).

51. The motif also occurs in Isa. 44:20; Mal. 3:21 [4:3]; Job 13:12, 30:19.

52. Cf. "'In the Image of God,' According to Rabbi Hayyim Volozhiner," *Beyond the Verse*, 151–167, and "Prayer Without Demand," in *The Levinas Reader*, ed. Seán Hand (Cambridge, Mass.: Basil Blackwell, 1989), 227–234. The classic mitnagdic-cum-kabbalistic text and its influence on Levinas is discussed in passing by Ira Stone in *Reading Levinas/Reading Talmud: An Introduction* (Philadelphia: Jewish Publication Society, 1998), and more substantively in the following: Catherine Chalier, "L'ame de la vie: Levinas, lecteur de R. Haim de Volozin," in *Emmanuel Levinas* (Paris: Editions de l'Herne, 1991), 387–398; Shaul Magid, "Deconstructing the Mystical: The Anti-Mystical Kabbalism in Rabbi Hayyim of Volozhin's *Nefesh Ha-Hayyim*," *Journal of Jewish Thought and Philosophy* 9 (1999): 21–67; and Oona Ajzenstat, *Driven Back to the Sources: The Premodern Sources of Levinas's Postmodernism*, 139–199. The best historiographic study of R. Hayyim is Alan Nadler's *The Faith of the Mithnagdim: Rabbinic Responses to Hasidic Rapture* (Baltimore: Johns Hopkins University Press, 1999), but see also Norman Lamm, *Torah Lishmah: Torah for Torah's Sake in the Works of Rabbi Hayyim of Volozhin and His Contemporaries* (Jersey City, N.J.: Ktav, 1989), and the *Kaphtziel* blog: http://kaphtziel .blogspot.com/2005/09/levinas-and-volozhin-essay.html.

53. The metaphor governs the contemporaneous essay in *Outside the Subject*, trans. Michael B. Smith (Stanford: Stanford University Press, 1994), "The Strings and the Wood: On the Jewish Reading of the Bible," 126–134.

54. Gerald Bruns, *Hermeneutics Ancient and Modern* (New Haven: Yale University Press, 1992), 210.

55. On this elusive figure, see Salomon Malka, *Monsieur Chouchani: L'enigme d'un maitre du XXe siècle* (Paris: J.C. Lattes, 1994); Warren Zev Harvey, "Chouchani on the Prophecy of Moses" (in Hebrew), in *Be-darkhei Shalom, Studies presented to Shalom Rosenberg*, B. Ish-Shalom (Jerusalem: Beit Morashah, 2007), 459–465; Shalom Rosenberg, "Uncollected Recollections of Shoshani" (in Hebrew), *'Amudim* (1995), 135–137;

Shmuel Wygoda, "Le maître et son disciple: Chouchani et Lévinas," *Cahiers d'études lévinassiennes* 1 (2002): 149–183; see also Geoffrey Cohen, "Finding Chouchani," www .jewdas.org/2009/06/finding-chouchani. I thank Warren Zev Harvey for the narrative behind the alias.

56. In a fairly obvious sense, Michael Fagenblat's *A Covenant of Creatures: Levinas's Philosophy of Judaism* is a book-length rejoinder to Moyn's argument about the role played by invention in Levinas's Jewish intellectual history. Both authors refer as well to Leora Batnitzky's *Leo Strauss and Emmanuel Levinas: Philosophy and the Politics of Revelation* (Cambridge: Cambridge University Press, 2006), which skeptically interrogates Levinas's allegiance to Fran Rosenzweig. Evenhanded reception of Moyn's book is perhaps best illustrated by Nathan Bracher in *H-France Review* 6, no. 88 (August 2006), www.h -france.net/vol6reviews/bracher.html, together with Moyn's response, www.h-france.net/ vol6reviews/moyn2.html. More critical reviews belong to Daniel T. Kline, *Shofar: An Interdisciplinary Journal of Jewish Studies* 26, no. 2 (Winter 2008): 178–181; and Martin Kavka, *Journal of the American Academy of Religion* 74, no. 4 (December 2006): 1003–1005.

57. The formula is invariant for all tractates, and a shortened form follows each and every chapter *within* a tractate. The term itself denotes both the celebration held on the completion or *siyyum* and the speech delivered on that occasion. See Daniel Sperber, *Why Jews Do What They Do: The History of Jewish Customs Throughout the Cycle of the Jewish Year* (Hoboken, N.J.: Ktav, 1999), 184–190, and Saul Lieberman, *Alei Ayin: Minhat Devarim li-Shelomoh Zalman Shoken ahare melot lo shiv'im shanah* (Tel Aviv: Schocken, 1948–52), 81 n. 33.

58. "On the Love of Torah," published in *The Shebuot Reader* (New York: Tebah Educational Services, 2009), 8–12. *Hullin* in the *Bavli* has been translated into English in the Soncino and Shottenstein editions and is also available in the single-authored translation in three volumes by Tsvee Zahavy as *The Talmud of Babylonia: An American Translation. XXX.A: Tractate Hullin* (Atlanta: Scholars Press, 1992–1994). See also Zahavy's book with Jacob Neusner, *How the Halakhah Unfolds: Hullin, Part One and Part Two* (Lanham, Md.: University Press of America, 2010).

59. On the same, relatively uncommon word in the Book of Esther 2:7, a *midrash* in *Breishit Rabbah* 30:8 states that Mordechai actually nursed Esther through male lactation.

60. On this figure, see especially Lisa Guenther, "'Like a Maternal Body': Emmanuel Levinas and the Motherhood of Moses," *Hypatia* 21, no. 1 (Winter 2006): 119–136. See also Stella Sandford, *The Metaphysics of Love: Gender and Transcendence in Levinas* (London: Athlone Press, 2000).

61. "Levinas's 'Ontology': 1935–1974," in *Emmanuel Levinas: Critical Assessments by Leading Philosophers*, ed. Claire Elise Katz and Lara Trout (New York: Routledge, 2005) 25–48.

62. Robert Alter, *Genesis: Translation and Commentary* (New York: Norton, 1997), 82.

63. Leviticus 17:13: "Any man of the Children of Israel and of the convert who dwells among them who will trap a wild beast or fowl that may be eaten, he shall spill its blood and cover it in the earth."

64. Rashi's comment explains that *Kisui hadam* accompanies the ritual slaughter of beast or fowl, which can then be consumed; but slaughter and consumption are still permitted even without the mitzvah of covering the blood with earth. Hence, unlike the other two mitzvoth, while it may certainly be fulfilled, no immediate benefit accrues from it.

65. "And furthermore, the rules of this chapter can have profound implications in then actual regulation by the rabbis of meat consumption in their communities. For these reasons, the chapter is considered to be on of the most difficult in the Talmud" (*The Talmud of Babylonia, Tractate Hullin, Chapters 3–6*, 11–12).

66. Although I leave it unexplored here, there are certainly Holocaust resonances for Levinas in the metaphor of "ashes," as well (as I have already implied in my footnote on Jacob Bronowski in the prologue). "Dust" in Genesis 3:14 (*ha-nahash*, the snake) and 3:19 (*ha-adam*, the man) already stand behind the word in Abraham's pronouncement in chapter 18. Further, as Levinas surely knew from liturgical practice, the brief supplement composed by the fourth-century Amora Mar Bar Rabina at the conclusion of the thrice-repeated daily prayer in Jewish rite, reads, *v'nafshi k'afar laqol t'hiyeh,* "and let my soul be like dust to everyone" (which, however, is supplicatory, and thus not exactly congruent with the affirmations of lowliness that Levinas finds especially meaningful).

67. The *Pesikta de Rav Kahana*, a fifth- or sixth-century compilation of *midrashei aggadah* that Levinas does not ever cite, makes the following point about the mitzvah's mystery and efficacy, with whose philosophical probity, however, Levinas might have well concurred: "Rabban Yoḥanan answered: 'By your lives, I swear: the corpse does not have the power by itself to defile, nor does the mixture of ash and water have the power to cleanse. The truth is that the purifying power of the Red Heifer is a decree of the Holy One. The Holy One said, 'I have set it down as a statute, I have issued it as a decree. You are not permitted to transgress My decree. *This is a statue of the Torah* (Numbers 19:1)." *Pesikta de Rav Kahana (Pesikta de-Rab Kahana),* trans. William G. Braude and Israel J. Kapstein (Philadelphia: Jewish Publication Society, 1975), *Piska* 4 ("the mystery and paradox of the Red Heifer"), 112.

68. Aside from remaining mute on the manifest (and appalling) primitiveness of the ceremony, Levinas omits a striking component of the ceremony, recorded in verses 21–23 of Numbers 5: "Then the priest shall make the woman swear this oath of imprecation, and the priest shall say unto the woman—May the LORD make you an imprecation and an oath in the midst of your people through the LORD's making your thigh sag and your belly swell. And this besetting water shall enter your innards to swell the belly and sag the thigh. And the woman shall say: 'Amen, Amen.'And the priest shall write these imprecations in a scroll, and wipe them out in the bitter water" (Alter translation, 708). As Levinas certainly knows, a midrashic tradition—to take one rich example, *Vayikra Rabbah*—explains the ceremony in terms of the radical lengths to which God himself will go in order to preserve *shalom bayit* (conjugal accord). That is, He will allow His own name to be blotted out and consumed in the expectation that the woman's fidelity is in fact unimpeachable. Moreover, according to rabbinic lore, a woman who successfully

survives the *sotah* ordeal, goes on to give birth to a son: the process is actually procreative. The trope of deinscription or erasure thus deeply resonates with the metaphorics of "dust and ashes," but Levinas, curiously, does not explore it.

69. *Beyond the Verse*, 161 on *Nefesh ha-Ḥayyim* 3:13–14. See also *Ruaḥ Ḥayyim* 1:1 (Ḥayyim Volozhiner's commentary on *Pirqei Avot*): " The Zohar notes that Abraham's name is doubled, but there is a pause between [the iterations] (Gen. 22:11), while Moshe's name is doubled without a pause (Ex. 3:4). This indicates that Moshe rose to a higher level than Abraham. As the Talmud notes, Abraham used the expression "I am dirt and ash," while Moshe said, "What are we?" (*Hullin* 89a on Gen. 18:27 and Ex. 16:8). It is with this additional level of humility that Moshe merited to be the one through whom the Torah was given." *Ruach Chaim*, trans. Chanoch Levi (New York: Feldheim Publishers, 2002), 34. The *Nefesh Ha-Ḥayyim* has been translated by R. Avraham Yaakov Finkel (New York: Judaica Press, 2009), and in a more complete version, including the sections to which Levinas alludes, as *The Soul of Life: The Complete Neffesh Ha-chayyim*, trans. Eliezer Lipa (Leonard) Moskowiz (Teaneck, N.J.: New Davar Publications, 2012).

70. See also his essay, "Levinas and Maimonides: From Metaphysics to Ethical Negative Theology," *Journal of Jewish Thought and Philosophy* 16, no. 1 (2008): 95–147.

71. The for-one-self resolutely critiqued by Abraham's speech acts (and by extension, by the communal rites that incorporate the material signifiers of those sayings-as-doings), is the same one-self also critiqued in Levinas's reading of *bShabbat* 88a–88b, "The Temptation of Temptation" where the self is, "at the same time, outside of everything and participating in everything . . . an ego, which, in engagement, is assured a permanent disengagement. The self is perhaps nothing other than that. An ego purely and simply engaged is naïve" (34).

72. Levinas quotes this formulation in his interview with Francoise Armengaud, "On Jewish Philosophy," *In the Time of Nations*, trans. Michael B. Smith (New York: Continuum, 2007), 181.

73. In the corrected translation by Caryl Emerson. See "The Tolstoy Connection in Bakhtin," *Rethinking Bakhtin: Extensions and Challenges*, ed. Caryl Emerson and Gary Saul Morson (Evanston, Ill.: Northwestern University Press, 1989), 156.

74. The conceit comes from the introduction to Boyarin's *Thinking in Jewish* (Chicago: University of Chicago Press, 1996), 3. In the appendix to his book, *Yidishe visnshaft un di postmodern* ("Yiddish Science and the Postmodern"), Boyarin enlists Levinas as the third of "three great Jewish thinkers of our century much of whose work can be seen as signposts leading toward" (195) this transitive intransitivity of "thinking in Jewish"; the other two are Jacques Derrida and Walter Benjamin.

75. He cites it again in "The Bible and the Greeks" from 1986, the essay "Peace and Proximity" from 1984, and in various interviews collected in *Is it Righteous to Be?* Admirably, Michael Morgan's *Discovering Levinas* begins by inquiring what might be the compelling attraction of Grossman's novel to the philosopher, and proceeds to read Levinas reading it, thus paying initial regard to Levinas as both practitioner and theorist of interpretation. Levinas's reference to Grossman is also taken up in Hent de Vries, "On

General and Divine Economy" and Michael Morgan, "Responding to Atrocity in the Twentieth Century," *The Cambridge Introduction to Levinas* (Cambridge University Press, 2011), 16–35.

5. Ethics of Reading II: Bakhtin and the Novel

1. Certainly at this fairly late date in Bakhtin's reception, a more rounded understanding has emerged regarding those influences (e.g., Kant, Hermann Cohen, Matvei Kagan, Bergson, Scheler, Marx), the interchange with colleagues (Medvedev, Voloshinov), the intellectual disagreements and resistances (Formalism, Marxism, material aesthetics, Russian Orthodoxy, the Russian intelligentsia, the Soviet authorities), and so on. Caryl Emerson's *The First Hundred Years of Mikhail Bakhtin* (Princeton: Princeton University Press, 1997) discusses the many reception-horizons of Bakhtin's published work. In the same year, the general introduction *Introducing Bakhtin* by Sue Vice (Manchester: Manchester University Press, 1997) was also published. Michael Holquist's *Dialogism: Bakhtin and His World* (London: Routledge, 2002) is more sophisticated about the early work, as is Caryl Emerson and Gary Morson, *Mikhail Bakhtin: Creation of a Prosaics* (Stanford: Stanford University Press, 1990). As of this date, *Mikhail Bakhtin* by Katrina Clark and Michael Holquist (Cambridge, Mass.: Harvard University Press, 1984), though in certain respects quite speculative, remains the only full-length biography in English. Numerous introductions to his thought and writings continue to be published, as well as ever more cutting-edge essay-collections across humanities and social sciences disciplines.

2. Compare, however, "I am more philosopher than [philologist], and remain so up to the present day. I am a философ ("philosopher"); I am a мыслите ("thinker")." From a 1973 interview with Vladimir Duvakin quoted in Alexandar Mihailovic, *Corporeal Worlds: Mikhail Bakhtin's Theology of Discourse* (Evanston, Ill.: Northwestern University Press, 1997), 12 and 87. And "philosophical anthropology" is one of the principal categories specified in "Notes Made in 1970–71," from *Speech Genres and Other Late Essays*, trans. Vern W. McGee (Austin: University of Texas Press, 1986), 155.

3. The *Annotated Bakhtin Bibliography*, now twelve years out of date, runs to almost 500 pages, and the sessions and topics at the International Mikhail Bakhtin Conference increase with every passing year: www.bakhtinconference2011.it/index.html. Some significant criticism and theory that export Bakhtinian concepts: Homi Bhabha, "DissemiNation," in *The Location of Culture* (London: Routledge, 1994), 139–147; Alexei Bogdanov, "*Ostranenie*, Kenosis, and Dialogue: The Metaphysics of Formalism according to Shklovsky," *Slavic and East European Journal* 49 (2005): 48–62; Wlad Godzich, "Correcting Kant: Bakhtin and Intercultural Interactions," *boundary 2* 18, no. 1 (1991): 5–17; Ken Hirschkop and David Shepherd, eds., *Bakhtin and Cultural Theory* (Manchester: Manchester University Press, 2001); Michael André Bernstein, *Bitter Carnival: Ressentiment and the Abject Hero* (Princeton: Princeton University Press, 1992); Zali Gurevitch, "Plurality in Dialogue: A Comment on Bakhtin," *Sociology* 34, no. 2

(2000): 243–263; Paul De Man, "Dialogue and Dialogism," *The Resistance to Theory* (Minneapolis: University of Minnesota Press, 1986), 106–114; K. G. Isupov, *M. M. Bakhtin—Pro Et Contra: Lichnost I Tvorchestvo M.M. Bakhtina V Otsenke Russkoi I Mirovoi Gumanitarnoi Mysli: Antologiia* (Saint Petersburg: Izd-vo Russkogo Khristianskogo gumanitarnogo inta, 2001); S. S. Konkin and L.S. Konkina, *Mikhail Bakhtin: stranitsy zhizni i tvorchestva* (Saransk: Mordovskoe knizhnoe izdvo, 1993); Vadim Kozhinov, *Bakhtin i ego chitateli* (Moskva); Kristeva, "Une poétique ruinée," in *Mikhail Bakhtin, La poétique de Dostoïevski* (Paris: Seuil, 1970), 5–27; Ladislav Matejka, "Deconstructing Bakhtin," in *Fiction Updated: Theories of Fictionality, Narratology, and Poetics*, ed. Calin Andrei Mihailescu and Walid Hamarneh (Toronto: University of Toronto Press, 1996), 257–266; Tzvetan Todorov, *Mikhail Bakhtin: The Dialogical Principle*, trans. Wlad Godzich (Minneapolis: University of Minnesota Press, 1985).

4. The early, metaphysical essays are particularly clotted with an academic (but also oddly literary) language quite at odds with both traditional philosophical discourse and the grounding and sometimes even subversive energies of the genre to which Bakhtin consistently defers: the novel and its discourse. That choice represents another point of tangency with Levinas who finds in Talmudic *aggadah* a language that is simultaneously profoundly "philosophical" and bracingly quotidian. On Bakhtin's stylistic peculiarities in these early works, see Daphna Erdinast-Vulcan, "Borderlines and Contraband: Bakhtin and the Question of the Subject," in *Poetics Today* 18, no. 2 (Summer, 1997): 251–269.

5. автор и гэрои в эстэтичэскои дэиатэльности, "Author and Hero in Aesthetic Activity," in *Art and Answerability: Early Philosophical Essays*, trans. Vadim Liapunov (Austin: University of Texas Press, 1990), 106, 155. These and other early essays along with the writings translated as *Speech Genres and Other Late Essays* were published in one volume in the original Russian, Естетики словесного творчества (The Aesthetics of Verbal Creation) (Moscow: Iskusstvo, 1979).

6. At the beginning of "From Notes Made in 1970–71," in *Speech Genres and Other Late Essays,* and speaking of "the writer" almost in the timbre of Roland Barthes, Bakhtin observes, "Literature has been completely secularized. The novel, deprived of style and setting, is essentially not a genre; it must imitate (rehearse) some extraartistic genre: the everyday story, letters, diary and so forth" (132). The earlier essay from 1941, "Epic and Novel," says: "The novelization of literature does not imply attaching to already completed genres a generic canon that is alien to them, not theirs. The novel after all has no canon of its own. It is, by its very nature, not canonic. It is plasticity itself" (39). The novel *novelizes*, in a word.

7. See *Creation of a Prosaics*, 70–71.

8. See *Corporeal Words*, 231–234.

9. The first term belongs to Alexandar Mihailovic, from *Corporeal Worlds: Mikhail Bakhtin's Theology of Discourse*, the most sophisticated inquiry into Bakhtin's religiosity and the role of doctrinal metaphor in his writing. It is superior to Ruth Coates's more journeyman study, *Christianity in Bakhtin: God and the Exiled Author*, which does for

Bakhtin (with arguable success) what Fagenblat attempts to do for Levinas insofar as it aims to decode an implicit subtext of soteriological *mythos* underpinning the work. The second phrase belongs to Graham Pechey, from the chapter "Philosophy and Theology," in *Mikhail Bakhtin: The Word in the World* (London: Routledge, 2007), 172, reprinted in *Bakhtin and Religion: A Feeling for Faith*, ed. Susan M. Felch and Paul J. Contino (Evanston, Ill.: Northwestern University Press, 2001), 47–62.

10. The early essays have received a number of treatments, not all of which harmonize. They were first introduced by Gary Saul Morson and Caryl Emerson in their introduction to *Rethinking Bakhtin: Extensions and Challenges*. In turn, Morson's account has been challenged by Michael Bernard-Donals in "Bakhtin and Phenomenology: A Reply to Gary Saul Morson," *South Central Review* 12, no. 2 (Summer 1995): 41–55. The two treatises are discussed at length by Michael Holquist in his introduction to their respective translations and in his *Dialogism*. Of particular importance to me in this chapter, however, is Ilya Kliger's "Heroic Aesthetics and Modernist Critique: Extrapolations from Bakhtin's 'Author and Hero in Aesthetic Activity,'" *Slavic Review* 67, no. 3 (Fall 2008): 551–566, which provides an extremely cogent analysis of Bakhtin's intervention in the "Kantian-modernist aesthetic situation."

11. Reliable gateways are the Morson-Emerson *Mikhail Bakhtin: Creation of a Prosaics* and *Introducing Bakhtin* by Sue Vice. Michael Holquist proposes affinities with likeminded philosophical projects (Buber, Sartre, Heidegger), along with correspondences to Bergson and Marx at the end of his introduction to *Art and Answerability*, xxxv–xxxix. For an argument about why "school" is more accurate than "circle" in describing Bakhtin's relations at various periods of his career to fellow scholars like Matvei Kagan, Lev Pumpianskii, P. N. Medvedev, and Valentin Voloshinov, see Alistair Renfrew, *Towards a New Materialist Aesthetics: Bakhtin, Genre, and the Fates of Literary Theory* (London: Legenda, 2006), x–xiii.

12. Pechey, *Mikhail Bakhtin*, 155. Peachey draws a very intriguing parallel between Bakhtin and Erich Auerbach, emphasizing the basal significance of the "Christian story" behind the advent of modernity, as well as the utility of *figura* and typology for understanding Bakhtin's own intellectual rapprochement between forms of early Christianity and secular modernity. Thus, "That hermeneutics and philology are intersecting disciplines, and that their best practitioners are acutely aware of the ethical force of their arguments in situations of international crisis, is nowhere made plainer than in the work of Auerbach and Bakhtin" (10). The figure of Edward Said, of course, suggests a spectral third party to this dialogue.

13. I take the phrase from Milan Kundera's *The Art of the Novel*, trans. Linda Asher (New York: Perennial, 2000), 5.

14. See the essays "Epic and Novel" and "From the Prehistory of Novelistic Discourse" in *The Dialogic Imagination: Four Essays*, trans. Caryl Emerson and Michael Holquist (Austin: University of Texas Press, 1981).

15. Meir Sternberg's *The Poetics of Biblical Narrative: Ideological Literature and the Drama of Reading* is perhaps the best example in a critical literature that deploys

contemporary literary approaches to the Bible for mounting an extremely sophisticated argument about why biblical discourse and novelistic narrative precede along asymptotic axes (see his introductory chapter, "Literary Text, Literary Approach," especially). But this would still not be Levinas's critique, principally because of the intermediating force for him of Talmudic discourse and rabbinic *midrash*, and because, more simply, he loves fiction differently than he loves Torah, e.g., "The Russian novel was my preparation for philosophy."

16. By contrast, a number of studies see intrinsic connections between Bakhtinian concepts and biblical discourse. See, for instance, Walter L. Reed, *Dialogues of the Word: The Bible as Literature According to Bakhtin* (New York: Oxford University Press, 1993); Roland Boer, ed., *Bakhtin and Genre Theory in Biblical Studies* (Atlanta: Society of Biblical Literature, 2007); and Barbara Green, ed., *Mikhail Bakhtin and Biblical Scholarship: An Introduction* (Atlanta: Society of Biblical Literature, 2000). Moshe Simon-Shoshan's *Stories of the Law: Narrative Discourse and the Construction of Authority in the Mishnah* (New York: Oxford University Press, 2012) can also be consulted for its typology of mishnaic narrative: exempla, case story, and etiologies.

17. "In dancing, I become 'bodied' in being to the highest degree; I come to participate in the being of others. What dances in me is my pr*esent-on-hand* being (that has been affirmed from the outside)—my *sophianic* being dances in me, the *other* dances in me. The moment of being-swayed, of being-possessed by being is manifestly experienced in dancing" (137). See also the treatment of the "lyrical hero an author," 167–172.

18. Besides my *Narrative Ethics* (1995), see David Patterson's "Bakhtin and Levinas: Signification, Responsibility, Spirit," *Literature and Spirit: Essays on Bakhtin and his Contemporaries* (Lexington: University of Kentucky Press, 1988); Augusto Ponzio's chapter "Humanism of the Other Man in Bakhtin and Levinas," in *Signs, Dialogue, and Ideology* (1993), (Philadelphia: John Benjamins, 1993); Jeffrey Nealon's "The Ethics of Dialogue: Bakhtin's Answerability and Levinas's Responsibility," *College English* 59, no. 2 (February 1997): 129–148, and *Alterity Politics: Ethics and Performative Subjectivity* (Durham, N.C.: Duke University Press, 1998); Michael Eskin's *Ethics and Dialogue: In the Works of Levinas, Bakhtin, Mandel'shtam, and Celan* (Oxford: Oxford University Press, 2000); Michael Gardiner's "Alterity and Ethics: A Dialogical Perspective," *Theory, Culture, and Society* 13 (1996): 121–143; Daphna Erdinast-Vulcan's "Between the Face and the Voice: Bakhtin Meets Levinas," in *Continental Philosophy Review* 41, no. 1 (2008): 43–58. This last essay should be read in company with "Borderline and Contraband: Bakhtin and the Question of the Subject," and "Bakhtin's Homesickness: A Late Reply to Julia Kristeva," *Textual Practice* 9, no. 2 (1995): 223–242, both of which treat the metaphysical and religious aspects of Bakhtin's early essays. See also Erdinast-Vulcan's "The I that Tells Itself: A Bakhtinian Perspective on Narrative Identity," *Narrative* 16, no. 1 (January 2008): 1–15.

19. "Aversive Thinking," in *Conditions Handsome and Unhandsome: The Constitution of Emersonian Perfectionism* (Chicago: University of Chicago Press, 1990), 57. Compare the postscript to *The World Viewed*, "More of the World Viewed," in which Cavell expresses

an earlier and quite different relationship to what Bakhtin would analyze as the natural condition of any word being "half someone else's": "There [in *Must We Mean What We Say*?] my hope for conviction from the reader was placed in my ability to motivate assertions, and objections to them, and to voice them in such a form and at such a time that the reader would have the impression that he was himself thinking them, had been about to have said them—not about to have said something generally along their lines, but as it were to find himself thinking those specific words just when and just as they were appearing to him" (163).

20. In her essay "The Tolstoy Connection To Bakhtin," Caryl Emerson makes the pertinent point that "At its most elevated level, of course, authorship is theological—a reenactment, writ small of supreme authority creating humanity" (154). This is Ruth Coates's argument, too, in *Christianity in Bakhtin: God and the Exiled Author* (Cambridge: Cambridge University Press, 1999), as she traces lineaments of the "exiled" God as author. But Cavell sees this, rather, as a function of the politics of interpretation, since reading aspires to its own supremacy, even if necessarily always belated and conflicted.

21. Some useful recent essay collections are Liisa Steinby and Tintti Klapuri, eds., *Bakhtin and His Others: (Inter)subjectivity, Chronotope, Dialogism* (London: Anthem Press, 2103); Karine Zbinden, ed., *Bakhtin Between East and West: Cross-Cultural Transmission* (London: Legenda, 2006); Michael Gardiner, ed., *Bakhtin and the Human Sciences* (Thousand Oaks, Calif.: Sage Publications, 1998); Jorgen Bruhn and Jan Lundquist, eds., *The Novelness of Bakhtin: Perspectives and Possibilities* (Copenhagen: Museum Tusculanum Press, 2001); Craig Brandist and Galin Tikhanov, eds. *Materializing Bakhtin: The Bakhtin Circle and Social Theory* (New York: St. Martins Press, 2000); David Shepherd, ed., *The Contexts of Bakhtin: Philosophy, Authorship, Aesthetics* (Amsterdam: Harwood Academic Publishers, 1998); and Amy Mandelker, ed., *Bakhtin in Contexts: Across the Disciplines* (Evanston, Ill.: Northwestern University Press, 1995).

22. Even if their logical thrust, as in *Toward a Philosophy of the Deed*, argues strenuously against теоретическое познание ("theoretical cognition" or theoreticism) as both methodology and worldview. See Holquist's introductions to *Art and Answerability,* xxxii and *Toward a Philosophy of the Act.*

23. The small pamphlet from which this directive comes was transcribed in the biography by S. S. Konkin and L. S. Konkina. *Mikhail Bakhtin: stranitsy zhizni i tvorchestva* (Saransk: Mordovskoe knizhnoe izdvo, 1993).

24. Is Bakhtin a nostalgist for bygone religious certainties in God and authorship, or does he belong to the vanguard of their secularist overturning? For in his last writings, Bakhtin returns to some of the ethical/aesthetic, quasi-religious questions posed but never fully resolved by the early ones. Daphna Erdinast-Vulcan ascribes such irresolution to a conceptual "homesickness"—"a metaphysical wound, an ache that will not go away" ("Borderline and Contraband," 262). While Bakhtin can be made to anticipate an eerily postmodern account of subjectivity as porous and borderline, he clearly remains drawn to a moral ground for identity and agency, to a bridge between ethics and metaphysics, to something like Levinas's commitment to exteriority, by turns post-Kantian, neo-Kantian,

and yet still Kantian. Let it be said that Bakhtin's dialogue with Kant in the early essays affords a testing ground for its own discoverable tension between *Dichtung* and *Darstellung*, that "certain literary 'crisis' in Kant" (19) so cleverly dissected by Jean-Luc Nancy in *The Discourse of the Syncope: Logodaedalus*, trans. Saul Anton (Stanford: Stanford University Press, 2008).

25. See the essay by Anthony Wall, "A Broken Thinker" in *Bakhtin/"Bakhtin": The Archives and Beyond* (Durham, N.C.: Duke University Press, 1999), 669–698, and Ken Hirschkop, "Bakhtin, Philosopher and Sociologist," *Face to Face: Bakhtin in Russia and the West*, ed. Carol Adlam, Rachel Falconer, Vitalii Makhlin, and Alistair Renfrew (Sheffield: Sheffield Academic Press, 1997), 54–67.

26. "But in fact there is no systematic theory of reading or the reader to be plucked read-formed from the diverse Bakhtinian legacy," writes David Shepherd in his often-cited, but now somewhat dated 1989 essay, "Bakhtin and the Reader," in *Bakhtin and Cultural Theory*, 136. Shepherd extrapolates dimensions of Bakhtin's arguments about discourse and intertextuality complementary to the state of reading theory in the late 1980s, which primarily means the work of Wolfgang Iser and Stanley Fish. The major contribution of the essay is to emphasize the interplay in Bakhtin's thought between literary text or speech genre and its various informing contexts (politics and ideology—institutional "sites of power" or perhaps what Georg Simmel called "social forms"), for various constituencies of empirical readers. But Shepherd's understanding of reading practice is primarily epistemological as opposed to performative, which limits its utility for an ethics of reading inflected through Bakhtinian categories. See also Judith Davidson, "Bakhtin as a Theory of Reading," *Center for the Study of Reading* (University of Illinois at Urbana-Champaign, August 1993).

27. "The World According to Globalization and Bakhtin," in *Materializing Bakhtin: The Bakhtin Circle and Social Theory*, ed. Craig Brandist and Galin Tihanov (New York: St. Martins Press, 2000), 3–19.

28. Consult the many articles in literary journals so titled, and the University of Sheffield Bakhtin Centre's Bakhtin Analytical Database: http://rother.shef.ac.uk/Bakhtin.

29. "The hero and the author/beholder—these are the fundamental constituents, the fundamental participants in the event of a work of art: they alone can be answerable, and they alone are capable of giving it the unity of an event and of bringing it into an essential communion with the unitary and unique event of being" (190). An inventory of Bakhtinian perspectives on authorship and authoring can be found in Giovanni Palmieri, "'The Author' According to Bakhtin . . . and Bakhtin the Author," *The Contexts of Bakhtin*, 45–56.

30. See, for example, the complex diagram Valerii Tiupa has constructed in order to accommodate the many vectors in Bakhtin's discursive field in "The Architectonics of Aesthetic Discourse," in ibid., 95–107.

31. See, for instance, Gary Saul Morson, "Who Speaks for Bakhtin?: A Dialogic Introduction," *Critical Inquiry* 10, no. 2 (December 1983): 225–243: "For Bakhtin, everything is 'pragmatics,' and semantic and syntactic codes are really 'context in rigor

mortis.'" Yet strictly, speaking, "linguistic/rhetorical" signifies neither ethical-linguistic in Kristeva's sense of a regulated system of language *altered* or (to retrieve Geoffrey Harpham's term) *shadowed* by semiotic rhythm ("the poetry that it presupposes"), nor ethical-rhetorical in James Phelan's sense of ethical-rhetorical *positioning* ("a concept that combines acting from and being placed in an ethical location") whereby readers' values and judgments are activated by connected currents of cognition, emotion, and desire. See Kristeva, "The Ethics of Linguistics" in *Desire in Language: A Semiotic Approach to Literature and Art*, trans. Alice Jardine (New York: Columbia University Press, 1980), 23–35 and James Phelan, "Sethe's Choice: *Beloved* and the Ethics of Reading," *Mapping the Ethical Turn: A Reader in Ethics, Culture, and Literary Theory*, ed. Todd F. Davis and Kenneth Womack (Charlottesville: University of Virginia Press, 2001), 93–109; and Heather Love, "Close but not Deep: Literary Ethics and the Descriptive Turn," *New Literary History* 41, no. 2 (Spring 2010): 371–391.

32. Although forming a continuous analysis, the readings are sufficiently different, that in the first case, the emphasis falls on an architectonic of aesthetic seeing as analogous to the answerable deed in life (a coming-to-consciousness), while in the second, what is privileged is the axiological center constituted by a given human being within an artistic whole. See *Toward a Philosophy of the Act*, 99.

33. "Only the value of mortal man provides the standards for measuring the spatial and temporal orders: space gains body as the possible horizon of mortal man and as his possible environment, and time possesses valuative weight and heaviness as the progression of mortal man's life" (65).

34. This applies to Bakhtin's concept of the "event," as well, as he indicates in a footnote to "Author and Hero": "The event of being is a phenomenological concept, for being presents itself to a living consciousness as an event, and a living consciousness actively orients itself and lives in it as an event" (188).

35. Bakhtin suffered from chronic osteomyelitis, eventually resulting in the amputation of his right leg (see the Clark and Holquist biography). It is tempting to ponder the afterlife of the aesthetic "consummation" and wholeness/unity tropes from the early essays of the 1920s (as well as the passages about the suffering person in need of the other's empathetic enframing) in connection with Bakhtin's own body history, from his leg-amputation in 1938 through the Rabelais book of the 1940s and his subsequent discussions of borders and boundaries in "The Problem of Speech Genres" and later essays. Thus, Emerson, in "Shklovsky's *ostranenie*, Bakhtin's *vnenakhodimost'* (How Distance Serves an Aesthetics of Arousal Differently from an Aesthetics Based on Pain)," *Poetics Today* 26, no. 4 (2005): 637–664: "It could be argued that Bakhtin's later, more famous constructs—the dialogic word and the carnival body—are in part variations on this primal imperative to displace, transcend, or recontextualize that which causes physical pain" (646). And also, "In all these situations (verbal utterance, luminous dying, cranial interaction, and the suffering body in need of the other's passionate gaze), getting outside the body means first of all getting to a place that no longer hurts" (647).

36. See Chapters 1 and 2 of Mihailovic's *Corporeal Words* and the first two chapters of Coates's *Christianity in Bakhtin*. "Perichoresis" denotes the mutual interpenetration within the triune structure of God the Father, the Son, and the Holy Spirit, developed in Patristic literature but revived recently by a number of Trinitarian theologians. The subsection "The Value of the Human Body in History" in "Author and Hero" (53–58) uses almost entirely religious examples. Yet, a tendentious appeal to a theologically "coded" language (as in Coates's analysis) need not exhaust the semantic horizon in these early essays. Thus, Augusto Ponzio and Susan Petrilli eschew a religious vocabulary and look instead to semiotics, borrowing, for example, the Peircian term "intercorporeity" in their analysis of Bakhtin (and Levinas) in *Semiotics Unbounded: Interpretive Routes Through the Open Network of Signs* (Toronto: University of Toronto Press, 2005).

37. This trajectory is particularly well mapped in Renfrew's *Towards a New Materialist Aesthetics: Bakhtin, Genre, and the Fates of Literary Theory* (London: Legenda, 2006).

38. *The Dialogic Imagination*, 250.

39. Ibid., 299–300. On this sentence, see also *Corporeal Words,* 31.

40. "Toward a Reworking of the Dostoevsky Book," in *Problems of Dostoevsky's Poetics,* trans. Caryl Emerson (Minneapolis: University of Minnesota Press, 1984), 287. Compare "Response to a Question from the *Novy Mir* Editorial Staff" (1970): "But one cannot draw an absolute boundary between body and meaning in the area of culture. . . . Therefore new discoveries of material bearers of meaning alter our semantic concepts, and they can also force us to restructure them radically. . . . It is only through the eyes of another culture that foreign culture reveals itself fully and profoundly" (*Speech Genres and Other Late Essays*, 6–7).

41. Mihailovic (68–69) explains an important distinction between incarnation and embodiment in Bakhtin, the latter being a partial preliminary version of the former's baseline indispensability for the deed as integrated with selfhood, undersigned and assimilated. Similarly as a calque for German *Einfühlung*, Baktin's Husserlian (or Schelerian) notion of вживание ("live-entering")—so crucial to the "Author and Hero" essay—represents a kinetic force and activeness through which one *exerts*, rather than merely projects, empathy (see 77–78). As kenotic self-emptying—a kenotics, Mihailovic emphasizes, that is also a kinetics—its direct analogue is the *bitul hayesh* Levinas analyzes in the *Nefesh Ha-Ḥayyim*. On the Scheler connection, see "From Phenomenology to Dialogue," in *Bakhtin and Cultural Theory*, ed. Ken Hirschkop and David G. Shepherd, 109–136).

42. "Philosophy by other means" was Bakhtin's formulation for the novel and its criticism, but it seems just as applicable to the philosophical vocation itself, which, in Bakhtin's hands, becomes creatively *altered*, or as he would say, dialogized. Levinas's appeal to the Talmud performs the same leverage.

43. On the textual history of this fragment (which, improbably enough, appeared in print fifty years after composition in a Soviet Academy of Sciences yearbook on technology and culture), see the introduction in the English translation by Holquist and the more extensive exposition by S. G. Bocharov in the Russian edition. Evidently, Bakhtin

planned the essay in four parts, of which only the first, phenomenological, section survives; the missing three treated, respectively, the participative subject, the ethics of politics, and religion. While the account of human agency in this text can certainly be read as both descriptive and deontological but not particularly embedded in cultural or historical realities (as a response, say, to Spengler), see the historicized corrective Ken Hirschkop provides in *Mikhail Bakhtin: An Aesthetic for Democracy* (Oxford: Oxford University Press, 1999).

44. The archetype for such communion of course is the figure of Christ, through the boundary-crossing events of incarnation and transubstantiation (Bakhtin's is not a suffering or crucified Christ). But, as Mihailovich correctly insists in my view, "What really interests Bakhtin in the figure of Christ is his interstitiality and liminality, his position of being poised between the states of conjunction with others and separation from them. Christ represents a sociological principle, which, as important as it is, most pointedly does not constitute a confessional frame of reference. The idea of specifically or denominationally Christian society . . . does not interest Bakhtin in the least" (80).

45. *Martin Eden* (New York: Penguin, 1994), 407.

46. *Mikhail Bakhtin and Walter Benjamin: Experience and Form* (New York: Palgrave Macmillan, 2007).

47. See in this connection Emerson's juxtaposition in "Shklovsky's *ostranenie*, Bakhtin's *vnenakhodimost'*" of Bakhtin and Vicktor Shklovsky—the former, Dostoyevskian in his tormented humanism and backward looking, and the latter, Tolstoyan and a fully "modernist humanist" (639).

48. "The Metropolis and Mental Life," in *On Individuality and Social Forms*, ed. Donald Levine (Chicago: University of Chicago Press, 1971), 324–339. Simmel, as it turns out, especially his distinction between *Erfahrung* and *Erlebnis* and its correlation in Bergsonian *Lebensphilosophie*, influenced both Benjamin and Bakhtin, as Beasley-Murray explains in his second chapter (Simmel is discussed by Voloshinov, if not specifically by Bakhtin, in *Marxism and the Philosophy of Language*).

49. See Beasley-Murray on the nuances here, 25–27.

50. Although laughter was so crucial and transcendent a concept to him, no photograph I have seen ever shows Bakhtin smiling.

51. Correlatively, reading reveals the poetics at work in Pascal's composition, its metrics, alliteration and assonance, and otherwise patterned form. A distinctly Nabokovian example from Mihailescu's essay: "Now the rhythm changes, *éternellement en joye*, although, under the influence of the previous lines, we hear its feminine rhymes (*jour* and *terre* are read as each having two syllables). But the new rhythm is broken by *exercice*, a word that echoes its anapestic predecessor *directeur*. In more than one sense, *exercice* lies at the center of the line: prosodically, it represents the caesura between two identical hemistiches. But as *exercice* breaks the (effeminate) harmony, it opens a different prosodic order in which it surrounds itself with a pair of peers, two anapestic sequences: *pour/un/jour* and *sur/la/terre*. The directed action (*exercice*) finds a place for itself in the new rhythmic order which it itself triggers" (11). Unsurprisingly, such *explication de texte* differs greatly

from the sort of plain-sense rendering we find in Marvin Richard O'Connell's *Blaise Pascal: Reasons of the Heart* (Grand Rapids, Mich.: Eerdmans, 1997), 90–103.

52. "Great works" are the brief focus in Bakhtin's 1970 interview with *Novy Mir*: "great works continue to live in the distant future. In the process of their posthumous life, they are enriched with new meanings, new significance: it is as though these works outgrow what they were in the epoch of their creation" (4). "Great time" is mentioned briefly in that essay and again in "Toward a Methodology for the Human Sciences" in *Speech Genres and Other Late Essays:* "The problem of remote contexts. The eternal renewal of meanings in all new contexts. Small time (the present day, the recent past, and the foreseeable—desired—future) and great time: infinite and unfinalized dialogue in which no meaning dies" (169). See also David Shepherd, "A Feeling for History? Bakhtin and 'The Problem of Great Time,'" *Slavonic and East European Review* 84, no. 1 (2006): 31–59, and William D. Lindsey, "'The Problem of Great Time': A Bakhtinian Ethics of Discourse," *Journal of Religion* 73, no. 3 (1993): 311–328.

53. Герои, in Bakhtin's usage, is not restricted to mimetic, individual character, but rather describes a certain projective energy of self, future-oriented and open-ended, that takes shape in narrative—especially modernist—but more generally embodies "collective, historical, in any case, suprapersonal process". See Kriger, "Heroic Aesthetics and Modernist Critique," 566. The most thorough, post-Bakhtinian analysis of intercharacter poetics belongs to Alex Woloch, *The One vs. the Many: Minor Characters and the Space of the Protagonist in the Novel* (Princeton: Princeton University Press, 2003). And for a very different, non-Bakhtinian take on premodernist subjectivity in the novel, see Nancy Armstrong, *How Novels Think: The Limits of Individualism from 1719 to 1900* (New York: Columbia University Press, 2006).

54. "The Problem of the Text in Linguistics, Philology, and the Human Sciences," *Speech Genres and Other Late Essays*, 126. The concept has loomed large in rhetorical approaches to Bakhtin, but see also Frank M. Farmer, "'Not Theory . . . but a Sense of Theory': The Superaddressee and the Contexts of Eden," *Symploke* 2, no. 1 (1994): 87–101, and Graham Pechey's discussion of it in the chapter "The Novel and Its Others" in *Mikhail Bakhtin*, 105–126. Unsubstantiated references to a third copy of the *Mémorial* that Pascal may have given to a close friend become more relevant in this respect, but no biography has provided proof, and the narrative recounted by Gilberte Pascal remains authoritative.

55. "What the other rightfully negates in himself, I rightfully affirm and preserve in him, and, in so doing, I give birth to his soul on a new axiological plane of being" (129).

56. To that degree, they resemble Bakhtin himself, who, in Erdinast-Vulcan's reading, smuggles contraband from philosophical to literary domains and back again. Bakhtin's subject, in this view, is amphibolous or double-voiced, as author-hero (aesthetic categories, or poetics) merge seamlessly into self-other (metaphysics), with a consequent blurring of ontological and epistemological differences, as well. See "Borderlines and Contraband," 253–258. Kriger's analysis aligns Bakhtin as well with an immanent critique of literary modernism, whose narrative poetics of the subject

inflates both ends of the bipolarity: to take the most obvious example, Joyce-Daedalus and Bloom.

57. "Only the inner body (the body experienced as heavy) is *given* to a human being himself; the other's outer body is not given but *set as a task*: I must actively produce it" (51).

58. It needs to be said that whenever Bakhtin deploys terms like "ethical" or "cognitive" or "religious" over against the "aesthetic," the distinctly relational interplay of author-and-hero, the noncoincidence of two connected consciousnesses, has been compromised in some way, and whatever agency or activity is effected fall short of the fully consummated and completed. Authors' primary obligation to their acts of creation is aesthetic; so, it seems, is that of readers, as well. On this point, and the correlative distinction to be made between "dialogism" (aesthetic) and "dialogue" (ethical-cognitive), see Bernard-Donals, "Bakhtin and Phenomenology," 44–45 and 47.

59. *Hermeneutics and the Human Sciences: Essays on Language, Action and Interpretation*, trans. John B. Thompson (Cambridge: Cambridge University Press, 1981), 112; see also *From Text to Action: Essays in Hermeneutics II*, trans. Kathleen Blamey and John B. Thompson (Evanston, Ill.: Northwestern University Press, 1991), and *Interpretation Theory: Discourse and the Surplus of Meaning*, trans. David Pellauer et al. (Fort Worth: Texas Christian University Press, 1976).

60. Selected passages have been transcribed in Bonesteel's *Henry Darger: Art and Selected Writings* and *Paper & Carriage no. 3*, ed. Joanna Zopor Mackenzie Picard, Caroline Picard, Chaz Reetz-Laiolo, and Shannon Stratton (Chicago: Green Lantern Press, 2008). See also Bonesteel's articles, "Henry Darger's Search for the Grail in the Guise of a Celestial Child," in *Third Person: Authoring and Exploring Vast Narratives,* ed. Pat Harrigan, Noah Wardrip-Fruin (Cambridge, Mass.: MIT Press, 2009), 253–266, and "Heroes and Villains: Henry Darger," *Raw Vision* 72. Other pertinent resources are the chapter on Darger in Charles Russell, *Groundwaters: A Century of Art by Self-Taught And Outsider Artists* (New York: Prestel Verlag, 2011), and the essay by Mary Trent, "'Many Stirring Scenes': Henry Darger's Engagement with American Mass Print Media," *American Art* 26 (Spring 2012): 74–101.

61. Darger's handwritten manuscripts show various strikethroughs and process errors, but the typescripts are remarkably meticulous. Nevertheless, he faced a practical problem: as he was constantly augmenting and revising the plot of his saga, the sequence of pages in the already bound volumes became difficult to alter, and at a certain point he seems to have abandoned hope of making the work fully cohere and conform to a definitive chronology. Simple materiality ultimately frustrated his authorial control over the vast scale of his narrative. (contrast the case of Dickinson's "envelope poems").

62. *Selected Writings Volume 4*, 338. In the *Kuntswerk* (1936) and *Kleine Geschichte der Photographie* (1931) essays, Benjamin characterizes aura as "a strange weave of space and time: the unique appearance [apparition, semblance] of a distance, however near it may be" (*SW* 2:518 and 3:104).

63. And Darger in fact *became* a waif, institutionalized in his own "Bleak House" after his father died in 1905, the Lincoln Asylum for Feeble-Minded Children in Lincoln

Illinois from which he finally escaped four years later. The buildings survive to this day, some used as a correctional center. See Anne E. Parsons, "From Asylum to Prison: The Story of the Lincoln State School," *Journal of Illinois History* 14 (Winter 2011): 242–260.

64. Charles Dickens, *Oliver Twist* (New York: Modern Library Classics, 2001), 75.

65. See Chapter 3.

66. Les W. Smith scrutinizes Bakhtin's phenomenology of confession at length in his *Confession in the Novel: Bakhtin's Author Revisited* (Cranbury, N.J.: Associated University Presses, 1996), 32ff.

67. Two books that make that demarcation are Greg M. Nielsen, *The Norms of Answerability: Social Theory Between Bakhtin and Habermas* (Albany: State University of New York Press, 2001), and the volume of four essays edited by Valerie Z. Nollan, *Bakhtin: Ethics and Mechanics* (Evanston, Ill.: Northwestern University Press, 2003).

68. See also the discussion of "artistic creation" in "The Problem of Content, Material, and Form in Verbal Art" (1924), collected in the same volume.

69. Bakhtin returns to this idea in "Toward a Methodology for the Human Sciences" (160–161), expressing it there as the distinction between the author-creator found only in the work and the "image" of the author.

70. Again, in "Toward a Methodology for the Human Sciences," Bakhtin distinguishes between real reader-listeners and the immanent, idealized version postulated by structuralism (165).

71. Especially in the choice of this term, Bakhtin, rather uncannily, inverts the progression of Barthes's famous formula (*de l'oeuvre au texte*) and keeps pace with a term (*oeuvre*) *that* Levinas retrieves often when discussing art and literature.

72. See Michael Holquist, "Answering as Authoring: Mikhail Bakhtin's Trans-Linguistics," *Critical Inquiry* 10, no. 2 (December 1983): 307–319.

73. *Time and Narrative Volume 3*, trans. Kathleen Blamey and David Pellauer (Chicago: University of Chicago Press, 1988).

74. In *Mikhail Bakhtin*, Pechey describes the complementarity of theology and aesthetics this way: "both are cognitive discourses which thematize that which is other that, or at least not wholly, cognitive; both are relatively logically ordered meta-languages whose object is either language incommensurably differently oriented and organized or beyond language altogether" (156). Thus, the "theologically-inflected aesthetics" of the "Author and Hero" treatise reveals itself at the same time to be an "ontologically inflected poetics" (165).

75. Bernard-Donals expands on this in position in Chapters 2 and 3 of *Mikhail Bakhtin: Between Phenomenology and Marxism* (Cambridge: Cambridge University Press, 1994)

76. In *Must We Mean What We Say? A Book of Essays* (Cambridge: Cambridge University Press, 2002). Cavell's distinction was already adumbrated by Wittgenstein in *On Certainty*, trans. Denis Paul and G. E. M. Anscombe (Oxford: Basil Blackwell, 1969), §378, p49e: "Knowledge in the end is based on acknowledgement."

77. "Knowing and Acknowledging," *Must We Mean What We Say?*, 263.

78. Cavell's remarks here are in deliberate echo of art historian Michael Fried's controversial critique of Clement Greenberg's theory of modernism, "Art and Object-

hood," in *Art and Objecthood: Essays and Reviews* (Chicago: University of Chicago Press, 1998), which Cavell understands as coinciding with his own sense of "acknowledgment": "I follow Michael Fried in speaking of this fact of modernist painting as an acknowledging of its conditions. Any painting may teach you what is true of all paintings. A modernist painting teaches you this *by* acknowledgment" (109). A long footnote to *The World Viewed* expands on the convergence around the idea of acknowledgment as "continuous discovery of mutual profit" (169). Fried's "notorious" and "infamous" argument, in particular his denigration of theater and theatricality as what fall outside the boundaries of a medium, along with Wittgensteinian notions of conventional practice ("forms of life') as parsed by Cavell, come under severe critique in Diarmuid Costello, "The Very Idea of a 'Specific' Medium: Michael Fried and Stanley Cavell on Painting and Photography as Arts," *Critical Inquiry* 34, no. 2 (Winter 2008): 274–312. The Cavell/Fried nexus is also the subject of Matthew Bowman, "Allegorical Impulses and the Body in Painting," *re•bus 1* (Spring 2008): 1–26. In *The World Viewed*, Cavell also continues a line of thought about modern art's "conditions of possibility," which he had previously explored in "Music Discomposed."

79. Compare his essay "The Fact of Television," in *Cavell on Film*, ed. William Rothman (Albany: State University of New York Press, 200), 59–86, where Cavell says, "What I have said they are principles of is the revelation (I habitually call this the acknowledgment) of an artistic medium. I specify this revelation in *The World Viewed*, by way of articulating what I call there 'the material basis' of film. I call the basis a succession of automatic world projections" (85).

80. Cleavage between thing and person or between thing and thing, coincidentally enough, lies at the heart of the Hebrew root meaning of קדושה ("holiness"), which, as something "set apart," signifies a modality of separation. See the interesting discussion of the trilateral root and its various morphological inflections in David Patterson, *Hebrew Language and Jewish Thought* (Routledge: New York, 2005), 195–200.

81. Franz Rosenzweig, *Understanding the Sick and the Healthy: A View of World, Man, and God*, trans. Nahum Glatzer (Cambridge, Mass.: Harvard University Press, 1999), 9–10. The passage also appears in Putnam's treatment of Rosenzweig and Wittgenstein in *Jewish Philosophy as a Guide to Life: Rosenzweig, Buber, Levinas, Wittgenstein* (Bloomington: Indiana University Press, 2008), 26–27.

82. In the 1978 essay "What Becomes of Things on Film," *Cavell on Film*, 1–10, Cavell expresses the thought anew this way: "Objects on film are always already displaced, *trouvé* (i.e., that we as viewers are already displaced before them)," 9.

6. Ethics of Reading III: Cavell and Theater/Cinema

1. *Little Did I Know: Excerpts from Memory* (Stanford: Stanford University Press, 2010) narrates certain details of familial lore at length, including Cavell's preparation for his *bar mitzvah*. In the essay "An Emerson Mood," included in the expanded edition of *Senses of Walden* (Chicago: University of Chicago Press, 1992), Cavell interprets Emerson's trope of marking "whim" on the lintels of the doorpost in "Self Reliance" as a

subliminal reference to the *mitzvah* of *mezuzah* of Ex. 12: 7, 23 and Deut. 6:29. Cavell discuss the episode of Jacob's beguiling of Isaac to receive a blessing (Gen. 27:22) in several places: "In the Meantime: Authority, Tradition, and the Future of the Disciplines," *Yale Journal of Criticism* 5, no. 2 (Spring 1992): 229–237; *Philosophical Passages: Wittgenstein, Emerson, Austin, Derrida* (Cambridge: Blackwell Publishers, 1995); and *A Pitch of Philosophy: Autobiographical Exercises* (Cambridge, Mass.: Harvard University Press, 1994). Finally, in the "overture" to *A Pitch of Philosophy*, Cavell recounts his reading of Gershom Scholem's correspondence with Benjamin in Jerusalem, prompting a family reverie about cultural inheritance; each section of the book begins with an epigraph from Scholem.

2. Overreading is the substance of Colin Davis's critique in his chapter on Cavell in *Critical Excess*. Cavell, of course, has his share or detractors: for his philosophizing, his prose style, and his accounts of medium and genre, in particular film and Shakespearean drama. See, for example, the admiring essay by Gerald Bruns, "Stanley Cavell's Shakespeare," *Critical Inquiry* 16, no. 3 (Spring 1990): 612–632, which prompted critical responses from both a Shakespearean and a philosopher in the following issue. See also the perspicuous essay by Jonathan Culler, "Bad Writing and Good Philosophy," in *Just Being Difficult: Academic Writing in the Public Arena*, ed. Jonathan Culler and Kevin Lamb (Stanford: Stanford University Press, 2003), 43–57.

3. See, for example, Maimonides's *Mishneh Torah*, Chap. 4:13. *bPesaḥim* 26a cites the same *mishnah* in the context of a discussion between Abaye and Rava about *issur hana'ah* (forbidden benefit); the phrase *kdei shelo yazunu 'eineihem* (so that they should not feast their eyes) is also deployed in a variant form in a parable about the king's garden in *bHagigah* 14b (following the famous parable, "four entered *pardes*") in which one is called upon to "look but not feast his eyes." As far as the actual structure is concerned, by the time of the rebuilt Second Temple, only the projection of bare rock known as "The Foundation Stone" was actually visible. The Ark of the Covenant itself, *keruvim* (cherubim), and *kapporet* ("Mercy Seat") of the First Temple were never replaced [*Mishnah Yoma* 5:2]. Literary critic Adam Kirsch briefly addresses the *tevot* from *bPesaḥim* 26a in "In the Shadow of the Divine, Reaping Unintended Benefits at the Edges of the Law," *Tablet Magazine* (July 23, 2013), www.tabletmag.com/jewish-life-and-religion/138527/adam-kirsch-daf-yomi-43.

4. Another very rough analogy that brings tevot and movie house somewhat closer to each other are "subway zoetropes," the most famous of which is probably Bill Brand's *Masstransitscope* (1980), which can be viewed on Manhattan-bound train from the De Kalb station in Brooklyn. See the website at www.bboptics.com/masstransiscope.html.

5. Three books and two essays discuss transits between Cavell's philosophy and Jewish tradition/identity: Rael Meyerowitz, *Transferring to America: Jewish Interpretations of American Dreams* (Albany: State University of New York Press, 1995); Susanne Klingenstein, *Enlarging America: The Cultural Work of Jewish Literary Scholars, 1930–1990* (Syracuse: Syracuse University Press, 1998); Bruce Rosenstock, *Philosophy and the Jewish Question: Mendelssohn, Rosenzweig, and Beyond* (New York: Fordham University Press,

2009); Emily Miller Budick, "Exodus, Discovery, and Coming Home to the Promised Land," *People of the Book: Thirty Scholars Reflect on Their Jewish Identity*, ed. Jeffrey Rubin Dorsky, Shelley Fisher Fishkin (Madison: University of Wisconsin Press, 1996), 217–230; and Thomas Elsaesser, "Presentation: Stanley Cavell and Cinema," *Come to Your Senses: ASCA Yearbook*, ed. Mieke Bal, Eloe Kingma (Amsterdam: ASCA 1999), 107–115. Peter Dula's *Cavell, Companionship, and Christian Theology* (Oxford: Oxford University Press, 2010) obviously pursues an alternate direction. See also Cavell's short essay-response to photographs by Frédéric Brenner, "Departures," in *Diaspora: Homelands in Exile (Voices)* ed. Frédéric Brenner (New York: HarperCollins, 2003), 133–151.

6. *Rashei tevot* ("word initials," or "abbreviations") and *sofei tevot* ("ends of words") are common usages of תבה in Modern Hebrew. In Sephardic synagogues, the *tevah* signifies not the Torah ark (as one might possibly guess) but rather the pulpit, the stand on the platform from which prayers are recited and the Torah is cantillated. See the essay "Sephardic Arks" in the column *On Language* by Philologos, *The Forward* (January 2, 2004) http://forward.com/articles/6047/sephardic-arks/.

7. This is not quite what Sergei Dolgopolski has in mind when he speaks of "The Talmud as Film" in the final chapter of his book, *The Open Past: Subjectivity and Remembering in the Talmud* (New York: Fordham University Press, 2013) whose focus is an analogy between montage and the Talmud's redaction by *stamm'aim* (editors).

8. *Cities of Words: Pedagogical Letters on a Register of the Moral Life* (Cambridge, Mass.: Harvard University Press, 2005), 400.

9. *Hearing Things: Voice and Method in the Writing of Stanley Cavell* (Chicago: University of Chicago Press, 1998), 151.

10. Cavell's rhetorical eccentricities have been duly noted. But when, for instance, he chooses to the anachronistic term "talkie" in *The World Viewed* to refer to sound film long after the advent of synchronized sound track in the late 1920s (unless he is referring strictly to sound films produced from, say, 1927 to 1933, which appears not to be the case since the preface mentions "Hollywood talkies of the 30's and 40's"), the reservations from "friends sympathetic to its issues" that he is gracious enough to concede in the appended chapter in the 1979 edition of *The World Viewed* ring home. On a related note, concurrent with the appended chapter, the "Foreword to the Enlarged Edition" contains three points of reference: (1) Cavell's insistence on his own "remembering a work" (rather than rescreening or otherwise checking it), (2) the visual beauty of Terence Malick's *Days of Heaven*, and (3) several remarks by Heidegger on "Being." Here, too, the book's hold on its own concerns and tightened focus are readily apparent.

11. *Making Trifles of Terrors: Redistributing Complicities in Shakespeare* (Stanford: Stanford University Press, 1997), xii. Berger's "acknowledgments" are an extended affidavit for the centrality of Cavell's concept for his literary thinking about Shakespearean drama.

12. The book is briefly mentioned by Cavell in his memoir (442) with regret over its unpopularity with readers. By contrast, *Pursuits of Happiness* has fared better both with Cavell's readership and, it appears, in his own remembrance. In his introduction to

Cavell on Film, Rothman notes that just "as *Must We Mean What We Say?* is curiously submerged within *The World on Film* . . . even as *The World on Film* is curiously submerged within Cavell's other books on film" (xvii). While Rothman also points out Cavell's listing of a number of Hollywood films from the 1990s in later essays like "The Good of Film" (2000), to indicate that his film criticism has remained up-to-date, more recent traditions in world cinema still fail to make it in to the discussion.

13. When Cavell once again laments in *The World Viewed* the passing of "those particular streets and carriages and chambers against and within which . . . the genres and types and individualities that have constituted the media of movies . . . had their being" (69), and asks "what new possibilities are now to be explored," his examples remain dedicated to US or American-inspired films which can be made to reside within his given ambit—as though his own *imaginative* camera remains similarly "fixed in that specific collection of human beings with which movies have been made." Cavell has written on then-Yugoslavian director Dusan Makavejev (in particular, his 1974 film, *Sweet Movie*), but even there, the angle of approach is mediated by Makavejev's essay on Bergman. And while Cavell has also written on Derrida, a book that might have mitigated this seeming bias in seeking to open Europe "onto that which is not, never was, and never will be Europe" (77), is Derrida's *The Other Heading: Reflections on Today's Europe,* trans. Pascale-Anne Brault and Michael B. Naas (Bloomington: Indiana University Press, 1992). The *AFI Film Readers* series on these various national and ethnocultural cinemas serve as excellent introductions.

14. Thus dated now seem references to character actors in films like *The Graduate* (1967) or *Bullitt* (1968), whom Cavell dismisses as not only unmemorable but ones who "*could* not become memorable" (76)—as, for instance, Robert Duvall, who appeared in the latter film and has since cemented his iconicity. Such judgments almost build in anachronism. Thus, the sorts of inquiry posed by Reed Miller in "A Lesson in Moral Spectatorship" *Critical Inquiry* 34, no. 4 (Summer 2008), 706–728, about the particularity of audience in dialogue with the kinesthetic affect of a certain *kind* of film (Spielberg's *Schindler's List*) falls outside the purview of Cavell's engagement with both specified features of the medium and a generalized notion of reception.

15. Cavell is forthright about the choice not to treat narrative poetics or diegesis: "My book contains next to nothing about the specific problems of cinematic narration or dramaturgy. My justification for this lack is nothing more than my sense that the problem of cinematic dramaturgy—of the ways in which its stories are comprehensibly related—can only correctly be investigated subsequent to an investigation of the medium of cinema itself" (209). For alternative approaches, see, among others, *Narration in the Fiction Film* (Madison: University of Wisconsin Press, 1988), *Making Meaning: Inference and Rhetoric in the Interpretation of Cinema* (Cambridge, Mass.: Harvard University Press, 1989), *Poetics of Cinema* (New York: Routledge, 2007), all by David Bordwell; and Sarah Kozloff, *Overhearing Film Dialogue* (Berkeley: University of California Press, 2000).

16. In a piece on *The French Connection* from 1971, Pauline Kael wrote, "I doubt if at any other time in American movie history there has been such a close relationship

between the life on the screen and the life of a portion of the audience," a sentiment to be placed in dialogue with Cavell's contemporaneous lament for lost companions (in front of the screen). "Urban Gothic," *The New Yorker*, October 30, 1971. An essay that praises Cavell's philosophical pragmatism and his willingness to let movies converse with each other, in contradistinction to a more "essentialist" streak in modern film criticism like that of critic David Thomson, is "Can Movies Think?" by Kent Jones, *Rouge* (October 2008), www.rouge.com.au/12/think.html. The following are also helpful resources: *Film as Philosophy: Essays in Cinema After Wittgenstein and Cavell*, ed. Rupert Read and Jerry Goodenough, (New York: Palgrave Macmillan, 2005), and *Thinking Through Cinema: Film as Philosophy*, ed. Murray Smith and Thomas E. Wartenberg (Malden, Mass.: Wiley-Blackwell, 2006).

17. "The Languages of Cinema," in *Nation, Language, and the Ethics of Translation* (Princeton: Princeton University Press, 2005), 79–88. The examples that Wood chooses from literary fiction to illustrate the machinery of observation, passages from Conan Doyle's "A Scandal in Bohemia" and Proust's *A la recherche de temps perdu*, uncannily speak to several of the issues Cavell raises.

18. See, among others, Michel Chion, *Audio-Vision: Sound on Screen*, trans. Claudia Gorbman (New York: Columbia University Press, 1994); Michael Cronin, *Translation Goes to the Movies* (New York: Routledge, 2009); Atom Egoyan and Ian Balfour, *Subtitles: On the Foreignness of Film* (New York: Alphabet City Media, 2007); Abe Mark Nornes, *Cinema Babel: Translating Global Cinema* (Minneapolis: University of Minnesota Press, 2007); Carol O'Sullivan, *Translating Popular Film* (New York: Palgrave Macmillan, 2011); and Ella Shohat and Robert Stam, "The Cinema After Babel: Language, Difference, Power," *Screen* 26, nos. 3–4 (1985): 35–58.

19. Yet, consider that chapter's initial discussion of animated film—which Cavell calls "cartoons" (referring only, however, to Disney productions), and which in his view do not merit classification as "movies," a judgment consistent with his dismissal of pop art in "A Matter of Meaning It," from *Must We Mean What We Say?*, 213–37. Again, timing was not exactly the book's best friend. *The Muppet Movie* (albeit puppetry), came out the same year as *The World Viewed*, computer animation (*Tron*, 1982) was released three years later, *Who Framed Roger Rabbit* (1988), was a mere decade away, stop-motion technology had already blurred the line between and acted and animated film (*Star Wars*, 1977), and soon afterwards began the quite ground-shifting development of computer graphics imaging in animated films produced by Pixar (*Toy Story*, 1995; *The Incredibles*, 2004; *Wall-E*, 2008). Together, these technological developments in the canvas of cinema would seem to correspond to Cavell's own specification of "not another instance of an art but a new medium within it" (103). Historically speaking, animated film festivals became popular in the 1960s and 1970s after the International Animated Film Association (ASIFA) was founded in 1960. While not devoted to feature films, the range of genres, styles, and technologies puts additional pressure on Cavell's shortsightedness here. But, as he says with perhaps less than fully intended prescience, "the moral of art, as of a life, is that you do not know in advance what may arise as a significant detail" (145). Diarmuid

Costello's cogent critique of the Cavell/Fried account of medium in "On the Very Idea of a 'Specific' Medium: Michael Fried and Stanley Cavell on Painting and Photography as Arts," bears notice in this regard. See also Paul Wells, *Understanding Animation* (New York: Routledge, 1998) and Paul Wells, Johnny Hardstaff, and Darryl Clifton, *Re-Imagining Animation: The Changing Face of the Moving Image* (Lausanne: AVA Publishing SA, 2008).

20. For these, see especially *The Claim of Reason: Wittgenstein, Skepticism, Morality, and Tragedy* (Oxford: Oxford University Press, 1982); *The Senses of Walden: An Expanded Edition,* including new: "Thinking of Emerson" and "An Emerson Mood" (Chicago: University of Chicago Press, 1992); *Pursuits of Happiness: The Hollywood Comedy of Remarriage* (Cambridge, Mass.: Harvard University Press, 1984); *Themes Out of School: Effects and Causes* (Chicago: University of Chicago Press, 1988); *In Quest of the Ordinary: Lines of Skepticism and Romanticism* (Chicago: Chicago University Press, 1988); *This New Yet Unapproachable America: Lectures After Emerson after Wittgenstein* (Chicago: University of Chicago Press, 1989); *Conditions Handsome and Unhandsome: The Constitution of Emersonian Perfectionism* (Chicago: University of Chicago Press, 1990); *Disowning Knowledge: In Seven Plays of Shakespeare* (Cambridge: Cambridge University Press, 2003).

21. Cavell remains intriguingly refractory to pairings on the model of what we have seen for the figures of Levinas and Bakhtin. Roger V. Bell, *Sounding the Abyss: Readings Between Cavell and Derrida* (Lanham, Md.: Lexington Books, 2004) and Paul Standish, "Education for Grownups, A Religion for Adults: Skepticism and Alterity in Cavell and Levinas" represent two exceptions. Gilles Deleuze's philosophy of film in *Cinema 1: The Movement-Image* and *Cinema 2: The Time-Image* is, in a certain sense, the "other" to Cavell's. They are discussed together in D. N. Rodowick, "An Elegy for Theory," *October* 121 (Summer 2007), 99–110. and "Ethics in Film Philosophy (Cavell, Deleuze, Levinas)," a proposed entry for the *Routledge Encyclopedia of Film*, http://isites.harvard.edu/fs/docs/icb.topic242308. files/RodowickETHICSweb.pdf.

22. Emerson's cautionary notes in "Self-Reliance" about the ingratiating nature of our reading could well be inscribed on this particular lintel, along with Cavell's own observations about the reading model in the "Divinity School Address" that "seeks to free us from the attachment to the person of the one who brings the message." One might call this the "acolyte effect," which has its reciprocal in Cavell's encomia for the films of Terence Malick (an exception to his sparse commentary on new Hollywood filmmakers of the 1970s), whose dissertation on Heidegger he directed at Harvard. Some examples are Steven G. Affeldt, "The Ground of Mutuality: Criteria, Judgment and Intelligibility in Stephen Mulhall and Stanley Cavell," *European Journal of Philosophy* 6, no. 1 (April 1998): 1–31; James Conant, "Stanley Cavell's Wittgenstein," *Harvard Review of Philosophy* XIII, no. 1 (2005): 51–65; and Conant, "On Bruns, on Cavell," *Critical Inquiry* 17, no. 3 (Spring 1991): 616–634. Rothman and Keane's approach—where "the authors are much too concerned with preserving, even weaving, [Cavell's] spell"—is subjected to sharp critique by Craig Tepper in his review, "The Cavell Cavil," *Film-Philosophy* 6, no. 12 (June 2002).

23. Fleming's book is *The State of Philosophy: An Invitation to a Reading in Three Parts of Stanley Cavell's "The Claim of Reason"* (Lewisburg, Pa.: Bucknell University Press, 1993). Mulhall's essay is collected in *Contending with Stanley Cavell*, ed. Russell B. Goodman (New York: Oxford University Press, 2005), 22–36. Rothman and Keane's book is *Reading Cavell's* The World Viewed*: A Philosophical Perspective on Film* (Detroit: Wayne State University Press, 2000). *The World Viewed* is referenced by a number of contemporary studies in film theory. Particularly helpful are D. N. Rodowick, *The Virtual Life of Film* (Cambridge, Mass.: Harvard University Press, 2007), and Garrett Stewart, *Between Film and Screen: Modernism's Photo Synthesis* (Chicago: University of Chicago Press, 2000), and *Framed Time: Toward a Postfilmic Cinema* (Chicago: University of Chicago Press, 2007). A bibliography of film studies informed by Cavell's work can be found at "'Why is this as it is?': The Question of Cavellian Film Studies," http://filmstudiesforfree.blogspot.com/2009 /09/why-is-this-as-it-is-question-of.html.

24. It was only in 1961 that Levinas received his *doctorat d'etat* for *Totality and Infinity*, supplemented by previously published philosophical works as a complementary thesis. What was published as a book, however, was not originally intended as a thesis. It was only in 1964, at the age of fifty-eight, that he received his first appointment as professor of philosophy, at the University of Poitiers. See "A Disparate Inventory" by Simon Critchley in *The Cambridge Companion to Levinas* (Cambridge: Cambridge University Press, 204), xiv–xxix. Bakhtin's osteomyelitis invalided him for much of his productive life. In the 1930s, he taught briefly at the Mordovian Pedagogical Institute in Saransk to which he was invited back in the 1950s as chair of the General Literature Department, and subsequently head of the Department of Russian and World Literature. It was not until 1951 that Bakhtin was eventually granted the qualification of *kandidat*, after having submitted his doctoral thesis on Rabelais in 1940. In 1961, Bakhtin's deteriorating health forced him to retire, and from then on until his death in 1975, he lived a mostly obscure, private life. By contrast, an academic apprenticeship divided between graduate study and teaching at both Berkeley and Harvard, with shorter stays at Julliard and UCLA and Princeton's Institute for Advanced Study, defines Cavell's early success. Having established a certain fame with his paper, "Must We Mean What We Say?" delivered in 1957 while still a graduate student, Cavell (in his thirties) was appointed to the Harvard philosophy department in 1963, where he has taught ever since.

25. The polyphonic and multigenre aspects of Cavell's thinking can be its most rewarding, I find. Of studies in this vein, Michael Fischer's *Stanley Cavell and Literary Skepticism* (Chicago: University of Chicago Press, 1989), comes at Cavell from the literary studies side of inquiry. See also Fischer's review-essay along these same lines: "Using Stanley Cavell," *Philosophy and Literature* 32, no. 1 (April 2008): 198–204, and the excellent book by James Guetti, *Wittgenstein and the Grammar of Literary Experience* (Athens: University of Georgia Press, 1993).

26. The phrase belongs to the Austrian novelist Robert Musil, from *The Enthusiasts*, trans. Andrea Simon (New York: Performing Arts, 1983), 19.

27. Cavell's analysis of the film medium carries over to other essays on related technologies like "The Fact of Television," *Daedalus* 111, no. 4 (1982), 75–96, (which I discuss later in the chapter) on the interplay between genre-as-medium (movies) and serial-episode or cycle (TV); "The Thought of Movies," *The Yale Review* 72, no. 2 (1983): 181–200, "What Becomes of Things on Film?" *Philosophy and Literature* 2, no. 2 (1984): 249–57, all collected in *Themes Out of School*; "What Photography Calls Thinking," *Raritan* 4, no. 4 (1985): 1–21; and "The Advent of Videos," in *Cavell on Film*, 167–173.

28. In "The Advent of Videos," Cavell meditates on their advantages (multiple screenings instead of a single screening) and disadvantages (pressure put upon the screen image by the television monitor image), but the essay (from 1988) was written just three years after the first Blockbuster opened and a decade before *Netflix* began distributing flat rate DVD-by-mail and on-demand internet streaming media. In "'What Becomes of Thinking on Film': Stanley Cavell in Conversation with Andrew Klevan," in *Film as Philosophy: Essays in Cinema After Wittgenstein and Cavell*, ed. Rupert Read and Jerry Goodenough (New York: Palgrave Macmillan, 2005), 167–209, Cavell offers some pungent observations on Turner's enterprise: "The reverse, the absolute negation of what one would mean by a film criticism that takes you to what is in plain view is, I judge, the familiar tendency to approach a film by producing an anecdote about it. This is familiar from the presentation of historical films on television, for example on the Turner Classics channel. The billionaire Turner has bought up an extraordinary, a priceless one would say, library of films. . . . Invariably, these films are introduced by way of anecdotes of casting or some amusing misadventure during the shooting of the film. But what is interesting to me is that this can be done. You can in fact interest a certain large audience of a film by giving some tiny anecdote about its making. The equivalent would be hard to find with a painting or a novel or a piece of music" (175). Interestingly, even though "Such anecdotes teach you nothing," Cavell finds a lesson in them from which he feels serious film criticism could benefit: "giv[ing] the audience a specific stake in the film. It breaks the smooth, hard, undifferentiated surface like a dive" (176).

29. Dave Boothroyd's "Touch, Time and Technics: Levinas and the Ethics of Haptic Communications," which I have already footnoted in the introduction, reflects on the particulars of this brave, new, partially disembodied world, but I stand by my claim here. See also Mark Paterson, *The Senses of Touch: Haptics, Affects and Technologies* (New York: Berg, 2007), M. B. N. Hansen, *New Philosophy for New Media* (Cambridge, Mass.: MIT Press, 2004) and *Bodies in Code: Interfaces with Digital Media* (London: Routledge, 2006) and Jerome McGann, *Radiant Textuality: Literature after the World Wide Web* (New York: Palgrave MacMillan, 2004). A dissenting view offering a "new ethics of perception" can be found in Paul Virilio's *Open Sky*, trans. Julie Rose (London: Verso, 2008).

30. "Stanley Cavell's Shakespeare," *Critical Inquiry* 16, no. 3 (Spring 1990): 612–632.

31. Cavell makes an odd move about midway through the essay, which I confess I cannot quite parse successfully, since it appears to contradict the climax of his argument and its transposition from reading a play to watching it. (I call this "slippage.") "What is the medium of this drama, how does it do its work upon us? My reading of *King Lear*

will have fully served its purpose if it provides data from which an unprejudicial description of its 'work' can be composed. One such description would be this: the medium is one which keeps all significance continuously before our senses, so that when it comes over us that we have missed it, this discovery will reveal our ignorance to have been willful, complicitous, a refusal to see. This is a fact of my experience in reading the play (it is not a fact of my experience in seeing the play, which may say something either about its performability or about the performances I have seen of it, or about the nature of performances generally)" (85). Gerald Bruns quotes this entire passage in his essay, "Cavell's Shakespeare" calling it "a highly condensed essay on reading (not watching) King Lear" (620). And in a subsequent essay on Cavell, "The Tragedy of Hermeneutic Experience," in *Rhetoric and Hermeneutics in Our Time: A Reader,* ed. Walter Jost and Michael J. Hyde (New Haven: Yale University Press, 1997), 73–89, Bruns once again explains that the failure described by Cavell here is not exegetical but rather one "of acknowledgment" (81). Significantly, however, he deletes entirely Cavell's parenthesis about performance and performability, which enables him to segue directly to the question of audience by way of Gadamer's analysis of "tragic effect." This rhetorical choice leads me to suspect that Bruns came to regard it as aporetic as well. See also David Hillman, "The Worst Case of Knowing the Other? Stanley Cavell and *Troilus and Cressida,*" *Philosophy and Literature* 32 (2008): 1–13, for some speculations about why, given a number of parallels with the themes he traces in other Shakespeare's tragedies, Cavell might have elected to avoid confronting *this* text.

32. Cavell contrasts this with tragedy by Ibsen and Racine: "In *Phédre* we are placed unprotected under heaven, examined by an unblinking light. In *Hedda Gabler*, we watch and wait, unable to avert our eyes, as if from as if from an accident or an argument rising at the next table in a restaurant, or a figure standing on the ledge of a skyscraper. In *King Lear* we are differently implicated, placed into a world not obviously unlike ours (as Racine's is, whose terrain we could not occupy) nor obviously like ours (as Ibsen's is, in whose rooms and rhythms we are, or recently were, at home), and somehow participating in their proceedings—not listening, not watching, not overhearing, almost as if dreaming it, with words and gestures that carry significance of that power and privacy and obscurity; and yet participating, as at a funeral or marriage or inauguration, confirming something; it could not happen without us. It is not a dispute or a story, but history happening, and we are living through it; later we may discover what it means, when we discover what life means" (97). This passage is parsed by Bruns in "On the Tragedy of Hermeneutic Experience," 85.

33. Compare Cavell's analysis of the spyglass in E. T. A. Hoffmann's "The Sandman" as a kind of cinematic apparatus before its time: "The glass is a death-dealing rhetoric machine, producing or expressing the consciousness of life in one case (Olympia's) by figuration, in the other (Clara's) by literalization, or say defiguration. One might also think of it as a machine of incessant animation, the parody of a certain romantic writing; and surely not unconnectedly as an uncanny anticipation of a movie camera. . . . Within the philosophical procedure of radical skepticism, the feature specifically allegorized by

the machine of the spyglass is skepticism's happening all at once, the world's vanishing at the touch, perhaps, of the thought that you may be asleep dreaming that you are awake, the feature Descartes expresses in his 'astonishment.'" *In Quest of the Ordinary*, 158.

34. For example, Cavell relates his mother's brief employment in the Fox movie palace in Sacramento (115). Although neither is listed among the film critics Cavell says he especially favors, two figures in close parallel in this regard are David Thomson, especially his books *Movie Man* (New York: Stein and Day, 1965) and *America in the Dark: Hollywood and the Gift of Unreality* (New York: William Morrow, 1977), and Stanley Kaufmann, whose criticism addresses both theater, e.g., *About the Theater* (Rhinebeck, N.Y.: Sheep Meadow Press, 2010) and film, e.g., *Regarding Film: Criticism and Comment* (New York: PAJ Publications, 2005).

35. In *Sounding the Abyss: Readings Between Cavell and Derrida* (82–83), Roger V. Bell makes the pertinent point that Cavell never invokes the "double" to Beckett's dramatic works, which is his fiction. Cavell includes a reading of Ibsen's play in *Conditions Handsome and Unhandsome.*

36. "A genre, as I use the notion in *Pursuits of Happiness,* and which I am here calling genre-as-medium, behaves according to two basic "laws" (or "principles"), one internal, the other external. Internally, a genre is constituted by members, about which it can be said that they share what you might picture as every feature in common. In practice, this means that, where a given member diverges, as it must, from the rest, it must "compensate" for this divergence. The genre undergoes continuous definition or redefinition as new members introduce new points of compensation. Externally, a genre is distinguished from other genres, in particular from what I call "adjacent" genres, when one feature shared by its members "negates" a feature shared by the members of another" (85). In *Contesting Tears: The Hollywood Melodrama of the Unknown Woman*, he refines this idea "to characterize groups of works in which members contest one another for membership, hence the power to define the genre" (13). Compare, however, Derrida's sense of the term.

37. Cavell has been taken to task for his insufficiently historicized treatment of this case, which is so obviously freighted with racial and racialized content. See, for example, Michael Bristol, *Big-Time Shakespeare* (London: Routledge, 1996), 198–199.

38. Pertinently, the essay that overtly names the centrality of ethics in Cavell's work, Stanley Bates's "Stanley Cavell and Ethics," in *Stanley Cavell*, ed. Richard Eldridge (Cambridge: Cambridge University Press, 2003), 15–47, passes over writings like *The World Viewed* and "The Avoidance of Love" in which an ethics of embodied presence—as a function of both genre and its formal demands—is obviously paramount. Bates addresses Cavell's film philosophy directly, however, in "Movies Viewed: Cavell on Medium and Motion Pictures," *Aesthetics: A Critical Anthology* ed. George Dickie, Richard Sclafani, and Ronald Roblin (New York: St Martin's Press, 1989), 576–582. Cavell's own equilibration between movies and the ethical is probably best summed up in his essay "The Good of Film," collected in *Cavell on Film,* 333–348.

39. "Their fate, up there, is that they must act, they are in the arena in which action is ineluctable. My freedom is that I am not now in the arena. Everything which can be done

is being done. The present in which action is alone possible is fully occupied. It is not that my space is different from theirs but that I have no space within which I can move. It is not that my time is different from theirs but that I have no present apart from theirs. The time in which that hint is laid, in which that knowledge is fixed, in which those fingers grip the throat, is all the time I have. There is no time in which to stop it" (109–110).

40. Similarly, in *Senses of Walden,* Thoreau's "building a house" becomes, in Cavell's gloss, an allegory for reading and writing, as "possessing a house," becomes, like writing of *Walden* itself, both an "experiment" and a "poetic exercise" (60–61). Compare Bakhin's concepts of "topographicality" and "topographic gesture" (as embodied within and for "the thoroughly accentuated space of the stage") in notes from 1944, published in Russianin 1992 and recently translated with commentary by Sergeiy Sandler as "Bakhtin on Shakespeare: Excerpt from 'Additions and Changes to *Rabelais*,'" *PMLA* vol. 129 no. 3 (May 2014).

41. Although Cavell is mentioned briefly and only for his reading of *Coriolanus,* Herbert Blau's *The Audience* (Baltimore: Johns Hopkins University Press, 1990), and his earlier texts of "theaterwork," *Blooded Thought: Occasions of Theater* (New York: Performing Arts Journal Publications, 1982) and *Take Up the Bodies: Theater at the Vanishing Point* (Urbana: University of Illinois Press, 1982), offer a deeper theorization of the audience question as it migrates from theater to cinema in Cavell's thought. For an appreciation of Blau's work, see also Mária Minich Brewer, "'The Thought of Performance': Theatricality, Reference, and Memory in Herbert Blau," *Journal of Dramatic Theory and Criticism* (Fall 2006): 97–113.

42. He makes similar moves where he refers to "the work" of theater (186) and the "basis of human existence" as theater, "even melodrama" (187) in his reading of *Hamlet,* "the origin" and "the magic" of theater (240, 241) in his reading of *Macbeth,* and Leontes's "theater of jealousy" (196) and theater as "contesting the distinction between saying and showing" (204) in his reading of *The Winter's Tale.* Anthony Cascardi's short essay "Cavell on Shakespeare," in Eldridge's *Stanley Cavell* does not address this element of Cavell's "philosophical criticism" on Elizabethan drama. By contrast, Lawrence Rhu's *Stanley Cavell's American Dream: Shakespeare, Philosophy, and Hollywood Movies* (New York: Fordham University Press, 2006) may be the best work to date on Cavell's film criticism and Shakespearean plays.

43. See Joel Snyder, "What Happens by Itself in Photographs?" *Pursuits of Reason: Essays in Honour of Stanley Cavell,* ed. Ted Cohen, Paul Guyer and Hilary Putnam (Lubbock: Texas Tech University Press, 1993), 361–373.

44. "This is not a wish for power over creation (as Pygmalion's was), but a wish not to need power, not to have to bear its burdens. It is, in this sense, the reverse of the myth of Faust . . . . It is as though the world's projection explains our forms of unknownness and of our inability to know. The explanation is not so much that the world is passing us by, as that we are displaced from our natural habitation within it, placed at a distance from it. The screen overcomes our fixed distance; it makes displacement appear as our natural condition" (40–41).

45. On this notion of candor and viewing, see Norton Batkin, "Photography, Exhibition, and the Candid," *Common Knowledge* 5, no. 2 (Fall 1996): 145–165.

46. For a consideration of Cavell in relation to Roland Barthes's *Camera Lucida* (which statements like this bear comparison with), see David Norman Rodowick's *The Virtual Life of Film*, in particular chapter 12, "An Ethics of Time," 73–89. Another intertext more pertinent to Cavell's intentions here might be Rousseau's *Letter to D'Alembert*, especially its famous assertion, "The more I think about it, the more I find that everything that is played in the theater is not brought nearer to us but made more distant" (269). See *Politics and the Arts: Letter to M. D'Alembert on the Theatre*, ed. and trans. Allan Bloom (New York: Free Press, 1960). Theater's positioning in relation to philosophy itself, from Plato to Shakespeare to Brecht, is the subject of part 1 of Freddie Rokem's *Philosophers and Thespians: Thinking Performance* (Stanford: Stanford University Press, 2010).

47. "The audience in a theater can be defined as those to whom the actors are present while they are not present to the actors. But movies allow the audience to be mechanically absent. The fact that I am invisible and inaudible to the actors, and fixed in position, no longer needs accounting for; it is not part of a convention I have to comply with; the proceedings do not have to make good the fact that I do nothing in the face of tragedy, or that I laugh at the follies of others. In viewing a movie my helplessness is mechanically assured: I am present not at something happening, which I must confirm, but at something that has happened, which I absorb (like a memory). In this, movies resemble novels, a fact mirrored in the sound of narration itself, whose tense is the past" (25–26).

48. Ludwig Wittgenstein, *Philosophical Investigations,* 4th edition, ed. and trans. P.M.S. Hacker and Joachim Schulte (Oxford: Wiley-Blackwell, 2009), 126.

49. As I quoted in a footnote to chapter one, "What is cinema's way of satisfying the myth? Automatically, we said. But what does that mean—mean mythically, as it were? It means satisfying it without my having to do anything, satisfying it *by* wishing. In a word, *magically,* I have found myself asking: How could film be art, since all the major arts arise in some way out of religion? Now I can answer: Because movies arise out of magic; from below the world" (39).

50. See the essays "The Thought of Movies" and "What Photography Calls Thinking" *Cavell on Film*, 87–108, 115–134.

51. From "'What Becomes of Thinking on Film': Stanley Cavell in Conversation with Andrew Klevan," *Film* as *Philosophy*, 182, 186.

52. Tertiary to Cavell's purposes but hardly unimportant is the whole promotional industry of film magazines, gossip columns (Winchell, Sullivan, Fidler, Parsons), celebrity appearances, and so on that moviegoers of his vintage consumed when they were not watching film but were still dreaming about movie stars. A related and even larger question concerns the social history of cinema itself—e.g., different social classes, ethnic, cultural, regional identities, spaces, and technologies. See, in this regard, archival resources on theatrical presentation like Douglas Gomery, *Shared Pleasures: A History Of*

Movie Presentation In The United States (Madison: University of Wisconsin Press, 1992), *Explorations in New Cinema History: Approaches and Case Studies,* ed. Richard Maltby, Daniel Biltereyst, and Philippe Meers (Oxford: Blackwell, 2011), and *Moviegoing in America: A Sourcebook in the History of Film Exhibition*, ed. Gregory A. Waller (London: Wiley-Blackwell, 2001). Social histories include Robert C. Allen, "From Exhibition to Reception: Reflections on the Audience in Film History, *Screen* 31, no. 4 (1990): 347–356; *Cinema, Audiences and Modernity: New Perspectives on European Cinema History*, ed. Daniel Biltereyst, Richard Maltby, and Philippe Meers (New York: Routledge, 2012); Kate Bowles, "Lost Horizon: The Social History of the Cinema Audience," *History Compass* 9, no. 11 (October 2011): 854–863; Richard Butsch, *The Making of American Audiences: From Stage to Television, 1750–1990* (Cambridge: Cambridge University Press, 2000) and "American Movie Audiences of the 1930s," *International Labor and Working-Class History* 59 (April 2001): 106–120; *Hollywood in the Neighborhood: Historical Case Studies of Local Moviegoing*, ed. Kathryn Fuller-Seeley (Berkeley: University of California Press, 2008); Kathryn H. Fuller, *At the Picture Show: Small-Town Audiences and the Creation of Movie Fan Culture* (Charlottesville: University of Virginia Press, 2001); *Hollywood Spectatorship: Changing Perceptions of Cinema Audiences*, ed. Melvyn Stokes and Richard Maltby (London: British Film Institute, 2008; *Going to the Movies: Holly-wood and the Social Experience of the Cinema* ed. Richard Maltby, Melvyn Stokes, and Robert C. Allen (Exeter: University of Exeter Press, 2008).

53. See, for example, the back-to-back essays by David Denby, "Has Hollywood Murdered the Movies?" and David Thomson, "Not Dead, Just Dying," *The New Republic*, October 4, 2012.

54. See Robert Gooding-Williams, "Aesthetics and Receptivity: Kant, Nietzsche, Cavell, and Astaire," in *The Claim to Community: Essays on Stanley Cavell and Political Theory,* ed. Andrew Norris and Thomas Dunn (Stanford: Stanford University Press, 2006), 236–262.

55. I am thinking of the famous passage that concludes "My Lost City," in *My Lost City: Personal Essays, 1920–1940* (Cambridge: Cambridge University Press, 2005): "Thus I take leave of my lost city. . . . All is lost save memory. . . . For the moment I can only cry out that I have lost my splendid mirage. Come back, come back, O glittering and white!" (113). Compare Luc Sante's afterword to *Low Life: Lures and Snares of Old New York* (Farrar, Straus and Giroux, 1991). whose original title as an essay in *The New York Review of Books* (November 6, 2003), "My Lost City," channels Fitzgerald.

56. Concertgoing and gallery/museumgoing raise issues of presence or presentness, too, of course, but their spaces do not enter into Cavell's analysis. The question of representation of the human across the arts—if it can be put this way, the dialectics of seeing, of audition, of speech, movement, and last, but not least, of reading—would seem to constitute Cavell's aesthetic inquiry, broadly framed. A general theory along the lines of what he has to say about video reproduction in "the Advent of Videos," or about copy vs. original in "The Fact of Television" might be helpful: "we need a theory of the reproduction, which can cover everything from a black-and-white half-page photograph in an art

book of a fresco a hundred times its size, to a duplicate cast of a statue" (94). But neither Cavell nor Levinas, nor even Bakhtin, attempted something so comprehensive.

57. See, for instance, Nussbaum, Rorty, Scarry, Sedgwick, Morson, Brooks. See also Gregory Currie, *Narratives and Narrators: A Philosophy of Stories* (New York: Oxford University Press, 2010); Dorrit Cohn, *Transparent Minds: Narrative Modes for Presenting Consciousness in Fiction* (Princeton: Princeton University Press, 1984); and Thomas Pavel, *Fictional Worlds* (Cambridge, Mass.: Harvard University Press, 1989). The work of Roland Barthes, of course, cuts across Cavell's in truly fascinating ways.

58. Kundera, "The Depreciated Legacy of Cervantes," in *The Art of the Novel*, 12.

59. *The Moviegoer* (New York: Vintage, 1998), 63. Lawrence Rhu makes brilliant use of Percy's novel in counterpoint with the many transcendentalist themes woven through *The World Viewed*, which I discovered it after I had made my own correlation between the two texts. What surely contributes to the superior inquiry of Rhu's book, *Stanley Cavell's American Dream*, in tracing the pleated strands of Shakespeare, philosophy, and movies, is its ability to address Cavell's work outside the echoing confines that limit most of his commentators, the contrapuntal insight, for example, to juxtapose Cavell and Walker Percy or Cavell and Harold Bloom.

60. See *Hearing Things*, 72–75.

61. Gould is particularly lucid on the generic difference between confession and autobiography, which bears comparison with Bakhtin's classifications in "Author and Hero": "The voice is discovered, or recovered, in the *act* of confession, or the passivity of being repressed" (79).

62. In a programmatic sense, "companions" is also a word that looks forward to Cavell's method for "doing" philosophy with reference to a restrictive cast(e) of characters, or what Deleuze and Guattari called a philosopher's *personnage conceptual*: "The conceptual persona is not the philosopher's representative but, rather, the reverse: the philosopher is only the envelope of his principal conceptual persona and of all the other personae who are the intercessors [*intercesseurs*], the real subjects of his philosophy. Conceptual personae are the philosopher's 'heteronyms,' and the philosopher's name is the simple pseudonym of his personae." Gilles Deleuze and Félix Guattari, *What Is Philosophy?* trans. Hugh Tomlinson and Graham Burchell (New York: Columbia University Press, 1994), 64.

63. "My claim about the aesthetic medium of television can now be put this way: its successful formats are to be understood as revelations (acknowledgments) of the conditions of monitoring, and by means of a serial-episode procedure of composition, which is to say, by means of an aesthetic procedure in which the basis of a medium is acknowledged primarily by the format rather than primarily by its instantiations" (86).

64. Actually, the scene features both Olsen *and* Johnson (an instance of Cavell's self-admitted misremembering the scenes he cites, based on one-time past screenings?). This film is particularly anarchic about "transgression of mechanical or conventional conditions upon which coherent narration in film has depended" (126). One of its ongoing gags is the byplay between Shemp Howard as Louie, the film's projectionist, and

his onscreen "cousins," Olsen and Johnson. At one point, after being hectored by them from within the film to rewind it (we see them screened through the booth's window) Louie yells back from the projection booth, "Hey what's the matter with you guys, don't you know you can't talk to me *and* the audience? . . . . This is screwy! The actors out there talking to me up here." The gag fuses elements of Keaton's silent comedy *Sherlock Jr.* with the famous vaudeville routine attributed to Joey Faye, "Slowly I turned," in which the dynamics of a told story (*l'énoncé*) are sabotaged and interrupted from within the frame of *énonciation*.

65. Compare the mythological framework here to Cavell's analysis of television as tied to "monitoring" rather than "viewing" (screening, projecting, exhibiting) the world: "The bank of monitors at which a door guard glances from time to time—one fixed, say, on each of the empty corridors leading from the otherwise unattended points of entry to the building—emblematizes the mode of perception I am taking as the aesthetic access to television. . . . As in monitoring the heart, or the rapid eye movements during periods of dreaming—say, monitoring signs of life—most of what appears is a graph of the normal, or the establishment of some reference or base line, a line, so to speak, of the uneventful, from which events stand out with perfectly anticipatable significance" ("The Fact of Television," 89).

66. It is worth keeping in mind that, as D. N. Rodowick has ably expressed the distinction, "ontology" in the subtitle of Cavell's book "indicates neither an essence of the medium nor an attempt to find its timeless or integral teleological direction. It expresses, rather, our being or being-in-the-world, not necessarily as film spectators, but rather as a condition expressed in photography and cinema as such" (*The Virtual Life of Film*, 63).

67. He mentions, for example, Gerald Bruns and also an unnamed colleague at the premiere of Claude Lanzmann's *Shoah*.

68. *Robert Frost: Collected Poems, Prose, and Plays* (New York: Library of America, 1995), 31.

69. In his seminal book *Robert Frost: The Work of Knowing* (New York: Oxford University Press, 1977), Richard Poirier writes, "Frost's speakers usually help create the structures that are to include them, and these, as in "Mowing" and "The Tuft of Flowers," are often equivalent to the structuring of the poems themselves" (40).

70. On the adaptation of book into film, see Jennifer Clement and Christian B. Long, "Hugo, Remediation, and the Cinema of Attractions, or, The Adaptation of Hugo Cabret," *Senses of Cinema* 63 (July 2012), http://sensesofcinema.com/2012/feature-articles/hugo-remediation-and-the-cinema-of-attractions-or-the-adaptation-of-hugo-cabret/.

71. In Joseph H. Smith and William Kerrigan, eds., *Cavell, Psychoanalysis, and Cinema* (Baltimore: Johns Hopkins University Press, 1987), 137–149.

72. In the same year that *Hugo* was released, another film that revived with a bygone moment in film history (albeit more artificially), Michel Hazanavicius's neo-silent film *The Artist*, makes a particular point in its opening scene of the audience's presence in movie houses and the peculiar bond between it and the medium.

73. Even if not crucial to the elements Cavell isolates, an important feature of cinema is the musical score that accompanies it. Whether played as a live soundtrack to a silent film, or synchronized as one more audio track in sound (and notwithstanding exceptions like Sergio Leone's *Once Upon a Time in the West* whose score the director asked to be played during filming), it is a convention of the form that only the audience hears it; it is designed *for* them.

74. The phrase belongs to Matt Patches, whose "The Spielberg Face: A Legacy" can be viewed at www.ugo.com/movies/the-spielberg-face-a-legacy. A more intricate video essay was created by Kevin B. Lee, viewable at www.fandor.com/blog/?p=9436.

75. See David Marshal, *The Surprising Effects of Sympathy: Marivaux, Diderot, Rousseau, and Mary Shelley* (Chicago: University of Chicago Press, 1988), and the excellent essay collection, *Literature and Sensation*, ed. Anthony Uhlmann, Helen Groth, Paul Sheehan, and Stephen McLaren (Newcastle upon Tyne: Cambridge Scholars, 2009), in particular the essays by Ben Denham, "Difficult Sense: The Neuro-physical Dimensions of the Act of Reading," 112–121, and Maria Angel and Angela Gibbs, "On Moving and Being Moved: The Corporeality of Writing in Literary Fiction and New Media Art," 162–171. *Empathy and the Novel* by Suzanne Keen (New York: Oxford University Press, 2007), as its title indicates, explores these questions in specific relation to the modern history of narrative fiction. See also the related volume of essays edited by Kate Flint, *The Feeling of Reading: Affective Experience and Victorian Literature* (Ann Arbor: University of Michigan Press, 2010) and Rae Greiner's survey in the spirit of Adam Smith, *Sympathetic Realism in Nineteenth-Century British Fiction* (Baltimore: Johns Hopkins University Press, 2012).

76. *Lettre a d'Alembert sur les spectacles,* avec une introduction et des notes par M. Léon Fontaine (Paris: Garnier Frères, 1889), 248–249. *Politics and the Arts: Letter to M. D'Alembert on the Theatre*, 111.

77. *The Catcher in the Rye* (New York: Penguin Books, 1994), 136.

78. *Cities of Words*, 400. The chapter on *Gaslight* also briefly remarks on the "nature of perception or reception of a film in relation, eventually, to . . . the presence of a communal audience present with the actors in a theater" (116).

79. Indeed, for Scorsese to have made a film in 3D conveys its own message about the evolving technology of film, quite beyond the list of devices that Cavell treats in his chapter, "Assertions in Technique," in *The World Viewed*, e.g., slow motion, freeze frame, flash insets, some of which just happen to be this particular director's trademarks.

80. See Martin Loiperdinger, "Lumiere's Arrival of the Train: Cinema's Founding Myth," *The Moving Image* 4, no. 1 (Spring 2004): 89–118. Cavell seems to comment on this cultural moment in his chapter on "Exhibition and Self-Reference," but, significantly, without Scorsese's directorial eye toward the audience *drama* of it: "We are told that people seeing the first moving pictures were amazed to see the motion in motion, as if by the novelty. But what movies did at first they can do at last: spare our attention wholly for *that* thing *now,* in the frame of nature, the world moving in the branch. In principle, anyone and everyone could be seeing it now. It is not novelty that has worn

off, but our interest in our own experience. Who can blame us for that? Our experience is so coarsened that we can be moved by it only through novelty, and that has lost interest" (122).

81. There is a real-life precedent to the myth, in fact. One year before the Lumiere film, on October 22, 1895, a train overran the buffer stop and derailed, just as depicted in Scorsese's film: "The engine careered across almost 100 feet (10 meters) of the station concourse, crashed through a two feet (0.6m) thick wall, across a terrace and sailed out of the station as it plummeted onto the street 30 feet (9m) below. This was the Place de Rennes which carried the tramway between the station and Place de l'Etoile. The falling locomotive just missed hitting one of the trams." From the website Danger Ahead: Historic Railway Disasters, http://danger-ahead.railfan.net/accidents/paris_1895.html.

82. The complex effects of this film are discussed along with the others for which Méliès became justly famous, e.g., the multiple Méliès heads in *La Mélomane* (1903) and *Un homme de têtes* (1898) in Elizabeth Ezra, *George Méliès* (Manchester: Manchester University Press, 2000). 2 DVDs are available, containing scenes from many of his films, *Georges Méliès: First Wizard of Cinema 1896–1913* (Flicker Alley–Blackhawk Films, 2008) and the follow-up disc, *Méliès Encore* (Flicker Alley-Blackhawk films, 2010). See also Richard Abel's authoritative history, *The Ciné Goes to Town: French Cinema, 1896–1914* (Berkeley: University of California Press, 1998) and Ian Christie, *The Last Machine: Early Cinema and the Birth of the Modern World* (London: British Film Institute, 1995).

83. In his *New Yorker review*, "Fantastic Voyages" (November 28, 2011), David Denby briefly compares it to James Cameron's *Avatar* (also in 3D), as "a fantasy of the mechanical world" as opposed to "a luscious purple-green spectacle—a fantasy of the natural world" (86).

84. The automaton in Seltzer's book is based on the early nineteenth-century Maillardet automaton, on display at the Franklin Institute in Philadelphia: www.fi.edu/learn/sci-tech/automaton/automaton.php?cts=instrumentation. For an extended treatment of the automaton as both object and allegory, see Kara Reilly, *Automata and Mimesis on the Stage of Theatre* (New York: Palgrave Macmillan, 2011).

85. *The New Yorker*, December 15, 1997.

86. See the interviews by James Rose, "Stephen and Timothy Quay" in the "Great Director" Series, *Senses of Cinema* 30 (February 12, 2004) and by André Habib, "Through a Glass Darkly—Interview with the Quay Brothers," *Senses of Cinema* 19 (March 13, 2002), www.sensesofcinema.com/2004/great-directors/quay_brothers and www.sensesof cinema.com/2002/19/quay. Another link to Scorsese's film becomes obvious in the following observation, from an article on the Quay Brothers and Bruno Schulz: "The material qualities and processes of photographic-based filmmaking are essential to the creation of the Quay's cinematic world. Unlike the encoded bits and bytes of digital filmmaking, photographic film relies on a transparent plastic material (such as celluloid or acetate) coated with a light-sensitive chemical (called emulsion) which when subjected to exposure to light forms a latent image of whatever is placed before the camera's lens. The actual physical presence of an object before the lens and the chemical processes of

film developing help to give the entire mise-en-scene of a Brothers Quay film an alchemic materiality—or, if you will, a life." James Fiumara, "The Thirteenth Freak Month: The Influence of Bruno Schulz on the Brothers Quay," *Kinoeye* 4, no. 5 (November 29, 2004).

87. As Denby expresses this thought, "No other work of art has demonstrated so explicitly how gears, springs, shutters, wheels, and tracks can generate wonders" (86–87). See also the essay by Kristin Thomson and David Bordwell, "*Hugo*: Scorsese's Birthday Present to Georges Méliès," on Bordwell's website *Observations on Film Art* (December 7, 2011), www.davidbordwell.net/blog/2011/12/07/hugo-scorseses-birthday-present-to -georges-melies.

88. "Philosophy and the Arrogation of Voice," *A Pitch of Philosophy*, 37. *Philosophical Passages: Wittgenstein, Emerson, Austin, Derrida* (Cambridge: Blackwell Publishers, 1995), 171.

89. *When We Were Orphans* (New York: Vintage, 2001), 336.

90. "Saturday 6 August, 1763: After we came out of the church, we stood talking for some time together of Bishop Berkeley's ingenious sophistry to prove the nonexistence of matter, and that every thing in the universe is merely ideal. I observed, that though we are satisfied his doctrine is not true, it is impossible to refute it. I never shall forget the alacrity with which Johnson answered, striking his foot with mighty force against a large stone, till he rebounded from it—'I refute it thus.'" James Boswell, *Life of Samuel Johnson* (Oxford: Oxford University Press, 1998), 333.

91. "From Notes Made in 1970–71," *Speech Genres and Other Essays*, 133–134. See also Zali Gurevitch, "Plurality in Dialogue," 257.

7. Abyss, Volcano, and the Frozen Swirl of Words: The Difficult and the Holy in Agnon, Bialik, and Scholem

1. Building on Carol Jacobs, "The Monstrosity of Translation," *Modern Language Notes* 6 (1975): 755–766, this was Paul de Man's famous gloss in his last published essay, "'Conclusions': Reading Walter Benjamin's 'The Task of the Translator,'" in *The Resistance to Theory* (Minneapolis: University of Minnesota Press, 1986): "if you enter the Tour de France and you give up, that is the *Aufgabe*—'er hat aufgegeben,' he doesn't continue in the race anymore," 80. De Man's detranslation of Harry Zohn's Englished Benjamin subsequently attracted its own critique, as for instance, in Valentine Cunningham, "Sticky Transfers," in *Aesthetics and Contemporary Discourse*, ed. Herbert Grabes (Tübingen: Gunter Narr Verlag, 1994), 325–354. See also Eve Tavor Bannet, "The Scene of Translation: After Jakobson, Benjamin, de Man, and Derrida," *New Literary History* 24, no. 3 (Summer 1993): 577–595, and "de Man on Benjamin" in Tom Cohen, Claire Colebrook, and J. Hillis Miller, *Theory and the Disappearing Future: On de Man, On Benjamin* (New York: Routledge, 2012).

2. Among its particular characteristics, Ashkenazi orthography distinguishes between the vowels *patakh* פַּתַ and *kamatz* קָמָץ as pronunciation distinguishes between the aspirated (without *dagesh*) and unaspirated *tav*.

3. For an excellent discussion of these nuances, see Miryam Segal, *A New Sound in Hebrew Poetry: Poetics, Politics, Accent* (Bloomington: Indiana University Press, 2010), especially the epilogue, "The Conundrum of the National Poet," 139–150. See also, by Ghil'ad Zuckermann, "'Abba, why was Professor Higgins trying to teach Eliza to speak like our cleaning lady?': Mizrahim, Ashkenazim, Prescriptivism and the Real Sounds of the Israeli Language," *Australian Journal of Jewish Studies* 19 (2005): 210–231; *Language Contact and Lexical Enrichment in Israeli Hebrew* (New York: Palgrave Macmillan, 2003); and *Language Revival and Multiple Causation: The Mosaic Genesis of the Israeli Language* (Oxford University Press, 2014); and finally, from the side of ethnography, Daniel Lefkowitz, *Words and Stones: The Politics of Language and Identity in Israel* (Oxford: Oxford University Press, 2004).

4. See Angel Sáenz-Badillos, *A History of the Hebrew Language*, trans. John Elwolde (Cambridge: Cambridge University Press, 1996).

5. Among a number of important works on this topic, see the classic essay by Baal Makhshoves, "*Tsvei Shprakhn—eyneyntsike literatur*" (Two Languages—One Literature), in *Geklibene verk* (New York: Tsiko-bikher, 1953): 112–123; Itamar Even-Zohar, "Polysystem Studies," *Poetics Today* 11, no. 1 (1990); Jordan Finkin, *A Rhetorical Conversation: Jewish Discourse in Modern Yiddish Literature* (Philadelphia: University of Pennsylvania Press, 2010); David E. Fishman, *The Rise of Modern Yiddish Culture* (Pittsburgh: University of Pittsburgh Press, 2010); Benjamin Harshav, *Language in a Time of Revolution* (Stanford: Stanford University Press, 1993); Chana Kronfeld, *On the Margins of Modernism: Decentering Literary Dynamics* (Berkeley: University of California Press, 1996); Anita Norich, "Hebraism and Yiddish: Paradigms of Modern Jewish Literary History," in *Modern Jewish Literatures: Intersections and Boundaries*, ed. Sheila E. Jelen, Michael Kramer, and L. Scott Lerner (Philadelphia: University of Pennsylvania Press, 2011), 327–342; Naomi Seidman, *A Marriage Made in Heaven: The Sexual Politics of Hebrew and Yiddish* (Berkeley: University of California Press, 2004); and Uriel Weinreich, *Languages in Contact: Findings and Problems* (The Hague: Mouton, 1964).

6. Barbara E. Mann, "Visions of Jewish Modernism," in *Modernism/Modernity* 13, no. 4 (2006): 673–699, at 682. See also Mann's related article "Toward an Understanding of Jewish Imagism," in *Religion & Literature* 30, no. 3, "Jewish Diasporism: The Aesthetics of Ambivalence" (Autumn 1998): 23–45. Dan Miron's *H. N. Bialik and the Prophetic Mode in Modern Hebrew Poetry* (Syracuse, N.Y.: Syracuse University Press, 2000) is the most dependable treatment of Bialik's poetics. See also the several chapters on Bialik, especially "Anthropological Betrayal: Bialik and the Jewish Book," in S. Daniel Breslauer, *Creating a Judaism without Religion: A Postmodern Jewish Possibility* (Lanham, Md.: University Press of America, 2001), and Breslauer's earlier study *The Hebrew Poetry of Ḥayyim Naḥman Bialik and a Modern Jewish Theology* (Lewiston: Edwin Mellen Press, 1991). Finally, for the "East/West" question around the modern revival of Hebrew, see Lital Levy, "From Baghdad to Bialik With Love: A Reappropriation of Modern Hebrew Poetry, 1933," in *Comparative Literature Studies* 42, no. 3 (2005): 125–154; and Sami Shalom Chetrit, "Revisiting Bialik: A Radical Mizrahi Reading of the Jewish National

Poet," *Comparative Literature* 62, no. 1 (2010): 1–21. Important criticism on Bialik in Hebrew includes Dov Sadan, *Hayim Naḥman Byalik ve-darkho bi-leshono u-leshonoteha* (Tel-Aviv: Hotsa'at ha-Kibuts ha-me'uḥad, 1989); Hillel Barzel, *Shirat ha-tehiyah: Ḥayim Naḥman Byalik* (Tel Aviv: Sifriyat po'alim, 1990); and Ziva Shamir, *Be-en 'alilah: sipure Byalik be-ma'gelotehem* (Tel Aviv: ha-Kibuts ha-me'uḥad, 1998).

7. I borrow the Bavel/Jerusalem dialectic from the essay by Simon Rawidowicz, "*Yerushalayim U-Bavel*" ("Babylon and Jerusalem"), translated in the essay collection *State of Israel, Diaspora, and Jewish Continuity: Essays on the "Ever-Dying People"* (Waltham, Mass.: Brandeis University Press, 1986). Each of the five essays collected in Bialik's *Revealment and Concealment: Five Essays* (Jerusalem: Ibis Editions, 2000) displays his profoundly dualistic temperament: whether as a matter of "Revealment and Concealment in Language," "The Sacred and Secular in Language," "*Halakhah* and *Aggadah*," or "Man and His Property" (unfinished at Bialik's death, but a preliminary analysis of how ownership can become a kind of servitude), Bialik's reflections are driven by the spirit of the fifth essay's title, "Jewish Dualism." As Zali Gurevitch puts it in "Eternal Loss," his afterword to the five essays: "For Bialik, loss, from the start, is everlasting. Every locale, every sense of the local for him, must also be a place of exile. Loss and longing are intertwined, as they are in the creative act, where exile is not only a curse but the very root of his being" (116).

8. "In the Seas of Youth," *Prooftexts* 21:1 (Winter, 2001), 57–70.

9. The word recalls the last sentence spoken by R. Ḥanina b. Teradyon, one of the Ten Martyrs, who, when wrapped in a Sefer Torah and burned alive on a pyre, cried *gevilim nisrafim ve-otiyot poreḥot* (Scrolls are burning, but the letters fly upward) (*bAvoda Zara* 18a).

10. "Hayim Nakhman Bialik's Poetry: An Introduction," in *Songs From Bialik: Selected Poems of Hayim Nakhman Bialik,* trans. Atar Hadari (Syracuse, N.Y.: Syracuse University Press, 2000), lx.

11. In "The Task of the Talmud: On Talmud as Translation," *Paratext and Megatext as Channels of Jewish and Christian Traditions: The Textual Markers of Contexualization*, ed. A. A. den Hollander, Ulrich Schmid, and Willem Smelik (Leiden: E. J. Brill, 2003), 82–108, Aryeh Cohen embeds the question of Hebrew/Aramaic (or both and Greek)—translation of and within the Talmud—within the larger frame of what he calls "the anxiety of Exile as a defining characteristic of Rabbinic/Talmudic thinking and legislating." And yet the scruple also resides in the Torah: ויקרא־לו לבן יגר שהדותא ויעקב קרא לו גלעד (And Lavan called it "Yegar-sahaduta" [in Aramaic]; but Yaakov called it "Galeid" [in Hebrew]) (Gen. 31:47). As befits a passage about boundary marking, here and exceptionally, the Bible records a word voiced in two languages—with the Aramaic ensconced, so to speak, within the text's capacity to "make the hands impure." In both tractates, *Shabbat* and *Megillah*, the Talmud stresses that scrolls with portions in Aramaic demand the same reverence and care as those written in *lashon haqodesh* (the holy tongue).

12. Built for him by the architect Yosef Minor in 1924–5. See the essay by Yonatan Dubosarsky, "Beit Bialik: The Home of Israel's National Poet," http://bit.ly/1cuVcrk.

13. That we also recognize such terms from their typographic avatars in the world of typesetting reminds us of the sometimes uncanny intersection of scriptural and secular vocabularies.

14. Two essays assess its achievement: Mark Kiel, "*Sefer ha'aggadah*: Creating a Classic Anthology for the People and by the People," *Prooftexts* 17, no. 2 (May 1997): 177–197, and Alan Mintz, "Sefer Ha-aggadah: Triumph or Tragedy?" in *History and Literature: New Readings of Jewish Texts in in Honor of Arnold J. Band*, ed. William Cutter and David C. Jacobson (Providence, R.I.: Brown Judaic Studies, 2002), 17–26.

15. The essay is discussed by David Biale in his section on Bialik in *Not in the Heavens: The Tradition of Jewish Secular Thought* (Princeton: Princeton University Press, 2011), 146–148 and stands behind the chapter "Beyond Language Pangs" in Chana Kronfeld in *On the Margins of Modernism* (Berkeley: University of California Press, 1996). It is given a politicized reading in Eyal Chowers, *The Political Philosophy of Zionism: Trading Jewish Words for a Hebraic Land* (Cambridge: Cambridge University press, 2012), 196ff. Bialik moved to Palestine in 1924; his last poems, an autobiographical series entitled *Yatmut* ("Orphanhood"), were composed in 1934, the year he died. See the biography by Sara Feinstein, *Sunshine, Blossoms and Blood: H. N. Bialik in His Time, a Literary Biography* (Lanham, Md.: University Press of America, 2005).

16. In Benjamin's usage of the term (subsequently adopted by Adorno and as first proposed in the *Trauerspiel* book and later refined in *The Arcades Project*), *Konstellation* describes both a dynamic interrelation among historical events rather than a strict linear flow, and a creative assemblage of textual fragments into an emergent whole. It is a much-discussed term in the critical literature; Graeme Gilloch, *Walter Benjamin: Critical Constellations* (Cambridge: Polity Press, 2002); Carol Jacobs, *In the Language of Walter Benjamin* (Baltimore: Johns Hopkins University Press, 1999); and the second part of Freddie Rokem, *Philosophers and Thespians: Thinking Performance* (Stanford: Stanford University Press, 2010).

17. The original thrust of these terms is temporal, with the aim of opening up still-present possibilities in past events, and thus pushing against closure and fixity. "Sideshadowing" is developed by Gary Saul Morson in "Sideshadowing and Tempics," in *New Literary History* 29, no. 4 (1998): 599–624, and *Narrative and Freedom: The Shadows of Time* (New Haven: Yale University Press, 1994); "backshadowing" is a term unpacked by Michael André Bernstein in *Foregone Conclusions: Against Apocalyptic History* (Berkeley: University of California Press, 1994) and "Victims-in-Waiting: Backshadowing and the Representation of European Jewry," *New Literary History* 29, no. 4 (Autumn 1998): 625–651.

18. The Hebrew here is the letter ׳ (*yod*), which corresponds to the Greek *iota*.

19. Several studies in Hebrew should be consulted: Zvi Luz and Ziva Shamir, ed., "*Al* Gilui ṿe-khisui ba-lashon: *'iyunim be-masato shel Biyalik*," (Ramat-Gan: Hotsa'at Universiṭat Bar-Ilan, 2001); Hillel Barzel and Hilel Ṿais, ed. *Halel li-Vyalik: 'iyunim ṿe-meḥḳarim be-yetsirat Ḥ. N. Byaliḳ* (Ramat-Gan: Hotsa'at Universiṭat Bar-Ilan, 1989); and Ziva Shamir, *Hashirah me'ayin timatse: "Art po'etika" bitsirat Byalik* (Tel Aviv: Papyrus, 1987).

20. Azzan Yadin, "A Web of Chaos: Bialik and Nietzsche on Language, Truth, and the Death of God," *Prooftexts* 21, no. 2 (Spring 2001): 179–203, focuses on Nietzsche's "On Truth and Lies in a Nonmoral Sense" and kabbalistic influences. Robert Alter's introduction to Bialik's essay in his anthology *Modern Hebrew Literature* (New York: Behrman House, 1975) emphasizes *kabbalah* and modernism, as does his seminal essay on Scholem that mentions Bialik as an influence, "Scholem and Modernism," in *Poetics Today* 15, no. 3 (Autumn 1994): 429–442; Arnold Band's "The Sacralization of Language in Bialik's Essays," in *Studies in Modern Jewish Literature* (Philadelphia: Jewish Publication Society, 2003), contextualizes the essay in relation to Ahad Ha'Am. Spinoza's *Theologico-Political Treatise*, trans. Samuel Shirley (Indianapolis: Hackett, 1998) from the section "In what respect Scripture is called Holy and the Word of God," is eerily similar: "Words acquire a fixed meaning solely from their use; if in accordance with this usage they are so arranged that readers are moved to devotion, then these words will be scared, and likewise this arrangement of words. But if these words at a later time fall into disuse so as to become meaningless, or if the book falls into disuse so as to become meaningless . . . then both words and book will be without sanctity" (146).

21. Jordan Finkin's *A Rhetorical Conversation* provides a useful linguistic analysis of this flow between rabbinic and secular idiolects, the classical religious heritage and modernist discourse.

22. Levinas mentions Bialik's name in passing in his interview with Myriam Anissi-mov included in *Is It Righteous to Be?*, 87, and briefly quotes him in the essay "The Diary of Leon Brunschvicg" in *Difficult Freedom*, 45. The two figures are brought together, albeit treated separately in S. Daniel Breslauer *Toward a Jewish (M)orality: Speaking of a Postmodern Jewish Ethics* (Westport, Conn.: Greenwood Press, 1998). Finally, the question of translation left implicit in this essay but in specific relation to Holocaust testimonies and Levinas's work generally is treated in Dorota Glowacka, "The Trace of the Untranslatable: Emmanuel Levinas and the Ethics of Translation," *PhaenEx* 7, no. 1 (2012): 1–29. The question of translating Levinas himself is not a small one, but see Nidra Poller's brief but eloquent "Translator's Note" to *Unforeseen History* (Champaign: University of Illinois Press, 2004), xxvii–xxviii.

23. Like his colleague Bialik, Micha Josef Berdyczewski (1865–1921) was a Ukrainian-born writer, also a polemical journalist, and also a student at the Volozhin yeshiva in his youth. He spent formative years in Berlin and Warsaw, and wrote short fiction and the novel, *Miryam*. See especially, William Cutter, "Language Matters," *Hebrew Studies* 39 (1998): 57–74; the brief contextualization by Dan Miron, "From Continuity to Contiguity: Thoughts on the Theory of Jewish Literature," in *Jewish Literatures and Cultures: Context and Intertext*, ed. Anita Norich and Yaron Z. Eliav (Providence, R.I.: Brown University Press, 2008), 9–36; Shachar Pinsker, "Intertextuality, Rabbinic Literature, and the Making of Hebrew Modernism" in the same volume, 201–228; and his *Literary Passports: The Making of Modernist Hebrew Fiction in Europe* (Stanford: Stanford University Press, 2011).

24. As quoted in Shachar Pinsker, *Literary Passports*, 282. See also Dan Miron, *Bodedim be-moadam* (Tel Aviv: Am Oved, 1987).

25. See especially the essays "*Halakhah* and *Aggadah*" and "The Sacred and Secular in Language," the early poems "Al saf bet hamidrash" ("On the Threshold of the House of Study") (1894) and "Hamtamid" ("The Talmud Scholar") (1897–98), and the long poems from 1905, "The Pool" and "Di fayer-megileh/Megilat ha-esh" ("The Scroll of Fire"). Using the latter poem especially, David C. Jacobson, *Modern Midrash: The Retelling of Traditional Jewish Narratives by Twentieth Century Hebrew Writers* (Albany: State University of New York Press, 1987), makes the case for Bialik as an exponent of "creative restoration," i.e., modern *midrash*.

26. Rather, as Arnold Band speculates in "The Sacralization of Language in Bialik's Essays," Bialik's influences here are Romanticist, probably by way of Schiller (293). See also "Revealment Within Concealment: The Role of Metaphor in Bialik's Essays," *Jerusalem Studies in Hebrew Literature* 10 (1988): 189–200.

27. See Azzan Yadin on these connections, especially the hypogrammatic allusion to the early medieval esoteric work, the *Sefer Yetsira* ("Book of Formation"), 191–192.

28. Yadin points to the passage that says, "We see with our very eyes that these words, and many like them, are tucked away in language—and nothing. . . . Their content has been wasted away, and their power over the soul has either dissipated or been *stored away*," the terminal verb in which, *nignaz*, recalls the אוֹר גָּנוּז *'or ganuz*, "the light that filled the world before the sun was created and was stored away for the righteous to enjoy in the Edenic hereafter" (197).

29. As the footnote to Levinas's text indicates, the trope of "turning and turning" surreptitiously cites *mishna* 5:2 from *Pirqei Avot* attributed to the convert Ben Bag Bag, "*Hafokh ba va-hafokh ba, d'hola ba*" (Turn it and turn it again, for everything is in it"). Franz Rosenzweig alludes to the same *mishna* at the end of his article on the Bible for the *Encyclopedia Judaica* and also in *The Star of Redemption*, as Michael Fishbane points out in "Speech and Scripture: The Grammatical Thinking and Theology of Franz Rosenzweig," in *The Garments of Torah*, 108 and 147.

30. "Neuhebräisch? Anläßlich der Übersetzung von Spinozas Kritik," written as a review of the new Hebrew translation of Baruch Spinoza's *Ethics* Hebrew by Jakob Klatzkin in *Zweistromland, Kleinere Schriften zu Glauben und Denken* (The Hague: Martinus Nijhoff, 1984), 723–729. It was translated under the title "Classical and Modern Hebrew" in Nahum Glatzer, *Franz Rosenzweig: His Life and Thought* (New York: Schocken, 1961), 263–271. See also Paul Mendes-Flohr, "Hebrew as a Holy Tongue: Franz Rosenzweig and the Renewal of Hebrew," *Hebrew in Ashkenaz: A Language in Exile*, ed. Lewis Glinert (Oxford: Oxford University Press, 1993), 222–241.

31. "Classical and Modern Hebrew," in *Franz Rosenzweig: His Life and Thought*, 268. "The holy language in the mouth of the people lacks the true characteristics of a sacred language, that is, separation from the colloquial, and so it never degenerated into anything like the magic sacredness of church Latin or the—of the Koran, which may be, which even should be, incomprehensible to the layman—al that is required of him is adherence in spirit and faith." (Obviously, while the example of Church Latin may be

well taken, as in *The Star of Redemption*, Rosenzweig's sense of a hermeneutic tradition in Islam complementary to the rabbinic remains undertheorized.)

32. Scholem translated Bialik's essay *"Halakhah and Aggadah"* in 1919. This particular affiliation, along with its resonance with Scholem's "Confession on the Subject of Our Language" and his essay "Der Name Gottes und die Sprachtheorie der Kabbala," is traced by Galili Shahar in "The Sacred and the Unfamiliar: Gershom Scholem and the Anxieties of the New Hebrew," *Germanic Review: Literature, Culture, Theory* 83, no. 4 (2008): 299–320. See also the review essay by Shachar Pinsker, "'Never Will I Hear the Sweet Voice of God': Religiosity and Mysticism In Modern Hebrew Poetry," *Prooftexts* 30, no. 1 (Winter 2010): 128–146.

33. "The Sacralization of Language in Bialik's Essays," 295.

34. See the account of this cultural moment in Allison Schacter, *Diasporic Modernisms: Hebrew and Yiddish in the Twentieth Century* (New York: Oxford University Press, 2012) and Dan Miron, *From Continuity and Contiguity.*

35. Once again, an opening to Rosenzweig reveals itself, this time, however, by way of Bialik. Compare, therefore, the assertion in the review-essay on the "New Hebrew": "Something holy that wants to turn its back on everything profane is made profane, and the profane of the first day hastens toward the seventh, which will make it holy" (266).

36. See the helpful discussion by Shahara in "The Sacred and the Unfamiliar," 312–316.

37. In the Hebrew poetry of medieval Andalus, the stylistic conceit is called *shibutz*. In his "Afterword" to his translation of Yehudah Halevi, Franz Rosenzweig refers to it as *Musivstil* ("mosaic") where *die Schrift* ("Scripture") prevails over *die Sprache* ("language"). See the translation by Barbara E. Galli, in *Franz Rosenzweig and Jehuda Halevi: Translating, Translations, and Translators* (Montreal: McGill Queens University Press, 1995), 177.

38. "Eternal Loss," the afterword to *Revealment and Concealment*, 132.

39. Like Abraham Heschel, Scholem wrote poetry, much of it in his youth. His poems have now been collected and translated in *The Fullness of Time: Poems,* trans. Richard Sieburth (Jerusalem: Ibis Editions, 2003). In their correspondence, Rosenzweig and Scholem actually exchanged translations of the poem, "HaMawdil" (*Havdalah*), as reproduced in an essay by Michael Brocke, "Franz Rosenzweig und Gerhard Gershom Scholem," *Juden in der Weimarer Republik*, ed. Walter Grab and Julius H. Schoeps (Berlin: Wissenschaftliche Buchgesellschaft, 1998), 127–48. One year after Scholem's letter to him was written, Rosenzweig, then almost completely paralyzed, published *Jehuda Halevi, Zweiundneunzig Hymnen und Dedichte*, translated into English by Barbara E. Galli, and more recently by Thomas A. Kovach, Eva Jospe, and Gilya Gerda Schmidt, *Ninety-Two Poems and Hymns of Yehuda Halevi* (Albany: State University of New York Press, 2000). See the excellent study by Mara Benjamin, "Building a Zion in German(y): Franz Rosenzweig on Yehudah Halevi," *Jewish Social Studies: History, Culture, Society* 13, no. 2 (Winter 2007): 127–154, and also the section on "Rosenzweig's Philosophy of Interpretation," in Barbara Galli's introduction to *Franz Rosenzweig and Jehuda Halevi: Translating, Translations, and Translators*, 322–359.

40. As Scholem puts it in "My Way to Kabbalah" (1974) in *On the Possibility of Jewish Mysticism In Our Time and Other Essays*, trans. Jonathan Chipman, ed. Avraham Shapira (Philadelphia: Jewish Publication Society 1997), "Having migrated from the ancient books to the mouths of babes and sucklings, its has given way to an extremely vital language, characterized by an anarchistic set of rules" (22).

41. These are Derrida's terms from "The Eyes of Language: The Abyss and the Volcano," trans. Gil Anidjar, *Acts of Religion* (New York: Routledge, 2002), 189–227.

42. Stéphane Mosès, "Une Lettre inédite de Scholem à Rozenzweig apropos de notre langue," *Archives de Science Sociales des Religions* 60, no. 1 (July–September 1985), to which Mosès appended his own commentary, "Langage et secularisation chez Gershom Scholem." The letter was translated first by Alexander Gelley, then by Martin Goldner (both versions appear in William Cutter's "Ghostly Hebrew, Ghastly Speech: Scholem to Rosenzweig, 1926," in *Prooftexts* 10, no. 3 (September 1990): 413–433; and by Ora Wiskind in "Scholem and Rosenzweig: The Dialectics of History," *History and Memory* 2, no. 2 (Winter 1990): 100–116. It appears in more recent English translation by Jonathan Chipman in Scholem's On the Possibility of Jewish Mysticism and Other Essays, 27–29, and by Gil Anidjar as the supplement to Derrida's "The Eyes of Language."

43. According to Lawrence Rosenwald, because Buber and Rosenzweig were "uncomfortable with *Übersetzen*," they "often preferred *Übertragen*," the latter of which idiomatically means "rendering" as opposed to "translation" and "to carry something over" vs. "to set something over." See his preface to the Buber-Rosenzweig collaboration, *Scripture and Translation*, trans. Lawrence Rosenwald with Everett Fox (Bloomington: Indiana University Press, 1994), x. Compare also Raḥel Katznelson's privileging of a "revolutionary" Hebrew whose exemplary writer "will always be more of a citizen of the world" when compared with one who writes in Yiddish ("a substitute homeland for us in the Diaspora") in her 1918 essay *Nedudei Lashon* (Language Migrations), a title in self-conscious echo of Bialik's *Ḥevlei Lashon*. Translated idiomatically as "Language Insomnia," it can be found in Benjamin Harshav, *Language in the Time of Revolution* (Stanford: Stanford University Press, 1993), 183–194. Naomi Seidman shifts the ground for these concerns to "translation performances shaped by asymmetrical relations between cultures" (253) in her essay, "Diaspora and Translation: The Migrations of Jewish Meanings," in Norich and Eliav, *Jewish Literatures and Cultures*, 245–258.

44. See Dana Hollander, *Exemplarity and Chosenness: Rosenzweig and Derrida on the Nation of Philosophy* (Stanford: Stanford University Press, 2008), 147–158. Rosenzweig's reflections on "the holiness of the holy language . . . which does not allow [a Jew's] life to take root in the soil of a language of his own" bring him quite close to Bialik here. His ordinary language "knows its real linguistic homeland is elsewhere, in the domain of holy language that is inaccessible to everyday speech" (321).

45. From *Der Stern der Erlösung (The Star of Redemption)*, trans. Barbara E. Galli (Madison: University of Wisconsin Press, 2005), 321, as cited in Hollander, 142.

46. "For German Jews still keep the treasures of Hebrew in their language and thought. "*Unsere Anklänge ans Hebräische sind unser gutes Recht*," the echo of Hebrew in

our language is our right, Rosenzweig writes in his 1921 lecture *Vom Geist der Hebräischen Sprache* (720). German Jews indeed speak German; their German, however, is still linked with Hebrew sources that endow German with theological horizons" (300). Shahara's explanation of Rosenzweig's commitment to the "hidden tradition" of Hebrew as inscribed within all languages should be compared with David Suchoff's superb revisionist monograph, *Kafka's Jewish Languages: The Hidden Openness of Tradition* (Philadelphia: University of Pennsylvania Press, 2011).

47. "To express it plainly and dryly to the point of blasphemy: the spirit of the center cannot grow in the direction of pure, uninhibited nationalism avid for its own development, no matter how much it would like to; just because of its focal character, it must constantly keep in sight the periphery which cannot be governed by nationalism but will always be constrained to regard the national as a function of the religious, and for very simple reasons based on the sociology of minorities" (*Franz Rosenzweig: His Life and Thought*, 269). These and other selections from Rosenzweig's review essay are also discussed by William Cutter in "Ghostly Hebrew, Ghastly Speech: Scholem to Rosenzweig, 1926." Rosenzweig reiterated this position to Martin Buber in a letter about their ongoing Bible translation, dated August 19, 1929, when Buber had taken up Scholem's position: "Even though in the firm of Buber and Rosenzweig your investment of working capital amounts to eighty percent and mine to only twenty, the goal and effectiveness of the work are determined by the goal and work contributed by me, the *galut* Jew." *Letters of Martin Buber: A Life of Dialogue*, trans. Richard Winston, Clara Winston, and Harry Zohn (Syracuse, N.Y.: Syracuse University Press, 1996), 378.

48. *Franz Rosenzweig, zum 25 December, 1926. Glueckwuensche zum 40. Geburtstag,* (*Congratulations to Franz Rosenzweig on His 40th Birthday: 25th December 1926*), trans. Martin Goldner (New York: Leo Baeck Institute of New York, 1987). The text is available also in a Hebrew translation in Scholem's *'Od Davar* (Tel Aviv: Am Oved, 1986). In her important essay "'Monolingualism' or the Language of God: Scholem and Derrida on Hebrew and Politics," *Modern Judaism* 29, no 2: 226–238, Annabel Herzog adds an important reference to Scholem's account, citing a letter from Benjamin to Scholem as quoted in Robert Alter's *Necessary Angels* that indicates an adjacent background for Scholem's thinking on Hebrew in 1925, one year before the contribution to the Rosenzweig portfolio was solicited (228). The Scholem-Rosenzweig-Benjamin nexus is expounded by Stéphane Mosès in *The Angel of History: Rosenzweig, Benjamin, Scholem*, trans. Barbara Harshav (Stanford: Stanford University Press, 2009).

49. Shahara's terms in "The Sacred and the Unfamiliar: Gershom Scholem and the Anxieties of the New Hebrew," 300. David Biale's authoritative study *Gershom Scholem. Kabbalah and Counter-History* (Cambridge; Mass.: Harvard University Press, 1979) takes the full measure of Scholem's intellectual trajectory and scholarship.

50. See the documents collected in Martin Buber, *A Land of Two Peoples: Martin Buber on Jews and Arabs*, ed. Paul Mendes-Flohr (Chicago: University of Chicago Press, 2005), and also the view from the United States, some three decades later, in David N.

Myers, *Between Jew and Arab: The Lost Voice of Simon Rawidowicz* (Waltham, Mass.: Brandeis University Press, 2008).

51. Need it be noted, with the corrective lenses of hindsight, that Scholem's sense of the linguistic situation in 1920s Palestine partakes, to borrow his own phrase, of *Wir freilich sprechen in Rudimenten* ("we freely speak in rudiments")? The cumulatively heteroglossial nature of Israeli society since that time that includes the ingathering of Arabic-speaking Mizrahi populations in 1948, successive waves of Amharic and Russian speaking immigrants, the perdurance of Yiddish among the *haredim*, not to mention the lingua franca of Arabic among 20 percent of the country's total population and the constantly changing nature of colloquial Hebrew itself (for instance, the increasingly common interpolations of American slang), *only further* introjects Scholem's expressed anxieties into his own personal phenomenology of *Unheimlichkeit*. Modern Hebrew abounds with portmanteau words, calques, and blendings that were inconceivable when Scholem addressed Rosenzweig in 1926. Scholem's attitude toward Hebrew is consistent with a cultural sensibility shared by a cadre of intellectuals in 1920s Palestine for which liberal nationalist self-identification and the aesthetic ideology of *Bildung* were basic features. Scholem, however, was distinguished by his preoccupation with language, "asserting that national sovereignty did not matter if only Hebrew were spoken in Jerusalem." See George Mosse, "Central European Intellectuals in Palestine," *Judaism* 45.2 (Spring, 1996), 134–142.

52. Derrida begins his essay on Scholem's text—"a reading that is as internal as possible" (198)—by noting, "This letter has no testamentary character, though it was found after Scholem's death, in his papers, in 1985. Here it is, nonetheless, arriving and returning to us, speaking *after* the death of its signatory. . . . One has at times the impression that a revenant proclaims to us the terrifying return of a ghost" (191). Later, he asks, "What does Scholem confess? What does he avow and in what sense is this an avowal or a confession—that is to say, at the same time, a recognition in the sense of an avowal and an avowal in the sense of a profession or faith?" (194).

53. He continues: "During the period when my path began to turn in the direction of Hebrew, German remained a living language for me, albeit to a certain degree a static one." He says that there were only three texts that he read and reread with "true atten-tiveness, with an open heart, and with spiritual tension": the Hebrew Bible, the *Zohar* and Kafka. "My Way to Kabbalah," *On the Possibility of Jewish Mysticism In Our Time and Other Essays*, 23.

54. Derrida also notes the cumulative effect of words like *Kraft, Macht,* and *Gewalt* as figures of linguistic "power and violence" (209). Later in the essay, he complicates the rhetoric of ensorcellment by referring to the letter's " *folie sacrée*" and its "*sacreé folie*" (sacred madness and damned madness).

55. As various commentaries note, and as Scholem's declaration, *Sprache ist Name* makes abundantly transparent, Benjamin's 1917 essay "On Language as Such and on the Language of Man" and its theory of language as naming and originary "magic" (exem-plified by the creation narrative in Genesis and *its* synergy between human and divine

acts of nomination), are deeply imprinted on Scholem's letter. Derrida does say, "This sacred language is 'con-juration' itself," (23), but he misses the *Jewishly* specific esoteric element here. Shahara's analysis is worth quoting at length: "Secular language can be understood as equivalent to the 'practical magic,' a vulgar misuse and a 'demonic' praxis of the sacred. This is how the 'demonic' character of the New Hebrew reveals itself: its enunciation of the holy names is to march on the path of apocalypse—a violent revelation of God's words. . . . The secular and the sacred cannot be discussed merely as oppositions or replacements, but rather they belong together. This is the paradox of secularization, namely the fact that the secular becomes a host, the medium in which the sacred is hidden. The forgetfulness of this treasure, the amnesia of spoken Hebrew, is a source for distortions that carry violent implications. Scholem thus calls the New Hebrew to recognize its own depth. He calls it to listen to its abyss, the void of language, and to hear the voice of its forgotten, lost traditions. His letter calls the New Hebrew to recognize its own demonic power, its creation and dangers, its apocalyptical path" (312).

56. It also, of course, addresses itself directly to Rosenzweig, who sustains his own conflicted relationship to the import of such "politicolinguistic" secularization. On this "not only *exterior* décor of a drama being played out by two German Jews who stand on the opposite sides of history, of eschatology, of the State of Israel" (194), see Michael Brenner, *The Renaissance of Jewish Culture in Weimar Germany* (New Haven: Yale University Press, 1996) and "A Tale of Two Families: Franz Rosenzweig, Gershom Scholem and the Generational Conflict around Judaism," *Judaism* 42.3 (1993), 349–361.

57. The distinction does come up in passing, however, for Derrida at the end of his essay, "Force of Law: The 'Mystical Foundation of Authority'" (*Acts of Religion*, 291–292), on Benjamin's "Critique of Violence," around "Greek" vs. "Jewish" discourses.

58. "'Monolingualism' or the Language of God: Scholem and Derrida on Hebrew and Politics," *Modern Judaism* 29, no. 2 (May 2009): 226–238.

59. "Desacralization and Disenchantment," in *Nine Talmudic Readings*, 141 and 152.

60. Robert Alter, *The Book of Psalms: A Translation with Commentary* (New York: Norton, 2007), 126. Herzog cites the entry of August 15, 1916, in *Lamentations of Youth: The Diaries of Gershom Scholem, 1913–1919*, trans. Anthony David Skinner (Cambridge, Mass.: Harvard University Press, 2007), 131, noting that Scholem mentions the verse in relation to the Shabbat *Minḥa* (Afternoon) Service.

61. In an equally illuminating essay on Scholem, Robert Alter provides yet another intertext, that of literary modernism. "Perhaps the most revelatory recurrent term in regard to Scholem's sensibility and worldview is 'abyss' because it is so frequently introduced as an interpretive metaphor. . . . The German term for abyss, *Abgrund,* can also mean simply 'basis,' but in Scholem's usage, it is almost always a close equivalent to the Hebrew *tehom*" (432). Scholem enlists Mann and Bely as modernist peers, but as far as this book is concerned, his most resonant allusion is to Conrad's *Nostromo* and his narrator's description of the *Golfo Placido* (434). See "Scholem and Modernism," 429–442.

62. Slavoj Žižek (and Friedrich Wilhelm Joseph von Schelling), *The Abyss of Freedom: Ages of the World* (Detroit: University of Michigan Press, 1997), 50, and "Neighbors and Other Monsters: A Plea for Ethical Violence," in *The Neighbor: Three Inquiries in Political Theology* ed. Kenneth Reinhard, Eric L. Santner, and Slavoj Žižek (Chicago: University of Chicago Press, 2005; Eric Santner, *On the Psychotheology of Everyday Life: Reflections on Freud and Rosenzweig* (Chicago: University of Chicago Press, 2001); Jacques Lacan, *The Seminar of Jacques Lacan: Book VII: The Ethics of Psychoanalysis 1959–1960*, trans. Dennis Porter (New York: Norton, 1997). See also Simon Critchley, "Das Ding: Lacan and Levinas," *Research in Phenomenology* 28, no. 1 (1998): 72–90.

63. *Monolingualism of the Other; or, The Prosthesis of Origin*, trans. Patrick Mensah (Stanford: Stanford University Press, 1998), 27. Because of the Scholem-Rosenzweig connection that comes to its uncanny crescendo in the *Berkenntnis*, Derrida's text is frequently paired with "The Eyes of Language essay," and is therefore referenced by both Hollander and Herzog. Each devotes space to the formulation of "monolingualism," which recurs often in Derrida's analysis. A context for the text's alternate title, however, appears only once in the book: "One can, of course, speak several languages. There are speakers who are competent in more than one language. Some even write several languages at a time (prostheses, grafts, translation, transposition). But do they not always do it with a view to an absolute idiom? And in the promise of a still unheard-of language? (67). It is subject to brief but mordant critique in Doris Sommer, *Bilingual Aesthetics: A New Sentimental Education* (Durham, N.C.: Duke University Press, 2004), 45, but neither Derrida's text nor Sommer's commentary addresses the question of the sacred. See also Gerhard Richter's pivoting of Derrida's text (by way of Benjamin) toward the figure of the *arrivant* and *langues d'arrivée*, the "homeless self [as] itself a prosthesis," in *Thought-images: Frankfurt School Writers' Reflections from Damaged Life* (Stanford: Stanford University Press, 2007).

64. *Franz Rosenzweig's The New Thinking*, trans. Alan Udoff, Barbara Ellen Galli (Syracuse, N.Y.: Syracuse University Press, 1999), 87. Rosenzweig's thoughts on this matter bear comparison with Bakhtinian formulations of "answer-word" and "addressivity" in his "Speech Genres" essay, e.g., "[Speech] does not know beforehand where it will emerge. It lets itself be given its cues from others; it actually lives by virtue of another's life, whether that others is the one who listens to a story, or is the respondent in a dialogue, or the participant in a chorus; while thinking is always a solitary business, even if it should happen in common, among several 'symphilosophers' . . . . In actual conversation, something really happens" (86).

65. Prior to *Monolingualism*, Derrida engaged the famous Benjamin essay at length in probably his most well known excursus on translation, "Des Tours de Babel." Among other points, Derrida calls attention to the Benjaminian trope of languages in *Verwand-schaft* [kinship, affinity] with each other as revealed through the act of translation itself. According to Derrida's reading, this latent possibility actualized by translation not only "holds for the literary text or the sacred text," but also "perhaps defines the essence of the literary and the scared at their common root"; they "do not lend themselves to thought

one without the other[,] they produce each other at the edge of the same limit" (*Acts of Religion*, 120, 123). It is in the same essay that Derrida speaks of the translator's task as the marrying of two languages to each other that thus seeks to "touch the untouchable" (in the hymenic sense) while nevertheless preserving a remnant that necessarily eludes final revelation and textual transmissibility: *die Übertragung.* On the vexing question of Derrida's own "translation" of both Benjamin and the Bible, see Bannet's "The Scene of Translation: After Jakobson, Benjamin, de Man, and Derrida," and Craig Bartholomew, "Babel and Derrida: Postmodernism, Language, and Biblical Interpretation," *Tyndale Bulletin* 49, no. 2 (1998): 305–328.

66. "If translation is a mode, then translatability must be essential to certain works" (153). This is the burden of Rodolphe Gasché's argument in "Saturnine Vision and the Question of Difference: Reflections on Walter Benjamin's Theory of Language," *Benjamin's Ground: New Readings of Walter Benjamin*, ed. Rainer Nägele (Detroit: Wayne State University Press, 1988), 83–104. See also Howard Caygill, *Walter Benjamin: The Colour of Experience* (London: Routledge, 1998).

67. This is the from the famous Harry Zohn translation. A more recent attempt by Steven Rendall, "'The Translator's Task,' Walter Benjamin (Translation)," *TTR: traduction, terminologie, redaction* 10, no. 2 (1997): 151–165, preserves some of the Benjaminian nuances Zohn omitted: "The translator's task consists in this: to find the intention toward the language into which the work is to be translated, on the basis of which an echo of the original can be awakened in it. . . . However, unlike a literary work, a translation does not find itself, so to speak, in middle of the high forest of the language itself; instead, from outside it, facing it, and without entering it, the translation calls to the original within, at that one point where the echo in its own language can produce a reverberation of the foreign language's work" (159). See, in this regard, Steven Rendall, "Notes on Zohn's Translation of Benjamin's '*Die Aufgabe des Übersetzers,*'" ibid., 191–206.

68. See, for instance, Martin Jay, "Politics of Translation: Siegfried Kracauer and Walter Benjamin on the Buber-Rosenzweig Bible," *Publications of the Leo Baeck Institute, Year Book XXI* (London: Secker & Warburg, 1976), 3–24, the section of Benjamin/Rosenzweig in Amit Pinchevski's *By Way of Interruption*, and Barbara Galli's to *Cultural Writings of Franz Rosenzweig*, "Translating as a Mode of Holiness," 3–57. Susan Ingram's review essay, "'The Task of the Translator': Walter Benjamin's Essay in English, a *Forschungsbericht,*" *TTR: traduction, terminologie, redaction* 10, no. 2 (1997): 207–233, catalogues many of the English treatments of Benjamin's essay.

69. "That is what is named from here on Babel: the law imposed by the name of God who in one stroke commands and forbids you to translate by showing *and* hiding from you the limit" (*Acts of Religion*, 132–133). And if "Babel" connotes not only the multiplicity of tongues but also the infiniteness and necessary incompleteness of interlinguistic relation, then the translator's task likewise becomes an infinite one—or in the essay's subsequent vocabulary of both "gift" and insolvent debt" (111).

70. Hollander notes Luther's injunction *die Worte steif zu behalten* ("to keep the words stiff"), *Exemplarity and Chosenness*, 144.

71. I borrow the idea of "detranslation" from "Making Room for the Hebrew: Luther, Dialectics, and the Shoah," *Journal of the American Academy of Religion* 69, no. 3 (2001): 551–576, Oona Ajzenstat (Eisenstadt)'s powerful reading of the essay's critique of Luther's dialectical renderings as presaging German culture but also therefore backshadowed by the Holocaust.

72. Martin Buber and Franz Rosenzweig, *Schrift und ihre Verdeutschung* ("Scripture and Its Germanization"), available in *Franz Rosenzweig, Der Mensch und sein Werk. Gesammelte Schriften. IV. Bd: Sprachdenken im Übersetzen. 2. Bd.: Arbeitspapiere zur Verdeutschung der Schrift*, ed. Rachel Bat-Adam (Dordrecht-Boston-Lancaster: Martinus Nijhoff, 1984). See also Batnitzky, "Rosenzweig's Aesthetic Theory and Jewish Unheimlichkeit," in *New German Critique* 77 (1999): 87–112, and the book-length treatment, *Idolatry and Representation: The Philosophy of Franz Rosenzweig Reconsidered* (Princeton: Princeton University Press, 2009). In *The Shape of Revelation: Aesthetics and Modern Jewish Thought* (Stanford: Stanford University Press, 2007), a book that connects the German Jewish philosophical tradition to early German modernism, Zachary Braiterman traces the Buber-Rosenzweig insistence on Scripture as an aesthetically unified whole, "like a work of art pressed against the limits of 'art'" (54), back to Schlegel's *"Ideen"* in his *Kritische Fragmente*.

73. "Wholly art" vs. "entire work of art" in Batnitzky, 100; Braiterman, 55. *"Ganz Kunstwerk"* is an expression Rosenzweig used in preparation for lectures at the *Lehrhaus* in 1921.

74. Rosenzweig's word is *"übersprungen"* (leaped over).

75. The formulation is quoted by both Barbara Galli in *Franz Rosenzweig and Jehuda Halevi: Translating, Translations, and Translators* (Montreal: McGill Queens University Press, 1995), 251, and Zachary Braiterman in *The Shape of Revelation* (Stanford: Stanford University Press, 2007), 7. Mara Benjamin's "Building a Zion in German(y): Franz Rosenzweig on Yehudah Halevi" is also extremely helpful here. The original is published in *Franz Rosenzweig, Der Mensch und sein Werk. Gesammelte Schriften. IV. Bd: Sprachdenken im Übersetzen. 1. Bd.: Fünfundzwanzig Hymnen und Gedichte*, ed. Rafael N. Rosenzweig (The Hague: Martinus Nijhoff, 1983).

76. "Making Room for Hebrew," 563. Scholem's text is "At the Completion of Buber's Translation of the Bible," in *The Messianic Idea in Judaism* (New York: Schocken, 1971), 314–319. See also Martin Jay, "Politics of Translation: Siegfried Kracauer and Walter Benjamin on the Buber–Rosenzweig Bible," *Permanent Exiles: Essays on the Intellectual Migration from Germany to America* (New York" Columbia University Press, 1986), 309 n. 90.

77. Rosenzweig deploys this conceit himself as "the *qer'iah*, the 'calling out'" in his short essay *"Die Schrift und das Wort"* when he speaks of the Bible's demand for a "pre-literary mode of reading" ("Scripture and Word: On the New Bible Translation," in *Scripture and Translation*, 40–46). In the 1961 commemorative address to Buber, Scholem said that the venture amounted to "an appeal to the reader: Go and learn Hebrew!" (315).

78. At the end of "Scripture and Word," Rosenzweig uses a metaphor distinct from Abyss, Void, Volcano, or the like: *das Tor* ["the gate"]. "Henceforth the gate into nocturnal silence that enveloped the human race in its origins, dividing each from each other, and all from what was outside and what was beyond—henceforth the gate is broken and cannot altogether be closed again: the gate of the word" (46).

79. The congruence here with Benjamin is noteworthy: "To set free in his own language the pure language spellbound in the foreign language, to liberate the language imprisoned in the work by rewriting it, is the translator's task" (163).

80. Marc Alain Ouaknin, *The Burnt Book: Reading the Talmud*, trans. Llewellyn Brown (Princeton: Princeton University Press, 1995), 73. Ouaknin also quotes Maurice Blanchot from "The Limit Experience" in *The Infinite Conversation*, trans. Susan Hanson (Minneapolis: University of Minnesota Press, 1993), 126, itself, a quotation from André Neher's *L'existence juive: Solitude et affrontements*: "a ferryman, the Hebrew Abraham not only invites us to go from one riverbank to the other but also to carry ourselves to wherever there is a passage to be achieved, while maintaining this between-two-banks that is the truth of passage." Gen. 14:13 identifies Abram as an *'ivri* ("he who crosses over"), which Rashi understands geographically in relation to the Euphrates but *Midrash Rabbah* glosses, Rosenzweig-like, as "the whole world stood on one side but Abram crossed over to the other."

81. Wittgenstein is enlisted as a Jewish philosopher in conjunction with Rosenzweig in the first section of Hilary Putnam's *Jewish Philosophy as a Way of Life*, 9–36.

82. To take some examples from Agnon's fiction: the tales "Lost" (*Hefker*), "The Document" (*Hate'udah*) and "Knots Upon Knots" (*Kishrei kesharim*) from *Sefer Ha-Ma'asim*" (*The Book of Deeds*) published in 1932 all depend on the metaphor of writing that has gone missing somehow to narrate a more general story about linguistic alienation. See Anne Golomb Hoffman, *Between Exile and Return: S. Y. Agnon and the Drama of Writing* (Albany: State University of New York Press, 1991), in particular her concluding discussion, along with Scholem's letter, of the fragment Agnon sent to Germany as part of Rosenzweig's *Die Gabe*.

83. On the entire passage, see Daniel Herwitz, "On the Exile of Words in the American Simulacrum: A Free Exercise in Wittgensteinian Cultural Critique," in *Borders, Exiles, Diasporas*, ed. Elazar Barkan and Marie-Denise Shelton (Stanford: Stanford University Press, 1998), 149–177.

84. In the manuscript TS 213 (the so-called *Big Typescript*) from the *Nachlass* (included as an appendix to *Wittgenstein on Mind and Language*, ed. David G. Stern (New York: Oxford University Press, 1995), the famous sentence reads alternately, "*Wir führen die Wörter von ihrer metaphysischen wieder auf ihre* so richtige *Verwendung* in der Sprache zurück.*"

85. Levinas makes the relevant point about this *sugya* that "the Scroll of Esther is the only book of the Bible whose dramatic action unfolds in the dispersion among the nations, the only book of the Diaspora" (45). Sergey Dolgopolski discussess the same folios along with their distinction between two writing idioms, *Targum* and *Miqra*, in

the chapter, "Talmud as Event" in his *What Is Talmud*, 158–170. He also emphasizes the Tosafists' commentary on *bMegillat* 7b citing comparisons between Esther and a doe in *bYoma*29a that "Esther, the book, and Esther, the person, sometimes become indistinguishable from one another, both conceptually and imaginatively" (130).

86. Not only its narrative sections, as Rosenzweig acknowledges later in the essay, in anticipation of theoretically informed current scholarship like Meir Sternberg's, but also its non-narrative genres, as well (141–142).

87. "At the Completion of Buber's Translation of the Bible," *The Messianic Idea in Judaism*, 318.

88. On metaphor in Levinas, see Annette Aronowicz, "The Sweet Life of Metaphor: Levinas' Reflections on Metaphor and Their Implications for Biblical Hermeneutics," in *Making a Difference: Essays on the Bible and Judaism in Honor of Tamara Cohn Eskenazi*, ed. David J. A. Clines, Kent Harold Richards, and Jacob L. Wright (Sheffield: Sheffield Phoenix Press, 2012), 9–19.

89. *"Prends l' éloquence et tords-lui son cou!"* from *L'art poétique* (1874).

90. The titular formulation of Gianni Vattimo's study in aesthetics and hermeneutics, *Art's Claim to Truth*, trans. Luca D'Isanto (New York: Columbia University Press, 2008).

91. *Artificial Paradises*, trans. Stacy Diamond (New York: Citadel Press, 1996), 157. Charles Baudelaire is writing about De Quincey's favored caduceus image in *Confessions of an English Opium Eater*.

92. As burden, the book often *attaches* itself. In "A Book That Was Lost," for example, an orphaned manuscript of commentary on Jewish law, saved from oblivion in western Ukraine when sent to the Ginzei Yosef Library in Palestine, is compared to a kite to which a child holds fast: "I knew that I made up the parcel in order to send it to Jerusalem, but for as long as it was in my hands, it bound me to Jerusalem. But if I let the parcel out of my hands, it would go up to Jerusalem while I stayed in Buczacz." *A Book That Was Lost and Other Stories*, ed. Alan Mintz and Anne Golomb Hoffman (New York: Schocken, 1995), 132.

93. Ibid., 445. This scene is discussed at length by Anne Golomb Hoffman in Chapter 8 of *Between Exile and Return* in the larger context of German Jewish collecting, 149–176. See also her article, "Topographies of Reading: Agnon through Benjamin," *Prooftexts* 21, no. 1 (Winter 2001): 71–89. Emile G. L. Schrijver's essay "The Transmission of Jewish Knowledge through MSS and Printed Books," in *The Oxford Companion to the Book*, ed. Michael F. Suarez and H. R. Woudhuysen (Oxford: Oxford University Press, 2010), 66–73, begins with an evocation of Agnon's own childhood memories as he stands before his grandfather's bookcase, in sentimental counterpoint to Bialik's "Lifnei aron ha-sefarim."

94. Ibid., 533. The character is based on a real figure whom Agnon knew: Saul Adler (1894–1966), who did indeed study tropical diseases in Sierra Leone between 1921 and 1924, injecting parasites into his own body. See Dan Laor, "An uncompromising search for truth," *Ha'aretz*, July 8, 2011.

95. Miron, *From Continuity to Contiguity*, 276. As Shachar Pinsker explains Miron's choice of terminology, "Thinking about relations between different phenomena in terms of contiguity might be traced to the philosophical theories of Hume and Wittgenstein, whose concept of 'family-resemblance' may serve as an alternative to essentialist definitions. Miron's new theory of Jewish literary thinking based on contiguity would focus on proximities, unregulated contacts, and moments of close adjacency, but not on the containment of one entity by another." "What is Jewish Literature?" in *The New Republic*, December 8, 2011.

96. Alan Mintz, *Sanctuary in the Wilderness: A Critical Introduction to American Hebrew Poetry* (Stanford: Stanford University Press, 2012), 76.

97. He eventually settled in Israel one year after statehood. His biography can be consulted in ibid., 298–306.

98. See the full treatment of the poem's philosophical and theological premises in Gideon Katz and Gideo Nevo, "Two Perspectives on Abraham Regelson's *Hakukot Oitiyotayich*," *Hebrew Studies* 48 (2007): 299–320.

99. Translated and discussed in Mintz, *Sanctuary in the Wilderness*, 68–109.

100. Quoted in ibid., 106.

101. See Chana Kronfeld's discussion of Bialik's essay in connection with Itamar Even-Zohar's "polysystem theory" in *On the Margins of Modernism*, 83–92.

Epilogue: The Book in Hand, Again

1. His absent interlocutor here is also Merleau-Ponty, as it will be Bergson in the essay's later sections. The particular work of Merleau-Ponty's that influenced this essay is *Signes*, from 1960. See the account of "Meaning and Sense" by Peter C. Blum, "Overcoming Relativism? Levinas's Return to Platonism," *Journal of Religious Ethics* 28, no. 1 (Spring 2000): 91–117, and Thomas W. Busch, "Ethics and Ontology: Levinas and Merleau-Ponty," *Man and World* 25, no. 2 (1992): 195–202.

2. Heidegger's famous etymologies serve Levinas as an example of how a word can open up depths and densities of meaning.

3. Levinas explains his use of "liturgical" according to "its first signification," which means "the exercise of an office that is not only gratuitous but requires from the executant an investment at a loss . . . . Further, this uncompensated work, whose result in the Agent's time is not banked on, this work insured only for patience . . . this liturgy is not placed as a cult beside 'works' and ethics. It is ethics itself" (28). The term is unpacked at length in Jeffrey Bloechl, *Liturgy of the Neighbor: Emmanuel Lévinas and the Religion of Responsibility* (Pittsburgh: Duquesne University Press, 2000).

4. A intriguing critique of the essay that connects it to Levinas's Eurocentrism can be found in Lin Ma, "All the Rest Must be Translated: Lévinas's Notion of Sense," *Journal of Chinese Philosophy* (2008): 599–612.

5. I would emphasize the participial constructions here, "reflecting" and "cutting" (not to mention their being staged in "the heart of the world"), as fore-echoing Judith

Butler's gloss on Merleau-Ponty in her famous essay, "Performative Acts and Gender Constitution." "As an intentionally organized materiality, the body is always an *embodying* of possibilities both conditioned and circumscribed by historical convention. In other words, the body is a historical situation, as Beauvoir has claimed, and is a manner of *doing, dramatizing,* and *reproducing* a historical situation" (521, my italics). In my example here, "the book in hand" collapses or conceals the participle—the holding, touching, fingering—that, in fact, transforms the act of reading into "a continual and incessant materializing of possibilities."

6. In the section "What Is Writing?" from *What Is Literature?,* just before he explains the reader's obligatory position relative to text and author—"the author's whole art is bent on obliging me to create what he discloses" (66)—Sartre says, almost in anticipation of Poulet, "You are perfectly free to leave that book on the table. But if you open it, you assume responsibility for it" (46). *What Is Literature and Other Essays,* trans. Bernard Frechtman (Cambridge, Mass.: Harvard University Press, 1988).

7. Section 1 of "The Book," www.schulzian.net/translation/sanatorium/book1.htm.

8. The vision endures even as the quasi-biblical Book, as sublime object of tactile reverence, reveals itself, rather, to be a random collection of magazine advertisements and personal announcements, the Book's "unofficial supplement, its tradesman's entrance full of litter and debris"; subsequently, it cedes to yet another "true book of Splendor," a "universal book, a compendium of all human knowledge; in allusions, naturally, in hints and insinuations": that is, a *stamp album.* For a postage stamp, the profile of Franz Joseph I, for example, represents not only "a symbol of the everyday" but "the determining of all possibilities, guarantor of the impassable borders in which the world is now and forever confined." (Sections III, VII, XXI and VI of "The Book." Israeli novelist David Grossman's Schulz-inspired *See Under: Love,* trans. Betsy Rosenberg [New York: Simon & Schuster, 1989]), echoes this motif in the form of a salvaged torn page from an old magazine, a children's story that its avid reader, Momik, decides is "the origin of every book and work of literature ever written[;] the books that came later were merely imitations of this page Momik had been lucky enough to find like a hidden treasure" (11).

9. Mary Ann Caws's translation: www.studiocleo.com/librarie/mallarme/prose.html.

10. Section V of "The Book." On the repeated figure of "the book" in Schulz, see Kris Van Heuckelom, "Artistic Crossover in Polish Modernism: The Case of Bruno Schulz's *Xięga Bałwochwalcza* (The Idolatrous Booke)," *Image [&] Narrative* (November 2006), www.imageandnarrative.be/inarchive/iconoclasm/heuckelom.htm.

11. The memorable phrase belongs to Maurice Blanchot from "Communication and the Work," *The Space of Literature,* trans. Ann Smock (Omaha: University of Nebraska Press, 1982), 196.

12. Stewart, an assiduous neologizer, coined the term "narratography" to describe a critical calibration of "the conjuring work" internal to the language in Victorian novels *as intoned, affective prose* in his monograph, *Novel Violence: A Narratography of Victorian Fiction* (Chicago: University of Chicago Press, 2009). The limits of both genre theory and narratology are weighed against an alternate approach that combines grammatical

stylistics (the "phrasal measures" of the prose in a sentence-by-sentence accounting) and what Stewart calls "media study" (using the analogy of narrative cinema). In effect, Stewart proposes that we approach reading Victorian novels the way Victorians did, word for word, sentence by sentence—which is not so radically dissimilar from the traditional rabbinic commentarial tradition for the Holy Scriptures.

13. Should one conduct a web search for "book as weapon" in expectation of finding literary examples, one will find instead an array of instructional videos (many tailored for women) on the art of self-defense, one of which is captioned as follows: "Books are good for more than reading! You may be able to use that Murakami novel to fend off an attack."

14. Thomas Hardy, *Poems Selected by Tom Paulin* (New York: Faber and Faber, 2005), 135. The poem is discussed in an essay by J. Hillis Miller of general pertinence here, "Hands in Hardy," *The Ashgate Research Companion to Thomas Hardy*, ed. Rosemarie Morgan (Surrey: Ashgate Publishing Company, 2010), 505–516.

15. "When one 'pays by check' in a commercial transaction so as to leave a trace of payment, the trace is inscribed in the very order of the world. However, the authentic trace disturbs the world's order. It is 'superimposed.' Its original significance is designed in the imprint left by the one who wanted to erase his traces in an attempt, for example, to accomplish the perfect crime. The one who left traces while erasing his traces didn't want to say or do anything by the traces he leaves . . . Being, as *leaving a trace,* is passing, leaving, absolving oneself" ("Signification and Sense," 41–42).

16. A romantic analogue can be found in Hardy's novel, *Tess of the D'Urbervilles* (Oxford: Oxford University Press, 2008), 151:

> "You needn't say anything, Izz," answered Retty. "For I zid you kissing his shade."
>   "What did you see her doing?" asked Marian.
>   "Why—he was standing over the whey-tub to let off the whey, and the shade of his face came upon the wall behind, close to Izz, who was standing there filling a vat. She put her mouth against the wall and kissed the shade of his mouth; I zid her, though he didn't."

17. "Work and the Body in Hardy and Other Nineteenth-Century Novelists," *Representations* 3 (Summer 1983): 91. Later in the essay, Scarry develops the argument by distinguishing between "the concussiveness of the interaction between the material creature and the material world" and "the largess of that interaction" (96). If *concussiveness* marks the site of imprint on the book passed through classmates' hands in Benjamin's Berlin classroom, then *largesse* is the generosity, the vulnerability, activated by reading itself—the book, for example, read under "high compulsion" by Canetti. The parenthetical reference to Arendt has in mind her famous distinction, borrowed from Locke, of "the labor of our body and the work of our hands." See *The Human Condition* (Chicago: University of Chicago Press, 1998), 79ff.

18. We could pose related questions of a programmatic kind. For example, do modernist or realist texts lend themselves more appositely to ethical criticism of one sort or another? Is lyric or narrative or dramatic discourse intrinsically more susceptible to such approaches? Centric vs. peripheral and marginal literary traditions? Fictions as

opposed to nonfictions? Such questions feel wrongly pitched, and should cede to the more pertinent drama of *staging* of a text, whether through the chemistry of commentary or the alchemy of critique. Given that Benjamin himself seems always to synthesize the two—the critic in his capacity as paleographer begins with a commentarial palimpsest, a blend of surfaces, inscriptions, and rubbings—such performative staging always has ethical potential because it seeks both to touch upon and to touch the work. Anson Rabinbach makes a similar point about Benjamin's own criticism when he locates its distinctly "sensuous aspect," in "Critique and Commentary/Alchemy and Chemistry: Some Remarks on Walter Benjamin," *New German Critique* 17 (Spring 1979): 3–14.

19. Letter to Oscar Pollak, dated January 27, 1904. *Letters to Family, Friends, and Editors,* trans. Richard and Clara Winston (New York: Schocken Books, 1977), 16.

20. "Jubilation Alley," *The Beauty Supply District* (New York: Pantheon Books, 2000), 51.

21. *Cheap Novelties: The Pleasure of Urban Decay* (New York: Penguin, 1991), 17. A brief account by Leona Christie of Katchor's lecture "On Graven Images in the Yiddish Press" may be relevant: www.printeresting.org/2011/04/28/ben-katchor-printmaker-as-saboteur/. Katchor's *The Cardboard Valise* (New York: Pantheon, 2011) most fully realizes this motif. The book of strips, about a valise containing a pile of books that have been rescued from discard, contains handles inside the covers, thus simulating a suitcase and making the text a remarkably reflexive object-as-container-of-objects. See also the essay by Nathalie op de Beeck, "Found Objects (Jem Cohen, Ben Katchor, Walter Benjamin)," *Modern Fiction Studies* 52:4 (2006), 807–831. Finally, Katchor's most recent and collection, *Hand Drying in America and Other Stories* (New York: Pantheon Books, 2013), features an endpaper, indicia-title-page narrative about the ecological price paid for any book published, which, noting that "the smell and texture of paper is [printed books'] last remaining physical pleasure," also affirms that "the environmental damage and human suffering associated with book production adds a new poignancy to the reader's pleasure."

22. As recorded by R. David Weiss Halivni in the chapter, "The Story of a *Bletl*" of his memoir, *The Book and the Sword: A Life of Learning in the Shadow of Destruction* (New York: Westview Press, 1997). "A text, like a human being, is only true to itself when it is more than itself" (92), Halivni's general maxim for Talmud study across the generations, captions this episode of luminous humanism "in the shadow of destruction." Compare both the Mayhew epigraph, as quoted in Price's *How to Do Things with Books in Victorian Britain* (260), along with her chapter on "it-narrative" for religious books; and also the description of a thirteenth-century folio of Tractate *Sanhedrin* that was used as a binding for a sixteenth-century Italian notarial register after the confiscation and burning of the Talmud in Italy in 1553, on which "the scars of the bookbinder's knife remain acutely evident as do the creases and other marks that remain after nearly four-hundred years of being folded into the binding" (182). *Printing the Talmud: From Bomberg To Schottenstein,* ed. Sharon Liberman Mintz and Gabriel M. Goldstein (New York: Yeshiva University Museum, 2006).

23. I refer specifically to a letter by Confederate soldier James Robert Montgomery and discussed by Drew Gilpin Faust in her *This Republic of Suffering: Death and the*

American Civil War (New York: Knopf, 2008), 16–17. See James R. Montgomery to A. R. Montgomery, May 10, 1864, CSA Collection, ESBL, and also John M. Coski, "Montgomery's Blood-Stained Letter Defines 'The Art of Dying'—and Living," *Museum of the Confederacy Magazine* (Summer 2006), 14.

24. Seth Rogovoy, "Ben Katchor," *The BerkshireWeb* (August 1, 2000), www.berk shireweb.com/rogovoy/interviews/feat000802.html, and Sam Adams, "Interview With Ben Katchor," *A.V. Club* (April 22, 2011), www. avclub.com/articles/ben-katchor,54962/.

25. "The Art of Fiction No. 173, Interviewed by Adam Begley," *Paris Review* 162 (Summer 2002): 30–60, at 41.

26. *Realism, Writing, and Disfiguration*, xiv, and quoted in "On Impressionism," 198.

27. "St. John of the Cross" by Francisco Antonio Gijón (1653–c. 1721) and unknown painter (possibly Domingo Mejías), National Gallery of Art, Washington, D.C. Where the bodily and writing/reading as a spiritual practices are both concerned, of course, St. John of the Cross casts a large shadow. See the introduction by Antonio T. de Nicolás to *St. John of the Cross/San Juan de La Cruz: Alchemist of the Soul: His Life, His Poetry (Bilingual), His Prose* (New York: Paragon House, 1989).

28. Darger's room and studio at 851 Webster St. in Chicago, a meager 17'6" × 13'9" × 9'8" space, have been recreated as "The Henry Darger Room Collection," housed within Intuit: The Center for Intuitive and Outsider Art. See the description at www.art.org/collection/henry-darger/. *Rodinsky's Room* by Rachel Lichtenstein and Iain Sinclair (London: Granta Books, 1999) and Benjamin Geissler, *The Picture Chamber of Bruno Schulz* (a mobile installation of the room in which the writer's last work was found) record similar instances of reclamation.

29. I borrow the term from Peter Sloterdijk's mammoth philosophical trilogy, *Sphären*, part one of which has appeared in English as *Bubbles: Spheres Volume I: Microspherology*, trans. Wieland Hoban (Cambridge, Mass.: MIT Press, 2011). Although Sloterdijk does not enlist the act of reading, let alone the cinema or theater, in his inventory of modern transformative self-training practices (elsewhere, in his *Elmauer Rede*, books as a medium of transmission are relegated to an obsolete mechanism of cultivating friendship), his account of "the anthropotechnic turn" in *You Must Change Your Life*, trans. Wieland Hoban (Malden, Mass.: Polity Press, 2013) offers a posthumanist model of secularized religiosity in respect to what I call rituals (his term would be "disciplines"). A vivid example of altered reading as "shared inside"—extreme rubbing the text, we might call it—are the remediated novels by Tom Phillips, *A Humument* (1966–2012) and Jonathan Safran Foer, *Tree of Codes* (2010). Both treat a prior literary work (in Philips's case, W. H. Mallock's 1882 novel *A Human Document* and in Foer's, Bruno Schulz's *The Street of Crocodiles*) by pruning or excavating it, erasing large portions of text and then fashioning from the whole a new narrative-as-palimpsest. In these instances, principled custodianship of the book-in-hand amounts to altering it in the very plainest sense. A cinematic version of this poetics of re-use can be seen in collage films of found footage like Bill Morrison's *Decasia: The State of Decay* (2002) or Peter Delpeut's *Lyrisch Nitraat* (1990), which "archive" fragments of decomposing nitrocellulose

silent film stock in an uncanny, reassembled afterlife. Of Delpeut's work, for example, a review in *Cinema Ramble* (June 3, 2012) offers the quasi-Schulzian observation "At times it even seems like these films are watching each other, providing a haunted fantasy of what films might get up to in an archive when they are discarded, forgotten and unobserved." See also Andre Habib, "Ruin, Archive and the Time of Cinema: Peter Delpeut's Lyrical Nitrate," *SubStance* 110 (35:2, 2006), 120–139.

30. The role that imagery plays for Levinas is not simple, especially if we cast him as iconoclast. See, therefore, the excellent article by Philippe Crignon, "Figuration: Emmanuel Levinas and the Image," trans. Nicole Simek and Zahi Zalloua, *Yale French Studies* 104 (2004): 100–125.

31. See Garret Stewart's book of the same name. George Steiner offers the definitive ekphrastic exposition of the Chardin painting in "The Uncommon Reader" from *No Passion Spent: Essays 1978–1995* (New Haven: Yale University Press, 1998), 1–19. On Rogado's painting, see "Training the Senses: Giacomo Santiago Rogado Revisits Enchantment," by Ursula Pia Jauch in *Giacomo Santiago Rogado: First Second Patience*, text by Magdalena Kröner, Konrad Bitterli, and Ursula Pia Jauch (Bielefeld: Kerber 2010).

32. For example, Anne Carson's elegiac *Nox* (New York: New Directions, 2010), a foldout book of sketches, family photos, and letters (and a high-culture analogue to magic's "blow book"), compels tactility as the very activity of reading.

33. *Profanations*, trans. Jeff Fort (New York: Zone Books, 2007), 73.

34. Derrida also comments on this double etymology in "Faith and Knowledge: The Two Sources of 'Religion' and the Limits of Reason Alone" in *Religion*, 16 and 34.

35. "There is no emergence of meaning," writes Hans Gumbrecht in *Production of Presence: What Meaning Cannot Convey* (Stanford: Stanford University Press, 2003), "that does not alleviate the weight of presence" (90).

36. The ceremonial effect of these concatenated names was dramatically brought home by witnessing the author himself publicly recite them, having chosen this same passage to conclude his formal remarks at the "Roth@80" conference in Newark, March 29, 2013. (The event was by chronicled by David Remnick in "Philip Roth's Eightieth-Birthday Celebration," *The New Yorker* [March 20, 2013], www.newyorker.com/online/blogs/books/2013/03/philip-roth-eightieth-birthday-celebration.html.) The specifically *material*, antisymbolic thrust of this scene of reading might also be compared with Ken Koltun-Fromm's observation in *Material Culture and Jewish Thought in America* on Roth's "Eli, the Fanatic" and *Patrimony*: "This is the lived reality of material life: not weighted signification of bodily performance, but the smell, touch, and physical sensation of things" (199). *The Human Stain* (2000) contains a vignette about the Vietnam Veterans Wall that foregrounds the same fusing of name and person at the level of material surface that Robert Pogue Harrison evokes in his essay "The Names of the Dead"; it is also one of several Roth texts (*Everyman* and *Patrimony*, for example) that feature graveyard scenes.

37. Martin Filler, "At the Edge of the Abyss," in *NYR Blog*, September 21, 2011, www.nybooks.com/blogs/nyrblog/2011/sep/21/at-the-edge-of-abyss-september-11-memorial/. David Henkin's *City Reading: Written Words and Public Spaces in Antebellum New York*

(New York: Columbia University Press, 1998) offers perhaps the most capacious local-historical background against which to consider what it means to both read *in* a city and *read* a city, whose quotidian text is signage in its myriad variety, the concatenation of urban texts "posted, circulated, fixed, and flashed in public view" (x).

38. *Gilgamesh*, trans. Stuart Kendall (New York: Contra Mundum Press, 2012), 2–4. The architectural embedding here is not incidental when one considers, with Régis Debray, that "The primordial book is taken to be edifying because its is an edifice. . . . One passes through it like a worshipper in a church or a king in his domain" (143–144). "The Book as Symbolic Object," in *The Future of the Book*, ed. Geoffrey Nunberg (Berkeley: University of California Press, 1997), 139–152.

39. From Henri Maldiney's essay "La Dimension du contact au regard du vivant et l'existant" as quoted in Derrida, *On Touching*, 146. See also Maldiney's "Flesh and Verb in the Philosophy of Maurice Merleau-Ponty," *Chiasms: Merleau-Ponty's Notion of Flesh*, ed. Fred Evans, Leonard Lawlor (Albany: State University of New York Press, 2000), 51–76.

40. In *A Book That Was Lost and Other Stories*, 132.

41. Stewart Ain, "A Burial for the Books," *New York Jewish Week*, January 8, 2013. The alternate fate for damaged holy books is the "burial" that is actually concealment (storage), known in Hebrew as *geniza* (evidently from the Persian *ganj*, meaning treasure). In their book, *Sacred Trash: The Lost and Found World of the Cairo Geniza* (New York: Schocken Books, 2011), Adina Hoffman and Peter Cole explain, "Implied in this idea is that these works, like people, are living things, possessing an element of the sacred about them—and therefore when they 'die' or become worn out, they must be honored and protected from profanation" (13). The most famous of such storage spaces is the "Cairo Geniza," located in the Ben Ezra Synagogue of Fustat and made famous by the research of Solomon Schechter in 1896. See Phyllis Lambert, ed., *Fortifications and the Synagogue: The Fortress of Babylon and the Ben Ezra Synagogue, Cairo* (Chicago: University of Chicago Press, 1994), especially the chapter by Charles Le Quesne, "The Geniza and the Scholarly Community," 237–243. "Threshold to the Sacred: The Ark Door of Cairo's Ben Ezra Synagogue," a 2013 exhibition on the Ben Ezra Synagogue at the Center for Jewish History, features a caption in which the tactile dimension here can be inadvertently glimpsed. "In the late 19th century, fragments from the Cairo Geniza began finding their way from the chamber, accessible by ladder through an opening in a wall of the women's gallery, into the hands of dealers, antiquarians, and scholars." The world of the Geniza, finally, is beautifully reconstituted by Simon Schama in *The Story of the Jews: Finding the Words 1000 BCE to 1492 CE* (London: The Bodley Head, 2013), a book whose very logic of organization—two sections titled, respectively, "*papyrus, potsherd, parchment*" and "*mosaic, parchment, paper*"—marks a fitting conclusion to this book's final endnote.

BIBLIOGRAPHY

Abel, Richard. *The Ciné Goes to Town: French Cinema, 1896–1914.* Berkeley: University of California Press, 1998.

Ackerman-Lieberman, Phillip, and Rakefet Zalashik, eds. *A Jew's Best Friend? The Image of the Dog Throughout Jewish History.* Brighton: Sussex Academic Press, 2012.

Adams, Sam. "Interview with Ben Katchor." *A.V. Club* (April 22, 2011). http://www .avclub.com/articles/ben-katchor,54962.

Adorno, Theodor. *Minima Moralia: Reflections on a Damaged Life.* Translated by E. F. N. Jephcott. New York: Verso, 2005.

Affeldt, Steven G. "The Ground of Mutuality: Criteria, Judgment and Intelligibility in Stephen Mulhall and Stanley Cavell." *European Journal of Philosophy* 6, no. 1 (April 1998): 1–31.

Agamben, Giorgio. *Homo Sacer: Sovereign Power and Bare Life.* Translated by Daniel Heller-Roazen. Stanford: Stanford University Press, 1998.

———. *The Open: Man and Animal.* Translated by Kevin Attell. Stanford: Stanford University Press, 2002.

———. *Profanations.* Translated by Jeff Fort. New York: Zone Books, 2007.

———. *The State of Exception.* Translated by Kevin Attell. Chicago: University of Chicago Press, 2005.

Agnon, S. Y. *A Book That Was Lost and Other Stories.* Edited by Alan Mintz and Anne Golomb Hoffman. New York: Schocken, 1995.

———. *Shira.* Translated by Zeva Shapiro. Syracuse: Syracuse University Press, 1996.

Aguirre, Benigno, and E. L. Quarantelli. "The Phenomenology of Death Counts in Disasters: The Invisible Dead in the 9/11 WTC Attacks." *International Journal of Mass Emergencies and Disasters* 26, no. 1 (March 2008): 19–39.

Ain, Stewart. "A Burial for the Books." *New York Jewish Week,* January 8, 2013.

Ajzenstat, Oona. *Driven Back to the Text: the Premodern Sources of Levinas's Postmodernism.* Pittsburgh: Duquesne University Press, 2001.

———. "Making Room for the Hebrew: Luther, Dialectics, and the Shoah." *Journal of the American Academy of Religion* 69, no. 3 (2001): 551–576.

Alexander, Christopher. *Pattern Language: Towns, Buildings, Construction.* New York: Oxford University Press, 1977.

Alford, C. Fred. *Levinas, the Frankfurt School, and Psychoanalysis*. Middletown, Conn.: Wesleyan University Press, 2003.

Allen, Robert C. "From Exhibition to Reception: Reflections on the Audience in Film History, *Screen* 31, no. 4 (1990): 347–356.

Allen, Valerie. "Difficult Reading." In *Levinas and Medieval Literature: The "Difficult Reading" of English and Rabbinic Texts*, edited by Ann W. Astell and J. A. Jackson, 15–34. Pittsburgh: Duquesne University Press, 2009.

———. "Levinas versus Levinas: Hebrew, Greek, and Linguistic Justice." *Philosophy & Rhetoric* 38, no. 2 (2005): 145–158.

Alter, Robert. *The Book of Psalms: A Translation with Commentary*. New York: Norton, 2007.

———. *Canon and Creativity: Modern Writing and the Authority of Scripture*. New Haven: Yale University Press, 2000.

———. *Genesis: Translation and Commentary*. New York: Norton, 1997.

———. *Modern Hebrew Literature*. New York: Behrman House, 1975.

———. *Necessary Angels: Tradition and Modernity in Kafka, Benjamin, and Scholem*. Cambridge, Mass.: Harvard University Press, 1991.

———. "Scholem and Modernism." *Poetics Today* 15, no. 3 (Autumn 1994): 429–442.

Altieri, Charles. "Lyrical Ethics and Literary Experience." In *Mapping the Ethical Turn: A Reader in Ethics, Culture, and Literary Theory*, edited by Todd F. Davis and Kenneth Womack, 30–58. Charlottesville: University of Virginia Press, 2001.

———. *The Particulars of Rapture: An Aesthetics of the Affects*. Ithaca, N.Y.: Cornell University Press, 2004.

Anderson, Benedict. *Imagined Communities: Reflections on the Origin and Spread of Nationalism*. London: Verso, 1991.

Anderson, Brooke Davis. *The Henry Darger Collection at the American Folk Art Museum*. New York: The American Folk Art Museum, 2001.

Anderson, Kurt. "Kids 'R' Us." *The New Yorker*, December 15, 1997.

Anderson, Mark M. "The Edge of Darkness: On W. G. Sebald." *October* 106 (Autumn 2003): 102–121.

Angel, Maria, and Angela Gibbs. "On Moving and Being Moved: The Corporeality of Writing in Literary Fiction and New Media Art." In *Literature and Sensation*, edited by Anthony Uhlmann, Helen Groth, Paul Sheehan, and Stephen McLaren, 162–171. Newcastle upon Tyne: Cambridge Scholars, 2009.

Anidjar, Gil. *The Jew, the Arab: A History of the Enemy*. Stanford: Stanford University Press, 2003.

———. "Secularism." *Critical Inquiry* 33, no. 1 (Autumn 2006): 52–57.

Anzieu, Didier. *The Skin Ego: A Psychoanalytic Approach to the Self*. Translated by Chris Turner. New Haven: Yale University Press, 1989.

Arac, Jonathan. "Criticism between Opposition and Counterpoint." *boundary 2* 25, no. 2 (Summer 1998): 55–69.

Arad, Michael. "Reflecting Absence." *Places: Forum of Design for the Public Realm* 21, no. 1 (Spring 2009): 42–52.

Arendt, Hannah. *The Human Condition*. Chicago: University of Chicago Press, 1998.

———. *The Origins of Totalitarianism*. New York: Harcourt, Brace, Jovanovich, 1973.

Aristotle. *De Anima/Perì Psūchēs*. Oxford: Clarendon Press, 1968.

Arizti, Bárbara, and Silvia Martínez-Falquina, eds. *On the Turn: The Ethics of Fiction in Contemporary Narrative in English*. Newcastle: Cambridge Scholars Publishing, 2007.

Armengaud, Françoise. "Ethique et esthétique: de l'ombre à l'oblitération." In *Cahiers de l'Herne: Emmanuel Levinas*, edited by Catherine Chalier and Miguel Abensour, 499–507. Paris: Herne, 1991.

———. "Faire ou ne pas faire d'images. Emmanuel Levinas et l'art d'oblitération," *Noesis* 3 (2000).

Armstrong, Nancy. *How Novels Think: The Limits of Individualism, 1719–1900*. New York: Columbia University Press, 2006.

Arnaldez, Roger. *Grammaire et theologie chez Ibn Hazm de Cordoue: Essai sur la struture et les conditions de la pens a musulmane*. Paris: J. Vrin, 1956.

Arnold, Matthew. *Poems 1840–1867*. London: Oxford University Press, 1940.

Aronowicz, Annette, and Michael Fagenblat. "Exchange on Michael Fagenblat's *A Covenant of Creatures*." *AJS Review* 35, no. 1 (April 2011): 105–124.

———. "The Little Man with the Burned Thighs: Levinas's Biblical Hermeneutic." In *Levinas and Biblical Studies*, 33–48. Atlanta: Society for Biblical Literature, 2003.

———. "The Sweet Life of Metaphor: Levinas' Reflections on Metaphor and Their Implications for Biblical Hermeneutics." In *Making a Difference: Essays on the Bible and Judaism in Honor of Tamara Cohn Eskenazi*, edited by David J. A. Clines, Kent Harold Richards, and Jacob L. Wright, 9–19. Sheffield: Phoenix Press, 2012.

Artaud, Antonin. *Collected Works Volume 1*. Translated by Victor Corti. New York: Calder, 1970.

Artese, Brian. *Testimony on Trial: Conrad, James and the Contest of Modernism*. Toronto: University of Toronto Press, 2012.

Asad, Talal. *Formations of the Secular: Christianity, Islam, Modernity*. Stanford: Stanford University Press, 2003.

Attridge, Derek. "On Knowing Works of Art." In *Inside Knowledge: (Un)doing Ways of Knowing in the Humanities*, edited by Carolyn Birdsall, Maria Boletsi, Itay Sapir, and Pieter Verstraete, 17–34. Cambridge: Cambridge University Press, 2009.

———. *The Singularity of Literature*. New York: Routledge, 2004.

Auster, Paul. *The Red Notebook: True Stories*. New York: New Directions, 2002.

Ayers, David. "Materialism and the Book." *Poetics Today* 24, no. 4 (Winter, 2003): 759–780.

Baal Makhshoves. "Tsvei Shprakhn—eyneyntsike literatur." In *Geklibene verk*, 112–123. New York: Tsiko-bikher, 1953.

Bakhos, Carol. *Current Trends in the Study of Midrash*. Leiden: Brill, 2006.

Bakhtin, Mikhail. *Art and Answerability*. Edited by Michael Holquist. Austin: University of Texas Press, 1990.

———. "Avtor i geroi v èsteticheskoi deiatel'nosti." *Èstetika slovesnogo tvorchestva.* Moscow: Iskusstvo, 1979.

———. *The Dialogic Imagination: Four Essays.* Edited by Caryl Emerson and Michael Holquist. Austin: University of Texas Press, 1981.

———. *Estetika slovesnogo tvorchestva.* Moscow: Iskusstvo, 1979.

———. "Iskusstvo i otvetstvennost'." *Voprosy literatury* 6 (1977): 307–308.

———. *K filosofi postupka. Filosofiia i sotsiologiia nauki i tekhniki (1984–85).* Moscow: Nauka, 1986.

———. "K metodologii literaturovedeniia." *Kontekst-1974* (Moscow, 1975), 203–212. Reprinted as "K metodologii gumaniternych nauk." In Bakhtin, *Èstetika slovesnogo tvorchestva*, 361–373.

———. *Problems of Dostoevsky's Poetics.* Translated by C. Emerson. Minneapolis: University of Minnesota Press, 1984.

———. *Problemy poetiki Dostoevskogo.* Moskva: Sovetskij pisatel', 1963.

———. *Problemy tvorchestva Dostoevskogo.* Leningrad: Priboj, 1929.

———. *Speech Genres & Other Late Essays.* Edited by Caryl Emerson and Michael Holquist. Austin: University of Texas Press, 1986.

———. *Toward a Philosophy of the Act.* Translated by Vadim Liapunov. Austin: University of Texas Press, 1993.Band, Arnold. "Revealment Within Concealment: The Role of Metaphor in Bialik's Essays." *Jerusalem Studies in Hebrew Literature* 10 (1988): 189–200.

———. "The Sacralization of Language in Bialik's Essays." *Studies in Modern Jewish Literature.* Philadelphia: Jewish Publication Society, 2003.

Bandler, Kenneth. "Jewish Youth Lead the Way in a Long Isolated Community." *Jewish Telegraph Agency*, January 7, 1996.

Banita, Georgiana. *Plotting Justice: Narrative Ethics and Literary Culture After 9/11.* Lincoln: University of Nebraska Press, 2012.

Bannet, Eve Tavor. "The Scene of Translation: After Jakobson, Benjamin, de Man, and Derrida." *New Literary History* 24, no. 3 (Summer 1993): 577–595.

Banon, David. *La lecture infinie. Les voies de l'interprétation midrachique. Préface d'Emmanuel Lévinas.* Paris: Éditions du Seuil, 1987.

———. "Une hermeneutique de la solicitation." *Emmanuel Levinas (Les Cahiers de la Nuit Surveillee 3)*, 99–115.

Barnes, Julian. *Flaubert's Parrot.* New York: Vintage, 1990.

Barthes, Roland. *Camera Lucida: Notes on Photography.* Translated by Richard Howard. New York: Farrar, Straus and Giroux, 1981.

———. "The Discourse of History." Translated by Stephen Bann. *Comparative Criticism* 3 (1981): 7–20.

———. *Roland Barthes.* Translated by Richard Howard. Berkeley: University of California Press, 1994.

———. *The Rustle of Language*. Translated by Richard Howard. New York: Farrar, Straus, and Giroux, 1986.

———. *Sade, Fourier, Loyola*. Baltimore: Johns Hopkins University Press, 1997.

———. "Textual Analysis of a Tale by Edgar Allan Poe." In *The Semiotic Challenge*, 261–293. Translated by Richard Howard. Oxford: Blackwell, 1988.

Bartholomew, Craig. "Babel and Derrida: Postmodernism, Language, and Biblical Interpretation." *Tyndale Bulletin* 49, no. 2 (1998): 305–328.

Barzel, Hillel. *Shirat ha-tehiyah: Hayim Nahman Byalik*. Tel Aviv: Sifriyat po'alim, 1990.

Barzel, Hillel, and Hilel Vais, eds. *Halel li-Vyalik: 'iyunim ve-mehkarim be-yetsirat H. N. Byalik*. Ramat-Gan: Hotsa'at Universitat Bar-Ilan 1989.

Baskin, Judith. *Midrashic Women: Formations of the Feminine in Rabbinic Literature*. Hanover, N.H.: Brandeis University Press, 2002.

Bates, Stanley. "Movies Viewed: Cavell on Medium and Motion Pictures." In *Aesthetics: A Critical Anthology*, edited by George Dickie, Richard Sclafani, and Ronald Roblin, 576–582. New York: St Martin's Press, 1989.

———. "Stanley Cavell and Ethics." In *Stanley Cavell*, edited by Richard Eldridge, 15–47. Cambridge: Cambridge University Press, 2003.

Batkin, Norton. "Photography, Exhibition, and the Candid." *Common Knowledge* 5, no. 2 (Fall 1996): 145–65.

Batnitzky, Leora. *Idolatry and Representation: The Philosophy of Franz Rosenzweig Reconsidered*. Princeton: Princeton University Press, 2009.

———. *Leo Strauss and Emmanuel Levinas: Philosophy and the Politics of Revelation*. Cambridge: Cambridge University Press, 2006.

———. "Rosenzweig's Aesthetic Theory and Jewish Unheimlichkeit." *New German Critique* 77 (1999): 87–112.

Batuman, Elif. "Kafka's Last Trial." *New York Times Magazine*, September 22, 2010.

Baudelaire, Charles. *Artificial Paradises*. Translated by Stacy Diamond. New York: Citadel Press, 1996.

Beasley-Murray, Tim. *Mikhail Bakhtin and Walter Benjamin: Experience and Form*. New York: Palgrave MacMillan, 2007.

Beaumont, Matthew. "Aleatory Realism: Reflections on the Parable of the Pier-Glass." *Synthesis* 3 (Winter 2011): 11–21.

Behar, Ruth. *An Island Called Home: Returning to Jewish Cuba*. New Brunswick, N.J.: Rutgers University Press, 2009.

Bell, Roger V. *Sounding the Abyss: Readings Between Cavell and Derrida*. Lanham, Md.: Lexington Books, 2004.

Belting, Hans. *Likeness and Presence: A History of the Image Before the Era of Art*. Chicago: University of Chicago Press, 1994.

Bennett, Jane. *Vibrant Matter: A Political Ecology of Things*. Durham, N.C.: Duke University Press, 2012.

Benjamin, Mara. "Building a Zion in German(y): Franz Rosenzweig on Yehudah Halevi." *Jewish Social Studies: History, Culture, Society* 13, no. 2 (Winter 2007): 127–154.

Benjamin, Walter. *The Arcades Project.* Translated by Howard Eiland and Kevin McLaughlin. Cambridge, Mass.: Harvard University Press, 1999.

———. *Berlin Childhood around 1900.* Translated by Howard Eiland. Cambridge, Mass.: Belknap Press of Harvard University Press, 2006.

———. *The Origin of German Tragic Drama.* Translated by John Osborne. London: Verso, 1998.

———. *Selected Writings, 1913–1926.* Translated by Marcus Paul Bullock and Michael William Jennings. Cambridge: Belknap Press of Harvard University Press, 1996.

———. *Selected Writings, 1927–1934, Volume 2, Part 2.* Edited by Michael William Jennings, Howard Eiland, and Gary Smith. Cambridge, Mass.: Harvard University Press, 2005.

———. *Selected Writings, Volume Three, 1935–1938.* Translated by Marcus Paul Bullock and Michael William Jennings. Cambridge, Mass.: Belknap Press of Harvard University Press, 2002.

———. *Selected Writings, Volume Four, 1938–1940.* Translated by Marcus Paul Bullock and Michael William Jennings. Cambridge, Mass.: Belknap Press of Harvard University Press, 2003.

———. "The Translator's Task." Translated by Steven Rendall. *TTR: traduction, terminologie, redaction* 10, no. 2 (1997): 151–165.

———. *The Work of Art in the Age of Its Technological Reproducibility, and Other Writings on Media.* Edited by Brigid Doherty, Michael W. Jennings, and Thomas Y. Levin. Cambridge, Mass.: Harvard University Press, 2008.

Benor, Sarah Bunin. *Becoming Frum: How Newcomers Learn the Language and Culture of Orthodox Judaism.* New Brunswick, N.J.: Rutgers University Press, 2012.

Benso, Sylvia. *The Face of Things: A Different Side of Ethics.* Albany: State University Press, 2000.

Berger, Harry. *Making Trifles of Terrors: Redistributing Complicities in Shakespeare.* Stanford: Stanford University Press, 1997.

Bergo, Bettina. *Levinas Between Ethics and Politics: For the Beauty That Adorns the Earth.* Dordrecht: Kluwer, 1999.

———. "Levinas's 'Ontology': 1935–1974." In *Emmanuel Levinas: Critical Assessments by Leading Philosophers*, edited by Claire Elise Katz and Lara Trout, 25–48. New York: Routledge, 2005.

———. "Levinas's Weak Messianism in Time and Flesh, or The Insistence of Messiah Ben David." *Journal for Cultural Research* 13, nos. 3–4 (2009): 225–248.

———. "A Site from Which to Hope? Notes on Sensibility and Meaning in Levinas and Nietzsche." *Levinas Studies* 3 (2008): 117–142.

———. "The Time and Language of Messianism: Levinas and Saint Paul." In *Levinas and the Ancients*, edited by Sylvia Benso and Brian Schroeder, 178–195. Bloomington: Indiana University Press, 2008.

Berkovits, Eliezer. *Not in Heaven: The Nature and Function of Halakhah.* New York, 1983.

Berman, Saul. "The Status of Women in Halakhic Judaism." *Tradition* (Fall 1973): 5–8.

Bernard-Donals, Michael F. *Mikhail Bakhtin: Between Phenomenology and Marxism.* Cambridge: Cambridge University Press, 1994.

———. "Bakhtin and Phenomenology: A Reply to Gary Saul Morson." *South Central Review* 12, no. 2 (Summer, 1995): 41–55.

———. "'Difficult Freedom': Levinas, Language, and Politics." *Diacritics* 35, no. 3 (Fall 2005): 62–77.

Bernasconi, Robert. "Different Styles of Eschatology: Derrida's Take on Levinas' Political Messianism." *Research in Phenomenology* 28, no. 1 (1998): 3–19.

———. "Extraterritoriality." *Lévinas Studies: An Annual Review 3.* Pittsburgh: Duquesne University Press, 2008: 61–77.

Bernstein, Michael André. *Bitter Carnival: Ressentiment and the Abject Hero.* Princeton: Princeton University Press, 1992.

———. *Foregone Conclusions: Against Apocalyptic History.* Berkeley: University of California Press, 1994.

———. "Victims-in-Waiting: Backshadowing and the Representation of European Jewry." *New Literary History* 29, no. 4 (Autumn 1998): 625–651.

Best, Stephen, and Sharon Marcus. "Surface Reading: An Introduction." *Representations* 108, no. 1 (Fall 2009): 1–21.

Bhabha, Homi. *The Location of Culture.* London: Routledge, 1994.

———. "Unpacking My Library Again." *The Journal of the Midwest Modern Language Association* 28, no. 1 (Spring 1995): 5–18.

Biale, David. *Gershom Scholem: Kabbalah and Counter-History.* Cambridge, Mass.: Harvard University Press, 1979.

———. *Not in the Heavens: The Tradition of Jewish Secular Thought.* Princeton: Princeton University Press, 2011.

Bialik, Hayyim Nahman. "Gilui v'khisui b'lashon." *Kol Kitvei Bialik.* Tel Aviv: Devir, 1953.

———. *Revealment and Concealment: Five Essays.* Jerusalem: Ibis Editions, 2000.

———. *Shirim, 1898/99–1933/34.* Edited by Dan Miron et al. Tel Aviv: Devir, 1990.

———. *Shirim be-yidish, shire yeladim, shire hakdashah.* Edited by Dan Miron et al. Tel Aviv: Devir, 2000.

———. *Songs from Bialik: Selected Poems of Hayim Nahman Bialik.* Translated by Atar Hadari. Albany: State University of New York Press, 2000.

Bielik-Robson, Agata. "The Promise of the Name: 'Jewish Nominalism' as the Critique of Idealist Tradition." *Bamidbar* 2, no. 1 (2012): 12–30.

Biesenbach, Klaus. *Henry Darger.* New York: Prestel Verlag, 2009.

Biltereyst, Daniel, Richard Maltby, and Philippe Meers, eds. *Cinema, Audiences and Modernity: New Perspectives on European Cinema History.* New York: Routledge, 2012.

Blair, Carole, Marsha S. Jeppeson, and Enrico Pucci. "Public Memorializing in Postmodernity: The Vietnam Veterans Memorial as Prototype." *Quarterly Journal of Speech* 77, no. 3 (August 1991): 263–289.

Blais, Allison, and Lynn Rasic. *A Place of Remembrance: Official Book of the National September 11 Memorial*. Washington, D.C: National Geographic Society, 2011.

Blanchot, Maurice. *Blooded Thought: Occasions of Theater*. New York: Performing Arts Journal Publications, 1982.

———. *The Infinite Conversation*. Translated by Susan Hanson. Minneapolis: University of Minnesota Press, 1993.

———. "Our Clandestine Companion." In *Face to Face with Levinas*, edited by Richard Cohen, 41–51. Albany: State University of New York Press, 1986.

———. *The Space of Literature*. Translated by Ann Smock. Omaha: University of Nebraska Press, 1982.

———. *Take Up the Bodies: Theater at the Vanishing Point*. Urbana: University of Illinois Press, 1982.

Blau, Herbert. *The Audience*. Baltimore: Johns Hopkins University Press, 1990.

Blau, R. Yitzchak. *Fresh Fruit and Vintage Wine: The Ethics and Wisdom of the Aggada*. Hoboken, N.J.: Ktav, 2009.

Bloechl, Jeffrey. *Liturgy of the Neighbor: Emmanuel Lévinas and the Religion of Responsibility*. Pittsburgh: Duquesne University Press, 2000.

Blum, Peter C. "Overcoming Relativism? Levinas's Return to Platonism." *Journal of Religious Ethics* 28, no. 1 (2000): 91–117.

Blumberg, Ilana M. *Houses of Study: A Jewish Woman Among Books*. Lincoln: University of Nebraska Press, 2007.

Boer, Roland, ed. *Bakhtin and Genre Theory in Biblical Studies*. Atlanta: Society of Biblical Literature, 2007.

Bogdanov, Alexei. "*Ostranenie*, Kenosis, and Dialogue: The Metaphysics of Formalism according to Shklovsky." *Slavic and East European Journal* 49 (2005): 48–62.

Boitani, Piero. *The Bible and Its Rewritings*. Translated by Anita Weston. New York: Oxford University Press, 1999.

Bonesteel, Michael. *Henry Darger: Art and Selected Writings*. New York: Rizzoli, 2001.

———. "Henry Darger's Search for the Grail in the Guise of a Celestial Child." In *Third Person: Authoring and Exploring Vast Narratives*, edited by Pat Harrigan and Noah Wardrip-Fruin, 253–266. Cambridge, Mass.: MIT Press, 2009.

Booth, Wayne. *The Company We Keep: An Ethics of Fiction*. Berkeley: University of California Press, 1989.

Boothroyd, Dave. "Time and Technics: Levinas and the Ethics of Haptic Communications." *Theory, Culture & Society* 26, nos. 2–3 (2009): 330–345.

Bordwell, David. *Making Meaning: Inference and Rhetoric in the Interpretation of Cinema*. Cambridge, Mass.: Harvard University Press, 1989.

———. *Narration in the Fiction Film*. Madison: University of Wisconsin Press, 1985.

———. *Poetics of Cinema*. New York: Routledge, 2007.

Borges, Jorge Luis. "The Approach to Al-Mu'Tasim." Translated by Andrew Hurley. In *Collected Fictions*, 82–87. New York: Penguin, 1998.

———. *Other Inquisitions: 1937–1952*. Austin: University of Texas Press, 2000.

Boswell, James. *Life of Samuel Johnson*. Oxford: The World's Classics, 1998.

Bourdieu, Pierre. *Rules of Art: Genesis and Structure of the Literary Field*. Translated by Susan Emanuel. Stanford: Stanford University Press, 1996.

Boustan, Ra'anan, S. Oren Kosansky, and Marina Rustow, eds. *Jewish Studies at the Crossroads of Anthropology and History: Authority, Diaspora, Tradition*. Philadelphia: University of Pennsylvania Press, 2011.

Bové, Paul A. *Edward Said and the Work of the Critic: Speaking Truth to Power*. Durham, N.C.: Duke University Press, 2000.

Bowles, Kate. "Lost Horizon: The Social History of the Cinema Audience." *History Compass* 9, no. 11 (October 2011): 854–863.

Bowman, Matthew. "Allegorical Impulses and the Body in Painting." *rebus* 1 (Spring 2008): 1–26.

Boyarin, Daniel. *Carnal Israel: Reading Sex in Talmudic Culture*. Berkeley: University of California Press, 1995.

———. *Intertextuality and the Reading of Midrash*. Bloomington: University of Indiana Press, 1990).

———. "Old Wine in New Bottles: Intertextuality and Midrash." *Poetics Today* 8, no. 3/4 (1987): 539–556.

———. "Take the Bible as Example: Midrash as Literary Theory." *Sparks of the Logos: Essays in Rabbinic Hermeneutics*. Leiden: Brill, 2003, 89–113.

Boyarin, Jonathan. *Jewishness and the Human Dimension*. New York: Fordham University Press, 2008.

———. *Thinking in Jewish*. Chicago: University of Chicago Press, 1996.

Bracher, Nathan. "Review of Samuel Moyn's *Origins of the Other: Emmanuel Levinas Between Revelation and Ethics*." *H-France Review* 6 (August 2006): 88.

Braiterman, Zachary. *The Shape of Revelation: Aesthetics and Modern Jewish Thought*. Stanford: Stanford University Press, 2007.

Brand, Bill. *Masstransitscope* (1980). www.bboptics.com/masstransiscope.html.

Brandist, Craig, and Galin Tihanov, eds. *Materializing Bakhtin: The Bakhtin Circle and Social Theory*. New York: St. Martins Press, 2000.

Bregman, Marc. "The Darshan: Preacher and Teacher of Talmudic Times." *The Melton Journal* 14 (1982): 3–10.

Brennan, Timothy. "The National Longing for Form." In *Nation and Narration*, edited by Homi Bhabha, 44–70. New York: Routledge, 1990.

Brenner, Michael. *The Renaissance of Jewish Culture in Weimar Germany*. New Haven: Yale University Press, 1996.

———. "A Tale of Two Families: Franz Rosenzweig, Gershom Scholem and the Generational Conflict around Judaism." *Judaism* 42.3 (1993): 349–361.

Breslauer, S. Daniel. *Creating a Judaism without Religion: A Postmodern Jewish Possibility*. Lanham, Md.: University Press of America, 2001.

———. *The Hebrew Poetry of Hayyim Nahman Bialik and a Modern Jewish Theology*. Lewiston, Maine: Edwin Mellen Press, 1991.

———. *Toward a Jewish (M)orality: Speaking of a Postmodern Jewish Ethics*. Westport, Conn.: Greenwood Press, 1998.

Brewer, Mária Minich. "'The Thought of Performance': Theatricality, Reference, and Memory in Herbert Blau." *Journal of Dramatic Theory and Criticism* (Fall 2006): 97–113.

Brocke, Michael. "Franz Rosenzweig und Gerhard Gershom Scholem." In *Juden in der Weimarer Republik*, edited by Walter Grab and Julius H. Schoeps, 127–148. Berlin: Wissenschaftliche Buchgesellschaft, 1998.

Brogan, Michael J. "Judaism and Alterity in Blanchot and Levinas." *Journal for Cultural and Religious Theory* 6, no. 1 (December 2004): 28–44.

Bronowski, Jacob. *The Ascent of Man*. London: BBC Books, 2011.

———. "Knowledge or Certainty." *The Ascent of Man: A Personal View*, episode 11. Ambrose Video Publishing, 2007.

Brooks, Peter. *Reading for the Plot: Design and Intention in Narrative*. Cambridge, Mass.: Harvard University Press, 1992.

Brooks, Peter, with Hilary Jewett. *The Humanities and Public Life*. New York: Fordham University Press, 2014.

Broyde, Michael J. "Defilement of the Hands, Canonization of the Bible, and the Special Status of Esther." *Judaism* 44, no. 1 (Winter 1995): 65–80.

Bruhn, Jorgen, and Jan Lundquist, eds. *The Novelness of Bakhtin: Perspectives and Possibilities*. Copenhagen: Museum Tusculanum Press, 2001.

Bruns, Gerald. "The Concepts of Art and Poetry in Emmanuel Levinas's writings." In *The Cambridge Companion to Levinas*, edited by Simon Critchley and Robert Bernasconi, 206–233. Cambridge: Cambridge University Press, 2002.

———. "Dialogue and the Truth of Skepticism." *Religion & Literature* 22, nos. 2/3 (Summer–Autumn 1990): 85–91.

———. *Hermeneutics Ancient and Modern*. New Haven: Yale University Press, 1992.

———. "Midrash and Allegory: The Beginnings of Scriptural Interpretation." In *The Literary Guide to the Bible*, edited by Robert Alter and Frank Kermode, 625–646. Cambridge, Mass.: Harvard University Press, 1987.

———. "The Tragedy of Hermeneutic Experience." In *Rhetoric and Hermeneutics in Our Time: A Reader*, edited by Walter Jost and Michael J. Hyde, 73–89. New Haven: Yale University Press, 1997.

Buber, Martin. *A Land of Two Peoples: Martin Buber on Jews and Arabs*. Edited by Paul Mendes-Flohr. Chicago: University of Chicago Press, 2005.

———. *Eclipse of God: Studies in the Relation Between Religion and Philosophy*. Amherst, N.Y.: Humanity Books, 1952.

———. *Letters of Martin Buber: A Life of Dialogue*. Translated by Richard Winston, Clara Winston, and Harry Zohn. Syracuse: Syracuse University Press, 1996.

Buckingham, Will. *Levinas, Storytelling and Anti-Storytelling*. London: Bloomsbury Academic, 2013.

Budick, Emily Miller. "Exodus, Discovery, and Coming Home to the Promised Land." In *People of the Book: Thirty Scholars Reflect on Their Jewish Identity*, edited by Jeffrey Rubin-Dorsky and Shelley Fisher Fishkin, 217–230. Madison: University of Wisconsin Press, 1996.

Bush, Andrew. *Jewish Studies: A Theoretical Introduction*. New Brunswick: Rutgers University Press, 2011.

———. "Teaching Continually: Beginning With Lévinas." In *Europe and Its Boundaries: Words and Worlds, Within and Beyond*, edited by Andrew Davison and Himadeep Muppidi, 5–24. Lanham, Maine: Lexington Books, 2009.

Butler, Judith. *Bodies That Matter: On the Discursive Limits of Sex*. New York: Routledge, 1993.

———. *Giving an Account of Oneself*. New York: Fordham University Press, 2005.

———. "On Edward Said, Emmanuel Levinas and the Idea of the Binational State." *Mita'am: A Review of Literature and Radical Thought* 10 (2007).

———. *Parting Ways: Jewishness and the Critique of Zionism*. New York: Columbia University Press, 2012.

———. "Performative Acts and Gender Constitution: An Essay in Phenomenology and Feminist Theory." *Theatre Journal* 40, no. 4 (December 1988): 519–531.

———. "Who Owns Kafka?" *London Review of Books* 33, no. 5 (March 3, 2011): 3–8.

Butsch, Richard. "American Movie Audiences of the 1930s." *International Labor and Working-Class History* 59 (April 2001): 106–120.

———. *The Making of American Audiences: From Stage to Television, 1750–1990*. Cambridge: Cambridge University Press, 2000.

Bynum, Caroline Walker. *Christian Materiality: An Essay on Religion in Late Medieval Europe*. Cambridge, Mass.: Zone Books, 2011.

Byrd, Jodi A. *The Transit of Empire: Indigenous Critiques of Colonialism*. Minneapolis: University of Minnesota Press, 2011.

Calarco, Matthew. "Faced by Animals." In *Radicalizing Levinas*, edited by Peter Atterton and Matthew Calarco, 113–128. Albany: State University of New York, 2010.

Calvino, Italo. *Mr. Palomar*. Translated by William Weaver. New York: Harcourt, Brace, 1985.

Camille, Michael. "The Book as Flesh and Fetish in Richard de Bury's *Philobiblion*." In *The Book and the Body*, edited by Dolores Warwick Frese and Katherine O'Brien O'Keeffe, 34–77. Notre Dame, Ind.: University of Notre Dame Press, 1997.

Canetti, Elias. *The Human Province*. Translated by Joachim Neugroschel. New York: Seabury Press, 1978.

Capuano, Peter J. "Handling the Perceptual Politics of Identity in *Great Expectations*." *Dickens Quarterly* 27, no. 3 (September 2010): 185–28.

Carmy, Shalom. "Polyphonic Diversity and Military Music: The Brisker Derekh and the Broader World of Jewish Thought." *Tradition* 34, no. 4 (2000): 6–31.

Carson, Anne. *Economy of the Unlost: Reading Simonides of Keos with Paul Celan*. Princeton: Princeton University Press, 2002.

———. *Nox.* New York: New Directions, 2010.

Caruana, John. "'Not Ethics, Not Ethics Alone, but the Holy': Levinas on Ethics and Holiness." *Journal of Religious Ethics* 34, no. 4 (2006): 561–583.

Castro, Brian. "Blue Max: A Tribute." *Heat* 3 (2002): 119–129.

Catling, Jo, and Richard Hibbitt, eds. *Saturn's Moons: W. G. Sebald—A Handbook.* Oxford: Legenda, 2011.

Cauchi, Mark. "The Secular to Come: Interrogating the Derridean Secular." *JCRT* 10, no. 1 (Winter 2009): 1–25.

Cavarero, Adriana. *For More Than One Voice: Toward a Philosophy of Vocal Expression.* Stanford: Stanford University Press, 2005.

Cave, Terence. *Recognitions: A Study in Poetics.* Oxford: Clarendon Press, 1988.

Cavell, Stanley. *Cavell on Film.* Edited by William Rothman. Albany: State University of New York Press, 2005.

———. *The Cavell Reader.* Edited by Stephen Mulhall. Oxford: Blackwell, 1996.

———. *Cities of Words: Pedagogical Letters on a Register of the Moral Life.* Cambridge, Mass.: Harvard University Press, 2005.

———. *The Claim of Reason: Wittgenstein, Skepticism, Morality, and Tragedy.* Oxford: Clarendon Press, 1979; Oxford: Oxford University Press, 1982.

———. *Conditions Handsome and Unhandsome: The Constitution of Emersonian Perfectionism.* Chicago: University of Chicago Press, 1990.

———. *Contesting Tears: The Hollywood Melodrama of the Unknown Woman.* Chicago: University of Chicago Press, 1996.

———. "Departures." In *Diaspora: Homelands in Exile (Voices),* edited by Frédéric Brenner, 133–151. New York: HarperCollins, 2003.

———. *Disowning Knowledge.* Cambridge: Cambridge University Press, 2003.

———. *In Quest of the Ordinary: Lines of Skepticism and Romanticism.* Chicago: University of Chicago Press, 1988.

———. "In the Meantime: Authority, Tradition, and the Future of the Disciplines." *Yale Journal of Criticism* 5, no. 2 (Spring 1992): 229–237.

———. *Little Did I Know: Excerpts from Memory.* Palo Alto: Stanford University Press, October 2010.

———. *Must We Mean What We Say? A Book of Essays.* Cambridge: Cambridge University Press, 2002.

———. *Philosophical Passages: Wittgenstein, Emerson, Austin, Derrida.* Oxford: Blackwell, 1995.

———. *Philosophy the Day After Tomorrow.* Cambridge, Mass.: Harvard University Press, 2006.

———. *A Pitch of Philosophy: Autobiographical Exercises.* Cambridge, Mass.: Harvard University Press, 1994.

———. *Pursuits of Happiness: The Hollywood Comedy of Remarriage.* Cambridge, Mass.: Harvard University Press, 1981.

———. *The Senses of Walden: An Expanded Edition.* Chicago: University of Chicago Press, 1992.

————. *Themes Out of School: Effects and Causes*. Chicago: University of Chicago Press, 1988.

————. *This New Yet Unapproachable America: Lectures after Emerson after Wittgenstein*. Chicago: University of Chicago Press, 1989.

————. "'What Becomes of Thinking on Film': Stanley Cavell in Conversation with Andrew Klevan." In *Film as Philosophy: Essays in Cinema After Wittgenstein and Cavell*, edited by Rupert Read and Jerry Goodenough, 167–209. New York: Palgrave Macmillan, 2005.

————. *The World Viewed: Reflections on the Ontology of Film*. Enlarged edition. Cambridge, Mass.: Harvard University Press, 1979.

Caygill, Howard. *Levinas and the Political*. London: Routledge, 2002.

————. *Walter Benjamin: The Colour of Experience*. London: Routledge, 1998.

Chalier, Catherine. "L'ame de la vie: Levinas, lecteur de R. Haim de Volozin." *Emmanuel Levinas*, 387–398. Paris: Éditions de l'Herne, 1991.

————. "The Voice and the Book." In *Making a Difference: Essays on the Bible and Judaism in Honor of Tamara Cohn Eskenazi*, edited by David J. A. Clines, Kent Harold Richards, and Jacob L. Wright, 60–72. Sheffield: Phoenix Press, 2012.

Chambers, Ross. *Loiterature*. Lincoln: University of Nebraska Press, 1999.

————. *Room for Maneuver: Reading (The) Oppositional (In) Narrative*. Chicago: University of Chicago Press, 1991.

Champagne, by Roland A. *The Ethics of Reading According to Emmanuel Lévinas*. Amsterdam: Editions Rodopi, 1998.

Chandler, James K. "About Loss: W. G. Sebald's Romantic Art of Memory." *The South Atlantic Quarterly* 102, no. 1 (Winter 2003): 235–262.

Chardin, Jean-Baptiste Siméon. *Le philosophe lisant* (1734). Musée du Louvre.

Chartier, Roger. *Inscription and Erasure: Literature and Written Culture from The Eleventh to the Eighteenth Century*. Translated by Arthur Goldhammer. Philadelphia: University of Pennsylvania Press, 2007.

————. "Laborers and Voyagers: From the Text to the Reader." *Diacritics* 22, no. 2 (Summer 1992): 49–61.

Chetrit, Sami Shalom. "Revisiting Bialik: A Radical Mizrahi Reading of the Jewish National Poet." *Comparative Literature* 62, no. 1 (2010): 1–21.

Chion, Michel. *Audio-Vision: Sound on Screen*. Translated by Claudia Gorbman. New York: Columbia University Press, 1994.

Chrétien, Jean-Louis. *The Ark of Speech*. Translated by Andrew Brown. New York: Taylor & Francis, 2003.

————. *The Call and the Response*. Translated by Anne A. Davenport. New York: Fordham University Press, 2004.

————. *Corps à corps: à l'écoute de l'oeuvre d'art*. Paris: Éditions de Minuit, 1997.

————. *Hand to Hand: Listening to the Work of Art*. Translated by Stephen E. Lewis. New York: Fordham University Press, 2003.

————. *L'appel et la réponse,* Paris: Éditions de Minuit, 1992.

————. *L'arche de la parole*. Paris: PUF, 1998.

Christie, Ian. *The Last Machine: Early Cinema and the Birth of the Modern World*. London: British Film Institute, 1995.

Christie, Leona. "On Graven Images in the Yiddish Press." www.printeresting.org/2011/04/28/ben-katchor-printmaker-as-saboteur/.

Ciocan, Cristan, and Georges Hansel. *Levinas Concordance*. Dordrecht: Springer, 2005.

Ciocan, Cristan, and Kascha Semon. "The Problem of Embodiment in the Early Writings of Emmanuel Levinas." *Levinas Studies* 4 (2009): 1–19.

Classen, Constance. *The Book of Touch*. Oxford: Berg, 2005.

———. *The Deepest Sense: A Cultural History of Touch*. Champaign: University of Illinois, 2012.

Claviez, Thomas. *Aesthetics and Ethics: Otherness and Moral Imagination from Aristotle to Levinas and from Uncle Tom's Cabin to House Made of Dawn*. Heidelberg: Universitätsverlag Winter, 2008.

Clement, Jennifer, and Christian B. Long. "Hugo, Remediation, and the Cinema of Attractions, or, The Adaptation of Hugo Cabret." *Senses of Cinema* 63 (July 2012).

Cohen, Aryeh. *Beginning/Again: Towards a Hermeneutics of Jewish Texts*. New York: Seven Bridges Press, 2000.

———. *Rereading Talmud: Gender, Law and the Poetics of Sugyot*. Providence, R.I.: Brown University Series in Jewish Studies, Scholars Press, 1988.

———. "Shabbat Parashat Be'Hukotai—17 Iyar 5771—Halfway to Sinai." http://ziegler.aju.edu/Default.aspx?id=7144.

———. "The Task of the Talmud: On Talmud as Translation." In *Paratext and Megatext As Channels of Jewish and Christian Traditions: The Textual Markers of Contextualization*, edited by A. A. den Hollander, Ulrich Schmid, and Willem Smelik, 82–108. Leiden: E. J. Brill, 2003.

———. Why Textual Reasoning?" *Journal of Textual Reasoning* 1, no. 1.

Cohen, Geoffrey. "Finding Chouchani." www.jewdas.org/2009/06/finding-chouchani.

Cohen, Richard A. *Ethics, Exegesis and Philosophy: Interpretation after Levinas*. Cambridge: Cambridge University Press, 2001.

Cohen, Tom, Claire Colebrook, and J. Hillis Miller. *Theory and the Disappearing Future: On de Man, On Benjamin*. New York: Routledge, 2012.

Cohen, William A. "Manual Conduct in Great Expectations." *ELH* 60 (1993): 217–259.

Cohn, Dorrit. *Transparent Minds: Narrative Modes for Presenting Consciousness in Fiction*. Princeton: Princeton University Press, 1984.

Cohn, Yehudah. *Tangled Up in Text: Tefillin and the Ancient World*. Providence, R.I.: Brown University, 2008.

Cole, J. R. *Pascal: The Man and his Two Loves*. New York: New York University Press, 1995.

Colebrook, Claire. "Derrida, Deleuze and Haptic Aesthetics." *Derrida Today* 2 (2009): 22–43.

Coleridge, Samuel Taylor. *Biographia Literaria: The Collected Works of Samuel Taylor Coleridge, Biographical Sketches of my Literary Life & Opinions*, volume 7. Edited by James Engell and Walter Jackson Bate. Princeton: Princeton University Press, 1985.

Collins, Paul. *Not Even Wrong: Adventures in Autism*. New York: Bloomsbury, 2004.

Conant, James. "On Bruns, on Cavell." *Critical Inquiry* 17, no. 3 (Spring, 1991): 616–634.

———. "Stanley Cavell's Wittgenstein." *Harvard Review of Philosophy* XIII, no. 1 (2005): 51–65.

Conner, Steven. "Review of Tobin Siebers's *The Ethics of Criticism*." *Textual Practice* 6, no. 2 (Summer 1992): 361–369.

Conrad, Joseph. *Lord Jim* and *Nostromo*. Edited by Robert D. Kaplan. New York: Modern Library, 2000.

———. *Youth/Heart of Darkness/The End of the Tether*. New York: Penguin Books, 1995.

Cooper, Sheila. "The Occluded Relations: Levinas and Cinema." *Film Philosophy* 11, no. 2 (August 2007): i–vii.

Coski, John M. "Montgomery's Blood-Stained Letter Defines 'The Art of Dying'—and Living." *Museum of the Confederacy Magazine* (Summer 2006): 14–30.

Costello, Diarmuid. "The Very Idea of a 'Specific' Medium: Michael Fried and Stanley Cavell on Painting and Photography as Arts." *Critical Inquiry* 34, no. 2 (Winter 2008): 274–312.

Courville, Mathieu E. *Edward Said's Rhetoric of the Secular*. New York: Continuum, 2010.

Cover, R. M. *The Supreme Court 1982 Term Foreword: Nomos and Narrative Harvard Law Review Association* (1983): 4–68.

Crignon, Philippe. "Figuration: Emmanuel Levinas and the Image." Translated by Nicole Simek and Zahi Zalloua. *Yale French Studies* 104 (2004): 100–125.

Crispe, Asher. "Out of Touch: A Phenomenology of Involvement without Interference in the Rabbinic and Philosophic Traditions." www. interinclusion.org/inspirations/out-of-touch.

Critchley, Simon. "Black Socrates? Questioning the Philosophical Tradition." In *Ethics, Politics, Subjectivity: Essays on Derrida, Levinas & Contemporary French Thought*, 122–142. London: Verso, 1990.

———. "Das Ding: Lacan and Levinas." *Research in Phenomenology* 28, no. 1 (1998): 72–90.

———. *The Ethics of Deconstruction: Derrida and Levinas*. Edinburgh: Edinburgh University Press, 1992.

———. "Persecution Before Exploitation—A Non-Jewish Israel?" *Theory and Event* 3, no. 4 (2000): 30–36.

———. *Very Little . . . Almost Nothing: Death, Philosophy and Literature*. London: Routledge, 2004.

Crombez, Thomas, and Katrien Vloeberghs, eds. *On the Outlook: Figures of the Messianic*. Cambridge: Cambridge University Press, 2007.

Cronin, Michael. *Translation Goes to the Movies*. New York: Routledge, 2009.

Crowley, John. "Unpacking *The Boston Review* (November–December 2011)." http://bit.ly/19jpoHR.

Culler, Jonathan. "Bad Writing and Good Philosophy." In *Just Being Difficult: Academic Writing in the Public Arena*, edited by Culler and Kevin Lamb, 43–57. Stanford: Stanford University Press, 2003.

Cummings, Brian. "The Book as Symbol." In *The Oxford Companion to the Book*, edited by Michael F. Suarez and H. R. Woudhuysen, 63–65. Oxford: Oxford University Press, 2010.

Cunningham, Valentine. *Reading After Theory*. Cambridge: Blackwell, 2002.

———. "Sticky Transfers." In *Aesthetics and Contemporary Discourse*, edited by Herbert Grabes, 325–354. Tübingen: Gunter Narr Verlag, 1994.

Cutter, William. "Ghostly Hebrew, Ghastly Speech: Scholem to Rosenzweig, 1926." *Prooftexts* 10, no. 3 (September, 1990): 413–433.

———. "Language Matters." *Hebrew Studies* 39 (1998): 57–74.

D'Agata, John. "Collage History of Art, by Henry Darger." In *Halls of Fame: Essays*, 159–168. Minneapolis: Graywolf Press, 2005.

Damrosch, David. "Secular Criticism Meets the World." *Al-Ahram Weekly* 769 (November 2005): 17–23.

Darger, Henry. *Art and Selected Writings*. In Michael Bonesteel. *Henry Darger: Art and Selected Writings*. New York: Rizzoli, 2001.

———. "Selections." In *Paper & Carriage 3*, edited by Joanna Zopor Picard, Caroline Picard Mackenzie, Chaz Reetz-Laiolo, and Shannon Stratton, 1–28. Chicago: Green Lantern Press, 2008.

Darnton, Robert. "What Is the History of Books?" *Daedalus* 111, no. 3 (Summer 1982): 65–83.

Davidson, Judith. "Bakhtin as a Theory of Reading." *Center for the Study of Reading*. University of Illinois at Urbana-Champaign (August 1993), 1–20.

Davies, Margaret. "Derrida and Law: Legitimate Fictions." In *Jacques Derrida and the Humanities: A Critical Reader*, edited by Tom Cohen, 213–237. Cambridge: Cambridge University Press, 2001.

Davis, Colin. *After Poststructuralism: Reading, Stories and Theory*. New York: Routledge, 2004.

———. *Critical Excess: Overreading in Derrida, Deleuze, Levinas, Žižek, and Cavell*. Stanford: Stanford University Press, 2010.

———. *Introduction to Levinas*. South Bend, Ind.: University of Notre Dame Press, 1997.

———. "Levinas and the Phenomenology of Reading." In *A Century with Levinas: Notes on the Margins of His Legacy*, edited by Cristian Ciocan, Adina Bozga, and Attila Szigeti, 275–292. Bucharest: Romanian Society for Phenomenology, 2006.

Davis, Diane. "Greetings: On Levinas and the Wagging Tail." *JAC: A Journal of Composition Theory* 29, no. 1 (2009): 711–748.

———. *Inessential Solidarity: Rhetoric and Foreigner Relations*. Pittsburgh: University of Pittsburgh Press, 2010.

Davy, Barbara Jane. "An Other Face of Ethics in Levinas." *Ethics & the Environment* 12, no. 1 (Spring 2007): 39–65.

De Boer, Theodore. *The Rationality of Transcendence: Studies in the Philosophy of Emmanuel Levinas*. Leiden: Brill, 1997.

De Bruyn, Dieter, and Kris Van Heuckelom. *(Un) Masking Bruno Schulz: New Combinations, Further Fragmentations, Ultimate Reintegrations*. Amsterdam: Editions Rodopi, 2009.

De Bury, Richard. *Philobiblion*. Translated by E. C. Thomas. New York: Cooper Square Publishers, 1966.

De Certeau, Michel. *The Practice of Everyday Life*. Translated by Steven Rendall. Berkeley: University of California Press, 1984.

De Lubac, Henri, S.J. *Medieval Exegesis: The Four Senses of Scripture, Volumes 1 and 2*. Translated by M. Sebanc and E. M. Macierowski. Grand Rapids, Mich.: Eerdmans, 1998–2000.

De Man, Paul. *The Resistance to Theory*. Minneapolis: University of Minnesota Press, 1986.

De Quincey, Thomas. *Confessions of an English Opium Eater*. New York: Penguin, 2003.

De Saint Cheron, Michaël. *Conversations with Emmanuel Levinas, 1983–1994*. Translated by Gary D. Mole. Pittsburgh: Duquesne University Press, 2010.

De Tocqueville, Alexis. *Democracy in America and Two Essays on America*. Translated by Gerald Bevan. New York: Penguin Books, 2003.

De Vries, Hent. "On General and Divine Economy: Talal Asad's Genealogy of the Secular and Emmanuel Levinas's Critique of Capitalism, Colonialism, and Money." In *Powers of the Secular Modern: Talal Asad and His Interlocutors*, 113–133. Stanford: Stanford University Press, 2006.

Debray, Régis. "The Book as Symbolic Object." In *The Future of the Book*, edited by Geoffrey Nunberg, 139–152. Berkeley: University of California Press.

Deleuze, Gilles. *Expressionism in Philosophy: Spinoza*. Translated by Martin Joughin. New York: Zone Books, 1990.

———. *The Fold: Leibnitz and the Baroque*. Translated by Tom Conley. Minneapolis: University of Minnesota Press, 1992.

Denby, David. "Fantastic Voyages." *The New Yorker*, November 28, 2011.

Denham, Ben. "Difficult Sense: The Neuro-physical Dimensions of the Act of Reading." In *Literature and Sensation*, edited by Anthony Uhlmann, Helen Groth, Paul Sheehan, and Stephen McLaren, 112–121. Newcastle upon Tyne: Cambridge Scholars, 2009.

Denham, Scott, and Mark McCulloh, eds. *W. G. Sebald: History, Memory, Trauma*. Berlin: Walter de Gruyter, 2006.

Deresiewicz, William. "The Shaman." *The New Republic*, September 14, 2011.

Derrida, Jacques. "All Ears: Nietzsche's Otobiography" In *The Ear of the Other: Otobiography, Transference, Translation: Texts and Discussions with Jacques Derrida*. Translated by Avital Ronell. Lincoln: University of Nebraska Press, 1988.

———. *Alterites: Derrida et Pierre-Jean Labarriere*. Paris: Osiris, 1986.

———. "And Say the Animal Responded?" In *Zoontologies: The Question of the Animal*. Edited by Cary Wolfe. Minneapolis: University of Minnesota Press, 2003.

———. *The Animal I Therefore Am*. Translated by David Wills. New York: Fordham University Press, 2008.

———. "At This Very Moment in This Work Here I Am." In *Re-Reading Levinas*, edited by Robert Bernasconi and Simon Critchley, 11–50. Bloomington: Indiana University Press, 1991.

———. "Des Tours de Babel." *Acts of Religion*. Translated by Gil Anidjar. London: Routledge, 2001.

———. *Dissemination*. Translated by Barbara Johnson. Chicago: University of Chicago Press, 1981.

———. "Ethics and Politics Today." *Negotiations*. Stanford: Stanford University Press, 2002.

———. "The Eyes of Language." *Acts of Religion*. Translated by Gil Anidjar. London: Routledge, 2001.

———. "Faith and Knowledge: The Two Sources of 'Religion' and the Limits of Reason Alone." In *Religion*, edited by Jacques Derrida and Gianni Vattimo, 1–78. Stanford: Stanford University Press, 1998.

———. *Geneses, Genealogies, Genres, and Genius: The Secrets of the Archive*. Translated by Beverley Bie Brahic. New York: Columbia University Press, 2008.

———. "The Law of Genre." Translated by Avital Ronell. *Critical Inquiry* 7, no. 1 (Autumn 1980): 55–81.

———. *Le toucher, Jean-Luc Nancy*. Paris: Galilée, 1998.

———. *Limited Inc*. Translated by Samuel Weber and Jeffrey Mehlman. Evanston, Ill.: Northwestern University Press, 1988.

———. *Monolinguism of the Other; Or the Prosthesis of Origin*. Translated by Patrick Mensah. Stanford: Stanford University Press, 1998.

———. *On the Name*. Translated by David Wood. Stanford: Stanford University Press, 1995.

———. *On Touching—Jean-Luc Nancy*. Translated by Christine Irizarry. Stanford: Stanford University Press, 2005.

———. *The Other Heading: Reflections on Today's Europe*. Translated by Pascale-Anne Brault and Michael B. Naas. Bloomington: Indiana University Press, 1992.

———. *Paper Machine*. Translated by Rachel Bowlby. Stanford: Stanford University Press, 2005.

———. "What Is a 'Relevant' Translation?" *Critical Inquiry* 27:2, 174–200.

———. *Writing and Difference*. Translated by Alan Bass. Chicago: University of Chicago Press, 1980.

Diamantides, M., ed. *Levinas, Law, and Politics*. New York: Routledge-Cavendish, 2007.

Dickens, Charles. *Great Expectations*. New York: Penguin Books, 2002.

———. *Oliver Twist*. New York: Modern Library Classics, 2001.

Dickinson, Emily. *The Complete Poems of Emily Dickinson*. New York: Back Bay Books, 1976.

Dimock, Wai Chee. "Genre as World System: Epic and Novel on Four Continents." *Narrative* 14, no. 1 (January, 2006): 85–101.

———. "A Theory of Resonance." *PMLA* 112, no. 5 (October 1997): 1060–1071.

Dolgopolski, Sergey. *The Open Past: Subjectivity and Remembering in the Talmud*. New York: Fordham University Press, 2013.

———. *What Is Talmud? The Art of Disagreement*. New York: Fordham University Press, 2003.

Donat, Alexander. *The Holocaust Kingdom: A Memoir*. New York: Holt, Rinehart, and Winston, 1965.

Döring, Tobias and Mark Stein, eds. *Edward Said's Translocations: Essays in Secular Criticism*. New York: Routledge, 2012.

Doss, Erika. "*De Oppresso Liber* and *Reflecting Absence*: Ground Zero Memorials and the War on Terror." *American Quarterly* 65, no. 1 (March 2013): 203–214.

Drabinski, John E. *Levinas and the Postcolonial*. Edinburgh: Edinburgh University Press, 2011.

Driever, Juliana. "Material (Un)reality." *Paper & Carriage* 3 (Spring 2008): 18–23.

Dubosarsky, Yonatan. "Beit Bialik: The Home of Israel's National Poet." www.mfa.gov.il.

Dula, Peter. *Cavell, Companionship, and Christian Theology*. Oxford: Oxford University Press, 2010.

Dunlap, David. "Constructing a Story, With 2,982 Names." *New York Times*, May 4, 2011.

Duttlinger, Carolin. "Imaginary Encounters: Walter Benjamin and the Aura of Photography." *Poetics Today* 29, no. 1 (2008): 79–101.

Dworkin, Ronald. *Religion Without God*. Cambridge: Harvard University Press, 2013.

Eaglestone, Robert. *Ethical Criticism After Levinas*. Edinburgh: Edinburgh University Press, 1997.

———. "Levinas, Ethics, and Translation." *Nation, Language, and the Ethics of Translation*. Edited by Sandra Bermann and Michael Wood. Princeton: Princeton University Press, 2005.

Edkins, Jenny. *Missing: Persons and Politics*. New York: Cornell University Press, 2011.

Edwards, Laurence L. "'Extreme Attention to the Real': Levinas and Religious Hermeneutics." *Shofar* 26, no. 4 (Summer 2008): 36–53.

Egoyan, Atom, and Ian Balfour. *Subtitles: On the Foreignness of Film*. New York: Alphabet City Media, 2007.

Eilberg-Schwartz, Howard. *People of the Body: Jews and Judaism from an Embodied Perspective*. Albany: State University of New York Press, 1992.

Einbinder, Susan. "Review of Leon J. Weinberger, trans, *Twilight of a Golden Age. Selected Poems of Abraham Ibn Ezra. AJS Review* 24, no. 2 (1999): 389–391.

Eliot, George. *Middlemarch*. New York: Penguin, 2003.

Elledge, Jim. *H*. Maple Shade, N.J.: Lethe Press, 2012.

———. *Henry Darger, Throw-Away Boy: The Tragic Life of an Outsider Artist*. New York: Overlook Press, 2013.

Elsaesser, Thomas. "Presentation: Stanley Cavell and Cinema." In *Come to Your Senses: ASCA Yearbook*, edited by Mieke Bal and Eloe Kingma, 107–115. Amsterdam: ASCA, 1999.

Emerson, Caryl. *The First Hundred Years of Mikhail Bakhtin*. Princeton: Princeton University Press, 1997.

———. "Shklovsky's *ostranenie*, Bakhtin's *vnenakhodimost*': How Distance Serves an Aesthetics of Arousal Differently from an Aesthetics Based on Pain." *Poetics Today* 26, no. 4 (2005): 637–664.

———. "The Tolstoy Connection in Bakhtin." In *Rethinking Bakhtin: Extensions and Challenges*, edited by Caryl Emerson and Gary Saul Morson, 149–172. Evanston, Ill.: Northwestern University Press, 1989.

Emerson, Caryl, and Gary Morson. *Mikhail Bakhtin: Creation of a Prosaics*. Stanford: Stanford University Press, 1990.

The Epic of Gilgamesh. Translated by Stuart Kendall. New York: Contra Mundum Press, 2012.

Erdinast-Vulcan, Daphna. "Bakhtin's Homesickness: A Late Reply to Julia Kristeva." *Textual Practice* 9, no. 2 (1995): 223–242.

———. "Between the Face and the Voice: Bakhtin Meets Levinas." *Continental Philosophy Review* 41, no. 1 (2008): 43–58.

———. "Borderlines and Contraband: Bakhtin and the Question of the Subject." *Poetics Today* 18, no. 2 (Summer, 1997): 251–269.

———. "The I That Tells Itself: A Bakhtinian Perspective on Narrative Identity." *Narrative* 16, no. 1 (January 2008): 1–15.

Ernst, Max. *Malningar, Collage, Frottage, Teckningar, Grafik, Bocker, Skulpturer, 1917–1969*. Stockholm: Moderna Museet, 1969.

Eskin, Michael. *Ethics and Dialogue: In the Works of Levinas, Bakhtin, Mandel'shtam, and Celan*. Oxford: Oxford University Press, 2000.

Esty, Jed. *Unseasonable Youth: Modernism, Colonialism, and the Fiction of Development*. Oxford: Oxford University Press, 2010.

Even-Zohar, Itamar. "Polysystem Studies." *Poetics Today* 11, no. 1 (1990).

Ezell, Margaret J. M., and Katherine O'Brien O'Keeffe. *Cultural Artifacts and the Production of Meaning: The Page, the Image, and the Body*. Ann Arbor: University of Michigan Press, 1994.

Ezra, Elizabeth. *George Méliès*. Manchester: Manchester University Press, 2000.

Fagenblat, Michael. *A Covenant of Creatures: Levinas's Philosophy of Judaism*. Stanford: Stanford University Press, 2011.

———. "Levinas and Maimonides: From Metaphysics to Ethical Negative Theology." *Journal of Jewish Thought and Philosophy* 16, no. 1 (2008): 95–147.

Fainhandler, Yeḥezkel. *Ginze ha-ḳodesh 'al hilkhot genizah u-khevod sefarim*. Jerusalem: Agudat Genizah Kelalit, 2002.

Fakhry, Majid. *A History of Islamic Philosophy*. New York: Columbia University Press, 2004.

Farmer, Frank M. "'Not Theory . . . but a Sense of Theory': The Superaddressee and the Contexts of Eden." *Symploke* 2, no. 1 (1994): 87–101.

Faur, José. *The Horizontal Society: Understanding the Covenant and Alphabetic Judaism Vol. 2.* Brighton: Academic Studies Press, 2008.

Faust, Drew Gilpin. *This Republic of Suffering: Death and the American Civil War.* New York: Knopf, 2008.

Feinstein, R. Moshe. "Including a Minor in Extraneous Circumstances." (Heb.) *Iggrot Moshe* (*Oraḥ Ḥayyim* vol. 2). New York: Noble Press, 1982.

Feinstein, Sara. *Sunshine, Blossoms and Blood: H.N. Bialik in His Time, a Literary Biography.* Lanham, Md.: University Press of America, 2005.

Felch, Susan M., and Paul J. Contino, eds. *Bakhtin and Religion: A Feeling for Faith.* Evanston, Ill.: Northwestern University Press, 2001.

Fiedorczuk, Julia. "'Thing Power': Bruno Schulz's 'Ecological' Poetics." UC Berkeley Conference on Ecopoetics (February 24, 2013). Unpublished conference paper.

Figueroa, Abel R. Castro. *Las religiones en Cuba: Un recorrido por la Revolución.* Guadalajara, 2009.

———. *Quo vadis, Cuba? Religión y revolución.* Bloomington: Palibrio, 2010.

Filler, Martin. "At the Edge of the Abyss." *NYR Blog*, September 21, 2011. www.nybooks .com/blogs/nyrblog/ 2011/sep/21/at-the-edge-of-abyss-september-11-memorial/.

Fincham, Gail. "The Dialogism of *Lord Jim*." In *Conrad and Theory*, edited by Andrew Gibson and Robert Hampson, 58–74. Atlanta: Rodopi B.V., 1998.

Fineman, Joel. "The History of the Anecdote: Fiction and Fiction." In *The New Historicism*, edited by Harold Aram Veeser, 49–76. New York: Routledge, 1989.

Finkelstein, Louis. "The Pharisees: Their Origin and Their Philosophy." *Harvard Theological Review* 22, no. 3 (July 1929): 185–261.

Finkielkraut, Alain. *The Wisdom of Love.* Translated by Kevin O'Neill and David Suchoff. Lincoln: University of Nebraska Press, 1997.

Finkin, Jordan. *A Rhetorical Conversation: Jewish Discourse in Modern Yiddish Literature.* Philadelphia: University of Pennsylvania Press, 2010.

Fischer, Michael. *Stanley Cavell and Literary Skepticism.* Chicago: University of Chicago Press, 1989.

———. "Using Stanley Cavell." *Philosophy and Literature* 32, no. 1 (April 2008): 198–204.

Fischer, Steven Roger. *A History of Reading.* London: Reaktion Books, 2003.

Fishbane, Michael. *Biblical Myth and Rabbinic Mythmaking.* New York: Oxford University Press, 2003.

———. *The Garments of Torah: Essays in Biblical Hermeneutics.* Bloomington: Indiana University Press, 1992.

Fishbane, Simcha. "The Symbolic Representation of the Sefer Torah." *Maqom Journal for Studies in Rabbinic Literature* 22 (Spring 2012), www.maqom.com/ journal/paper35 .pdf.

Fishman, David E. *The Rise of Modern Yiddish Culture*. Pittsburgh: University of Pittsburgh Press, 2010.

Fitzgerald, F. Scott. *My Lost City: Personal Essays, 1920–1940*. Cambridge: Cambridge University Press, 2005.

Fiumara, James. "The Thirteenth Freak Month: The Influence of Bruno Schulz on the Brothers Quay." *Kinoeye* 4, no. 5 (November 29, 2004).

Flatley, Jonathan. *Affective Mapping: Melancholia and the Politics of Modernism*. Cambridge, Mass.: Harvard University Press, 2008.

Flaubert, Gustave. *The Letters of Gustave Flaubert: 1857–1880*. Translated by Francis Steegmuller. Cambridge, Mass.: Harvard University Press, 1980.

Fleming, James Dougal. *Milton's Secrecy: And Philosophical Hermeneutics*. London: Ashgate, 2008.

Fleming, Richard. *The State of Philosophy: An Invitation to a Reading in Three Parts of Stanley Cavell's "The Claim of Reason."* Lewisburg, Pa.: Bucknell University Press, 1993.

Flint, Kate. *The Feeling of Reading: Affective Experience and Victorian Literature*. Ann Arbor: University of Michigan Press, 2010.

Fogel, Aaron. *Coercion to Speak: Conrad's Poetics of Dialogue*. Cambridge, Mass.: Harvard University Press, 1985.

Foucault, Michel. *The Government of Self and Others: Lectures at the College de France, 1982–1983*. Translated by Graham Burchell. New York: Palgrave Macmillan, 2010.

Fraade, Steven D. *From Tradition to Commentary: Torah and Its Interpretation in the Midrash Sifre to Deuteronomy*. Albany: State University of New York Press, 1998.

———. *Legal Fictions: Studies of Law and Narrative in the Discursive Worlds of Ancient Jewish Sectarians and Sages*. Leiden: Brill, 2011.

———. "Nomos and Narrative Before *Nomos and Narrative*." *Yale Journal of Law and the Humanities* 17, no. 1 (2005): 81–96.

Fraenkel, Yonah. *Darkhei ha-Agadah ve-ha-Midrash*. Givatayim: Yad latalmud, 1991.

Franck, Didier. *Flesh and Body: On the Phenomenology of Husserl*. Translated by Joseph Rivera and Scott Davidson. London: Bloomsbury Academic, 2014.

Frank, David A. "Arguing with God, Talmudic Discourse, and the Jewish Countermodel: Implications for the Study of Argumentation." *Argumentation and Advocacy* 41 (Fall 2004): 71–86.

Fredman, Stephen. "'How to Get Out of the Room That Is the Book?' Paul Auster and the Consequences of Confinement." *Postmodern Culture* 6, no. 3 (May 1996).

Freedberg, David. *The Power of Images: Studies in the History and Theory of Response*. Chicago: University of Chicago Press, 1989.

Fried, Michael. "Almayer's Face: On 'Impressionism' in Conrad, Crane, and Norris." *Critical Inquiry* 17, no. 1 (Autumn 1990): 193–236.

———. *Art and Objecthood: Essays and Reviews*. Chicago: University of Chicago Press, 1998.

———. *Courbet's Realism*. Chicago: University of Chicago Press, 1997.

————. *Realism, Writing, Disfiguration: On Thomas Eakins and Stephen Crane*. Chicago: University of Chicago Press, 1987.

Friedlander, Judith. *Vilna on the Seine: Jewish Intellectuals in France*. New Haven: Yale University Press, 1990.

Friedman, Shamma. *Five Sugyot From the Babylonian Talmud*. The Jerusalem: Society for the Interpretation of the Talmud, 2002.

————. "The Holy Scriptures Defile the Hands—The Transformation of a Biblical Concept in Rabbinic Theology." In *Minhah le-Nahum: Biblical and Other Studies Presented to Nahum M. Sarna in Honour of his 70th Birthday*, edited by M. Brettler and M. Fishbane, 117–132. Sheffield: JSOT Press, 1993.

————. "Literary Development and History in the Aggadic Narrative of the Babylonian Talmud: A Study Based Upon B.M. 83b–86a." In *Community and Culture Essays in Jewish Studies in Honor of the 90th Anniversary of the Founding of Gratz College*, 67–80. Philadelphia: Jewish Publication Society, 1987.

Frost, Gary. "Reading by Hand: How Hands Prompt the Mind." http://futureofthebook.com/hand/.

Frost, Robert. *Robert Frost: Collected Poems, Prose, and Plays*. New York: Library of America, 1995.

Fuller, Kathryn H. *At the Picture Show: Small-Town Audiences and the Creation of Movie Fan Culture*. Charlottesville: University of Virginia Press, 2001.

Fuller-Seeley, Kathryn. *Hollywood in the Neighborhood: Historical Case Studies of Local Moviegoing*. Berkeley: University of California Press, 2008.

Fung, Stanislaus, and Mark Jackson. "Dualism and Polarism: Structures of Architectural and Landscape Architectural Discourse in China and the West." *Interstices* 4 (1997): 84–91.

Furstenberg, Yair. "The Agon with Moses and Homer: Rabbinic Midrash and the Second Sophistic." *Homer and the Bible in the Eyes of Ancient Interpreters*, edited by Maren R. Niehoff. Leiden: Brill, 2012), 299–328.

————. *Hand Purity and Eating in a State of Purity: A Chapter in the Development of Halakhah*. Diss. Jerusalem: Hebrew University, 2005 [Hebrew].

Gardiner, Michael. "Alterity and Ethics: A Dialogical Perspective." *Theory, Culture, and Society* 13 (1996): 121–143.

Gardiner, Michael, ed. *Bakhtin and the Human Sciences*. Thousand Oaks, Calif.: Sage Publications, 1998.

Gasché, Rodolphe. "Saturnine Vision and the Question of Difference: Reflections on Walter Benjamin's Theory of Language." In *Benjamin's Ground: New Readings of Walter Benjamin*, edited by Rainer Nägele, 83–104. Detroit: Wayne State University Press, 1988.

Gauchet, Marcel. *The Disenchantment of the World: A Political History of Religion*. Translated by Oscar Burge. Princeton: Princeton University Press, 1997.

Geissler, Benjamin. The Picture Chamber of Bruno Schulz: The Final Work of a Genius. http://bit.ly/1caiSBd.

Gellrich, Jesse M. *The Idea of the Book in the Middle Ages: Language Theory, Mythology and Fiction*. Ithaca, N.Y.: Cornell University Press, 1985.

Gibbs, Robert. *Correlations in Rosenzweig and Levinas*. Princeton: Princeton University Press, 1992.

———. "The Disincarnation of the Word: The Trace of God in Reading Scripture." In *The Exorbitant: Emmanuel Levinas Between Jews and Christians*, edited by Kevin Hart and Michael A. Signer, 41. New York: Fordham University Press, 2010.

———. *Why Ethics? Signs of Responsibilities*. Princeton: Princeton University Press, 2000.

Gibson, Andrew. *Postmodernity, Ethics and the Novel: From Leavis to Levinas*. London: Routledge, 1999.

Gillespie, Vincent. *Looking in Holy Books: Essays on Late Medieval Religious Writing in England*. Turnhout: Brepols, 2012.

Gilloch, Graeme. *Walter Benjamin: Critical Constellations*. Cambridge: Polity Press, 2002.

Gilman, Sander. *The Jew's Body*. New York: Routledge, 1991.

Girgus, Sam B. *Levinas and the Cinema of Redemption: Time, Ethics, and the Feminine*. New York: Columbia University Press, 2010.

Gitelman, Lisa. *Scripts, Grooves, and Writing Machines: Representing Technology in the Edison Era*. Stanford: Stanford University Press, 1999.

Glowacka, Dorota. "The Trace of the Untranslatable: Emmanuel Levinas and the Ethics of Translation." *PhaenEx* 7, no. 1 (2012): 1–29.

Godzich, Wlad. "Correcting Kant: Bakhtin and Intercultural Interactions." *boundary 2* 18, no. 1 (1991): 5–17.

Gold, Moshe. "Those Evil Goslings, Those Evil Stories: Letting the Boys Out of Their Caves." In *Levinas and Medieval Literature: The "Difficult Reading" of English and Rabbinic Texts*, edited by Ann W. Astell and J. A. Jackson, 281–304. Pittsburgh: Duquesne University Press, 2009.

Goldberg, Jonathan. *Writing Matter: From the Hands of the English Renaissance*. Stanford: Stanford University Press, 1990.

Goldziher, Ignaz. *The Zahiris, Their Doctrine and Their History: A Contribution to the History of Islamic Theology*. Translated by Wolfgang Behn. Leiden: E. J. Brill, 1971.

Gomery, Douglas. *Shared Pleasures: A History of Movie Presentation in the United States*. Madison: University of Wisconsin Press, 1992.

Gonzalez, Francisco J. "Levinas Questioning Plato on Eros and Maieutics." In *Levinas and the Ancients*, edited by Sylvia Benso and Brian Schroeder, 40–61. Bloomington: Indiana University Press, 2008.

Goodhart, Sandor. "'A Land that Devours Its Inhabitants': Midrashic Reading, Emmanuel Levinas, and Medieval Literary Exegesis." In *Levinas and Medieval Literature: The "Difficult Reading" of English and Rabbinic Texts*, edited by Ann Astell and Justin Jackson, 227–254. Pittsburgh: Duquesne University Press, 2009.

Gooding-Williams, Robert. "Aesthetics and Receptivity: Kant, Nietzsche, Cavell, and Astaire." In *The Claim to Community: Essays on Stanley Cavell and Political Theory*, edited by Andrew Norris and Thomas Dunn, 236–262. Stanford: Stanford University Press, 2006.

Goodman, Martin. "Sacred Scripture and 'Defiling the Hands.'" *Jewish Theological Studies* 41, no. 1 (1990): 99–107.

Gopnik, Adam. "The Real Work: Modern Magic and the Meaning of Life." *The New Yorker*, March 17, 2008.

Gouhier, Henri. "Le memorial est-il un texte mystique?" In *Blaise Pascal: Commentaires*, 48–57. Paris: J. Vrin, 1984.

Gould, Timothy. *Hearing Things: Voice and Method in the Writing of Stanley Cavell*. Chicago: University of Chicago Press, 1998.

Gourgouris, Stathis. *Lessons in Secular Criticism* (Thinking Out Loud: The Sydney Lectures in Philosophy and Society). New York: Fordham University Press, 2012.

Greaney, Michael. *Conrad, Language, and Narrative*. Cambridge: Cambridge University Press, 2002.

Green, Barbara, ed. *Mikhail Bakhtin and Biblical Scholarship: An Introduction*. Atlanta: Society of Biblical Literature, 2000.

Greenblatt, Stephen. *Renaissance Self-Fashioning: From More to Shakespeare*. Chicago: University of Chicago Press, 1980.

———. "Resonance and Wonder." In *Exhibiting Cultures: The Poetics and Politics of Museum Display*, edited by Ivan Karp and Steven D. Lavine, 42–56. Washington: Smithsonian Institution Press, 1991.

———. *The Swerve: How the World Became Modern*. New York: Norton, 2011.

Greenwood, Daniel J. H. "Akhnai: Legal Responsibility in the World of the Silent God." *Utah Law Review* (1997): 309–358.

Greiner, Rae. *Sympathetic Realism in Nineteenth-Century British Fiction*. Baltimore: Johns Hopkins University Press, 2012.

Griswold, Charles L., and Stephen S. Griswold. "The Vietnam Veterans Memorial and the Washington Mall: Philosophical Thoughts on Political Iconography." *Critical Inquiry* 12, no. 4 (Summer 1986): 688–719.

Gritz, David. *Lévinas face au beau*. Paris: Editions de l'eclat: 2004.

Gross, Kenneth. *Shylock Is Shakespeare*. Chicago: University of Chicago Press, 2006.

Grossman, David. *See Under: Love*. Translated by Betsy Rosenberg. New York: Simon & Schuster, Inc., 1989.

Guenther, Lisa. "*Le flair animal*: Levinas and the Possibility of Friendship." *PhaenEx: Journal of Existential and Phenomenological Theory and Culture* 2, no. 2 (Fall–Winter 2007): 216–238.

———. "'Like a Maternal Body': Emmanuel Levinas and the Motherhood of Moses." *Hypatia* 21, no. 1 (Winter 2006): 119–136.

Guetti, James. *Wittgenstein and the Grammar of Literary Experience*. Athens: University of Georgia Press, 1993.

Gumbrecht, Hans. *Production of Presence: What Meaning Cannot Convey*. Stanford: Stanford University Press, 2003.

Gurevitch, Zali. "Plurality in Dialogue: A Comment on Bakhtin." *Sociology* 34, no. 2 (2000): 243–263.

Habib, André. "Ruin, Archive and the Time of Cinema: Peter Delpeut's *Lyrical Nitrate*." *SubStance* # 110, vol. 35, no. 2 (2006): 120–139.

———. "Through a Glass Darkly: Interview with the Quay Brothers." *Senses of Cinema* 19 (2004) and 30 (2009). http://sensesofcinema.com/2002/feature-articles/quay; http://www.sensesofcinema.com/2004/great-directors/quay_brothers.

Hägglund, Martin. *Radical Atheism: Derrida and the Time of Life*. Stanford: Stanford University Press, 2008.

Halberstam, Chaya T. *Law and Truth in Biblical and Rabbinic Literature* Bloomington: Indiana University Press, 2010.

Halbertal, Moshe. "Beyond Naturalism." *The New Republic* (October 21, 2013), 60–63.

———. *People of the Book: Canon, Meaning, Authority*. Cambridge, Mass.: Harvard University Press, 1997.

Hale, Dorothy J. "Fiction as Restriction: Self-Binding in New Ethical Theories of the Novel." *Narrative* 15, no. 2 (May 2007): 187–206.

Halivni, David Weiss. *Book and the Sword: A Life of Learning in the Shadow of Destruction*. New York: Westview Press, 1997.

———. *The Formation of the Babylonian Talmud*. Translated by Jeffrey L. Rubenstein. New York: Oxford University Press, 2013.

———. *Iyunim Behithavot Hatalmud*. Jerusalem: Magnes Press, 2008.

———. *Mekorot Umasorot*. Jerusalem: Magnes Press, 1968.

———. *Peshat and Derash: Plain and Applied Meaning in Rabbinic Exegesis*. Oxford and New York: Oxford University Press, 1991.

Hall, Dewey W. "Signs of the Dead: Epitaphs, Inscriptions, and the Discourse of the Self." *ELH* 68, no. 3 (Fall 2001): 655–677.

Halpern, Moyshe-Leyb. "Freg ikh bay mayn liber froy." In Benjamin Harshav, *The Meaning of Yiddish*. Berkeley: University of California Press, 1990.

Hammer, Espen. *Stanley Cavell: Skepticism, Subjectivity, and the Ordinary*. Cambridge: Blackwell, 2002.

Hampson, Robert. *Cross-Cultural Encounters in Joseph Conrad's Malay Fiction*. New York: Palgrave, 2000.

Hand, Seán. "Taking Liberties: Re-situating *Difficile liberté*." *Modern Judaism* 31, no. 1 (2011): 1–22.

Handelman, Susan. *Fragments of Redemption: Jewish Thought and Literary Theory in Benjamin, Scholem, and Levinas*. Bloomington: Indiana University Press, 1991.

———. "Fragments of the Rock: Contemporary Literary Theory and the Study of Rabbinic Texts—A Response to David Stern." *Prooftexts* 5, no. 1 (January 1985): 75–95.

Haney, David P., and Donald R. Wehrs, eds. *Levinas and Nineteenth-Century Literature: Ethics and Otherness from Romanticism Through Realism*. Newark: University of Delaware Press, 2009.

Hansel, Joëlle. "Beyond Phenomenology: Levinas's Early Jewish Writings." In *Levinas Studies: An Annual Review* 5, 5–17. Pittsburgh: Duquesne University Press, 2010.

Hansen, M. B. N. *Bodies in Code: Interfaces with Digital Media*. London: Routledge, 2006.

———. *New Philosophy for New Media*. Cambridge, Mass.: MIT Press, 2004.

Hansen, Miriam Bratu. "Benjamin's Aura." *Critical Inquiry* 34 (Winter 2008): 336–375.

Hanssen, Beatrice. *Walter Benjamin's Other History: Of Stones, Animals, Human Beings, and Angels*. Berkeley: University of California Press, 2000.

Haran, Menachem. *The Biblical Collection: Its Consolidation to the End of the Second Temple Times and Changes of Form to the End of the Middle Ages*. Jerusalem: Bialik Institute and Magnes Press, 1996.

Hardy, Thomas. *Poems Selected by Tom Paulin*. New York: Faber and Faber, 2005.

Harpham, Geoffrey. *Shadows of Ethics: Criticism and the Just Society*. Durham, N.C.: Duke University Press, 1999.

Harris, Robert D. "Medieval Jewish Exegesis." *A History of Biblical Interpretation*, edited by A. Hauser and D. Watson, 2:141–170. Grand Rapids, Mich.: Erdmanns, 2009.

Harrison, Robert Pogue. *The Dominion of the Dead*. Chicago: University of Chicago Press, 2003.

———. "The Names of the Dead." *Critical Inquiry* 24, no. 1 (1997): 176–190.

Harshav, Benjamin. *Language in a Time of Revolution*. Stanford: Stanford University Press, 1993.

———. *The Meaning of Yiddish*. Berkeley: University of California Press, 1990.

Hart, William D. *Edward Said and the Religious Effects of Culture*. Cambridge: Cambridge University Press, 2000.

Hartman, David. *A Living Covenant: The Innovative Spirit in Traditional Judaism*. New York: Jewish Lights Publications, 1998.

Hartman, Geoffrey. *The Third Pillar: Essays in Judaic Studies*. Philadelphia: University of Pennsylvania Press, 2011.

Harvey, Warren Zev. "Levinas on the Vocation of Jewish Philosophy." In *Emmanuel Levinas: Prophetic Inspiration and Philosophy*, edited by Irene Kajon, Emilio Baccarini, Francesca Brezzi, and Joelle Hansel, 77–83. Florence: LaGiuntina, 2008.

———. "Shushani al nevuat Moshe Rabeinu." In *Be-darkhei Shalom*, edited by B. Ish-Shalom, 459–465. Jerusalem: Beit Morashah, 2007.

Hauptman, Judith. *Development of the Talmudic Sugya: Relationship Between Tannaitic and Amoraic Sources*. Lanham, Md.: University Press of America, 1987.

———. *Rereading the Mishnah: A New Approach to Ancient Jewish Texts*. Tübingen: Mohr Siebeck, 2005.

Hawkins, Peter S. "Naming Names: The Art of Memory and the NAMES Project AIDS Quilt." *Critical Inquiry* 19, no. 4 (Summer 1993): 752–780.

Hayes, Christine. "The 'Other' in Rabbinic Literature." In *The Cambridge Companion to the Talmud and Rabbinic Literature*, edited by Charlotte E. Fonrobert and Martin S. Jaffee, 243–278. Cambridge: Cambridge University Press, 2007.

Hayot, Eric. *Literary Worlds*. Oxford: Oxford University Press, 2012.

Hayyim ben Yitzchok Ickovits of Volozhin. *Nefesh Hachaim*. Translated by Rabbi Avraham Yaakov Finkel. New York: Judaica Press, 2009.

———. *Ruach Chaim*. Translated by Chanoch Levi. New York: Feldheim, 2002.

———. *The Soul of Life: The Complete Neffesh Ha-chayyim*. Translated by Eliezer Lipa (Leonard) Moskowiz. Teaneck, N.J.: New Davar Publications, 2012.

Henkin, David M. *City Reading: Written Words and Public Spaces in Antebellum New York*. New York: Columbia University Press, 1998.

Henricksen, Bruce. *Nomadic Voices: Conrad and the Subject of Narrative*. Urbana: University of Illinois Press, 1992.

Hervieu-Léger, Danièle. *Religion as a Chain of Memory*. Translated by Simon Lee. New Brunswick: Rutgers University Press, 2000.

Herwitz, Daniel. "On the Exile of Words in the American Simulacrum: A Free Exercise in Wittgensteinian Cultural Critique." In *Borders, Exiles, Diasporas*, edited by Elazar Barkan and Marie-Denise Shelton, 149–177. Stanford: Stanford University Press, 1998.

Herzog, Annabel. "'Monolingualism' or the Language of God: Scholem and Derrida on Hebrew and Politics." *Modern Judaism* 29, no. 2 (May 2009): 226–238.

Heschel, Abraham Joshua. *Heavenly Torah: As Refracted Through the Generations*. Translated by Gordon Tucker. New York: Continuum, 2006.

Hetherington, Kevin. "The Unsightly: Touching the Parthenon Frieze." *Theory, Culture & Society* 19 (December 2002): 187–205.

Hillman, David. "The Worst Case of Knowing the Other? Stanley Cavell and *Troilus and Cressida*." *Philosophy and Literature* 32 (2008): 1–13.

Hirsch, Marianne. *Family Frames: Photography, Narrative, and Postmemory*. Cambridge, Mass.: Harvard University Press, 1997.

———. *The Generation of Postmemory: Writing and Visual Culture After the Holocaust*. New York: Columbia University Press, 2012.

Hirschkop, Ken. "Bakhtin, Philosopher and Sociologist." In *Face to Face: Bakhtin in Russia and the West*, edited by Carol Adlam, Rachel Falconer, Vitalii Makhlin, and Alistair Renfrew, 54–67. Sheffield: Sheffield Academic Press, 1997.

———. *Mikhail Bakhtin: An Aesthetic for Democracy*. Oxford: Oxford University Press, 1999.

Hirschkop, Ken, and David Shepherd, eds. *Bakhtin and Cultural Theory*. Manchester: Manchester University Press, 2001.

Hitchcock, Peter. "The World According to Globalization and Bakhtin." In *Materializing Bakhtin: The Bakhtin Circle and Social Theory*, edited by Craig Brandist and Galin Tikhanov, 3–19. New York: St. Martins Press, 2000.

Hochberg, Gil Z. "Edward Said: 'The Last Jewish Intellectual': On Identity, Alterity, and the Politics of Memory." *Social Text* 24, no. 2 (Summer 2006): 47–65.

Hoffman, Adina, and Peter Cole. *Sacred Trash: The Lost and Found World of the Cairo Geniza.* New York: Schocken Books, 2011.

Hoffman, Anne Golomb. *Between Exile and Return: S. Y. Agnon and the Drama of Writing.* Albany: State University of New York Press, 1991.

———. "Topographies of Reading: Agnon through Benjamin." *Prooftexts* 21, no. 1 (Winter 2001): 71–89.

Holden, Terence. *Levinas, Messianism and Parody.* New York: Continuum, 2011.

Holdrege, Barbara A. *Veda and Torah: Transcending the Textuality of Scripture.* Albany: State University of New York Press, 1996.

Hollander, Dana. *Exemplarity and Chosenness: Rosenzweig and Derrida on the Nation of Philosophy.* Stanford: Stanford University Press, 2008.

Holquist, Michael. "Answering as Authoring: Mikhail Bakhtin's Trans-Linguistics." *Critical Inquiry* 10, no. 2 (December 1983): 307–319.

———. *Dialogism: Bakhtin and His World.* London: Routledge, 2002.

Holquist, Michael, and Katrina Clark. *Mikhail Bakhtin.* Cambridge, Mass.: Harvard University Press, 1984.

Homer. *The Odyssey.* Translated by Robert Fitzgerald. New York: Farrar, Straus and Giroux, 1998.

———. *The Odyssey.* Translated by Robert Fagles. New York: Penguin, 1997.

———. *The Odyssey.* Translated by Stephen Mitchell. New York: Atria Books, 2013.

Howe, LeAnne. *Shell Shakers.* San Francisco: Aunt Lute Books, 2001.

Hughes, Aaron W. *The Texture of the Divine: Imagination in Medieval Islamic and Jewish Thought.* Bloomington: Indiana University Press, 2003.

Hughes, Robert. *Ethics, Aesthetics, and the Beyond of Language.* Albany: State University of New York Press, 2001.

Hume, David. *Enquiries Concerning Human Understanding and Concerning the Principles of Morals.* Edited by L. A. Selby-Bigge. Oxford: Clarendon Press, 1902.

Hussein, Abdirahman. *Edward Said: Criticism and Society.* London: Verso, 2002.

Husserl, Edmund. *Ideas Pertaining to a Pure Phenomenology and to a Phenomenological Philosophy. Second Book: Studies in the Phenomenology of Constitution*, Translated by R. Rojcewicz and A. Schuwer. Dordrecht: Kluwer, 1989.

Ibn Ezra, Abraham. *Selected Poems: Twilight of a Golden Age.* Translated by Leon J. Weinberger. Tuscaloosa: University of Alabama Press, 1997.

Ibn Ḥaviv, R. Yaaqov ben Shelomo. *Ein Yaakov: The Ethical and Inspirational Teachings of the Talmud.* Translated by Avraham Yaakov Finkel. Lanham, Md.: Jason Aronson, 1999.

Idel, Moshe. *Absorbing Perfections: Kabbalah and Interpretation.* New Haven: Yale University Press, 2002.

Ingram, Susan. "'The Task of the Translator': Walter Benjamin's Essay in English, a *Forschungsbericht*." *TTR: traduction, terminologie, redaction* 10, no. 2 (1997): 207–233.

Inman, Arthur C. *The Inman Diary: A Public and Private Confession.* Edited by Daniel Aaron. Cambridge, Mass.: Harvard University Press, 1985.

Ishiguro, Kazuo. *When We Were Orphans*. New York: Vintage, 2001.

Isupov, K. G. *M. M. Bakhtin—Pro et Contra: Lichnost I Tvorchestvo Bakhtina V Otsenke Russkoi I Mirovoi Gumanitarnoi Mysli: Antologiia*. Saint Petersburg: Izd-vo Russkogo Khristianskogo gumanitarnogo inta, 2001.

Jacobs, Carol. *In the Language of Walter Benjamin*. Baltimore: Johns Hopkins University Press, 1999.

———. "The Monstrosity of Translation." *Modern Language Notes* 6 (1975): 755–766.

Jacobs, Louis. *Structure and Form in the Babylonian Talmud*. Cambridge: Cambridge University Press, 1991.

Jacobson, David C. *Modern Midrash: The Retelling of Traditional Jewish Narratives by Twentieth Century Hebrew Writers*. Albany: State University of New York Press, 1987.

Jager, Colin. "Romanticism/Secularization/Secularism." *Literature Compass* 5, no. 4 (2008): 791–806.

James, Henry. *Eight Tales from the Major Phase: In the Cage and Others*. New York: Norton, 1958.

James, Ian. "Incarnation and Infinity." In *Re-treating Religion: Deconstructing Christianity with Jean-Luc Nancy*, edited by Alena Alexandrova, Ignaas Devisch, Laurens ten Kate, and Aukje van Rooden, 246–260. New York: Fordham University Press, 2012.

Jameson, Fredric. *The Political Unconscious: Narrative as a Socially Symbolic Act*. Ithaca, N.Y.: Cornell University Press, 1981.

Jastrow, Marcus. *Sefer Ha-Milim: Dictionary of the Targumim, Talmud Bavli, Talmud Yerushalmi, and Midrashic Literature*. New York: Judaica Press, 1992.

Jauch, Ursula Pia. "Training the Senses: Giacomo Santiago Rogado Revisits Enchantment." In *Giacomo Santiago Rogado: First Second Patience*. Bielefeld: Kerber 2010.

Jay, Martin. *Permanent Exiles: Essays on the Intellectual Migration from Germany to America*. New York: Columbia University Press, 1986.

———. "Politics of Translation: Siegfried Kracauer and Walter Benjamin on the Buber-Rosenzweig Bible." In *Publications of the Leo Baeck Institute, Year Book XXI*, 3–24. London: Secker & Warburg, 1976.

Jay, Ricky. *The Magic Magic Book*. New York: Whitney Museum Library Associates, 1994.

Johnson, Barbara. *Persons and Things*. Cambridge, Mass.: Harvard University Press 2008.

Jonas, Hans. *The Phenomenon of Life: Toward a Philosophical Biology*. Evanston, Ill.: Northwestern University Press, 2001.

Jones, Kent. "Can Movies Think?" *Rouge* (October 2008). www.rouge.com.au/12/think.html.

Jonsson, AnnKatrin. *Ethics and the Modernist Subject in Joyce's Ulysses, Woolf's The Waves and Barnes's Nightwood*. New York: Peter Lang, 2006.

Juffé, Michel. "Lévinas as (mis)Reader of Spinoza." Translated by Beatriz Bugni. *Levinas Studies* 2 (2007): 153–173.

Julius, Anthony. *Transgressions: The Offenses of Art*. London: Thames and Hudson, 2002.

Kael, Pauline. "Urban Gothic." *The New Yorker*, October 30, 1971.

Kafka, Franz. *Letters to Family, Friends, and Editors*. Translated by Richard and Clara Winston. New York: Schocken Books, 1977.

Kahane, Ahuvia. "Homer and the Jews in Antiquity." In *Textus: Studies of the Hebrew Bible Project*, edited by Michael Segal and Noam Mizrahi, 25:75–114. Jerusalem: Hebrew University Press, 2010.

Kamenetz, Rodger. *Burnt Books: Rabbi Nachman of Bratslav and Franz Kafka*. New York: Schocken, 2010.

Kant, Immanuel. *Anthropology from a Pragmatic Point of View*. Translated by Robert B. Louden. Cambridge: Cambridge University Press, 2006.

Karavanta, Mina, and Nina Morgan. *Edward Said and Jacques Derrida: Reconstellating Humanism and the Global Hybrid*. Newcastle: Cambridge Scholars Publishing, 2008.

Katchor, Ben. *The Beauty Supply District*. New York: Pantheon Books, 2000.

———. *The Cardboard Valise*. New York: Pantheon Books, 2011.

———. *Cheap Novelties: The Pleasure of Urban Decay*. New York: Penguin Books, 1991.

———. *Hand Drying in America and Other Stories*. New York: Pantheon Books, 2013.

Katz, Claire Elise. *Levinas and the Crisis of Humanism*. Bloomington: Indiana University Press, 2013.

Katz, Gideon, and Gideo Nevo. "Two Perspectives on Abraham Regelson's *Hakukot Oitiyotayich*." *Hebrew Studies* 48 (2007): 299–320.

Katznelson, Raḥel. "Nedudei Lashon." In *Language in the Time of Revolution*, edited by Benjamin Harshav, 183–194. Berkeley: University of California Press, 1993.

Kaufmann, Stanley. *About the Theater*. Rhinebeck, N.Y.: Sheep Meadow Press, 2010.

———. *Regarding Film: Criticism and Comment*. New York: PAJ Publications, 2005.

Kavka, Martin. "Is There a Warrant for Levinas's Talmudic Readings?" *Journal of Jewish Thought and Philosophy* 14, no. 1 (2006): 153–173.

———. *Jewish Messianism and the History of Philosophy*. Cambridge: Cambridge University Press, 2004.

———. "Recollection, Zakhor, Anamnesis: On Ira Stone's *Reading Levinas/Reading Talmud*." *Cross Currents* 49: 4 (1999): 523–536.

———. "Review of Samuel Moyn's *Origins of the Other: Emmanuel Levinas Between Revelation and Ethics*." *Journal of the American Academy of Religion* 74, no. 4 (December, 2006): 1003–1005.

Kearney, Richard. "Levinas and the Ethics of Imagining." In *Between Ethics and Aesthetics: Crossing the Boundaries*, edited by Dorota Glowacka and Stephen Boos, 85–96. Albany: State University of New York Press, 2002.

Keen, Suzanne. *Empathy and the Novel*, New York: Oxford University Press, 2007.

Kellner, Menachem. *Maimonides on the "Decline of the Generations" and the Nature of Rabbinic Authority*. Albany: State University of New York Press, 1996.

Kendall, Tim. "'Joy, Fire, Joy': Blaise Pascal's 'Memorial' and the Visionary Explorations of T. S. Eliot, Aldous Huxley and William Golding." *Literature and Theology* 11, no. 3 (1997): 299–212.

Kermode, Frank. "Novels: Recognition and Deception." *Critical Inquiry* 1, no. 1 (September 1974): 103–121.

Kertész, André. *On Reading.* New York: Norton, 2008.

Kiel, Mark. "Sefer ha'aggadah: Creating a Classic Anthology for the People and by the People." *Prooftexts* 17, no. 2 (May 1997): 177–197.

Kimmelman, Michael. "The New Ground Zero: Finding Comfort in the Safety of Names." *New York Times*, August 31, 2003.

Kirsch, Adam. "Appreciating the Talmud's Sublime Devotion to Torah for Its Own Sake." *Tablet Magazine*, July 26, 2013. www.tabletmag.com/jewish-life-and-religion/137870/kirsch-daf-yomi-42/2.

———. "In the Shadow of the Divine, Reaping Unintended Benefits at the Edges of the Law." *Tablet Magazine*, July 23, 2013. www.tabletmag.com/jewish-life-and-religion/138527/adam-kirsch-daf-yomi-43.

Kirshenblatt-Gimblett, Barbara. "The Cut That Binds: The Western Ashkenazic Torah Binder as Nexus between Circumcision and Torah." In *Celebration, Studies in Festivity and Ritual*, edited by Victor Witter Turner, 136–146. Washington, D.C.: Smithsonian Institution Press, 1982.

Kitcher, Philip. *The Ethical Project.* Cambridge, Mass.: Harvard University Press, 2011.

Klawans, Jonathan. *Impurity and Sin in Ancient Judaism.* Oxford: Oxford University Press, 2000.

Kleinberg-Levin, David Michael. *Gestures of Ethical Life: Reading Hölderlin's Question of Measure After Heidegger.* Stanford: Stanford University Press, 2005.

Kliger, Ilya. "Heroic Aesthetics and Modernist Critique: Extrapolations from Bakhtin's 'Author and Hero in Aesthetic Activity.'" *Slavic Review* 67, no. 3 (Fall 2008): 551–566.

Kline, Daniel T. "Review of Samuel Moyn's *Origins of the Other: Emmanuel Levinas Between Revelation and Ethics*." *Shofar: An Interdisciplinary Journal of Jewish Studies* 26, no. 2 (Winter 2008): 178–181.

Klingenstein, Susanne. *Enlarging America: The Cultural Work of Jewish Literary Scholars, 1930–1990.* Syracuse: Syracuse University Press, 1998.

Kolakowski, Leszek. *God Owes Us Nothing: A Brief Remark on Pascal's Religion and on the Spirit.* Chicago: University of Chicago Press, 1995.

Koltun-Fromm. *Material Culture and Jewish Thought in America.* Bloomington: Indiana University Press, 2010.

Konkin, S. S., and L.S. Konkina. *Mikhail Bakhtin: stranitsy zhizni i tvorchestva.* Saransk: Mordovskoe knizhnoe izdvo, 1993.

Konner, Melvin. *The Jewish Body.* New York: Random House, 2009.

Kozhinov, Vadim. *Bakhtin i ego chitateli. Razmyshleniia i otchasti vospominaniia,"* *Dialog, Karnaval, Kronotop* 2–3 (1993): 120–134.

Kozloff, Sarah. *Overhearing Film Dialogue*. Berkeley: University of California Press, 2000.

Kraemer, David Charles. *The Mind of the Talmud: An Intellectual History of the Bavli*. New York: Oxford University Press, 1990.

Kraman, Cynthia. "The Wound of the Infinite: Rereading Levinas through Rashi's Commentary on the *Song of Songs*." In *Levinas and Medieval Literature: The "Difficult Reading" of English and Rabbinic Texts*, edited by Ann W. Astell and J. A. Jackson, 207–226. Pittsburgh: Duquesne University Press, 2009.

Kreilkamp, Ivan. *Voice and the Victorian Storyteller*. Cambridge: Cambridge University Press, 2005.

Krishnan, Sanjay. "Animality and the Global Subject in Conrad's *Lord Jim*." In *Reading the Global: Troubling Perspectives on Britain's Empire in Asia*, 133–164. New York: Columbia University Press, 2007.

Kristeva, Julia. "The Ethics of Linguistics." In *Desire in Language: A Semiotic Approach to Literature and Art*, 23–35. New York: Columbia University Press, 1980.

———. *"Une poétique ruinée."* In *Mikhaïl Bakhtin, La poétique de Dostoïevski*, 5–27. Paris: Seuil, 1970.

Kronfeld, Chana. *On the Margins of Modernism: Decentering Literary Dynamics*. Berkeley: University of California Press, 1996.

Krumbein, R. Elyakim. *"Netillat Yadayim*—Washing Hands Before Eating Bread." Translated by R. Eliezer Kwass. *Daf Kesher* 136, no. 2(1996): 68–70.

Kugel, James. "Two Introductions to Midrash." *Prooftexts* 3, no. 3 (1983): 131–155.

Kundera, Milan. *The Art of the Novel*. Translated by Linda Asher. New York: Perennial, 2000.

Lacan, Jacques. *The Seminar of Jacques Lacan: Book VII: The Ethics of Psychoanalysis 1959–1960*. Translated by Dennis Porter. New York: Norton, 1997.

Lambert, Phyllis, ed. *Fortifications and the Synagogue: The Fortress of Babylon and the Ben Ezra Synagogue, Cairo*. Chicago: University of Chicago Press, 1994.

Lamm, Norman. *Torah Lishmah: Torah for Torah's Sake in the Works of Rabbi Hayyim of Volozhin and His Contemporaries*. Jersey City, N.J.: Ktav Publishers, 1989.

Lancaster, Irene. *Deconstructing the Bible: Abraham ibn Ezra's Introduction to the Torah*. New York: Routledge, 2007.

Landes, Donald A. *"Le Toucher* and the Corpus of Tact: Exploring Touch and Technicity with Jacques Derrida and Jean-Luc Nancy." *L'Esprit Créateur* 47, no. 3 (2007): 80–92.

Lanksy, Aaron. *Outwitting History: The Amazing Adventures of a Man Who Rescued a Million Yiddish Books*. Chapel Hill, N.C.: Algonquin Books, 2005.

Laor, Dan. "An uncompromising search for truth." *Ha'aretz*, July 8, 2011.

Latour, Bruno. *We Have Never Been Modern*. Translated by Catherine Porter. Cambridge, Mass.: Harvard University Press, 1993.

Lawton, Philip. "Levinas' Notion of the 'There Is.'" In *Emmanuel Levinas: Critical Assessments of Leading Philosophers*, edited by Claire Katz, 249–259. New York: Routledge, 2004.

Lefkowitz, Daniel. *Words and Stones: The Politics of Language and Identity in Israel.* Oxford: Oxford University Press, 2004.

Legrand, Pierre. *Derrida and Law.* London: Ashgate, 2009.

Lehman, Marjorie. *The En Yaaqov: Jacob ibn Habib's Search for Faith in the Talmudic Corpus.* Detroit: Wayne State University Press, 2012.

Leibowitz, Yeshayahu. *Sihot al Pirke Avot ve-al ha-Rambam.* Jerusalem: Schocken, 1979.

Leiman, Sid Z. *The Canonization of Hebrew Scripture: The Talmudic and Midrashic Evidence.* New Haven: Connecticut Academy of Arts and Sciences, 1991.

Lentricchia, Frank. "How to Do Things with Wallace Stevens." In *Close Reading: The Reader,* edited by Andrew DuBois and Frank Lentricchia, 136–156. Durham, N.C.: Duke University Press Books, 2002.

Lerner, Kiyoko, Nathan Lerner, and David Berglund. *Henry Darger's Room.* Tokyo: Imperial Press, 2007.

Lescourret, Marie-Anne. *Emmanuel Levinas.* Paris: Flammarion, 1994.

Levi, Primo. *If This is a Man.* Translated by Stuart Woolf. London: Orion Press, 1959.

Levina, Marina, and Grant Kien, eds. *Post-Global Network and Everyday Life.* New York: Peter Lang, 2010.

Levinas, Emmanuel. *A l'heure des nations.* Paris: Éditions de Minuit, 1988.

———. *Alterity and Transcendence.* Translated by Michael B. Smith. New York: Columbia University Press, 2000.

———. *Autrement qu'être ou Au-delà de l'essence.* Paris: Le Livre de Poche, 2004.

———. *Beyond the Verse: Talmudic Readings and Discourses.* Translated by Gary Mole. New York: Continuum, 2007.

———. "The Contemporary Criticism of the Idea of Value and the Prospects for Humanism." In *Value and Values in Evolution,* edited by Edward A. Maziarz, 179–187. New York: Gordon and Breach, 1979.

———. *Difficile liberté: Essais sur le judaïsme.* Paris: Le Livre de Poche, 2003.

———. *Difficult Freedom: Essays on Judaism.* Translated by Seán Hand. Baltimore: Johns Hopkins University Press, 1997.

———. *Du sacré au saint: Cinq nouvelles lectures talmudiques.* Paris: Éditions de Minuit, 1977.

———. *Ethics and Infinity.* Translated by Richard A. Cohen. Pittsburgh: Duquesne University Press, 1985.

———. *Existence and Existents.* Translated by Alphonso Lingis. Pittsburgh: Duquesne University Press, 2001.

———. *Humanism of the Other.* Translated by Nidra Poller. Chicago: University of Chicago Press, 2005.

———. *In the Time of Nations.* Translated by Michael B. Smith. New York: Continuum, 2007.

———. *Is It Righteous to Be? Interviews with Emmanuel Levinas.* Stanford: Stanford University Press, 2001.

———. *L'au-delà du verset.* Paris: Éditions de Minuit, 1982.

———. "The Meaning of Religious Practice." Translated by Peter Atterton, Matthew Calarco, and Joelle Hansel. *Modern Judaism* 25, no. 3 (October 2005): 285–289.

———. *Nine Talmudic Readings.* Translated by Annette Aronowicz. Bloomington: Indiana University Press, 1990.

———. "Nom d'un chien; ou le droit naturel." In *Celui qui nepeut se servir de mots: à Bram Van Velde.* Montpellier: Éditions Fata Morgana, 1975.

———. *Noms propres.* Paris: Fata Morgana, 1976.

———. *Of God Who Comes to Mind.* Translated by Bettina Bergo. Stanford: Stanford University Press, 1998.

———. *Otherwise Than Being or Beyond Essence.* Translated by Alphonso Lingis. Pittsburgh: Duquesne University Press, 1998.

———. *Outside the Subject.* Translated by Michael B. Smith. Stanford: Stanford University Press, 1994.

———. *Oeuvres. Tome 1, Carnets de captivité suivi de Ecrits sur la captivité et Notes philosophiques diverses.* Edited by Rodolphe Calin and Catherine Chalier. Paris: Grasset/Imec, 2009.

———. "The Paradox of Morality: An Interview with Emmanuel Levinas." With Tamra Wright, Peter Hughes, and Alison Ainley. In *The Provocation of Levinas: Rethinking the Other,* edited by Robert Bernasconi and David Wood, 168–180. New York: Routledge & Kegan Paul, 1988.

———. *Proper Names.* Translated by Michael B. Smith. Stanford: Stanford University Press, 1997.

———. *Quatre lectures talmudiques.* Paris: Éditions de Minuit, 2005.

———. *Totalité et infini: Essai sur l'extériorité.* The Hague: M. Nijhoff. 1961.

———. *Totality and Infinity.* Pittsburgh: Duquesne University Press, 1980.

———. "The Trace of the Other." Translated by Alphonso Lingis. In *Deconstruction in Context: Literature and Philosophy,* edited by Mark Taylor, 345–359. Chicago: University of Chicago Press, 1986.

———. *Unforeseen History.* Translated by Nidra Poller. Champaign: University of Illinois Press, 2004.

———. "Useless Suffering." In *Entre Nous: Thinking-of-the-Other,* 91–102. Translated by Michael Bradley Smith and Barbara Harshav. New York: Columbia University Press, 2000.

Levinas, Emmanuel, and Richard Kearney. "Dialogue with Emmanuel Levinas." In *Face to Face with Levinas,* edited by Richard A. Cohen, 13–34. Albany: State University of New York Press, 1986.

Levine, Nachman. "'The Oven of Achnai' Re-Deconstructed." *Hebrew Studies* (November 2004): 1–11.

Levine, Samuel J. "*Halacha* and *Aggada*: Translating Robert Cover's *Nomos and Narrative.*" *Utah Law Review* 465 (1998): 465–504.

Levy, Lital. "From Baghdad to Bialik with Love: A Reappropriation of Modern Hebrew Poetry, 1933." *Comparative Literature Studies* 42, no. 3 (2005): 125–154.

Levy, Ze'ev. *From Spinoza to Lévinas: Hermeneutical, Ethical, and Political Issues in Contemporary Jewish Philosophy*. New York: Peter Lang, 2009.

Lezama Lima, José. *Obras completas: Tratados en La Habana*. Havana: Editorial Letras Cubanas, 2009.

Lichtenstein, R. Aharon. "The Conceptual Approach to Torah Learning: The Method and Its Prospects." In *Lomdut: The Conceptual Approach to Jewish Learning*, edited by R. Yosef Blau, 1–44. Jersey City, N.J.: Ktav, 2006.

Lichtenstein, R. Mosheh. "'What' Hath Brisk Wrought: The Brisker *Derekh* Revisited." In ibid., 167–188.

Lieberman, Saul. *Alei Ayin: Minhat Devarim li-Shelomoh Zalman Shoken aḥare melot lo shiv'im shanah*. Tel Aviv: Schocken, 1948–52.

Liebersohn, Harry. "Discovering Indigenous Nobility: Tocqueville, Chamisso, and Romantic Travel Writing." *American Historical Review* 99, no. 3 (June 1994): 746–766.

Lim, Timothy H. "The Defilement of the Hands as a Principle Determining the Holiness of Scriptures." *Journal of Theological Studies* 61, no. 2: 501–515.

Lin Ma. "All the Rest Must Be Translated: Lévinas's Notion of Sense." *Journal of Chinese Philosophy* (2008): 599–612.

Lindsey, William D. "'The Problem of Great Time': A Bakhtinian Ethics of Discourse." *Journal of Religion* 73, no. 3 (1993): 311–328.

Liu, Alan. "The End of the End of the Book: Dead Books, Lively Margins, and Social Computing." *Michigan Quarterly Review* 48 (2009): 499–520.

Llewelyn, John. "Am I Obsessed by Bobby? (Humanism of the Other Animal)." In *Rereading Levinas*, edited by Robert Bernasconi and Simon Critchley, 234–246. Bloomington: Indiana University Press, 1991.

———. *Emmanuel Levinas: The Genealogy of Ethics*. London: Routledge Press, 1995.

———. *The Middle Voice of Ecological Conscience: A Chiasmic Reading of Responsibility in the Neighbourhood of Levinas, Heidegger, and Others*. London: Macmillan, 1991.

———. "Responsibility with Undecidability." In *Appositions of Jacques Derrida and Emmanuel Levinas*, 17–36. Bloomington: Indiana University Press, 2002.

Loiperdinger, Martin. "Lumiere's Arrival of the Train: Cinema's Founding Myth." *The Moving Image* 4, no. 1 (Spring 2004): 89–118.

London, Jack. *John Barleycorn, or, Alcoholic Memoirs*. New York: Century, 1913.

———. *Martin Eden*. New York: Penguin Books, 1994.

Long, Jonathan James. *W.G. Sebald: Image, Archive, Modernity*. New York: Columbia University Press, 2007.

Lorberbaum, Yair. "Reflections of the Halakhic Status of Aggadah." *Dine Yisrael* 24 (2007): 29–64.

———. *Tzelem Elohim: Halakha v'Aggadah*. Jerusalem: Schocken Press, 2004.

Lothe, Jakob, Jeremy Hawthorn, and James Phelan, eds. *Joseph Conrad: Voice, Sequence, History, Genre*. Columbus: Ohio State University Press, 2008.

Louden, Bruce. *Homer's Odyssey and the Near East*. Cambridge: Cambridge University Press, 2011.

Louie, Miriam Ching. "The 9/11 Disappeareds." *The Nation*, December 3, 2001.

Love, Heather. "Close but not Deep: Literary Ethics and the Descriptive Turn." *New Literary History* 41, no. 2 (Spring 2010): 371–391.

Loye, Tobias Percival Zur. "History of a Natural History: Max Ernst's Histoire Naturelle, Frottage, and Surrealist Automatism." Ph.D. dissertation, University of Oregon, 2010.

Luz, Zvi, and Ziva Shamir, eds. *ʿAl gilui ṿe-khisui ba-lashon: ʿiyunim be-masato shel Biyaliḳ.* Ramat-Gan: Hotsaʾat Universiṭat Bar-Ilan 2001.

Lyotard, Jean-François. "Levinas's Logic." In *Face to Face with Levinas*, edited by Richard Cohen, 117–158. Albany: State University of New York Press, 1986.

MacGregor, John. *Henry Darger: In the Realms of the Unreal.* New York: Delano Greenidge Editions, 2002.

Mack, Michael. "Spinoza's Non-Humanist Humanism." In *Spinoza Beyond Philosophy*, edited by Beth Lord, 28–47. Edinburgh: Edinburgh University Press, 2012.

Magid, Shaul. "Deconstructing the Mystical: The Anti-Mystical Kabbalism in Rabbi Hayyim of Volozhin's *Nefesh Ha-Hayyim*." *Journal of Jewish Thought and Philosophy* 9 (1999): 21–67.

Magness, Jodi. "Scrolls and Hand Impurity." In *The Dead Sea Scrolls: Texts and Contexts*, edited by Charlotte Hempel, 89–98. Leiden: Brill, 2010.

Maimon, Moshe ben (Maimonides). *Pirkei Avot/Shemoneh Perakim of the Rambam/The Thirteen Principles of Faith.* Translated by R. Elihayu Touger. New York: Moznaim, 1994.

Malcolm, Janet. "Depth of Field: Thomas Struth's Way of Seeing." *The New Yorker*, September 26, 2011.

Malka, Salomon. *Emmanuel Levinas: His Life and Legacy.* Translated by Michael Krigel. Pittsburgh: Duquesne University Press, 2006.

———. *Monsieur Chouchani: L'enigme d'un maitre du XXe siècle.* Paris: J.C. Lattes, 1994.

Maltby, Richard, Daniel Biltereyst, and Philippe Meers, ed. *Explorations in New Cinema History: Approaches and Case Studies.* Oxford: Blackwell, 2011.

Maltby, Richard, Melvyn Stokes, and Robert C. Allen, eds. *Going to the Movies: Hollywood and the Social Experience of the Cinema.* Exeter: University of Exeter Press, 2008.

Mandel, Paul. "Between Byzantium and Islam: the Transmission of a Jewish Book in the Byzantine and Early Islamic Periods." In *Transmitting Jewish Traditions: Orality, Textuality and Cultural Diffusion*, edited by Yaakov Elman and Israel Gershoni, 74–106. New Haven: Yale University Press, 2000.

Mandelker, Amy, ed. *Bakhtin in Contexts: Across the Disciplines.* Evanston, Ill.: Northwestern University Press, 1995.

Mandell, Hinda. "In Curious Pursuit of the Original Owners of 'Mein Kampf.'" *The Forward*, September 12, 2012.

Mandelstam, Osip. *The Noise of Time: Selected Prose.* Translated by Clarence Brown. Evanston, Ill.: Northwestern University Press, 2002.

Manderson, Desmond. *Essays on Levinas and Law: A Mosaic.* New York: Palgrave Macmillan, 2009.

———. *Proximity, Levinas and the Soul of Law.* Toronto: McGill-Queen's University Press, 2006.

Manguel, Alberto. *A History of Reading.* New York: Viking, 1996.

Mann, Barbara E. "Toward an Understanding of Jewish Imagism." *Religion & Literature* 30, no. 3 (Autumn 1998): 23–45.

———. "Visions of Jewish Modernism." *Modernism/modernity* 13, no. 4 (2006): 673–699.

Marder, Michael. "Breathing 'to' the Other: Levinas and Ethical Breathlessness." *Levinas Studies* 4 (2009): 91–110.

Marion, Jean-Luc. "Metaphysics and Phenomenology: A Relief for Theology." Translated by Thomas A. Carlson. *Critical Inquiry* 20, no. 4 (Summer 1994): 572–591.

Markell, Patchen. *Bound Recognition.* Princeton: Princeton University Press, 2003.

Markowski, Michal Paweł. "Text and Theater: The Ironic Imagination of Bruno Schulz." In *(Un)masking Bruno Schulz: New Combinations, Furthe Fragmentations, Ultimate Regenerations*, edited by Dieter De Bruyn and Kris van Heuckelom, 435–450. Amsterdam: Editions Rodopi, 2009.

Marshal, David. *The Surprising Effects of Sympathy: Marivaux, Diderot, Rousseau, and Mary Shelley.* Chicago: University of Chicago Press, 1988.

Martin, Douglas. "Robert Shields, Wordy Diarist, Dies at 89." *New York Times*, October 29, 2007.

Massumi, Brian. *Parables for the Virtual: Movement, Affect, Sensation.* Durham, N.C.: Duke University Press, 2002.

Mastroianni, Dominic. "Astonishing Politics: Levinas, Emerson, and Thinking Beyond Virility." *Comparative Literature* 66, no. 3 (Summer, 2014).

Maszewski, Zbigniew. "Bianca Looks from above the Book: Readings on the Margin of Bruno Schulz's Ex-Libris for Stanisław Weingarten." *Text Matters* 2, no. 2 (2012): 130–143.

Matejka, Ladislav. "Deconstructing Bakhtin." In *Fiction Updated: Theories of Fictionality, Narratology, and Poetics*, edited by Calin Andrei Mihailescu and Walid Hamarneh, 257–266. Toronto: University of Toronto Press, 1996.

Matson, John. "Commemorative Calculus." *Scientific American*, September 7, 2011.

McCole, John. *Walter Benjamin and the Antinomies of Tradition.* Ithaca, N.Y.: Cornell University Press, 1993.

McDade, John. "Divine Disclosure and Concealment in Bach, Pascal and Levinas." *New Blackfriars* 85 (2004): 121–132.

McDonald, Henry. "Aesthetics as First Ethics: Levinas and the Alterity of Literary Discourse." *Diacritics* 38, no. 4 (Winter 2008): 15–41.

McDonald, Lee Martin. *The Biblical Canon: Its Origin, Transmission, and Authority.* Grand Rapids, Mich.: Baker Academic, 2011.

McDonald, Lee Martin, and James A. Sanders. *The Canon Debate.* Peabody, Mass.: Hendrickson, 2007.

McEwan, Ian. "The Art of Fiction No. 173." *Paris Review* 162 (Summer 2002): 30–60.

McGann, Jerome. *Radiant Textuality: Literature after the World Wide Web*. New York: Palgrave Macmillan, 2004.

———. *The Textual Condition*. Princeton: Princeton University Press, 1991.

McGowan, Todd. *The Fictional Christopher Nolan*. Austin: University of Texas Press, 2012.

McKee, Jesse O. and Jon A. Schlenker. *The Choctaws: Cultural Evolution of a Native American Tribe*. Jackson: University Press of Mississippi, 1980.

McKim, Joel. "Agamben at Ground Zero: A Memorial Without Content." *Theory, Culture & Society* 25 (September 2008): 83–103.

Meir, Ephraim. *Levinas's Jewish Thought: Between Jerusalem and Athens*. Jerusalem: Hebrew University Magnes Press, 2008.

Méliès, Georges. *Georges Méliès: First Wizard of Cinema 1896–1913*. Flicker Alley–Blackhawk Films, 2008.

———. *Méliès Encore*. Flicker Alley–Blackhawk Films, 2010.

Mendes Flohr, Paul. "Hebrew as a Holy Tongue: Franz Rosenzweig and the Renewal of Hebrew." In *Hebrew in Ashkenaz: A Language in Exile*, edited by Lewis Glinert, 222–241. Oxford: Oxford University Press, 1993.

Merleau-Ponty, Maurice. *Phenomenology of Perception*. Translated by Colin Smith. London: Routledge, 2002.

Meskin, Jacob. "Critique, Tradition, and the Religious Imagination: An Essay on Levinas' Talmudic Readings." *Judaism* (Winter 1998): 91–106.

———. "The Role of Lurianic Kabbalah in the Early Philosophy of Emmanuel Levinas." *Levinas Studies* 2 (2007): 49–77.

Mesnard, Jean. "La maison où Pascal écrivit le 'Mémorial.'" *Revue d'Histoire littéraire de la France* 55, no. 1 (January–March 1955): 51–55.

Metzger, David D. 'Bobby Who?' *JAC* 31, nos. 1–2 (2011): 273–283.

Meyerowitz, Rael. *Transferring to America: Jewish Interpretations of American Dreams*. Albany: State University of New York Press, 1995.

Michelfelder, Diane. "Derrida and the Question of the Ear." In *The Question of the Other: Essays In Contemporary Continental Philosophy*, edited by Arleen B. Dallery and Charles E. Scott, 47–54. Albany: State University of New York Press, 1989.

———. "Toward a New Understanding of the Work of Emmanuel Levinas." *Modern Judaism* 20, no. 1 (February 2000): 78–102.

Mihailescu, Calin. "*Corpus Epochalis*: Mysticism, Body, History." *Surfaces* 1 (1991): 4–34.

Mihailovic, Alexandar. *Corporeal Worlds: Mikhail Bakhtin's Theology of Discourse*. Evanston, Ill.: Northwestern University Press, 1997.

Milikowsky, Chaim. "Reflections on Hand-Washing, Hand-Purity and Holy Scripture in Rabbinic Literature." In *Purity and Holiness: The Heritage of Leviticus*, edited by M. J. H. M. Poorthuis and J. Schwartz, 149–162. Leiden: Brill, 2000.

Miller, Barry. *The Fullness of Being: A New Paradigm for Existence: A New Paradigm for Existence*. Notre Dame, Ind.: University of Notre Dame Press, 2002.

Miller, D. A. "Hitchcock's Hidden Pictures." *Critical Inquiry* 37, no. 1 (Autumn 2010): 106–130.

Miller, J. Hillis. *Charles Dickens: The World of His Novels*. Cambridge, Mass.: Harvard University Press, 1958.

———. *The Conflagration of Community: Fiction Before and After Auschwitz*. Chicago: University of Chicago Press, 2011.

———. "The Critic as Host." *Critical Inquiry*, 3, no. 3 (Spring 1977): 439–447.

———. *For Derrida*. New York: Fordham University Press, 2009.

———. "Hands in Hardy." In *The Ashgate Research Companion to Thomas Hardy*, edited by Rosemarie Morgan, 505–516. Surrey: Ashgate, 2010.

———. "Optic and Semiotic in Middlemarch." In *The Worlds of Victorian Fiction*, edited by Jerome H. Buckley, 125–145. Cambridge, Mass.: Harvard University Press, 1975.

———. *Reading for Our Time: Adam Bede and Middlemarch Revisited*. Edinburgh: Edinburgh University Press, 2012.

———. *Theory Now and Then*. Durham, N.C.: Duke University Press, 1991.

Miller, Reed. "A Lesson in Moral Spectatorship." *Critical Inquiry* 34, no. 4 (Summer 2008): 706–728.

Milosz, Czeslaw. *The Collected Poems, 1931–1987*. New York: Ecco Press, 1988.

Mintz, Alan. L. "In the Seas of Youth." *Prooftexts* 21, no. 1 (Winter, 2001): 57–70.

———. *Sanctuary in the Wilderness: A Critical Introduction to American Hebrew Poetry*. Stanford: Stanford University Press, 2012.

———. "Sefer Ha-aggadah: Triumph or Tragedy?" In *History and Literature: New Readings of Jewish Texts in in Honor of Arnold J. Band*, edited by William Cutter and David C. Jacobson, 17–26. Providence, R.I.: Brown University Judaic Studies, 2002.

Mintz, Sharon Liberman, and Gabriel M. Goldstein, eds. *Printing the Talmud: From Bomberg to Schottenstein*. New York: Yeshiva University Museum, 2006.

Miron, Dan. *Bodedim be-moadam*. Tel Aviv: Am Oved, 1987.

———. "From Continuity to Contiguity: Thoughts on the Theory of Jewish Literature." In *Jewish Literatures and Cultures: Context and Intertext*, edited by Anita Norich and Yaron Z. Eliav, 9–36. Providence, R.I.: Brown University Press, 2008.

———. *From Continuity to Contiguity: Toward a New Jewish Literary Thinking*. Stanford: Stanford University Press, 2010.

———. *H. N. Bialik and the Prophetic Mode in Modern Hebrew Poetry*. Syracuse: Syracuse University Press, 2000.

Mishnayot Kehati: Massechet Tevul Yom/Yadayim/Uktzin Vol 21b. Edited by Pinhas Kehati. Translated by Edward I. Levin. New York: Feldheim, 2005.

Mitchell, W. J. T. *What Do Pictures Want? The Lives and Loves of Images*. Chicago: University of Chicago Press, 2005.

Montaigne, Michel de. "The Language of Animals: An Apology of Raymond Sebond." *Selected Essays*. Translated by Charles Cotton. New York: Modern Library, 1949.

Moon, Michael. *Darger's Resources*. Durham, N.C.: Duke University Press, 2012.

Moreno Márquez, César A. "The Curvature of Intersubjective Space: Sociality and Responsibility in the Thought of Emmanuel Levinas." *Analecta Husserliana* 22 (1987): 343–352.

Moretti, Franco. "Conjectures on World Literature." *New Left Review* 1 (January–February 2000): 54–68.

Morgan, Michael. *Discovering Levinas*. Cambridge: Cambridge University Press, 2010.

Morson, Gary Saul. *Narrative and Freedom: The Shadows of Time*. New Haven: Yale University Press, 1994.

———. "Sideshadowing and Tempics." *New Literary History* 29, no. 4 (1998): 599–624.

———. "Who Speaks for Bakhtin? A Dialogic Introduction." *Critical Inquiry* 10, no. 2 (December 1983): 225–243.

Moses, Michael Valdez. "Disorientalism: Conrad and the Imperial Origins of Modernist Aesthetics." In *Modernism and Colonialism: British and Irish Literature, 1899–1939*, edited by Richard Begam and Michael Valdez Moses, 43–69. Durham, N.C.: Duke University Press, 2007.

Mosès, Stéphane. *The Angel of History: Rosenzweig, Benjamin, Scholem*. Translated by Barbara Harshav. Stanford: Stanford University Press, 2009.

———. "Une lettre inédite de Scholem à Rosenzweig apropos de notre langue." *Archives de Science Sociales des Religions* 60, no. 1 (July–September 1985).

Moyaert, Paul. "Lacan on Neighborly Love: The Relation to the Thing in the Other Who Is My Neighbor." *Epoché: A Journal for the History of Philosophy* 4, no. 1 (1996): 1–31.

Moyn, Samuel. "Emmanuel Levinas's Talmudic Readings: Between Tradition and Invention." *Prooftexts* 23 (2003): 338–364.

———. *Origins of the Other: Emmanuel Levinas Between Ethics and Revelation*. Ithaca, N.Y.: Cornell University Press, 2005.

Mufti, Amir. "Auerbach in Istanbul: Edward Said, Secular Criticism, and the Question of Minority Culture." *Critical Inquiry* 25, no. 1 (Autumn 1998): 95–125.

Mulhall, Stephen. "On Refusing to Begin." In *Contending with Stanley Cavell*, edited by Russell B. Goodman, 22–36. New York: Oxford University Press, 2005.

Murdoch, Iris. *The Sovereignty of Good*. London: Routledge and Kegan Paul, 1970.

Musil, Robert. *The Enthusiasts*. Translated by Andrea Simon. New York: Performing Arts, 1983.

Myers, David N. *Between Jew and Arab: The Lost Voice of Simon Rawidowicz*. Waltham, Mass.: Brandeis University Press, 2008.

Nabokov, Vladimir. *Lectures on Literature*. New York: Harcourt Brace Jovanovich, 1980.

Nadler, Alan. *The Faith of the Mithnagdim: Rabbinic Responses to Hasidic Rapture*. Baltimore: Johns Hopkins University Press, 1999.

Nancy, Jean-Luc. *Being Singular Plural*. Translated by Robert Richardson and Anne O'Byrne. Stanford: Stanford University Press, 2000.

———. *The Birth to Presence*. Translated by Brian Holmes et al. Stanford: Stanford University Press, 1993.

———. *Corpus*. Translated by Richard A. Rand. New York: Fordham University Press, 2008.

———. *The Discourse of the Syncope: Logodaedalus*. Translated by Saul Anton. Stanford: Stanford University Press, 2008.

———. "Exscription." *Yale French Studies* 78 (1990): 47–64.

———. *The Inoperative Community*. Translated by Simona Sawhnee. Minneapolis: University of Minnesota Press, 1991.

———. *La communauté désoeuvrée*. Paris: Christian Bourgois, 1983.

———. *La comparution*/The Compearance: From the Existence of 'Communism' to the Community of 'Existence.'" Translated by Tracy B. Strong. *Political Theory* 20, no. 3 (August, 1992): 371–398.

———. "Le partage, l'infini et le jardin." *Libération*, 2000.

———. *Noli me tangere: On the Raising of the Body*. Translated by Sarah Clift, Pascale- Anne Brault, and Michael Naas. New York: Fordham University Press, 2008.

———. *On the Commerce of Thinking: Of Books and Bookstores*, trans. David Wills. New York: Fordham University Press, 2009.

Nealon, Jeffrey Thomas. *Alterity Politics: Ethics and Performative Subjectivity*. Durham, N.C.: Duke University Press, 1998.

———. "The Ethics of Dialogue: Bakhtin's Answerability and Levinas's Responsibility." *College English* 59, no. 2 (February 1997): 129–148.

Neher, André. *L'existence juive: Solitude et affrontements*. Paris: Seuil, 1962.

Nelson, Robert J. *Pascal: Adversary and Advocate*. Cambridge, Mass.: Harvard University Press, 1982.

Nelson, Victoria. *The Secret Life of Puppets*. Cambridge, Mass.: Harvard University Press, 2001.

Neusner, Jacob. *Eliezer ben Hyrcanus: The Tradition and the Man Vol II*. Leiden: E. J. Brill, 1973.

———. *A History of the Mishnaic Law of Purities, Part 19: Tebul Yom and Yadayim*. Eugene, Ore.: Wipf & Stock, 2007.

New, Melvyn, ed. *In Proximity: Levinas and the Eighteenth Century*. Lubbock: Texas Tech University Press, 2001.

Newton, Adam Zachary. *The Elsewhere, On Belonging at a Near Distance: Reading Literary Memoir from East Central Europe and the Levant*. Madison: University of Wisconsin Press, 2002.

———. *Facing Black and Jew: Literature as Public Space in 20th Century America*. Cambridge: Cambridge University Press, 1998.

———. *The Fence and the Neighbor: Yeshayahu Leibowitz, Emmanuel Levinas and Israel Among the Nations*. Albany: State University of New York Press, 2001.

———. *Narrative Ethics*. Cambridge, Mass.: Harvard University Press, 1995.

———. "The *SARL* of Criticism: Sonority, Arrogation, Letting-Be." *American Literary History* 13, no. 4 (Winter 2001): 603–637.

Nielsen, Greg M. *The Norms of Answerability: Social Theory Between Bakhtin and Habermas*. Albany: State University of New York Press, 2001.

Nolan, Christopher. *The Prestige*. Warner Bros.–Touchstone Pictures, 2006.

Nollan, Valerie Z., ed. *Bakhtin: Ethics and Mechanics*. Evanston, Ill.: Northwestern University Press, 2003.

Noonan, Sarah. "Bodies of Parchment: Representing the Passion and Reading Manuscripts in Late Medieval England." Ph.D. dissertation, Washington University, 2010.

Norich, Anita. "Hebraism and Yiddish: Paradigms of Modern Jewish Literary History." In *Modern Jewish Literatures: Intersections and Boundaries*, edited by Sheila E. Jelen, Michael Kramer, and L. Scott Lerner, 327–342. Philadelphia: University of Pennsylvania Press, 2011.

Nornes, Abe Mark. *Cinema Babel: Translating Global Cinema*. Minneapolis: University of Minnesota Press, 2007.

Nunberg, Geoffrey, ed. *The Future of the Book*. Berkeley: University of California Press, 1996.

Nussbaum, Martha. *Love's Knowledge: Essays on Philosophy and Literature*. New York: Oxford University Press, 1990.

———. *Poetic Justice: The Literary Imagination and Public Life*. Boston: Beacon Press, 1995.

Ochs, Peter. *The Return to Scripture in Judaism and Christianity: Essays in Postcritical Scriptural Interpretation*. Mahwah, N.J.: Paulist Press, 1993.

O'Connell, Marvin Richard. *Blaise Pascal: Reasons of the Heart*. Grand Rapids, Mich.: Eerdmans, 1997.

Olin, Margaret. "Touching Photographs: Roland Barthes's 'Mistaken' Identification." *Representations* 80 (Fall 2002): 99–118.

O'Brien, Flann. *The Best of Myles*. Normal, Ill.: Dalkey Archive, 1999.

Otten, Thomas J. *A Superficial Reading of Henry James: Preoccupations with the Material World*. Columbus: Ohio State University Press, 2006.

Ouaknin, M. A. *The Burnt Book: Reading the Talmud*. Translated by Llewellyn Brown. Princeton: Princeton University Press, 1995.

Oz, Amos, and Fania Oz-Salzberger. *Jews and Words*. New Haven: Yale University Press, 2012.

Pagis, Dan. *The Selected Poetry of Dan Pagis*. Translated by Stephen Mitchell. Berkeley: University of California Press, 1989.

Palmieri, Giovanni. "'The Author' According to Bakhtin . . . and Bakhtin the Author." In *The Contexts of Bakhtin: Philosophy, Authorship, Aesthetics*, 45–56. Amsterdam: Harwood, 1998.

Palumbo-Liu, David. *The Deliverance of Others: Reading Literature in the Global Age*. Durham, N.C.: Duke University Press, 2012.

Pardes, Ilana. *The Biography of Ancient Israel: National Narratives in the Bible*. Berkeley: University of California Press, 2002.

Park, Ed. "The Outsiders: John MacGregor Unlocks Henry Darger's Unreal Realms." *The Village Voice*, April 16, 2002.

Parker, David. *Ethics, Theory and the Novel*. Cambridge: Cambridge University Press, 1994.

Parsons, Anne E. "From Asylum to Prison: The Story of the Lincoln State School." *Journal of Illinois History* 14 (Winter 2011): 242–260.

Pascal, Blaise. *Le mémorial*. Translated by Elizabeth T. Knuth. Edited by Olivier Joseph. www.users.csbsju.edu/~eknuth/pascal.html.

———. *The Memorial*. Translated by A. J. Krailsheimer. London: Penguin Classics, 1966.

———. *Pensées*. Translated by A. J. Krailsheimer. London: Penguin Classics, 1995.

Paterson, Mark. *The Senses of Touch: Haptics, Affects and Technologies*. New York: Berg, 2007.

Patt, Lise, ed. *Searching for Sebald: Photography after W.G. Sebald*. Los Angeles: Institute of Cultural Inquiry Press, 2007.

Patterson, David. "Bakhtin and Levinas: Signification, Responsibility, Spirit." In *Literature and Spirit: Essays on Bakhtin and His Contemporaries*, 98–127. Lexington: University of Kentucky Press, 1988.

———. *Hebrew Language and Jewish Thought*. Routledge: New York, 2005.

Pattison, George. *Thinking about God in an Age of Technology*. Oxford: Oxford University Press, 2005.

Paumgarten, Nick. "The Names," *The New Yorker*, May 16, 2011.

Pavel, Thomas. *Fictional Worlds*. Cambridge, Mass.: Harvard University Press, 1989.

Pechey, Graham. *Mikhail Bakhtin: The Word in the World*. London: Routledge, 2007.

Penney, D., and P. Stastny. *The Lives They Left Behind: Suitcases from a State Hospital Attic*. New York: Bellevue Literary Press, 2009.

Percy, Walker. *The Moviegoer*. New York: Vintage, 1998.

Perelmuter, Rosa. "Yiddish in Cuba: A Love Story." *Hispanófila: Ensayos de Literatura* 157 (2009): 117–132.

Pesikta de Rav Kahana (Pesikta de-Rab Kahana). Translated by William G. Braude and Israel J. Kapstein. Philadelphia: Jewish Publication Society, 1975.

Peters, Gary. "The Rhythm of Alterity: Levinas and Aesthetics." *Radical Philosophy* 82 (March–April 1997): 9–16.

Phelan, James. *Experiencing Fiction: Judgments, Progressions, and the Rhetorical Theory of Narrative*. Columbus: Ohio State University Press, 2007.

———. "Sethe's Choice: *Beloved* and the Ethics of Reading." In *Mapping the Ethical Turn: A Reader in Ethics, Culture, and Literary Theory*, edited by Todd F. Davis and Kenneth Womack, 93–109. Charlottesville: University of Virginia Press, 2001.

Phillips, Tom. *A Humument: A Treated Victorian Novel* (5th edition). London: Thames and Hudson, 2012.

"Philologos." "Sephardic Arks." *The Forward*, January 2, 2004.

———. "Studying or Learning?" *The Forward*, March 30, 2007.

Pinchevski, Amit. *By Way of Interruption: Levinas and the Ethics of Communication* Pittsburgh: Duquesne University Press, 2005.

Pinsker, Shachar. "Intertextuality, Rabbinic Literature, and the Making of Hebrew Modernism." In *Jewish Literatures and Cultures: Context and Intertext*, edited by Anita Norich and Yaron Z. Eliav, 201–228. Providence, R.I.: Brown University Press.

———. *Literary Passports: The Making of Modernist Hebrew Fiction in Europe*. Stanford: Stanford University Press, 2011.

———. "'Never Will I Hear the Sweet Voice of God': Religiosity and Mysticism in Modern Hebrew Poetry." *Prooftexts* 30, no. 1 (Winter 2010): 128–146.

———. "What Is Jewish Literature?" *The New Republic*, December 8, 2011.

Poirié, Francois. *Emmanuel Levinas. Qui êtes-vous?* Lyon: La Manifacture, 1987.

Poirier, John C. "Why Did the Pharisees Wash Their Hands?" *Journal of Jewish Studies* 47 (1996): 217–233.

Poirier, Richard. *Robert Frost: The Wortk of Knowing*. New York: Oxford University Press, 1977.

Polakow-Suransky, Sasha. "The Invisible Victims: Undocumented Workers at the World Trade Center." *The American Prospect, Online Edition* 12, no. 21 (December 3, 2001), http://prospect.org/article/invisible-victims.

Polan, Dana. Review of Edward Said's *The World, the Text and the Critic. Poetics Today* 6, no. 3 (1985): 537–538.

Polansky, Ronald. *Commentary on Aristotle's De Anima*. Cambridge: Cambridge University Press, 2008.

Ponzio, Augusto. *Man as a Sign: Essays on the Philosophy of Language*. Translated by Susan Petrilli. New York: Mouton de Gruyter, 1990.

———. *Signs, Dialogue, and Ideology*. Translated by Susan Petrilli. Philadelphia: John Benjamins Publishing, 1993.

Ponzio, Augusto, and Susan Petrilli. *Semiotics Unbounded: Interpretive Routes Through the Open Network of Signs*. Toronto: University of Toronto Press, 2005.

Popek, Michael. *Forgotten Bookmarks: A Bookseller's Collection of Odd Things Lost Between the Pages*. New York: Perigee Books, 2011.

Poulet, Georges. "New and Old History." *New Literary History* 1, no. 1 (October 1969): 53–68.

Price, Daniel M. *Touching Difficulty: Sacred Form from Plato to Derrida*. Aurora, Colo.: Davies Group, 2009.

Price, Leah. *How to Do Things with Books in Victorian Britain*. Princeton: Princeton University Press, 2012.

———. *Unpacking My Library: Writers and Their Books*. New Haven: Yale University Press, 2011.

Priest, Christopher. *The Prestige*. New York: Tom Doherty Associates, 1995.

Proust, Marcel. *On Reading Ruskin*. Translated by Jean Autret and William Burford. New Haven: Yale University, 1971.

Putnam, Hilary. *Jewish Philosophy as a Guide to Life: Rosenzweig, Buber, Levinas, Wittgenstein.* Bloomington: Indiana University Press, 2008.

Rabinbach, Anson. "Critique and Commentary/Alchemy and Chemistry: Some Remarks on Walter Benjamin." *New German Critique* 17 (Spring 1979): 3–14.

Rawidowicz, Simon. *State of Israel, Diaspora, and Jewish Continuity: Essays on the "Ever-Dying People."* Waltham, Mass.: Brandeis University Press, 1986.

Read, Rupert, and Jerry Goodenough, eds. *Film as Philosophy: Essays in Cinema After Wittgenstein and Cavell.* New York: Palgrave Macmillan, 2005.

Reed, Walter L. *Dialogues of the Word: The Bible as Literature According to Bakhtin.* New York: Oxford University Press, 1993.

——. *An Exemplary History of the Novel.* Chicago: University of Chicago Press, 1981.

Reilly, Kara. *Automata and Mimesis on the Stage of Theatre.* New York: Palgrave Macmillan, 2011.

Reiter, Paul. "Comparative Literature in Exile: Said and Auerbach." In *Exile and Otherness: New Approaches to the Experience of the Nazi Refugees,* edited by Alexander Stephan, 21–30. Bern: Peter Lang, 2005.

Remnick, David. "Philip Roth's Eightieth-Birthday Celebration." *The New Yorker* (March 20, 2013).

Rendall, Steven. "Notes on Zohn's Translation of Benjamin's '*Die Aufgabe des Übersetzers.*'" *TTR: traduction, terminologie, redaction* 10, no. 2 (1997): 191–206.

Renfrew, Alistair. *Towards a New Materialist Aesthetics: Bakhtin, Genre, and the Fates of Literary Theory.* London: Legenda, 2006.

Rhu, Lawrence. *Stanley Cavell's American Dream: Shakespeare, Philosophy, and Hollywood Movies.* New York: Fordham University Press, 2006.

Rich, Nathaniel. "Storm of Creativity." *The New Republic,* January 5, 2005.

Richter, Gerhard. *Thought-images: Frankfurt School Writers' Reflections from Damaged Life.* Stanford: Stanford University Press, 2007.

Ricoeur, Paul. *The Course of Recognition.* Translated by David Pellauer. Cambridge, Mass.: Harvard University Press, 2005.

——. *From Text to Action: Essays in Hermeneutics II.* Translated by Kathleen Blamey and John B. Thompson. Evanston, Ill.: Northwestern University Press, 1991.

——. *Hermeneutics and the Human Sciences: Essays on Language, Action and Interpretation.* Translated by John B. Thompson. Cambridge: Cambridge University Press, 1981.

——. *Interpretation Theory: Discourse and the Surplus of Meaning.* Translated by David Pellauer et al. Fort Worth: Texas Christian University Press, 1976.

——. *Oneself as Another.* Translated by Kathleen Blamey. Chicago: University Of Chicago Press, 1995.

——. *Time and Narrative, Volume 3.* Translated by Kathleen Blamey and David Pellaver. Chicago: University of Chicago Press, 1988.

Roberts, Jonathan. "Wordsworth's Apocalypse." *Literature and Theology* 20, no. 4 (December 2006): 361–378.

Robbins, Bruce. "Said and Secularism." In *Edward Said and Jacques Derrida: Reconstellating Humanism and the Global Hybrid*, edited by Mina Karavantas and Nina Morgan, 140–157. Cambridge: CSP, 2008.

———. *Secular Vocations: Intellectuals, Professionalism, Culture*. London: Verso, 1993.

———. "Secularism, Elitism, Progress, and Other Transgressions: On Edward Said's 'Voyage In.'" *Social Text* 40 (1994): 25–37.

Robbins, Jill. *Altered Reading: Levinas and Literature*. Chicago: University of Chicago Press, 1999.

———. "An Inscribed Responsibility: Levinas's *Difficult Freedom*." *Modern Language Notes* 106 (1991): 1052–1062.

———. *Prodigal Son/Elder Brother: Interpretation and Alterity in Augustine, Petrarch, Kafka, Levinas*. Chicago: University of Chicago Press, 1991.

Rodowick, D. N. "An Elegy for Theory." *October* 121 (Summer 2007): 99–110.

———. "Ethics in Film Philosophy (Cavell, Deleuze, Levinas)." http://isites. harvard .edu/fs/docs/icb.topic242308.files/RodowickETHICSweb.pdf.

———. *The Virtual Life of Film*. Cambridge, Mass.: Harvard University Press, 2007.

Rogers, Ben. "Pascal's Life and Times." In *The Cambridge Companion to Pascal*, edited by Nicholas Hammond, 4–19. Cambridge: Cambridge University Press, 2003.

Rogovoy, Seth. "Ben Katchor." *The Berkshire Web* (August 1, 2000), www.berkshireweb .com/rogovoy/interviews/feat000802.html.

Rojtman, Betty. *Black Fire on White Fire: An Essay on Jewish Hermeneutics from Midrash to Kabbalah*. Translated by Steven Randall. Berkeley: University of California Press, 1998.

Rokem, Freddie. *Philosophers and Thespians: Thinking Performance*. Stanford: Stanford University Press, 2010.

Rooney, Ellen. "Live Free or Describe: The Reading Effect and the Persistence of Form." *differences* 21, no. 3 (2010): 112–139.

Rorty, Richard. *Contingency, Irony, and Solidarity*. Cambridge: Cambridge University Press, 1989.

Rosenberg, Shalom. "Uncollected Recollections of Shoshani" (in Hebrew). *'Amudim* (1995): 135–137.

Rosenstock, Bruce. *Philosophy and the Jewish Question: Mendelssohn, Rosenzweig, and Beyond*. New York: Fordham University Press, 2009.

Rosenzweig, Franz. *Der Stern der Erlösung*. Translated by Barbara E. Galli. Madison: University of Wisconsin Press, 2005.

———. "Die Schrift und Luther." In *Das Problem des Übersetzens*, 220–248. Edited by H. J. Störig. Darmstadt, 1963.

———. *Franz Rosenzweig and Jehuda Halevi: Translating, Translations, and Translators*. Translated by Barbara E. Galli. Montreal: McGill Queens University Press, 1995.

———. *Franz Rosenzweig, Der Mensch und sein Werk. Gesammelte Schriften. IV. Bd: Sprachdenken im Übersetzen. 1. Bd.: Fünfundzwanzig Hymnen und Gedichte*. Edited by Rafael N. Rosenzweig. The Hague: Martinus Nijhoff, 1983.

————. *Franz Rosenzweig, Der Mensch und sein Werk. Gesammelte Schriften. IV. Bd: Sprachdenken im Übersetzen. 2. Bd.: Arbeitspapiere zur Verdeutschung der Schrift.* Edited by Rachel Bat-Adam. Martinus. The Hague: Nijhoff, 1984.

————. *Franz Rosenzweig: His Life and Thought.* Edited by Nahum Glatzer. New York: Schocken, 1961.

————. *Franz Rosenzweig's "The New Thinking."* Translated by Alan Udoff and Barbara Ellen Galli. Syracuse: Syracuse University Press, 1999.

————. "Neuhebräisch? Anlässlich der Übersetzung von Spinozas Kritik." In *Zweistromland, Kleinere Schriften zu Glauben und Denken*, 723–729. The Hague: Martinus Nijhoff, 1984.

————. *Ninety-Two Poems and Hymns of Yehuda Halevi.* Translated by Thomas A. Kovach, Eva Jospe, and Gilya Gerda Schmidt. Albany: State University of New York Press, 2000.

————. *On Jewish Learning.* Edited by N. N. Glatzer. Madison: University of Wisconsin Press, 2002.

————. *Understanding the Sick and the Healthy: A View of World, Man, and God.* Translated by Nahum Glatzer. Cambridge, Mass.: Harvard University Press, 1999.

Rosenzweig, Franz, and Martin Buber. "Scripture and Luther." In *Scripture and Translation*, 47–69. Translated by Lawrence Rosenwald with Everett Fox. Bloomington: Indiana University Press, 1994.

Rosner, Fred. *Encyclopedia of Medicine in the Bible and the Talmud.* Northvale, N.J.: Jason Aronson, 2000.

Roth, Laurence. "Unpacking my Father's Bookstore." In *Modern Jewish Literatures: Intersections and Boundaries*, edited by Sheila E. Jelen, Michael P. Kramer, and L. Scott Lerner, 280–302. Philadelphia: University of Pennsylvania Press, 2011.

Roth, Philip. *Goodbye, Columbus.* New York: Vintage, 1994.

————. *Sabbath's Theater.* New York: Houghton Mifflin, 1995.

Rothman, William, and Marian Keane. *Reading Cavell's The World Viewed: A Philosophical Perspective on Film.* Detroit: Wayne State University Press, 2000.

Rousseau, Jean Jacques. *On the Origin of Language.* Translated by John H. Moran and Alexander Gode. Chicago: University of Chicago Press, 1986.

————. *Politics and the Arts: Letter to M. D'Alembert on the Theatre.* Edited and translated by Allan Bloom. New York: Free Press, 1960.

Rubenstein, Jeffrey L. *The Culture of the Babylonian Talmud.* Baltimore: Johns Hopkins University Press, 2003.

————. *Talmudic Stories: Narrative Art, Composition, and Culture.* Baltimore: Johns Hopkins University Press, 1999.

Rubin, Andrew. "Techniques of Trouble: Edward Said and the Dialectics of Cultural Philology." *The South Atlantic Quarterly* 102, no. 4 (Fall 2003): 861–876.

Ruiz, Albor. "Giving a Voice to Immigrant Victims of 9/11 and Aiding Families." *New York Daily News*, September 11, 2011.

Rundquist, Leisa. "Pyre: A Poetics of Fire and Childhood in the Art of Henry Darger." Ph.D. dissertation, University of North Carolina, 2007.

Runia, David T. *Philo and the Church Fathers: A Collection of Papers.* Leiden: Brill, 1995.

Russell, Charles. *Groundwaters: A Century of Art by Self-Taught and Outsider Artists.* New York: Prestel Verlag, 2011.

Russo, Teresa G., ed. *Recognition and Modes of Knowledge: Anagnorisis from Antiquity to Contemporary Theory.* Edmonton: University of Alberta Press, 2013.

Rustow, Marina, and A. I. Baumgarten. "Judaism and Tradition: Continuity, Change, and Innovation." *Jewish Studies at the Crossroads*, 207–237.

Sacks, Oliver. *A Leg to Stand On.* New York: Touchstone, 1984.

Sadan, Dov. *Ḥayim Naḥman Byaliḳ ve-darkho bi-leshono u-leshonoteha.* Tel Aviv: Hotsa'at ha-Kibuts ha-me'uḥad, 1989.

Saenger, Paul. *Space Between Words: The Origins of Silent Reading.* Stanford: Stanford University Press, 1997.

Sáenz-Badillo, Ángel. "Abraham ibn Ezra and the Twelfth-Century European Renaissance." In *Hebrew Language and Jewish Culture*, edited by Martin F. J. Baasten and Reiner Munk, 1–20. Dordrecht: Springer, 2007.

———. *A History of the Hebrew Language.* Translated by John Elwolde. Cambridge, England: Cambridge University Press, 1996.

Sagi, Avi. *The Open Canon: On the Meaning of Halakhic Discourse.* Translated by Batya Stein. New York: Continuum Books, 2007.

Said, Edward. "Adorno as Lateness Itself." In *Adorno: A Critical Reader*, edited by Nigel Gibson and Andrew Rubin, 193–208. Oxford: Blackwell, 2002.

———. *Beginnings: Intention and Method.* New York: Columbia University Press, 1985.

———. "Diary." *The London Review of Books* 22, no. 11 (1 June 2000): 42–43.

———. *Edward Said: A Critical Reader.* Edited by Michael Sprinker. Oxford: Wiley-Blackwell, 1993.

———. *Freud and the Non-European.* London: Verso, 2003.

———. *Humanism and Democratic Criticism.* New York: Columbia University Press, 2004.

———. "An Interview with Edward Said." In *Conrad in the Twenty-First Century: Contemporary Approaches and Perspectives*, edited by Carola M. Kaplan, Peter Mallios, and Andrea White, 283–304. New York: Routledge, 2005.

———. *On Late Style: Music and Literature Against the Grain.* New York: Pantheon Books, 2006.

———. *Orientalism.* New York: Vintage, 1978.

———. *Reflections on Exile and Other Essays.* Cambridge, Mass.: Harvard University Press, 2000.

———. *The World, the Text, and the Critic.* Cambridge, Mass.: Harvard University Press, 1983.

Saint-Cheron, Michaël de. *Conversations with Emmanuel Lévinas, 1983–1994.* Pittsburgh: Duquesne University Press, 2010.

Saitō, Tamaki. *Beautiful Fighting Girl.* Translated by J. Keith Vincent and Dawn Lawson. Minneapolis: University of Minnesota Press, 2011.

Salinger, J. D. *The Catcher in the Rye.* New York: Penguin Books, 1994.

Salter, James. "The Art of Fiction 133." *The Paris Review* (1993).

Samet, R. Elchanan. "The Sin of the Spies." *The Israel Koschitzky Virtual Beit Midrash,* www.vbm-torah.org/parsha.60/37shelah.htm.

Sandford, Stella. *The Metaphysics of Love: Gender and Transcendence in Levinas.* London: Athlone Press, 2000.

Sante, Luc. *Low Life: Lures and Snares of Old New York.* New York: Farrar, Straus and Giroux, 1991.

Santner, Eric. *On Creaturely Life: Rilke, Benjamin, Sebald.* Chicago: University of Chicago Press, 2006.

———. *The Psychotheology of Everyday Life: Reflections on Freud and Rosenzweig.* Chicago: University of Chicago Press, 2005.

Sartre, Jean-Paul. *What Is Literature? and Other Essays.* Translated by Bernard Frechtman. Cambridge, Mass.: Harvard University Press, 1988.

Scarry, Elaine. *Dreaming by the Book.* Princeton: Princeton University Press, 2001.

———. "On Vivacity: The Difference between Daydreaming and Imagining-Under-Authorial-Instruction." *Representations* 52 (Autumn 1995): 1–26.

———. "Poetry Changed the World: Injury and the Ethics of Reading." *Boston Review* (July–August 2012).

———. "Work and the Body in Hardy and Other Nineteenth-Century Novelists." *Representations* 3 (Summer 1983): 90–123.

Schacter, Allison. *Diasporic Modernisms: Hebrew and Yiddish in the Twentieth Century.* New York: Oxford University Press, 2012.

Schama, Simon. *The Story of the Jews: Finding the Words 1000 BCE–1492 CE.* London: The Bodley Head, 2013.

Schmiedgen, Peter. "Art and Idolatry: Aesthetics and Alterity in Levinas." *Contretemps* 3 (July 2002): 148–160.

Scholem, Gershom. "At the Completion of Buber's Translation of the Bible." In *The Messianic Idea in Judaism,* 314–319. New York: Schocken, 1971.

———. "Bekenntnis über unsere Sprache." *Franz Rosenzweig, zum 25 Dezember, 1926. Glückwünsche zum 40. Geburtstag.* Translated by Martin Goldner. New York: Leo Baeck Institute of New York, 1987.

———. *Lamentations of Youth: The Diaries of Gershom Scholem 1913–1919.* Translated by Anthony David Skinner. Cambridge, Mass.: Harvard University Press, 2007.

———. "My Way to Kabbalah." *On the Possibility of Jewish Mysticism in Our Time and Other Essays.* Translated by Jonathan Chipman. Edited by Avraham Shapira. Philadelphia: Jewish Publication Society 1997.

———. *'Od Davar.* Tel Aviv: Am Oved, 1986.

———. *Origins of the Kabbalah.* Translated by Allan Arkush. Princeton: Princeton University Press, 1987.

Schrijver, Emile G. L. "The Transmission of Jewish Knowledge through MSS and Printed Books." In *The Oxford Companion to the Book*, edited by Michael F. Suarez and H. R. Woudhuysen, 66–73. Oxford: Oxford University Press, 2010.

Schulte Nordholt, Annelise. "Tentation esthétique et exigence éthique: Lévinas et l'oeuvre littéraire." *Études littéraires* 31, no. 3 (1999): 69–85.

Schulz, Bruno. *The Cinnamon Shops*. Translated by John Curran Davis. www.schulzian .net/translation/shops/krokodyli.htm.

———. *Letters and Drawings of Bruno Schulz*. Translated by Walter Arndt. New York: Harper & Row, 1988.

Schwartz, Baruch, J. David P. Wright, Jeffrey Stackert, and Naphtali S. Meschel, eds. *Perspectives on Purity and Purification in the Bible*. New York: T&T Clark, 2008.

Scorsese, Martin, and John Logan. *Hugo*. Paramount Pictures, 2011.

Searle, John. "Reiterating the Differences: A Reply to Derrida." *Glyph* 2 (1977): 198–208.

Sebald, W. G. *The Emigrants*. Translated by Michael Hulse. New York: New Directions, 1992.

Secunda, Shai. *The Iranian Talmud: Reading the Bavli in Its Sassanian Context*. Philadelphia: University of Pennsylvania Press, 2013.

Sedgwick, Eve Kosofsky. *Epistemology of the Closet*. Berkeley: University of California Press, 1990.

Segal, Eliezer. "Midrash and Literature: Some Medieval Views." *Prooftexts* 11, no. 1 (January 1991): 57–65.

Segal, Miryam. *A New Sound in Hebrew Poetry: Poetics, Politics, Accent*. Bloomington: Indiana University Press, 2010.

Segedin, Leo. "Henry Darger: The Inside of an Outsider." www.leopoldsegedin.com/ essay_detail_darger.cfm.

Seidman, Naomi. "Diaspora and Translation: The Migrations of Jewish Meanings." In *Jewish Literatures and Cultures: Context and Intercontext*, edited by Anita Norich and Yaron Z. Eliav, 245–258. Providence, R.I.: Brown University Press, 2008.

———. *A Marriage Made in Heaven: The Sexual Politics of Hebrew and Yiddish*. Berkeley: University of California Press, 2004.

Selznick, Brian. *The Invention of Hugo Cabret*. New York: Scholastic Books, 2007.

Septimus, Zvi. "Trigger Words and Simultexts: The Experience of Reading the Bavli." In *Wisdom of Bat Sheva: In Memory of Beth Samuels*, edited by Barry Scott Wimpfheimer, 163–185. Jersey City, N.J.: Ktav, 2009.

Serpell, C. Namwali. "Of Being Bridge." *The Comparatist* 36 (May 2012): 4–23.

———. *Seven Modes of Uncertainty*. Cambridge, Mass.: Harvard University, 2014.

Serres, Michel. *The Five Senses: A Philosophy of Mingled Bodies*. Translated by Margaret Sankey and Peter Cowley. New York: Continuum, 2008.

Shahar, Galil. "The Sacred and the Unfamiliar: Gershom Scholem and the Anxieties of the New Hebrew." *The Germanic Review: Literature, Culture, Theory* 83, no. 4 (2008): 299–320.

Shamir, Ziva. *Be-en 'alilah: sipure Byaliḳ be-ma'gelotehem.* Tel Aviv: Ha-Ḳibuts ha-me'uḥad, 1998.

———. *Hashirah me'ayin timatse: "Art po'etika" bitsirat Byalik.* Tel Aviv: Papyrus, 1987.

Sharpe, Matthew. "Aesthet(h)ics: On Levinas' Shadow." *Colloquy: Text Theory Critique* 9 (2005): 29–47.

Shatz, David. "The Biblical and Rabbinic Background to Medieval Jewish Philosophy." *The Cambridge Companion to Medieval Jewish Philosophy*, edited by Daniel H. Frank and Oliver Leaman, 16–37. Cambridge: Cambridge University Press, 2003.

Shaw, Lytle. "The Moral Storm." *Cabinet Magazine* 3 (Summer 2001).

Shepherd, David, ed. *The Contexts of Bakhtin: Philosophy, Authorship, Aesthetics.* Amsterdam: Harwood Academic Publishers, 1998.

———. "A Feeling for History? Bakhtin and 'The Problem of Great Time.'" *Slavonic and East European Review* 84, no. 1 (2006): 31–59.

Sherman, Daniel J. "Naming and the Violence of Place." In *Terror, Culture, Politics: Rethinking 9/11*, edited by Daniel J. Sherman and Terry Nardin, 121–148. Bloomington: Indiana University Press, 2006.

Shohat, Ella, and Robert Stam. "The Cinema After Babel: Language, Difference, Power." *Screen* 26, nos. 3–4 (1985): 35–58.

Sicker, Martin. *An Introduction to Judaic Thought and Rabbinic Literature.* New York: Praeger, 2007.

Siebers, Tobin. *The Ethics of Criticism.* Ithaca: Cornell University Press, 1988.

Simmel, Georg. "The Metropolis and Mental Life." In *On Individuality and Social Forms*, edited by Donald Levine, 324–339. Chicago: University of Chicago Press, 1971.

———. "Two Essays (The Handle and the Ruin)." Translated by Rudolph H. Weingartner. *Hudson Review* 11, no. 3 (Autumn 1958): 371–385.

Simon-Shoshan, Moshe. *Stories of the Law: Narrative Discourse and the Construction of Authority in the Mishnah.* New York: Oxford University Press, 2012.

Sloterdijk, Peter. *Bubbles: Spheres Volume I: Microspherology.* Translated by Wieland Hoban. Cambridge, Mass., MIT Press, 2011.

———. "Rules for the Human Zoo: A Response to the *Letter on Humanism*." Translated by Mary Varney Rorty. *Environment and Planning D: Society and Space* 27 (2009): 12–28.

———. *You Must Change Your Life.* Translated by Wieland Hoban. Malden, Mass.: Polity Press, 2013.

Smith, Adam. *The Theory of Moral Sentiments.* Oxford: Clarendon Press, 1976.

Smith, Joseph H., and William Kerrigan, eds. *Cavell, Psychoanalysis, and Cinema.* Baltimore: Johns Hopkins University Press, 1987.

Smith, Kenneth Clay. "The Book as Material Instrument: London Literary Publishing, 1885–1900." Ph.D. dissertation, Indiana University, 2006.

Smith, Les W. *Confession in the Novel: Bakhtin's Author Revisited.* Cranbury, N.J.: Associated University Presses, 1996.

Smith, Murray, and Thomas E. Wartenberg, eds. *Thinking Through Cinema: Film as Philosophy.* Malden, Mass.: Wiley-Blackwell, 2006.

Snart, Jason Allen. *The Torn Book: Unreading William Blake's Marginalia*. Cranbury, N.J.: Rosemont, 2006.

Snyder, Joel. "Benjamin on Reproducibility and Aura: A Reading of 'The Work of Art in the Age of its Technical Reproducibility.'" In *Benjamin: Philosophy, Aesthetics, History*, edited by Gary Smith, 158–174. Chicago: University of Chicago Press, 1989.

———. "What Happens by Itself in Photographs?" In *Pursuits of Reason: Essays in Honour of Stanley Cavell*, edited by Ted Cohen, Paul Guyer, and Hilary Putnam, 361–373. Lubbock: Texas Tech University Press, 1993.

Söffner, Jan. "On Nostalgia (and Homer)." In *Habitus in Habitat I: Emotion and Motion*, edited by Sabine Flach, Daniel Margulies, and Jan Söffner, 81–91. Bern: Peter Lang, 2011.

Soloveitchik, Rabbi Joseph B. "A Yid iz Geglaykhn tzu a Seyfer Toyre." Translated by Shaul Seidler-Feller. In *Beit Yosef Shaul*, edited by R. Elchanan Asher Adler, 17–67. New York: Rabbi Isaac Elchanan Theological Seminary, 1994.

———. *An Exalted Evening: The Seder Night*. New York: Ktav, 2009.

———. "On the Love of Torah." In *The Shebuot Reader*, 8–12. New York: Tebah Educational Services, 2009.

Sommer, Doris. *Bilingual Aesthetics: A New Sentimental Education*. Durham, N.C.: Duke University Press, 2004.

———. *Proceed with Caution, When Engaged by Minority Writing in the Americas*. Cambridge, Mass.: Harvard University Press, 1999.

Speina, Jerzy. "Bankructwo realnosci: Proza Brunona Schulza." *Towarzystwo Naukowe w Toruniu: Prace Wydzialu Filologicznego-Filozoficznego* 24, no. 1 (1974).

Sperber, Daniel. *Why Jews Do What They Do: The History of Jewish Customs Throughout the Cycle of the Jewish Year*. Hoboken, N.J.: Ktav, 1999.

Spinoza, Benedict. *Theologico-Political Treatise*. Translated by Samuel Shirley. Indianapolis: Hackett, 1998.

Stallybrass, Peter. "Books and Scrolls: Navigating the Bible." In *Books and Readers in Early Modern England: Material Studies*, edited by Jennifer Andersen and Elizabeth Sauer, 42–79. Philadelphia: University of Pennsylvania Press, 2004.

Standish, Paul. "Education for Grown-Ups, a Religion for Adults: Skepticism and Alterity in Cavell and Levinas." *Ethics and Education* 2, no. 1 (2007): 73–91.

Stanford Encyclopedia of Philosophy. Online edition. http://plato.stanford.edu.

Stein, Dina. *Textual Mirrors: Reflexivity, Midrash, and the Rabbinic Self*. Philadelphia: University of Pennsylvania Press, 2012.

Steinby, Liisa, and Tintti Klapuri, eds. *Bakhtin and His Others: (Inter)subjectivity, Chronotope, Dialogism*. London: Anthem Press, 2103.

Stern, David. "Literary Criticism or Literary Homilies? Susan Handelman and the Contemporary Study of Midrash." *Prooftexts* 5, no. 1 (January 1985): 96–103.

———. "Rabbinics and Jewish Identity: An American Perspective." In *Jewish Thought and Jewish Belief*, edited by Daniel J. Lasker, 7–26. Bersheva: Ben Gurion University Press, 2012.

Sternberg, Meir. *The Poetics of Biblical Narrative: Ideological Literature and the Drama of Reading*. Bloomington: Indiana University Press, 1987.

Stewart, Garrett. *Between Film and Screen: Modernism's Photo Synthesis*. Chicago: University of Chicago Press, 2000.

———. *Bookwork: Medium to Object to Concept to Art*. Chicago: University of Chicago Press, 2011.

———. *Framed Time: Toward a Postfilmic Cinema*. Chicago: University of Chicago Press, 2007.

———. *The Look of Reading: Book, Painting, Text*. Chicago: University of Chicago Press, 2006.

———. *Novel Violence: A Narratography of Victorian Fiction*. Chicago: University Of Chicago Press, 2009.

———. "Painted Readers, Narrative Regress." *Narrative* 11, no. 2 (May 2003): 125–176.

Stewart, Susan. *On Longing: Narratives of the Miniature, the Gigantic, the Souvenir, the Collection*. Durham, N.C.: Duke University Press, 1993.

Stokes, Mark. *Revolutions of the Night: The Enigma of Henry Darger*. Quale Films, 2012.

Stokes, Melvyn, and Richard Maltby, eds. *Hollywood Spectatorship: Changing Perceptions of Cinema Audiences*. London: British Film Institute, 2008.

Stone, Ira. *Reading Levinas/Reading Talmud: An Introduction*. Philadelphia: Jewish Publication Society, 1998.

Stow, Kenneth. *Jewish Dogs: An Image and Its Interpreters*. Stanford: Stanford University Press, 2006.

Stow, Simon. *Republic of Readers? The Literary Turn in Political Thought and Analysis*. Albany: State University of New York Press, 2007.

Strack, Hermann, and Gunter Stemberger. *Introduction to the Talmud and Midrash*. Minneapolis: Fortress Press, 1996.

Sturken, Marita. "The Aesthetics of Absence: Rebuilding Ground Zero." *American Ethnologist* 31, no. 3 (2004): 311–325.

———. "The Wall, the Screen, and the Image: The Vietnam Veterans Memorial." *Representations* 35 (Summer 1991): 118–142.

Suarez, Michael, and H. R. Woudhuysen, eds. *The Oxford Companion to the Book*. Oxford: Oxford University Press, 2010.

Suchoff, David. "Family Resemblances: Ludwig Wittgenstein as a Jewish Philosopher." *Bamidbar* 1 (2012): 74–89.

———. *Kafka's Jewish Languages: The Hidden Openness of Tradition*. Philadelphia: University of Pennsylvania Press, 2011.

Sussman, Henry. *Around the Book: Systems and Literacy*. New York: Fordham University Press, 2010.

Swartz, Michael D. "Jewish Visionary Tradition in Rabbinic Literature." In *The Cambridge Companion to the Talmud and Rabbinic Literature*, edited by Charlotte E. Fonrobert and Martin S. Jaffee, 198–221. Cambridge: Cambridge University Press, 2007.

Swiss, Jamy Ian. *Devious Standards*. Seattle: Hermetic Press, 2011.

———. *Shattering Illusions*. Seattle: Hermetic Press, 2002.

Talmud. Soncino Edition (English). Edited by Rabbi Isidore Epstein. New York: Bloch, 1990.

Talmud Bavli. Translated and edited by Adin Steinsaltz. Jerusalem: Ha- Makhon ha-Yiśre'eli le-Firsumim Talmudiyim, 1989–2010.

———. *Tractate Chagigah*. Hebrew/English Schottenstein Edition. New York: Mesorah Publications, 2002.

———. *Tractate Chullin*. Hebrew/English Schottenstein Edition. New York: Mesorah Publications, 2003.

———. *Tractate Megillah*. Hebrew/English Schottenstein Edition. New York: Mesorah Publications, 1991.

———. *Tractate Shabbos Vols. 1 and 3*. Hebrew/English Schottenstein Edition. New York: Mesorah Publishers, 2003.

Talmud Bavli Koren: Tractate Shabbat Vols. 2 and 3. Hebrew/English Steinsaltz Edition. Jerusalem: Koren, 2012.

Talmud Yerushalmi (Jerusalem Talmud). Tractates Šabbat and 'Eruvin. Edited by Heinrich W. Guggenheimer. Berlin: Walter de Gruyter, 2012.

Taragin, R. Moshe. "Is Megillat Esther Patterned after a Sefer Torah?" *Yeshivat Har Etzion Israel Koschitzky Virtual Beit Midrash*, www.vbm-torah.org/archive/metho67/13metho.htm.

Taussig, Michael. *Mimesis and Alterity: A Particular History of the Senses*. New York: Routledge, 1992.

Taylor, Charles. *A Secular Age*. Cambridge, Mass.: Harvard University Press, 2007.

———. *Modern Social Imaginaries*. Durham, N.C.: Duke University Press, 2003.

Tepper, Craig. "The Cavell Cavil." *Film-Philosophy* 6, no. 12 (June 2002).

Theriault, Kim Servart. "Re-membering Vietnam: War, Trauma, and 'Scarring Over' After 'The Wall.'" *Journal of American Culture* 26, no. 4 (December 2003): 421–431.

Theroux, Alexander. "Interview With Ben Katchor." *Bomb* 88 (Summer 2004): 30–35.

Thomson, David. *America in the Dark: Hollywood and the Gift of Unreality*. New York: William Morrow, 1977.

———. *Movie Man*. New York: Stein and Day, 1965.

Thomson, Kristin, and David Bordwell. "*Hugo*: Scorsese's Birthday Present to Georges Méliès." *Observations on Film Art* (December 7, 2011).

Tiupa, Valerii. "The Architectonics of Aesthetic Discourse." In *The Contexts of Bakhtin*, 95–107. London: Routledge, 1998

Todorov, Tzvetan. *Mikhail Bakhtin: The Dialogical Principle*. Translated by Wlad Godzich. Minneapolis: University of Minnesota Press, 1985.

Toumayan, Alain P. *Encountering the Other: The Artwork and the Problem of Difference in Blanchot and Levinas*. Pittsburgh: Duquesne University Press, 2004.

Trent, Mary. "'Many Stirring Scenes': Henry Darger's Reworking of American Visual Culture." *American Art* 26 (Spring 2012): 74–101.

Twersky, Isidore, ed. *A Maimonides Reader*. Springfield, N.J.: Behrman House, 1972.

Twersky, Isidore, and J. M. Harris, eds. *Rabbi Abraham ibn Ezra: Studies in the Writings of a Twelfth-Century Jewish Polymath*. Cambridge, Mass.: Harvard University Press, 1993.

Underhill, Karen. "Ecstasy and Heresy: Buber, Schulz, and Jewish Modernity." In *(Un) Masking Bruno Schulz: New Combinations, Further Fragmentations, Ultimate Reintegrations*, edited by Dieter de Bruyn and Kris Van Heuckelom, 27–47. Amsterdam: Editions Rodopi, 2009.

Urbach, Ephraim E. *The Sages: Their Concepts and Beliefs*. Translated by Israel Abrahams. Cambridge, Mass.: Harvard University Press, 1987.

Valéry, Paul. *Leonardo Poe Mallarmé*. Translated by M. Cowley and J. R. Lawler. Princeton: Princeton University Press, 1972.

Van Heuckelom, Kris. "Artistic Crossover in Polish Modernism: The Case of Bruno Schulz's *Xiega Balwochwalcza* (The Idolatrous Booke)." *Image & Narrative* (November 2006), www.imageandnarrative.be/inarchive/iconoclasm/heuckelom.htm.

Vattimo, Gianni. *Art's Claim to Truth*. Translated by Luca D'Isanto. New York: Columbia University Press, 2008.

Vattimo, Gianni, and Jacques Derrida. *Religion*. Translated by David Webb et al. Stanford: Stanford University Press, 1998.

Verbeek, Peter-Paul. *What Things Do: Philosophical Reflections on Technology, Agency, and Design*. Philadelphia: University of Pennsylvania Press, 2005.

Vice, Sue. *Introducing Bakhtin*. Manchester: Manchester University Press, 1997.

Vinokur, Val. *The Trace of Judaism: Dostoevsky, Babel, Mandelstam, Levinas*. Evanston, Ill.: Northwestern University Press, 2009.

Virilio, Paul. *Open Sky*. Translated by Julie Rose. London: Verso, 2008.

Wall, Anthony. "A Broken Thinker." In *Bakhtin/"Bakhtin": The Archives and Beyond*, 669–698. Durham, N.C.: Duke University Press, 1999.

Waller, Gregory A. *Moviegoing in America: A Sourcebook in the History of Film Exhibition*. London: Wiley-Blackwell, 2001.

Walzer, Michael, Menachem Lorberbaum, Noam J. Zohar, and Yair Lorberbaum, eds. *The Jewish Political Tradition*. New Haven: Yale University Press, 2000–2003.

Watson, Cal. "The Metaphysics of Wreckage: An Introduction to the Autobiography of Henry Darger." In *Henry Darger*, edited by Klaus Biesenbach, 277–281. New York: Prestel Verlag, 2009.

———. "Recollecting Turbulence: Catastrophe and Sacrifice in the 'History of My Life' by Henry Darger." Ph.D. dissertation, City University of New York, 2012.

Watson, Stephen. "Levinas, the Ethics of Deconstruction, and the Remainder of the Sublime." *Man and World* 21 (1988): 35–64.

Watts, Linda. "Reflecting Absence or Presence? Public Space and Historical Memory at Ground Zero." *Space and Culture* 12 (November 2009): 412–418.

Weber, Samuel. "Mass Mediauras, or: Art, Aura and Media in the Work of Walter Benjamin." In *Mass Mediauras: Form, Technics, Media*, edited by Samuel Weber and Alan Cholodenko, 75–207. Stanford: Stanford University Press, 1996.

Weinreich, Uriel. *Languages in Contact: Findings and Problems.* The Hague: Mouton, 1964.

Weiskel, Thomas. *The Romantic Sublime: Studies in the Structure and Psychology of Transcendence.* Baltimore: Johns Hopkins University Press, 1976.

Weiss, Avraham. "Women and *Sifrei Torah.*" *Tradition* 20, no. 2 (Summer 1982): 106–118.

Weiss, Raymond L. *Maimonides' Ethics: The Encounter of Philosophic and Religious Morality.* Chicago: University of Chicago Press, 1991.

Wellek, René, and Austin Warren. *Theory Of Literature: New Revised Edition.* New York: Harcourt Brace, 1984.

Wells, Paul. *Understanding Animation.* New York: Routledge, 1998.

Wells, Paul, Johnny Hardstaff, and Darryl Clifton. *Re-Imagining Animation: The Changing Face of the Moving Image.* Lausanne: AVA Publishing SA, 2008.

Welz, Claudia. "A Wandering Dog as the 'Last Kantian in Nazi Germany': Revisiting the Debate on Levinas's Supposed Antinaturalistic Humanism." *Levinas Studies* 6 (2011): 65–88.

Werner, Marta L. "Helen Keller and Anne Sullivan: Writing Otherwise." *Interval(le)s* II.2–III.1 (Fall 2008–Winter 2009): 958–996.

Williamson, Colin. "The Blow Book, Performance Magic, and Early Animation: Mediating the Living." *Animation* 6 (2011): 111–126.

Wimpfheimer, Barry. *Narrating the Law: A Poetics of Talmudic Legal Stories.* Philadelphia: University of Pennsylvania Press, 2011.

Winner, Langdon. *The Whale and the Reactor: A Search for Limits in an Age of High Technology.* Chicago: University of Chicago Press, 1986.

Wiskind, Ora. "Scholem and Rosenzweig: The Dialectics of History." *History and Memory* 2, no. 2 (Winter 1990): 100–116.

Wittgenstein, Ludwig. *On Certainty.* Translated by Denis Paul and G. E. M. Anscombe. Oxford: Basil Blackwell, 1969.

———. *Philosophical Investigations.* Translated by P. M. S. Hacker and Joachim Schulte. Oxford: Wiley-Blackwell, 2009.

———. *Wittgenstein on Mind and Language.* Edited by David G. Stern. New York: Oxford University Press, 1995.

Wolin, Richard. *Walter Benjamin: An Aesthetic of Redemption.* Berkeley: University of California Press, 1994.

Woloch, Alex. *The One vs. the Many: Minor Characters and the Space of the Protagonist in the Novel.* Princeton: Princeton University Press, 2003.

Wolterstorff, Nicholas. *Divine Discourse: Philosophical Reflections on the Claim That God Speaks.* Cambridge: Cambridge University Press, 1995.

Wood, James. *The Broken Estate: Essays on Literature and Belief.* New York: Picador, 2010.

———. "Shelf Life." *The New Yorker,* November 7, 2011.

Wood, Michael. "The Languages of Cinema." In *Nation, Language, and the Ethics of Translation,* 79–88. Princeton: Princeton University Press, 2005.

Wordsworth, William. *The Prelude: The Four Texts (1798, 1799, 1805, 1850).* Edited by Jonathan Wordsworth. New York: Penguin, 1995.

———. *Prose Works*. Edited by W. J. B. Owen and Jane Worthington Smyser. Oxford: Clarendon, 1974.

Wright, Tamra. *The Twilight of Jewish Philosophy: Emmanuel Lévinas' Ethical Hermeneutics*. Amsterdam: Harwood, 1999.

Wygoda, Shmuel. "Le maître et son disciple: Chouchani et Lévinas." *Cahiers d'études lévinassiennes* 1 (2002): 149–183.

———. "A Phenomenological Outlook at the Talmud: Levinas as Reader of the Talmud." http://ghansel.free.fr/wygoda.html.

Wyschogrod, Edith. "The Art in Ethics, Aesthetics, Objectivity, and Alterity in the Philosophy of Levinas." In *Ethics as First Philosophy: The Significance of Emmanuel Levinas for Philosophy, Literature, and Religion*, edited by Adriaan Theodoor Peperzak, 137–149. London: Routledge, 1995.

———. *Crossover Queries: Dwelling with Negatives, Embodying Philosophy's Others*. New York: Fordham University Press, 2006.

———. "Ethics as First Philosophy: Levinas Reads Spinoza." *The Eighteenth Century* 40, no. 3 (Fall 1999): 195–205.

———. *An Ethics of Remembering: History, Heterology, and the Nameless Others*. Chicago: University of Chicago Press, 1998.

Yadin, Azzan. *Scripture as Logos: Rabbi Ishmael and the Origins of Midrash*. Philadelphia: University of Pennsylvania Press, 2004.

———. "A Web of Chaos: Bialik and Nietzsche on Language, Truth, and the Death of God." *Prooftexts* 21, no. 2 (Spring, 2001): 179–203.

Yager, Susan. "Levinas, Allegory, and Chaucer's *Clerk's Tale*." In *Levinas and Medieval Literature: The "Difficult Reading" of English and Rabbinic Texts*, edited by Ann W. Astell and J. A. Jackson, 35–56. Pittsburgh: Duquesne University Press, 2009.

Yalkut Shimoni: Midrash al Torah, Neviim u-Khetuvim. Jerusalem: Yarid ha-Sefarim, 2006.

Yerushalmi, Yosef Ḥayyim. *Freud's Moses: Judaism Terminable and Interminable*. New Haven: Yale University Press, 1993.

Young, James E. *At Memory's Edge: After-Images of the Holocaust in Contemporary Art and Architecture*. New York: Littauer Foundation, 2000.

———. "The Counter-Monument: Memory against Itself in Germany Today." *Critical Inquiry* 18, no. 2 (Winter, 1992): 267–296.

———. *The Texture of Memory: Holocaust Memorials and Meaning*. New Haven: Yale University Press, 1994.

Yu, Jessica. *In the Realms of the Unreal*. Diorama Films, 2003.

Zahavy, Tsvee, and Jacob Neusner. *How the Halakhah Unfolds: Hullin, Part One and Part Two*. Lanham, Md.: University Press of America, 2010.

———. *The Talmud of Babylonia: An American Translation. XXX.A: Tractate Hullin*. Brown Judaic Studies. Atlanta: Scholars Press, 1994.

Zbinden, Karine, ed. *Bakhtin Between East and West: Cross-Cultural Transmission*. London: Legenda, 2006.

Ziarek, Ewa Płonowska. *The Rhetoric of Failure: Deconstruction of Skepticism, Reinvention of Modernism*. Albany: State University of New York Press, 1996.

Ziegler, Aharon. "Counting a Minor in a Minyan." *Halakhic Positions of Rabbi Joseph B. Soloveitchik: Volume III*. Lanham, Md.: Rowman & Littlefield, 2004.

Žižek, Slavoj, and Friedrich Wilhelm Joseph von Schelling. *The Abyss of Freedom: Ages of the World*. Detroit: University of Michigan Press, 1997.

———. "Neighbors and Other Monsters: A Plea for Ethical Violence." In *The Neighbor: Three Inquiries in Political Theology*, edited by Kenneth Reinhard, Eric L. Santner, and Slavoj Žižek, 134–190. Chicago: University of Chicago Press, 2005.

Zornberg, Avivah Gottleib. *The Particulars of Rapture: Reflections on Exodus*. New York: Schocken Books, 2001.

Zuckermann, Ghil'ad. "'Abba, why was Professor Higgins trying to teach Eliza to speak like our cleaning lady?' Mizrahim, Ashkenazim, Prescriptivism and the Real Sounds of the Israeli Language." *Australian Journal of Jewish Studies* 19 (2005): 210–231.

———. *Language Contact and Lexical Enrichment in Israeli Hebrew*. New York: Palgrave Macmillan, 2003.

———. *Language Revival and Multiple Causation: The Mosaic Genesis of the Israeli Language*. New York: Oxford University Press, 2014.

Zwiep, Irene E. "From *Perush* to *Be'ur*: Authenticity and Authority in Eighteenth-Century Jewish Interpretation." In *Hebrew Language and Jewish Culture*, edited by Martin F. J. Baasten and Reiner Munk, 257–270. Amsterdam: Springer, 2007.

INDEX OF PROPER NAMES

INDEX OF TOPICS AND WORKS